THE
NATURE AND DESTINY
OF MAN

The Nature and Destiny of Man

of Man

A CHRISTIAN INTERPRETATION

I. HUMAN NATURE
II. HUMAN DESTINY

One Volume Edition

By

Reinhold Niebuhr

GIFFORD LECTURES

New York · CHARLES SCRIBNER'S SONS

To my wife

URSULA

who helped, and

To my children

CHRISTOPHER *and* ELIZABETH

*who frequently interrupted me
in the writing of these pages*

THE NATURE AND DESTINY OF MAN

OF MAN

I.   HUMAN NATURE

II. HUMAN DESTINY

PREFACE

THE publication of the two series of Gifford lectures on *The Nature and Destiny of Man* in this single volume calls for a new preface. I should like to say a word of gratitude to the reading public whose continued interest warrants the republication of this work. A decade of tragic human history has intervened between the delivery of these lectures at the University of Edinburgh and the present moment. Not a few achievements and frustrations of this decade might yield valuable insights upon the issues discussed in this volume or prompt a real revision of some of the judgements arrived at. Furthermore the debate to which the thesis of this work has been subjected by both sympathetic and critical readers has been of sufficient profit to the author to tempt him to change an emphasis here, or attempt a clarification there, or to correct an obviously faulty judgement or make a defense of a challenged position. But the temptation must be resisted, if for no other reason than that an adequate fulfillment of such tasks would require a new volume. The volumes are therefore presented as originally written with no more than corrections of obvious typographical errors.

It is gratifying to note that the relevance of Christian thought and doctrine, for the understanding of human nature, is more widely recognized than when these pages were first written. Perhaps it may be claimed, therefore, that experiences of our recent history have supplied a measure of substantiation for the thesis attempted in this work.

REINHOLD NIEBUHR

Union Theological Seminary
New York

THE TWO VOLUMES, which comprise the author's first and second series of Gifford Lectures, were published separately. Because the two series properly belong together, and for convenience to the reader, they are here bound together in a single volume.

The page numbers of Volume II have not been changed in this combined volume so that references given in other current works will cause no confusion to readers.

CONTENTS

THE NATURE AND DESTINY OF MAN

II. HUMAN DESTINY

xiii

THE
NATURE AND DESTINY
OF MAN

I. Human Nature

CHAPTER I

MAN AS A PROBLEM TO HIMSELF

Man has always been his own most vexing problem. How shall he think of himself? Every affirmation which he may make about his stature, virtue, or place in the cosmos becomes involved in contradictions when fully analysed. The analysis reveals some presupposition or implication which seems to deny what the proposition intended to affirm.

If man insists that he is a child of nature and that he ought not to pretend to be more than the animal, which he obviously is, he tacitly admits that he is, at any rate, a curious kind of animal who has both the inclination and the capacity to make such pretensions. If on the other hand he insists upon his unique and distinctive place in nature and points to his rational faculties as proof of his special eminence, there is usually an anxious note in his avowals of uniqueness which betrays his unconscious sense of kinship with the brutes. This note of anxiety gives poignant significance to the heat and animus in which the Darwinian controversy was conducted and the Darwinian thesis was resisted by the traditionalists. Furthermore the very effort to estimate the significance of his rational faculties implies a degree of transcendence over himself which is not fully defined or explained in what is usually connoted by "reason." For the man who weighs the importance of his rational faculties is in some sense more than "reason" and has capacities which transcend the ability to form general concepts.

If man takes his uniqueness for granted he is immediately involved in questions and contradictions on the problem of his virtue. If he believes himself to be essentially good and attributes the admitted evils of human history to specific social and historical causes he involves himself in begging the question; for all these specific historical causes of evil are revealed, upon close analysis, to be no more than particular consequences and historical configurations of evil tendencies in man himself. They cannot be understood at all if a capacity for, and inclination toward, evil in man himself is not presupposed. If, on the other hand, man comes to pessimistic conclusions about himself, his capacity for such judgments would seem to negate the content of the judgments. How can man be "essentially" evil if he knows himself to be so? What is the character of the ultimate subject, the quintessential "I," which passes such devastating judgments upon itself as object?

If one turns to the question of the value of human life and asks whether life is worth living, the very character of the question reveals that the questioner must in some sense be able to stand outside of, and to transcend the life which is thus judged and estimated. Man can reveal this transcendence more explicitly not only by actually committing suicide but by elaborating religions and philosophies which negate life and regard a "lifeless" eternity, such as Nirvana, as the only possible end of life.

Have those who inveigh so violently against otherworldliness in religion, justified as their criticisms may be, ever fully realized what the error of denying life implies in regard to the stature of man? The man who can negate "life" must be something other than mere vitality. Every effort to dissuade him from the neglect of natural vitality and historic existence implies a vantage point in him above natural vitality and history; otherwise he could not be tempted to the error from which he is to be dissuaded.

Man's place in the universe is subject to the same antinomies. Men

have been assailed periodically by qualms of conscience and fits of
dizziness for pretending to occupy the centre of the universe. Every
philosophy of life is touched with anthropocentric tendencies. Even
theocentric religions believe that the Creator of the world is interested in saving man from his unique predicament. But periodically
man is advised and advises himself to moderate his pretensions and
admit that he is only a little animal living a precarious existence on
a second-rate planet, attached to a second-rate sun. There are moderns who believe that this modesty is the characteristic genius of
modern man and the fruit of his discovery of the vastness of inter-
stellar spaces; but it was no modern astronomer who confessed,
"When I consider thy heavens, the work of thy fingers, the moon
and the stars, which thou hast ordained; What is man that thou art
mindful of him?" (Ps. 8:4). Yet the vantage point from which man
judges his insignificance is a rather significant vantage point. This
fact has not been lost on the moderns whose modesty before the
cosmic immensity was modified considerably by pride in their discovery of this immensity. It was a modern, the poet Swinburne, who
sang triumphantly:

The seal of his knowledge is sure, the truth and his spirit are wed; . . .
Glory to Man in the highest! for man is the master of things,

thereby proving that the advance of human knowledge about the
world does not abate the pride of man.

   While these paradoxes of human self-knowledge are not easily
reduced to simpler formulæ, they all point to two facts about man:
one of them obvious and the other not quite so obvious. The two are
not usually appreciated with equal sympathy. The obvious fact is
that man is a child of nature, subject to its vicissitudes, compelled by
its necessities, driven by its impulses, and confined within the brevity
of the years which nature permits its varied organic form, allowing
them some, but not too much, latitude. The other less obvious fact
is that man is a spirit who stands outside of nature, life, himself, his
reason and the world. This latter fact is appreciated in one or the

other of its aspects by various philosophies. But it is not frequently appreciated in its total import. That man stands outside of nature in some sense is admitted even by naturalists who are intent upon keeping him as close to nature as possible. They must at least admit that he is *homo faber,* a tool-making animal. That man stands outside the world is admitted by rationalists who, with Aristotle, define man as a rational animal and interpret reason as the capacity for making general concepts. But the rationalists do not always understand that man's rational capacity involves a further ability to stand outside himself, a capacity for self-transcendence, the ability to make himself his own object, a quality of spirit which is usually not fully comprehended or connoted in *"ratio"* or *"νοῦς"* or "reason" or any of the concepts which philosophers usually use to describe the uniqueness of man.

How difficult it is to do justice to both the uniqueness of man and his affinities with the world of nature below him is proved by the almost unvarying tendency of those philosophies, which describe and emphasize the rational faculties of man or his capacity for self-transcendence to forget his relation to nature and to identify him, prematurely and unqualifiedly, with the divine and the eternal; and of naturalistic philosophies to obscure the uniqueness of man.

II

THE CLASSICAL VIEW OF MAN

Though man has always been a problem to himself, modern man has aggravated that problem by his too simple and premature solutions. Modern man, whether idealist or naturalist, whether rationalist or romantic, is characterized by his simple certainties about himself. He has aggravated the problem of understanding himself because these certainties are either in contradiction with each other or in contradiction with the obvious facts of history, more particularly of contemporary history; and either they have been controverted by that history or they are held in defiance of its known facts. It is not unfair

to affirm that modern culture, that is, our culture since the Renaissance, is to be credited with the greatest advances in the understanding of nature and with the greatest confusion in the understanding of man. Perhaps this credit and debit are logically related to
each other.

Fully to appreciate the modern conflicts in regard to human nature, it is necessary to place the characteristically modern doctrines
of man in their historic relation to the traditional views of human
nature which have informed western culture. All modern views of
human nature are adaptations, transformations and varying compounds of primarily two distinctive views of man: (*a*) The view of
classical antiquity, that is of the Græco-Roman world, and (*b*) the
Biblical view. It is important to remember that while these two
views are distinct and partly incompatible, they were actually
merged in the thought of medieval Catholicism. (The perfect expression of this union is to be found in the Thomistic synthesis of
Augustinian and Aristotelian thought.) The history of modern culture really begins with the destruction of this synthesis, foreshadowed
in nominalism, and completed in the Renaissance and Reformation.
In the dissolution of the synthesis, the Renaissance distilled the classical elements out of the synthesis and the Reformation sought to free
the Biblical from the classical elements. Liberal Protestantism is an
effort (on the whole an abortive one) to reunite the two elements.
There is, in fact, little that is common between them. What was common in the two views was almost completely lost after modern
thought had reinterpreted and transmuted the classical view of man
in the direction of a greater naturalism. Modern culture has thus
been a battleground of two opposing views of human nature. This
conflict could not be resolved. It ended in the more or less complete
triumph of the modernized classical view of man, a triumph which
in this latter day is imperilled not by any external foe but by confusion within its own household. To validate this analysis of the matter requires at least a brief preliminary analysis of the classical and
the Christian views of human nature.

The classical view of man, comprised primarily of Platonic, Aristotelian and Stoic conceptions of human nature, contains, of course,
varying emphases but it may be regarded as one in its common
conviction that man is to be understood primarily from the standpoint of the uniqueness of his rational faculties. What is unique in
man is his *νοῦς*. Νοῦς may be translated as "spirit" but the primary
emphasis lies upon the capacity for thought and reason. In Aristotle
the *nous* is the vehicle of purely intellectual activity and is a universal
and immortal principle which enters man from without. Only one
element in it, the "passive" in distinction to the "active" *nous* becomes involved in, and subject to, the individuality of a particular
physical organism. How completely the Aristotelian *nous* is intellectual may best be understood by Aristotle's explicit denial of its
capacity for self-consciousness. It does not make itself its own object
except in making things known the object of consciousness: "No mind
knows itself by participation in the known; it becomes known by
touching and knowing, so that the same thing is mind and object
of mind."[1] This definition is the more significant when contrasted
with Aristotle's conception of divine consciousness which expresses
itself only in terms of self-knowledge.

In Plato the *nous* or *logistikon* is not as sharply distinguished from
the soul as in Aristotle. It is, rather, the highest element in the soul,
the other two being the spirited element ($\theta\upsilon\mu\omega\epsilon\iota\delta\acute{\epsilon}\varsigma$) and the ap-
petitive element ($\dot{\epsilon}\pi\iota\theta\upsilon\mu\eta\tau\iota\kappa\acute{o}\nu$). In both Plato and Aristotle "mind"
is sharply distinguished from the body. It is the unifying and or-
dering principle, the organ of *logos,* which brings harmony into
the life of the soul, as *logos* is the creative and forming principle of
the world. Greek metaphysical presuppositions are naturally determinative for the doctrine of man; and since Parmenides Greek
philosophy had assumed an identity between being and reason on
the one hand and on the other had presupposed that reason works
upon some formless or unformed stuff which is never completely
tractable. In the thought of Aristotle matter is "a remnant, the

[1] *Physics,* 20.

non-existent in itself unknowable and alien to reason, that remains after the process of clarifying the thing into form and conception. This non-existent neither is nor is not; it is 'not yet,' that is to say it attains reality only insofar as it becomes the vehicle of some conceptual determination."[2]

Plato and Aristotle thus share a common rationalism; and also a common dualism which is explicit in the case of Plato and implicit and covert in the case of Aristotle.[3] The effect of this rationalism and dualism has been determinative for the classical doctrine of man and for all modern doctrines which are borrowed from it. The consequences are: (*a*) The rationalism practically identifies rational man (who is essential man) with the divine; for reason is, as the creative principle, identical with God. Individuality is no significant concept, for it rests only upon the particularity of the body. In the thought of Aristotle only the active *nous,* precisely the mind which is not involved in the soul, is immortal; and for Plato the immutability of ideas is regarded as a proof of the immortality of the spirit. (*b*) The dualism has the consequence for the doctrine of man of identifying the body with evil and of assuming the essential goodness of mind or spirit. This body-mind dualism and the value judgments passed upon both body and mind stand in sharpest contrast to the Biblical view of man and achieve a fateful influence in all subsequent theories of human nature. The Bible knows nothing of a good mind and an evil body.

While Stoicism, as a monistic and pantheistic philosophy, sharply diverges from the Aristotelian and Platonic concepts in many respects, its view of human nature betrays more similarities than differences. The similarities are great enough, at any rate, to constitute it a part of the general "classical" picture of man. The Stoic reason is

[2]*Cf.* Werner Jaeger, *Aristotle,* Ch. VIII.
[3]Despite Aristotle's naturalism, his psychology is dependent upon Plato's and it may be wrong to speak of his dualism as covert. It was fairly explicit. He believed that life without the body was the soul's normal state and that its sojourn in the body was a severe illness. *Cf.* Jaeger, *ibid.,* p. 51.

more immanent in both the world process and in the soul and body of man than in Platonism; yet man is essentially reason. Even the dualism is not completely lacking. For while Stoicism is not always certain whether the reason which governs man must persuade him to emulate nature as he finds it outside of his reason or whether it, being a special spark of the divine reason, must set him against the impulses of nature, it arrives on the whole at convictions which do not qualify the classical concepts essentially.[4] The emphasis upon human freedom in its psychology overcomes the pantheistic naturalism of its metaphysics; and its completely negative attitude toward the passions and the whole impulsive life of man set reason in contrast to the impulses of the body, however much it conceives reason as basically the principle of harmony within the body.

Obviously, the Platonic, Aristotelian and Stoic conceptions which define the "classical" view of man do not exhaust Greek speculations about human nature. Modern vitalism and romanticism have their antecedents in the earlier Dionysian religion, in Heraclitus' conception of ultimate reality as Flux and Fire and more particularly in the development of the Dionysian theme in Greek tragedy.[5] Subsequent mysticism is anticipated in Orphism and Pythagoreanism.

[4]The confusion in Stoic thought between the reason in man and the reason in nature, a confusion which was perpetuated constantly in eighteenth-century borrowings from Stoicism, is clearly revealed in Diogenes Laërtius' account of Zeno's thought. He writes: "When rational animals are endowed with reason in token of a more complete superiority, life in them in accordance with nature is rightly understood to mean life in accordance with reason. For reason is like a craftsman, shaping impulses and desires. Hence Zeno's definition of the end is to live in conformity with nature, which means to live a life of virtue; for it is virtue to which nature leads. On the other hand a virtuous life is one which conforms to our experience of the course of nature, our human natures being parts of universal nature." Diogenes Laërtius VII, 85.

[5]Nietzsche in his *Birth of Tragedy* claims the Greek dramatists too unreservedly for his vitalistic philosophy. The significance of the tragedies lies in the unresolved conflict between the Olympian and Dionysian, the rational and the vitalistic, principles in Greek thought. Significantly Zeus, the god of order and measure, remains the ultimate arbiter in the Greek tragedies.

Even more significant for developments in contemporary culture, Democritus and Epicurus interpreted man, in accordance with their naturalism and materialism, not as standing outside of nature by the quality of his unique reason, but as wholly a part of nature. This Greek materialism was no less rationalistic than Platonism or Aristotelianism but it reduced the immanental reason in the world to mechanical necessity and sought to understand man in terms of this mechanism. It was by combining Stoic with Democritan and Epicurean naturalism that modern culture arrived at concepts which were to express some of its most characteristic interpretations of man, as primarily a child of nature.

It must be observed that while the classical view of human virtue is optimistic when compared with the Christian view (for it finds no defect in the centre of human personality) and while it has perfect confidence in the virtue of the rational man, it does not share the confidence of the moderns in the ability of all men to be either virtuous or happy. Thus an air of melancholy hangs over Greek life which stands in sharpest contrast to the all-pervasive optimism of the now dying bourgeois culture, despite the assumption of the latter that it had merely restored the classical world view and the Greek view of man. "There is nothing, methinks, more piteous than a man, of all things that creep and breathe upon the earth," declares Zeus in the *Iliad,* and that note runs as a consistent strain through Greek thought from Homer to the Hellenistic age. Primarily it was the brevity of life and the mortality of man which tempted the Greeks to melancholy. They were not dissuaded from this mood either by Plato's assurance of immortality nor yet by Epicurus' counsel that death need not be feared, since there was nothing on the other side of the grave.

Aristotle confessed that "not to be born is the best thing and death is better than life," and gave it as his opinion that melancholy was a concomitant of genius. The philosophers were optimistic in their confidence that the wise man would be virtuous; but, alas, they had no confidence that the many could be wise. The Stoic Chryssipus could conceive happiness only for the wise and was certain that most men were fools. The Stoics tended on the one hand to include all men in the brotherhood of man on the ground that they all had the spark of divine reason; but on the other hand they pitied the multitude for having no obvious graces of rationality. Thus their equalitarianism rapidly degenerated into an aristocratic condescension not very different from Aristotle's contempt for the slave as a "living tool." Seneca, despite his pious universalism, prays "forgive the world: they are all fools."

Neither Greek nor Roman classicists had any conception of a meaning in human history. History was a series of cycles, a realm of endless recurrences. Aristotle maintained that the arts and sciences were lost and found again not once but an infinite number of times.[6] Zeno envisaged the end of the world as a huge conflagration which would destroy the world's body. This pessimism about both man and his history is the natural consequence of the mind-body dualism which characterizes Greek thought far beyond the limits of Platonism. It culminated invariably in the conviction that the body is a tomb ($\sigma\hat{\omega}\mu\alpha-\sigma\hat{\eta}\mu\alpha$)[7] a conviction which makes neo-Platonism the logical consummation of Greek thought.

The pessimism of Greek tragedy is somewhat different from that of the philosophers and most nearly approaches the Christian interpretation of life. But, unlike Christian thought, it has no answer for the problem it presents. In Æschylus and Sophocles the capricious jealousy of Zeus against mortal men of Homeric legend had been transmuted into the justified jealousy of the ultimate principle of law and order against the lawlessness of human passions. But, unlike the philosophers, the dramatists see human passions as something more than mere impulses of the body. The principle of order and measure, represented by Zeus, is constantly defied by vitalities in human life which are creative as well as destructive. The tragedy

[6]*Cf.* S. H. Butcher on "The Melancholy of the Greeks," in *Some Aspects of the Greek Genius.*
[7]*Cf.* E. Bevan, *Stoics and Sceptics,* p. 100.

of human history consists precisely in the fact that human life cannot be creative without being destructive, that biological urges are enhanced and sublimated by dæmonic spirit and that this spirit cannot express itself without committing the sin of pride. The heroes of Greek tragedy are always being counselled to remember their mortality and to escape νέμεσις ·by observing a proper restraint. But the ὕβρις which offends Zeus is an inevitable concomitant of their creative action in history. The tragic heroes are heroes precisely because they disregard this prudent advice of moderation. In that sense Greek tragedy is an explication of Nietzsche's observation: "Every doer loves his deed much more than it deserves to be loved; and the best deeds are born out of such an excess of love that they could not be worthy of it, even though their worth be very great."[8] The various vitalities of human history are moreover not only in conflict with Zeus but in conflict with each other. There is no simple resolution of the conflict between the state and the family, usually symbolized as a conflict between man and woman, the latter representing the community of blood and family in contrast to the political community (as in *Iphigenia at Aulis* and in *Antigone*). The conflict in Greek tragedy is, in short, between Gods, between Zeus and Dionysus; and not between God and the devil, nor between spirit and matter. The spirit of man expresses itself in his vital energies as well as in the harmonizing force of mind; and while the latter, as the rational principle of order, is the more ultimate (here the dramatists remain typically Greek) there can be creativity in human affairs only at the price of disturbing this order.

Thus life is at war with itself, according to Greek tragedy. There is no solution, or only a tragic solution for the conflict between the vitalities of life and the principle of measure. Zeus remains God. But one is prompted to both admiration and pity toward those who defy him. It is significant that this profound problem, posed by Greek tragedy, was never sensed by the moderns who revived classicism and ostensibly built their view of man upon Greek thought.

[8]*Kritik und Zukunft der Kultur,* Ch. IV, Par. 13.

They may have understood or misunderstood Plato and Aristotle: but the message of Æschylus and Sophocles was neither understood nor misunderstood. It was simply neglected, except as the minor romantic note in modern culture appreciated and partly misunderstood it.

III

THE CHRISTIAN VIEW OF MAN

The Christian view of man, which modern culture ostensibly rejects in its entirety but by which its estimate of human nature is influenced more than it realizes, will be more fully analysed in this book. At this point we must anticipate subsequent elaborations briefly by distinguishing the Christian view from the classical doctrine of man. As the classical view is determined by Greek metaphysical presuppositions, so the Christian view is determined by the ultimate presuppositions of Christian faith. The Christian faith in God as Creator of the world transcends the canons and antinomies of rationality, particularly the antinomy between mind and matter, between consciousness and extension. God is not merely mind who forms a previously given formless stuff. God is both vitality and form and the source of all existence. He creates the world. This world is not God; but it is not evil because it is not God. Being God's creation, it is good.

The consequence of this conception of the world upon the view of human nature in Christian thought is to allow an appreciation of the unity of body and soul in human personality which idealists and naturalists have sought in vain. Furthermore it prevents the idealistic error of regarding the mind as essentially good or essentially eternal and the body as essentially evil. But it also obviates the romantic error of seeking for the good in man-as-nature and for evil in man-as-spirit or as reason. Man is, according to the Biblical view, a created and finite existence in both body and spirit. Obviously a view which depends upon an ultra-rational presupposition is immediately endangered when rationally explicated; for reason which seeks to bring all things into terms of rational coherence is tempted to make one known thing the principle of explanation and to derive all other things from it. Its most natural inclination is to make itself that ultimate principle, and thus in effect to declare itself God. Christian psychology and philosophy have never completely freed themselves from this fault, which explains why naturalists plausibly though erroneously regard Christian faith as the very fountain source of idealism.

This is also the reason why the Biblical view of the unity of man as body and soul has often seemed to be no more than the consequence of primitive Hebraic psychology. In Hebrew thought the soul of man resides in his blood and the concept of an immortal mind in a mortal body remains unknown to the end. It is true that certain distinctions are gradually made. At first both *ruach* and *nephesh* mean little more than "breath"; but they are gradually distinguished and *ruach* becomes roughly synonymous with spirit or *nous* and *nephesh* with soul or *psyche*. But, unlike Greek thought, this distinction does not lead to dualistic consequences. The monism of the Biblical view is something other than the failure to differentiate *physis, psyche* and *nous,* which characterized Greek thought before Anaxagoras; nor is it merely the consequence of an undeveloped psychology. It is ultimately derived from the Biblical view of God as the Creator and of the Biblical faith in the goodness of creation.

The second important characteristic of the Christian view of man is that he is understood primarily from the standpoint of God, rather than the uniqueness of his rational faculties or his relation to nature. He is made in the "image of God." It has been the mistake of many Christian rationalists to assume that this term is no more than a religious-pictorial expression of what philosophy intends when it defines man as a rational animal. We have previously alluded to the fact that the human spirit has the special capacity of standing continually outside itself in terms of indefinite regression. Consciousness is a capacity for surveying the world and determining action from a governing centre. Self-consciousness represents a further degree of transcendence in which the self makes itself its own object in such a way that the ego is finally always subject and not object. The rational capacity of surveying the world, of forming general concepts and analysing the order of the world is thus but one aspect of what Christianity knows as "spirit." The self knows the world, insofar as it knows the world, because it stands outside both itself and the world, which means that it cannot understand itself except as it is understood from beyond itself and the world.

This essential homelessness of the human spirit is the ground of all religion; for the self which stands outside itself and the world cannot find the meaning of life in itself or the world. It cannot identify meaning with causality in nature; for its freedom is obviously something different from the necessary causal links of nature. Nor can it identify the principle of meaning with rationality, since it transcends its own rational processes, so that it may, for instance, ask the question whether there is a relevance between its rational forms and the recurrences and forms of nature. It is this capacity of freedom which finally prompts great cultures and philosophies to transcend rationalism and to seek for the meaning of life in an unconditioned ground of existence. But from the standpoint of human thought this unconditioned ground of existence, this God, can be defined only negatively. This is why mystic religions in general, and particularly the neo-Platonic tradition in western culture, have one interesting similarity with Christianity and one important difference in their estimate of human nature. In common with Christianity they measure the depth of the human spirit in terms of its capacity of self-transcendence. Thus Plotinus defines *nous* not as Aristotle defines it. For him it is primarily the capacity for self-knowledge and it has no limit short of the eternal. Mysticism and Christianity agree in understanding man from the standpoint of the eternal. But since mysticism leads to an undifferentiated ultimate reality, it is bound to regard particularity, including individuality, as essentially evil. All mystic religions therefore have the characteristic of accentuating individuality inasfar as individuality is inherent in the capacity for self-consciousness emphasized in mysticism and is something more than mere bodily particularity; but all mystic philosophies ultimately lose the very individuality which they first emphasize, because they sink finite particularity in a distinctionless divine ground of existence.

God as will and personality, in concepts of Christian faith, is thus the only possible ground of real individuality, though not the only possible presupposition of self-consciousness. But faith in God as will and personality depends upon faith in His power to reveal Himself. *Caillet, Pascal, p. 142.* The Christian faith in God's self-disclosure, culminating in the revelation of Christ, is thus the basis of the Christian concept of personality and individuality. In terms of this faith man can understand himself as a unity of will which finds its end in the will of God. We thus have in the problem of human nature one of the many indications of the relation of general and special revelation, which concerns theology so perennially. The conviction that man stands too completely outside of both nature and reason to understand himself in terms of either without misunderstanding himself, belongs to general revelation in the sense that any astute analysis of the human situation must lead to it. But if man lacks a further revelation of the divine he will also misunderstand himself when he seeks to escape the conditions of nature and reason. He will end by seeking absorption in a divine reality which is at once all and nothing. To understand himself truly means to begin with a faith that he is understood from beyond himself, that he is known and loved of God and must find himself in terms of obedience to the divine will. This relation of the divine to the human will makes it possible for man to relate himself to God without pretending to be God; and to accept his distance from God as a created thing, without believing that the evil of his nature is caused by this finiteness. Man's finite existence in the body and in history can be essentially affirmed, as naturalism wants to affirm it. Yet the uniqueness of man's spirit can be appreciated even more than idealism appreciates it, though always preserving a proper distinction between the human and divine. Also the unity of spirit and body can be emphasized in terms of its relation to a Creator and Redeemer who created both mind and body. These are the ultra-rational foundations and presuppositions of Christian wisdom about man.

This conception of man's stature is not, however, the complete Christian picture of man. The high estimate of the human stature implied in the concept of "image of God" stands in paradoxical juxtaposition to the low estimate of human virtue in Christian thought. Man is a sinner. His sin is defined as rebellion against God. The Christian estimate of human evil is so serious precisely because it places evil at the very centre of human personality: in the will. This evil cannot be regarded complacently as the inevitable consequence of his finiteness or the fruit of his involvement in the contingencies and necessities of nature. Sin is occasioned precisely by the fact that man refuses to admit his "creatureliness" and to acknowledge himself as merely a member of a total unity of life. He pretends to be more than he is. Nor can he, as in both rationalistic and mystic dualism, dismiss his sins as residing in that part of himself which is not his true self, that is, that part of himself which is involved in physical necessity. In Christianity it is not the eternal man who judges the finite man; but the eternal and holy God who judges sinful man. Nor is redemption in the power of the eternal man who gradually sloughs off finite man. Man is not divided against himself so that the essential man can be extricated from the nonessential. Man contradicts himself within the terms of his true essence. His essence is free self-determination. His sin is the wrong use of his freedom and its consequent destruction.

Man is an individual but he is not self-sufficing. The law of his nature is love, a harmonious relation of life to life in obedience to the divine centre and source of his life. This law is violated when man seeks to make himself the centre and source of his own life. His sin is therefore spiritual and not carnal, though the infection of rebellion spreads from the spirit to the body and disturbs its harmonies also. Man, in other words, is a sinner not because he is one limited individual within a whole but rather because he is betrayed by his very ability to survey the whole to imagine himself the whole.

The fact that human vitality inevitably expresses itself in defiance of the laws of measure can be observed without the presuppositions of the Christian faith. The analysis of this fact in Greek tragedy has already been observed. But it is impossible without the presuppositions of the Christian faith to find the source of sin within man himself. Greek tragedy regards human evil as the consequence of a conflict between vitality and form, between Dionysian and Olympian divinities. Only in a religion of revelation, whose God reveals Himself to man from beyond himself and from beyond the contrast of vitality and form, can man discover the root of sin to be within himself. The essence of man is his freedom. Sin is committed in that freedom. Sin can therefore not be attributed to a defect in his essence. It can only be understood as a self-contradiction, made possible by the fact of his freedom but not following necessarily from it.

Christianity, therefore, issues inevitably in the religious expression of an uneasy conscience. Only within terms of the Christian faith can man not only understand the reality of the evil in himself but escape the error of attributing that evil to any one but himself. It is possible of course to point out that man is tempted by the situation in which he stands. He stands at the juncture of nature and spirit. The freedom of his spirit causes him to break the harmonies of nature and the pride of his spirit prevents him from establishing a new harmony. The freedom of his spirit enables him to use the forces and processes of nature creatively; but his failure to observe the limits of his finite existence causes him to defy the forms and restraints of both nature and reason. Human self-consciousness is a high tower looking upon a large and inclusive world. It vainly imagines that it is the large world which it beholds and not a narrow tower insecurely erected amidst the shifting sands of the world.

It is one of the purposes of this volume to analyse the meaning of the Christian idea of sin more fully and to explain the uneasy conscience expressed in the Christian religion. It must suffice at this point to record the fact that the Christian view of human nature is involved in the paradox of claiming a higher stature for man and of taking a more serious view of his evil than other anthropology.

IV

THE MODERN VIEW OF MAN

The modern view of man is informed partly by classical, partly by Christian and partly by distinctively modern motifs. The classical element tends to slip from the typical classical, Platonic and Aristotelian rationalism to a more naturalistic rationalism. That is, the Epicurean and Democritan naturalism, which remained subordinate in the classical period of Greek thought, becomes dominant in the modern period. This modern naturalism is in accord with the Christian concept of man as "creature" but it contradicts the Christian concept of man as "image of God" which the early Renaissance emphasized in opposition to the Christian idea of man as creature and man as sinner. The curious compound of classical, Christian and distinctively modern conceptions of human nature, involved in modern anthropology, leads to various difficulties and confusions which may be briefly summarized as follows: (*a*) The inner contradictions in modern conceptions of human nature between idealistic and naturalistic rationalists; and between rationalists, whether idealistic or naturalistic, and vitalists and romanticists. (*b*) The certainties about human nature in modern culture which modern history dissipates, particularly the certainty about individuality. (*c*) The certainties about human nature, particularly the certainty about the goodness of man, which stands in contradiction to the known facts of history.

(*a*) One of the unresolved antinomies in modern culture is the contradictory emphasis of the idealists and the naturalists. The former are inclined to protest against Christian humility and to disavow both the doctrine of man's creatureliness and the doctrine of his sinfulness. This was the mood of the Renaissance, the thought of which upon this issue was determined by Platonic, neo-Platonic and Stoic conceptions. Bruno is concerned to establish the infinity of human self-consciousness; and the infinity of space is merely an interesting analogue of this infinity of spirit in his pantheistic system. He prizes the achievements of Copernican astronomy because Copernicus "emancipated our knowledge from the prison house in which, as it were, it saw stars only through small windows." In the same manner Leonardo da Vinci is more concerned to prove that the mathematical method which unlocks nature's mysteries and discloses her regularities and dependable recurrences is a fruit and symbol of the greatness of the human mind, than that it is a tool of nature's mastery. Petrarch sees nature as a mirror in which man beholds his true greatness.

Yet there was a minor note in the Renaissance which finally led to the naturalistic rationalism of the eighteenth century. It expresses itself in Francis Bacon's primary interest in nature, and in Montaigne's effort to understand man in the variety of his natural differentiations. Bacon is afraid lest the "unquietness of the human spirit," that is the very hankering after infinity which Bruno praises as the true mark of humanity, will "interfere most mischievously in the discovery of causes," that is, with the sober inductive processes of science. Thus modern culture slips from the essential Platonism of the early Renaissance to the Stoicism of Descartes and Spinoza and the seventeenth century generally and then to the more radical, materialistic and Democritan naturalism of the eighteenth century. Modern man ends by seeking to understand himself in terms of his relation to nature, but he remains even more confused about the relation of reason in nature and reason in man than the Stoics were. The thought of the French enlightenment is a perfect exposition of this confusion. The idealistic reaction to this naturalism is to be found in German idealism, where, with the exception of Kant, reason and being are more unqualifiedly equated than in Platonism. Descartes, the fountain source of modern culture, manages to conceive of man purely in terms of thought, nature in terms of mechanics and to find no organic unity between the two, thus bearing within himself both the contradictions and the extravagances of modernity.

In terms of social history, this course of modern thought from an idealistic protest against the Christian conception of man as creature and as sinner to the naturalistic protest against man as the "image of God" may be interpreted as the anti-climactic history of bourgeois man. The middle-class world begins with a tremendous sense of the power of the human mind over nature. But having destroyed the ultimate reference by which medieval man transcended nature spiritually, even while acknowledging his dependence practically, the bourgeois and technical world ends by seeking asylum in nature's dependabilities and serenities. Modern capitalism really expresses both attitudes at the same time. The spirit of capitalism is the spirit of an irreverent exploitation of nature, conceived as a treasure-house of riches which will guarantee everything which might be regarded as the good life. Man masters nature. But the social organization of capitalism at least theoretically rests upon the naive faith that nature masters man and that her pre-established harmonies will prevent the human enterprise from involving itself in any serious catastrophes (physiocratic theory).

The conflict between idealistic and naturalistic rationalists is complicated by a further factor: the protest of the romantic naturalists who interpret man as primarily vitality and who find neither a pale reason nor a mechanical nature an adequate key to man's true essence. This romantic interpretation of man is in some respects the newest element in modern anthropological doctrines, for it is only partially foreshadowed in either classical or Christian thought. Its bitterest fruit is modern fascism. Marxist thought complicates the pattern further; for it interprets man, as he is, primarily in vitalistic terms and rightly discounts the pretenses of rational man who does

not know his own finiteness; but the man who is to be will build
a society which will be governed by the most remarkable rational
coherence of life with life and interest with interest. The conflict between rationalists and romanticists has become one of the most fateful
issues of our day, with every possible religious and political implication. Modern man, in short, cannot determine whether he shall understand himself primarily from the standpoint of the uniqueness of his
reason or from the standpoint of his affinity with nature; and if
the latter whether it is the harmless order and peace of nature or
her vitality which is the real clue to his essence. Thus some of the
certainties of modern man are in contradiction with one another;
and it may be questioned whether the conflict can be resolved within
terms of the presuppositions with which modern culture approaches
the issues.

(*b*) The concept of individuality in modern culture belongs to that
class of certainties of modern man about himself which his own history has gradually dissipated. The tremendous emphasis upon individuality in the Renaissance is clearly a flower which could have
grown only on Christian soil, since the classical culture, to which the
Renaissance is an ostensible return, lacked this emphasis completely.
The Italian Renaissance avails itself primarily of neo-Platonic conceptions to establish its idea of the dignity and the liberty of man.
But these conceptions would not yield the idea of individuality if
Christian ideas were not presupposed. The Renaissance is particularly intent upon establishing the freedom of the human spirit in
opposition to Christian doctrines of divine predestination.[1]

Pico della Mirandola extols the freedom of the human spirit in
concepts drawn from Platonism. God said to man, according to Pico:
"You alone are not bound by any restraint, unless you will adopt it
by the will which we have given you. I have placed you in the centre

---

[1]Some or the important documents in this cause were: Manetti's *De
dignitate, ex excellentia hominis;* Valla's *De libero arbitrio;* Pompanazzi's *De fato, libero arbitrio et predestinatione;* and Pico della Mirandola's *Oratio de hominis dignitate.*

of the world that you may the easier look about and behold all that is in it. I created you a creature, neither earthly nor heavenly, neither mortal nor immortal, so that you could be your own creator and choose whatever form you may assume for yourself."

While classical thought was used by the Renaissance to challenge the Christian idea of man's dependence and weakness, by emphasis upon his uniqueness and the freedom of his spirit, classicism was obviously not able to suggest the concept of individuality which the Renaissance held so dear. This idea must be regarded as partly a Christian inheritance and partly a consequence of the emergence of the bourgeois individual from the historical and traditional cohesions, patterns and restraints of the medieval world. This bourgeois individual felt himself the master of his own destiny and was impatient with both the religious and the political solidarities which characterized both classical and medieval life. Speaking in social terms one may say that he lost this individuality immediately after establishing it by his destruction of the medieval solidarities. He found himself the artificer of a technical civilization which creates more enslaving mechanical interdependencies and collectivities than anything known in an agrarian world. Furthermore no one can be as completely and discreetly an individual as bourgeois individualism supposes, whether in the organic forms of an agrarian or the more mechanical forms of a technical society.

Considered in terms of philosophical issues bourgeois individualism had an insecure foundation, not only in the Platonism and neo-Platonism in which it first expressed itself but also in the later naturalism of the eighteenth and nineteenth centuries. Idealism begins by emphasizing man's freedom and transcendence over nature but ends by losing the individual in the universalities of rational concepts and ultimately in the undifferentiated totality of the divine. Naturalism begins by emphasizing natural variety and particularity. Thus it was Montaigne's interest to picture the multifarious forms of social and moral custom under the influence of the diversities of geography. But variety in nature comes short of individuality. There is no place for individuality in either pure mind or pure nature. As the idealists lose individuality in the absolute mind, so the naturalists lose it in "streams of consciousness" when dealing with the matter psychologically, and in "laws of motion" when thinking sociologically. Thus the individualism of the Renaissance and of the eighteenth century is dissipated culturally, just as bourgeois libertarian idealism disintegrates politically and succumbs to fascist and Marxist collectivism. A genuine individuality can be maintained only in terms of religious presuppositions which can do justice to the immediate involvement of human individuality in all the organic forms and social tensions of history, while yet appreciating its ultimate transcendence over every social and historical situation in the highest reaches of its self-transcendence. The paradox of man as creature and man as child of God is a necessary presupposition of a concept of individuality, strong enough to maintain itself against the pressures of history, and realistic enough to do justice to the organic cohesions of social life.

(c) The final certainty of modern anthropology is its optimistic treatment of the problem of evil. Modern man has an essentially easy conscience; and nothing gives the diverse and discordant notes of modern culture so much harmony as the unanimous opposition of modern man to Christian conceptions of the sinfulness of man. The idea that man is sinful at the very centre of his personality, that is in his will, is universally rejected. It is this rejection which has seemed to make the Christian gospel simply irrelevant to modern man, a fact which is of much more importance than any conviction about its incredibility. If modern culture conceives man primarily in terms of the uniqueness of his rational faculties, it finds the root of his evil in his involvement in natural impulses and natural necessities from which it hopes to free him by the increase of his rational faculties. This essentially Platonic idea manages to creep into many social and educational theories, even when they are ostensibly naturalistic and not Platonic. On the other hand, if it conceives of man primarily in terms of his relation to nature, it hopes to rescue man

from the dæmonic chaos in which his spiritual life is involved by
beguiling him back to the harmony, serenity and harmless unity of
nature. In this the mechanistic rationalist and the Rousseauistic romantic of the French enlightenment seem to stand on common
ground. Either the rational man or the natural man is conceived as
essentially good, and it is only necessary for man either to rise from
the chaos of nature to the harmony of mind or to descend from the
chaos of spirit to the harmony of nature in order to be saved. The
very fact that the strategies of redemption are in such complete contradiction to each other proves how far modern man is from
solving the problem of evil in his life.

A further consequence of modern optimism is a philosophy of
history expressed in the idea of progress. Either by a force immanent
in nature itself, or by the gradual extension of rationality, or by the
elimination of specific sources of evil, such as priesthoods, tyrannical
government and class divisions in society, modern man expects to
move toward some kind of perfect society. The idea of progress is
compounded of many elements. It is particularly important to consider one element of which modern culture is itself completely oblivious. The idea of progress is possible only upon the ground of
a Christian culture. It is a secularized version of Biblical apocalypse
and of the Hebraic sense of a meaningful history, in contrast to the
meaningless history of the Greeks. But since the Christian doctrine
of the sinfulness of man is eliminated, a complicating factor in the
Christian philosophy is removed and the way is open for simple
interpretations of history, which relate historical process as closely as
possible to biological process and which fail to do justice either to
the unique freedom of man or to the dæmonic misuse which he
may make of that freedom.

There are of course pessimistic reactions to this optimism about
both the individual and the total human enterprise. In the mechanistic naturalism of Hobbes and the romantic naturalism of Nietzsche
a thoroughgoing pessimism is elaborated. One of the modern fruits
of Nietzschean thought is Freudian pessimism. Here we have no

good opinion about human nature; yet there is no uneasy conscience in this pessimism. The egotism and the will-to-power which Christian thought regards as the quintessence of sin and which, in the view of bourgeois liberalism, is a defect to be sloughed off by a new education or a new social organization, is regarded as normal and normative. Hobbes accepts and Nietzsche glorifies the will-to-power. In Hobbes a political vantage point against individual egotism is gained but none against the collective egotism, embodied in the state. In Nietzsche's transvaluation of values, the characteristics of human life which make for conflict between life and life are raised to the eminence of the ideal. The fateful consequences in contemporary political life of Hobbes's cynicism and Nietzsche's nihilism are everywhere apparent.

By way of validating the relevance of the Christian conception of man as a possible source of light for the confusion of modernity, we must consider the problems of modern culture, briefly sketched here, more fully in the three following chapters.

1. Man's problem has been to determine whether he is basically Rational or natural.

2. The classical view of Plato elevates reason and scorns the body

3. The Christian view holds that both man's reason and his creatureliness are redeemed as created of God

4. Modern man tends to elevate Reason but also may elevate man as a creature. In either case he has rejected the Christian view. Idea of progress.

CHAPTER II

THE PROBLEM OF VITALITY AND FORM
IN HUMAN NATURE

ALL creatures express an exuberant vitality within the limits of certain unities, orders and forms. Animal existence exhibits a uniform and resolute will to survive; but the strategy of that will, whether for the individual or the species, expresses itself variously according to the particular form of existence within the species and genus. Vitality and form are thus the two aspects of crea‧ tion. Human existence is obviously distinguished from animal life by its qualified participation in creation. Within limits it breaks the forms of nature and creates new configurations of vitality. Its transcendence over natural process offers it the opportunity of interfering with the established forms and unities of vitality as nature knows them. This is the basis of human history, with its progressive alteration of forms, in distinction from nature which knows no history but only endless repetition within the limits of each given form.

Since man is deeply involved in the forms of nature on the one hand and is free of them on the other; since he must regard determinations of sex, race and (to a lesser degree) geography as forces of ineluctable fate, but can nevertheless arrange and rearrange the vitalities and unities of nature within certain limits, the problem of human creativity is obviously filled with complexities. Four terms

26

must be considered in his situation: (1) The vitality of nature (its impulses and drives); (2) the forms and unities of nature, that is, the determinations of instinct, and the forms of natural cohesion and natural differentiation; (3) the freedom of spirit to transcend natural forms within limits and to direct and redirect the vitalities; (4) and finally the forming capacity of spirit, its ability to create a new realm of coherence and order. All these four factors are involved in human creativity and by implication in human destructiveness. Creativity always involves both vitality and form (in the phrase of Schiller, the *Formtrieb* and the *Stofftrieb,* though the identification of vitality with purely natural dynamic, *Stofftrieb,* betrays Schiller's romantic bias). Nature and spirit both possess resources of vitality and form. The resources of nature may be more negative. The vitalities of nature and its forms may be the indispensable presuppositions of human creativity rather than its active agents; but they cannot be disregarded. In the same manner all the four elements are involved in human destructiveness, though again the vitalities and the unities of nature may play a more negative part in human destructiveness than those of spirit. The natural impulse of sex is, for instance, an indispensable condition of all higher forms of family organization as it is the negative force of destructive sex aberrations. In the same way the natural cohesion of tribe and race is the foundation of higher political creations as also the negative determinant of interracial and international anarchy.

Modern culture, particularly in its controversies between rationalists and romanticists, has illumined various aspects of the problem of vitality and form and of the relative contributions of nature and spirit to both form and vitality. But it has not been able to arrive at any satisfactory solution of the problem because its interpretations of man were derived from metaphysical theories, idealistic and naturalistic, in which one aspect of reality was made the principle of interpretation of the whole. Its theories of man conformed to these metaphysical theories. The idealists identified spirit too simply with reason and reason too simply with God. In idealism the essential man is therefore the rational man and his reason is either the source of both vitality and form or it is the source of the order and form which transmutes the anarchic vitality of nature into genuine creativity. The possibility of spiritual destructiveness cannot be envisaged because spirit as reason is regarded as the very principle of order.

In opposition to idealistic rationalism romanticism emphasizes either the primary importance of natural vitality as a source of human creativity or the significance of the natural unities and forms as sources of order and virtue. But romanticism does not recognize to what degree the freedom of the spirit has entered into the natural vitalities which it extols and to what degree nature's unities and cohesions are subject to necessary revision by human freedom. The problem of vitality and form is thus a cause of never-ceasing debate in which half-truths are set against half-truths. Modern culture is unable to escape the confusion arising from these misconceptions. This confusion must be regarded as part of the decadence of a Christian civilization which, in its uncorrupted form, had a principle of interpretation which transcended both form and vitality. The God of the Christian faith is the creator of the world. His wisdom is the principle of form, the *logos*. But creation is not merely the subjection of a primitive chaos to the order of *logos*. God is the source of vitality as well as of order. Order and vitality are a unity in Him. Even the *logos,* identified with the second person of the Trinity in Christian faith, is more than *logos*. The Christ is the redeemer who reveals God in His redemptive vitality, above and beyond the revelation of the created order. "The world was made by Him" indeed. He is the pattern, the logos of creation. But He is also the revelation of the redemptive will which restores a fallen world to the pattern of its creation.

Concomitant with this faith in the unity of God's will and wisdom, man is interpreted as a unity of will in which human vitality, natural and spiritual, is set under the ordering will of God. No pattern of human reason but only the will of God can be the principle of the form and order to which human life must be conformed. In that sense the Christian faith is set against all idealism and participates in the romantic and materialistic protest against it. The forms, unities and patterns of human reason are themselves involved in historical relativity according to Christianity. The pretension that they are not, is, in the view of Christian faith, one of the primary proofs of the sinfulness of the human spirit which, in its pride, claims unconditioned validity for its systems of logical coherence and rational unities.

On the other hand, natural vitality is not evil of itself; and redemption does not therefore consist in a rational enervation of or transcendence over natural impulse. This emphasis of Christianity is largely responsible for the superior vigour of historical action revealed by western civilization in contrast to the Orient. Romantic vitalism must be regarded as a decadent form of this vitality or as a primitivistic emphasis upon natural forms and unities, once the Christian unity of vitality and form had been destroyed. It must also be regarded as partially a justified protest against the classical view of human nature, a view which insinuated itself into Christian culture. This rationalized Christianity failed to do justice to the natural vitalities in man and tended to attribute all creativity too simply to the capacities of human reason. The romantic protest against classicism pretends to be primarily a protest against Christianity. This was inevitable because idealistic versions of Christianity had become the vehicles of the classical tradition in the Christian era. Nevertheless there are elements in Biblical Christianity which embody what is true in romanticism and refute what is false in idealism and rationalism.

When these elements are separated from the Christian tradition the romantic protest tends to become nihilistic and primitivistic. It degenerates into a nihilistic defiance of all form and order and makes vitality self-justifying. Or it seeks to make primitive and natural forms of order and cohesion the only possible principles of harmony. This ambiguous character of romanticism and vitalism adds to the tragedy of our era; for it aggravates social anarchy in the effort to arrest it. The gradual transmutation of Nazi racialism and primitivism into an imperialism which consciously and unconsciously disavows its earlier theories of racial cohesion, proves how impossible it is for man, in his freedom, to return to the harmless unities of nature or early society.

II

THE RATIONALISTIC VIEW OF HUMAN NATURE

We have previously noted the abiding influence of Platonism upon the classical view of man, and traced the tendency of the classical view to insinuate itself into both the Christian and the naturalistic view of man. In a sense Platonism draws the most obvious and immediately plausible conclusion about the character of human creativity. Since man is creative because he has the capacity to form and reform the impulses of nature into new and more inclusive patterns, the most obvious conclusion is to identify his creative capacity with reason and to define creativity as the capacity to give form and order to a previously given and assumed vitality of nature. Ideally the soul is the natural principle of order in the body. But in the *Phædo* Plato admits that the soul "is almost always opposing and coercing the elements of which she is believed to be composed, in all sorts of ways throughout life, sometimes more violently with the pains of medicine and gymnastics; sometimes more gently; now threatening, now admonishing the desires, passions, fears as if talking to a thing which is not herself." This inner conflict is an obvious fact which proves that man alone, among all animals, stands in contradiction to himself. The possibility for this contradiction is given by the self-transcendence of the human spirit, the fact that man is not only soul, as unity of the body, but spirit, as capacity to transcend both the body and soul. But Plato does not recognize that the anarchic impulses which the "soul" brings into subjection are more than mere bodily impulses. They are impulses which have been given their freedom by the fact that man is spirit as well as nature. Plato thus falsely identifies anarchy with bodily impulse. Answering the question "Whence come wars and fightings and factions?" he answers erroneously, "Whence but from the body and the lusts of the body."

This theory of human nature is of course in harmony with the Platonic metaphysics, according to which creation consists of the activity of divine reason which coerces the formless stuff, previously given, into the order of its ideas and forms. In this aspect of his thought Plato lays the foundation for all those forms of western rationalism in which spirit is identified with reason; and creativity is equated with the capacity to discipline a previously given vitality into order. The relation of reason to impulse is negative. Plato speaks of the "ten thousand cases of opposition of the soul to the things of the body." It is this side of classical thought which prompts the romantic charge that reason enervates and destroys the instincts.

In the Platonic doctrine of ἔρως, we have, however, a different emphasis. *Eros* represents the natural vitalities sublimated rather than repressed by reason. Plato's "intellectual love" is a sublimation and not a repression of natural vitality and desire. In his famous figure of the charioteer and the two horses, representing the three aspects of the soul, reason as the charioteer drives the steeds toward divine beauty "not clogged with the pollutions of mortality." This represents a positive rather than negative relation between reason and nature, though it must be admitted that one of the steeds in Plato's simile is a "crooked lumbering animal, put together anyhow" and so recalcitrant that the charioteer is forced "with a still more violent wrench to drag the bit out of the teeth of the wild steed, cover his abusive tongue and jaws with blood and force his legs and haunches to the ground."[1] In the *Symposium* the relation of intellectual love to natural desire is explained in the following terms: "Those who are pregnant in the body only betake themselves to women and beget children—this is the character of their love; their offsprings will, as they hope, pre-

[1]This simile is recorded in the *Phædrus*.

serve their memory and give them the blessedness and immortality which they desire in the future. But souls which are pregnant—for there certainly are men who are more creative in their souls than in their bodies—conceive that which is proper for the soul to conceive or contain. And what are these conceptions? wisdom and virtue in general." The error in the Platonic analysis is nicely betrayed in the observation that men, who are supposedly pregnant in body only, nevertheless beget children "to preserve their memory and give them the blessedness of immortality," an ambition which hardly belongs to the realm of pure physical impulse.

The Platonic *eros* doctrine has the virtue, however, of qualifying the purely negative definitions of the relation of reason to nature in Platonism and of recognizing nature as a source of vitality subject to rational sublimation. The basic forms of idealism in modern culture, derived from Kant and from Hegel, are either more dualistic or more monistic than Platonism, as qualified by its doctrine of *eros*. In Kantian thought reason furnishes both the forms and the vitality of human creativity; and the vitality of the sensible world is not admitted into the realm of human creativity. The intelligible world furnishes the forms in terms of those universally applicable canons of reason to which the will of man must submit. It furnishes the vitality also; for the vital force of moral action is a reverence for law which borrows nothing from natural vitality but is generated out of the resources of the intelligible world. Kantian idealism throws the impulses of nature more completely into an outer darkness than any form of Greek classicism.

Hegelian idealism on the other hand derives the total dynamic of life, spiritual and natural, from the operations of reason. In Hegelian panlogism, *logos* is, as it were, both *logos* and *eros*. Reason transmutes and tames all the vitalities of human existence. Hegelianism is thus a rationalized version and corruption of the Christian view of the unity of human life and of the dynamic quality of historic existence. In it the Christian idea of divine creation and providence is reduced to categories of rationality; and the Christian concept of the unity of body and soul is interpreted in terms which make all natural impulses derivatives of rational processes.

It is significant that Hegelian idealism arouses the protest of Marxism rather than romanticism. For Marxism is not concerned, as is romanticism, to emphasize the vitality of natural impulses against the peril of their enervation by mind. Its interest is rather to assert the creative power of subrational dynamics, as expressed particularly in collective economic activity, against the imperial pretensions of reason to be the sole source of creativity, pretensions which achieve their most typical expression in Hegelianism.

III

THE ROMANTIC PROTEST AGAINST RATIONALISM

The history of modern culture is, as we have noted, the story of a running debate between those who interpret man as reason and those who seek to explain him in terms of his relation to nature. But the latter history of this culture is not so much a debate between these two schools of thought as a rebellion of romanticism, materialism and psychoanalytic psychology against the errors of rationalism, whether idealistic or naturalistic, in its interpretation of human nature. In this revolt the older naturalism of bourgeois liberalism is more frequently on the side of classicism than on the side of the more robustious modern naturalists of romantic, materialistic and psychoanalytic persuasion. At best it stands between the battle lines. It had never suspected the depth and complexity of vital impulse below the level of reason with which romantic naturalism is concerned.

(*a*) The romantic protest takes various forms. In one of its aspects it is an assertion of the vitalities of nature against the peril of enervation through rational discipline. In this aspect romanticism is concerned to prove, in the words of Schiller, that *Fleiss in den Formen kann zuweilen die massive Wahrheit des Stoffes vergessen lassen.*[1]

[1] In *Letters on the Æsthetic Education of Mankind.*

The final form of this protest is achieved in the thought of Nietzsche, who asserts the "wisdom of the body," the will-to-power (the vitality of what he assumes to be physical impulse), against the discipline of reason. In Nietzsche the romantic protest achieves nihilistic proportions because he regards vitality as self-justifying and sets the robust expression of instincts against all possible forms and disciplines. Originally he was primarily concerned with the protagonism of the "Dionysian" urge against the rational disciplines of a "Socratic" culture.[2] His protests were subsequently directed more and more against Christian discipline, which he probably understood primarily as Schopenhauer interpreted it, and against every type of form and discipline.[3] No complete moral nihilism is of course possible. Some recognition of the principle of form and order is inevitable even in the most consistent vitalism. In Nietzsche this is done in minimal terms by his insistence that the will-to-power of his superman will create aristocratic societies of higher worth than the rationalized societies in which the morality of "herd animals" has gained ascendancy.

(*b*) Another aspect of the romantic-materialistic revolt, and one in which Marxism takes a more primary role than romanticism, is the discovery of the dishonesty of reason in its pretension of mastery over, or creation of, the vital impulses of physical life. This note is somewhat in conflict with the romantic fear of the enervation of impulsive spontaneity and vitality through rational discipline. The gravamen of its charge is that the conscious life of man is the instrument and prostitute of profound unconscious urges for which it provides rationalizations rather than disciplines.

In Freud these impulses are interpreted in individualistic and

[2]In his *Birth of Tragedy*.

[3]To choose but one among many similar reiterations, Nietzsche wrote: "Consciousness of values as norms of conduct is a sickliness and evidence that real morality, that is instinctive certainty of action, has gone to the devil. Strong nations and periods do not reflect about their rights, about principles or actions or about instinct and reason." *Works XV*, p. 166.

sexual terms; in Marx the impulses which the mind rationalizes and for which it provides "ideologies" are regarded as basically collective and economic. They are expressed in the productive relations of society which, according to Marxist doctrine, are the basis upon which the superstructure of culture and philosophy, of religion and morals, is reared. Every cultural achievement is thus but a rationalization of a given equilibrium of power in society in which the dominant class, which controls the equilibrium, fashions philosophical, moral and legal systems to justify its rule and maintain its privileges.

Marx has nothing in common with the simple hedonism of Freudianism. He does not believe that the basic impulses of man's subrational nature are primarily determined by a pleasure-pain strategy. He contends rather that men do seek the good but that they define the good in terms of their own interest. He thus recognizes, as no hedonist can, the profound paradox of human spirituality and morality: that the interests of the self cannot be followed if the self cannot obscure these interests behind a façade of general interest and universal values. This fact, which in Christian theology is regarded as the element of inevitable dishonesty in original sin, becomes in Marxism a tool of class conflict. It is used to transvalue the values of the dominant class and destroy their prestige. Marxism thus tentatively discovers and finally dissipates a valuable insight into human nature. It dissipates the insight because it fails to recognize that there is an ideological element in all human rational processes which reveals itself not only in the spirituality of the dominant bourgeois class, and not only in the rationalization of economic interest; but which expresses itself in all classes and uses every circumstance, geographic, economic and political, as an occasion for man's assertion of universal significance for his particular values. This defect in human life is too constitutional to be eliminated by a reorganization of society; a fact which constitutes the basic refutation of the utopian dreams of Marxism.

The errors in the Marxist analysis must not, however, obscure its genuine and necessary contribution to the understanding of man.

Marxist materialism is a necessary reaction to Hegelian rationalism and to every form of human pretension which glorifies rational man as essential man.

While romanticism is primarily concerned to assert the vitality of nature and to preserve it against the peril of enervation, there are also elements in romanticism which relate it to the Marxist and the Freudian criticisms of reason's pretended mastery over vital impulse. Nietzsche understands the dishonest pretensions of rational consciousness very well. He writes: "Do not deceive yourself: what constitutes the chief characteristic of modern souls and modern books is not the lying, but the innocence which is part and parcel of their intellectual dishonesty. . . . Our cultured men of today, our 'good' men do not lie, that is true; but it does not redound to their honour. The real lie, the genuine, determined honest lie (on whose value you can listen to Plato) would prove too tough and strong an article for them by a long way; it would be asking them to do what people have been forbidden to ask them to do, to open their eyes to their own selves, and to learn to distinguish between 'true' and 'false' in their own selves."[4]

Nietzsche's understanding of the hidden lie, of man's capacity for self-deception, relates him not only to Marx and Freud but to the Christian conception of original sin. But a tentative affinity of thought at this point is quickly transmuted into conflict when Nietzsche seeks to overcome the hidden lie by the robust and "honest" lie. This element in Nietzsche's thought is partly responsible for the brazen dishonesty of contemporary fascist politics. It is needless to point out that the "honest" lie represents no real gain. The dishonest pretensions of human nature are not cured by disavowing the value of truth. We solve no problem by disavowing values to which we are only partially loyal and for which we pretend a greater loyalty than we actually give. We must return to this problem when we consider the problem of sin and truth in terms of the Christian faith (Vol. II, Ch. 7).

[4] *Genealogy of Morals, Third Essay,* Par. 19.

(c) Another aspect of the romantic protest against rationalism and idealism, chronologically prior to those previously considered, disputes the claim of reason to be the organizing and forming principle of human life. In this school of romantic thought the unities and forms of nature are emphasized against the disintegrating and divisive tendencies of conscious reason. Bergson, as a modern representative of this school of romanticism, calls attention to the perfect unity of the primitive tribe and of the ant-hill, in which natural impulse guarantees social cohesion. He regards primitive religion as "a precaution against the danger man runs as soon as he thinks at all of thinking of himself alone," as a "defensive reaction against the dissolvent power of intelligence."[5]

Bergson sees that the unities of natural impulse in primitive life are too narrow. He therefore seeks a way of escape in mystical religion from the closed morality and "static religion" of primitive life. Significantly "static religion" is, for Bergson, a substitute for purely natural organic cohesion, after heightened individual self-consciousness has intervened to destroy this cohesion. His absolute distinction between "closed" religion and "open," that is mystical, religion, the one serving the purpose of preserving the narrow unities and forms of nature, and the other breaking these forms and creating universal forms and values, advances his thought beyond usual romantic primitivism but betrays the inability of romanticism to understand the paradox of the form-creating and form-destroying capacity of human spirituality.[6] The static, that is, tribal, religion of Bergson's conception develops imperial tendencies and pretensions of universality which point to the anarchic and dæmonic capacities of even primitive man. On the other hand Bergson's mystical religion must either forswear all historical interest, as classical mysticism does, or run the danger of insinuating partial and relative historical values into its devotion to the universal. Man is, in other words, never pure nature or pure

---

[5] *Two Sources of Religion and Morality*, pp. 112, 113.
[6] *Cf.* for profound analysis of this paradox, Paul Tillich, *The Interpretation of History*, Part II, Ch. 1.

spirit. All his activities in history are involved in the paradox of creativity and destructiveness, arising from his ability: (*a*) to affirm and to break the unities and forms of natural cohesion; (*b*) to affirm them excessively so that they become forces of anarchy; (*c*) to create higher rational unities and realms of coherence but to corrupt these in turn by insinuating partial and narrow loyalties into them.

In the romanticism of Schopenhauer the protest against the divisiveness of self-conscious reason results in an ascetic rather than primitivistic morality. The unity of vitality (the world as will), which Schopenhauer sets against the diversification and disunity of conscious and rational existence, is not the narrow unity of life with life in primitive social forms but the absolute unity of vitality in the noumenal world, before reason has objectified it into separate entities of will. For Schopenhauer the dæmonic fury of human egotism, its tendency to destroy all forms and unities, is created by the effort of the whole vitality of life, the primal and undifferentiated will, to pour itself through the too narrow vehicle of a single individuality. He writes: "Therefore the will everywhere manifests itself in the multiplicity of individuals. But this multiplicity does not concern the will itself but only its phenomena. The will itself is present whole and undivided in every one of these, and beholds around it the innumerable repeated images of its own nature; but this nature itself, the actual real, it finds only in its inner self. Therefore every one desires everything for himself, desires to possess or at least to control everything." Thus "every individual, though vanishing altogether and diminished to nothing in a boundless world, yet makes itself the centre of the world, has regard for its existence and well-being before anything else in the world—is ready to annihilate the world to maintain its own self, this drop in the ocean, a little longer."[7] For this disease Schopenhauer has no other cure but the denial of the will-to-live, its turning upon itself. He does not however explain from what vantage point the will can gain a fulcrum upon its in-

[7] *The World as Will and Idea* (*English and Foreign Philosophical Library*), p. 428.

dividual expression and press individuality back into its primal and undivided unity. His system of thought leads to essentially Buddhist conclusions; but the Occidental-Christian emphasis upon vitality is too strong to allow these conclusions to emerge in unqualified terms. His redeemed world is undifferentiated will and not, as in Oriental thought, a world in which all vitality has been destroyed.

Obviously the romanticism of Schopenhauer and that of Nietzsche have nothing in common except their common definition of life as being primarily will. In the one case individual vitality is expressed in defiance of all forms and in the other individual vitality is destroyed because its expression in human life is believed to lead inevitably to just such dæmonic fury as Nietzsche glorifies. The negativism which Nietzsche falsely regards as the genius of Christianity is therefore really the Schopenhauerian Buddhistic variant of Christianity.

The contrast between Nietzsche and Schopenhauer sharply focuses the two contrasting strategies of the romantic attack upon rationalism. In Nietzsche the unities and forms which reason creates are regarded either as spurious masters or as perils of the original vitality in man. In Schopenhauer reason is seen as the divisive and disintegrating force of a noumenal unity and form. In other types of romanticism this original unity is conceived as a characteristic of primitive life. The fact that romanticism, in various schools of thought, charges rational self-consciousness with completely contradictory tendencies: with the enervation on the one hand and the accentuation of the natural vitalities on the other; with the creation of too broad and too narrow forms for the expression of the will-to-live or the will-to-power, proves the impossibility of penetrating to the paradox of human spirituality from the perspective of romanticism.

IV

THE ERRORS OF ROMANTICISM

But romanticism errs not only in the contradictory criticisms which it levels at rationalism in general and idealism in particular. It also errs in interpreting the vitality of man, of which it constitutes itself the champion. Its error consists not so much in reducing that vitality to bio-mechanical proportions as bourgeois naturalism tends to do. Its basic error lies in its effort to ascribe to the realm of the biological and the organic what is clearly a compound of nature and spirit, of biological impulse and rational and spiritual freedom. Man is never a simple two-layer affair who can be understood from the standpoint of the bottom layer, should efforts to understand him from the standpoint of the top layer fail. If rationalism tends to depreciate the significance, power, inherent order and unity of biological impulse, romanticism tends to appreciate these without recognizing that human nature knows no animal impulse in its pure form.

Every biological fact and every animal impulse, however obvious its relation to the world below man, is altered because of its incorporation into the human psyche. The freedom of man consists not only, as it were, of the windows of mind which look out from his second story; but also of vents on every level which allow every natural impulse a freedom which animals do not know. Romanticism is therefore wrong in ascribing either the unity or the vitality of animal impulse in man to pure nature. The unity of social cohesion even in the primitive tribe is differentiated from the unity of the wolf pack. Pride of self and contempt of the other is required to maintain it; and social convention enters into the mechanics of its social solidarity. Man has difficulty in controlling the vital force of the sex impulse not because nature has endowed it with an impetus beyond the requirements of human life; on the contrary the sex impulse is controlled with difficulty because it is not imbedded in a total order of natural process in man as in animal life. Each physical impulse, freed of the restraints which hedge it about in nature, can therefore develop imperial tendencies of its own. The difficulty which man experiences in bringing his various impulses into some kind of harmony is therefore not caused by the recalcitrance of nature but occasioned by the freedom of spirit. Even the so-called inertia of nature has spiritual qualities. The anarchy of narrow loyalties in the field of inclusive unities, created by rational freedom, is always partly the consequence, not of the inertia of nature but of the freedom which enables man to accentuate and emphasize natural unities of family and tribe and use them as vehicles of his pride.

The vitality of the total, organized personality is as filled with spiritual factors as the force of specific and particular impulses. Nietzsche seeks to equate his basic concept of vitality, the will-to-power, with purely natural impulse by interpreting the whole of nature as an area of conflict between competing wills.[1] Nietzsche's Zarathustra says: "I am body through and through and nothing else besides. Soul is only a word for something in the body. . . . There is more intelligence in your body than in the highest wisdom. . . . The creating body created the spirit as a tool of its will." Yet pure nature knows no will-to-power. It is informed by the will-to-live, that is by each organism's impulse to survive. The romantic definition of basic natural vitality as "will" is obviously an error prompted by interpreting nature through categories of uniquely human vitality, in which spirit has given natural impulse a conscious organization and direction unknown in animal existence.

Nietzsche's insistence that wisdom, courage and strength are to be found in the purely biological impulses may be a consciously perverse symbolism, prompted by his hatred of rationalism. For in his first great work, *The Birth of Tragedy,* he deliberately relates his interpretation of life to the Dionysian, the form-defying ambitions and lusts of the spirit, which Greek tragedy seeks to interpret. Dionysus is a god. He is spirit and not flesh. The pride and ambition which defy the rule of Zeus in Greek drama are obviously "fruits of the spirit" and Nietzsche makes no effort to interpret them otherwise.

[1]He writes: "Physiologists must beware of regarding the impulse of survival as the basic drive of organic life. All life desires above all to express its power. Life is itself will-to-power. The impulse of survival is only an indirect and frequent consequence of this will." *Kritik und Zukunft der Kultur,* Ch. IV, Par. 13.

One must suspect that, unlike other romantics, Nietzsche sees the distinction between pure physical impulse and lusts of the spirit clearly enough, but obscures it for polemic purposes.

Rousseau, in contrast to later romantics, also knows this distinction. He recognizes pride and the will-to-power as the spiritual corruption of a simpler animal egoism which he defines with a strikingly unbiological term as "self-respect." He would separate this simple animal impulse of survival "which leads every animal to look to its own preservation" from "the purely relative and factitious feeling which arises in the state of society and leads each individual to make more of himself than any other," in other words, from the very will-to-power which later romantics interpret in purely biological terms. But he imagines that reason "can modify by compassion" the natural impulse of survival and thus "create humanity and virtue" and fails to see that the same capacities of spirit would transmute the will-to-live into a will-to-power.[2]

In this interpretation of human vitalities in purely biological terms, Freudian psychology is in perfect accord with romanticism. The basic biological impulses, according to Freudian psychology, are sexual. But the *id* which is their abode is described as "a chaos, a cauldron of seething excitement." It has "no organization and no unified will, only an impulsion to obtain satisfaction for the instinctual needs according to the pleasure principle."[3] The instinctual drives of the *id* may not be highly organized but they have remarkably subtle strategies for escaping the censor of the conscious ego. They are in other words armed with the guile of spirit. The "little we know about it (the *id*) we have learned from the study of dreamwork," Freud declares (p. 103). This is a significant admission which reveals the basic error in Freudian psychology. How remarkable that the world of dreams, that curious twilight zone between consciousness and unconsciousness should be the portal of entry into the meaning of purely biological impulses. Here Freud might have learned

[2] *Social Contract* (*Everyman's Edition*), p. 197.
[3] Freud, *New Introductory Lectures on Psychoanalysis*, p. 104.

something from Job, who seeks to flee into the simplicity of simple biological existence from the strains of self-consciousness. He seeks this asylum in sleep: "But when I said my bed will comfort me, my couch will ease my complaint, then thou scarest me with visions and terrifiest me with dreams." Dreams reveal something quite different from purely biological impulses. Or can it be supposed that animals are troubled by the Œdipus complex and suffer from a guilty conscience because incestuous impulses struggle for expression in the depths of their unconscious?

The whole of Freudian psychology, not in what it declares but in what it implies, is really a striking proof of how remarkably spirit and nature, animal impulse and spiritual freedom, are compounded in human existence. The *id* reveals subtleties and strategies which do not belong to nature; and on the other hand Freud warns that we must remember that "parts of the ego and the super-ego are unconscious" (p. 105). Freudianism pretends to explain all the complexities of man's spirit in biological terms but fails to explain how biological impulses should have become transmuted into such highly complex spiritual phenomena.[4]

V

ROMANTIC ELEMENTS IN MARXISM

The Marxist interpretation of man's subrational life is of course sharply distinguished from the romantic one. Since the emphasis lies not so much upon the impulses of individuals but upon the common

---

[4]An interesting admission by Freud of an error he had made in his calculations points much further than Freud realizes. In reporting on his analysis of the Œdipus complex he declares: "Let it suffice to say that, to our astonishment, the result was the reverse of what we had expected. It is not repression that creates anxiety; it is there first and creates repression" (*Ibid.*, p. 120). If Freud could have realized how basic a concomitant of human freedom anxiety is, and how little it has to do with "external danger" it would have become apparent that all the aberrations with which he deals are not the consequence of the repressions of his "super-ego" but arise out of the very character of human freedom. A

drives of social classes, and since these drives are interpreted primarily in economic terms, the interpretation of man's infrarational life avails itself of materialistic rather than biological concepts. It is never pure nature which furnishes the vitality of historical action, according to Marxist theory. "In nature," declares Engels, "insofar as we disregard the reaction of man upon it, there exist only unconscious blind agents which influence one another and through whose reciprocal interplay general laws assert themselves. . . . On the other hand in social history the active agents are always endowed with consciousness, are always men working toward definite ends, with thought and passion. . . . But this difference does not alter the fact that the course of history obeys general laws. . . . Out of the conflicts of innumerable individual wills and acts there arises in the social world a situation which is quite analogous to that in the unconscious and natural one. The ends of actions are willed; but the results, which really flow from these actions, are not willed, or, insofar as the results seem to agree with the willed ends, ultimately they turn out to be quite contrary to the desired consequences."[1]

This description of historical process, the accuracy of which can

---

modern and very intelligent Freudian, Karen Horney, seeks to prove that both the "will-to-power" which Alfred Adler regards as the basic impulse and the libidinal impulse in Freud must be regarded as derivatives from a more basic anxiety. "Neither Freud nor Adler has recognized the rôle which anxiety plays in bringing about such drives" (*The Neurotic Personality of Our Time*," p. 187). Miss Horney regards Freud's theory as too narrowly biological: "He tends to attribute sociological phenomena to psychic factors and these primarily to biological factors" (p. 28). But Miss Horney in turn has a purely sociological explanation for anxiety: "Modern culture is economically based upon the principle of competition. . . . The potential hostile tension between individuals results in constant generation of fears" (p. 284). In substituting this socio-economic interpretation of the root of anxiety for a purely biological one, Miss Horney comes only slightly nearer to the truth. Modern psychoanalysts might learn much about the basic character of anxiety and its relation to human freedom from the greatest of Christian psychologists, Soren Kierkegaard, who devoted a profound study to this problem: *Der Begriff der Angst*.

[1] F. Engels, *Ludwig Feuerbach* (Duncker ed.), p. 56.

hardly be denied, assigns the vital propulsion of historical creativity to conscious human will and associates the principle of form and direction with a higher suprahuman logic which overrules the wills of men. This logic, the dialectic of history, which must be regarded as a rationalized and mechanized version of the Christian concept of providence, brings Marxism into terms of analogy with Stoic rationalism; but with the difference that its rationalized providence is a law of history and not of nature. It therefore does not make the harmony and unity of nature a premature goal of human activity. Or, stated in other words, Marxism remains within terms of Hegelian rationalism up to this point. It does not deny a rational principle of form. It objects, however, to the Hegelian derivation of the propulsive power of history from pure reason. The propulsive power lies in the dynamics of historical economic relations. Reduced to biological proportions, that would mean in the impulse of hunger. But significantly Marxism does not reduce the vitality of human history to such proportions. It is never simply the hunger impulse, but some organization of society, designed to satisfy it, which determines human thought. "It is precisely the changes in nature brought about through men and not nature as such alone which is the most essential and primary foundation of human thought," declares Engels.[2]

Beginning with this assumption that the vital force of history is an impulse of nature, previously organized and formed by human consciousness in history, Marxism seeks to do justice to both natural vitality and rational freedom in its interpretation of human action and history. It finally fails in this effort only because its metaphysical presuppositions do not allow it to interpret human nature in terms which are consistent with its conception of the relation of natural necessity and spiritual freedom in its social philosophy.

In its social philosophy Marxism is obviously far from interpreting materialism in terms of mechanism. It does not fail to do justice to the element of freedom in human consciousness. "According to the

[2] In *Dialectik und Natur,* quoted by Sidney Hook in *Toward an Understanding of Karl Marx,* p. 165.

materialistic conception of history," Engels writes, "the production and reproduction of life constitutes in the last instance the determining factor of history. Neither Marx nor I ever maintained more. Now when some one comes along and distorts this to mean that the economic factor is the *sole* determining factor, he is converting the former proposition into a meaningless, abstract and absurd phrase."[3] Though increasing misery is, on the one hand, the source of the proletariat's rising revolutionary will, Lenin protests against "subservience to the spontaneity of the labor movement," against "belittling the role of the conscious element" and insists that revolutionists must be judged by the quality of their revolutionary will rather than by their economic circumstance.[4] In the same spirit, Engels recognizes that historical factors, into which conscious human decisions have entered, become in turn determining factors in history, together with purely economic causes. He writes: "An historical factor, once it has been brought into the world by another, ultimately economic fact, is able to react upon its surroundings and even affect its own causes."[5]

According to such interpretations Marxism knows nothing of a simple vitality of nature but only vitalities which are formed partly by a superhuman historical logic and partly by human consciousness itself.

But this position is not consistently maintained. Rational consciousness which plays such a role in historical decisions is nevertheless debased into the role of a mere tool of unconscious forces. Marx declares: "The phantasmagorias in the brains of men are necessary supplements . . . of their material life-processes as empirically establishable and bound up with material premises. Morals, religion, metaphysics and other ideologies and the forms of consciousness corresponding to them here no longer retain a look of independence. They have no history, they have no development; but men in developing

[3]From letter to J. Bloch, quoted by Hook, *ibid.,* p. 179.
[4]Lenin, *Works,* Vol. IV (Engl. trans.), p. 122.
[5]In letter to F. Mehring, quoted by Hook, *ibid.,* p. 342.

their material production and their material intercourse, alter along with this reality of theirs, their thought and the product of their thought. It is not consciousness which determines life but life which determines consciousness."[6]

If the role of consciousness is inconsistently emphasized and depreciated in Marxist social theory, Marxist psychology and epistemology have the virtue of complete consistency, in the interest of materialistic determinism. Its epistemology is crudely sensationalistic and the psychology reduces rational processes to biological dimensions. Engels declares: "Our consciousness and thought, however supernatural they may seem, are only evidences of a material bodily organ, the brain. Matter is not a product of mind but mind is itself the highest product of matter."[7]

Marxism consequently has at least one characteristic in common with the older liberalism. It reveals a voluntarism, however qualified, in its social theory which its psychology does not support. Within the limits of its philosophy it cannot conceive of the real freedom and transcendence of the human spirit. It introduces sufficient inconsistency into its social theory to give a fairly true picture of historical events, falsified only to the degree in which it uses mechanical concepts to comprehend the paradox of historical freedom and historical destiny. But in its view of man's stature, it is forced to deny the depth of spirit in the structure of human personality. It is consequently unable to understand the real character of human evil. The greed of the dominant bourgeoisie, which symbolizes the principle of evil in Marxist theory, is obviously something more than organized hunger. The possessive impulse is itself more spiritual than physical; and it is obviously only the tool for the lust of power in many instances. But Marxism has no understanding of the will-to-power. That is why it can hope for a complete social harmony as soon as the physical needs of all men are equally satisfied—and can construct a new society in Russia in which the will-to-power of a

[6] *Capital* (*Modern Library*), p. 8.
[7] *Ludwig Feuerbach*, p. 64.

new oligarchy expresses itself without social restraint and with tragic fury.

Marxism understands the spiritual character of dishonesty as little as the spiritual character of the possessive and the power impulse. Its great insights into the ideological character of all cultural enterprises are vitiated by its interpretation of consciousness as merely the reflection and the product of material conditions. Marxism, in other words, attributes the human tendency to hide egoistic interests behind ideals of supposedly general validity, to the mere finiteness of the human mind, its dependence upon its environment. But it fails thereby to explain why the human spirit should feel under the necessity of making such pretensions. Why does not man merely seek his own interest as animals do? Precisely because his spirit transcends his impulses of survival sufficiently to envisage a more general realm of value than his own life, he must seem to be loyal to this more inclusive realm even when he is not. The same spiritual capacity which necessitates dishonesty also adds an element of conscious deception to the errors of unconscious dishonesty. Engels recognizes a part of this truth, but only a part, in the words: "Ideology is a process which of course is carried on with the consciousness of the so-called thinkers, but with a false consciousness. The real driving force which moves it remains unconscious; otherwise there would be no ideology."[8] Engels is right in seeing that there is a true consciousness beyond the false consciousness, though that insight does not agree with the general Marxist position that all consciousness is merely the reflection of the balance of interest in which a man stands. But he is wrong in assuming that the rationalization of interest is possible only if it remains unconscious. It is both conscious and unconscious. Marxist political polemic, incidentally, constantly implies a denial of this definition of completely unconscious rationalization, by treating the ideologies of the foe with a moral scorn which only conscious wrongdoing deserves.

[8] In letter to F. Mehring, quoted by Hook, *op. cit.,* p. 341.

VI

THE SOCIAL BASIS OF CONFLICTING THEORIES

The ambiguous and equivocal position of the older rationalistic naturalism in the conflict between idealism and romanticism, psychoanalysis and materialism, has been previously mentioned, and attributed to the covert rationalism in this naturalism. But neither the neutrality of the older naturalism nor the fury of the attack from the more recent romantic and materialistic type of naturalism can be understood in purely cultural terms. The real dynamic of the struggle must be explained in socio-economic terms. The naturalism which dominated eighteenth-century thought was the philosophical expression of rising middle-class life. This class, in the period of its revolt against feudalism, made naturalistic philosophy a vehicle of its appreciation of the vitalities of nature and the relativities of history against the conservatism of a Christian-classical rationalism. This feudal conservatism used the idea of immutable and perennially valid rational-social forms as a support for the society which it had established and the reconstruction of which it resisted. But these same middle classes have now become the dominant forces in modern society, at least in what is still left of bourgeois civilization. They have therefore allowed their sense of vitality and relativity, their understanding of man in his relation to the processes of nature and history, to be subordinated to the rationalistic sense of established form. Since this bourgeois rationalism was indebted to Stoic and Epicurean, rather than Platonic, rationalism from the very beginning, it had never had a strong sense of tension between natural vitality and rational discipline. The real tensions of life were obscured in its thought. It lacked all sense of the tragic while it was rising to power; and it could not consequently be expected to appreciate the tragic conflicts of life, particularly the paradox of creativity and destruction, in the period of its triumph. For this reason the Nietzschean and Marxist protest against both Christianity and rationalism has more affinities with the essential insights of Christianity than the less obviously anti-Christian thought of the bourgeois world.

The romantic and materialistic protest against the pretensions of rational man as essential man and against the perils of the enervation of vitality by reason is borne by the two classes in modern society: the lower middle classes and the industrial workers, who are forced by historical necessity to challenge the economic and political supremacy of the higher middle classes. The lower middle classes express themselves in various forms of romanticism culminating in fascist politics; while the industrial workers gravitate naturally toward the philosophy of materialism and communist politics. These protests gain in plausibility as the power and the prestige of the bourgeois civilization decays; for the truth embodied in a culture maintains itself, and hides the error in which all historical truth is involved, more by the prestige and stability of the civilization in which it is incarnated than by the inherent plausibility of its ideas.

Unfortunately, in spite of the important truths about human nature and history which romanticism and materialism have discovered, these philosophies are becoming instruments of a deepening decadence on the one hand and of abortive regeneration on the other. They do not see the problem of human nature in sufficient depth and therefore remain in the confusion, and sometimes accentuate the errors, in which modern culture has been involved from the beginning. Romanticism asserts both the vitality of nature and its primitive and organic unities against the universalities of rationalism. It therefore either defies every principle of form and order (as in Nietzscheanism) or it emphasizes primitive and inadequate natural forms of unity (*Blut und Boden*). It thus becomes an instrument of decadence, hastening the destruction of bourgeois civilization without offering a way to a new order. Significantly the lower middle classes (individualists who desperately flee from their isolation into unities of race and nation, and persons without a sense of history who rediscover history in terms of primitive tribalism) are the instruments of this decadence.

Marxist materialism on the other hand contains a genuine principle of construction. It is itself a type of rationalism; for it believes in the forming and creative capacity of reason, though not of human reason. The creative human force in history lies below the level of reason in the vital impulses which are expressed in the dynamic of class relations. But it believes that these vital impulses are under the simple control of a higher logic, a dialectic of history. Under the illusion that it can tame the destructiveness of man by a simple change in social organization, that it can purge human creativity of its destructiveness, it prompts modern rebels against an established social and cultural order to a dæmonic fury, assuring them that their destruction will result in a new society in which the vital forces of human existence will be brought under, and remain within, the forming power of a dialectical suprahuman historical logic. If romanticism leads in politics to primitivistic tribalism and concomitant anarchy, Marxist materialism believes that the anarchy of class conflict in modern society can be guided, by those who understand its underlying logic, into a resolution of all conflict.

It is not altogether strange that Marxist politics should result in political realities in Russia, not too distinguishable from the fruits of fascism. For in both cases the paradoxical relation of the creative and the destructive forces in human life is not fully understood; nor is the relation of form to vitality in human creativity fully comprehended. The romantic fascist, conscious of the element of pretension in the culture of bourgeois rationalism, dispenses with all norms and rational principles of order, insisting upon the self-justifying character of the romantic-natural order of race and blood, if only it is expressed with sufficient vitality. The Marxist rebel, also conscious of the element of pretension in the social standards of the rationalist, but oblivious to the inevitability of a degree of pretension in all forms of human spirituality including his own, blandly hopes for a new social order in which human creativity will express itself without destructiveness; and human vitality will be captured and contained in a perfect social harmony. The provisional cynicism of the Marxist is thus given a moral sanction and façade of a too simple principle of universal form and order; just as the deeper cynicism of the romanticist, unable to exist in terms of pure nihilism, is compounded with a too primitive and narrow principle of natural cohesion and order. In both cases the moral façade allows human impulses to express themselves without sufficient discipline. Hence the similarity in the political fruits of these two creeds. It must be admitted, however, that the moral cynicism and nihilism of romantic fascism is more unqualifiedly destructive than the provisional cynicism and ultimate utopianism of communism.

It might be added that the insights of Freudian psychology, considered in terms of social history, may be regarded as elaborations of the basic romantic-materialistic protest against rationalistic interpretations of human nature and history. In the Freudian protest those aspects of a common rebellion are emphasized which are available to the members of the dominant social classes rather than to the lower middle class and proletarian rebels. In Freudianism the dark labyrinths of man's unconscious impulses are illumined in such a way that he loses confidence in the pretensions of rational man and the disciplines of culture and civilization. Since these insights are expressed within the terms of the given social order and do not envisage moral or political alternatives, they lead to a deeper pessimism which despairs not of a particular civilization or culture but of civilization itself. This may be the consequence of the sense of impotence of individuals who are socially too bound to their culture and civilization to allow themselves to envisage alternatives. It may also be a way of deflecting insights into the pretensions of a particular historical form and discipline so that the individual who is still attached to it socially and benefits from its privileges, need not undergo the pain of seeking socio-moral alternatives. In *Civilization and Its Discontents* Freud arrives at conclusions almost as nihilistic in their implications as Nietzsche's. He believes that the discipline of the super-ego (significantly regarded not as transcendent spirit but as a social construct) leads inevitably to complexes and aberrations. Provisionally inclined to draw anarchistic conclusions from these premises, Freud is ultimately unable either to deny the necessity of social discipline or to find a real cure for the psychopathic aberrations which are, in his opinion, inevitable concomitants of such discipline. This insoluble problem leads him into the cul-de-sac of pessimism.

In a sense his pessimistic conclusions reveal the basic spiritual problem of the upper middle classes as clearly as Marxism reveals that of the proletarian classes and fascism that of the lower middle classes. Freudianism is a typical product of the uneasy conscience of that portion of the upper middle class which has discovered the realm of chaos under the pretenses and partial achievements of rational order and discipline, but is unable or unwilling to find a basic solution for the problem which it has discovered.

The fact is, that it is not possible to solve the problem of vitality and form, or fully to understand the paradox of human creativity and destructiveness within the limits of the dimension in which modern culture, whether rationalistic or romantic, views this problem. Within those limits modern culture is forced to choose between four equally untenable viewpoints: (*a*) It exalts destructive fury because it is vital, as in fascism; or (*b*) it imagines a harmony of vital forces in history which the facts belie, as in liberalism; or (*c*) it admits the dishonest pretensions of rational discipline and the reality of human destructiveness provisionally but hopes for a complete change in the human situation through a revolutionary reorganization of society, as in Marxism; or (*d*) it despairs of any basic solution for the problem of vitality and discipline and contents itself with palliatives, as in Freudianism.

CHAPTER III

INDIVIDUALITY IN MODERN CULTURE

INDIVIDUALITY is a fruit of both nature and spirit. It is the product of nature because the basis of selfhood lies in the particularity of the body. The self is most obviously separated from other selves by the simple fact that it is grounded in a physical organism which maintains its discrete existence and has its particular and dated history. Yet nature rises only gradually to the reality of individuality. In the inorganic world substances or forces are integrated and disintegrated so as to produce capriciously "unique" events (the upheaval of a particular mountain, for instance, and its gradual corrosion) but no unique or irreproducible unities. The inorganic world is thus subject to recurrences which can be charted with mathematical exactitude; hence the intimate relation between physics and mathematics.

In the organic world nature rises to the particularity of organisms, characterized by an interdependent and indestructible unity. The plant lives as a unity and its death means the destruction of that particular unity, its component elements sinking back into the inorganic world. On a still higher level animal life achieves a higher measure of discrete particularity, through an organism with a specific centre of unified interdependence, a central nervous system. Through this nervous system the animal achieves a higher degree of separation from its environment; yet its actions are governed by instincts which bind the individual animal to the general characteristics of the species. Variations in colour, size and, possibly, temper are capricious rather than significant and are subject to predictable recurrences. In animal life it is the species rather than the individual which is really unique. The particular animal merely expresses through endless repetition the special life-strategy of the species.

Genuine individuality, embodying both discreteness and uniqueness, is a characteristic of human life. It must consequently be regarded as the product of spirit as well as of nature. Nature supplies particularity but the freedom of the spirit is the cause of real individuality. Man, unlike animal existence, not only has a centre but he has a centre beyond himself. Man is the only animal which can make itself its own object. This capacity for self-transcendence which distinguishes spirit in man from soul (which he shares with animal existence), is the basis of discrete individuality, for this self-consciousness involves consciousness of the world as "the other." The animal knows its particular needs and the particular objects in its environment which satisfy those needs. Its consciousness therefore does not transcend the natural process in which it is involved. Animal consciousness is merely the expression of a central organic unity of an organism in relation to its immediate environment. Human consciousness involves the sharp distinction between the self and the totality of the world. Self-knowledge is thus the basis of discrete individuality.

Human capacity for self-transcendence is also the basis of human freedom and thereby of the uniqueness of the individual. Human consciousness not only transcends natural process but it transcends itself. It thereby gains the possibility for those endless variations and elaborations of human capacities which characterize human existence. Every impulse of nature in man can be modified, extended, repressed and combined with other impulses in countless variations. In consequence no human individual is like another, no matter how similar their heredity and environment. To a certain degree man is free to reject one environment for another. If he dislikes the spiritual environment of the twentieth century he may consciously choose to live by the patterns of the thirteenth century. If he finds his physical environment uncongenial he has the capacity to modify it. The pride of modern man has sometimes tempted him to forget that there are limits of creatureliness which he cannot transcend and that there are inexorable forces of nature which he cannot defy. It is nevertheless important to remember that human spirituality is sharply distinguished from animal existence by the measure of human freedom and the consequent degree of discrete and unique individuality in man.

Human individuality, being a product of spirit as well as of nature, is subject to development. Primitive man is inserted with comparative frictionless harmony into the "primeval we" of group life.[1] He emerges from this group consciousness only gradually as an individual. But what emerges is an original endowment, present from the beginning. The uniqueness of this special endowment is proved not only by the fact that it develops in human life only but by the character of primitive existence. The primitive community is forced to establish certain common usages and methods of restraining natural impulse whereas animal existence, having no freedom, faces no problem of achieving unity. The lack of social freedom in a primitive community is a testimony of the inchoate freedom of primitive man. This freedom makes for a wide variety of the expression of impulses. Since the primitive community lacks the intelligence to achieve unity within variety it must insist upon uniformity, enforcing standards which may have emerged at first by pure historical caprice but which are gradually submitted to crude pragmatic tests of usefulness.[2]

[1]Cf. *inter alia,* Fritz Kunkel, *Charakter, Einzelmensch und Gruppe.*
[2]Efforts to explain the emergence of "mind," that is of human freedom, in purely sociological terms are self-contradictory, sometimes to an amusing degree. Thus Professor George H. Mead, who elaborates a social behaviourist viewpoint, widely held in America, reasons in his *Mind, Self and Society:* "[Our view] must be clearly distinguished from

īī

THE CHRISTIAN SENSE OF INDIVIDUALITY

It would be impossible at this point to trace the development of individuality through the centuries of early civilization. What is important for us is that both the idea and the fact of individuality achieve their highest development in the Christian religion and that modern culture, beginning with the Renaissance, seeks to raise the idea of individuality beyond the limits set for it in the Christian faith by the law of love on the one hand and by the idea of the creatureliness of man on the other; and ends by losing the idea and the fact altogether.

Before tracing this remarkable self-destruction of individuality in modern culture it is necessary to anticipate later chapters by a brief exposition of the Christian view of the individual. Christianity is responsible for a heightened sense of individuality because, according to the Christian faith, the human spirit in its freedom is finally bound only by the will of God, and the secret of its heart is only fully known and judged by the divine wisdom. This means that human life has an ultimate religious warrant for transcending the

the partially social view of mind. According to this view, mind can get expression only within or in terms of an organized social group, yet it is nevertheless in some sense a native endowment, a congenital or hereditary biological attribute of the individual organism. . . . According to this latter view the social process presupposes and in a sense is the product of mind; in direct contrast is our opposite view that mind presupposes and is the product of the social process. The advantage of our view is that it enables us to give a detailed account of, and actually to explain the genesis and development of mind" (p. 224). This viewpoint, which has nothing to commend it but rigorous consistency, sacrifices its consistency when Professor Mead explains in a footnote: "Hence it is only in human society, only within the peculiarly complex context of social relations and interactions which the human central nervous system makes physiologically possible, that minds arise or can arise; and thus also human beings are evidently the only biological organisms which are or can be self-conscious or possessed of selves." P. 235.

custom of tribes, rational rules of conduct, and all general and abstract norms of behaviour. Yet Christian morality at its best is not antinomian because it is bound to the will of God as revealed in Christ: "All things are yours but ye are Christ's," said St. Paul. In the mysticism of Plotinus we find something of the same sense of the transcendence of the human spirit. But mysticism results only in an immediate heightening of the sense of man's spiritual uniqueness and in an ultimate loss of the uniqueness of the individual. Unique individuality is identified with natural creatureliness in mysticism and is therefore regarded as the very root of evil which must be overcome. In the words of Meister Eckhardt: "Thou must be pure in heart; and only that heart is pure which has exterminated creaturehood."[1] According to the Christian faith each individual life is subjected to the will of God. It is this obedience to the divine will which establishes the right relation between the human will in its finiteness and the whole world order as ruled by God. According to mysticism, even when interpreted in Meister Eckhardt's semi-Christian sense, virtue can be achieved only by the annihilation of the individual's will: "The poor man is not he who wants to do the will of God but he who lives in such a way as to be free of his own will and from the will of God, even *as he was when he was not.*"[2] Mysticism in other words insists on the full dimension of height in the human spirit but identifies unique individuality with a creatureliness which must be overcome. Ultimately the individual is absorbed into the divine. In various nature religions the human spirit may transcend a given circumstance but it is bound to the spirit of its tribe, nation, culture or era. Thus only Christianity (and Judaism inasfar as it participates in the prophetic-Biblical tradition and does not allow itself to be bound to a law of a nation) sees and establishes the human spirit in its total depth and uniqueness.

Naturally this heightened sense of individuality is not without its

[1]*Meister Eckhardt,* comp. by Franz Pfeiffer, trans. by C. deB. Evans, Vol. I. p. 48.
[2]*Ibid.,* p. 220.

perils. If the religious sense of responsibility to God and contrite humility before God is weakened, Christian individuality may become the source of anarchy. This may explain some of the cruel and dæmonic aspects of the history of western Christendom.

During the whole period of medieval Catholicism Christian individuality never came to a consistent expression. This was partly due to socio-economic causes. The agrarian-feudal economy of medievalism was in still intimate relation to the previous tribal unity of the Teutonic tribes; and social complexity had not yet forced the full emergence of individual consciousness. On the other hand the Catholic religion prevented the emergence of a high sense of individuality, partly by the amalgam of Greek rationalism in its theology which subjected the individual to the universal rules of the natural law; and partly by its religious authoritarianism which interposed the religious institution between the soul and God. Since the will of God which transcended all rational abstractions was nevertheless completely interpreted by an historic institution, involving casuistic applications of general norms to specific situations, the individual always remained conscious of the general categories, social, moral and political of which he was an exemplar. He never expressed himself fully as an individual.

The modern sense of individuality therefore begins on the one hand in Protestantism and on the other hand in the Renaissance. From the standpoint of the typical modern, Protestantism and Renaissance are merely two different movements in the direction of individual freedom, the only difference between them being that the latter is a little more congenial to the modern spirit than the former. The real significance of the two movements lies in the fact that one represents the final development of individuality within terms of the Christian religion and the other an even further development of individuality beyond the limits set in the Christian religion, that is, the development of the "autonomous" individual. It is this autonomous individual who really ushers in modern civilization and who is completely annihilated in the final stages of that civilization.

The heightened sense of individuality in Protestantism is expressed theologically in the Reformation principle of the "priesthood of all believers." The emphasis lies not so much upon the individual's capacity to know the truth as upon his indivisible responsibility to God, and upon an assurance of mercy for his sins which no institution can mediate, if individual faith is wanting. Involved in this conception is a strong sense of the peril of meaninglessness in the freedom of human spirituality which only the individual's direct relation to God can overcome. Luther puts the matter in a typically robust illustration: "When you lie upon your deathbed you cannot console yourself by saying 'The pope said thus and so.' The devil can drill a hole through that assurance. Suppose the pope were wrong? Then you will be defeated. Therefore you must be able to say at all times: 'This is the word of God.'"

The Protestant Christian sense of the individual's immediate responsibility to God implies and develops a strong anti-legalism; not only because it is felt that no particular external norm can guarantee the quality of motives which prompt the conforming deed, but also because legal and rational moral norms are regarded as inadequate guides of virtue amidst the infinite possibilities of good and evil which every action presents in both its internal and external facets. Protestantism significantly places the rational concept of the "natural law" in a more insignificant position than in Catholic thought. It has too strong a sense of the individual occasion, and the uniqueness of the individual who faces the occasion, to trust in general rules. The will of God is the norm, the life of Christ is the revelation of that will, and the individual faces the awful responsibility of seeking to do God's will amidst all the complexities of human existence with no other authoritative norm but that ultimate one.

Despite the religious profundity of this conception of a human spirit, which transcends all circumstances and norms so much as to be responsible to no one but God, Protestantism has frequently contributed to the anarchy of modern life by its inability to suggest and to support relative standards and structures of social virtue and political justice. It has thus indirectly contributed to the romantic defiance of all rational and traditional norms in the sphere of politics and morals. In that sense the profoundest expression of Christian individuality is itself partly responsible for the anarchy of modern life. The individual who is admonished, "All things are yours but ye are Christ's," may, in a period of religious decay, easily lose the sense of ultimate religious responsibility expressed in the words, "But ye are Christ's," and remember only the law-defying implications of the first part of the dictum: "All things are yours."

III

THE IDEA OF INDIVIDUALITY IN THE RENAISSANCE

If Protestantism represents the final heightening of the idea of individuality within terms of the Christian religion, the Renaissance is the real cradle of that very unchristian concept and reality: the autonomous individual. The Renaissance emphasis upon individual autonomy is partly a reaction to Catholic authoritarianism. Its part in the emancipation of learning from the tyranny of religious dogmatism is so great that most of the uncritical devotees of the "scientific spirit" of modernity have not discerned the peril in this idea of autonomy. Ostensibly Renaissance thought is a revival of classicism, the authority of which is either set against the authority of Christianity or used to modify the latter. Yet classic thought has no such passion for the individual as the Renaissance betrays. The fact is that the Renaissance uses an idea which could have grown only upon the soil of Christianity. It transplants this idea to the soil of classic rationalism to produce a new concept of individual autonomy, which is known in neither classicism nor Christianity.

The nexus between the Christian and the Renaissance individual is not the Protestant idea of the individual's sole responsibility to God but the medieval mystical idea of the infinite potentialities of the human spirit. A straight line leads from Meister Eckhardt to Nicholas of Cusa, one of the great creative spirits of the Renaissance, via the "Brothers of the Common Life" and John Ruysbroek.[1] To the mystics who followed Eckhardt, Christ was the symbol of the divine potentialities of man. "The Father," wrote Eckhardt, "is begetting his Son unceasingly and furthermore I say he begets me his Son, his very own Son." There is no upper limit for the potentiality of the human spirit: "The just soul is like to God, by the side of God, on a level with God, not under nor yet over."[2]

In the thought of Eckhardt this divine potentiality does not make for individuality but ultimately destroys it. How the Renaissance transmutes the idea of man's divine potentiality into the concept of individuality and uniqueness is beautifully illustrated in the prayer of Nicholas of Cusa: "Thy true countenance is without any limitations and has neither quantitative nor qualitative, neither temporal nor spacial qualities; for it is the absolute form, the countenance of countenances. . . . Every countenance which gazes into Thine own therefore beholds something not different from its own because it beholds its own truth. . . . O Lord, how wonderful is Thy countenance which must be conceived as youthful by the youth, as mature by the man and as old by the old. In every countenance the countenance of countenances is veiled as in a mystery. Unveiled it cannot be seen until man enters that secret and dark stillness which is beyond all countenances and in which nothing is left of the knowledge and concept of countenances."[3] This is a remarkable sentiment of a Christian mystic standing at the threshold of the Renaissance. He feels and expresses no opposition to Christian thought; yet the Renaissance emphasis upon unique individuality breaks the bounds of both Christian and mystic thought. The prophetic-Biblical note of God as the judge of men "whose thoughts are not our thoughts" is wholly lost in the contemplation of God who is the fulfillment of each unique human individuality but not the judge of its sin. The

[1]*Cf.* Ernst Cassierer, *Individuum und Kosmos in der Philosophie der Renaissance,* p. 35.
[2]*Op. cit.,* Vol I, p. 162.
[3]From *De visione Dei,* Ch. 6. Quoted from Cassierer, *op. cit.,* p. 34.

mystic concept of an eternity which finally swallows up all individuality is significantly retained as an afterthought.

Giordano Bruno is less Christian and more neo-Platonic than Cusa and his primary interest is in the divine potentiality of the human spirit rather than its uniqueness. His concern is to assert that man "becomes a god through intellectual contact with that transcendent object and has no thought but of divine things and shows himself insensible by that which ordinary men feel most of all."[4] But in him also the mystical doctrine of the divine potentiality of the human spirit is subtly made the bearer of the new doctrine of the uniqueness of human individuality: "Poetry is not born in rules; rules are derived from poetry. But how are true poets to be recognized? By their song."[5] Bruno arrives at the idea of a completely autonomous individual; and this idea inspires his resistance to authoritarianism. The source of the soul's duty lies in the soul's own nature. And this nature is not some general law of rationality as in Stoic or Kantian thought. An inner light guides every man. Since for Bruno infinity of space is a symbol of the infinite potentialities of the soul, it might be supposed that the doctrine of immortality would be important for his thought. His attitude toward the hope of immortality is, however, ambiguous. Here his pantheism overcomes his strong sense of individuality, just as Nicholas of Cusa crowns his view of the fulfillment of each individuality in the divine with a mystic vision of "dark stillness" which swallows up all individuality.

On this point the Renaissance anticipates the tendency of later rationalism to destroy the concept of individuality; and proves that it has a less tenable ground for this concept than the Biblical religion. In Biblical religion the idea of individuality is preserved in the hope of the resurrection. The thoroughly unrational idea of the "resurrection of the body" has the virtue of expressing a dark and unconscious recognition of the sources of individuality in nature as well as in spirit. Without the particularity of the body the spirit of man is easily lost in the universality of divine spirit, in the undifferentiated being

[4]William Boulting, *Giordano Bruno*, p. 178.   [5]*Ibid.*, p. 180.

of eternity. Naturally a consistent rationalism finds it impossible to affirm eternal significance for the particularities which have emerged in temporal existence.

The Renaissance concept of individuality, rooted in the idea of the greatness and the uniqueness of man, naturally implies his liberty. It was therefore one of the primary interests of Renaissance thinkers to prove that divine foreknowledge does not circumscribe human liberty of action or invalidate man's creative role in history. The freedom of the will was a problem of primary interest to the thinkers of the Italian Renaissance.[6]

The Renaissance emphasis upon individuality is obviously not prompted by any simple set of ideas, for it presses various philosophies into its service. The sober, sceptical and earth-bound Montaigne expresses the idea as fully as the God-intoxicated Bruno. Montaigne's primary interest is in the endless variety and relativity of forms in which human life expresses itself. He is scornful of every effort to bring these multifarious forms under general categories, whether moral, legal or rational. Montaigne's sense of individuality is partly an extension of this interest in variety. Human beings exhibit an endless diversity: "Plutarke saith in some place that he findes no such great difference between beast and beast, as he findeth diversitie between man and man. . . . I could finde in my heart to endeare upon Plutarke; and say there is more difference between such and such a man than there is diversitie between such a man and such a beast."[7] In a sense Montaigne pays tribute to individualization inasfar as it is the fruit of natural history, of the diversity of geographic and historical circumstances; while the leaders of the Italian Renaissance are primarily interested in the individualization of spirit, in the mystery of introspection and the art of self-portraiture. Yet Montaigne is equally interested with Petrarch and the Italian Renaissance in the art of autobiography, boasts that, "I present myself standing

[6] Two treatises of Italian thinkers are particularly devoted to this theme: Pompanazzi's *De fato, libero arbitrio et praedestinatione* (1436) and Valla's *De libero arbitrio* (1520).

[7] *The Essays of Montaigne*, trans. by John Florio, Book I, Ch. XLII.

up and lying down, front and back, right and left and in all my
natural attitudes,"[8] and justifies the importance of such a study by
the conviction that "every man has in himself the whole form of
human nature."[9] The idea, despite Montaigne's naturalism, is really
derived from a combination of nominalistic and mystic thought and
we find it more fully elaborated in the romanticism of a later period,
in Goethe's and Schleiermacher's view of the individual as a revelation of the universal.

IV

BOURGEOIS CIVILIZATION AND INDIVIDUALITY

Since the Renaissance doctrine of individuality avails itself of various
philosophical and theological ideas, Christian and classic, pantheistic
and naturalistic, mystic and nominalistic, we cannot attribute the
emergence of the doctrine to the potency of any of these ideas. Its
cultural roots lie, paradoxically, to a larger degree in the Christian
religion itself than in the classical influences which corroded the
medieval form of the Christian religion. But this does not answer the
question why this particular emphasis should have come to expression at just this time and should have dominated the culture of
modernity until a recent date. The answer must be found in the
social rather than in the purely cultural history of the era. The rise
of the sense of individuality corresponds with the emergence of
the commercial, the bourgeois classes. The Italian city states were
the seed-plot of bourgeois culture. While the rest of Europe was still
under the dominance of the landed aristocrat, the Italian cities provided the rising business man with the opportunity of forming his
own culture; and it is significant that the forms of this culture
anticipated in many particulars the culture of the Enlightenment
which signalized the triumph of the business man in the rest of
Europe.

The business man developed a form of economic power which

---

[8]*Ibid.*, Book III, Ch. 8.   [9]*Ibid.*, Book III, Ch. 2.

depends upon individual initiative and resourcefulness rather than upon hereditary advantages; and which creates dynamic rather than static social relationships. It naturally sees human history as a realm of human decisions rather than of inexorable destiny. In the same way it regards nature as an instrument rather than the master of the human will. The rise of the natural sciences was at first merely a by-product of this sense of human self-reliance, for nature was regarded merely as the mirror of the greatness of 'man. But as science gradually contributed to man's actual mastery of natural forces it gave a new impetus of its own to the idea of human self-sufficiency.

This pride and power of man, who surprises himself by the influence of his decisions upon history and the power of his actions upon nature, who discovers himself as a creator, is subtly merged with the Christian idea of the significance of each man in the sight of God. It is indeed a this-worldly version of the latter. That is proved by the fact that neither the non-Christian nations nor the Catholic nations, in the culture of which Christianity was modified by classical influences, participated in any large degree in the dynamics of modern commercial-industrial civilization. It is proved also by the bewildering complexity of interactions between Protestant religious individualism and the secular individualism of bourgeois culture. The modern individual could not have arisen in any but a Christian culture; yet the progress of his thought destroys the Christian basis of individuality; and the development of his civilization destroys the social and economic basis for the effectiveness of individual initiative, resourcefulness and decisive action.

The social and economic destruction of individuality is a consequence of the mechanical and impersonal elaborations of a commercial culture which reach their culmination in the development of an industrial civilization. Modern industrialism pushes the logic of impersonal money and credit relationships to its final conclusion. The processes of production and exchange, which remain imbedded in the texture of personal relationships in a simpler economy, are gradually emancipated and established as a realm of automatic and rationalized relations in which the individual is subordinated to the process. The same historical dynamic, which corrodes the traditional social unities, loyalties and inertias of medieval agrarianism and thus allows the business man to emerge and assume a creative role in history, continues the process of corrosion until communities and nations are bound together primarily by ties of mechanical inter-dependence and tempted to conflict by the frictions which this inter-dependence entails.

Inevitably the early vision of capitalistic philosophers (Adam Smith) of a process of production and exchange which would make for automatic harmony of interests is not realized. Man controls this process just enough to disturb its harmony. The men who control and own the machines become the wielders of social power on a vaster scale and of more dynamic quality than previous history has known. They cannot resist the temptations of power any more than the older oligarchies of history. But they differ from previous oligar-chies in that their injustices are more immediately destructive of the very basis of their society than the injustices of a less dynamic age. Modern society is consequently involved in processes of friction and decay which threaten the whole world with disaster and which seem to develop by a kind of inexorable logic of their own, defying all human efforts to arrest the decay.

The bourgeois individuals who initiated the age with such blithe confidence in the power of human decisions over historical fate see an historical process unfold in which individuals appear as hapless and impotent victims of an ineluctable destiny. Most of their de-cisions tend, in fact, to aggravate the difficulties of modern society; for those who hold significant economic and social power make decisions in the interest of maintaining their power so that the de-cisions fall into a general pattern of social anarchy. Thus the bour-geois individual who emerges from the social cohesions, restraints and inertias of medievalism and imagines himself master of nature and history, perishes ingloriously in the fateful historical necessities and the frantically constructed tribal solidarities of the age of decay.

The lower middle classes fashion this solidarity out of corrupted forms of romanticism; and the proletarian class conceives a philosophy of history which supplants the bourgeois sense of historical mastery with a sense of submission to historical destiny. Unfortunately this class is sufficiently corrupted by the mechanism of the age to deny what is true as well as what is false in bourgeois individualism. Therefore it conceives of historical destiny in mechanical terms and tries to comprehend history in terms of "laws of motion."

V

THE DESTRUCTION OF INDIVIDUALITY IN NATURALISM

The mistake of the Renaissance was to overestimate the freedom and the power of man in history. This power and freedom in history is ambiguous. His actions and decisions are less unique than he imagines them to be. That is proved by the fact that the character of his decisions can be averaged statistically and predicted with fair exactitude according to the circumstances in which they are made. His privileges and securities, or lack of them, his mode of work, whether rural or urban, are fairly determinative in prompting his decisions. They are, moreover, less potent in determining historical direction than the Renaissance had assumed. They are in each instant compounded with, modified, and frequently overruled by partly conscious and partly unconscious hopes, fears and strivings of his fellow creatures. Frequently his own conscious decisions are overruled by his own unconscious fears. In such a moment the individual remains individual only in the highest reaches of transcendent spirit, where he is able to defy historical fate and appeal to a realm of meaning in which his life has a significance which history denies. Yet his ability to make decisions in history depends upon this same sphere of transcendence. Any individual who is completely immersed in historical process is naturally forced to accept the moral, political and religious norms which the caprices of that process make definitive at a given moment. His ability to challenge the victory of a culture or civilization depends upon a measure of freedom over its presuppositions and credos. Frequently, and possibly usually, this means complete dependence upon some competing philosophy of life and history. This dependence may sustain him as long as his own cause still promises a measure of success. An irrevocable defeat of a socio-historical cause which gives meaning to the life of the individual must create a complete sense of meaninglessness unless the individual is sustained by a religion which interprets such defeats from the aspect of the eternal.

If, however, the eternity to which the individual flees is an undifferentiated realm of being, which negates all history and denies its significance, the individual is himself swallowed up in that negation, as the logic of mysticism abundantly proves. Consequently it is only in a prophetic religion, as in Christianity, that individuality can be maintained. This faith alone does justice to both the natural and the spiritual bases of individuality. Since it takes history seriously, it affirms the significance of the distinctive character achieved by each individual within the tensions of historical existence, tensions which have their root in natural, geographic, economic, racial, national and sexual conditions. But since it interprets history from the standpoint of the eternal (*i.e.* since it sees the source and end of history beyond history) it gives the individual a place to stand within a world of meaning, even when and if the particular historical movement into which he is integrated should fail completely.

No philosophy or religion can change the structure of human existence. That structure involves individuality in terms of both the natural fact of a particular body and the spiritual fact of self-transcendence. But religions and philosophies have an important bearing upon the possibility of the ego, maintaining itself in such a position of transcendence. Naturalistic philosophies may (and in modern nationalism do) destroy individuality by emphasizing consanguinity and other natural forces of social uniformity as the only basis of meaning; spiritualistic philosophies may on the other hand prompt the transcendent ego (spirit) to flee from history with all its perils of particularity and its uncertain vicissitudes into a realm of meaning which negates history and individuality. Both the concept and reality of individuality are a characteristic product of the Christian faith because it is only within terms of that faith that an individual may stand both inside and outside of history. He stands inside because his faith affirms the meaningfulness of history and he stands outside because his faith asserts that history is borne by an eternal will.

The history of modern culture has a peculiar pathos because the same Renaissance tendencies which had asserted and modified the Christian idea of individuality in such a way as to accentuate the individual's historic power and freedom unduly finally led to the destruction of any genuine concept of individuality. Since this cultural destruction of individuality was both antecedent to and synchronous with the development of a mechanical civilization, it may have contributed to, and in turn been influenced by, the latter's practical annihilation of individual freedom and uniqueness.

The logic of this annihilation can be simply stated. The naturalistic portion of modern culture seeks to reduce the whole dimension of spirit in man to an undifferentiated "stream of consciousness" if indeed it does not seek to reduce consciousness itself to purely mechanical proportions. Idealism on the other hand is interested in spirit as mind; but it generally dissipates the distinctive qualities of human selfhood in the abstract universalities of mind. Between them the reality of selfhood remains in constant peril.

Beginning with Thomas Hobbes a fairly consistent denial of the significance of selfhood, certainly of transcendent individuality, runs through the empirical and naturalistic tradition. In Hobbes's sensationalistic psychology and materialistic metaphysics there is no place for human individuality. His individuals are animal natures whose egohood consists in the impulse of survival. Human reason serves the purpose of extending this impulse beyond the limits known in nature, thus creating conflict between equally valid claims of various individuals; but there is no rational transcendence over impulse where these claims might be arbitrated. They must therefore be suppressed and arbitrated by a political power, which is the sole source of all morality. Fear of mutual destruction prompts the historical decision, the social contract, by which government comes into being. But this decision lies significantly in a mythical past. This philosophy may be regarded as symbolic of the curious vagary of naturalistic thought which, throughout subsequent ages, interprets human history as the consequence of pure human decisions without having an individual with sufficient transcendence over the social process to make significant decisions.

John Locke is sufficiently influenced by Cartesian thought to define the self as a "thinking thing" and to insist on personal identity as a reality: "The self is that conscious thinking thing whatever substance made of (whether spiritual or material, simple or compounded, it matters not) which is sensible or conscious of pleasure or pain, capable of happiness or misery and so is concerned for itself so far as that consciousness extends. . . . This consciousness is annexed to and the affection of one individual immaterial substance."[1] His concern is to prove that it is consciousness and "not numerical substance" which accounts for identity. This description of consciousness would apply with equal validity to animal consciousness, *i.e.,* to any organism with a central nervous system. But Locke's theory of self-consciousness follows Descartes, in insisting upon self's intuitive awareness of itself: "If I doubt all other things that very doubt makes me perceive my own existence and will not suffer me to doubt that."[2] This awareness of the existence of the self is hardly an adequate description of the whole dimension and uniqueness of human self-consciousness. It is nevertheless a recognition of human uniqueness found in neither Hobbes nor Hume, particularly when Locke's argument for the existence of God as related to his idea of the thinking self is taken into consideration. The idea of self-awareness does not, however, enter into Locke's conception of personal identity from which he explicitly subtracts the element of self-tran-

[1] *An Essay Concerning Human Understanding,* Book II, Ch. 25.
[2] John Locke, *ibid.,* Book IV, Ch. 9.

scendence involved in memory: "Could we suppose any spirit stripped wholly of all its memory or consciousness of past actions" this "would make no variation in personal identity."[3] It is perfectly true that this would make no difference in the identity of what may be called the "empirical ego," the self as involved in the unity of the body. But it is precisely the pure or transcendent ego, which stands above consciousness as the consciousness of consciousness and which expresses itself in terms of memory and foresight, which is the real centre of human personality.

David Hume, in this as in other respects, purges Locke's thought of Cartesian elements in the interest of a purer empiricism and denies the possibility of any awareness of the ego: "When I enter most intimately into what I call myself I always stumble on some particular perception or other, of heat or cold, light or shade, pain or pleasure. I can never catch myself at any time without a perception and can never observe anything but the perception."[4] This observation may be regarded as a valid criticism of Descartes' conception of a pure ego which subsists within itself without relations. The ego is always the centre of relations so that it is perfectly correct to observe, "I do not catch myself without a perception"; but Hume's final conclusion, "and can never observe anything but a perception," is obviously not a logical deduction from the former observation; nor is it in accord with the facts. Yet even if Hume were correct in his interpretation of the empirical ego as a stream of impressions it would still be pertinent to inquire into the nature of the "I" which he implies when he says: "When I enter most intimately into what I call myself." It is reality of that "I" as subject which challenges the validity of all purely empirical interpretations of the ego.[5]

However great may be the achievements of modern psychology, it is not unfair to say that the psychological systems which remain within the confines of the naturalistic tradition never get beyond

[3]*Ibid.,* Book II, Ch. 25.
[4]David Hume, *A Treatise of Human Nature,* Vol. I, Part IV, Sec. 6.
[5]*Cf.* C. D. Broad, *The Mind and Its Place in Nature,* Ch. 6.

the varying interpretations of Hobbes, Locke and Hume. Behaviouristic psychology is an elaboration of Hobbes's position. The position
of Locke is taken by all "dynamic" psychologists who emphasize the
initiative of the ego and the unity of its processes. Of those who follow Hume it may suffice to present one particularly illustrious example: William James. James denies both the unity of consciousness
and the transcendent ego: "If there were no passing states of consciousness, then indeed we might suppose an abiding principle, absolutely one with itself, to be the ceaseless thinker in each of us. But
if the states of consciousness be accorded as realities no such 'substantial' identity in the thinker need be supposed. Yesterday's and
today's states of consciousness have no substantial identity, for when
one is here the other is irrevocably gone. . . . The logical conclusion
seems to be that the states of consciousness are all that psychology
needs to do her work with. Metaphysics or theology may prove the
soul to exist; but for psychology the hypothesis of such a substantial principle of unity is superfluous."[6]

James's assurance, that the hypothesis of a substantial principle of
unity is superfluous, is an interesting example of an ever recurring
effort of psychology as a natural science (and of all natural science
for that matter) to affirm its character as a pure science by its
metaphysical scepticism. But, unfortunately, this scepticism leads to
implied metaphysical credos. An object which has both surface and
depth cannot be correctly interpreted in terms of one dimension
when it has in fact two. That is why science which is only science
cannot be scientifically accurate. This is particularly true of *Geistes-
wissenschaft* in contrast to physical science. It is more particularly
true of psychology which deals with a dimension of depth in the
human spirit, transcending the scientific method. Every rigorous
effort to remain within the confines of pure science reduces psychology to physiology, and physiology to bio-mechanics. The ultimate
unity and transcendence of the human ego are indeed beyond pure

[6]*Psychology, Briefer Course,* p. 203. James sums up his position in the
succinct phrase: "The thoughts themselves are the thinkers." P. 216.

science. Yet it is a necessary undertaking to inquire into the realities of that region "beyond."[7]

Psychological theory of the past decades exhibits, of course, a wide variety of schools which range from mechanistic to organismic interpretations, and from atomistic and behaviouristic interpretations of consciousness to interpretations which emphasize configurative wholeness (*Gestalt* psychology). It is interesting, however, that naturalistic psychology rises with difficulty to the concept of organic unity in consciousness and only occasionally makes the self and self-consciousness an object of particular study.[8] The real profundities of self-consciousness, the complex problems of personality, in the breadth of its relations to the world of nature and history on the one hand and in the depth of its dimension as self-conscious ego on the other, are the concern of only those schools of psychology which frankly leave the confines of natural science and regard psychology as a cultural science, which means that their psychological investigations are guided and prompted by philosophical and therefore semi-religious presuppositions.

VI

THE LOSS OF THE SELF IN IDEALISM

Long before the emergence of a particular "cultural science" emphasis in psychology, philosophy had of course dealt with the problems

[7]This is a fact more generously recognized in European than in American psychological schools. *Cf.* G. E. Stout, *Manual of Psychology:* "The last word about freedom lies with neither psychology nor ethics. Its full discussion involves an examination of the relation of thought and will of the individual mind and the reality of the universe. This relation is utterly inexplicable from the point of view of any finite science. The more closely and conscientiously we seek to explain it by the ordinary categories of any special science the more plain it becomes that so regarded it is a miracle, indeed the miracle of miracles. Psychology cannot explain how it is possible that an individual can consciously mean or intend something." P. 735.

[8]One of the few studies of self-consciousness is by M. W. Calkins, *A First Book in Psychology.*

of human consciousness and sought to interpret the nature of the human spirit and its relation to nature, history and the universe. The significant fact from the standpoint of our study is that, while naturalistic philosophies tend to reduce the human ego to a stream of consciousness in which personal identity is minimal, idealistic philosophies tend in varying degrees to identify consciousness with mind and to equate the highest reaches of conscious mind with a divine or absolute mind, or at least with some socially or politically conceived universal mind.

The self is primarily an active rather than contemplative organic unity. But it is more than an organic unity. It has the spiritual capacity of transcending both the natural process in which it is immersed and its own consciousness. As consciousness is the principle of transcendence over process, so self-consciousness is the principle of transcending consciousness. Idealistic philosophy always has the advantage over naturalism in that it appreciates this depth of human spirit. But it usually sacrifices this advantage by identifying the universal perspective of the self-transcendent ego with universal spirit. Its true self therefore ceases to be a self in a true sense and becomes merely an aspect of universal mind. This self of idealistic rationalism is both less and more than the real self. It is less in the sense explained by Kierkegaard: "The paradox of faith is this that the individual is higher than the universal, that the individual determines his relation to the universal by his relation to the absolute, not his relation to the absolute by his relation to the universal."[1] In idealism the true self is that reason which relates the self to the universal. But since the true self in idealistic thought is neither more nor less than this universal reason, the actual self is really absorbed in the universal. The actual self is, however, less, as well as more, than reason; because every self is a unity of thought and life in which thought remains in organic unity with all the organic processes of finite existence. Failure to recognize this latter fact falsifies the prob-

[1]From *Fear and Trembling,* quoted by W. Lowrie, *Kierkegaard,* p. 264.

lem of sin in all idealistic philosophy. Sin becomes the inertia of man's "animal nature" in contrast to the universalities of mind.[2] Idealism fails to recognize to what degree finiteness remains a basic characteristic of human spirituality. The self has in other words a narrower natural base and a higher and narrower pinnacle of spirit than the breadth of perspective of its rational processes. The self is a narrow tower with a wide view. In idealism the self is lost in the breadth of its view; and the breadth of its view is identified with ultimate reality. Idealism conceives the self primarily as reason and reason primarily as God.[3]

It could not be maintained that all forms of idealism lose the individual in universal mind. There are pluralistic forms of idealism with a strong sense of individuality as for instance those of Leibnitz and Herbart. There are furthermore forms of idealism strongly under the influence of Christian theism in which the pantheistic tendencies of idealism are challenged.[4] Yet the indictment is true with reference to all forms of absolute idealism. In Kant's critical idealism the self is not lost in universality but maintains a shadowy existence between the universality of the intelligible self and the particu-

[2]Bosanquet uses the betraying phrase "animal nature" consistently. See, inter alia, *Philosophical Theory of the State,* p. 143.

[3]James Ward defines reason as follows: "Reason is concerned with the world in its totality either as being a system or as having a meaning." *The Realm of Ends,* p. 418. The error of all rationalism is to identify "totality as being a system" with "totality as having a meaning." The system in totality, its "logos," is the structure and coherence as analysed by reason. The Christian faith asserts that totality cannot be comprehended or exhausted in this structure and that therefore meaning cannot be identified with rational coherence. The validity of this distinction is attested by the fact that the self stands outside its own rational processes sufficiently to ask whether its reason can comprehend the structure of reality and whether that structure includes the totality of reality. In terms of our simile the self is a high tower which not only looks at the world to understand its "what" but beyond the world to inquire into its "why." The former may give clues to the latter but can give no final answer in regard to the "why."

[4]As for instance in James Ward's profound theistic pluralism expounded in *The Realm of Ends.*

larity of the empirical (*i.e.,* the sensible) self. It exists by virtue of its acceptance of the moral law of the intelligible self.[5] It is the unvarying tendency of idealistic thought thus to translate the Christian moral paradox "who loseth his life will find it" into an ontological one and to claim that true selfhood and true individuality are something quite other than actual selfhood and individuality. Bosanquet states the logic of absolute idealism perfectly in the words: "God, it has been said, could only impart Himself by imparting a self; and we may urge the complementary truth that the self can only be a self by being THE self."[6] This conclusion is arrived at in steps which may be most succinctly stated in a series of brief quotations: (1) "We want to think of the individual primarily as mind."[7] (2) "The best general description of mind is to call it a world; and a world which constitutes a mind is not limited according to hard and fast rules—there are many conditions under which a single mind is constituted by and controls more bodies than one."[9] (3) The individual is therefore "a world that realizes, in a limited matter, the logic and the spirit of the whole, and in principle there is no increase of comprehension and no transformation of the self, that is inconceivable as happening to him."[9] (4) "Individuality is positive and constructive; and if self-consciousness is negative against the idea of the self, individuality must not be construed in analogy with it. . . . Its exclusiveness judged by the principle of its self-identity is a defect."[10]

It is instructive to observe how near Bosanquet's rationalism is to the classical mystical belief that selfhood as such is evil. Mysticism hopes that the self will be swallowed up into an undifferentiated divine unity and Bosanquet hopes it will be lost in the attainment of a rationality "beyond the reflective consciousness of self

---

[5]Hegel's theory of the transmutation of the individual of "unhappy consciousness" to the "changeless consciousness" which is its "true self" is analysed more fully in Ch. IV.

[6]Bernard Bosanquet, *The Principle of Individuality and Value,* p. 342.

[7]*Ibid.,* p. 282.   [9]*Ibid.,* p. 288.

[8]*Ibid.,* p. 287.   [10]*Ibid.,* pp. 285-6.

and not-self." In terms of the Christian faith man always remains a creature and there is, therefore, no possibility of achieving a position "beyond the reflective consciousness of self and not self." The ideal possibility is a loving relationship between the self and the other self in which alienation but not discrete identity is transcended.

The impossibility of doing justice to the Christian idea of self-hood within terms of absolute idealism is perfectly illustrated in Josiah Royce's heroic efforts to do so in his *The World and the Individual,* particularly because he tries so desperately to preserve an adequate concept of individuality. Royce rightly insists that he does not lose the self as mysticism does; and most of his polemic is directed against the mystic doctrine of an ultimate undifferentiated reality in which all individuality is lost. His Absolute is a mosaic which requires the variety of individuality for its richness. But by individuality Royce means merely particularity and not the distinctive depth of spirit which distinguishes human individuality from the particularity of nature: "Any finite idea is so far a self; and I can, if you please, contrast my present self with my past or my future self, with yesterday's hopes or with tomorrow's deeds, quite as genuinely as with your inner life or with the whole society of which I am a member, or with the whole of life of which our experience of nature is a hint, or, finally with the life of God in its entirety."[11] Finite self-hood is thus in the same category as any finite reality while ultimate selfhood is nothing short of the Absolute. For the Absolute is defined as "our very own selfhood in fulfillment."[12] Royce is less concerned about the exclusive aspect of self-consciousness, as a root of evil, than is Bosanquet. He writes: "But if one persists in asking, 'What has sundered us from the Absolute and narrowed our consciousness as it is narrowed?' my only general answer is, Such narrowness must find its place within the Absolute life in order that the Absolute may be complete. One needs then no new principle to explain why, as Plotinus asked, the souls fell away from God. From the point of view of the Absolute the finite beings never fall away. They are

[11]*The World and the Individual,* Book II, p. 273.   [12]*Ibid.,* p. 302.

where they are, namely in and of the Absolute Unity."[13] Put in terms of Christian doctrine, Royce's view is that each man is Christ from the perspective of God while he is both creature and sinner only from his own perspective. Or it might be fairer to say that in his view man's finiteness is sinful only as its exclusiveness and discreteness have not yet been transcended in a rational perspective which logically culminates in God's perspective.[14] Thus universal mind is the "Christ" of redemption.

The logic of idealism in annihilating individuality probably achieves its most consistent (and absurd) expression in the thought of the Italian idealist, Gentile—who "denies reality to the thinking personality."[15] Thus the circle is completed and the idealist agrees with the radical empiricist that "the thoughts themselves are the thinkers."

That the idealistic denial of individuality has immediate socio-political as well as ultimate cultural significance in the history of western civilization is proved by the fact that it has made a tremendous contribution of dubious worth to the modern deification of the state. Whenever idealism seeks to escape the undifferentiated Absolute of mysticism and desires to prove that it is a counsel of historical action rather than pure contemplation, its rational universal becomes embodied in that very dubious god, the modern state. In the words of Bosanquet: "The idea is that in it [the state] or by its help, we find at once discipline and expansion, the transfiguration

[13]*Ibid.*, p. 303.

[14]How little, despite his fervent Christian piety, Royce understands the basic presuppositions of the Christian view of man is revealed in his equating of the Biblical and the Platonic view of man: "The two doctrines which, in European history, have most insisted upon the duality of our higher and our lower selfhood, *viz.* the ethical teachings of Plato and the Gospel of the Christian church, have agreed in insisting that the higher self is a resultant of influences which belong to the eternal world and which the individual man is powerless to initiate. In Plato's account of the process of the soul's release from its own lower nature, the eternal Ideas appear as the supernatural source of truth and goodness. . . . Christianity has emphasized, in all its essential teachings, a similar source and meaning in speaking of the higher self." *Ibid.*, p. 251.

[15]Roger Holmes, *The Idealism of Giovanni Gentile*, p. 175.

of partial impulses and something to do and care for such as the nature of the human self demands. If, that is to say, you start with a human being as he is in fact and try to devise what will furnish him with an outlet and a stable purpose capable of doing justice to his capacities, a satisfying object of life, you will be driven by the necessity of the facts as far as the state and perhaps further."[16] The state in its inclusiveness and stability represents the "real will" of man against his momentary and fragmentary will. The irony of this deification of the state by Hegel and his followers is that the whole dæmonic fury of the state, as a partial historical force, more universal than the individual but less universal in either value or extent than it claims to be, is not recognized by the same idealists who are so very sensitive to the fragmentary and finite aspects of individual existence. In Bosanquet's thought this tremendous problem of the sinfulness of the state as a partial reality which claims absolute value is both expressed and veiled in the innocent qualification, "you will be driven by the necessity of the facts as far as the state, AND PERHAPS FURTHER." A great deal further, one is bound to say, and not probably but certainly.[17]

From the Christian point of view the whole pathos of original sin expresses itself in the pretensions of idealistic thought. The individual is sacrificed to the rational universal conceived in either political or trans-historical terms, for fear that anything less than this total immolation will result in the chaos of particularity and the sin of "exclusive consciousness." But human pride manages to reclaim the supposedly divine and universal reason as not only some universal humanity but as a very particular type of universality conforming to the prejudices and perspectives of the philosopher who conceives

[16]*The Philosophical Theory of the State,* p. 140.
[17]E. F. Carritt calls attention to the frequency of similar qualifying clauses in Bosanquet's thought upon the state, declaring that his thought differs from Hegel's primarily "by the insertion of these rather puzzling qualifications." They are puzzling, for if taken seriously they invalidate the whole thesis on the state held by this school of idealism. *Morals and Politics,* p. 160.

it. James Ward describes this anti-climactic note in Hegel's thought with nice irony: "The earth, he says, is the truth of the solar system —the sun, the moon and the stars are only conditions for the earth which they serve. Among the continents of the earth Europe, by virtue of its physical characteristics, forms its consciousness, its rational part, and the centre of Europe is Germany. With his own philosophy he has the sublime assurance to think that philosophy closes; and in the restoration of Prussia under Stein he thought the culmination of the world's history was attained."[18]

VII

THE LOSS OF THE SELF IN ROMANTICISM

Naturalism loses the individual because it does not view life in sufficient depth to comprehend the self-transcendent human spirit. This spirit is a reality which does not fit into the category of natural causality which is naturalism's sole principle of comprehending the universe. Idealism on the other hand discovers the human spirit in its height of transcendence over natural process, but loses it again because the uniqueness and arbitrariness of individuality do not conform to its pattern of rationality, which is its sole principle of interpreting reality. It is instructive in this connection that even a pluralistic philosophy such as Leibnitz's, with its emphasis upon individuality, can find a place for the individual only by seeing it as a microcosmic type of the macrocosm. This interpretation allows a monist such as Christian Wolff, with a slight shift of emphasis, to reabsorb the individual into, and identify him with the universal. In the words of Kierkegaard's criticism of the idealistic passion for a universal system: "Before the system completes itself, every scrap of existence must have been swallowed up in the eternal; there must not be the slightest remainder; not even so much as a bit of dingle-dangle represented by the Herr Professor who writes the system."[1]

[18]*The Realm of Ends,* p. 180.
[1]From "Unscientific Postscript" as trans. by David E. Swenson in *Anthology of Modern Philosophy,* edited by D. S. Robinson, p. 649.

Within the alternatives of naturalism and idealism the modern man therefore faces either the submergence of both his individuality and his spirit in natural causality or the submergence of his individuality and the deification of his spirit in the universality of reason. Confronted with annihilation through either abasement or deification it is natural that modern culture should have sought for another way out. It found this way in romanticism.

Beginning with Paracelsus in the period of the Renaissance, romanticism has played a subordinate role in the history of modern culture only to emerge in these latter days as the conqueror over rationalism. (The political form and tool of romanticism is fascism.) Romanticism was originally par excellence the champion of the individual. It seemed to understand him in terms of both the particularity of his physical existence and the unique self-knowledge of his spiritual life, because the romantic tradition is curiously compounded of Rousseauistic primitivism and Christian pietism. It seeks, speaking symbolically, wisdom in the body rather than the mind (Nietzsche). But it does not reduce man's physical existence to bio-mechanical proportions. On the contrary it means by body: feeling, imagination and will; which it prefers to spirit, particularly to spirit conceived as mind. The romantic quarrel with rationalism is really a quarrel of the soul (psyche) in its intimate union with the body, against spirit conceived as ratio. But through its union with Christian pietism romanticism emphasizes the self-transcendence of this soul to such a degree that its body-soul is really spirit in its particularity and individuality in contrast to spirit as rational and universal. This "spiritual" emphasis is frequently more implicit than explicit. Nietzsche, for instance, extols animal cruelty; but the cruelty he values is not known among animals but only among men with their spiritual endowments. Furthermore he explicitly rejects the animal's impulse of self-preservation and substitutes the spiritual "will-to-power"[2] as the basic vitality of existence.

From the standpoint of the vicissitudes of the idea of individuality

[2]*Beyond Good and Evil*, p. 20.

in modern culture the significance of romanticism is that it exalts the individual more unqualifiedly, but also loses him more quickly and completely than any form of rationalism. The process of this romantic destruction of individuality can be briefly summarized as follows: Individuality is directly related to the eternal source of meaning and given unqualified significance, while idealism ascribes significance to the individual only as he is related to a rational universal value of history. Sooner or later the romantic thinker must, however, recoil from the pretension of this purely individual self-deification; and all but Nietzsche do recoil. They seek to increase the plausibility and reduce the pretension of this self-glorification by looking for the "larger individual"; which they find in the unique nation. This collective individual then supplants the single individual as the centre of existence and the source of meaning. In the pursuit of seeking something larger than a person as his centre, the romanticist meets the absolute idealist who is intent upon finding something a little more domestic and manageable than the Absolute as the source of value. Thus they both discover the nation, approaching it from different sides but agreeing in its deification. The fact that race or nation is a form of universality which seems small enough to be regarded by the romantic as a fruit of natural cohesion (consanguinity) and large enough to seem to the idealist a characteristic product of reason, unites these two forces, romanticism and idealism, behind the single historical reality of the nation. This is the cultural, though not the socio-political, history of modern nationalism in a nutshell. The compound of Nietzschean and Hegelian philosophy in modern nationalistic hysterias is an expression of this strange unity. In the earlier history of romanticism the two elements were combined in the thought of Fichte.

This brief summary requires further explication. The romantic tradition, we have said, is compounded of Rousseauistic primitivism on the one hand and Christian pietism on the other. From Rousseau it derives its emphasis on the non-rational forces in human personality, upon emotion, imagination and will. From pietism it takes the sense of the individual's unmediated relation to God; which it secularizes so that the individual is not only directly related to God, as the source and centre of meaning, but becomes himself self-justifying and autonomous.

The romantic sense of individuality is primarily derived from what the pietist, Spener, termed the "spiritual priesthood." This pietist version of the Protestant principle of the priesthood of all believers differs slightly but significantly from the original. Luther's religious individualism emphasized the person's unique relation of faith and responsibility to God.[3] The pietists emphasized, rather, the possibility of a direct and unmediated experience of unity between the believer and God. "Every individual," said Zinzendorf, "experiences the Saviour himself and does not merely repeat what he has heard from his neighbor."[4] This sense of individuality in pietism represents a compound of Protestant and mystic doctrines. But it is more Protestant than mystic because the union of the individual with God is achieved through the grace of God rather than man's own mystic discipline. It is through "the overwhelming greatness and power of the Lord" that the individual rises "from the natural state to the state of grace" (Francke). Pietistic individualism is therefore not subject to the peril of mystic dissipation of individuality. On the other hand it easily transgresses the bounds which orthodox Protestantism sets between creature and Creator. Zinzendorf's assurance, "I am a part of the body of Christ," analogous to Meister Eckhardt's "Christ is born in me" becomes the basis of the romantic doctrine of individuality. Schleiermacher, who represents the historical nexus between pietism and romanticism, states this doctrine in the words: "Thus there dawned upon me what is now my highest intuition. I saw clearly that each man is meant to represent humanity in his own way, combining its elements uniquely so that it may reveal itself in every mode, and all that can issue from its womb be made actual in the

[3]Luther said: "Just as no one can go to Hell or Heaven for me, so no one can believe for me and so no one can open or close Heaven or Hell for me and no one can drive me either to believe or disbelieve."

[4]Otto Uttendoerfer, *Zinzendorf's Weltbetrachtung,* p. 305.

fullness of unending space and time. . . . But tardily and only with great difficulty does man reach the full knowledge of his individuality. He does not always dare to look toward it as his ideal but prefers to turn his eyes upon the good which he possesses in common with humanity. Clinging to this common element with love and gratitude he often doubts whether he should separate his individual self from it."[5]

One might imagine that romanticism thus possessed an ideal understanding of the natural and the spiritual sources of individuality, the particularity of the body and the ultimate self-transcendence of the human spirit. But individuality has an even shorter life in romanticism than in rationalism. In rationalism the whole history of an era is required to dissipate the Renaissance emphasis upon individuality. In romanticism individuality is emphasized and lost in the life of practically each romantic thinker. Rousseau quickly subordinates the will of the individual to the mystically conceived general will, regarded as the real will of the individual. The German romantics are interested in originality and uniqueness rather than in individuality, despite their protestations. Schleiermacher explains that by "individuals" he means not solely persons but also collective individuals, such as races, nations and families. "It is precisely individuality," wrote Schlegel, "which is the eternal and original thing in men. . . . The cultivation and development of this individuality, as one's highest vocation, would be a divine egoism."[6] But Schlegel finds in the uniqueness of the landscape of his homeland as significant an expression of individuality as in individual personality. Herder, Lavater, Haman and Novalis were interested in the æsthetic implications of this doctrine of the significance of variety. "The more personal, local, peculiar (*eigentuemlich*) of its own time a poem is," said Novalis, "the nearer it stands to the centre of poetry."[7]

The romantic doctrine led to complete relativism in morals, religion and politics. "Why," said Schleiermacher, "in the province of

[5]*Monologen*, II. Trans. by Horace L. Friess (Open Court Publ. Co.).
[6]*Athaneum*, III, 15.
[7]Quoted by Arthur O. Lovejoy, *The Great Chain of Being*, p. 307.

morals does this pitiable uniformity prevail which seeks to bring the highest human life within the compass of a single lifeless formula?"[8] a sentiment which betrays the affinity between Schleiermacher and Nietzsche and foreshadows the latter's doctrine of the autonomous and self-justifying superman with his contempt for the morality of the herd.

The romantic relativism in religion and politics is particularly instructive because it clearly reveals the romantic logic, leading to the self-destruction of the concept of individuality. The religious relativism of the romantics reveals how far they have departed from the Christian faith. In Christianity the unique individual finds the contingent and arbitrary aspect of his existence tolerable because it is related to, judged and redeemed by the eternal God, who transcends both the rational structure and the arbitrary facts of existence in the universe. In romantic religion the unique and arbitrary character of existence does not find its limit and fulfillment in an eternal world of meaning but expresses itself in terms of limitless pretension. "Every man," said Lavater, "has his own religion just as he has his own face and every one has his own God just as he has his own individuality."[9] While Schleiermacher does not follow this position through to such an explicit polytheism, he thinks in the same terms. "If you want to grasp the idea of religion as a factor in the infinite and progressive development of the World Spirit then you must give up the vain and empty desire for one religion," he declares.[10] This means that the only meaning of life is that there should be a variety of meaning. This untenable position, beginning in relativism, ends in nihilism. Here again Nietzsche follows the logic, suggested by Schleiermacher, to its consistent conclusion: "The world seen from within, the world defined and designated according to its 'intelligible character,' would simply be the 'Will to Power' and nothing else. What? Does this not mean in popular language:

[8]*Reden ueber die Religion*, II.
[9]*Antworten auf wichtige und wuerdige Fragen und Briefe weiser und guter Menschen*, Vol. I, p. 66.
[10]*Reden ueber die Religion*, p. 36.

God is disproved but not the devil? On the contrary, my friends! On the contrary! And who the devil also compels you to speak popularly?"[11]

If religious relativism is the natural and logical expression of the romantic doctrine of individuality with its premium upon uniqueness and variety as such, its worship of the unique race and nation is an inevitable effort to reduce the pretension and absurdity of this polytheism, an effort which leads tragically to the complete annihilation of the idea of individuality in personal terms. An individual cannot bear to make himself the centre of meaning without qualification. Inevitably he must seek support from something greater and more inclusive than himself. Schleiermacher follows this idea perfectly in supplementing his conception of individuality. A few months after the battle of Jena he wrote to a friend: "Remember that the individual cannot stand alone, cannot save himself, if that in which each and all of us are rooted—German freedom and German feeling—be lost; and it is these that are threatened."[12]

The whole pathos of the unique individual projecting himself into eternity in one moment and in the next seeking for a simple historical companionship which will give his life meaning, is expressed in Schleiermacher's confession: "Here alone [in nationality] can you make yourself completely understood; here you can turn to a common feeling and to common ideas; for your ideas are welcomed by your brothers because they are the same as yours."[13] In other words national self-worship is a more plausible form of self-glorification than mere emphasis upon individual uniqueness. The nation, said Schleiermacher, is the largest form of individuality as the person is the smallest. Yet in this largest form one finds oneself writ large, for the ideas of "your brothers are the same as yours." Following the same thought Herder rather regretted that Christianity had supplanted the more primitive polytheistic religions of the nations fearing that

[11]*Beyond Good and Evil*, p. 52.
[12]Fredericka Rowan, *Life of Schleiermacher as Unfolded in His Autobiography and Letters*, Vol. II, p. 55.
[13]*Predigten*, Vol. I, p. 230.

with them "they lost their spirit and character, yes, I might say, their language, their heart, their country and their history."[14]

While Nietzsche maintains a more resolute individualism and bravely asserts the autonomous individual against every type of universality, including the relative universality of the nation, it is significant that in these latter days even his version of romanticism has been subtly compounded with nationalistic furies. There is a peculiar irony in the fact that his doctrine, which was meant as an exposure of the vindictive transvaluation of values engaged in by the inferior classes, should have itself become a vehicle of the pitiful resentments of the lower middle classes of Europe in their fury against more powerful aristocratic and proletarian classes.

In the heyday of romanticism when the individuality of the nation begins to devour the individuality of the person, an effort is still made to remain within terms of a nationalistic polytheism and not to claim ultimate value for the national uniqueness which the individual appreciates simply because it is his own. Herder states this doctrine held by all the classical romanticists: "Ministers might deceive each other, political machines might be set against each other until one destroys the other. Not so with fatherlands. They lie peacefully side by side and aid each other as families. It is the grossest barbarity of human speech to speak of fatherlands in bloody battle with each other."[15] Unfortunately the barbarity which Herder deplores belongs inevitably to human history and not merely to human speech, and precisely because it is not possible to appreciate and preserve particularity and uniqueness, whether individual or national, without either bringing it into relation with, and subordination to, an ultimate centre and source of meaning or allowing the particular and the unique value to become itself an imperialistic centre of ultimate meaning.[16]

The full force of this development has become apparent only in

[14]K. Pinson, *Pietism as a Factor in the Rise of German Nationalism*, p. 92.
[15]Pinson, *op. cit.*, p. 101.
[16]Professor Lovejoy describes this development accurately: "A type of national culture valued at first because it was one's own, and because the

our own day. But it betrayed itself even in the heyday of classical romanticism. Thus Schleiermacher neatly anticipates the anti-Semitism of modern German fascism with the idea that, once a people has arrived at a high stage of development, "it is disgraceful for it to embrace within it anything alien to it, no matter how excellent that may be in itself, for its particular character it has received from God Himself."[17] This domestic imperialism is in strange contradiction with Schleiermacher's boast: "This *is* the very thing of which I chiefly boast, that my love and friendship always have so high a source that they have never been blended with any vulgar sentiment, have never been the offspring of habit or tender feeling but ever an act of purest freedom oriented toward the individuality of other human beings. . . . Wherever I notice an aptitude for individuality, inasmuch as love and sensitiveness its highest guarantees are present, there also I find an object of my love."[18]

In the thought of Fichte, who represents a watershed between rationalism and romanticism, the universalism of rationalism becomes compounded with the nationalistic particularism of romanticism and issues in a dubious spiritual national imperialism. For Fichte conscience is the voice of the universal and the eternal in man: "Thus do I approach that Infinite Will; and the voice of conscience in my soul, which teaches me in every situation of life what I have here to do, is the channel through which again His influence descends upon me. That voice made audible by my environment and translated into my language is the oracle of the Eternal world which announces to me how I am to perform my part in the order of the spiritual universe, or in the Infinite Will who is

---

conservation of differences was recognized as good for humanity as a whole, came in time to be conceived of as a thing which one had the mission to impose upon others, or to diffuse over as large a part of the world as possible. Thus the wheel ran full circle; what may be called a particularistic uniformitarianism, a tendency to seek to universalize things originally valued because they were not universal, found expression in poetry, in a sort of philosophy in the policies of great states and the enthusiasm of their populations." *The Great Chain of Being,* p. 313.

[17]*Predigten,* Vol. IV, p. 75.   [18]*Monologen,* p. 46.

Himself that order."[19] On one side of his thought the demands of the Eternal drive Fichte into otherworldliness: "My sensuous existence may, in the future, assume other forms but they are just as little true to life as its present forms. By that resolution I lay hold on eternity and cast off this earthly life and all other forms of sensuous life which may yet lie before me in futurity, and place myself far above them. I become the sole source of my own being and its phenomena, and henceforth, unconditioned by anything about me, I have a life in myself."[20]

On this side of Fichte's thought he belongs in the category of the idealists, previously discussed, who transmute the human ego into virtual divinity, to unconditioned reality. But the vicissitudes of his contemporary Germany prompt Fichte to follow the romantics in their emphasis upon the nation as the largest individuality of history. Conscious of the very relative character of national existence in comparison with the infinite will which is, for him, the true source of value, Fichte conveniently discovers that only Germans can love their nation especially, without treason to the heavenly vision of the universal, because Germany as the birthplace of philosophy is a true instrument of universal values.[21]

[19]Fichte, *The Vocation of Man,* trans. by William Smith (Open Court Publ. Co.), p. 152.

[20]*Ibid.,* p. 142.

[21]*Cf.* "The German patriot wishes that this purpose be attained first of all among the Germans and that from them it spread to the rest of mankind. The German can desire this, for in his midst philosophy has had its origin and it is developed in his language. It may be assumed that in that nation which has had the wisdom to conceive philosophy there should also rest the ability to understand it. Only the German can desire this, for only he, through the possession of philosophy and the possibility given thereby to understand it, can comprehend that this is the immediate purpose of mankind. This purpose is the only possible patriotic goal. Only the German can therefore be a patriot. Only he can, in the interest of his nation, include all mankind. Since the instinct of Reason has become extinct and the era of Egotism has begun, every other nation's patriotism is selfish, narrow, hostile to the rest of mankind." Quoted by H. C. Engelbrecht in *Johann Gottlieb Fichte,* p. 98 (Columbia University Press).

Romanticism is, in short, nearer to the Christian faith and a more perverse corruption of it than idealistic philosophies. It understands, with Christianity, the unique and arbitrary character of historical existence and knows that the rational universalities of philosophical systems can neither fully contain nor comprehend the unique quality of the givenness of things nor yet themselves fully transcend the contingency and irrationality of existence. With Christianity, it consequently discovers the subtle self-deception and hypocrisy of rationalistic cultures, which manage to insinuate their own particular values into the supposed impartial and objective universal values of their philosophy. (The relation of democracy to bourgeois culture for instance.) It is this penetration into the dishonesty of rational idealists which establishes affinities between Nietzsche and classical Christianity, despite his strictures against the "bad conscience" which Christianity prompts. On the other hand romanticism, at least in its fully developed Nietzschean form, substitutes brutality for hypocrisy and asserts the particular and unique, whether individual or collective, in nihilistic disregard of any general system of value.

The simple fact is that both the obviously partial and unique and the supposedly universal values of history can be both appreciated and judged only in terms of a religious faith which has discovered the centre and source of life to be beyond and yet within historical existence. This is the God who is both Creator and Judge revealed in Biblical faith. Romanticism understands the fact of the goodness of creation in all of its particularity and individuality; but it has no perspective beyond creation. Idealism seeks a rational point of vantage beyond the created forms and thus has an inchoate conception of God as judge. But the judge turns out to be man's own reason. The individuality of man is tenable only in a dimension of reality in which the highest achievements of his self-knowledge and self-consciousness are both known and judged from a source of life and truth beyond him.

The idea of individuality which is the most unique emphasis of modern culture, is thus a tragically abortive concept, which cannot be maintained as either fact or as idea within the limits of the cultural presuppositions of modernity. The social history of modern life moves from the individualism of the early commercial period to the collectivism of industrialism. The individual who emancipates himself from the social solidarities of agrarian feudalism and the religious authoritarianism of medievalism is, within a brief span of history, subjected to the mechanical solidarities of industrial collectivism. His revolt against this collectivism betrays him into the even more grievous tyranny of primitive racialism and imperial nationalism.

The cultural history of modern man gives him no resource to modify or to defy this tendency. In idealism the individual is able to transcend the tyrannical necessities of nature only to be absorbed in the universalities of impersonal mind. In the older naturalism, the individual is able for a moment to appreciate that aspect of individuality which the variety of natural circumstances creates; but true individuality is quickly lost because nature knows nothing of the self-transcendence, self-identity and freedom which are the real marks of individuality. In romantic naturalism the individuality of the person is quickly subordinated to the unique and self-justifying individuality of the social collective. Only in Nietzschean romanticism is the individual preserved; but there he becomes the vehicle of dæmonic religion because he knows no law but his own will-to-power and has no God but his own unlimited ambition.

Without the presuppositions of the Christian faith the individual is either nothing or becomes everything. In the Christian faith man's insignificance as a creature, involved in the process of nature and time, is lifted into significance by the mercy and power of God in which his life is sustained. But his significance as a free spirit is understood as subordinate to the freedom of God. His inclination to abuse his freedom, to overestimate his power and significance and to become everything is understood as the primal sin. It is because man is inevitably involved in this primal sin that he is bound to meet God first of all as a judge, who humbles his pride and brings his vain imagination to naught.

CHAPTER IV

THE EASY CONSCIENCE OF MODERN MAN

OUR introductory analysis of modern views of human nature
has established the complacent conscience of modern man
as the one unifying force amidst a wide variety of anthropological conceptions. In the words of T. E. Hulme: "All thought since
the Renaissance, in spite of its apparent variety, forms one coherent
whole. . . . It all rests on the same conception of the nature of man
and all exhibits the same inability to recognize the meaning of the
dogma of original sin. In this period not only have its philosophy, its
literature and its ethics been based upon this new conception of man
as fundamentally good, as sufficient, as the measure of things; but a
good case can be made out for regarding many of its characteristic
economic features as springing entirely from this central abstract
conception."[1]

The most surprising aspect of the modern man's good conscience
is that he asserts and justifies it in terms of the most varied and
even contradictory metaphysical theories and social philosophies.
The idealist Hegel and the materialist Marx agree in their fundamental confidence in human virtue, disagreeing only in their conception of the period and the social circumstances in which and the
method by which his essential goodness is, or is to be, realized. The

[1]*Speculations*, p. 52.

93

romantic naturalist Rousseau agrees with the rationalistic naturalists of the French enlightenment, though in the one case the seat of virtue is found in natural impulse unspoiled by rational disciplines and in the other case it is reason which guarantees virtue. Among the rationalistic naturalists again there is agreement upon this point whether they are hedonistic or Stoic in their conceptions and whether they believe that reason discovers and leads to a natural harmony of egoistic impulses or that it discovers and affirms a natural harmony of social impulses.

The whole Christian drama of salvation is rejected ostensibly because of the incredible character of the myths of Creation, Fall, Atonement, etc., in which it is expressed. But the typical modern is actually more certain of the complete irrelevance of these doctrines than of their incredibility. He is naturally not inclined to take dubious religious myths seriously, since he finds no relation between the ethos which informs them and his own sense of security and complacency. The sense of guilt expressed in them is to him a mere vestigial remnant of primitive fears of higher powers, of which he is happily emancipated. The sense of sin is, in the phrase of a particularly vapid modern social scientist, "a psychopathic aspect of adolescent mentality."

The universality of this easy conscience among moderns is the more surprising since it continues to express itself almost as unqualifiedly in a period of social decay as in the eighteenth- and nineteenth-century heyday of a bourgeois culture. The modern man is involved in social chaos and political anarchy. The Marxist escape from this chaos has developed in Russia into a political tyranny of unparalleled proportions. Contemporary history is filled with manifestations of man's hysterias and furies; with evidences of his dæmonic capacity and inclination to break the harmonies of nature and defy the prudent canons of rational restraint. Yet no cumulation of contradictory evidence seems to disturb modern man's good opinion of himself. He considers himself the victim of corrupting institutions which he is about to destroy or reconstruct, or of the confusions of ignorance which an adequate education is about to overcome. Yet he continues to regard himself as essentially harmless and virtuous. The question therefore arises how modern man arrived at, and by what means he maintains, an estimate of his virtue in such pathetic contradiction with the obvious facts of his history.

One possible and plausible answer is that the great achievement of modern culture, the understanding of nature, is also the cause of the great confusion of modern man: the misunderstanding of human nature. Nature is a one-dimensional world of seemingly necessary effects consequent upon particular causes. Though a profounder observation may reveal that no observable cause is a sufficient explanation of a subsequent effect and that each effect is but one of many possible consequences in the causal chain, this metaphysical scruple, pointing to a realm of freedom even in nature, has given but slight pause to a culture which is primarily informed by the methods and presuppositions of physical science. Whatever the ultimate problem of the relation of *nous* to *physis,* of spirit to nature, the modern man is certain that the two scientific methods of detailed empirical observation and mathematical calculation give him knowledge of the unique and particular event on the one hand and of the regularities and dependable recurrences of nature on the other.

The two methods are the sources of his two sometimes conflicting and sometimes mutually supporting assurances of security. The empirical method points to nature as a realm of order, having its own laws which cannot be fathomed by a priori deductions. Let man disavow his proud pretensions and follow the course of nature patiently! Here modern culture follows Epicurean naturalism. The mathematical method, on the other hand, impresses man with his own powers of reason and with the marvellous coincidence of rational calculation and natural process, prompting a new Stoic identification of reason and nature. Nature and reason are thus the two gods of modern man, and sometimes the two are one. In either case man is essentially secure because he is not seriously estranged from the realm of harmony and order. Either it is nature which is itself that harmony; in which case mere ignorance has tempted man to stray from her innocency and the return to it is easy. Or if, on the other hand, nature is regarded as a realm of chaos, the realm of reason is an easily accessible asylum from, and force of conquest over, the conflicts and disharmonies of nature. A culture which underestimates the problem of freedom and necessity in nature is bound to depreciate the reality of freedom in man. The modern man is, in short, so certain about his essential virtue because he is so mistaken about his stature. He tries to interpret himself in terms of natural causality or in terms of his unique rationality; but he does not see that he has a freedom of spirit which transcends both nature and reason. He is consequently unable to understand the real pathos of his defiance of nature's and reason's laws. He always imagines himself betrayed into this defiance either by some accidental corruption in his past history or by some sloth of reason. Hence he hopes for redemption, either through a program of social reorganization or by some scheme of education.

II

THE EFFORT TO DERIVE EVIL FROM SPECIFIC

HISTORICAL SOURCES

The inclination of modern man to find the source of evil in his life in some particular event in history or some specific historical corruption is a natural consequence of his view of himself in a simple one-dimensional history. But this modern error merely accentuates a perennial tendency of the human heart to attribute wrong-doing to temptation and thus to escape responsibility for it. Every man has at some time or other repeated the excuse of the first man: "The woman whom thou gavest to be with me, she gave me of the tree and I did eat." The important point in all these explanations is that they fail to explain why the particular sources of evil in history, bad priests, evil rulers, and ruling classes, should have had the power and the inclination to introduce evil into history. In the eighteenth century human evil was variously attributed to the corrupting influence of religion or to tyrannical governments and ignorant legislators who had disturbed the harmony of nature. In the nineteenth century Marx traced the self-alienation of man from his true essence to the rise of the class organization in society. Each of these explanations has the virtue of throwing light upon the character of particular social evils and may point the way to their mitigation or elimination. But none of them explain how an evil which does not exist in nature could have arisen in human history.

The belief that priests and their religion were the source of social evil was a natural conviction of a generation which was forced to contend against the religious sanction of established social injustice. The eighteenth century regarded religion as the source of both political tyranny and social conflict. Holbach wrote: "History points out some of these vice-regents of deity who in the exacerbations of their delirious rage have insisted upon displacing him by exalting themselves into gods, exacting the most obsequious worship, who have inflicted the most cruel torment upon those who have opposed themselves to their madness." This self-deification of the religious leader is also the source of political tyranny, according to Holbach: "Theology—far from being useful to the human species, is the true source of all those sorrows which afflict the earth—of those governments which oppress him."[1] In the same spirit Helvetius protests against the fanaticism of religion and the social conflict which results from it: "What does the history of religions teach us? That religions have kindled the torch of intolerance everywhere. They have filled the plains with corpses, bathed the countryside in blood, destroyed cities, devastated empires. Religions have never improved men. Their improvement is the work of law. Religions determine our beliefs but laws determine our habits and customs."[2] The eighteenth century saw quite truly that there is a religious element in all tyranny and fanaticism. But it attributed this fact to the corruptions of par-

[1] *System of Nature*, Vol. III, pp. 60, 152.
[2] *De l'Homme*, Section VII, Cd. I.

ticular historical religions. It ought to have asked why it is that man is prompted and tempted to claim a dignity and eminence which no man ought to possess; and to affirm a finality for his convictions which no relative human judgment deserves. The world of pure nature knows nothing of priest-kings or fanatic prophets. "Nature interrogated by princes," declares Holbach, "would teach them that they are men and not gods";[3] but it does not seem to occur to him to inquire why men should have both the capacity and the inclination to claim divinity for themselves and infallibility for their opinions, the very inclination which Christianity defines as original sin. One of the instructive and pathetic aspects of contemporary history is that the same modern man who hoped for emancipation from tyranny and fanaticism by the destruction of historic religion, should in this latter day of modernity be drawn to the worship of Hitlers and Stalins and a whole variety of new priest-kings who manage to assert their ridiculous pretensions without the benefit of clergy. A particular manifestation of evil in human history cannot be regarded as the source of a general evil inclination. It is, on the contrary, but the fruit and consequence of a profounder root of evil.

The naturalists of the eighteenth century, following Epicurus, thought they could beguile man from his fears, hatreds, ambitions and fanatic furies by dwelling on the serenity and harmony of nature and upon its freedom from those ultimate perils which men fear most. They thought it possible to destroy the depth of human spirituality by proving that there is no depth in nature. They did not realize that, even if the spirits with which the human imagination peoples the world of nature were purely figments of the imagination, it would still be important to know why the imagination of man runs riot in this way and why it is impossible for men to enjoy the bovine serenity of the animal world. Epicurus thought he could exorcize the fear of death by proving that there is no peril on the other side of the grave, since death for man is merely the dissolution which all nature knows. But Epicurus overlooked the significance

[3] *Op. cit.*, p. 109.

of the fact that man should inevitably fear death while animals do not.

These eighteenth-century savants did not realize that man cannot, by taking thought, reduce himself to the proportions of nature and that he does not have the freedom to destroy his freedom over natural process, any more than he has the freedom to overcome his precarious dependence upon nature. Human fears arise precisely in this situation of strength and weakness; and the boundless character of human ambitions is the consequence of man's effort to hide his weakness, deny his dependence and insignificance and thus to quiet his fears.

Modern culture makes exactly the same mistake in dealing with the problems of government as in dealing with the fanaticism and fury of historic religions. It attributes evils to specific historical causes without inquiring how such particular causes could have arisen. The eighteenth century attributed tyranny and injustice to governments as well as to historic religions; and it was never very clear about the relation between the political and the religious sources of injustice. Furthermore in attributing social evil to the machinations of "bad governors" and "evil legislators," it assumes a voluntarism in its social theory which its deterministic psychology denies. While it reduces human freedom to such minimal proportions as will conform to its naturalism, its social theory assumes man's mastery over his social destiny. It fails to understand how every social decision is modified and circumscribed by natural circumstances and historical tendencies, beyond the control of human decision. There is a peculiar pathos in the social contract theories of government, which dominate the thought of the seventeenth and eighteenth centuries. They all attribute a more absolute freedom to man in history than the obvious facts of history justify; and certainly more freedom than is justified by their own philosophy.

This paradox is most striking in the thought of the father of modern empirical naturalism, Thomas Hobbes. When analysing human nature Hobbes is intent upon reducing man's uniqueness to

a minimum. Reason merely extends the natural will to live: "Reason
is no less of the nature of man than passion, and it is the same in
all men, because all men agree in the will to be directed and governed in the way to that which they desire to attain, namely their
own good which is the work of reason."[4] The freedom of man is not
distinguished in essence from that of animal life: "Neither is the
freedom of willing and not willing greater in man than in other
living creatures. . . . Such a liberty as is found free of necessity is
found in neither men nor in beasts. But if by liberty we mean the
faculty or power of doing what they will, then certainly that liberty
is to be allowed to both and both may equally have it."[5]

Human history begins nevertheless with an act of decision. For
Hobbes this decision, the social contract, is intended to avoid anarchy
by the creation of an absolute government, to the authority of which
all social decisions are submitted. The primary purpose of government, created by the social contract, is to establish precisely the kind
of sovereignty which the French naturalists regard as the "Fall" in
history, the error from which man must retrace his way back to
nature.

Hobbes ostensibly regards the peril of anarchy as a peril of nature.
He meets this peril by a free decision of human history, which involves him in the contradiction of assuming a distinction between
historical man and natural man in his social philosophy which he
denies in his psychology. Furthermore the peril of anarchy is really
in human history rather than in nature. Hobbes is forced to admit
this in spite of his psychological denial of human freedom. He
writes: "It is true that certain living creatures as bees and ants live
sociably with one another . . . and therefore some may perhaps desire
to know why mankind cannot do the same." He answers this question by admitting that "men are continually in competition for
honour and dignity and consequently . . . there ariseth envy and hatred
and finally war" and that "these creatures having not as man the use

[4]*Elements of Law,* IV.
[5]*Elements of Philosophy,* Part IV, Ch. 25, Part 12.

of reason, do not see, or think they see, any fault in the administration of their common business."[6] This difficulty in the thought of Hobbes perfectly illustrates the conflict between the voluntarism of modern social theory and the determinism of its psychology, a contradiction which becomes a permanent source of confusion in modern thought. Man actually has a greater degree of freedom in his essential structure and less freedom in history than modern culture realizes.

Beginning with John Locke the idea of the social contract is appropriated for democratic rather than.absolutistic theories of civil government. In the opinion of Locke the autocratic government defined by Hobbes is still in the realm of nature, and he requires a different social contract in order to establish democratic government, in which the power of the ruler is brought under social control. Locke finds the condition of nature "inconvenient" rather than anarchic and his natural law is not abrogated by civil law. Rather civil law must be regarded as a "proper remedy for the inconvenience of the state of nature which must certainly be great where men may be judges in their own cases." Whatever the explicit presuppositions of this democratic theory, Locke's real concern is for what Christian theology would call the peril of sin in human society but which Locke defines as the "inconvenience" of a state of nature. Since the peril arises from the fact that men "are judges in their own cases" it is not a peril of nature but of human freedom. In democratic theory, government is thus, as in Christian thought, a dyke against sin; the only difference being that Locke wrongly attributes sin to nature rather than to freedom. Unlike either Hobbes or most Christian theologians, Locke rightly fears the perils of tyranny more than the perils of anarchy. But with Hobbes, and unlike Christianity, he falsely ascribes the perils of social life to "nature." He seeks to overcome these perils, whether of tyranny or anarchy, by decisions in history. These decisions have a freedom ascribed to them which neither naturalism's own psychology nor the facts of history validate,

[6]*Leviathan,* Part II, Ch. 17.

and they have a degree of virtue attributed to them which history belies. In spite of himself the democratic naturalist thus trusts reason rather than nature in his effort to overcome human evil by new political institutions.

The French enlightenment partially follows the democratic doctrines of Locke's empiricism; but on the whole it is informed by a simpler naturalism. It ascribes political injustice to some error in history by which tyrannical governments have been established; and it hopes to return to justice by a return from history to nature. The nature to which it wishes to return is usually conceived more in Epicurean and Democritan than Stoic terms; which is to say that it regards nature as a realm of necessity in which the will-to-live of competing organisms is held in a simple harmony. This harmony can be restored, once the interference of governments is eliminated. "Moralists continually declaim against the badness of men," declares Helvetius, "but this shows how little they understand the matter. . . . The thing to complain of is not the badness of men but the ignorance of legislators who have always put the interests of individuals in opposition with general interest." In this theory the natural egoism of man is regarded as harmless so long as bad rulers and legislators do not interfere with the balance of competing egotistic impulses as it exists in nature. It is, of course, not explained how man happens to have the freedom to interfere with nature's laws. He is told that he must not and cannot interfere with nature; but none of these guides to a new morality seems to understand that if man cannot interfere it is superfluous to advise him that he must not. The contradiction is vividly revealed in the words of Diderot: "It would be very singular that all planets, all nature, should obey eternal laws and that there should be a little animal five feet high, who in contempt of these laws could act as he pleased, solely according to his caprice."

The logic of this position finally leads to a fully developed "physiocratic" theory; and it is this theory which Adam Smith ultimately elaborated into the philosophy of modern capitalism. The theory moves in the general direction of anarchism, as is evident in the thought of W. Godwin and others. The idea is that if only government will not interfere with the operation of natural laws in the economic sphere justice will be established through a harmony pre-established in nature. It is instructive that while modern political life can boast of genuine advances in justice, through the equaliza-tion of political power advocated by the democrats, modern economic life was allowed to develop cruel and iniquitous disproportions of power through the *laissez-faire* theories advocated by the physio-crats. Whatever their errors, the democrats started with more realistic assumptions than the physiocrats. Both were equally wrong how-ever in attributing social sin merely to social institutions and in hoping for a sinless man in a just society. W. Godwin, who, like Condorcet, mixed democratic and physiocratic theories in his thought, expressed this hope in the words: "All men would be fearless [in the new society] because they would know that there would be no legal snares lying in wait for their lives. They would be courageous because no man would be pressed to earth that another might enjoy immoderate luxury—jealousy and hatred would cease, because they are the offsprings of injustice."[7]

Profoundly as Marxism is distinguished from eighteenth-century liberalism in its social philosophy, its view of human nature is strik-ingly similar. It merely derives human evil, not from faulty political organization but from a prior fault in economic organization. Tyrannical governments are the consequence and the instruments of class domination. Man was alienated from his natural goodness at that period in history when the equalitarian and communistic or-ganization of the primitive tribe grew into the class organizations of the more advanced societies. The final elimination of classes will restore the natural goodness of man and thus obviate the necessity of coercion and, therefore, the need of the state. The Marxist theory of human consciousness, its virtual reduction of conscious behaviour to the "laws of motion" of the physical world, makes it difficult to

[7] *Enquiry Concerning Political Justice*, Vol. II, p. 29.

understand by what capacity man escaped from the restrictions of the primitive "we-consciousness" of the early tribe and how he achieved the ability and inclination to lord it over his fellow man. In the Marxist theory of man's alienation from his true communal essence there is an implicit, though not explicit, affinity with the doctrines of Rousseau. Social evil is attributed not so much to a specific evil in the history of man as to the elaborations of civilization itself. But the Marxist, unlike the romanticist, seeks to go forward rather than backward to a new innocency, a distinction which probably establishes the primary difference between communist and fascist social theories.

III

NATURE AS A SOURCE OF VIRTUE

The hope of modern culture of eliminating human wrong-doing through the political and economic reorganization stands in more or less confused relation with its other hope of eliminating social evil by more individual methods of return to the simple harmony of nature. The modern naturalist, whether romantic or rationalistic, has an easy conscience because he believes that he has not strayed very far from, and can easily return to, the innocency of nature. The most consistent naturalism from the ethical point of view is the naturalism of romanticism. For Rousseau and his followers the way back to nature was the method of throttling and destroying the uniquely human elaborations of nature in the freedom of man. "Retire to the woods," he declared, "there to lose sight and remembrance of the crimes of your contemporaries and be not apprehensive of degrading your species by renouncing its advances in order to renounce its vices." This romantic primitivism has the one advantage over rationalism of recognizing that the freedom of the so-called rational man is not harmless and that it is not easily conformed to the order of either nature or reason. But it fails to recognize that the freedom of man is the source of all his creativity as well as of his vices. It therefore seeks abortively to turn human history back upon itself by "renouncing its advances in order to renounce its vices." It is both more profound and more perverse than the more rationalistic-mechanistic forms of naturalism. It is profound because it understands, as the other naturalists do not, that there is a wide gulf between the purely natural impulse of survival and the distinctively human and spiritual impulse of pride and power, or, in the language of Rousseau, between "the natural feeling which leads every animal to look to its own preservation" and the "factitious feeling which arises in the state of society which leads every individual to make more of himself than any other." This difference between the natural will-to-live and the spiritual will-to-power remains an unexplored mystery to non-romantic forms of naturalism.

The perversity of romantic naturalism consists in its primitivistic effort to regain the innocency of nature. Rousseau does not, of course, remain true to a consistent primitivism. His theory of social contract does not conform to his injunction, "retire to the woods." It is, rather, an effort to reconstitute the harmony of nature on a new level of historical decision. He thinks it possible to compound all individual wills into a frictionless harmony of a "general will" upon this new level. There is significantly no clarity in his thought about the character of this general will. Is it the will of the majority? Or does it merely represent some ideal possibility of perfect harmony between life and life? This lack of clarity reveals the inability of romanticism to understand the nature of human freedom. It does not realize that there is no definition of a general and unifying purpose at which any society may arrive, which the individual does not transcend sufficiently to be able to criticize. He is not only able to criticize it and to seek to amend it; but he may feel under a high sense of obligation to do so.

Practically Rousseau's "general will" becomes merely the will of the majority. Since there is no principle of criticism in his philosophy for this general will, his conception of the general will becomes an instrument of tyranny in the hands of a given and momentary majority. This tyranny of the majority is easily transmuted into the tyranny of a minority, which uses the instruments of modern democracy to give its purposes the semblance of majority consent. Thus Rousseau's too simple solution of a perplexing problem contributes to the emergence of modern political dæmonries. The relation between the primitive and the demonic in the history of modern culture is a significant revelation of the danger which arises when human freedom is not understood. Every effort to return by a too simple route to the harmony and harmlessness of nature inevitably results in dæmonic politics in which human ambitions and lusts defy the restraints of both nature and reason.

The naturalism of Rousseau's rationalistic contemporaries offers the individual an even simpler way back to the harmlessness of nature. Nature is governed by the impulse of survival and no distinction is made in this rationalism between this impulse and human ambitions. "It is the essence of man to love himself," writes Holbach, "to tend to his own conservation, to seek to render his own existence happy; thus interest and desire is the only motive of all actions."[1] It is the business of reason to discover or to rediscover the "necessary" harmonious relations which exist in nature by virtue of this egoism, to "teach that everything is necessary" to "take for the basis of morality the necessity of things."[2] The only prerequisite for achieving this harmlessness of nature is the elimination of precisely the government which Hobbes institutes in order to overcome the chaos of conflicting egoistic desires. With naive inconsistency Holbach implies the reality of human freedom while he ostensibly denies it. The same man who is asked to base his morality on the "necessity of things" is scolded: "Thou wicked unfortunate who art everywhere in continual contradiction with thyself."[3]

In the simple hedonistic naturalism of Holbach and Helvetius reason simply leads man back to the laws of nature and its harmony but it is not explained how he could ever have departed from them.

[1] *System of Nature*, Vol. II, p. 8.
[2] *Ibid.*, Vol. III, p. 91.   [3] *Ibid.*, Vol. III, p 91.

In the more sophisticated hedonism of the nineteenth century reason so directs the desire for happiness that it includes the general welfare in the interest of the agent. The hedonism of nineteenth-century utilitarianism assumes the harmlessness not of the egoist as such but of the prudent egoist. This utilitarianism really transcends both hedonism and naturalism. The reason of which James Mill speaks completely transcends the self-interest of individuals. He is convinced that "every man possessed of reason is accustomed to weigh evidence and to be guided and determined by its preponderance" and that "the greater number will judge right and that the greatest force of evidence wherever it is, will produce the greatest impression."[4] In John Stuart Mill the obligation toward the general welfare is held within a hedonistic scheme only with the greatest difficulty. This naturalism is Stoic rather than Epicurean, despite its protestations. It is still the philosophy of an easy conscience but it regards reason rather than nature as the seat of virtue. That this virtue is not as perfect as had been assumed dawns upon the last of the great utilitarians, Jeremy Bentham, who discovers the "principle of self-preference," that is, the principle that "man prefers his own happiness to that of all sentient beings put together."[5] Against this egoistic tendency Bentham is forced to set political rather than purely rational restraint. He does this by inventing the "principle of the artificial identification of interest," which means that he will use government to distribute rewards and punishments in such a way as to counteract the tendency of the individual to seek his own advantage at the expense of the general welfare.

The other possibility of reason improving upon nature and thus achieving the virtue of man is that it will favour the social as against the egoistic impulses. There seems to be in reason a principle of selection which enables it to choose between various forces of nature. Thus David Hume declares: "that a man had but bad grace who delivers a theory however true, which, he must confess, leads to practice dangerous and pernicious. Why rake into those corners

[4]*Liberty of the Press*, p. 22.   [5]*Works*, Vol. X, p. 80.

of nature which spread a nuisance all around? Why dig up the pestilence from the pit in which it is buried?"[6]

The function of reason is to select and affirm the social and generous impulses as against the more egoistic ones. Hume writes: "It is sufficient for our present purposes if it be allowed, what surely without the greatest absurdity cannot be disputed, that there is some benevolence, however small, infused into our bosom, some spark of friendship for humankind, some particle of the dove kneaded into our frame along with elements of the wolf and the serpent. Let these generous sentiments be supposed ever so weak . . . they must still direct the determinations of *our mind* and, where everything else is equal, produce a cool preference of what is useful and serviceable to mankind above what is pernicious. . . . Avarice, ambition, vanity and all passions vulgarly though improperly comprised under the denomination of self-love are here excluded from our theory concerning the origin of morals, not because they are too weak but because they have not a proper direction for that purpose."[7] It must be noted that, in conformity with the classical tradition, the antisocial impulses in man are attributed to nature (wolf and serpent) and not to the unique freedom of the human spirit. Furthermore Hume is quite complacent about the possibility of checking egotism by education. He thinks that though "we are naturally partial to ourselves and to our friends we are capable of learning the advantages of a more equitable conduct."[8]

The belief that human virtue is guaranteed by the rational preference for the benevolent as against the egoistic impulses becomes a definite strand in modern thought. Saint Simon erected his structure of a "New Christianity" upon it and Auguste Comte made it the cornerstone of his positivist sociology. Comte imagined he had found a new path to virtue by exploiting and extending parental affection: "The love of his family leads Man out of the original state of self-love and enables him to attain finally a sufficient measure of social

[6]*General Principles of Morals,* Sec. VI, Part 2.
[7]*Ibid.,* Sec. IX.   [8]*Ibid.,* Sec. III, Part 1.

love." The family "completes the training by which nature prepares us for universal sympathy."[9] Comte failed to observe that his great discovery was vitiated by the fact that the family is also the source of that "alteregoism" which is a more potent source of injustice than the egotism of the individual. He realizes that rational discipline may extend social sympathy; but he does not see that human imagination may not only extend the boundaries which nature sets but may also impart such an intensity to the narrow loyalties, within the bounds of natural consanguinity, as to transmute them into forces of anarchy within the general community.

In all forms of naturalism in which reason is regarded as a secondary resource of virtue, as the eye without which natural impulse might be too blind to achieve "harmony between the parts," there is some difficulty in defining a consistent relation between reason and impulse. Sometimes it is regarded as a transcendent perspective which is able to prefer benevolence to self-love and the social to the egoistic impulses. Sometimes it holds a balance between them. In the thought of Bishop Butler it is not clear whether it is the business of reason to maintain such a balance or to find the identity between self-love and social harmony. Sometimes it is the business of reason to extend the impulse of self-preservation beyond itself until it includes the "general weal." All these interpretations, though usually claiming to be naturalistic, are inconsistently so because they fail to be consistently hedonistic. They introduce some criterion of reason as the norm of conduct and fail to maintain the pleasure principle consistently as either the norm or the motive of conduct.

The fact that such a great proportion of modern thought since the eighteenth century preserves man's good opinion of himself in terms of a dubious naturalism which is not certain whether virtue is to be found in reason or in nature nor how the two are related to each other, is indicative of the degree to which modern man's easy conscience is derived from a false estimate of his transcendence over nature.

[9] *A General View of Positivism*, pp. 100, 102.

The thought of a typical naturalistic philosopher of the twentieth century, John Dewey, advances remarkably little beyond the perplexities and confusions of the previous centuries. He has the same difficulty in finding a vantage point for reason from which it may operate against the perils of nature and the same blindness toward the new perils of spirit which arise in the "rational" life of man. Dewey is in fact less conscious of the social perils of self-love than either Locke or Hume. In his thought the hope of achieving a vantage point which transcends the corruptions of self-interest takes the form of trusting the "scientific method" and attributing antisocial conduct to the "cultural lag," that is, to the failure of social science to keep abreast with technology. "That coercion and oppression on a large scale exist no honest person can deny," he declares. "But these things are not the product of science and technology but of the perpetuation of old institutions and patterns untouched by the scientific method. The inference to be drawn is clear."[10] The failures of the past and present are due to the fact that the scientific method "has not been tried at any time with use of all the resources which scientific material and the experimental method now put at our disposal."[11] The subordination of intelligence to party passion is attributed to faulty social theories which represent "a kind of political watered-down version of the Hegelian dialectic" and the true liberal must make it clear that this "method has nothing in common with the procedure of organized co-operative inquiry which has won the triumphs of science in the field of physical nature."[12]

Professor Dewey has a touching faith in the possibility of achieving the same results in the field of social relations which intelligence achieved in the mastery of nature. The fact that man constitutionally corrupts his purest visions of disinterested justice in his actual actions seems never to occur to him. Consequently he never wearies in looking for specific causes of interested rather than disinterested action. As an educator, one of his favourite theories is that man's

---

[10]*Liberalism and Social Action*, p. 82.
[11]*Ibid.*, p. 51.   [12]*Ibid.*, p. 71.

betrayal of his own ideals in action is due to faulty educational techniques which separate "theory and practice, thought and action." He thinks this faulty pedagogy is derived from the "traditional separation of mind and body" in idealistic philosophy.[13] In common with his eighteenth-century precursors, he would use the disinterested force of his "freed intelligence" to attack institutional injustices and thus further free intelligence. Despotic institutions represent "relationships fixed in a pre-scientific age" and are the bulwark of anachronistic social attitudes. On the other hand "lag in mental and moral patterns provide the bulwark of the older institutions."[14]

No one expresses modern man's uneasiness about his society and complacency about himself more perfectly than John Dewey. One half of his philosophy is devoted to an emphasis upon what, in Christian theology, is called the creatureliness of man, his involvement in biological and social process. The other half seeks a secure place for disinterested intelligence above the flux of process; and finds it in "organized co-operative inquiry." Not a suspicion dawns upon Professor Dewey that no possible "organized inquiry" can be as transcendent over the historical conflicts of interest as it ought to be to achieve the disinterested intelligence which he attributes to it. Every such "organized inquiry" must have its own particular social locus. No court of law, though supported by age-old traditions of freedom from party conflict, is free of party bias whenever it deals with issues profound enough to touch the very foundation of the society upon which the court is reared. Moreover, there can be no "free co-operative inquiry" which will not pretend to have achieved a more complete impartiality than is possible for human instruments of justice. The worst injustices and conflicts of history arise from these very claims of impartiality for biased and partial historical instruments. The solution at which Professor Dewey arrives is therefore an incredibly naive answer to a much more ultimate and perplexing problem than he realizes. It could only have arisen in a

[13]Joseph Ratner, *Philosophy of John Dewey*, p. 381.
[14]John Dewey, *Liberalism and Social Action*, p. 76.

period of comparative social stability and security and in a nation in which geographic isolation obscured the conflict of nations, and great wealth mitigated the social conflict within a nation.

IV

THE OPTIMISM OF IDEALISM

Modern naturalism expresses its confidence in the goodness of man either by finding a harmony of nature, conceived in mechanistic or vitalistic terms, to which he can flee from the tensions and conflicts of freedom; or by placing its trust in some principle of order and harmony in reason in which it really has no right to believe within the limits of its naturalistic presupposition. Idealistic rationalism, on the other hand, has a much more simple approach to its moral optimism. Its confidence in the goodness of man rests upon a sharp distinction between nature and reason, between *nous* and *physis*. The order and inner coherence of reason is regarded as a safe retreat from the chaos of natural impulse; and the power of reason is considered sufficient to master and coerce natural vitality and transmute it into a higher realm of coherence. Such an interpretation of human nature has the advantage of recognizing the total dimension of the human spirit; but it makes the mistake of dividing the human *psyche* too absolutely and of identifying spirit and reason too completely. Its dualism prevents it from understanding the organic relation between nature and reason and the dependence of reason upon nature. Its identification of reason and spirit obscures the fact that human freedom actually transcends the capacities which are usually known as "rational." In other words it repeats the errors of Greek classicism. Consequently it finds a premature security for the freedom of man in the inner coherence of reason and does not see to what degree man may, in his freedom, violate, corrupt and prostitute the canons of reason in his own interest. Its rejection of Christian pessimism rests upon its belief that the rational man is also the good man.

Professor Alfred N. Whitehead, despite the qualified character of his idealism, offers a striking example of this idealistic optimism. He distinguishes between "speculative reason" and "pragmatic reason" and regards the former as the source of virtue and the latter as the root of evil. This distinction is reminiscent of Aristotle's distinction between the active and the passive *nous*. According to Whitehead, the former is the reason "which Plato shares with God," while the latter is the reason which "Ulysses shares with the foxes": "The short-range function of reason characteristic of Ulysses is reason criticizing and emphasizing subordinate purposes of nature which are agents of final causation. This is reason as a pragmatic agent. . . . The other function of reason was connected with the life work of Plato. In this function reason is enthroned above the practical tasks of the world. . . . It seeks with disinterested curiosity an understanding of the world. . . . In this function reason serves only itself. This is speculative reason." Evil arises from the "massive obscurantism of human nature" and this obscurantism in turn is defined as "the inertial resistance of practical reason with its millions of years behind it, to interference with its fixed methods arising from recent habits of speculation."[1]

Thus Whitehead, from the standpoint of a quasi-idealistic theory, believes the root of evil to lie in the inertia of that very intelligence, that pragmatic and short-range rational relation to natural impulses which, in the opinion of Professor Dewey, is man's sole rational possession. Yet both arrive at a "cultural lag" theory of human evil and both hope for a society which will ultimately be governed purely by rational suasion rather than force.[2] Their arrival at this common goal by contrasting methods is indicative of the power of moral optimism in modern culture. The rationalistic naturalists are forced to construct a very shaky and inadequate point of reference from which they can operate against the confusion of natural impulse. In Professor Dewey's case this is the device of a "free cooperative

[1] *The Function of Reason*, pp. 23–30.
[2] *Cf.* Whitehead, *Adventures of Ideas*, Ch. 5; John Dewey, *Philosophy and Civilization*.

inquiry," which is involved in the natural-historical process and yet somehow has a vantage point of pure disinterestedness above it. The purer rationalist splits the human spirit into a speculative and a pragmatic intelligence; and he assumes that the former has a vantage point of pure disinterestedness which no type of human intelligence ever possesses.

Idealism always has the provisional advantage over naturalism that it sees the human spirit in a deeper dimension than a pure naturalism. The proof that this is an advantage is given by the fact that naturalism is always forced to contradict itself to explain the facts of human history. The human spirit obviously transcends natural process too much to be bound by the harmony of natural necessity. This is proved both by the character of human creativity and by the emergence of a distinctively historical rather than natural chaos and destruction. The rationalist realizes that the human spirit is *nous* and not *physis*. But he immediately sacrifices his provisional advantage by identifying *nous* with *logos,* spirit with rationality. He believes therefore that the human spirit has a certain protection against the perils of its freedom within its own law-giving rationality. The possible evil of human actions is recognized but it is attributed to the body or, more exactly, to the *psyche,* that is, to the vitality of a particular form of existence.

For Spinoza, for instance, the "Fall" signifies the fact that human reason is unable to control passions completely; "for if he [Adam] had the power to make right use of his reason it was not possible for him to be deceived ... accordingly we must conclude that it was not in the first man's power to make right use of his reason but that, like us, he was subject to passions."[3] Of the three great rationalists of the seventeenth century, Spinoza, Descartes, and Leibnitz, Spinoza had the least confidence in the ability of reason to control passions and he made it a point to criticize Descartes' simple faith in the completely rational man. This realism prompted in him a provisional agreement with the Christian doctrines of humility: "For inasmuch as men

[3] *A Political Treatise,* Ch. 2, Part 8.

rarely live according to the dictates of reason . . . humility and repentance . . . work more good than evil. For if men who are powerless in mind should also become equally proud they would be
shamed with nothing."⁴ But this provisional uneasiness about man
is overcome in Spinoza's thought by the admixture of Epicurean or
hedonistic naturalism in his Stoic pantheism. So completely are natural necessity and rationality identified in his thought that he is
finally unable to condemn even the actions of unreason: "For man,
be he learned or ignorant, is part of nature and everything by which
man is determined to action ought to be referred to the power of
nature. . . . For man whether guided by reason or mere desire does
nothing save in accordance with the laws of nature, this is by natural right. But most people believe that the ignorant rather disturb
than follow the course of nature. . . . Experience however teaches us
but too well that it is no more in our power to have a sound mind
than a sound body. Next, inasmuch as everything, as far as in it lies,
strives to preserve its own existence, we cannot at all doubt, were it
as much in our power to live by the dictates of reason as to be led
by blind desire, all would live by reason and order their lives wisely,
which is far from being the case."⁵ In these words Spinoza becomes
almost the most perfect representative of modern culture, for he
manages to express its confidence in both nature and reason and its
slight preference for the latter over the former. He fails to understand, of course, that human egotism is something more than the
natural impulse of every organism "to preserve its own existence,"
that it has a power which defies both nature and reason; and that
the possession of a sound mind and a sound body is not completely a
matter of natural necessity in the life of man, for man is free to perfect and to destroy both physical health and mental capacity.

   Leibnitz's pluralistic rationalism arrives at remarkably similar
optimistic conclusions in spite of a tremendous difference in philosophical presuppositions. For him natural necessity and rational

⁴Spinoza, *Ethics,* Part IV, Prop. LIV.
⁵*A Political Treatise,* Ch. II, par. 5–6.

universality are not in conflict, because God as a divine clock-maker has ordained that the two clocks, soul and body, should achieve a perfect coincidence in each unit. Thus "souls which act according to the laws of final causes" and "bodies which act according to the laws of efficient causes" though belonging to two realms are "in harmony with each other." The harmony is not quite perfect and what is called sin is to be regarded as "the inertia of matter," the friction between the two realms. But even this is not evil. On the contrary it is a prerequisite virtue; for without it, the soul could not express its true genius as a citizen of the heavenly city.

In the thought of German idealism, Christian conceptions of the freedom of human self-consciousness are merged with classical distinctions between the rational self and the self which is involved in natural process. In Hegel there is a profound understanding of the problems of self-consciousness which must be attributed to the Christian rather than the classical background. He nevertheless arrives at the conclusion that the highest self which knows itself is identical with universal reason. "Reason," he declares, "is the highest union of consciousness with self-consciousness, of the knowing of an object and the knowing of itself. It is the certitude that its determinations are just as much objective, *i.e.*, determinations of the essence of things as they are subjective thoughts." The ultimate heights of the human spirit are thus identical with God. "The knowing reason is therefore not the mere subjective certitude, but also truth; because Truth consists in the harmony or rather unity of certitude and Being, or of certitude and objectivity." But the self which is thus on the one hand identical with divine reason is on the other hand involved in change and particularity which leads to the "unhappy consciousness" which is "explicitly aware of its own doubleness," of "its own contradiction." It regards the "changeless consciousness as the true self" and "the other the multiform and fickle as the false self."[6] The sense of sin in Hegel, expressed in his term of "contrite" or "unhappy" consciousness is thus the sense of conflict

[6]Hegel, *Phenomenology of Mind,* trans. by J. B. Baillie, Vol. I, p. 201.

between what Professor Hocking calls "the self which is in the world and the self which contemplates the world from a point not within the world."[7] Sin, for Hegel, is thus practically identical with the emergence of man from the innocency of nature and is a prelude to virtue. Sin is a necessary and inevitable assertion of individuality against universality. But since the divided self "is aware of the Changeless, *i.e.*, of the True Self its task must be one of self-deliverance," a task which is accomplished by achieving a unity of the twofold consciousness in which it discovers that "its individuality is reconciled with the Universal." In a sense, sin, for Hegel, performs an even more positive function than in the thought of Leibnitz. Without the sinful assertion of individuality man would not express the freedom which distinguishes him from nature, nor would he be able to find the ultimate synthesis of universality and individuality which is true virtue. The self-consciousness which separates the self and distinguishes it from the world is a necessary element in the logic of consciousness by which the self ultimately finds itself in unity with the world.

Whatever the uniqueness of Hegel's thought and its admitted profundity in analysing the position of the self in the realms of both nature and spirit, it exhibits the uniform tendency of all idealism to be essentially complacent about the perils of the freedom of the human spirit. It is certain that spirit and rationality are really identical and that the laws of the latter control the freedom of the former. In Hegel this idea is accentuated because in his thought rationality is not only the principle of form but also a self-moving vitality and creativity. The full peril of Hegel's complacency is revealed in his estimate of the virtue of the state. He regards the state as the true universal in which the rational self emancipates itself from its particular self: "It provides for the reasonable will—insofar as it is in the individual only implicitly the universal will—coming to a consciousness and an understanding of itself and being found."[8]

[7] W. E. Hocking, *Thoughts on Death and Life*, p. 72.

[8] Hegel, "Philosophy of Mind," from *Encyclopedia of the Phil. Sciences*, Section II, par. 539.

Thus the belief that the individual must and can come to his true self in the universal and that this must be achieved in history leads Hegel to appreciate the morality of man most highly at precisely the point at which it is most dubious, that is in his collective will. It is at that very point at which the elimination of individual particularity in the collective ego creates a false sense of universality. The fact that the collective will of the nation remains, from the ultimate perspective, a particular will, in conflict with other wills, is obscured. Hegel does not deny that "the national spirit contains nature-necessity" and "labours under contingency" but he believes that the spirit which "thinks in universal history" thereby "lays hold of its concrete universality."[9] Yet it is in precisely this relation of the nation to universal history that the sinful pretensions of the national spirit are most fully revealed. It is just at that point that imperialism is compounded, being composed of the universalism of spirit and the will-to-live of the finite organism. Hegelian state worship is a rather pathetic fruit of idealism's unjustified confidence in the universality and virtue of reason. This reason, which remains involved in the contingencies of history becomes most dæmonic at the very point at which it pretends to have transcended all natural contingency, *i.e.,* at the point of collective particularity.

In Kant's critical idealism there is no such temptation to confound the universal and particular in history because he has no scheme for rising from nature to spirit by way of the self-sublimation of the individual ego. On the contrary in Kant a great gulf is fixed between the intelligible self and the sensible self, roughly synonymous with Hegel's "changeless" and "multiform" self, or the self which is reason and the self which is in nature. The gulf is so absolute that "if the determination of the will takes place in conformity indeed with the moral law—but not for the sake of the law, then the action possesses legality but not morality."[10] In consequence all natural vital forces in the life of man are ruled out of the field of ethics. Only respect

[9]Hegel, *ibid.,* par. 552.
[10]T. K. Abbott, *Kant's Theory of Ethics,* par. 7.

for law is an adequate moral motive, a basis for moral goodwill. Thus, in general compliance with the classical tradition, it is man's involvement in the natural process which is the cause of evil in him. The sensible self is essentially evil from the perspective of the intelligible self. Kant is thus able to arrive at provisionally pessimistic conclusions about man and declares: "Man is indeed unholy enough." But the intelligible self is holy and man must therefore "regard humanity in his own person as holy." The basis of human worth "is nothing less than a power which elevates man above himself (as a part of the world of sense). . . . This power is nothing but personality, that is, freedom and independence of the mechanism of nature, yet regarded also as a faculty of a being which is subject to special laws, namely, purely practical laws given by its own reason."[11]

This reason of the intelligible self is not as unqualifiedly identified with either God or the active self as in absolute idealism. God stands beyond it as an ultimate unity of essence and existence. On the other hand the intelligible self, though defined as the reason of the self, seems to have a more transcendent position than the self which wills obedience to the law of reason. It would appear that the self which is the lawgiver is really abstract reason, not to say abstract logic, since its primary function is to prevent contradiction within the sphere of morals. The self which obeys is primarily will; but since no vital urges of the sensible self are allowed to enter that will, it is a will generated by reason. The Kantian self is thus involved in a hierarchy of existence consisting of the self in nature, the self as rational will transcending nature, the rational or intelligible self which is the lawgiver and God who is the ultimate nexus between reason and nature. But this complexity of structure does not modify the general approach of rationalism to the problem of man. Man is cut in two. The part which is immersed in natural process is essentially evil and the part which is subject to reason is essentially good. But the freedom of man is always freedom from nature and not freedom from reason. In Kant "freedom is the *ratio essendi* of the moral

[11]*Ibid.*, par. 7.

law while the moral law is the *ratio cognoscendi* of freedom." It is thus inconceivable that the human spirit in its freedom should defy reason. Non-rational actions and immoral actions are the consequence of natural inclinations and passions which defy the laws of reason.[12]

It would not be profitable for our purposes to trace the various configurations of idealistic thought in modern culture. Whatever their variations, they are derivations from either Hegel or Kant. Sometimes, as in Fichte, they achieve a greater sense of the total unity of the human psyche by an admixture of romantic motifs. But the general emphasis remains the same. They see the problem of human freedom more clearly than naturalism. They are deeply conscious of the paradox of man's involvement in nature and transcendence over natural process. But they are never able to define sin in terms of a violation of the good within freedom itself. They cannot define sin as spiritual because they regard spirit as essentially good. They fail to see the paradox of evil arising out of freedom not as an essential or necessary consequence but as an alogical fact.

The easy conscience of modern culture is practically unanimous, but not quite. It may be more correct to say that there are practically no exceptions to the easy conscience but there are exceptions to the

---

[12]In the basic trends of his thought Kant exhibits the moral complacency of the rational man which modern idealism shares with all forms of rationalism. It is necessary, however, to call attention to the fact that Kant had a theory of sin in his *Religion Within the Limits of Reason Alone* which stands in complete contradiction to his general system and which can only be explained as the evidence of the influence of pietistic Christian thought upon him, an influence which did not, however, change the general system of his ethics and could not have done so without completely shattering it. Kant's theory is expounded under the caption of "The Radical Evil." Radical evil, for Kant, is man's inclination to corrupt the imperatives of morality so that they become a screen for the expression of self-love. "This evil is radical," he declares, "because it corrupts the very basis of all maxims." In analysing the human capacity for self-deception and its ability to make the worse appear the better reason for the sake of providing a moral façade for selfish actions, Kant penetrates into spiritual intricacies and mysteries to which he seems to remain completely blind in his *Critique of Practical Reason*.

general moral optimism. For there are pessimists about human nature, who are nevertheless of easy conscience, because they do not hold man himself responsible for the evils in human nature. Hobbes is a pessimist in regard to the individual; but he is completely complacent about the moral qualities of the state, which he introduces to overcome the chaos of individual life. Most of the other pessimists stand in the romantic tradition. Rousseau's romanticism is provisionally pessimistic; yet it becomes the very fountain of optimism in modern educational theory. Nietzsche's pessimism is thoroughgoing but even he is able to erect an ultimate optimism upon his conception of the superman, who transmutes the will-to-power into an instrument of social creativity and order. Freud's pessimism is most thoroughgoing, but he finds no conscience to appeal to. His "superego" performs the functions of Hobbes's state; but it cannot be given an unconditioned function of discipline, because it is feared that discipline will lead to new disorders in the unconscious life of the individual.

The romantic pessimism which culminates in Freud may be regarded as symbolic of the despair which modern man faces when his optimistic illusions are dispelled; for under the perpetual smile of modernity there is a grimace of disillusion and cynicism.

This undercurrent of romantic pessimism and cynicism does not, however, deflect the main stream of optimism. The fact that modern man has been able to preserve such a good opinion of himself, despite all the obvious refutations of his optimism, particularly in his own history, leads to the conclusion that there is a very stubborn source of resistance in man to the acceptance of the most obvious and irrefutable evidence about his moral qualities. This source of resistance is not primarily modern but generally human. The final sin of man, said Luther truly, is his unwillingness to concede that he is a sinner. The significant contribution of modern culture to this perennial human inclination lies in the number of plausible reasons which it was able to adduce in support of man's good opinion of himself. The fact that many of these reasons stand in contradiction to each other did not shatter modern man's confidence in them; for he could always persuade himself of the truth of at least one of them and it never occurred to him that they might all be false.

Yet they were all false. Whether they found the path from chaos to order to lead from nature to reason or from reason to nature, whether they regarded the harmony of nature or the coherence of mind as the final realm of redemption, they failed to understand the human spirit in its full dimension of freedom. Both the majesty and the tragedy of human life exceed the dimension within which modern culture seeks to comprehend human existence. The human spirit cannot be held within the bounds of either natural necessity or rational prudence. In its yearning toward the infinite lies the source of both human creativity and human sin. In the words of the eminent Catholic philosopher Étienne Gilson: "Epicurus remarked, and not without reason, that with a little bread and water the wise man is the equal of Jupiter himself. . . . The fact is, perhaps, that with a little bread and water a man ought to be happy but precisely is not; and if he is not, it is not necessarily because he lacks wisdom, but simply because he is a man, and because all that is deepest in him perpetually gainsays the wisdom offered. . . . The owner of a great estate would still add field to field, the rich man would heap up more riches, the husband of a fair wife would have another still fairer, or possibly one less fair would serve, provided only she were fair in some other way. . . . This incessant pursuit of an ever fugitive satisfaction springs from troubled deeps in human nature. . . . The very insatiability of human desire has a positive significance; it means this: that we are attracted by an infinite good."[13]

The fact that man can transcend himself in infinite regression and cannot find the end of life except in God is the mark of his creativity and uniqueness; closely related to this capacity is his inclination to transmute his partial and finite self and his partial and finite values into the infinite good. Therein lies his sin.

[13]*The Spirit of Medieval Philosophy*, pp. 270–272.

CHAPTER V

THE RELEVANCE OF THE CHRISTIAN VIEW
OF MAN

Our analysis of modern interpretations of human nature has [SUMMARY] led to the conviction that the modern mind arrives at contradictory conclusions about the relation of vitality to form in human nature; that the perennial debate between rationalists and romanticists, the one depreciating and the other glorifying the power and the virtue of subrational vitalities, is the historic evidence of this contradiction; that the modern mind fails to find a secure foundation for the individuality which it ostensibly cherishes so highly; and that its estimates of human virtue are too generous and optimistic to accord with the known facts of human history.

In analysing the modern failure in each of these areas of thought we have suggested that the difficulty arises from the lack of a principle of interpretation which can do justice to both the height of human self-transcendence and the organic unity between the spirit of man and his physical life. The modern mind interprets man as either essentially reason, without being able to do justice to his non-rational vitalities, or as essentially vitality without appreciating the extent of his rational freedom. Its metaphysics fails to comprehend the unity of mind and nature, of freedom and necessity, in the actual life of man. In similar fashion it dissipates the sense of individuality, upon which it insists with so much vehemence in the early Renaissance, because it cannot find a foundation in either nature, historical social structure, or universal mind for this individuality. It lacks an anchor or norm for the free individual who transcends both the limitations of nature and the various social concretions of history. Its inability to estimate the evil in man realistically is partly due to the failure of modern culture to see man in his full stature of self-transcendence. The naturalist sees human freedom as little more than the freedom of *homo faber* and fails to appreciate to what degree the human spirit breaks and remakes the harmonies and unities of nature. The idealist, identifying freedom with reason and failing to appreciate that freedom rises above reason, imagines that the freedom of man is secure, in the mind's impetus toward coherence and synthesis. Neither naturalism nor idealism can understand that man is free enough to violate both the necessities of nature and the logical systems of reason.

All three errors of modern estimates of man, therefore, point to a single and common source of error: Man is not measured in a dimension sufficiently high or deep to do full justice to either his stature or his capacity for both good and evil or to understand the total environment in which such a stature can understand, express and find itself. One might define this total environment most succinctly as one which includes both eternity and time; but the concept of eternity without further definition may be too ambiguous to clarify the point at issue. The eternity which is part of the environment of man is neither the infinity of time nor yet a realm of undifferentiated unity of being. It is the changeless source of man's changing being. As a creature who is involved in flux but who is also conscious of the fact that he is so involved, he cannot be totally involved. A spirit who can set time, nature, the world and being *per se* into juxtaposition to himself and inquire after the meaning of these things, proves that in some sense he stands outside and beyond them.

This ability to stand outside and beyond the world, tempts man to megalomania and persuades him to regard himself as the god around and about whom the universe centres. Yet he is too obviously involved in the flux and finiteness of nature to make such pretensions plausibly. The real situation is that he has an environment of eternity which he cannot know through the mere logical ordering of his experience. The rational faculty by which he orders and interprets his experience (sometimes erroneously regarded as the very eternity in which finiteness rests) is itself a part of the finite world which man must seek to understand. The only principle for the comprehension of the whole (the whole which includes both himself and his world) is therefore inevitably beyond his comprehension. Man is thus in the position of being unable to comprehend himself in his full stature of freedom without a principle of comprehension which is beyond his comprehension.

This is the situation which gives perennial rise to mystic faiths in both east and west, though the east is more addicted to mysticism than the west. The mystic, being conscious of standing somehow beyond the flux of events in the finite world, and fearful lest his finite effort to comprehend this eternal world merely obscure the concept of the eternal with finite perspectives, restricts himself to a purely negative definition of the eternal world. It is everything the finite world is not; or rather it is not anything which the finite world is. He thus arrives at a concept of an undifferentiated eternal unity. With this as his principle of criticism for the finite world, he is forced to regard the finite world as a corruption of, or emanation from, the undifferentiated unity of eternity. Since his own particularized existence is a part of this corrupt finite world the pure mystic, who begins by lifting self-consciousness out of the flux of temporal events, must end by negating his own conscious life as part of the temporal world and by seeking absorption into eternity.

II

INDIVIDUAL AND GENERAL REVELATION

The character of Biblical religion must be understood in contrast to this tendency toward self-immolation in mysticism. It is a religion which neither reduces the stature of man to the level of nature, nor yet destroys it in an empty and undifferentiated eternity. Biblical religion is variously defined, in distinction from other religions, as a prophetic or as an apocalyptic religion, or as a religion of revelation. In a religion of revelation, the unveiling of the eternal purpose and will, underlying the flux and evanescence of the world, is expected; and the expectation is fulfilled in personal and social-historical experience.[1]

From the standpoint of an understanding of human nature, the significance of a religion of revelation lies in the fact that both the transcendence of God over, and his intimate relation to, the world are equally emphasized. He is more completely transcendent than the eternity of mystic faith. Mysticism always regards the final depth of human consciousness as in some sense identical with the eternal order, and believes that men may know God if they penetrate deeply enough into the mystery of their own being. But on the other hand the transcendent God of Biblical faith makes Himself known in the finite and historical world. The finite world is not, because of its finiteness, incapable of entertaining comprehensible revelations of the incomprehensible God. The most important characteristic of a religion of revelation is this twofold emphasis upon the transcendence of God and upon His intimate relation to the world. In this divine transcendence the spirit of man finds a home in which it can understand its stature of freedom. But there it also finds the limits of its freedom, the judgment which is spoken against it and, ultimately, the mercy which makes such a judgment sufferable.

[1]John Oman defines the difference between mystical and apocalyptic religions as follows: "In the former case the eternal is sought as the unchanging by escape from the evanescent; in the latter it is looked for in the evanescent as a revelation of the increasing purpose in its changes." . . . "A mystical religion is, as it should always be understood scientifically, one that seeks the eternal behind the illusion of the evanescent; but in using 'apocalyptic' for any religion which looks for a revealing in the evanescent the term is extended from its customary use, which is for a religion which expects this in sudden catastrophic form, to one which expects it in any form." *The Natural and the Supernatural,* pp. 403–409.

God's creation of, and relation to, the world on the other hand prove that human finiteness and involvement in flux are essentially good and not evil. A religion of revelation is thus alone able to do justice to both the freedom and the finiteness of man and to understand the character of the evil in him.

The revelation of God to man is always a twofold one, a personal-individual revelation, and a revelation in the context of social-historical experience. Without the public and historical revelation the private experience of God would remain poorly defined and subject to caprice. Without the private revelation of God, the public and historical revelation would not gain credence. Since all men have, in some fashion, the experience of a reality beyond themselves, they are able to entertain the more precise revelations of the character and purpose of God as they come to them in the most significant experiences of prophetic history. Private revelation is, in a sense, synonymous with "general" revelation, without the presuppositions of which there could be no "special" revelation. It is no less universal for being private. Private revelation is the testimony in the consciousness of every person that his life touches a reality beyond himself, a reality deeper and higher than the system of nature in which he stands.

St. Paul speaks of this experience of God when he declares that even without a further revelation men are "without excuse" if they do not glorify God as God but become vain in their imagination and make themselves God (Romans 1:20). The experience of God is not so much a separate experience, as an overtone implied in all experience.[2] The soul which reaches the outermost rims of its own consciousness, must also come in contact with God, for He impinges upon that consciousness.

---

[2] Professor John Baillie writes very truly: "No matter how far back I go, no matter by what effort of memory I attempt to reach the virgin soil of childish innocence, I cannot get back to an atheistic mentality. As little can I reach a day when I was conscious of myself but not of God as I can reach a day when I was conscious of myself but not of other human beings." *Our Knowledge of God,* p. 4.

Schleiermacher describes this experience of God as the experience of "unqualified dependence." This is one of its aspects but not its totality. It is one of its aspects because there is, in all human consciousness, at least a dim recognition of the insufficient and dependent character of all finite life, a recognition which implies the consciousness of the reality upon which dependent existence depends. An equally important characteristic of the experience of God is the sense of being seen, commanded, judged and known from beyond ourselves. This experience is described by the Psalmist in the words: "O Lord, thou hast searched me, and known me. Thou knowest my downsitting and mine uprising, . . . and art acquainted with all my ways" (Ps. 139). The Psalmist exults in this relation between God and man and rightly discerns that the greatness and uniqueness of man is as necessary as the greatness of God for such a relationship: "I am fearfully and wonderfully made: marvellous are thy works; and that my soul knoweth right well." If any one should maintain that this sense of the impingement of God upon human life is a delusion by which man glorifies himself, one might call attention to the fact that in the book of Job exactly the same experience is described by one who is not grateful for it but protests against it. The constant demands and judgments of God seem to him to place life under an intolerable strain: "What is man, that thou shouldest magnify him? and that thou shouldest set thine heart upon him? and that thou shouldest visit him every morning, and try him every moment?" He feels that the divine demands are too exacting for human weakness: "let me alone; for my days are vanity," and he looks forward to the day when death will make the visitations of God impossible: "for now shall I sleep in the dust; and thou shalt seek me in the morning, but I shall not be" (Job 7:16–21). This impious protest against the ever-present accusing God is perhaps a more perfect validation of the reality of the experience than any pious words of gratitude for it.

The experience so described is in some sense identical or associated with what is usually called "conscience." The actual nature of conscience is, of course, variously defined in various philosophies. It may be regarded as the social obligations and judgments which all men must face. Or it may be defined as the obligation and judgment under which the rational or intelligible self places the empirical, the sensible or the partial self. The significance of the Biblical interpretation of conscience lies precisely in this, that a universal human experience, the sense of being commanded, placed under obligation and judged is interpreted as a relation between God and man in which it is God who makes demands and judgments upon man. Such an interpretation of a common experience is not possible without the presuppositions of the Biblical faith. But once accepted the assumption proves to be the only basis of a correct analysis of all the factors involved in the experience; for it is a fact that man is judged and yet there is no vantage point in his own life, sufficiently transcendent, from which the judgment can take place. St. Paul describes the three levels of judgment under which men stand, and the relativity of all but the last level in the words: "But to me it is a very small thing that I should be judged of you, or of man's judgment: yea, I judge not mine own self. For I know nothing by myself; yet am I not hereby justified: but he that judgeth me is the Lord" (1 Cor. 4:3-4).

It might be argued that the content of a personal experience which can be defined only through the aid of a more historical revelation of the nature of the divine, which enters this experience, while this historical revelation can gain credence only if the personal experience is presupposed, is so involved in a logical circle as to become incredible. But the fact is that all human knowledge is also so involved. All common human experience requires more than the immediate experience to define the character of the object of experience. The reality of the object of experience is not in question, but the exact nature of the reality touched is not clear until it is defined by insights which transcend the immediate perception of the object. If the reality touched is something more than a mere "object" but is itself subject, that is, if its character cannot be fully revealed to us, except as it takes the initiative, the principle of interpretation must be something more than merely the general principles of knowledge which illumine a particular experience. The principle of interpretation must be a "revelation."

Our approach to other human personalities offers an illuminating analogy of the necessity and character of "revelation" in our relation to God. We have various evidence that, when dealing with persons, we are confronting a reality of greater depth than the mere organism of animal life. We have evidence that we are dealing with a "Thou" of such freedom and uniqueness that a mere external observation of its behaviour will not only leave the final essence of that person obscure but will actually falsify it, since such observation would debase what is really free subject into a mere object. This person, this other "Thou" cannot be understood until he speaks to us; until his behaviour is clarified by the "word" which comes out of the ultimate and transcendent unity of his spirit. Only such a word can give us the key by which we understand the complexities of his behaviour. This word spoken from beyond us and to us is both a verification of our belief that we are dealing with a different dimension than animal existence; and also a revelation of the actual and precise character of the person with whom we are dealing.

In the same way, the God whom we meet as "The Other" at the final limit of our own consciousness, is not fully known to us except as specific revelations of His character augment this general experience of being confronted from beyond ourselves.

In Biblical faith these specific revelations are apprehended in the context of a particular history of salvation in which specific historical events become special revelations of the character of God and of His purposes. Without the principle of interpretation furnished by this "special revelation" the general experience or the general revelation involved in conscience becomes falsified, because it is explained merely as man facing the court of social approval or disapproval or as facing his own "best self." In that case, whatever the provisional verdict, the final verdict always is, "I know nothing against myself" and the conclusion drawn from this verdict must be and is, "I am thereby justified." But this conclusion is at variance with the actual facts of the human situation, for there is no level of moral achievement upon which man can have or actually has an easy conscience.

The fact that a culture which identifies God with some level of human consciousness, either rational or super-rational, or with some order of nature, invariably falsifies the human situation and fails to appreciate either the total stature of freedom in man or the complexity of the problem of evil in him, is the most telling negative proof for the Biblical faith. Man does not know himself truly except as he knows himself confronted by God. Only in that confrontation does he become aware of his full stature and freedom and of the evil in him. It is for this reason that Biblical faith is of such importance for the proper understanding of man, and why it is necessary to correct the interpretations of human nature which underestimate his stature, depreciate his physical existence and fail to deal realistically with the evil in human nature, in terms of Biblical faith.

III

CREATION AS REVELATION

The general revelation of personal human experience, the sense of being confronted with a "wholly other" at the edge of human consciousness, contains three elements, two of which are not too sharply defined, while the third is not defined at all. The first is the sense of reverence for a majesty and of dependence upon an ultimate source of being. The second is the sense of moral obligation laid upon one from beyond oneself and of moral unworthiness before a judge. The third, most problematic of the elements in religious experience, is the longing for forgiveness. All three of these elements become more sharply defined as they gain the support of other forms of revelation. The first, the sense of dependence upon a reality greater and more ultimate than ourselves, gains the support of another form of "general" revelation, the content of which is expressed in the concept of the Creator and the creation. Faith concludes that the same "Thou"

who confronts us in our personal experience is also the source and
Creator of the whole world. The second element in personal religion,
the experience of judgment, gains support from the prophetic-Biblical
concept of judgment in history. The whole of history is seen as
validation of the truth in the personal experience that God stands
over against us as our judge. The third element, the longing for
reconciliation after this judgment (and it must be regarded provisionally as a longing rather than an assurance), becomes the great
issue of the Old Testament interpretation of life. The question is:
is God merciful as well as just? And if He is merciful, how is His
mercy related to His justice? This is the question which hovers over
the whole of Biblical religion. Because Christian faith believes the
final answer to this ultimate question to be given in Christ, it regards the revelation in Christ a final revelation, beyond which there
can be no further essential revelation. For this reason it speaks of
Christ "as the express image of his person." Here the whole depth
and mystery of the divine are finally revealed.

In these three types of revelation God becomes specifically defined
as Creator, Judge and Redeemer. It is significant that each term
represents a definition of divine transcendence in increasingly specific
and sharply delineated terms; and yet in each the relation of God
to the world is preserved. They must be studied in order.

To speak of God as Creator of the world, is to regard the world in
its totality as a revelation of His majesty and self-sufficient power.
This revelation still belongs in the category of "general" revelation
though it has been transferred from the inner to the outer world. It
is this transfer which St. Paul effects in his argument that "they are
without excuse" if "they" do not know God, "because," he declares,
"that which may be known of God is manifest *in* them, for God hath
showed it unto them." This God who is manifest *in* them further
establishes Himself, "for the invisible things of him from the creation
of the world are clearly seen, being understood by the things that
are made, even his eternal power and Godhead" (Romans 1:19–20).
The fact that the world is not self-derived and self-explanatory and

self-sufficing but points beyond itself, is used as evidence for the doctrine of Creation and to point to the glory of the Creator. In a sense St. Paul is making use of the cosmological argument at this point, but not in such a way as to be subject to the Kantian criticism. It is not assumed that the reality of God can be proved by the fact that the contingent and dependent character of all finite being implies that the whole of the sensible world "rests upon some intelligible being that is free from all empirical conditions and itself contains the ground of the possibility of all appearances."[1] Rather the creation is contemplated as pointing to a Creator, already known in man's moral experience. Martin Buber accurately describes the process by which Biblical faith arrives at its concept of the Creator. He says: "The polytheist constructs a god out of every divine appearance, that is out of every mystery of the world and of existence; but the monotheist recognizes in all these mysteries the same God whom he experienced in personal confrontation. . . ."[2]

The Biblical doctrine of the Creator, and the world as His creation, is itself not a doctrine of revelation, but it is basic for the doctrine of revelation. It expresses perfectly the basic Biblical idea of both the transcendence of God and His intimate relation to the world. The doctrine is expressed in a "mythical" or supra-rational idea. Genetically the idea of creation is related to primitive concepts in which God is pictured as fashioning the world as the potter moulds his clay. The Bible retains this "primitive" concept because it preserves and protects the idea of the freedom of God and His transcendence. These are lost or imperilled by the more rational concept of "first cause" (which takes the place of God in naturalistic philosophies), and of the concept of a form-giving *nous,* which creates by forming the previously formless stuff or matter (which is the basic conception of divinity in idealistic philosophies).

The doctrine of creation preserves the transcendence and freedom of God without implying that the created world is evil because it

---

[1] *Cf.* Immanuel Kant, *Critique of Pure Reason,* Book II, Ch. ii, par. 4.
[2] *Koenigtum Gottes,* p. 91.

is not God. On the contrary Biblical religion consistently maintains the goodness of creation precisely on the ground that it is created by God. In this doctrine of the goodness of creation the foundation is laid for the Biblical emphasis upon the meaningfulness of human history. History is not regarded as evil or meaningless because it is involved in the flux of nature, and man is not regarded as evil because he is dependent upon a physical organism. The doctrine of creation escapes the error of the naturalists who, by regarding causality as the principle of meaning, can find no place for human freedom and are forced to reduce man to the level of nature. It escapes the error of the rationalists who make *nous* into the ultimate principle of meaning, and are thereby tempted to divide man into an essentially good reason, which participates in or is identified with the divine, and an essentially evil physical life.

To reject the principle of natural causation as the final principle of interpreting the unity of the world is not to interpret the world merely from the standpoint of man's internal problem or to read psychic attributes of man into nature. The fact is, that the relation of things to each other in the chain of natural causation is not an adequate explanation of their specific givenness. This irrational givenness must be regarded either as merely chance or caprice, or the order of the world must be related to a more ultimate realm of freedom. There is, in other words, a gain for an adequate cosmology, if man uses concepts in his interpretations of the cosmos which he won first of all in measuring the dimension of his own internal reality. Even nature is better understood if it is measured in a dimension of depth which is initially suggested by the structure of human consciousness, and by the experience of a reality more ultimate than his own, which impinges upon his freedom.

In the same manner the doctrine of creation corrects mistakes in rationalistic and idealistic cosmologies. These cosmologies are forced to presuppose some unformed stuff, some realm of chaos, which *nous* fashions into order, and to identify this forming process with creation. The Biblical doctrine of creation derives both the formless stuff and the forming principle from a more ultimate divine source, which it defines as both *logos* and as creative will, as both the principle of form and the principle of vitality. The supra-rational character of this doctrine is proved by the fact that, when pressed logically, it leads to the assertion that God creates *ex nihilo,* the idea at which all logical concepts of derivation must end—and begin.

The only metaphysical system which can be compared with the Biblical idea of Creator and creation, in terms of the dimension of depth which it assigns to the world, is the system of mysticism. One may speak of a mystical metaphysics because there is a remarkable unity and unanimity in mystical interpretations of life and reality, whether they develop in east or west and whether it be Plotinus or Buddha who elaborates the philosophy in detail. In all of them the finite world is regarded as illusory, or evil; in all of them the eternal world is regarded as a realm of undifferentiated unity from which the particularity, individuality and insufficiency of the finite world have been expunged; all of them place *nous, logos,* reason or form, which for the rationalists represents the eternal principle within flux, into the category of the finite, while they seek for a more ultimate and undifferentiated unity than "contrasting thoughts"; all of them seek to arrive at this unity of the divine and eternal by a rigorous discipline of introversion which assumes that the unity of consciousness above the level of sense experience but also above the level of reason, is identical with the divine. Brahman and Atman are one.

Mysticism, which is therefore closest to Biblical religion in measuring the depth of reality and the height of human consciousness, is also in sharpest contrast to the Biblical concept of Creator and creation. The contrast is threefold. (1) In contrast to the creative will and wisdom of the divine in the Biblical conception of God, it defines God in terms of negation.[3] (2) In contrast to the Biblical doc-

[3]Mercer in *Nature Mysticism* describes the mystic process of defining the eternal and divine as follows: "By a ruthless process of abstraction they have abjured the world of sense to vow allegiance to a mode of being about which nothing can be said without denying it . . . it embraces everything and remains pure negation—leave us not alone with the abso-

trine of the goodness of creation, the finite, differentiated and particularized world is regarded as either illusory or evil. The human ego, as finite and particularized reality, is evil by virtue of being an ego; and salvation consists essentially in the destruction of individuality. (3) Despite this ultimate destruction of individuality, mysticism makes for a provisional deification of man, since it believes that God is identical with the deepest level of human consciousness. This is in contrast to the Biblical doctrine of the creatureliness of man and to the sharp Biblical distinction between Creator and creature.

The Biblical doctrine of Creator and creation is thus the only ground upon which the full height of the human spirit can be measured, the unity of its life in body and soul be maintained and the essential meaningfulness of its history in the finite world asserted, and a limit set for its freedom, and self-transcendence.

IV

HISTORICAL AND SPECIAL REVELATION

Faith in the transcendent God, as revealed in personal experience and in the character of the whole creation, is the ground upon which the Biblical historical revelation is built up; and this revelation is concerned with the two other attributes of God to man, His judgment and His mercy. This historical revelation is by no means simply the history of man's quest for God or the record of man's increasingly adequate definitions of the person of God, interpretations to which modern liberal thought has sometimes reduced Biblical revelation. It is rather the record of those events in history in which faith discerns the self-disclosure of God. What it discerns are actions of God which clarify the confrontation of man by God in the realm

---

lute of orthodox mysticism lest we perish of inanition." P. 10. Rufus Jones recognizes this tendency in mysticism but, like most Christian mystics, he regards it as an aberration rather than as a constitutional weakness of mysticism. *Studies in Mystical Religion.* Ch. 6.

of the personal and individual moral life. In personal life the moral experience consists of the sense of moral obligation as being laid upon man not by himself, nor yet by his society but by God; as a judgment upon man for failing in his obligation; and finally as the need for reconciliation between man and God because of the estrangement resulting from man's rebellion against the divine will.

In the history of revelation the counterpart of the sense of moral obligation is the covenant relation between God and His people. In this covenant we have the basic Biblical idea of the character of human history. It is not regarded as evil by reason of being involved in finiteness. Its ideal possibility is that a particular nation, Israel, should serve not its own purpose but the will of God, according to the covenant between God and His people. But the prophetic consciousness discerns that this ideal possibility is not fulfilled. Israel fails to fulfill its special mission not by reason of any inertia of nature, or any finiteness of mind, or any inability to comprehend the divine mission. On the contrary the basis of the sin of Israel, according to the prophets, lies in the temptation of the nation to identify itself too completely with the divine will of which it is only an historical instrument. Israel makes this mistake particularly; but the prophets discern the same mistake in each of the great empires who become executors of divine judgment upon Israel.

The real evil in the human situation, according to the prophetic interpretation, lies in man's unwillingness to recognize and acknowledge the weakness, finiteness and dependence of his position, in his inclination to grasp after a power and security which transcend the possibilities of human existence, and in his effort to pretend a virtue and knowledge which are beyond the limits of mere creatures. The whole burden of the prophetic message is that there is only one God ("I am the first, and I am the last; and beside me there is no God." Is. 44:6) and that the sin of man consists in the vanity and pride by which he imagines himself, his nations, his cultures, his civilizations to be divine. Sin is thus the unwillingness of man to acknowledge his creatureliness and dependence upon God and his effort to make his

own life independent and secure. It is the "vain imagination" by
which man hides the conditioned, contingent and dependent character of his existence and seeks to give it the appearance of unconditioned reality. The second Isaiah laughs at the idol makers who
transmute a perishable tree into the image of man and worship this
totem as God.[1] The God who protests against this idolatry discloses
Himself as the one "who made the earth and created man upon it,"
who is "the Lord and there is none else beside me" (Is. 45).

In condemning the pride of Babylon the second Isaiah shows a
remarkable insight into the fact that the mystery and height of human self-consciousness are among the elements of temptation which
betray man into his pride: "thou hast said, None seeth me. Thy
wisdom and thy knowledge, it hath perverted thee; and thou hast
said in thine heart, I am, and none else beside me" (Is. 47:10). Man,
in other words, always transcends the world and contains the world
within himself in the process of knowledge. He overestimates the
completeness of his knowledge and even more the self-sufficiency of
his existence. Ezekiel castigates the pride and self-sufficiency of the
various princes and nations of the world in the same vein: "Say unto
the prince of Tyrus . . . because thine heart is lifted up, and thou
hast said, I am God, I sit in the seat of God in the midst of the seas;
yet thou art a man, and not God, though thou set thine heart as the
heart of God; . . . Behold, therefore I will bring strangers upon
thee, . . . Wilt thou yet say before him that slayeth thee, I am God?
but thou shalt be a man, and no God, in the hand of him that
slayeth thee" (Ez. 28:2–9).

The catastrophes of history by which God punishes this pride, it

---

[1]The words of the prophet are filled with profound religious insight.
He declares: "He heweth him down cedars, and taketh the cypress and
the oak—he burneth part thereof in the fire; with part thereof he eateth
flesh; he roasteth roast and is satisfied: yea, he warmeth himself, and
saith, Aha, I am warm, I have seen the fire: and the residue thereof he
maketh a god, even his graven image, he falleth down unto it, and
worshippeth it, and prayeth unto it, and saith, Deliver me; for thou art
my god" (Is. 44:14–17).

must be observed, are the natural and inevitable consequences of men's effort to transcend their mortal and insecure existence and to establish a security to which man has no right. One aspect of this human pride is man's refusal to acknowledge the dependent char-acter of his life. Thus Egypt exists by the beneficences of nature in terms of the Nile's rhythmic seasons, but, according to Ezekiel, she imagines herself the author of this source of her wealth: "Behold, I am against thee, Pharaoh, king of Egypt, the great dragon that lieth in the midst of his rivers, which hath said, My river is mine own, and I have made it for myself" (Ezek. 29:3). One might write pages on the relevance of this prophetic judgment upon the self-sufficiency of modern man whose technical achievements obscure his dependence upon vast natural processes beyond his control and accentuate the perennial pride of man in his own power and security.

Psalm 49 sees the human problem in terms of this same prophetic insight. It inveighs against those "who trust in their wealth and boast themselves in the multitude of their riches" observing that "none of them can by any means redeem his brother nor give to God a ransom for him," and insisting that no special strength can emancipate man from common human frailty: "Their secret thought is that their houses shall continue forever. . . . Nevertheless man, being in honour, abideth not. He is like a beast that perisheth. Like sheep they are all laid in the grave. . . . Be not afraid when one is made rich and the glory of his house is increased. For when he dieth he shall carry nothing away." Jesus' parable of the rich fool stands squarely in this whole Biblical interpretation of sin. The rich fool imagines himself secure for many years by reason of his filled granaries. He declares: "Soul, thou hast much goods laid up for many years; take thine ease, eat, drink and be merry. But God said unto him, Thou fool, this night thy soul shall be required of thee: then whose shall those things be, which thou hast provided?" (Lk. 12:19–20).

The most classical definition of sin in the New Testament, that of St. Paul, is conceived in terms of perfect consistency with this prophetic interpretation. The sin of man is that he seeks to make himself God: "For the wrath of God is revealed from heaven against all ungodliness and unrighteousness of men, who hold the truth in unrighteousness; . . . because that when they knew God, they glorified him not as God, neither were thankful; but became vain in their imaginations, and their foolish heart was darkened. Professing themselves to be wise, they became fools, and changed the glory of the incorruptible God into an image made like to corruptible man, and to birds, and to four-footed beasts, and creeping things" (Romans 1:18–23).

The serious view which the Bible takes of this sin of man's rebellion against God naturally leads to an interpretation of history in which judgment upon sin becomes the first category of interpretation. The most obvious meaning of history is that every nation, culture and civilization brings destruction upon itself by exceeding the bounds of creatureliness which God has set upon all human enterprises. The prophets discern this fact of judgment most clearly in regard to Israel itself. The first of the great prophets, Amos, transmutes an inchoate Messianic hope into the expectation of doom: "The day of the Lord will be darkness and not light." But Hebraic prophecy soon extends the conception of judgment to apply not only to Israel but to all nations, including those great empires which God used, for the moment, as executors of judgment upon Israel. They all fall prey to the same temptation of pride and all finally face the same doom. Since the prophets were never wholly successful in convincing Israel that this was the right interpretation of history, a good deal of prophetic literature represents the conflict between the sense of impending doom in prophetic thought and the optimism and the complacency of the nation. During and after the exile this prophetic interpretation of history faced, and was deflected by, the complication of a new problem. The question arose why, if God punishes Israel for its sin, does He use, as instruments of judgment, nations which are more wicked than Israel? This problem has its peculiar and poignant relevance to the historical situation of our own day.

While the course of historical events does not inevitably yield the prophetic interpretation of events, it is significant that history does justify such an interpretation, once faith in the God of the prophets is assumed. It is, in fact, impossible to interpret history at all without a principle of interpretation which history as such does not yield. The various principles of interpretation current in modern culture, such as the idea of progress or the Marxist concept of an historical dialectic, are all principles of historical interpretation introduced by faith. They claim to be conclusions about the nature of history at which men arrive after a "scientific" analysis of the course of events; but there can be no such analysis of the course of events which does not make use of some presupposition of faith, as the principle of analysis and interpretation.

For Biblical faith, God is revealed in the catastrophic events of history as being, what each individual heart has already dimly perceived in its sense of being judged: as the structure, the law, the essential character of reality, as the source and centre of the created world against which the pride of man destroys itself in vain rebellion.

The God who judges and condemns man is not some capricious tyrant whose will and "law" are irrelevant to the structure of the universe. Yet He is not merely "natural law." It is because He transcends the "laws of nature" in His freedom that He can set a law for man, who in his limited way transcends the "laws of nature" and cannot be bound by them. The relation of the freedom of God to the structure of the universe must be considered more fully later. The important point at the present moment is to record the emphasis of Biblical faith upon history as a revelation of the wrath of God upon the sinful pride of man.

But this interpretation leaves an important and ultimate problem unsolved. The further question is whether there is a resource in the heart of the Divine which can overcome the tragic character of history and which can cure as well as punish the sinful pride in which man inevitably involves himself. The Messianic prophecies of the Old Testament are all concerned with that problem in some form or

other. After Amos the prophets all look forward to a final triumph
of God over the sinfulness of man. This problem of the relation of
mercy to judgment becomes obscured, as we shall see in later chapters, by the subordinate question, why Israel, which has a special
historical relation to God, should suffer more than other nations.
The Messianic hope was deflected by this issue and finally expressed
itself primarily as the hope of Israel's vindication over its foes, or at
least the hope of the vindication of the righteous over the unrighteous.

From the standpoint of Christian faith the life and death of Christ
become the revelation of God's character with particular reference
to the unsolved problem of the relation of His judgment to His
mercy, of His wrath to His forgiveness. Christian faith sees in the
Cross of Christ the assurance that judgment is not the final word
of God to man; but it does not regard the mercy of God as a forgiveness which wipes out the distinctions of good and evil in history
and makes judgment meaningless. All the difficult Christian theological dogmas of Atonement and justification are efforts to explicate
the ultimate mystery of divine wrath and mercy in its relation to
man. The good news of the gospel is that God takes the sinfulness
of man into Himself; and overcomes in His own heart what cannot
be overcome in human life, since human life remains within the
vicious circle of sinful self-glorification on every level of moral advance.

This is rightly regarded as the final revelation of the personality
of God. It is final because it is the revelation of God's freedom in
the highest reaches of its transcendence. The judgment of God is
always partly the effect of the structure of reality upon the vitalities
of history which defy that structure. For this reason Greek tragedy
can arrive at conclusions about judgment in history so similar to
the prophetic interpretation. But Greek tragedy has no word about
history to transcend its conception of *nemesis* and its prophecy of
doom. In Biblical faith the longing for divine mercy accompanies
the expectation of judgment, though Old Testament faith is not clear

on just how the mercy of God is to triumph over His wrath, or how the reconciliation between man and God is to be effected, once judgment has taken place.

Christian faith regards the revelation in Christ as final because this ultimate problem is solved by the assurance that God takes man's sin upon Himself and into Himself and that without this divine initiative and this divine sacrifice there could be no reconciliation and no easing of man's uneasy conscience. This revelation is final not only as a category of interpreting the total meaning of history but also as a solution for the problem of the uneasy conscience in each individual. We have previously observed that God as Creator upon whom all life depends and God as Judge who stands over against man is not unknown to each individual in terms of that "general" revelation which is mediated by common human experience. We have also noted that the longing, though not the assurance, of forgiveness and reconciliation is a part of this common experience. The assurance of faith that the nature and character of God are such that He has resources of love and redemption transcending His judgments, is not something which may be known in terms of "general" revelation. It is the most distinctive content of special revelation. It must be observed that, once this character of God is apprehended in terms of special revelation, common human experience can validate it.

There are tentative assurances of divine mercy in the Old Testament. But they do not come to grips with the issue of the relation of mercy to judgment. The characteristic expressions about the mercy of God in the Old Testament are, that He will "cover" our sins, that He will not "remember" them and that He will "blot them out." Sometimes the problem is obscured as in later apocalypse, by the feeling of the righteous that the final revelation of God must consist in His vindication of the righteous rather than in His mercy to sinners.

The difficult conception of the "suffering servant" as the Messiah and messenger of God, suffering for the sins of the guilty though himself guiltless, and revealing thereby not simply the beauty of vicarious suffering in history but the very character of the divine, is thus rightly regarded by Christian faith as the ultimate revelation of God. We shall consider later to what degree Christ himself re-fashioned the Messianic hope and how he disappointed the Messianic dream at certain levels in order to fulfill it at its highest level, at a level at which it was not completely conscious of itself.[2]

It could not be claimed that this interpretation of the Christian revelation is consistently held in Christianity itself. There have al-ways been interpretations of the revelation in Christ, from early Hellenistic Christianity to certain modern forms of Catholic and Anglican thought in which the Incarnation is regarded, not so much as the bearer of the revelation of divine mercy, as the assurance that the gulf between the finite and the eternal, between man and God, between history and superhistory is not unbridgeable. "The word of God became man," said Clement, the early church father, "in order that thou mayest become a god."[3]

This type of Christian faith may be regarded as standing, gen-erally, under the influence of Platonism and Hellenism. For it the problem of human existence is not primarily the problem of sin but the problem of finiteness. Its concern is to prove that God can speak to man and make Himself known, a proposition which Hebraic-Biblical faith has never doubted, since it rests upon the very pre-supposition of such a relationship between God and man. This type of Christianity does not give a Greek or Platonic answer to the prob-lem of time and eternity but it is Greek in regarding this problem as primary. The answer which it gives is a triumph over Greek dual-ism. In Greek thought the tendency is always to regard history as meaningless or evil by reason of its involvement in time and nature. In Hebraic thought it is fully understood that there could be no history at all if human action and existence did not stand in the dimension of eternity as well as of time. For this reason the content of revelation is not primarily the assurance that God can speak to man but rather the assurance that His final word to man is not one of judgment but of forgiveness and mercy. The primary problem of

[2]In Vol. II, Chs. 1, 2.   [3]*Protrepticus,* i.8

human existence is believed to be not man's involvement in nature but the tragic consequence of his effort to extricate himself from nature, finiteness and time by his own effort. This issue must be more fully discussed in the second volume of this study.

The modern liberal Protestant interpretation of Christianity is usually removed one further step from the Biblical faith. In this modern interpretation even the time-eternity issue, which dominates Catholic thought, is not taken seriously; and the problem of sin is not understood at all. This version of Christian faith is obviously informed by, and is an accommodation to, the general presuppositions of modern culture. The optimism of this culture makes the central message of the gospel, dealing with sin, grace, forgiveness and justification, seem totally irrelevant. The naturalism of the culture also reduces the time and eternity problem to meaninglessness.

In consequence the Christology of this type of Christianity is primarily interested in rejecting the rationally absurd orthodox doctrine of the two natures of Christ. Modern liberal Christianity does not understand that this rationally absurd doctrine contains the basic affirmation of the Christian faith in regard to the relation of time and eternity, and that the doctrine is rationally absurd merely because the relevance between time and eternity was stated in terms of Greek philosophy in which it is not possible to state it, since this philosophy assumes an absolute gulf between the "passible" and the "impassible." Since the orthodox doctrine is rejected, the Christ of orthodox faith is transmuted into the "historic Jesus" who "incarnates values worthy of our highest devotion." The whole problem whether there can be anything in the flux of history which is worthy of our highest devotion and by what criterion we are to determine that it has this special eminence and significance is not clearly recognized, because the ethical naturalism, which informs this thought, assumes that nature yields certain ethical values which gradually culminate in human history.

Sometimes modern liberal versions of Christianity become uneasy about the special significance assigned to Jesus. They realize that they are perpetuating an estimate of his significance which is not compatible with their philosophical and theological presuppositions and which is no more than an attenuated form of the orthodox faith. In that case the effort is made to maintain some contact with the traditional faith by affirming simply that Jesus was a very, very, very good man but that of course a better man might appear, at a future date, in which case the loyalty of the faithful would be transferred to him. These moderns do not understand that they cannot transcend the relativities of history by the number of superlatives which they add to their moral estimate of Jesus and that they have not faced the problem of the nature of the criterion by which they judge Jesus to be good and by which they might regard some future character of history to be superior to him. They do not see that all historical judgments are based upon an explicit or implicit assumption about the character of history itself; and that there can be no judgment about the character of history which does not rest upon a further assumption about the relation of history to eternity.

In terms of the study of human nature, the difficulty with all these modern, presumably more credible, interpretations of Christ is that they do not recognize the full stature and freedom of man. Standing in his ultimate freedom and self-transcendence beyond time and nature, he cannot regard anything in the flux of nature and history as his final norm. Man is a creature who cannot find a true norm short of the nature of ultimate reality. This is the significance of the historic doctrine of Christ as the "second Adam." The same Christ who is accepted by faith as the revelation of the character of God is also regarded as the revelation of the true character of man. Christ has this twofold significance because love has this double significance. "God is love," which is to say that the ultimate reality upon which the created world depends and by which it is judged is not an "unmoved mover" or an undifferentiated eternity, but the vital and creative source of life and of the harmony of life with life. But the essence of human nature is also love, which is to say that for man, who is involved in the unities and harmonies of nature but who also transcends them in his freedom, there can be no principle of harmony short of the love in which free personality is united in freedom with other persons. But the coerced unities of nature and the highly relative forms of social cohesion established by historic "laws" are inadequate as final norms of human freedom. The only adequate norm is the historic incarnation of a perfect love which actually transcends history, and can appear in it only to be crucified.[4]

In distinction to modern, and usually covertly naturalistic, versions of Christian revelation the Hellenistic versions (in which the relation of time and eternity in the Incarnation are emphasized) have the merit of insisting upon the true dimension in which human life stands. It stands in the dimension of eternity as well as time. Hellenistic Christianity may be regarded as a partial triumph of the Christian faith over Hellenism. The doctrine of the Incarnation, the belief that God has become man and the hope that man can become divine, is asserted against the dualism of non-Christian and Platonic Hellenism, according to which a great gulf is fixed between the flux of nature and history and the perfection and calm of the eternal order.

But Hellenistic Christianity (and with it the whole of the Catholic tradition insofar as it subordinates all other problems to the time-eternity issue) exhausts itself in maintaining this Biblical emphasis against the dualism and pessimism of Greek thought. It therefore neglects the more basic issue of Biblical religion. This issue is not the finiteness of man but his sin, not his involvement in the flux of nature but his abortive efforts to escape that flux. The issue of Biblical religion is not primarily the problem of how finite man can know God but how sinful man is to be reconciled to God and how history is to overcome the tragic consequences of its "false eternals," its proud and premature efforts to escape finiteness.

It is in answer to this central problem of history, as Biblical faith conceives it, that God speaks to man in the Incarnation; and the content of the revelation is an act of reconciliation in which the judgment of God upon the pride of man is not abrogated, in which

[4]This issue will be dealt with more fully in Vol. II, Ch. 3.

the sin of man becomes the more sharply revealed and defined by the knowledge that God is Himself the victim of man's sin and pride. Nevertheless the final word is not one of judgment but of mercy and forgiveness.

This doctrine of Atonement and justification is the "stone which the builders rejected" and which must be made "the head of the corner." It is an absolutely essential presupposition for the understanding of human nature and human history. It is a doctrine which, as we shall see, was subordinated to the "time-eternity" implications of the doctrine of the Incarnation in patristic Christianity. It was qualified by that same doctrine in medieval Catholicism, so that Catholicism failed to understand the full seriousness of human sin or the full tragedy of human history. It emerged with elemental force in the Protestant Reformation, to become the central truth of the Christian religion. But it quickly lost its central position, so that modern liberal Protestantism knows less of its meaning or significance than the Middle Ages did.

Why this Biblical-Protestant interpretation of human nature should have had such a short life is one of the ancillary problems which must engage our attention. If medieval Catholicism united Biblical and classical Greek interpretations of human nature, and if the modern period begins by the destruction of this synthesis, the Renaissance emphasizing the classical element in the synthesis while the Reformation abstracted the Biblical element from it, the subsequent history of modern culture marks the virtual triumph of the Renaissance viewpoint over Reformation doctrine; and finally the disintegration of the Renaissance viewpoint. In this disintegration the Platonic and idealistic elements in classicism give way to Stoic and finally to Epicurean forms of naturalism.

Thus modern views of man tend to eliminate the very elements in the classical-Renaissance view which are most closely related to the Biblical view. Having eliminated the time-eternity dimension in measuring human nature, they naturally regard with uncomprehending contempt or fury those aspects of th Biblical view which introduce a further complexity into the time-eternity dimension, the complexity of sin.

We shall seek in Volume II of this study to determine how modern culture succeeded so completely in neglecting or destroying those Biblical insights into human nature which the Reformation rescued from the medieval synthesis. Is the pride of modern man a new version of the old human pride which finds the conclusions of Biblical religion too damaging to human self-esteem? Or did the Reformation make a serious error in its transmission of Biblical insights? Before seeking to answer these questions in the second half of this study, we must address ourselves to the task of explicating the meaning of the Biblical doctrine of man.

CHAPTER VI

MAN AS IMAGE OF GOD AND AS CREATURE

THE Christian view of man is sharply distinguished from all alternative views by the manner in which it interprets and relates three aspects of human existence to each other: (1) It emphasizes the height of self-transcendence in man's spiritual stature in its doctrine of "image of God." (2) It insists on man's weakness, dependence, and finiteness, on his involvement in the necessities and contingencies of the natural world, without, however, regarding this finiteness as, of itself, a source of evil in man. In its purest form the Christian view of man regards man as a unity of God-likeness and creatureliness in which he remains a creature even in the highest spiritual dimensions of his existence and may reveal elements of the image of God even in the lowliest aspects of his natural life. (3) It affirms that the evil in man is a consequence of his inevitable though not necessary unwillingness to acknowledge his dependence, to accept his finiteness and to admit his insecurity, an unwillingness which involves him in the vicious circle of accentuating the insecurity from which he seeks escape.

In analysing these three elements in the Christian view of man we shall seek, on the one hand, to trace the various efforts within the Christian faith, to state the logic of this Biblical doctrine clearly against the constant peril of confusing admixtures from other, partially contradictory, views of man. On the other hand we must seek to validate the Christian view by measuring the adequacy of its answer for human problems which other views have obscured and confused.

II

BIBLICAL BASIS OF THE DOCTRINES

The Biblical doctrine that man was made in the image of God and after His likeness is naturally given no precise psychological elaboration in the Bible itself. Nor does Biblical psychology ever achieve the careful distinctions of Greek thought. As in early Greek thought, spirit and soul are not at first carefully distinguished in the Bible. *Ruach* and *nephesh*, both meaning "breath" and "wind," are used interchangeably in the Old Testament and they connote the Hebraic sense of the unity of body and soul rather than any special idea of the transcendence of spirit. It is important for an understanding of this Hebraic sense of man's complete unity that the locus of *nephesh* is believed to be in the blood. Gradually however the term *ruach* becomes the more specific designation of man's organ of relation to God, in distinction to *nephesh* which achieves a connotation identical with "soul" or ψυχή, of the life principle in man (*Vis vitalis*). The prophets for instance are always said to be animated by the *ruach* of God.[1] The New Testament distinction between ψυχή and πνεῦμα is practically identical with that of the later writings in the Old Testament, πνεῦμα expressing the same concept as *ruach*. Thus it is distinguished as spirit from soul, but not absolutely for "spirit is never something separate beside the soul. . . . Spirit and soul are never separated from each other as soul and body. They may be distinguished but not separated: and when distinguished, spirit is the principle of the soul."[2] While the distinction between

---

[1] *Cf.* H. Wheeler Robinson, *The Christian Doctrine of Man*, pp. 20 and 65; also *Realencyklopaedie fuer Protestantische Theologie und Kirche*, Vol. VI, p. 452.

[2] *Realencyklopaedie*, Vol. VI, p. 453.

soul and spirit is not absolute yet the πνεῦμα, which the New Testament uses almost exclusively to designate spirit in distinction to the more rationalistic νοῦς of Greek philosophy, designates the relative God-likeness of man to such a degree that some commentators advance the plausible, though not conclusive, opinion, that the Pauline psychology assumes no natural πνεῦμα in man but only as a special charismatic gift from God.[3] While St. Paul uses the word πνεῦμα to designate the spirit of man as a natural endowment, it must be admitted that Pauline psychology generally juxtaposes πνεῦμα to σάρξ in terms which are prompted by his doctrine of salvation and in which πνεῦμα means something more than a natural capacity and σάρξ means the principle of sin rather than the body. The Biblical psychology, minus the Genesis doctrine of the image of God in man, does not therefore lay the full foundation for the subsequent Christian view of man but it does fit into the general outline of subsequent emphases by not making too sharp a distinction between body and soul and between soul and spirit, and by not defining spirit in terms of such sharp intellectualistic connotations as are found in Greek philosophy. The Hebraic sense of the unity of body and soul is not destroyed while, on the other hand, spirit is conceived of as primarily a capacity for and affinity with the divine.

This latter emphasis is made explicit through the attempts of Christian theology to define what is meant by the "image of God." These attempts, particularly in the early period of strong Platonic influence and in the latter Middle Ages, when Aristotle shared with Augustine and the Bible the position of ultimate arbiter of theological truth, sometimes define the "imago Dei" in terms which do not advance beyond the limits of the Aristotelian conception of man as a

---

[3]Cf. *inter alia*, Weiss, *The History of Primitive Christianity*, Vol. II, p. 479. Holtzmann held a similar view. The view is not conclusive because St. Paul speaks distinctively of the spirit of man in 1 Cor. 2:11 and 5:3.

For a comprehensive analysis of the Biblical concept of πνεῦμα in the New Testament and for definitions and connotations of "spirit" in Christian thought *see*, Edwyn Bevan, *Symbolism and Belief*, Chs. 7 and 8.

rational creature. Yet even in the most Platonic and Aristotelian forms of Christianity some suggestions of the "imago Dei" as an orientation of man toward God, some hint of the Christian understanding of man's capacity for indeterminate self-transcendence are given.[4]

Augustine is, in this as in other doctrines, the first Christian theologian to comprehend the full implications of the Christian doc-

[4]Gregory of Nyssa defines the image of God in man thus: "The Godhead is mind and word for 'in the beginning was the Word'...humanity too is not far removed from these; you see in yourself word and understanding, an imitation of the very Mind and Word" (Par. V, "On the Making of Man"). And again: "Thus the soul finds its perfection in that which is intellectual and rational; everything which is not may indeed share the name of soul but it is not really soul but a certain vital energy associated with the name of soul" (Par. XV). The implications of this essential Platonism are fully stated: "All the peculiar conditions of brute creation are blended with the intellectual part of the soul. To them belongs anger, to them belongs fear, to them all those opposing activities within us, everything but the faculty of reason and thought. That alone, the choice product, as has been said of all our life, bears the stamp of the Divine image" ("On the Soul and the Resurrection"). Yet Gregory introduces a more Biblical element into this rationalism with the observation: "Again God is love and the fount of love; ... the fashioner of our nature has made this to be our feature too; ... thus if this be absent the whole stamp of the likeness is transformed." Par. XI in the *Nicene and Post-Nicene Fathers, Second Series,* Vol. V, pp. 390–442.

Origen's Platonism completely destroys the Biblical sense of the unity of man. For him the image of God in man, the ψυχή λογική is really a fallen supernal spirit who expiates his pre-existent fall by his life in a physical body.

In Thomas Aquinas intellectualistic and Biblical conceptions of the "image of God" are compounded, with the Aristotelian elements achieving predominance. The image of God is defined as "primarily intellectual nature"; but "secondly we may consider the image of God in man as regards its accidental qualities so far as to observe imitation of God consisting in the fact that man proceeds from man as God from God; and also in the fact that the whole human soul is in the whole human body and again in every part, as God is in regard to the whole world." Nevertheless, this consideration does not shake his dominant rationalism which is strong enough to prompt him to challenge Augustine's assertion that man rather than the angels is made in the image of God. "We must grant," he writes, "that absolutely speaking the angels are

trine of man.[5] Augustine was and remained sufficiently under the influence of neo-Platonism to define the image of God in what seems at first glance to be terms of pure rationalism. He declares: "For not in the body but in the mind was man made in the image of God. In his own similitude let us seek God; in his own image recognize the Creator."[6] Or again: "It is in the soul of man, that is, in his rational or intellectual soul, that we must find that image of the Creator which is immortally implanted in its immortality. . . .

---

more to the image of God than man is, though in some respects man is more like God." *Summa theologiae,* Part I, Question 93, Art. 3.

In regard to the image of God as man's relation of virtuous obedience and love to God, Aquinas holds that this could not have belonged to man's original nature or it could not have been destroyed by the Fall. Since man does not possess it now it must be regarded as a supernatural endowment which man lost in the Fall: "The rectitude [of the primitive state] consisted in his reason being subject to God, the lower powers to reason and the body to the soul; and the first subjection was the cause of both the second and the third. Now it is clear that such a subjection was not from nature; otherwise it would have remained after sin. . . . Hence it is clear that also the primitive subjection by virtue of which reason was subject to God was not merely a natural gift but a supernatural endowment of grace." *Summa,* Part I, Question 95, Art. 1.

This official Catholic doctrine of a *donum superadditum* given to man beyond his natural endowments and lost in the Fall, leaving him thus with his natural virtues unimpaired, is very confusing. Ostensibly it is a supernatural virtue which is destroyed, but the capacity for it is the same as that which leads to sin, namely man's self-transcendent spirit. The structure of man is therefore altered after the Fall. He has become an essentially Aristotelian man. He has a capacity for natural virtue which is subject to the limitations of man immersed in finiteness. He lacks the capacity for the eternal. If this were true he would also lack the capacity for the sinful glorification of himself.

[5] Calvin rightly points to Augustine's profundity in distinction to the inconsistencies and obscurities in the doctrine of man in the early fathers. He says: "Although the Greeks beyond all others and among them particularly Chrysostom have exceeded all bounds in extolling the ability of the human will, yet such are the variations, fluctuations or obscurities of all the fathers, except Augustine, upon this subject that scarcely anything certain can be concluded from their writings." *Institutes,* Book II, Ch. 2, par. 4.

[6] In *Joan. Evang.,* XXIII, 19.

Although reason or intellect be at one time dormant within it, at another appears to be small and at another great, yet the human soul is never anything but rational and intellectual. Hence if it is made after the image of God in respect to this, that it is able to use reason for the understanding and beholding of God, then from the very moment when that nature so marvellous and so great began to be, whether this image be so worn down as to be almost none at all, whether it be obscure and defaced or bright and beautiful, assuredly it always is."[7] But it is immediately apparent that Augustine means by "the rational and intellectual soul" something more than the capacity for discursive reasoning, the ability to form "general concepts." Here his neo-Platonic heritage comes to the aid of his Biblical faith: for the νοῦς of Plotinus represents the capacity for self-knowledge and introspection. Augustine is primarily interested in the capacity of transcendence to the point of self-transcendence in the human spirit. The human memory is of particular importance to him as a symbol of man's capacity to transcend time and finally himself: "When I enter there [the place of memory] I require what I will to be brought forth and something instantly comes; others must be longer sought after, which are fetched as it were out of some inner receptacle. . . . Nor yet do the things themselves enter in; only the images of the things perceived are there in readiness, for thought to recall. . . . For even while I dwell in darkness and silence, in my memory I can produce colours if I will . . . yea I discern the breath of lilies from violets, though smelling nothing. . . . These things I do in the vast court of my memory. . . . There also I meet with myself, and recall myself and when and where and what I have done and under what feelings. . . . Out of the same store do I myself with the past continually combine fresh likenesses of things, which I have experienced, have believed; and thence again infer future actions, events and hopes, and all these again I reflect on, as present. I will do this or that, say I to myself, in that great receptacle of my mind, stored with images of things so many and so great, and this or that might be."

[7]From *De trin.*, XIV, 4, 6.

His description of the capacity to transcend temporal process, and of the ultimate power of self-determination and self-transcendence stir a sense of amazement in Augustine and the conviction that the limits of the self lie finally outside the self. He concludes his hymn of praise to memory with the words: "Great is the force of memory, excessive great, O my God; a large and boundless chamber; who ever sounded the bottom thereof? yet is this a power of mine and belongs to my nature; nor do I myself comprehend all that I am. *Therefore is the mind too strait to contain itself.* And where should that be which it containeth not of itself? Is it without it and not within? and how then does it not comprehend itself? A wonderful admiration surprises me, amazement seizes me upon this." He returns again and again to the power of self-transcendence as the most remarkable aspect of his power of transcendence: "When then I remember memory, memory itself is through itself, present with itself; but when I remember forgetfulness there are present both memory and forgetfulness." . . . "Great is the power of memory, a fearful thing, O my God, a deep and boundless manifoldness; and this thing is the mind and this am I myself. What am I then, O my God? What nature am I?"

The conclusions at which Augustine arrives in the contemplation of this mystery of human self-transcendence are of tremendous importance for the understanding of man's religious nature. He concludes that the power of transcendence places him so much outside of everything else that he can find a home only in God: "I dive on this side and on that, as far as I can and there is no end. So great is the force of memory, so great is the force of life, even in the mortal life of man. What shall I do then, O Thou my true life my God? I will pass beyond this power of mine which is called memory; yea, I will pass beyond it that I may approach unto Thee, O sweet Light. . . . And where shall I find Thee? If I find Thee without my memory then do I not retain Thee in my memory. And how shall I find Thee if I remember Thee not?"[8]

[8]*Confessions,* Book X, par. 7-17.

Those final questions are of particular significance because they mark the watershed between neo-Platonic and Christian thought in Augustine's mind. As a neo-Platonist Augustine sought God in the mystery of self-consciousness; and there are passages in his earlier writings in which he is still close to the deification of self-consciousness: "Descend into thyself; go into the secret chamber of thy mind. If thou be far from thyself, how canst Thou be near to God?"[9] Or again: "If thou dost find that nature is mutable, rise above thyself. But when thou transcendest thyself, remember that thou raisest thyself above the rational soul; strive therefore to reach the place where the very light of reason is lit."[10] Indeed it must be admitted that Augustine's interest in, and emphasis upon, the mysteries and majesties of the human spirit are not derived solely from the insights of the Christian religion. They are so remarkable because he was able to exploit what mysticism and Christianity, at their best, have in common: their understanding that the human spirit in its depth and height reaches into eternity and that this vertical dimension is more important for the understanding of man than merely his rational capacity for forming general concepts. This latter capacity is derived from the former. It is, as it were, a capacity for horizontal perspectives over the wide world, made possible by the height at which the human spirit is able to survey the scene.

However, Augustine's Biblical faith always prompts him finally to stop short of the mystic deification of self-consciousness. Man's powers point to God; but they cannot comprehend him: "Insofar as concerns the nature of man there is in him nothing better than the mind or reason. But he who would live blessedly ought not to live according to them; for then he would live according to man, whereas he ought to live according to God."[11] Or again: "We are speaking of God. Is it any wonder that Thou dost not comprehend? For if Thou dost comprehend, He is not God. . . . To reach God by the mind in any measure is a great blessedness; but to comprehend Him

[9]In *Joan. Evang.*, XXIII, 10.   [10]*De vera relig.*, XXXIX, 72.
[11]*Retract.*, I, i, 2. Quoted by Przywara, *Augustinian Synthesis*, p. 23.

is altogether impossible."[12] At this very point Augustine's strong
Christian emphasis upon revelation saves him from the ultimate
perils of mysticism. Human life points beyond itself. But it must not
make itself into that beyond. That were to commit the basic sin of
man. It can, therefore, understand the total dimension in which it
stands only by making faith the presupposition of its understanding:
"For although, unless he understands somewhat, no man can believe
in God, nevertheless by the very faith whereby he believes, he is
helped to the understanding of greater things. For there are some
things which we do not believe unless we understand them; and
there are other things which we do not understand unless we believe
them."[13]

When some of Augustine's earlier lapses into neo-Platonism are
discounted, it must be recognized that no Christian theologian has
ever arrived at a more convincing statement of the relevance and
distance between the human and divine than he. All subsequent statements of the essential character of the image of God in man are
indebted to him, particularly if they manage to escape the shallows
of a too simple rationalism.[14]

Under the influence of Augustinian ideas Christian theology consistently interprets the image of God in terms of the rational faculties
of the soul, but includes among these the capacity of rising to the
knowledge of God and (when unspoiled by sin) of achieving blessedness and virtue by reason of subjecting its life to the Creator. Calvin
writes: "Though the soul is not the whole man yet there is no
absurdity in calling him the image of God with relation to the soul:
although I retain the principle . . . that the image of God includes
all the excellence in which the nature of man surpasses all the other

---

[12]*Serm. (de script. N. T.),* CXVII, iii, 5.

[13]In *Ps.* 118, *Serm.* xviii, 3.

[14]It is significant that Karl Barth, who stands, of course, in the general
Augustinian tradition but who is interested to prove that revelation from
God to man has practically no points of contact with man except those
which it itself creates, finds Augustine's definitions of the image of God
in man very inconvenient and criticizes them severely. Cf. *Doctrine of
the Word of God,* p. 281.

species of animals. This term therefore denotes the integrity which Adam possessed when he was endued with right understanding, when he had affections regulated by reason, and all his senses governed in proper order and when in the excellence of his nature he truly resembled the excellence of his Creator."[15] It will be noted that here Calvin defines the image of God in terms of both a unique structure of human nature and of an original and now lost perfection of character. Calvin makes clear that by the reason of the soul he means capacities which include the self-determination of the will and the quality of transcendence which Augustine has analysed: "God hath furnished the soul of man with a mind capable of discerning good from evil, just from unjust; and of discovering by the light of reason what ought to be pursued and avoided. . . . To this He hath annexed the will on which depends the choice. The primitive condition of man was ennobled with those eminent faculties; he possessed reason, understanding, prudence and judgment not only for the government of his life upon earth but to enable him to ascend even to God and eternal felicity."[16] Nor does Calvin omit to do justice to the Hebraic-Biblical sense of the unity of man in his whole nature, body and soul: "Though the principal seat of the divine image was in the mind and heart, or in the soul and its faculties, yet there was no part of man, not even the body, which was not adorned with some rays of his glory."[17]

Though the Protestant Reformation must be regarded, generally, as a revival of Augustinianism both in its view of the human situa-

[15]*Institutes,* Book I, Ch. 15, par. 3.

[16]*Institutes,* Book I, Ch. 15, par. 8.

[17]*Institutes,* Book I, Ch. 15, par. 3. In the same chapter Calvin, following some of the early fathers, points to man's upright position as an aspect of the image of God in him: "I admit that external form, as it distinguishes from brutes, also exalts us more nearly to God: nor will I vehemently contend with any one who would understand by the image of God that

> 'While the mute creation downward bend
> Their sight, and to their earthly mother tend,
> Man looks aloft and with expectant eyes
> Beholds his own hereditary skies.' " (Ovid)

tion and its interpretation of the plan of God to meet that situation, it could hardly be claimed that Martin Luther adds any significant insights to the Augustinian view of the image of God in man. Luther is so concerned to re-establish the Augustinian doctrine of original sin against the semi-Pelagianism of Catholicism that all his interpretations of the image of God are coloured by his eagerness to prove that, whatever the image is, it is now lost: "Wherefore when we now attempt to speak of the image we speak of a thing un-known, an image which we have not only not experienced, but the contrary to which we have experienced all our lives and experience still. Of this image therefore all we now possess are the mere words 'image of God.' . . . But there was in Adam an illumined reason, a true knowledge of God and a will the most upright to love both God and his neighbour."[18] In a sense Luther offers more important indirect than direct, more implicit than explicit, evidence of the fact that some concept of the image of God and of a state of perfection before the Fall is an inevitable consequence of "natural theology," of man's capacity and inclination to transcend his present state of im-perfection and sin and posit a state of perfection which must be realized. For, though Luther insists that "the image is so marred and obscured by sin" and is "so utter leprous and unclean" that we cannot even in thought "reach a comprehension of it," he proceeds, nevertheless, to seek to comprehend and define it, largely in terms of contrast to the present state of sin. He declares that though we only "retain the name and the semblance and, as it were, the naked title of an original dominion—the reality of which is now almost

[18]In *Commentary on Genesis.* Luther usually defines the image of God purely in terms of contrast to the present state of sin. He, more than any Reformation theologian, is confused by the mythical aspects of the state of perfection before the Fall, though all of them accepted the historicity of this state. He allows his imagination to run riot in pictur-ing this state of perfection and insists that it included remarkable attri-butes of physical perfection as well as of mental and spiritual endow-ments. Adam "had powers of vision exceeding those of a lynx" and "handled lions and bears, being stronger than they, as we handle the young of any animal." (*Ibid.*)

wholly lost . . . still it is good for us to know and to think upon this state of things that we may sigh after that day which shall come." The consequence of his definition by contrast is the conclusion that the image of God is something more than the "powers of the soul, memory and mind or intellect and will." He believes that even the scholastic definition of "man's memory being adorned with hope, his intellect with faith and his will with love" is not enough. "The image of God is something far different from this. . . . The image of God created in Adam was a workmanship, the most beautiful, the most excellent, the most noble, . . . his intellect was most clear, his memory most complete and his will the most sincere, accompanied by a most charming security, without any fear of death and without any care or anxiety whatever."[19] Luther's extravagant descriptions of the state of perfection before the Fall are so obviously prompted by the desire to accentuate man's present state of sin, misery and death, and they are, compared with both Augustine and Calvin, so inexact that his thought is not very helpful in interpreting the real import of the Christian conception of the image of God. They may be regarded rather as evidence of a partial corruption of the paradox that Christianity measures the stature of man more highly and his virtue more severely than any alternative view. In the case of Luther the "uneasy conscience" of Christianity erupts so vehemently and is set so uncompromisingly against the moralism of Catholic scholasticism that it is in danger of obscuring insights into the dimension and structure of the human spirit without which the uneasy conscience of man becomes an absurdity.

Without going into further historical analysis it will suffice to assert by way of summary that the Biblical conception of "image of God" has influenced Christian thought, particularly since Augustine (when not under a too strong Platonic or Aristotelian influence), to interpret human nature in terms which include his rational faculties but which suggest something beyond them. The ablest non-

[19] All quotations from his *Commentary on Genesis,* Part IV, II, V, 26 ff.

theological analysis of human nature in modern times, by Heidegger, defines this Christian emphasis succinctly as "the idea of 'transcendence,' namely that man is something which reaches beyond itself— that he is more than a rational creature."[20] Max Scheler, following the Biblical tradition, proposes to use the word "spirit" (*Geist*) in distinction to the Greek *nous* to denote this particular quality and capacity in man, because it must be "a word which, though including the concept of reason, must also include, beside the capacity of thinking ideas, a unique type of comprehension for primeval phenomena (*Urphaenomenen*) or concepts of meaning and furthermore a specific class of emotional and volitional capacities for goodness, love, contrition and reverence." "The nature of man," he declares, "and that which could be termed his unique quality transcend that which is usually called intelligence and freedom of choice and would not be reached if his intelligence and freedom could conceivably be raised to the *n*th degree. . . . Between an intelligent monkey and an Edison, merely as technical intelligence, only a difference of degree, though a great degree, exists. It is the quality of the human spirit on the other hand to lift itself above itself as living organism and to make the whole temporal and spatial world, including itself, the object of its knowledge."[21]

The freedom of which Scheler speaks is something more (and in a sense also something less) than the usual "freedom of choice" so important in philosophical and theological theory. Man is self-deter-

[20]Martin Heidegger, *Sein und Zeit*, p. 49.

[21]Max Scheler, *Die Stellung des Menschen im Kosmos*, pp. 46–47. Scheler obviously overstates his case in this statement. The technical intelligence of an Edison depends upon capacities for abstractions and generalizations which are derived from a more ultimate ability "to make the whole temporal and spatial world including itself the object of its knowledge." If this were not so the monkey ought to be able to approximate Edison's technical intelligence in degree. The distinction between the two is qualitative and not merely quantitative. But Scheler is right in his emphasis upon the final dimension of "spirit" in contrast to mere reason. What is ordinarily meant by "reason" does not imply "spirit," but "spirit" does imply "reason."

mining not only in the sense that he transcends natural process in such a way as to be able to choose between various alternatives presented to him by the processes of nature but also in the sense that he transcends himself in such a way that he must choose his total end. In this task of self-determination he is confronted with endless potentialities and he can set no limit to what he ought to be, short of the character of ultimate reality. Yet this same man is a creature whose life is definitely limited by nature and he is unable to choose anything beyond the bounds set by the creation in which he stands. This paradox of human freedom is succinctly stated by Kierkegaard: "Truth [in the human situation] is exactly the identity of choosing and determining and of being chosen and determined. What I choose I do not determine, for if it were not determined I could not choose it; and yet if I did not determine it through my choice I would not really choose it. It is: if it were not I could not choose it. It is not: but becomes reality through my choice, or else my choice were an illusion. . . . I choose the Absolute? What is the Absolute? I am that myself the eternal personality. . . . But what is this myself? . . . It is the most abstract and yet at the same time the most concrete of all realities. It is freedom."[22]

This excellent statement of the paradox by Kierkegaard is partly confused by his identification of the self with the Absolute and with "eternal personality." In Christian faith the place of Christ as both the revelation of the character of God and of the essential nature of man (the "second Adam") does justice to the fact that man can find his true norm only in the character of God but is nevertheless a creature who cannot and must not aspire to be God. The God who is his norm is God as He is revealed in a character of human history, that is, in Christ. Christ is at once an historical character and more than an historical character. His life transcends the possibilities of history but it remains relevant to all historical striving, for all historical goals can be expressed only in supra-historical terms. If stated in purely historical terms they will embody some contingency of

[22]*Entweder Oder Band,* II, p. 182.

nature and history and set a false limit for the human spirit. This aspect of Christian Christology is not understood by naturalistic versions of the Christian faith in which the "Jesus of history" becomes the norm of life. These versions do not understand the total stature of freedom in which human life stands and are therefore not able to appreciate the necessity of a trans-historical norm of historical life.

The perfect love of the life of Christ ends on the Cross, after having existed in history. It is therefore supra-historical, not in the sense of setting up a non-historical eternity as the goal of human life; but in the sense that the love which it embodies is the point where history culminates and ends.[23]

Implicit in the human situation of freedom and in man's capacity to transcend himself and his world is his inability to construct a world of meaning without finding a source and key to the structure of meaning which transcends the world beyond his own capacity to transcend it. The problem of meaning, which is the basic problem of religion, transcends the ordinary rational problem of tracing the relation of things to each other as the freedom of man's spirit transcends his rational faculties.[24]

This problem is not solved without the introduction of a principle of meaning which transcends the world of meaning to be interpreted. If some vitality of existence, or even some subordinate principle of coherence is used as the principle of meaning, man is involved in idolatry. He lifts some finite and contingent element of existence into the eminence of the divine. He uses something which

[23]This problem of the relation of Christology to the Christian conception of human freedom will be considered more fully in Vol. II, Ch. 3.

[24]Max Scheler defines this distinction as follows: "A problem of reason would be the following: 'I have a pain in my arm. Where did it come from and how may I be rid of it?' To determine that is a task of science. But I may use the pain in my arm to reflect upon the fact that the world is tainted with pain, evil and sorrow. Then I will ask: What is pain, evil and sorrow essentially and of what nature is the ground of all existence, making pain as such, without reference to my particular pain, possible?" *Op. cit.,* p. 60.

itself requires explanation as the ultimate principle of coherence and meaning. The most obvious forms of idolatry are those in which the world of meaning is organized around a centre of natural or historical vitality, such as the life of a tribe or nation, which is patently contingent and not ultimate. More covert forms of idolatry are achieved if a subordinate principle of coherence and meaning is regarded as the ultimate principle. The causal sequences of nature represent one such subordinate principle. If the effort is made to comprehend the meaning of the world through the principle of natural causation alone, the world is conceived in terms of a mechanistic coherence which has no place for the freedom which reveals itself in human consciousness. Rational principles of coherence represent another, somewhat higher, and yet inadequate system of meaning. Every effort to identify meaning with rationality implies the deification of reason. That such an identification represents idolatry and that the laws of reason and logic are incapable of fully comprehending the total meaning of the world, is attested by the fact that life and history are full of contradictions which cannot be resolved in terms of rational principles. Furthermore a mind which transcends itself cannot legitimately make itself the ultimate principle of interpretation by which it explains the relation of mind to the world. The fact of self-transcendence leads inevitably to the search for a God who transcends the world. Augustine accurately describes the logic of this procedure in the words: "I dive on this side and on that as far as I can see and there is no end. . . . I will pass beyond this power of mine which is called memory; yea I will pass beyond it that I may approach unto Thee."

Though the religious faith through which God is apprehended cannot be in contradiction to reason in the sense that the ultimate principle of meaning cannot be in contradiction to the subordinate principle of meaning which is found in rational coherence yet, on the other hand religious faith cannot be simply subordinated to reason or made to stand under its judgment. When this is done the reason which asks the question whether the God of religious faith is plausible has already implied a negative answer in the question because it has made itself God and naturally cannot tolerate another. The usual procedure in purely rational and intellectual judgments upon religion is to find the God of religious faith essentially identical with the god of reason, with the distinction that religious faith is regarded as a somewhat crude form of apprehending what reason apprehends more purely.

The real situation is that man who is made in the image of God is unable, precisely because of those qualities in him which are designated as "image of God," to be satisfied with a god who is made in man's image. By virtue of his capacity for self-transcendence he can look beyond himself sufficiently to know that a projection of himself is not God. This does not mean that he will not commit idolatry and make God in his own image. Man is constantly tempted to the sin of idolatry and constantly succumbs to it because in contemplating the power and dignity of his freedom he forgets the degree of his limitations. Yet the rigorous efforts of mystic religions to escape the sin of idolatry and to overcome the error of defining God in finite and contingent terms attest to a transcendent perspective in the human spirit from which the sin of idolatry is apprehended.

The ability to be conscious of and uneasy about the sin of idolatry, which is revealed in mystic spirituality, does not, of course, solve the problem of man's self-transcendence on the one hand and finiteness on the other. Without the presuppositions of the Christian faith, men run into the Charybdis of life-denial and acosmism in the effort to escape the Scylla of idolatry. Either they make some contingent and relative vitality or coherence into the unconditioned principle of meaning or they negate the whole of temporal and historical existence because it is involved in contingency.

To understand the paradoxical approach of Christian faith to the problem of human freedom and finiteness, it is necessary to set the doctrine of man as creature in juxtaposition to the doctrine of man as *imago Dei.*

III

THE DOCTRINE OF MAN AS CREATURE

The Christian view of the goodness of creation is solidly anchored in a very simple word of Scripture: "And God saw every thing that he had made, and behold, it was very good" (Gen. 1:31). The doctrine does not of course depend merely upon the authority of this estimate of creation in Genesis. The whole Biblical interpretation of life and history rests upon the assumption that the created world, the world of finite, dependent and contingent existence, is not evil by reason of its finiteness.

It must be admitted that sometimes the authority of this simple dictum in Genesis was all that prevented Christian faith from succumbing to dualistic and acosmic doctrines which pressed in upon the Christian church. Nevertheless Christianity has never been completely without some understanding of the genius of its own faith that the world is not evil because it is temporal, that the body is not the source of sin in man, that individuality as separate and particular existence is not evil by reason of being distinguished from undifferentiated totality, and that death is no evil though it is an occasion for evil, namely the fear of death.

The Biblical view is that the finiteness, dependence and the insufficiency of man's mortal life are facts which belong to God's plan of creation and must be accepted with reverence and humility. In one of the most beautiful Biblical expositions of the glory and majesty of God the brevity of man is presented merely as a contrast to and proof of that majesty: "All flesh is grass and all the goodliness thereof is as the flower of the field; The grass withereth, the flower fadeth: . . . but the word of our God shall stand forever." Even man's collective and national life, which so frequently offers him the illusion of an immortality and eternity transcending his individual finiteness, is rightly seen to be involved in the same finiteness: "Behold, the nations are as a drop of a bucket, and are counted as the small dust of the balance: . . . all nations before him are as nothing; and they are counted to him less than nothing" (Is. 40). The fragmentary character of human life is not regarded as evil in Biblical faith because it is seen from the perspective of a centre of life and meaning in which each fragment is related to the plan of the whole, to the will of God. The evil arises when the fragment seeks by its own wisdom to comprehend the whole or attempts by its own power to realize it. All Biblical theism contains the suggestion that God's will and wisdom must be able to transcend any human interpretation of its justice and meaning, or it would be less than the centre of that inclusive meaning which alone can comprehend the seeming chaos of existence into a total harmony. This surely is the significance of the message of the Book of Job. Job seeks to comprehend the justice of God by human standards, is thwarted and baffled and then finally overwhelmed by God's display of all the mysteries and majesties of creation which are obviously beyond human comprehension. These divine arguments are introduced by the challenging question, "Where wast thou when I laid the foundations of the earth?" and they finally reduce Job to contrite submission: "Therefore have I uttered that I understood not; things too wonderful for me, which I knew not. . . . I have heard of thee by the hearing of the ear: but now mine eye seeth thee. Wherefore I abhor myself, and repent in dust and ashes" (Job 42:3, 5, 6).

Jesus compares the impotence and dependence of man to that of the lower creation: "Which of you by taking thought can add one cubit to his stature?" (Mt. 6:27). Significantly this observation is a part of a general analysis of the human situation, the purpose of which is to affirm that both man and the lower creatures have their existence by and in God's providence. It may be observed, by way of anticipating later expositions of the cause of evil in human life, that Jesus' injunction, "Therefore I say unto you be not anxious" contains the whole genius of the Biblical view of the relation of finiteness to sin in man. It is not his finiteness, dependence and weakness but his anxiety about it which tempts him to sin.

The New Testament may contain fewer striking passages on the brevity and impotence of man and the created world than the Old Testament, but there is no change of emphasis with one exception to be noted later. As in the first chapter of Hebrews, the consistent emphasis is upon the brevity and dependence of all temporal existence in contrast to the majesty and eternity of God. But this contrast is never given a moral connotation. The created world is a good world, for God created it.[1]

It is important to recognize how basic the Christian doctrine of the goodness of creation is for a conception of man in which human finiteness is emphasized but not deprecated. In the Biblical view the contrast between the created world and the Creator, between its dependent and insufficient existence and His freedom and self-sufficiency, is absolute. But this contrast never means that the created world is evil by reason of the particularization and individualization of its various types of existence. It is never a corruption of an original divine unity and eternity, as in neo-Platonism; nor is it evil because of the desire and pain which characterize all insufficient and dependent life, as in Buddhism.[2]

The whole import of the Christian doctrine of creation for the

---

[1] The passage in Hebrews reads: "Thou, Lord, in the beginning hast laid the foundation of the earth; and the heavens are the work of thy hands: They shall perish; but thou remainest; and they all shall wax old as doth a garment; and as a vesture shalt thou fold them up, and they shall be changed: but Thou art the same, and thy years shall not fail" (Hebrews 1:10–12). The passage is a quotation from Ps. 102. The Psalms offer a wide variety of expositions of the same theme.

[2] Augustine strikingly expounds the dialectical emphasis in the Christian doctrine of creation, the emphasis upon both its dependence and goodness: "And what is this? I asked the earth and it answered me 'I am not He'; and whatsoever are in it confessed the same. I asked the sea and the deeps and the living creeping things, and they answered: 'We are not God, seek above us.' . . . I asked the sun, moon, stars. 'Nor (say they) are we the God whom thou seekest.' And I replied to all things that encompass the door of my flesh: 'Ye have told me of my God that ye are not He; tell me something of Him.' And they cried with a loud voice: 'He made us.' . . . I asked the whole frame of the world about my God: and it answered me 'I am not He but He made me.'" *Confessions,* Book X, par. 9.

Christian view of man is really comprehended in the Christian concept of individuality. The individual is conceived of as a creature of
infinite possibilities which cannot be fulfilled within terms of this
temporal existence. But his salvation never means the complete
destruction of his creatureliness and absorption into the divine.[3] On
the other hand, though finite individuality is never regarded as of
itself evil, its finiteness, including the finiteness of the mind, is never
obscured. The self, even in the highest reaches of its self-consciousness, is still the finite self, which must regard the pretensions of universality, to which idealistic philosophies for instance tempt it, as a
sin. It is always a self, anxious for its life and its universal perspectives qualified by its "here and now" relation to a particular body.
Though it surveys the whole world and is tempted to regard its
partial transcendence over its body as proof of its candidature for
divinity, it remains in fact a very dependent self. This is not to say
that men informed by this interpretation will not commit the same
pretensions as other mortals. Half of Christianity has always been
influenced by Platonic concepts; but even if this were not the case,
the pride of man would express itself even in defiance of a faith
which discounted it. Yet it is important to recognize that Christianity
in its authentic and Biblical form is not subject to the charge of
"idealism" so frequently levelled at it by materialists and naturalists.
It knows of the finiteness of the self and of its involvement in all
the relativities and contingencies of nature and history. The presuppositions of its faith make it possible to realize that the self in
the highest reaches of its self-consciousness is still the mortal and
finite self. In this, as in other instances, Kierkegaard has interpreted

---

[3]Augustine rejects mystic doctrines of the deification of man with the
words: "I am of the opinion that the creature will never become equal
with God, even when so perfect a holiness is accomplished within us as
that it shall be quite incapable of receiving an addition. No, all who
maintain that our progress is to be so complete that we shall be changed
into the substance of God, and that we shall thus become what He is
should look well to it how they build up their opinion; upon myself I
must confess that it produces no conviction." *Treatise on Nature and
Grace*, Ch. 38. *Anti-Pelagian Works*, Vol. I, p. 266.

the true meaning of human selfhood more accurately than any modern, and possibly than any previous, Christian theologian. He writes: "The determining factor in the self is consciousness, *i.e.* self-consciousness. The more consciousness, the more self; the more consciousness the more will; the more will, the more self. . . . The self is the conscious synthesis of the limited and the unlimited which is related to itself and the task of which is to become a self, a task which can be realized only in relation to God. To become a self means to become concrete. But to become concrete means to be neither limited nor unlimited, for that which must become concrete is a synthesis. Therefore development consists in this: that in the eternalization of the self one escapes the self endlessly and in the temporalization of the self one endlessly returns to the self."[4]

One must not claim that Christian thought and life have consistently preserved the Biblical insights on the basic character and the essential goodness of the finiteness, dependence and insufficiency of the self. On the contrary Christianity from the very beginning incorporated some of the errors of idealism and mysticism, including their mistaken estimates of the human situation, into its own thought; and has never completely expelled them. The greatest of the early Christian theologians, who dominated the centuries before Augustine, Origen, combined Platonism with Christianity by interpreting the myth of the Fall as pointing to a pre-existent defection of man from God, the punishment for which was his involvement in mutability and finiteness. For him therefore sex, as the consequence of this mutability, was the particular symbol of sin. It is interesting to note that, on the whole Greek side of Christianity, sex is regarded as a special symbol and consequence of sin, not only because sexual lust is seen as a vivid form of sensuality, but also because generation is so obviously a necessity of finite existence; because the incompleteness of man and woman, one without the other, is the most striking example of the insufficiency and dependence of one life upon the other and the most vivid illustration of a qualifica-

[4]*Die Krankheit zum Tode* (Diederich Verlag), p. 27.

tion and modification of an abstractly ideal human nature by natural circumstance and necessity. The idea of bi-sexuality as a consequence of the Fall is a frequent doctrine of Hellenistic Christianity, particularly in its more heretical forms.[5] It is interesting to note that the most brilliant modern exponent of Greek orthodox mysticism, Nikolai Berdyaev, clings to this same interpretation of sex.[6] Duns Scotus had the same view of the significance of bi-sexuality.

The identification of sin and evil with the mutability of the temporal world and with the ignorance of the finite mind is very general in the pre-Augustinian period of Christianity. Justin Martyr taught that sin was ignorance; and Clement defined it as "the weakness of matter" and as "the involuntary impulse of ignorance." Gregory of Nyssa tried desperately, though not too successfully, to harmonize Hellenistic and Biblical views of the nature of evil. He wrote: "It is not allowable to ascribe our constitutional liability to passion to that human nature which was fashioned in the divine likeness; but as brute life first entered the world, and man, for the reason already mentioned, took something of their nature (I mean their mode of generation), he accordingly took at the same time a share of the other attributes contemplated in that nature." . . . "Thus our love of pleasure took its beginning from our being made like to the irrational creation." To this Gregory adds the Biblical idea: "and was increased by the transgression of men, becoming the parent of so many varieties of sins, arising from pleasure, as we cannot find among animals."[7] Gregory's thoroughly Platonic conception of the relation of the soul to the body is vividly expressed in his metaphor of the gold and the alloy, a type of metaphor common to dualistic forms

---

[5] *The Poimandres,* one of the tractates of the Hermetica, has this version of the Fall. Greek thought tends to follow Plato's suggestion in the *Symposium* upon this point. Philo could not conceive of a bi-sexual creature as made in God's image. *Cf.* C. H. Dodd, *The Bible and the Greeks,* p. 165.

[6] *The Destiny of Man,* p. 299.

[7] *On the Making of Man,* XVIII. *Nicene and Post-Nicene Fathers,* Sec. Series, Vol. V.

of Christianity from his day to our own: "Just as those who refine gold from the dross which it contains not only get this base alloy to melt in the fire but are obliged to melt the pure gold along with the alloy and then while this last is being consumed the pure gold remains, so while evil is being consumed in the purgatorial fire, the soul which is welded to this evil must inevitably be in this fire too until the *spurious material alloy* is consumed and annihilated by the fire."[8]

Irenæus' conception of the relation of natural finiteness to the soul is revealed in his belief that the one would be sloughed off to free the other: "We blame Him because He did not make us Gods at the beginning but men first and Gods afterwards. . . . He was aware of the results of human infirmity; but in his love and power He shall subdue the substance of the nature He created. For it was necessary that nature should be exhibited first and afterwards that the mortal part should be subdued by the immortal and finally that man should be made after the image and likeness of God, having received the knowledge of good and evil."[9] On its Hellenistic side, Christianity exhibits many similarities with the Greek cults of immortality and the mystery religions. Salvation is frequently defined as the ultimate deification of man, through Christ's conquest of human mortality.

While it is not Biblical to regard finiteness, as such, as evil it must be admitted that there is strong Biblical support for the conception of death as evil. In Pauline theology death is the consequence of sin. The difference between this idea and the Hellenistic identification of finiteness and sin is trenchantly expressed in the words of Augustine: "It is by sin that we die, and not by death that we sin,"[10] an exposition of the Pauline words in Romans 5:12: "Thus sin came into the world by one man and death came in by sin."

While there is a profound difference between attributing sin to mortality and deriving mortality from sin, the Pauline interpretation of death nevertheless lends itself to dualistic interpretations. It is not

[8]*On the Soul and the Resurrection, op. cit.*
[9]*Treatise Against Heresies,* IV, 38.4. Irenæus was not a Hellenist but yet deeply indebted to the rationalistic Apologists.
[10]*Anti-Pelagian Works,* Vol. I, p. 150.

at all clear that St. Paul consistently regards physical death as the consequence of sin. At any rate he frequently uses the concept of death symbolically to designate spiritual death, as for instance when he speaks of the man who is "dead in trespasses and sins" (Eph. 2:1). Furthermore his classical assertion that the "sting of death is sin" (1 Cor. 15:56) can hardly be interpreted to mean that mortality as such is the consequence of sin. On the contrary, it seems in complete accord with the general Biblical view of the relation of sin to mortality. In this view mortality, insecurity and dependence are not of themselves evil but become the occasion of evil when man seeks in his pride to hide his mortality, to overcome his insecurity by his own power and to establish his independence. The ideal possibility would be that a man of perfect faith would not fear death because of his confidence that "neither life nor death . . . shall be able to separate us from the love of God which is in Christ Jesus our Lord." But since unbelief is the very basis of sin, it is impossible for sinful man to anticipate his end with equanimity. Thus sin is "the sting of death"; and the obvious mark of that sting is fear.

Despite St. Paul's symbolic use of the term death and despite the profound observation in 1 Corinthians 15, it is probable that St. Paul followed the rabbinic teaching of his day in the belief that death was the consequence of Adam's sin.[11] It is frequently assumed that St. Paul merely interpreted the Genesis account of God's curse upon Adam after the Fall. But it must be observed that this account assumes the mortality of man and does not include it as one of the several punishments which Adam must endure.[12]

Certainly the words "for dust thou art" are most naturally re-

---

[11]The Book of Wisdom asserts: "God created man for incorruption but by the envy of the devil death entered into the world" (ii:23–24).

[12]Gen. 3:17-19: "Cursed is the ground for thy sake; in sorrow shalt thou eat bread all the days of thy life; thorns also and thistles shall it bring forth to thee and thou shalt eat the herb of the field; in the sweat of thy face shalt thou eat bread, till thou return unto the ground; for out of it wast thou taken; for dust thou art, and unto dust shalt thou return."

garded as the statement of a fact and not as the promise of future punishment. The concluding words "and to dust shalt thou return" might be made to yield an implied promise of punishment. If so interpreted they would mean that though man arose from the dust, he would not, but for his sin, have returned to it.

This is precisely the interpretation which became dominant in orthodox Christianity. Athanasius puts this doctrine in classical form: "For man, indeed, is by nature mortal as being made of the things that are not. But yet by reason of the similitude to Him that is, he would have repelled his natural corruption and remained incorruptible, as the Book of Wisdom says: 'The giving heed unto Thy laws is the assurance of incorruption.' But being incorruptible, *i.e.*, immortal, he would have lived for the future as God; for this also the Holy Scripture signifies, I suppose, when it says: 'I said ye are gods and ye are all the sons of the Most Highest; but ye die like men and fall like one of the princes. . . . But men turning away from the things that are eternal, and by the counsel of the devil turning to the things that are corruptible, became to themselves a cause of the corruption which is death; being indeed, as I said before, by nature corruptible yet by grace of the participation of the Word they would have avoided what was according to nature, if they had remained perfect."[13]

This interpretation has the merit of seeking to explain the basic paradox of human existence: man's involvement in finiteness and his transcendence over it. But it confuses the paradox by the belief that, if sin had not intervened, man would have of himself transcended mortality. Such an interpretation obscures man's organic relation to nature and could be made meaningful only if it were assumed that sin had introduced death into the whole of nature. But such an assumption becomes almost identical with the Hellenistic belief that nature and finiteness are themselves evil. The orthodox doctrine, rooted in Pauline theology, therefore has affinities with Hellenistic dualism, despite the important distinction that it regards

[13]*De incarnatione verbi Dei,* Par. 5.

death as the consequence of sin and not sin as the consequence of death.[14]

It can hardly be denied that the Pauline authority, supporting the idea that physical death is a consequence of sin, introduced a note into Christian theology which is not fully in accord with the total Biblical view of the finiteness of man. The dominant note in the Biblical view of death is that it illustrates the difference between the majesty of God and the weakness and dependence of man as creature. This does not mean that physical death is accepted as the final word about the fate of man. We shall have occasion to deal with the

[14]The doctrine that death is the consequence of sin is of course variously stated; but it remains a consistent doctrine of Christian orthodoxy. Irenæus' version is: "But God set a bound to his state of sin by interposing death and thus causing sin to cease, putting an end to it by the dissolution of the flesh, which should take place upon the earth, so that man, ceasing at length to live to sin, and by dying to it, might begin to live to God." *Against Heresies,* Book III, xxiii, 6.

Gregory of Nyssa thinks that God created man as mortal in anticipation of his sin: "But as he perceived in our created nature the bias towards evil and the fact that after its voluntary fall from equality with the angels it would require fellowship with the lower nature, he mingled for this reason with his own image, an element of the irrational—transferring I say to man the special attribute of the irrational formation." *On the Making of Man,* Ch. XXI.

Aquinas' version is: "For man's body was indissoluble not by reason of any intrinsic vigour of immortality but by reason of a supernatural force given by God to the soul whereby it was enabled to preserve the body from corruption so long as it remained itself subject to God. . . . This power of preserving the body was not natural to the soul but was a gift of grace. And though man recovered grace as regards the remission of guilt and the merit of glory; yet he did not recover immortality the loss of which was an effect of sin." *Summa theologiae,* Part I, Question 97, Art. 1.

Martin Luther's view is similar upon this point: "Adam, if he had not sinned, would yet have lived a corporeal life, a life which would have needed meat, drink and rest; a life which would have grown, increased and generated until God would have translated him to that spiritual life in which he would have lived without natural animality if I may so express it. . . . And yet he would have been a man with body and bones and not a pure spirit as angels are." *Commentary on Genesis,* III. 5, 7.

significance of the Biblical hope of the resurrection in the second volume[15] of this treatise. Ideally the hope of the resurrection, this Christian confidence in the fulfillment of life beyond the limitations of temporal existence, does not stand in contradiction to the Biblical interpretation of the temporal order as essentially good and not evil. The Pauline view, even though lacking complete consistency, has the general effect of obscuring the sharp line of demarcation between the classical and the Christian view of the temporal world.

The distinctively Christian doctrine that sin has its source not in temporality but in man's willful refusal to acknowledge the finite and determinate character of his existence is the third element in the Christian doctrine of man and must now be considered more fully.

[15]Vol. II, Chs. 9 and 10.

CHAPTER VII

MAN AS SINNER

I N EVERY religion," declared Albrecht Ritschl, the most authoritative exponent of modern liberal Christianity, "what is sought with the help of the superhuman power reverenced by man is a solution of the contradiction in which man finds himself as both a part of nature and a spiritual personality claiming to dominate nature."[1] It is perfectly true that this problem of finiteness and freedom underlies all religion. But Ritschl does not appreciate that the uniqueness of the Biblical approach to the human problem lies in its subordination of the problem of finiteness to the problem of sin. It is not the contradiction of finiteness and freedom from which Biblical religion seeks emancipation. It seeks redemption from sin; and the sin from which it seeks redemption is occasioned, though not caused, by this contradiction in which man stands. Sin is not caused by the contradiction because, according to Biblical faith, there is no absolute necessity that man should be betrayed into sin by the ambiguity of his position, as standing in and yet above nature. But it cannot be denied that this is the occasion for his sin.

Man is insecure and involved in natural contingency; he seeks to overcome his insecurity by a will-to-power which overreaches the limits of human creatureliness. Man is ignorant and involved in the

[1] *Justification and Reconciliation*, p. 199.

limitations of a finite mind; but he pretends that he is not limited. He assumes that he can gradually transcend finite limitations until his mind becomes identical with universal mind. All of his intellectual and cultural pursuits, therefore, become infected with the sin of pride. Man's pride and will-to-power disturb the harmony of creation. The Bible defines sin in both religious and moral terms. The religious dimension of sin is man's rebellion against God, his effort to usurp the place of God. The moral and social dimension of sin is injustice. The ego which falsely makes itself the centre of existence in its pride and will-to-power inevitably subordinates other life to its will and thus does injustice to other life.

Sometimes man seeks to solve the problem of the contradiction of finiteness and freedom, not by seeking to hide his finiteness and comprehending the world into himself, but by seeking to hide his freedom and by losing himself in some aspect of the world's vitalities. In that case his sin may be defined as sensuality rather than pride. Sensuality is never the mere expression of natural impulse in man. It always betrays some aspect of his abortive effort to solve the problem of finiteness and freedom. Human passions are always characterized by unlimited and demonic potencies of which animal life is innocent. The intricate relation between pride and sensuality must be considered more fully presently. First we must analyse the relation of sin to the contradiction of finiteness and freedom.

II

TEMPTATION AND SIN

While the Bible consistently maintains that sin cannot be excused by, or inevitably derived from, any other element in the human situation it does admit that man was tempted. In the myth of the Fall the temptation arises from the serpent's analysis of the human situation. The serpent depicts God as jealously guarding his prerogatives against the possibility that man might have his eyes opened and become "as God, knowing good and evil." Man is tempted, in other words, to break and transcend the limits which God has set for him. The temptation thus lies in his situation of finiteness and freedom. But the situation would not be a temptation of itself, if it were not falsely interpreted by "the serpent." The story of the Fall is innocent of a fully developed satanology; yet Christian theology has not been wrong in identifying the serpent with, or regarding it as an instrument or symbol of, the devil. To believe that there is a devil is to believe that there is a principle or force of evil antecedent to any evil human action. Before man fell the devil fell. The devil is, in fact, a fallen angel. His sin and fall consists in his effort to transcend his proper state and to become like God. This definition of the devil's fall is implied in Isaiah's condemnation of Babylon, in which the pride of Babylon is compared or identified with "Lucifer's" pride: "How art thou fallen from heaven, O Lucifer, son of the morning! how art thou cut down to the ground. For thou hast said in thine heart, I will ascend into heaven, I will exalt my throne above the stars of God. Yet thou shalt be brought down to hell."[1]

It is not necessary to trace the intricate relation between Old Testament satanology and its source in Babylonian and Persian myths. The importance of Biblical satanology lies in the two facts that: (1) the devil is not thought of as having been created evil. Rather his evil arises from his effort to transgress the bounds set for his life, an effort which places him in rebellion against God. (2) The devil fell before man fell, which is to say that man's rebellion against God is not an act of sheer perversity, nor does it follow inevitably from the situation in which he stands. The situation of finiteness and freedom in which man stands becomes a source of temptation only when it is falsely interpreted. This false interpreta-

---

[1]Is. 14:12, 13, 15. In the Slavonic Enoch the fall of the devil is similarly described: "And one from out of the order of angels, having turned away with the order that was under him, conceived an impossible thought, to place his throne higher than the clouds above the earth that he might become equal in rank with my [God's] power. And I threw him out from the height with his angels, and he was flying continually in the air above the bottomless [abyss]." II Enoch, XXIX, 4.

tion is not purely the product of the human imagination. It is suggested to man by a force of evil which precedes his own sin. Perhaps the best description or definition of this mystery is the statement that sin posits itself, that there is no situation in which it is possible to say that sin is either an inevitable consequence of the situation nor yet that it is an act of sheer and perverse individual defiance of God.

But what is the situation which is the occasion of temptation? Is it not the fact that man is a finite spirit, lacking identity with the whole, but yet a spirit capable in some sense of envisaging the whole, so that he easily commits the error of imagining himself the whole which he envisages? Let us note how quickly a mere analysis of the "situation" yields a definition of sin as error rather than as evil. Sin is not merely the error of overestimating human capacities. St. Paul rightly insists that "their foolish heart was darkened" and that "they became vain in their imagination." Neither the devil nor man is merely betrayed by his greatness to forget his weakness, or by his great knowledge to forget his ignorance. The fact is that man is never unconscious of his weakness, of the limited and dependent character of his existence and knowledge. The occasion for his temptation lies in the two facts, his greatness and his weakness, his unlimited and his limited knowledge, taken together. Man is both strong and weak, both free and bound, both blind and far-seeing. He stands at the juncture of nature and spirit; and is involved in both freedom and necessity. His sin is never the mere ignorance of his ignorance. It is always partly an effort to obscure his blindness by overestimating the degree of his sight and to obscure his insecurity by stretching his power beyond its limits.

This analysis proves the impossibility of either eliminating the element of conscious perversity from sin or of reducing it merely to error. But it also reveals that both freedom and necessity, both man's involvement in nature and his transcendence over it must be regarded as important elements in the situation which tempts to sin. Thus man is, like the animals, involved in the necessities and contingencies of nature; but unlike the animals he sees this situation and anticipates its perils. He seeks to protect himself against nature's contingencies; but he cannot do so without transgressing the limits which have been set for his life. Therefore all human life is involved in the sin of seeking security at the expense of other life. The perils of nature are thereby transmuted into the more grievous perils of human history. Or again: man's knowledge is limited by time and place. Yet it is not as limited as animal knowledge. The proof that it is not so limited is given by the fact that man knows something of these limits, which means that in some sense he transcends them. Man knows more than the immediate natural situation in which he stands and he constantly seeks to understand his immediate situation in terms of a total situation. Yet he is unable to define the total human situation without colouring his definition with finite perspectives drawn from his immediate situation. The realization of the relativity of his knowledge subjects him to the peril of scepticism. The abyss of meaninglessness yawns on the brink of all his mighty spiritual endeavours. Therefore man is tempted to deny the limited character of his knowledge, and the finiteness of his perspectives. He pretends to have achieved a degree of knowledge which is beyond the limit of finite life. This is the "ideological taint" in which all human knowledge is involved and which is always something more than mere human ignorance. It is always partly an effort to hide that ignorance by pretension.

In short, man, being both free and bound, both limited and limitless, is anxious. Anxiety is the inevitable concomitant of the paradox of freedom and finiteness in which man is involved. Anxiety is the internal precondition of sin. It is the inevitable spiritual state of man, standing in the paradoxical situation of freedom and finiteness.[2] Anxiety is the internal description of the state of temptation. It must not be identified with sin because there is always the ideal

[2]Kierkegaard says: "Anxiety is the psychological condition which precedes sin. It is so near, so fearfully near to sin, and yet it is not the explanation for sin." *Der Begriff der Angst*, p. 89. Kierkegaard's analysis of the relation of anxiety to sin is the profoundest in Christian thought.

possibility that faith would purge anxiety of the tendency toward sinful self-assertion. The ideal possibility is that faith in the ultimate security of God's love would overcome all immediate insecurities of nature and history. That is why Christian orthodoxy has consistently defined unbelief as the root of sin, or as the sin which precedes pride.[3] It is significant that Jesus justifies his injunction, "Be not anxious" with the observation, "For your heavenly Father knoweth that ye have need of these things." The freedom from anxiety which he enjoins is a possibility only if perfect trust in divine security has been achieved. Whether such freedom from anxiety and such perfect trust are an actual possibility of historic existence must be considered later. For the present it is enough to observe that no life, even the most saintly, perfectly conforms to the injunction not to be anxious.

Yet anxiety is not sin. It must be distinguished from sin partly because it is its precondition and not its actuality, and partly because it is the basis of all human creativity as well as the precondition of sin. Man is anxious not only because his life is limited and dependent and yet not so limited that he does not know of his limitations. He is also anxious because he does not know the limits of his possibilities. He can do nothing and regard it perfectly done, because higher possibilities are revealed in each achievement. All human actions stand under seemingly limitless possibilities. There are, of course, limits but it is difficult to gauge them from any immediate perspective. There is therefore no limit of achievement in any sphere of activity in which human history can rest with equanimity.[4]

It is not possible to make a simple separation between the creative

[3]Martin Luther, in conformity with the general Christian tradition and quoting Sirach 10: 14, writes in his *Treatise on Christian Liberty:* "The wise man has said: The beginning of all sin is to depart from God and not trust Him." Luther frequently defines the state of perfection before the Fall as being completely free of all anxiety. Here, as frequently in Luther's thought, he overstates the case. Ideally anxiety is overcome by faith but a life totally without anxiety would lack freedom and not require faith.

[4]Heidegger calls attention to the significant double connotation of the word "Care," *Sorge, cura,* that is a double connotation revealed in many

and destructive elements in anxiety; and for that reason it is not possible to purge moral achievement of sin as easily as moralists imagine. The same action may reveal a creative effort to transcend natural limitations, and a sinful effort to give an unconditioned value to contingent and limited factors in human existence. Man may, in the same moment, be anxious because he has not become what he ought to be; and also anxious lest he cease to be at all.

The parent is anxious about his child and this anxiety reaches beyond the grave. Is the effort of the parent to provide for the future of the child creative or destructive? Obviously it is both. It is, on the one hand, an effort to achieve the perfection of love by transcending the limits of finiteness and anticipating the needs of the child beyond the death of the parent. On the other hand, as almost every last will and testament reveals, it betrays something more than the perfection of love. It reveals parental will-to-power reaching beyond the grave and seeking to defy death's annulment of parental authority.

The statesman is anxious about the order and security of the nation. But he cannot express this anxiety without an admixture of anxiety about his prestige as a ruler and without assuming unduly that only the kind of order and security which he establishes is adequate for the nation's health. The philosopher is anxious to arrive at the truth; but he is also anxious to prove that his particular truth is the truth. He is never as completely in possession of the

---

languages. He writes: "The perfection of man, his becoming what in his freedom he can become according to his ultimate possibility, is a capacity of care or anxiety (*Sorge*). But just as basically care points to his being at the mercy of an anxious world, of his contingency (*Geworfenheit*). This double connotation of *cura* points to a basic structure in man of contingency and potentiality" (*geworfenen Entwurfs*). *Sein und Zeit,* p. 199.

This double connotation, according to Heidegger, is clearly revealed if *Sorgfalt* is juxtaposed to *Sorge,* that is care as carefulness to care as anxiety. Unfortunately the English language makes the distinction between *Angst* and *Sorge* impossible. Both of them must be translated as *anxiety.*

truth as he imagines. That may be the error of being ignorant of one's ignorance. But it is never simply that. The pretensions of final truth are always partly an effort to obscure a darkly felt consciousness of the limits of human knowledge. Man is afraid to face the problem of his limited knowledge lest he fall into the abyss of meaninglessness. Thus fanaticism is always a partly conscious, partly unconscious attempt to hide the fact of ignorance and to obscure the problem of scepticism.

Anxiety about perfection and about insecurity are thus inexorably bound together in human actions and the errors which are made in the search for perfection are never due merely to the ignorance of not knowing the limits of conditioned values. They always exhibit some tendency of the agent to hide his own limits, which he knows only too well. Obviously the basic source of temptation is, therefore, not the inertia of "matter" or "nature" against the larger and more inclusive ends which reason envisages. It resides in the inclination of man, either to deny the contingent character of his existence (in pride and self-love) or to escape from his freedom (in sensuality). Sensuality represents an effort to escape from the freedom and the infinite possibilities of spirit by becoming lost in the detailed processes, activities and interests of existence, an effort which results inevitably in unlimited devotion to limited values. Sensuality is man "turning inordinately to mutable good" (Aquinas).

Anxiety, as a permanent concomitant of freedom, is thus both the source of creativity and a temptation to sin. It is the condition of the sailor, climbing the mast (to use a simile), with the abyss of the waves beneath him and the "crow's nest" above him. He is anxious about both the end toward which he strives and the abyss of nothingness into which he may fall. The ambition of man to be something is always partly prompted by the fear of meaninglessness which threatens him by reason of the contingent character of his existence. His creativity is therefore always corrupted by some effort to overcome contingency by raising precisely what is contingent to absolute and unlimited dimensions. This effort, though universal, cannot be regarded as normative. It is always destructive. Yet obviously the destructive aspect of anxiety is so intimately involved in the creative aspects that there is no possibility of making a simple separation be-tween them. The two are inextricably bound together by reason of man being anxious both to realize his unlimited possibilities and to overcome and to hide the dependent and contingent character of his existence.

When anxiety has conceived it brings forth both pride and sen-suality. Man falls into pride, when he seeks to raise his contingent existence to unconditioned significance; he falls into sensuality, when he seeks to escape from his unlimited possibilities of freedom from the perils and responsibilities of self-determination, by immers-ing himself into a "mutable good," by losing himself in some natural vitality.

III

THE SIN OF PRIDE

Biblical and Christian thought has maintained with a fair degree of consistency that pride is more basic than sensuality and that the latter is, in some way, derived from the former. We have pre-viously considered the Biblical definition of basic sin as pride and have suggested that the Pauline exposition of man's self-glorification ("they changed the glory of the incorruptible God into an image made like unto corruptible man") is really an admirable summary of the whole Biblical doctrine of sin.[1]

[1] Again it cannot be claimed that Christian thought is absolutely con-sistent in regarding pride as the basic sin. Wherever the classical view of man predominates, whether in early Greek theology, or medieval or modern liberal thought, the tendency is to equate sin with sensuality. The definition of sin as pride is consistently maintained in the strain of theology generally known as Augustinian.

Augustine defines sin as follows: "What could begin this evil will but pride, that is the beginning of all sin? And what is pride but a perverse desire of height, in forsaking Him to whom the soul ought solely to cleave, as the beginning thereof, to make the self seem the beginning. This is when it likes itself too well. . . ." *De civ. Dei,* Book XII, Ch. 13.

Or again: "What is pride but undue exaltation? And this is undue

This Biblical definition is strictly adhered to in that strain of
Christian theology which manages to maintain the Biblical viewpoint against the influence of the rationalist-classical view of man,

---

exaltation, when the soul abandons Him to whom it ought to cleave as
its end and becomes a kind of end in itself." *De civ. Dei,* Book XIV,
Ch. 13.

Pascal's definition is: "This I is hateful. . . . In one word it has two
qualities: It is essentially unjust in that it makes self the centre of everything and it is troublesome to others in that it seeks to make them subservient; for each I is the enemy and would be the tyrant of all others."
Faugère, Vol. I, p. 197.

In Luther, pride and self-love are used synonymously (*Superbia et
amor sui*). Original sin is sometimes defined as the lust of the soul in
general (*Universa concupiscentia*) (Weimer edition III. 215), which expresses itself in the turning of the soul from God to the creature.
Luther's definition of concupiscence is not in opposition to or sharp
distinction from sin as pride. Both have their source in *caro,* which for
Luther has the exact connotation of the Pauline σάρξ. It is not the
"body" as symbol of man's finiteness but "flesh" as symbol of his sinfulness. Stomph defines Luther's conception as follows: "With 'self as
flesh' Luther means that the sinner desires himself just as he is, though
he does not see himself just as he is and does not expressly will himself
as such." M. A. H. Stomph, *Die Anthropologie Martin Luthers,* p. 73.

Thomas Aquinas derives sensuality from a more basic self-love: "The
proper and direct cause of sin is to be considered on the part of the ad-
herence to a mutable good, in which respect every sinful act proceeds
from inordinate desire for some temporal good. Now the fact that some
one desires a temporal good inordinately is due to the fact that he loves
himself inordinately." *Summa,* Part I, Third Number, Question 77,
Art. 4.

Calvin consistently holds to the Pauline definition of sin given in Romans 1. Sin is pride and not ignorance: "They worship not Him but
figments of their own brains instead. This pravity Paul expressly re-
marks: 'Professing themselves wise they became fools.' He had before
said 'they became vain in their imaginations.' But lest any should ex-
culpate them, he adds that they were deservedly blinded, because, not
content with the bounds of sobriety, but arrogating themselves more
than was right they wilfully darkened and even infatuated themselves
with pride, vanity and perverseness. Whence it follows that their folly
is inexcusable, which originates not only in a vain curiosity but in false
confidence and in immoderate desire to exceed the limits of human
knowledge." *Institutes,* Book I, Ch. 4.

in which sin tends to to be identified with ignorance or the passions of the body. The Biblical view colours the definitions of Christian rationalists so that when they define sin primarily as sensuality, they recognize, at least, that this sensuality is not merely the expression of physical impulse but represents an inordinate quality made possible by the freedom of the spirit.[2] We are not at present concerned with the emphasis of Christian theology upon the inexcusable character of this pride and the insistence that sin is rooted in an evil will and not in some antecedent weakness of man.[3] Our present interest is to relate the Biblical and distinctively Christian conception of sin as pride and self-love to the observable behaviour of men. It will be convenient in this analysis to distinguish between three types of pride, which are, however, never completely distinct in actual life: pride of power, pride of knowledge and pride of virtue.[4] The third type, the pride of self-righteousness, rises to a form of spiritual pride, which is at once a fourth type and yet not a specific form of pride at all but pride and self-glorification in its inclusive and quintessential form.

(*a*) "Of the infinite desires of man," declares Bertrand Russell, "the chief are the desires for power and glory. They are not identical though closely allied."[5] Mr. Russell is not quite clear about the relation of the two to each other, and the relation is, as a matter of fact, rather complex. There is a pride of power in which the human ego assumes its self-sufficiency and self-mastery and imagines itself secure against all vicissitudes. It does not recognize the contingent and dependent character of its life and believes itself to be the author of its own existence, the judge of its own values and the master of its own destiny. This proud pretension is present in an

---

[2]Gregory of Nyssa for instance analyses anger as follows: "Thus the arising of anger in us is indeed akin to the impulses of brutes; but it grows by the alliance of thought." *On the Making of Man*, XVIII, 4.

[3]This aspect of the problem of sin will be considered in Ch. 9.

[4]This is a traditional distinction in Christian thought. *Cf.* Mueller, *On the Christian Doctrine of Sin*, Vol. I, p. 177.

[5]*Power. A New Social Analysis*, p. 11.

inchoate form in all human life but it rises to greater heights among those individuals and classes who have a more than ordinary degree of social power.[6] Closely related to the pride which seems to rest upon the possession of either the ordinary or some extraordinary measure of human freedom and self-mastery, is the lust for power which has pride as its end. The ego does not feel secure and therefore grasps for more power in order to make itself secure. It does not regard itself as sufficiently significant or respected or feared and therefore seeks to enhance its position in nature and in society.

In the one case the ego seems unconscious of the finite and determinate character of its existence. In the other case the lust for power is prompted by a darkly conscious realization of its insecurity.[7] The first form of the pride of power is particularly characteristic of individuals and groups whose position in society is, or seems to be, secure. In Biblical prophecy this security is declared to be bogus and those who rest in it are warned against an impending doom. Thus the second Isaiah describes the pride of Babylon in the words: "Thou saidst, I shall be a lady forever; so that thou dost not lay these things to thy heart." The impending doom is defined as a revelation of the weakness and insecurity of Babylon: "Thy nakedness shall be uncovered; yea, thy shame shall be seen."[8] In the same

[6]"Every man would like to be God," declares Mr. Russell, "if it were possible; some few find it difficult to admit the impossibility." *Ibid.*, p. 11.

[7]In modern international life Great Britain with its too strong a sense of security, which prevented it from taking proper measures of defense in time, and Germany with its maniacal will-to-power, are perfect symbols of the different forms which pride takes among the established and the advancing social forces. The inner stability and external security of Great Britain has been of such long duration that she may be said to have committed the sin of Babylon and declared, "I shall be no widow and I shall never know sorrow." Germany on the other hand suffered from an accentuated form of inferiority long before her defeat in the World War. Her boundless contemporary self-assertion which literally transgresses all bounds previously known in religion, culture and law is a very accentuated form of the power impulse which betrays a marked inner insecurity.

[8]Is. 47:3–7. See also Rev. 18:7; Zeph. 2:15.

[handwritten margin note: One form of pride is that sense of power which cannot envision vissicitude of any sort.]

way the first Isaiah warns the rulers of Israel who are described as "the crown of pride" that their "glorious beauty is a fading flower." He declares that in the day of judgment the "Lord of hosts" will be vindicated and will be "for a crown of glory and for a diadem of beauty" (Is. 28:1–5). In other words <u>history invariably shatters the</u> <u>illusions of those who overestimate the power of human life and in</u> <u>the day of judgment God is revealed as the true source and end of</u> <u>life as the "crown of glory."</u> In Ezekiel's prophecies of doom upon the nations of the earth, they are constantly accused of having foolishly overestimated their security, independence and self-mastery. Egypt, for instance, is accused of imagining herself the creator of the river Nile and saying, "My river is my own, I have made it for myself." In the doom which overtakes this pride the real source and end of life will be revealed: "They shall know that I am the Lord" (Ez. 30:8).

The second form of the pride of power is more obviously prompted by the sense of insecurity. It is the sin of those, who knowing themselves to be insecure, seek sufficient power to guarantee their security, inevitably of course at the expense of other life. It is particularly the sin of the advancing forces of human society in distinction to the established forces. Among those who are less obviously secure, either in terms of social recognition, or economic stability or even physical health, the temptation arises to overcome or to obscure insecurity by arrogating a greater degree of power to the self. Sometimes this lust for power expresses itself in terms of man's conquest of nature, in which the legitimate freedom and mastery of man in the world of nature[9] is corrupted into a mere exploitation of nature. Man's sense of dependence upon nature and his reverent gratitude toward the miracle of nature's perennial abundance is destroyed by his arrogant sense of independence and his greedy effort to overcome

[margin handwritten note: The other kind of pride comes from inferiority seeking in power to find its security. p. 198, n. 9]

[9] A legitimate mastery is symbolically expressed in the words of Genesis 1:26: "Let us make man in our image, after our likeness: and let them have dominion over the fish of the sea, and over the fowl of the air, and over the cattle, and over all the earth, and over every creeping thing that creepeth upon the earth."

the insecurity of nature's rhythms and seasons by garnering her stores with excessive zeal and beyond natural requirements. Greed is in short the expression of man's inordinate ambition to hide his insecurity in nature. It is perfectly described in Jesus' parable of the rich fool who assures himself: "Soul, thou hast much goods laid up for many years; take thine ease, eat, drink, and be merry." Significantly this false security is shattered by the prospect of death, a vicissitude of nature which greed cannot master. God said to the rich fool, "This night thy soul shall be required of thee" (Luke 12: 19–20).

Greed as a form of the will-to-power has been a particularly flagrant sin in the modern era because modern technology has tempted contemporary man to overestimate the possibility and the value of eliminating his insecurity in nature. Greed has thus become the besetting sin of a bourgeois culture. This culture is constantly tempted to regard physical comfort and security as life's final good and to hope for its attainment to a degree which is beyond human possibilities. "Modern man," said a cynical doctor, "has forgotten that nature intends to kill man and will succeed in the end."[10]

Since man's insecurity arises not merely from the vicissitudes of

[10]Bertrand Russell makes the mistake of assuming that economic desires are never inordinate unless they are the servants of social pride and power. He writes: "The desire for commodities, when separated from power and glory, is finite, and can be fully satisfied by a modest competence. . . . When a moderate degree of comfort is assured, both individuals and communities will pursue power and glory rather than wealth: they may seek wealth as a means to power, or they may forego an increase of wealth to secure an increase of power but in the former as in the latter case the fundamental motive is not economic." *Power*, p. 12. Mr. Russell rightly criticizes the too simple Marxian interpretation of the primacy of economic motives. But his own interpretation is faulty because he regards the desire for "power and glory" in purely social terms. Greed may indeed be the servant of the desire for social power, since money is one form of "power over men." But the economic motive may be inordinate even when no power over men is sought after. The typical miser seeks absolute security and not social recognition. He wants power over his fate and not over his fellowmen.

nature but from the uncertainties of society and history, it is natural that the ego should seek to overcome social as well as natural insecurity and should express the impulse of "power over men" as well as "power over matter." The peril of a competing human will is overcome by subordinating that will to the ego and by using the power of many subordinated wills to ward off the enmity which such subordination creates. The will-to-power is thus inevitably involved in the vicious circle of accentuating the insecurity which it intends to eliminate. "Woe to thee," declares the prophet Isaiah, "that spoilest, and thou wast not spoiled; and dealest treacherously, and they dealt not treacherously with thee! when thou shalt cease to spoil, thou shalt be spoiled" (Is. 33:1). The will-to-power in short involves the ego in injustice. It seeks a security beyond the limits of human finiteness and this inordinate ambition arouses fears and enmities which the world of pure nature, with its competing impulses of survival, does not know.

The school of modern psychology which regards the will-to-power as the most dominant of human motives has not yet recognized how basically it is related to insecurity, Adler attributes it to specific forms of the sense of inferiority and therefore believes that a correct therapy can eliminate it. Karen Horney relates the will-to-power to a broader anxiety than the specific cases of the sense of inferiority which Adler enumerates. But she thinks that the will-to-power springs from the general insecurities of a competitive civilization and therefore holds out hope for its elimination in a co-operative society.[11] This is still far short of the real truth. The truth is that man is tempted by the basic insecurity of human existence to make himself doubly secure and by the insignificance of his place in the total scheme of life to prove his significance. The will-to-power is in short both a direct form and an indirect instrument of the pride which Christianity regards as sin in its quintessential form.

We have provisionally distinguished between the pride which does not recognize human weakness and the pride which seeks power in

[11] *The Neurotic Personality of Our Time.*

order to overcome or obscure a recognized weakness; and we have
sought to attribute the former to the more established and traditionally respected individuals and groups, while attributing the latter to
the less secure, that is, to the advancing rather than established
groups in society. This distinction is justified only if regarded as
strictly provisional. The fact is that the proudest monarch and the
most secure oligarch is driven to assert himself beyond measure
partly by a sense of insecurity. This is partly due to the fact that the
greater his power and glory, the more the common mortality of
humankind appears to him in the guise of an incongruous fate.
Thus the greatest monarchs of the ancient world, the Pharaohs of
Egypt, exhausted the resources of their realm to build pyramids,
which were intended to establish or to prove their immortality. A
common mortal's fear of death is thus one prompting motive of the
pretensions and ambitions of the greatest lords.[12]

But furthermore, the more man establishes himself in power and
glory, the greater is the fear of tumbling from his eminence, or losing
his treasure, or being discovered in his pretension. Poverty is a peril
to the wealthy but not to the poor. Obscurity is feared, not by those
who are habituated to its twilight but by those who have become

[12]Bertrand Russell doubts whether fear or anxiety could be regarded
as the root of the will-to-power among the great leaders of mankind. He
is inclined to believe that a "hereditary position of command" is a more
plausible basis for it. He would, in other words, sharply separate the
pride which does not know its own weakness and the pride which compensates for a recognized weakness. He cites Queen Elizabeth as one
whose will-to-power was prompted by an hereditary position rather than
by fear (*op. cit.*, p. 20). Yet a modern historian makes this interesting
observation upon the fears which harassed Elizabeth: "Strong as was her
sense of public duty, it failed her here [in dealing with the problem
of her succession]. Her egotism blinded her to the dangers to which
her failure to discuss the subject was likely to expose the state. The
thought that her dignities must, by the efflux of time, pass to another
seems only to have suggested to her the insecurity of her own tenure of
them and the coming extinction of her own authority. Such a prospect
she could not nerve herself to face." J. K. Laughton in *The Cambridge
Modern History*, Vol. III, p. 359.

accustomed to public acclaim. Nor is this sense of insecurity of the powerful and the great to be wholly discounted as being concerned with mere vanities. Life's basic securities are involved in the secondary securities of power and glory. The tyrant fears not only the loss of his power but the possible loss of his life. The powerful nation, secure against its individual foes, must fear the possibility that its power may challenge its various foes to make common cause against it. The person accustomed to luxury and ease actually meets a greater danger to life and mere existence in the hardships of poverty than those who have been hardened by its rigours. The will-to-power is thus an expression of insecurity even when it has achieved ends which, from the perspective of an ordinary mortal, would seem to guarantee complete security. The fact that human ambitions know no limits must therefore be attributed not merely to the infinite capacities of the human imagination but to an uneasy recognition of man's finiteness, weakness and dependence, which become the more apparent the more we seek to obscure them, and which generate ultimate perils, the more immediate insecurities are eliminated. Thus man seeks to make himself God because he is betrayed by both his greatness and his weakness; and there is no level of greatness and power in which the lash of fear is not at least one strand in the whip of ambition.

(*b*) The intellectual pride of man is of course a more spiritual sublimation of his pride of power. Sometimes it is so deeply involved in the more brutal and obvious pride of power that the two cannot be distinguished. Every ruling oligarchy of history has found ideological pretensions as important a bulwark of authority as its police power. But intellectual pride is confined neither to the political oligarchs nor to the savants of society. All human knowledge is tainted with an "ideological" taint. It pretends to be more true than it is. It is finite knowledge, gained from a particular perspective; but it pretends to be final and ultimate knowledge. Exactly analogous to the cruder pride of power, the pride of intellect is derived on the one hand from ignorance of the finiteness of the human mind and on the other hand from an attempt to obscure the known conditioned character of human knowledge and the taint of self-interest in human truth.

The philosopher who imagines himself capable of stating a final truth merely because he has sufficient perspective upon past history to be able to detect previous philosophical errors is clearly the victim of the ignorance of his ignorance. Standing on a high pinnacle of history he forgets that this pinnacle also has a particular locus and that his perspective will seem as partial to posterity as the pathetic parochialism of previous thinkers. This is a very obvious fact but no philosophical system has been great enough to take full account of it. Each great thinker makes the same mistake, in turn, of imagining himself the final thinker. Descartes, Hegel, Kant, and Comte, to mention only a few moderns, were so certain of the finality of their thought that they have become fair sport for any wayfaring cynic. Not the least pathetic is the certainty of a naturalistic age that its philosophy is a final philosophy because it rests upon science, a certainty which betrays ignorance of its own prejudices and failure to recognize the limits of scientific knowledge.

Intellectual pride is thus the pride of reason which forgets that it is involved in a temporal process and imagines itself in complete transcendence over history. "It is this appearance of independent history of state constitutions, systems of law, of ideologies in every special field which above all has blinded so many people," declares Friederich Engels.[13] Yet intellectual pride is something more than the mere ignorance of ignorance. It always involves, besides, a conscious or subconscious effort to obscure a known or partly known taint of interest. Despite the tremendous contribution of Marxist thought in the discovery of the ideological taint in all culture, it is precisely the element of pretense which it fails to understand. Its too simple theory of human consciousness betrays it here. Thus Engels declares: "The real driving force which moves it [ideology] remains

[13]From a letter to F. Mehring, quoted by Sidney Hook, *Toward an Understanding of Karl Marx*, p. 341.

unconscious otherwise it would not be an ideological process."[14] But the real fact is that all pretensions of final knowledge and ultimate truth are partly prompted by the uneasy feeling that the truth is not final and also by an uneasy conscience which realizes that the interests of the ego are compounded with this truth.

Sometimes this root of insecurity in intellectual pride is revealed in the pathetic pretense of an individual thinker; sometimes the thinker hides and exposes not his own insecurity but that of an age, a class or a nation. Descartes' intellectual pride was something more than the ignorance of his ignorance. That was disclosed when he resented the reminder of a friend that his *"Cogito, ergo sum,"* the keystone of his philosophical arch, was derived from Augustinian thought.[15] Schopenhauer's pride was more than the consequence of his inability to measure the limits of his system. It was compensation for his lack of recognition in competition with more widely acclaimed idealistic thinkers. In the case of such men as Hegel and Comte, individual and representative pride is curiously mingled. Hegel not only proclaimed the finality of his own thought but regarded his contemporary Prussian military state as the culmination of human history. Comte believed his philosophy to be final not only as a philosophy but as a religion; and with pathetic national pride he predicted that Paris would be the centre of the new universal culture which he would found.[16]

A particular significant aspect of intellectual pride is the inability of the agent to recognize the same or similar limitations of perspective in himself which he has detected in others. The Marxist detection of ideological taint in the thought of all bourgeois culture is significantly unembarrassed by any scruples about the conditioned character of its own viewpoints. "Socialist thought," declares Karl Mannheim, "which hitherto has unmasked all its adversaries' utopias as ideologies, never raised the problem of determinateness about its

[14]*Ibid.*, p. 341.
[15]*Cf.* Etienne Gilson, *Unity of Philosophical Experience*, p. 157.
[16]Auguste Comte, *Catechism of Positive Religion*, p. 211.

own position. It never applied this method to itself and checked its own desire to be absolute."[17] The fanaticism which springs from this blindness becomes particularly tragic and revealing when it is expressed in conflict between various schools of Marxist thought as for instance between the Stalinists and Trotskyites. Each is forced to prove and to believe that the opponent is really a covert capitalist or fascist, since ideological taint in genuine proletarian thought is inconceivable. The proud achievement of Marxism in discovering the intellectual pride and pretension of previous cultures therefore ends in a pitiful display of the same sin. It has no inkling of the truth of the Pauline observation: "For wherein thou judgest another, thou condemnest thyself; for thou that judgest doest the same things" (Romans 2:1).

The Marxist pride may, as in other instances of similar pride, be regarded as merely the fruit of the ignorance of ignorance. The Marxist has mistakenly confined ideological taint to economic life and therefore erroneously hopes for a universal rational perspective when economic privileges would be equalized. But one has the right to suspect that something more than ignorance is involved. The vehemence with which the foe is accused of errors of which the self regards itself free betrays the usual desperation with which the self seeks to hide the finiteness and determinateness of its own position from itself.

There is in short no manifestation of intellectual pride in which the temptations of both human freedom and human insecurity are not apparent. If man were not a free spirit who transcends every situation in which he is involved he would have no concern for unconditioned truth and he would not be tempted to claim absolute validity for his partial perspectives. If he were completely immersed in the contingencies and necessities of nature he would have only his own truth and would not be tempted to confuse his truth with *the* truth. But in that case he would have no truth at all, for no particular event or value could be related meaningfully to the

[17]*Ideology and Utopia*, p. 225.

whole. If on the other hand man were wholly transcendent he would not be tempted to insinuate the necessities of the moment and the vagaries of the hour into the truth and thus corrupt it. Nor would he be prompted to deny the finiteness of his knowledge in order to escape the despair of scepticism which threatens him upon the admission of such ignorance. Yet the ignorance of ignorance which underlies every attempt at knowledge can never be described as a mere ignorance. The ignorance presupposes pride, for there is always an ideal possibility that man should recognize his own limits. This implicit pride becomes explicit in the conscious efforts to obscure the partiality of the perspective from which the truth is apprehended. The explicit character of this pride is fully revealed in all cases in which the universalistic note in human knowledge becomes the basis of an imperial desire for domination over life which does not conform to it. The modern religious nationalist thus declares in one moment that his culture is not an export article but is valid for his nation alone. In the next moment he declares that he will save the world by destroying inferior forms of culture.

The insecurity which hides behind this pride is not quite as patent as the pride, yet it is also apparent. In the relations of majority and minority racial groups for instance, for which the negro-white relation is a convenient example, the majority group justifies the disabilities which it imposes upon the minority group on the ground that the subject group is not capable of enjoying or profiting from the privileges of culture or civilization. Yet it can never completely hide, and it sometimes frankly expresses the fear that the grant of such privileges would eliminate the inequalities of endowment which supposedly justify the inequalities of privilege.[18] The pretension of pride is thus a weapon against a feared competitor. Sometimes it is intended to save the self from the abyss of self-contempt which always yawns before it.[19]

[18] *Cf.* Paul Levinson, *Race, Class and Party,* for striking examples of this sense of insecurity in the dominant group.

[19] An interesting example of pride as defense against self-contempt is offered by an historian of the French Directory. He writes: "These

(c) All elements of moral pride are involved in the intellectual pride which we have sought to analyse. In all but the most abstract philosophical debates the pretension of possessing an unconditioned truth is meant primarily to establish "my good" as unconditioned moral value. Moral pride is revealed in all "self-righteous" judgments in which the other is condemned because he fails to conform to the highly arbitrary standards of the self. Since the self judges itself by its own standards it finds itself good. It judges others by its own standards and finds them evil, when their standards fail to conform to its own. This is the secret of the relationship between cruelty and self-righteousness. When the self mistakes its standards for God's standards it is naturally inclined to attribute the very essence of evil to non-conformists. The character of moral pride is perfectly described in the words of St. Paul: "For I bear them record that they have the zeal of God, but not according to knowledge. For they, being ignorant of God's righteousness and going about to establish their own righteousness, have not submitted themselves unto the righteousness of God" (Romans 10:2–3). Moral pride is the pretension of finite man that his highly conditioned virtue is the final righteousness and that his very relative moral standards are absolute. Moral pride thus makes virtue the very vehicle of sin, a fact which explains why the New Testament is so critical of the righteous in comparison with "publicans and sinners." This note in the Bible distinguishes Biblical moral theory from all simple moralism, including Christian moralism. It is the meaning of Jesus' struggle with the pharisees, of St. Paul's insistence that man is saved "not by works

---

profiteers were also doctrinaires and they clung to their doctrines with the greater tenacity because only thus could they escape the self-contempt which otherwise they would have felt in their secret hearts. They were under no illusion as to the life they were leading, the system of government they had established or the persons they employed to maintain it. But sunk though they were in foulness they cling to the shadow of an ideal aim. . . . They asked nothing better than to be stigmatized as sectaries, illuminati and fanatics, for in that case people would forget to call them 'rotten.' " Pierre Gaxotte, *The French Revolution*, p. 390.

lest any man should boast," in fact of the whole Pauline polemic
against the "righteousness of works"; and it is the primary issue in
the Protestant Reformation. Luther rightly insisted that the unwillingness of the sinner to be regarded as a sinner was the final form
of sin.[20] The final proof that man no longer knows God is that he
does not know his own sin.[21] The sinner who justifies himself does
not know God as judge and does not need God as Saviour. One
might add that the sin of self-righteousness is not only the final sin
in the subjective sense but also in the objective sense. It involves us
in the greatest guilt. It is responsible for our most serious cruelties,
injustices and defamations against our fellowmen. The whole history
of racial, national, religious and other social struggles is a commentary on the objective wickedness and social miseries which result from self-righteousness.

Spiritual pride.

(*d*) The sin of moral pride, when it has conceived, brings forth
spiritual pride. The ultimate sin is the religious sin of making the
self-deification implied in moral pride explicit. This is done when
our partial standards and relative attainments are explicitly related
to the unconditioned good, and claim divine sanction. For this reason
religion is not simply as is generally supposed an inherently virtuous
human quest for God. It is merely a final battleground between God
and man's self-esteem. In that battle even the most pious practices
may be instruments of human pride. The same man may in one
moment regard Christ as his judge and in the next moment seek
to prove that the figure, the standards and the righteousness of
Christ bear a greater similarity to his own righteousness than to that
of his enemy. The worst form of class domination is religious class
domination in which, as for instance in the Indian caste system, a
dominant priestly class not only subjects subordinate classes to social
disabilities but finally excludes them from participation in any universe of meaning. The worst form of intolerance is religious in-

[20]*Superbus primo est excusator sui ac defensor, justificator,* Weimar
ed. of *Works,* Vol. 3, p. 288.

[21]*Nescimus, quid Deus, quid justitia, denique quid ipsum peccatum
sit.* ibid., Vol. 2, p. 106.

tolerance, in which the particular interests of the contestants hide behind religious absolutes.[22] The worst form of self-assertion is religious self-assertion in which under the guise of contrition before God, He is claimed as the exclusive ally of our contingent self. "What goes by the name of 'religion' in the modern world," declares a modern missionary, "is to a great extent unbridled human self-assertion in religious disguise."[23]

Christianity rightly regards itself as a religion, not so much of man's search for God, in the process of which he may make himself God; but as a religion of revelation in which a holy and loving God is revealed to man as the source and end of all finite existence against whom the self-will of man is shattered and his pride abased. But as soon as the Christian assumes that he is, by virtue of possessing this revelation, more righteous, because more contrite, than other men, he increases the sin of self-righteousness and makes the forms of a religion of contrition the tool of his pride.

Protestantism is right in insisting that Catholicism identifies the church too simply with the Kingdom of God. This identification, which allows a religious institution, involved in all the relativities of history, to claim unconditioned truth for its doctrines and un-

---

[22]One example is worth quoting, the manifesto of Philip of Spain against William of Nassau: "Philip by the grace of God, King of Castile . . . whereas William of Nassau, a foreigner in our realm once honoured and promoted by the late emperor and ourselves, has by sinister practices and arts gained over malcontents, lawless men, insolvents, innovators, and especially those whose religion was suspected, and has instigated these heretics to rebel, to destroy sacred images and churches and to profane the sacraments of God . . . with a view of exterminating by impieties our Holy Catholic faith . . . whereas the country can have no peace with this wretched hypocrite . . . we empower all and every to seize the person and property of this William of Nassau as an enemy of the human race and hereby on the word of a king and minister of God promise any one . . . who will deliver him dead or alive . . . the sum of 25,000 crowns in gold . . . and we will pardon him of any crime if he has been guilty and give him a patent of nobility."

[23]Henrik Kraemer, The Christian Message in the Non-Christian World, p. 212.

conditioned moral authority for its standards, makes it just another tool of human pride. For this reason Luther's insistence that the pope is Anti-Christ was religiously correct. A vicar of Christ on earth is bound to be, in a sense, Anti-Christ. The whole contemporary political situation yields evidence of the perils of the Catholic doctrine of the church. Everywhere the church claims to be fighting the enemies of God without realizing to what degree these enemies are merely the rebels against a corrupt feudal civilization.

But as soon as the Protestant assumes that his more prophetic statement and interpretation of the Christian gospel guarantees him a superior virtue, he is also lost in the sin of self-righteousness. The fact is that the Protestant doctrine of the priesthood of all believers may result in an individual self-deification against which Catholic doctrine has more adequate checks. The modern revival of Reformation theology may be right in regarding the simple moralism of Christian liberalism as just another form of pharisaism. But the final mystery of human sin cannot be understood if it is not recognized that the greatest teachers of this Reformation doctrine of the sinfulness of all men used it on occasion as the instrument of an arrogant will-to-power against theological opponents.[24] There is no final guarantee against the spiritual pride of man. Even the recognition in the sight of God that he is a sinner can be used as a vehicle of that very sin.[25] If that final mystery of the sin of pride is not recognized the meaning of the Christian gospel cannot be understood.

It must be added that it is not necessary to be explicitly religious in order to raise moral pride to explicit religious proportions. Stalin

[24]Luther's attitude toward Schwenkfeld for instance and Calvin's against Castellio and Servetus. It may not be amiss to call attention to the fact that Karl Barth engaged in theological controversy with Emil Brunner some years ago on the theological issues raised in this chapter. He feared that Brunner's pamphlet on "Nature and Grace" conceded too much to the natural goodness of men. His own answer, entitled *Nein,* is informed by a peculiar quality of personal arrogance and disrespect for the opponent.

[25]"Discourses on humility are a source of pride to the vain," declares Pascal, "and of humility in the humble." *Pensées,* 377.

can be as explicit in making unconditioned claims as the pope; and a French revolutionist of the eighteenth century can be as cruel in his religious fervour as the "God-ordained" feudal system which he seeks to destroy. We have previously dwelt upon the fallacious hope of modern culture, that the elimination of religion might result in the elimination of religious intolerance. Religion, by whatever name, is the inevitable fruit of the spiritual stature of man; and religious intolerance and pride is the final expression of his sinfulness. A religion of revelation is grounded in the faith that God speaks to man from beyond the highest pinnacle of the human spirit; and that this voice of God will discover man's highest not only to be short of the highest but involved in the dishonesty of claiming that it is the highest.

IV

THE RELATION OF DISHONESTY TO PRIDE

Our analysis of man's sin of pride and self-love has consistently assumed that an element of deceit is involved in this self-glorification. This dishonesty must be regarded as a concomitant, and not as the basis, of self-love. Man loves himself inordinately. Since his determinate existence does not deserve the devotion lavished upon it, it is obviously necessary to practice some deception in order to justify such excessive devotion. While such deception is constantly directed against competing wills, seeking to secure their acceptance and validation of the self's too generous opinion of itself, its primary purpose is to deceive, not others, but the self. The self must at any rate deceive itself first. Its deception of others is partly an effort to convince itself against itself. The fact that this necessity exists is an important indication of the vestige of truth which abides with the self in all its confusion and which it must placate before it can act. The dishonesty of man is thus an interesting refutation of the doctrine of man's total depravity.

The Biblical analysis of sin is filled with references to the function of deception in the economy of sin. Jesus speaks of the devil as the father of lies (John 8:44). St. Paul declares that the self-glorification of man is a process of changing "the truth of God into a lie" (Romans 1:25) and, with psychological astuteness, he regards the blindness of self-deception not as the consequence of ignorance but ignorance as the consequence of sin. They "became vain in their imaginations and their foolish heart was darkened." They "hold the truth in unrighteousness."[1]

The dishonesty which is an inevitable concomitant of sin must be regarded neither as purely ignorance, nor yet as involving a conscious lie in each individual instance. The mechanism of deception is too complicated to fit into the category of either pure ignorance or pure dishonesty.[2]

A certain degree of inevitable ignorance may be said to constitute the temptation to deception. This natural illusion may be defined as the tendency of the self as knower, finding its self-consciousness at the very centre of the world which it beholds, to believe itself to be the whole world, an error of solipsism which philosophy finds difficulty in avoiding. Yet the self as a determinate existence is obviously not the centre of the world. Furthermore, the self as self-knower may mistake its capacity for self-transcendence as the proof of having a position as ultimate judge, transcending all things.[3] Yet the self,

[1] Other Biblical passages which deal with the deceptions of sin are: Hebrews 3:13; Romans 7:11; Rev. 12:9; II Cor. 11:3 and Gen. 3:13, in which the deception of the serpent in the myth of the Fall is recorded.

[2] Philip Leon, in an invaluable study of human egotism, analyses self-deception as follows: "The self-deceiver does not believe . . . what he says or he would not be a deceiver. He does believe what he says or he would not be deceived. He both believes and does not believe . . . or he would not be self-deceived." *The Ethics of Power*, p. 258.

[3] In Isaiah 47 the sin of Babylon is defined as consisting in the two claims: "I am and none else beside me" and "None seeth me," which may be regarded as succinct definitions of the illusions of the self as centre of the world and of the self as transcending the world, in the one case leading to the denial of the existence of other life and in the other case to a denial of a higher court of judgment. Significantly these illusions are attributed on the one hand to the very greatness of the human mind: "Thy wisdom and thy knowledge, it hath perverted thee," and on the other to dishonesty: "Thou hast trusted thy wickedness."

though standing outside itself and the world, is obviously a finite existence within the world. The pretensions of the self therefore can be maintained only by wilful deception, for which Tertullian had the very accurate description of "willing ignorance."[4] This deception does not require a conscious act of dishonesty in each individual instance. The deception of sin is rather a general state of confusion from which individual acts of deception arise. Yet the deception never becomes so completely a part of the self that it could be regarded as a condition of ignorance. In moments of crisis the true situation may be vividly revealed to the self, prompting it to despairing remorse or possibly to a more creative contrition. The despair of remorse is essentially the recognition of the lie involved in sin without any recognition of either the truth or the grace by which the confusion of dishonesty might be overcome.

Modern psychology and Marxist social analyses have fully substantiated the Christian doctrine of the lie involved in sin, up to a certain point. Marxism cannot see the whole truth about the lie because its materialist conception of consciousness prevents it from understanding the self in all the complexities of its self-transcendence.[5] The psychologists also have had a great deal to say about "ra-

[4]"Such is the power of earthly pleasures, that to retain the opportunity of still partaking of them it [the self] contrives to prolong a willing ignorance and bribes knowledge to play a dishonest part." *De spectaculis,* Ch. 1.

[5]Harold Laski, for instance, declares: "I fully admit that statesmen at any given time are likely to be as sincere as their critics in the belief that they devote the machinery of state to the highest ends they know. My point is the wholly different one that what they can know is set by the economic relationships which the state exists to maintain. . . . The history of British exploitation in Africa is sufficient proof of that. We have set up admirable principles of stewardship through which to guard the interests of the native races there; but immediately gold is discovered on native reserves we can exhaust the resources of human reason to discover grounds on which to invade those preserves. We can even persuade ourselves to believe that the native ought to accept our view that it is for his benefit that we are above all concerned. . . . But these men are sincere; they are seeking to do their best; they genuinely will the good of the whole community. Of course they are and do; this book will have

tionalization" defined by a recent psychologist as "an attempt to make conduct appear sensible and in conformity with custom and social expectation."[6] Their difficulty is usually that they cannot imagine any but a social norm to which the self pretends to conform. They consequently regard deception as primarily intent on social approval; and derive self-deception from this prior social deception.[7]

The real nature of the lie involved in all sinful self-love can be fully understood only in terms of the Christian understanding of the self-transcendent and yet determinate self; and the Christian distinction between the sinful state of the self which denies its limitations and an essential self, whose knowledge of the truth can never be so completely obscured as to make the lies, in which the sinful self involves itself in the process of its self-glorification, either superfluous or wholly convincing. The sinful self needs these deceptions because it cannot pursue its own determinate ends without paying tribute to the truth. This truth, which the self, even in its sin, never wholly obscures, is that the self, as finite and determinate, does not deserve unconditioned devotion. But though the deceptions are needed they are never wholly convincing because the self is the only ego fully privy to the dishonesties by which it has hidden its own interests behind a façade of general interest.

The desperate effort to deceive others must, therefore, be regarded as, on the whole, an attempt to aid the self in believing a pretension it cannot easily believe because it was itself the author of the decep-

---

been written wholly in vain if it suggests that I cast any doubt on the motives of statesmen." *The State in Theory and Practice,* pp. 101–164.

Mr. Laski is a very astute social analyst, who is evidently trying to maintain his convictions within the bounds of Marxist presuppositions. But he does not quite succeed. "Are likely to be as sincere as their critics." How sincere is that? Such a qualified sincerity is adequate ground for casting suspicion upon the motives of statesmen.

[6]L. F. Shaffer, *The Psychology of Adjustment,* p. 168.

[7]Thus the quoted author continues: "Not only are they [drives regarded as inferior or blameworthy] not acknowledged in polite society but the individual becomes so conditioned that he will not admit them to himself." *Ibid.,* p. 169.

tion. If others will only accept what the self cannot quite accept, the self as deceiver is given an ally against the self as deceived. All efforts to impress our fellowmen, our vanity, our display of power or of goodness must, therefore, be regarded as revelations of the fact that sin increases the insecurity of the self by veiling its weakness with veils which may be torn aside. The self is afraid of being discovered in its nakedness behind these veils and of being recognized as the author of the veiling deceptions. Thus sin compounds the insecurity of nature with a fresh insecurity of spirit.

CHAPTER VIII

MAN AS SINNER (*Continued*)

THE egotism of man has been defined and illustrated thus far without a careful discrimination between group pride and the pride and egotism of individuals. This lack of discrimination is provisionally justified by the fact that, strictly speaking, only individuals are moral agents, and group pride is therefore merely an aspect of the pride and arrogance of individuals. It is the fruit of the undue claims which they make for their various social groups. Nevertheless some distinctions must be made between the collective behaviour of men and their individual attitudes. This is necessary in part because group pride, though having its source in individual attitudes, actually achieves a certain authority over the individual and results in unconditioned demands by the group upon the individual. Whenever the group develops organs of will, as in the apparatus of the state, it seems to the individual to have become an independent centre of moral life. He will be inclined to bow to its pretensions and to acquiesce in its claims of authority, even when these do not coincide with his moral scruples or inclinations.

A distinction between group pride and the egotism of individuals is necessary, furthermore, because the pretensions and claims of a collective or social self exceed those of the individual ego. The group is more arrogant, hypocritical, self-centred and more ruthless in the pursuit of its ends than the individual. An inevitable moral tension between individual and group morality is therefore created. "If," said the great Italian statesman, Cavour, "we did for ourselves what we do for our country, what rascals we would be." This tension is naturally most apparent in the conscience of responsible statesmen, who are bound to feel the disparity between the canons of ordinary morality and the accepted habits of collective and political behaviour. Frederick the Great was not, as statesmen go, a man of unique moral sensitivity. His confession of a sense of this tension is therefore the more significant. "I hope," said he, "that posterity will distinguish the philosopher from the monarch in me and the decent man from the politician. I must admit that when drawn into the vortex of European politics it is difficult to preserve decency and integrity. One feels oneself in constant danger of being betrayed by one's allies and abandoned by one's friends, of being suffocated by envy and jealousy, and is thus finally driven to the terrible alternative of being false either to one's country or to one's word."[1]

The egotism of racial, national and socio-economic groups is most consistently expressed by the national state because the state gives the collective impulses of the nation such instruments of power and presents the imagination of individuals with such obvious symbols of its discrete collective identity that the national state is most able to make absolute claims for itself, to enforce those claims by power and to give them plausibility and credibility by the majesty and panoply of its apparatus. In the life of every political group, whether nation or empire, which articulates itself through the instrument of a state, obedience is prompted by the fear of power on the one hand and by reverence for majesty on the other. The temptation to idolatry is implicit in the state's majesty. Rationalists, with their simple ideas of government resting purely upon the consent of the governed, have never appreciated to what degree religious reverence for majesty is implicit in this consent. The political history of man begins with tribal polytheism, can be traced through the religious pretensions of empires with their inevitable concomitants of imperial religions and

---

[1] Quoted by F. Meinecke, *Die Idee der Staatsraison*, p. 377.

their priest-kings and god-kings, and ends with the immoderate and idolatrous claims of the modern fascist state. No politically crystallized social group has, therefore, ever existed without entertaining, or succumbing to, the temptation of making idolatrous claims for itself. Frequently the organs of this group pride, the state and the ruling oligarchy which bears the authority of the state, seek to detach themselves from the group pride of which their majesty is a symbol and to become independent sources of majesty. But this inversion is possible only because the original source of their majesty lies in something which transcends their individual power and prestige, namely the pride and greatness of the group itself.

Sinful pride and idolatrous pretension are thus an inevitable concomitant of the cohesion of large political groups. This is why it is impossible to regard the lower morality of groups, in comparison with individuals, as the consequence of the inertia of "nature" against the higher demands of individual reason. It is true of course that the group possesses only an inchoate "mind" and that its organs of self-transcendence and self-criticism are very unstable and ephemeral compared to its organs of will. A shifting and unstable "prophetic minority" is the instrument of this self-transcendence, while the state is the organ of the group's will. For this reason the immorality of nations is frequently regarded as in effect their unmorality, as the consequence of their existence in the realm of "nature" rather than the realm of reason. "I treat government not as a conscious contrivance," wrote Professor Seeley in a sentiment which expresses the conviction of many modern political scientists, "but as an half-instinctive product of the effort of human beings to ward off from themselves certain evils to which they are exposed."[2]

---

[2]*Political Science,* p. 129. I have interpreted the behaviour of nations primarily from this viewpoint in a previous work, declaring: "Since there can be no ethical action without self-criticism and no self-criticism without the rational capacity for self-transcendence, it is natural that national attitudes can hardly approximate the ethical. . . . The nation is a unity held together much more by force and emotion than by mind." *Moral Man and Immoral Society,* p. 88.

Such an interpretation has a measure of validity but it certainly does not do justice to the "spiritual" character of national pride, nor to the contribution which individuals, with all their rational and spiritual faculties, make to pride of groups and the self-deification of nations. The most conducive proof that the egotism of nations is a characteristic of the spiritual life, and not merely an expression of the natural impulse of survival, is the fact that its most typical expressions are the lust-for-power, pride (comprising considerations of prestige and "honour"), contempt toward the other (the reverse side of pride and its necessary concomitant in a world in which self-esteem is constantly challenged by the achievements of others); hypocrisy (the inevitable pretension of conforming to a higher norm than self-interest); and finally the claim of moral autonomy by which the self-deification of the social group is made explicit by its presentation of itself as the source and end of existence.

It cannot be denied that the instinct of survival is involved in all these spiritual manifestations of egotism; but that is equally true of individual life. We have previously noted that the fear of death is a basic motive of all human pretensions. Every human self-assertion, whether individual or collective, is therefore involved in the inconsistency of claiming, on the one hand, that it is justified by the primary right of survival and, on the other hand, that it is the bearer of interests and values larger than its own and that these more inclusive values are the justification of its conflict with competing social wills. No modern nation can ever quite make up its mind whether to insist that its struggle is a fight for survival or a selfless effort to maintain transcendent and universal values. In the World War both claims were constantly made; and it is significant that even modern Germany, though it has constructed a primitive tribal religion which makes the power and pride of the nation a self-justifying end, nevertheless feels constrained to pretend that its expected victory in Europe is desired as a triumph of a high type of (Aryan) culture over an allegedly inferior and decadent form of (Jewish or liberal) culture. The nation claims (or the claim is made for it) that it is the instrument of a value more universal than its contingent self, because, like the individual, the determinateness of its life is too obvious to be denied, at least by modern man. But the claim that it is itself the final and ultimate value, the cause which gives human existence meaning, is one which no individual can plausibly make for himself. It is plausible, though hardly credible, only because the social unit, particularly the nation, to which the individual belongs, transcends the individual life to such a degree in power, majesty, and pseudo-immortality that the claim of unconditioned value can be made for it with a degree of plausibility.

The significance of this claim is that through it human pride and self-assertion reach their ultimate form and seek to break all bounds of finiteness. The nation pretends to be God. A certain ambiguity which envelops this claim has already been noted. It is on the one hand a demand of a collective will and mind upon the individual. The social group asks for the individual's unconditioned loyalty, asserting that its necessities are the ultimate law of the individual's existence. But on the other hand it is a pretension which the individual makes for himself, not as an individual but as a member of his group. Collective egotism does indeed offer the individual an opportunity to lose himself in a larger whole; but it also offers him possibilities of self-aggrandizement beside which mere individual pretensions are implausible and incredible. Individuals "join to set up a god whom each then severally and tacitly identifies with himself, to swell the chorus of praise which each then severally and tacitly arrogates to himself."[3] It may be that such group pride represents a particular temptation to individuals who suffer from specific forms of the sense of inferiority. The relation of modern fascist nationalism to the insecurity and sense of inferiority of the lower middle classes is therefore significant. But it hardly can be denied that extravagant forms of modern nationalism only accentuate a general character of group life and collective egotism; and that specific forms of inferiority feeling for which this pride compensates

[3]Philip Leon, *The Ethics of Power*, p. 140.

only accentuate the general sense of inferiority from which all men suffer. Collective pride is thus man's last, and in some respects most pathetic, effort to deny the determinate and contingent character of his existence. The very essence of human sin is in it. It can hardly be surprising that this form of human sin is also most fruitful of human guilt, that is of objective social and historical evil. In its whole range from pride of family to pride of nation, collective egotism and group pride are a more pregnant source of injustice and conflict than purely individual pride.

The pride of nations is, of course, not wholly spurious. Their claim to embody values which transcend their mere existence has foundations in fact. It is the very character of human life, whether individual or collective, that it incarnates values which transcend its immediate interests. A particular nation or group of nations may actually be the bearers of a "democratic civilization" or of a communist one. Men are not animals and never fight merely for existence, because they do not have a mere animal existence. Their physical life is always the base for a superstructure of values which transcends physical life.

The pride of nations consists in the tendency to make unconditioned claims for their conditioned values. The unconditioned character of these claims has two aspects. The nation claims a more absolute devotion to values which transcend its life than the facts warrant; and it regards the values to which it is loyal as more absolute than they really are. Nations may fight for "liberty" and "democracy" but they do not do so until their vital interests are imperiled. They may refuse to fight and claim that their refusal is prompted by their desire to "preserve civilization." Neutral nations are not less sinful than belligerent ones in their effort to hide their partial interests behind their devotion to "civilization." Furthermore the civilization to which they claim loyalty does not deserve such absolute devotion as the nation asks for it.

This does not mean that men may not have to make fateful decisions between types of civilization in mortal combat. The moralists who contend that the imperfection of all civilizations negates every obligation to preserve any of them suffer from a naive cynicism. Relative distinctions must always be made in history. But these necessary distinctions do not invalidate the general judgment upon the collective life of man, that it is invariably involved in the sin of pride.

Prophetic religion had its very inception in a conflict with national self-deification. Beginning with Amos, all the great Hebrew prophets challenged the simple identification between God and the nation, or the naive confidence of the nation in its exclusive relation to God. The prophets prophesied in the name of a holy God who spoke judgment upon the nation; and the basic sin against which this judgment was directed was the sin of claiming that Israel and God were one or that God was the exclusive possession of Israel.[4] Judgment would overtake not only Israel but every nation, including the great nations who were used for the moment to execute divine judgment upon Israel but were also equally guilty of exalting themselves beyond measure (Is. 47; Jer. 25:15; Ez. 24-39).

This insight of Biblical religion stands in sharpest contrast to the simple identification of morals and politics in the thought of Plato and Aristotle and their inability to find any perspective from which to judge the relative character and contingent achievements of their Greek city-state. In this realm of thought Greek philosophy must be regarded as no more than a rationalized form of tribal religion. It does not achieve a vantage point from which to criticize the most pretentious and the most plausible form of human pride. This is natural enough, because there is no such vantage point in man himself. The conviction that collective pride is the final form of sin is possible only within terms of a religion of revelation in the faith of which a voice of God is heard from beyond all human majesties

---

[4]*Cf.* Amos 7:16, 17: "Hear thou the word of the Lord: Thou sayest prophesy not against Israel, and drop not thy word against the house of Isaac. Therefore thus saith the Lord: Thy wife shall be an harlot in the city, and thy sons and thy daughters shall fall by the sword, etc."

and a divine power is revealed in comparison with which the "nations are as a drop of a bucket" (Is. 40:15).[5]

This genius of prophetic faith enables Augustine in the Christian era to view the destruction of the Roman Empire without despair and to answer the charge that Christianity was responsible for its downfall with the assertion that, on the contrary, destruction is the very law of life of the "city of this world" and that pride is the cause of its destruction. "But because it [the earthly city] is not a good which acquits the possessors of all troubles, therefore this city is divided in itself into wars, altercations and appetites of bloody and deadly victories. For any part of it that wars against another desires to be the world's conqueror, whereas indeed it is vice's slave. And if it conquer it extols itself and so becomes its own destruction."[6] There are suggestions of a similar perspective upon national pride in Stoic universalism. But the presuppositions of its pantheism betray Stoicism into a doctrine of ἀπάθεια which condemns human vitality indiscriminately and renders it incapable of a discriminate judgment upon the pride and self-will of man. With the exception of Stoicism, prophetic Christianity and qualifiedly Judaism[7] have alone been able

[5]There are of course universalistic notes in both Aristotle and Plato (particularly in the *Timæus*) and Stoic universalism will be considered presently. However none of the classical philosophers conceive of the universal value as standing in contradiction to particular values of Greek culture and civilization, which seem to them final. They think of the universal as the extension of their particular viewpoint, just as a modern communist is a universalist in his hope that communism may become the basis of a world civilization.

The first word to be spoken against a nation and its rulers from within that nation was spoken by a prophet, Amos. He pronounced the judgment of the "Holy One of Israel" against Israel. The difference between the prophetic faith in a God who transcends the nation and whose judgments may condemn a nation and its rulers and the universalistic overtones in high philosophies is very considerable. This difference makes nonsense of the claims of the rationalists that only reason is able to emancipate men of excesive devotion to the parochial and the partial.

[6]*De civ. Dei*, Book XV, Ch. 4.

[7]One must say "qualifiedly Judaism" because post-exilic Judaism exhausted its spiritual resources in maintaining the integrity of a nation,

to find a certain and secure vantage point from which to oppose the self-glorification of nations. This does not, of course, prevent many forms of historic Christianity from playing the part of the court chaplain to the pride of nations. Yet the word of Augustine against the pretensions of empire is one which is possible only in terms of the presuppositions of the Christian faith: "Set justice aside and what are kingdoms but large robber bands, and what are robber bands but little kingdoms? . . . Excellent and elegant was the pirate's answer to the great Macedonian Alexander, who had taken him. The king asking him how he durst molest the seas so, he replied with a free spirit 'How darest thou molest the whole world? But because I do it with a little ship only I am called a thief; thou doing it with a great navy art called a conqueror.' "[8]

Unfortunately this prophetic insight of Augustine's was partially obscured by his identification, however qualified, of the city of God with the historic church, an identification which was later to be stripped of all its Augustinian reservations to become the instrument of the spiritual pride of a universal church in its conflict with the political pride of an empire. This identification had the merit of introducing a religio-political institution into the world which actually placed a check upon the autonomy of nations; but at the price of developing in that institution dangerous similarities with the old Roman Empire, and of establishing the pope as a kind of spiritualized Cæsar. The conflict between Papacy and Empire therefore revealed a curiously ironic quality from beginning to end. The pot called the kettle black. Pope and emperor levelled the charge of

---

scattered among the nations of the earth. Its historic faith became too much a necessity of its racial existence to maintain the prophetic words, spoken against the nation, at their full vigour. Judaism has frequently elaborated moral ideals of relatively universal value, in cooperation with the general tendencies of a liberal culture, more successfully than historic Christianity. It has been "prophetic" in its passion for justice but not usually "prophetic" in its understanding of the basic character of collective pride as a cause of injustice.

[8] *De civ. Dei,* Book IV, Ch. 4.

Anti-Christ at each other; and both were justified in doing so because each saw in the other the sin of pretension, the exaltation above his measure, which defines the Anti-Christ.[9] This was a struggle between two political forces one of which had distilled political power from the principle of sanctity while the other had exalted power to the proportions of sanctity.

The fact that human pride insinuated itself into the struggle of the Christian religion against the pride and self-will of nations merely proves how easily the pride of men can avail itself of the very instruments intended to mitigate it. The church, as well as the state, can become the vehicle of collective egotism. Every truth can be made the servant of sinful arrogance, including the prophetic truth that all men fall short of the truth. This particular truth can come to mean that, since all men fall short of the truth and since the church is a repository of a revelation which transcends the finiteness and sinfulness of men, it therefore has the absolute truth which other men lack.

The element of sinful human pretension which entered into the medieval Christian opposition to the pride of nations made the rise of the new nation, beginning with the Renaissance and Reformation, appear in the light of emancipation from religious tyranny. Even so pious a Catholic as Dante had foreshadowed this interpretation by his opposition to the political ambitions of the papacy. Thus the Renaissance ushered in a period in which not only individuals but

[9]Gregory VII, the founder of the medieval political papacy, indicted Emperor Henry IV as Anti-Christ, and was in turn accused by the German bishops of megalomania. And who is to determine how much personal and clerical pride and how much genuine passion for the "city of God" was mixed into the compound of motives which actuated Gregory's policies?

At the very end of the medieval period Gregory IX and Frederick II charged each other with being Anti-Christ. The emperor insisted that the pope was a false vicar of Christ and therefore the Anti-Christ and the pope made the same charge against the emperor; and not without reason because the emperor proclaimed himself a new Messiah, as the primeval norm of all good, as the ideal man. *Cf.* Alois Demph, *Sacrum Imperium,* pp. 190 and 324 ff.

also nations were to defy all bounds of creatureliness in the name of liberty. Machiavelli fashioned the doctrine of the moral autonomy for the state as Bruno and others conceived it for the individual. Significantly Luther, through the exigencies of religious warfare, was more intent upon challenging the pride of the pope than the arrogance of kings. The pope for him was Anti-Christ but kings ruled by divine right. Thus Protestantism, in spite of its more prophetic conception of the inevitability of sinful pride in all the activities of mankind, allowed a vent for political arrogance of which the rising nation was to take full advantage.

As a consequence a culture, schooled by the Renaissance on the one hand and the Reformation on the other, has resulted in a contemporary period of decadence in which the collective will of man, particularly as embodied in the nation, has achieved heights of sinful pretension never before equalled. The nation is god. The naive polytheism of early empires and their consequent unconscious glorification of themselves as the centre and end of existence has given way to a sophisticated self-glorification of the nation which consciously defies the obvious fact that it is not the whole of existence. This net result is partly a reaction to the error and sin which had crept into Christianity's testimony against the nations, that is, its deification of the historic church. But the very extravagence of modern nationalism must be regarded as partly a reaction to the truth in Christianity rather than the error of the church. It is only within terms of a Christian civilization, though a decadent one, that collective egotism can reach such desperate proportions. For conscious defiance of a known law is bound to be desperate. Here, in the realm of collective behaviour, is a striking commentary on the truth of the Pauline observation: "For I had not known lust, except the law had said, thou shalt not covet. But sin, taking occasion by the commandment, wrought in me all manner of concupiscence. For without the law sin was dead" (Romans 7:7–8).

The pride of nations and the arrogance of self-deification of collective man are the more extravagant for being expressed in and against a Christian culture in which it must consciously negate and defy the highest insights of the faith which formed the culture of the western world.

The most dæmonic form of nationalism today is expressed against rather than in a Christian culture. The German Nazis were quite right in regarding the Christian faith as incompatible with their boundless national egoism. While Christianity may itself be made the tool of nationalism, the Christian faith, if it retains any vitality, is bound to mediate some word of divine judgment upon the nation, which the Nazis find intolerable. No nation is free of the sin of pride, just as no individual is free of it. Nevertheless it is important to recognize that there are "Christian" nations, who prove themselves so because they are still receptive to prophetic words of judgment spoken against the nation. It may be that only a prophetic minority feels this judgment keenly. But there is a genuine difference between nations which do not officially destroy the religious-prophetic judgment against the nation and those which do. While all modern nations, and indeed all nations of history, have been involved in the sin of pride, one must realize, in this as in other estimates of human sinfulness, that it is just as important to recognize differences in the degree of pride and self-will expressed by men and nations, as it is to know that all men and nations are sinful in the sight of God. Here, as in individual life, the final sin is the unwillingness to hear the word of judgment spoken against our sin. By that criterion, the modern fascist nations have achieved a dæmonic form of national self-assertion which is more dangerous even than that of the ancient religious empires because it is expressed within and against the insights of a Christian culture.

II

THE EQUALITY OF SIN AND THE INEQUALITY OF GUILT

Orthodox Christianity has held fairly consistently to the Biblical proposition that all men are equally sinners in the sight of God. The Pauline assertion: "For there is no difference: for all have sinned, and come short of the glory of God" (Romans 3:22, 23) is an indispensable expression of the Christian understanding of sin. Yet it is quite apparent that this assertion imperils and seems to weaken all moral judgments which deal with the "nicely calculated less and more" of justice and goodness as revealed in the relativities of history. It seems to inhibit preferences between the oppressor and his victim, between the congenital liar and the moderately truthful man, between the debauched sensualist and the self-disciplined worker, and between the egotist who drives egocentricity to the point of sickness and the moderately "unselfish" devotee of the general welfare. Though it is quite necessary and proper that these distinctions should disappear at the ultimate religious level of judgment, yet it is obviously important to draw them provisionally in all historic judgments. The difference between a little more and a little less justice in a social system and between a little more and a little less selfishness in the individual may represent differences between sickness and health, between misery and happiness in particular situations. Theologies, such as that of Barth, which threaten to destroy all relative moral judgments by their exclusive emphasis upon the ultimate religious fact of the sinfulness of all men, are rightly suspected of imperilling relative moral achievements of history. In this connection it is significant that Germany, with its Augustinian-Lutheran theological inheritance, has had greater difficulty in achieving a measure of political sanity and justice than the more Pelagian, more self-righteous and religiously less profound Anglo-Saxon world.

Orthodox Catholicism answered this problem of relative moral judgments by incorporating into its system of ethics the whole Stoic concept of the natural law, including its distinction between a relative and an absolute natural law, by which rational norms of justice were made definitive for the Christian conception of virtue and vice. The difficulty with this impressive structure of Catholic ethics, finally elaborated into a detailed casuistic application of general moral standards to every conceivable particular situation, is that it constantly insinuates religious absolutes into highly contingent and historical moral judgments. Thus the whole imposing structure of Thomistic ethics is, in one of its aspects, no more than a religious sanctification of the relativities of the feudal social system as it flowered in the thirteenth century. The confusion between ultimate religious perspectives and relative historical ones in Catholic thought accounts for the fury and self-righteousness into which Catholicism is betrayed when it defends feudal types of civilization in contemporary history as in Spain for instance.

Orthodox Protestantism, both Calvinistic and Lutheran, rightly discerned the perils of moralism and self-righteousness in the rigidities of the natural law; and therefore allowed natural law theories an only subordinate place in its system of thought. In one instance it was prompted by Biblical authority (the Pauline doctrine of the divine ordinance of government in Romans 13) to qualify its aversion to absolute moral judgments in the field of historical relativity. It gave government and the principle of order an absolute preference over rebellion and political chaos. This one exception had morally catastrophic consequences. It tended to ally the Christian church too uncritically with the centres of power in political life and tempted it to forget that government is frequently the primary source of injustice and oppression. Happily Calvin in his later years, and more particularly the later Calvinists, discovered that it was as important to place the ruler under the judgment of God as to regard him as an instrument of God for checking individual sin. This important Calvinistic discovery bore rich consequences in the relation of Calvinistic piety to the democratic movements toward social justice in the seventeenth and eighteenth centuries.

The mistake of Catholic moral casuistry to derive relative moral judgments too simply from the presuppositions of its natural law and the opposite tendency of orthodox Protestantism to efface all moral distinctions of history in the light of a religious conviction of the undifferentiated sinfulness of all men persuade us to walk warily in relating the Biblical truth that all men are sinners to the other truth that there is nevertheless an ascertainable inequality of guilt among men in the actualities of history. Guilt is distinguished from sin in that it represents the objective and historical consequences of sin, for which the sinner must be held responsible. It is the guilt of the sinner that his self-love results in the consequence of broken or unhappy homes, of children made unhappy by the tyranny of their parents, of peoples destroyed by wars which were prompted by the vanity of their rulers, of the poverty of the victims of greed and the unhappiness of the victims of jealousy and envy. Guilt is the objective consequence of sin, the actual corruption of the plan of creation and providence in the historical world.

Obviously men who are equally sinful in the sight of God may also be equally guilty in a specific situation. The equality of their sin must, in fact, lead to the general assumption that their guilt is more equal than it will seem to be upon cursory analysis. Two nations involved in perennial war may thus be equally guilty, even though only one was responsible for the latest act of provocation. A ruthless father may be more equally guilty of the waywardness of his son than a superficial analysis would reveal. An abandoned wife may share equal guilt with her faithless husband though the overt act of desertion was his alone. The Christian doctrine of the sinfulness of all men is thus a constant challenge to re-examine superficial moral judgments, particularly those which self-righteously give the moral advantage to the one who makes the judgment. There is no moral situation in which the Pauline word does not apply: "Therefore thou art inexcusable, O man, whosoever thou art that judgest: for wherein thou judgest another, thou condemnest thyself; for thou that judgest doest the same things" (Romans 2:1).

Yet men who are equally sinners in the sight of God need not be equally guilty of a specific act of wrong-doing in which they are involved. It is important to recognize that Biblical religion has emphasized this inequality of guilt just as much as the equality of sin. A primary source of orthodox Lutheranism's inability to deal effectively with specific moral issues in history is its blindness to the prophetic note in Scriptures in which those who are particularly guilty of moral wrong-doing are constantly singled out. Specially severe judgments fall upon the rich and the powerful, the mighty and the noble, the wise and the righteous (that is, those who are tempted to spiritual pride by their attainment of some relative, socially approved standard of righteousness, the Pharisees). The strictures of the prophets against the mighty, accusing them of pride and injustice, of both the religious and the social dimensions of sin, are consistently partial. Prophetic judgment is levelled at those "which oppress the poor, which crush the needy" (Amos 4:1), those who "lie upon beds of ivory, and stretch themselves upon their couches, and eat the lambs out of the flock, and the calves out of the midst of the stall" (Amos 6:4), who "swallow up the needy, even to make the poor of the land to fail" (Amos 8:4).

The simple religious insight which underlies these prophetic judgments is that the men who are tempted by their eminence and by the possession of undue power become more guilty of pride and of injustice than those who lack power and position. The injustice of the powerful and the pride of the eminent are assumed as a matter of course and they are threatened with judgment: "For the day of the Lord of hosts shall be upon every one that is proud and lofty, and upon every one that is lifted up . . . and the loftiness of man shall be bowed down, and the haughtiness of men shall be made low: and the Lord alone shall be exalted in that day" (Is. 2:12, 17, also Is. 26:5). While the religious dimension of sin, pride, is always the primary concern of the prophets, they see much more clearly than most historic Christianity has seen, that an inevitable concomitant of pride is injustice. The pride which makes itself the source and end of existence subordinates other life to its will and despoils it of its rightful inheritance. Therefore Isaiah continues: "The Lord will enter into judgment with the ancients of his people, and the princes thereof; for ye have eaten up the vineyard; the spoil of the poor is in your houses. What mean ye that ye beat my people to pieces, and grind the faces of the poor? saith the Lord God of hosts" (Is. 3:14, 15). Nor do the prophets hesitate to draw the conclusion that the poor shall be exalted as the powerful are abased: "The meek also shall increase their joy in the Lord, and the poor among men shall rejoice in the Holy One of Israel" (Is. 29:19). The judgment upon the powerful and proud and the promise to the poor and needy is not only an ultimate judgment in the sight of God. The promised judgment is one which reveals itself in history: "Thus saith the Lord, Even the captives of the mighty shall be taken away, and the prey of the terrible shall be delivered: for I will contend with him that contendeth with thee, and I will save thy children" (Is. 49:25).

The prophetic note of moral discrimination between rich and poor, between the powerful and the weak, the proud and the meek is maintained in the New Testament, beginning with Mary's *Magnificat:* "He hath put down the mighty from their seats, and exalted them of low degree. He hath filled the hungry with good things; and the rich he hath sent empty away" (Lk. 1:52 ff.). St. Paul's judgment that "not many wise men after the flesh, not many mighty, not many noble, are called" (1 Cor. 1:26) stands in this same prophetic tradition; and significantly it adds the wise to the mighty and the noble, as standing particularly under the judgment of God. And rightly so; for the pride of the wise and the pretensions of the spiritual leaders of culture and civilization may be more productive of evil than the simpler will-to-power of the mighty and the noble. In the teachings of Jesus this prophetic note of moral discrimination is maintained without reservation. His blessings upon the poor and his woes upon the rich in the beatitudes, as recorded in St. Luke, have sometimes been found inconvenient, and commentators have been happy to prefer the seemingly less rigorous and more ambiguous blessings upon the "poor in spirit" in the version of the beatitudes as recorded in St. Matthew. But the Aramaic word which Jesus probably used had a highly significant double connotation. It meant both "poor" and "humble."[1] The very use of the word therefore would have given support to the anti-aristocratic tradition which fashioned the word. The "poor of the land" were unable to maintain

[1]The Hebrew word *amē ha-ares.*

the meticulous observances of Pharisaic righteousness. They were therefore outcastes by the rules which the moral aristocracy had fashioned and which had become instruments of their power and social prestige rather than guides to good conduct. To prefer these poor and humble men to the conventionally good and self-righteous men was to strengthen rather than weaken the prophetic anti-aristocratic tradition. The good are added to the mighty, noble and wise as standing particularly under the judgment of God.

If one realizes to what degree every civilization, as a system of power, idealizes and rationalizes its equilibrium of power and how these rationalizations invariably include standards of morals which serve the moral and spiritual pride of the ruling oligarchy, it is apparent that an attack upon Pharisaism is really an attack upon the final and most confusing and dishonest pretension of power.

The anti-aristocratic emphasis of the Bible has been interpreted by certain types of sectarian Christianity and by modern secular radicalism in too simple politico-moral terms. Jesus is reduced in this type of thought to the stature of a leader of a proletarian revolt against the rich. The same emphasis has, on the other hand, been too simply obscured by most types of conventional Christianity. These have been anxious to regard the humility of spirit which Jesus extolled as a spiritual grace which transcended all social, political and economic circumstances and might be absent or present among rich or poor alike. Biblical religion is too concerned with the ultimate and perennial human situation to permit a simple political interpretation of its anti-aristocratic tendencies. It is on the other hand too realistic to obscure the fact that socio-economic conditions actually determine to a large degree that some men are tempted to pride and injustice, while others are encouraged to humility.

This Biblical analysis agrees with the known facts of history. Capitalists are not greater sinners than poor labourers by any natural depravity. But it is a fact that those who hold great economic and political power are more guilty of pride against God and of injustice against the weak than those who lack power and prestige. Gentiles are not naturally more sinful than Jews. But Gentiles, holding the dominant power in their several nations, sin against Semitic minority groups more than the latter sin against them. White men sin against Negroes in Africa and America more than Negroes sin against white men. Wherever the fortunes of nature, the accidents of history or even the virtues of the possessors of power, endow an individual or a group with power, social prestige, intellectual eminence or moral approval above their fellows, there an ego is allowed to expand. It expands both vertically and horizontally. Its vertical expansion, its pride, involves it in sin against God. Its horizontal expansion involves it in an unjust effort to gain security and prestige at the expense of its fellows. The two forms of expansion cannot be sharply distinguished because, as previously noted, spiritual pretension can be made an instrument of power in social conflict, and dominant power, measured socially, inevitably seeks to complete its structure by spiritual pretensions.

A too simple social radicalism does not recognize how quickly the poor, the weak, the despised of yesterday, may, on gaining a social victory over their detractors, exhibit the same arrogance and the same will-to-power which they abhorred in their opponents and which they were inclined to regard as a congenital sin of their enemies. Every victim of injustice makes the mistake of supposing that the sin from which he suffers is a peculiar vice of his oppressor. This is the self-righteousness of the weak in distinction to the self-righteousness of the powerful; and it cannot be denied, as Nietzsche observed, that it is a vehicle of vindictive passions. Such a form of moral pride among the weak will accentuate their arrogance when the fortunes of history transmute their weakness into strength. This fact explains the unique fury and the insufferable moral and spiritual arrogance of the new Russian oligarchy, which believes that the very sins of power which it exemplifies by its arrogance are the peculiar vices of capitalism. But the mistakes of a too simple social radicalism must not obscure the fact that in a given historical situation the powerful man or class is actually more guilty of injustice and pride than those who lack power.

The fact that men of intellectual, spiritual and moral eminence should fall under the same judgment as the men of power according to the Bible will seem particularly offensive to most moralists. It is at this point that the anti-aristocratic tendencies of Biblical religion stand in sharpest contrast to all forms of rationalism which assume that the intelligent man is also the good man, and which do not recognize to what degree reason may be the servant of passion; and that the genuine achievements of mind and conscience may also be new occasions for expressing the pride of sinful man. "If any man stand, let him take heed lest he fall" is a warning which is as relevant to bishops, professors, artists, saints and holy men as to capitalists, dictators and all men of power. Every one who stands is inclined to imagine that he stands by divine right. Every one who has achieved a high form of culture imagines that it is a necessary and final form of culture. It is the man who stands, who has achieved, who is honoured and approved by his fellowmen who mistakes the relative achievements and approvals of history for a final and ultimate approval.

It is at this point that the Biblical insight into the sinfulness of all human nature actually supports rather than contradicts the prophetic strictures against the wise, the mighty, the noble and the good. For without understanding the sinfulness of the human heart in general it is not possible to penetrate through the illusions and pretensions of the successful classes of every age. If one did not know that all men are guilty in the sight of God it would not be easy to discern the particular measure of guilt with which those are covered who are able to obscure the weakness and insecurity of man so successfully by their power, and the sinfulness of man by their good works. Aristotelian and Platonic thought, with all of its derivatives, will continue to persuade kings that they are philosophers and philosophers that they are kings; and will tempt them to hide their will-to-power behind their virtues and to obscure their injustices behind their generosities. It is only by an ultimate analysis from beyond all human standards that the particular guilt of the great and the good men of history is revealed.

III

SIN AS SENSUALITY

Without question Biblical religion defines sin as primarily pride and self-love and classical Christian theology remains fairly true to this conception, though on its Hellenistic side Christianity is always tempted to regard sin as basically lust and sensuality. But this defini- tion of sin as pride, which history and experience have amply veri- fied, raises the problem of the relation of sensuality to selfishness. Is it merely a form of selfishness? Or a consequence of selfishness? Or does it betray characteristics which must prompt the conclusion that sensuality is a distinctive form of sin, to be sharply distinguished from self-love?

A provisional distinction must certainly be made. If selfishness is the destruction of life's harmony by the self's attempt to centre life around itself, sensuality would seem to be the destruction of har- mony within the self, by the self's undue identification with and devotion to particular impulses and desires within itself. The sins of sensuality, as expressed for instance in sexual license, gluttony, ex- travagance, drunkenness and abandonment to various forms of physical desire, have always been subject to a sharper and readier social disapproval than the more basic sin of self-love. Very fre- quently the judge, who condemns the profligate, has achieved the eminence in church or state from which he judges his dissolute brethren, by the force of a selfish ambition which must be judged more grievously sinful than the sins of the culprit. Yet Christian cul- tures have usually not deviated from the severer condemnations which non-Christian cultures have visited upon the sins of sensuality. The reason for this aberration is obviously the fact that sensuality is a more apparent and discernible form of anarchy than selfishness.

The compliance of conventional Christian morality with this essential identification of sin and sensuality has given modern critics of Christianity a partial justification for their belief that Christianity encourages prurience in its judgment of sexual problems and a cruel self-righteousness on the part of the self-possessed and respectable members of the community toward those who have fallen into obvious forms of sin. Yet the fact is that only the more Hellenistic and rationalistic forms of Christianity, with which modern critics of Christianity have more kinship than with the main body of Christian tradition, have ever defined sin as primarily sensuality or been inclined to identify sensuality particularly with sexual license.

Origen, the greatest of Hellenistic theologians, had beside his theory of a pre-historic Fall which resulted in man's involvement in the material world another theory of an actual historic Fall in which the serpent is represented as having seduced Eve and as having physically infected her, and in which original sin is defined as an inclination "to ignominy and wantonness."[1] As a consequence Origen consistently regarded all sex activity as inherently wrong and as the ground and origin of all actual sins. Clement of Alexandria defined the Fall as a falling "under the power of pleasure, for by the serpent pleasure creeping on its belly is in a figure signified."[2] Gregory of Nyssa, as noted in another chapter, not only identifies sin with the love of pleasure but derives it from "our being made like unto the irrational creation" though he admits that something is added to animal passion in human life, for it (the love of pleasure) "was increased by the transgression of man becoming the parent of so many varieties of sins arising from pleasure as we can not find among animals."[3] Gregory, following the general views of Platonism in regard to sex, attributed the bi-sexuality of man to the Fall. Such an interpretation is obviously unscriptural since the Genesis account of creation regards bi-sexuality as a part of the original creation: "Male and female created he them." Gregory overcame this difficulty by suggesting that God created man bi-sexually in anticipation of the Fall. Gregory's morbid attitude toward sex is expressed in extrava-

---

[1] *Cf.* N. P. Williams, *The Ideas of the Fall and Original Sin,* p. 227.
[2] *Protrepticus,* XI. iii.
[3] *On the Making of Man,* XVIII, 4.

gant terms in his treatise *De Virginitate*. It is unnecessary to make an exhaustive analysis of the writings of the Greek Fathers to establish the conclusion that the tendency of Greek thought to attribute evil to animal passion has tempted Hellenistic Christianity to a fairly consistent identification of sin with the love of pleasure, with sensuality and lust and prompted it to make sexual life the particular symbol of this lust.[4]

The Pauline-Augustinian theological tradition interprets the relation of sensuality to sin fairly consistently in the light of the first chapter of Paul's epistle to the Romans. Here lust, particularly unnatural lust, is described as a consequence of and punishment for the more basic sin of pride and self-deification. Because men changed the glory of the incorruptible God into the image of corruptible man, and because they "worshipped and served the creature rather than the Creator," therefore "God gave them up unto vile passions, for their women changed the natural use into that which is against nature . . . and even as they refused to have God in their knowledge God gave them up unto a reprobate mind, to do those things which are not fitting, being filled with all unrighteousness, fornication, wickedness, covetousness, maliciousness, etc." (Romans 1:26–30). In enumerating the various forms of sin, St. Paul makes no clear distinction between anti-social vices (selfishness) and lust, but in this instance his thought obviously is that the sins of lust (more particularly unnatural lust) are fruits of the more primal sin of rebellion against God.[5]

Augustine follows the Pauline interpretation literally and, quoting

[4]N. P. Williams, an Anglo-Catholic theologian, curiously seeks to establish the implausible thesis that a morbid attitude toward sex is a characteristic of the Pauline-Augustinian, or in his terms, of the "African" or "twice-born" theology and that it is inconsistent with the "Hellenic" viewpoint. Cf. *The Ideas of the Fall and of Original Sin*, p. 273.

[5]In cataloguing the various vices and sins, St. Paul sometimes enumerates anti-social and sensual sins separately and sometimes lists them indiscriminately, without a clear distinction between them. *Cf.* 1 Cor. 5:10–11; 11 Cor. 12:20; Gal. 5:19–21; Eph. 5:3–5; Col. 3:5–8.

from the first chapter of Romans the words "and receiving in themselves that recompense of their error which was due" (v. 27), declares that "these things were not only sins in themselves but punishment for sins." He continues. "Here now let our opponents say: 'Sin
ought not to have been punished in this way that the sinner through
his punishment should commit more sins.' Perhaps he may say in
answer: God does not compel men to do these things; He only leaves
those alone who deserve to be forsaken."[6]

Sensuality as a secondary consequence of man's rebellion against
God is explained in more explicit terms by Augustine in the following words: "When the first man transgressed the law of God, he
began to have another law in his members which was repugnant to
his mind; then he felt evil of disobedience when he experienced in
the rebellion of his own flesh a most righteous retribution recoiling
on himself.—For it certainly was not just and right that obedience
should be rendered by his servant, that is, his body to him who had
not obeyed his own Lord and Master."[7] Whatever Augustine may
say about the passions of the flesh and however morbidly he may
use sex as the primary symbol of such passions, his analyses always
remain within terms of this general statement. He never regards
sensuality as a natural fruit of the man's animal nature: "We should
therefore wrong our Creator in imputing our vices to our flesh: the
flesh is good, but to leave the Creator and live according to this
created good is mischief."[8]

The Thomistic version of the Pauline-Augustinian interpretation

[6]*Treatise on the Nature of Grace,* Chs. 24 and 25.
[7]*On Marriage and Concupiscence,* Ch. 7.
[8]*De civ. Dei,* Book XIV, Ch. v. Or again: "If any man say that flesh
is the cause of the viciousness of the soul, he is ignorant of man's nature,
for the corruptible body does not burden the soul.—For this corruption
that is so burdensome to the soul is the punishment for the first sin and
not the cause. The corruptible flesh made not the soul to sin, but the
sinning soul made the flesh corruptible; from which corruption although
there arise some incitements to sin, and some vicious desires, yet are not
all sins of an evil life to be laid to the flesh, otherwise we shall make the
devil, who has no flesh, sinless." *De civ. Dei,* Book XIV, Ch. 3.

of sensuality as the consequence of and punishment for sin is fairly true to the original. St. Thomas writes: "God bestowed this favour upon man in his primitive state, that as long as his mind was subject to God, the lower powers of his soul would be subject to his rational mind, and his body to his soul. But inasmuch as through sin man's mind withdrew from subjection to God, the result was that neither were his lower powers wholly subject to his reason; and from this there followed so great a rebellion of carnal appetite against reason that neither was the body subject to the soul; whence arose death and other bodily defects."[9] Though St. Thomas defines original sin as concupiscence he still insists that concupiscence is a consequence of self-love: "Every sinful act proceeds from inordinate desire of a mutable good. Now the fact that some one desires a temporal good inordinately is due to the fact he loves himself inordinately."[10]

The Lutheran interpretation does not differ materially from the Thomistic one, except that Luther eliminates the implicit Aristotelian emphasis upon reason as the master of the body. For Luther, as for St. Thomas, sin is essentially lust (*concupiscentia* or *cupiditas*) but he does not mean by this the natural desires and impulses of physical life. Lust is the consequence of man's turning from God, which results in the corruption of his heart and will with evil desire.[11] This evil desire includes both self-love and sensuality. It is the preference of the self and that which pertains to the self (*se et quae sua*) instead of God. Thus while Luther, as St. Thomas, uses the word lust as the inclusive term for sin, he follows the general tradition in regarding lust, in the narrower sense of sinful pleasure, as a consequence of man's turning from God, of his disobedience and pride. Sensuality is, in effect, the inordinate love for all creaturely and mutable values which results from the primal love of self, rather than love of God.

If we discount Hellenistic theology with its inclination to make

[9] *Summa theologiae*, Part II (Second Part), Question 164, Art. 1.
[10] *Summa*, Part II (First Part), Question 77, Art. 4.
[11] *Mala inclinatio cordis, inordinatio in volunte.*" Werke, *Weimarausgabe*, Vol. III, 453.

sensuality the primary sin and to derive it from the natural inclinations of the physical life, we must arrive at the conclusion that Christian theology in both its Augustinian and semi-Augustinian (Thomistic) forms, regards sensuality (even when it uses the words *concupiscentia* or *cupiditas* to denote sin in general) as a derivative of
the more primal sin of self-love. Sensuality represents a further
confusion consequent upon the original confusion of substituting the
self for God as the centre of existence. Man, having lost the true
centre of his life, is no longer able to maintain his own will as the
centre of himself. While we accept this general analysis it must be
pointed out that the explanations of the relation of sensuality to
self-love are unsatisfactory, partly because they are too vague and
partly because they are partially contradictory. They do not give a
precise or psychologically convincing account of how self-love results
in the further consequence of sensuality. Inasfar as the explanation
is precise it suffers from the contradiction that on the one hand the
self is said to have lost control over the impulses of the body while
on the other hand its undue gratification of these impulses is regarded as merely a further form of self-love. This inconsistency raises
an interesting question.

The question is: does the drunkard or the glutton merely press
self-love to the limit and lose all control over himself by his effort to
gratify a particular physical desire so unreservedly that its gratification comes in conflict with other desires? Or is lack of moderation
an effort to escape from the self? And does sexual license mean
merely the subordination of another person to the ego's self-love,
expressed in this case in an inordinate physical desire; or does un-
disciplined sex life represent an effort on the part of a disquieted and
disorganized self to escape from itself? Is sensuality, in other words,
a form of idolatry which makes the self god; or is it an alternative
idolatry in which the self, conscious of the inadequacy of its self-
worship, seeks escape by finding some other god?

The probable reason for the ambiguous and equivocal answers to
this question in the whole course of Christian theology is that there

is a little of both in sensuality. An analysis of various forms of sensuality may prove the point. Luxurious and extravagant living, the gratification of various sensual desires without limit, is on the one hand a form of self-love. Sometimes its purpose is to display power and to enhance prestige.[12] Sometimes it is not so much the servant of pride as the consequence of the freedom which power secures. Freed of the restraints, which poverty places upon all forms of expansive desires, the powerful individual indulges these desires without restraint. But sometimes luxurious living is not so much an advertisement of the ego's pride or even a simple and soft acquiescence with the various impulses of the physical life, as it is a frantic effort to escape from self. It betrays an uneasy conscience. The self is seeking to escape from itself and throws itself into any pursuit which will allow it to forget for a moment the inner tension of an uneasy conscience. The self, finding itself to be inadequate as the centre of its existence, seeks for another god amidst the various forces, processes and impulses of nature over which it ostensibly presides.

Drunkenness exhibits the same ambivalence of purpose. The drunkard sometimes seeks the abnormal stimulus of intoxicating drink in order to experience a sense of power and importance which normal life denies him. This type of intoxication represents a pathetic effort to make the self the centre of the world to a degree which normal reason with its consciousness of the ego's insignificance makes impossible. But drunkenness may have a quite different purpose. It may be desired not in order to enhance the ego but to escape from it.[13] It would not be inaccurate to define the first purpose of

[12]*Cf.* Thorstein Veblen, *Theory of the Leisure Class.*

[13]A modern psychoanalyst explains this twofold function of addiction to alcohol as follows: " 'Alcoholics' are almost invariably jolly, sociable, talkative fellows—who indeed seem obliged to make themselves well liked and are skillful in doing so. It takes very little penetration to discover, however, that this inordinate wish to be loved which compels them to be at so much pains to be charming . . . bespeaks a great underlying feeling of insecurity, a feeling which must constantly be denied, compensated for or anesthetized. . . . Such feelings of insecurity and inferiority

intoxication as the sinful ego-assertion which is rooted in anxiety and unduly compensates for the sense of inferiority and insecurity; while the second purpose of intoxication springs from the sense of guilt, or a state of perplexity in which a sense of guilt has been compounded with the previous sense of insecurity. The tension of this perplexity is too great to bear and results in an effort to escape consciousness completely. Thus drunkenness is merely a vivid form of the logic of sin which every heart reveals: Anxiety tempts the self to sin; the sin increases the insecurity which it was intended to alleviate until some escape from the whole tension of life is sought.

It has been previously noted that in all forms of Christian thought sexual passion is regarded as a particularly vivid form of, or at least occasion for, sensuality. The modern fashion is to deride this characteristic of Christian thought as morbid and as leading to an accentuation of sexual passion by its prurient repression. While it must be admitted that Christian thought on sex has frequently been unduly morbid and that dualistic forms of Christianity have regarded sex as evil of itself, there are nevertheless profound insights into the problem of sex in the Christian interpretation of sin, which modern thought has missed completely.

Both modern and traditional Christian thought would agree that sexual passion is a particularly powerful impulse which has expressed itself more vigorously throughout human history than the physical function of procreation requires. The usual modern explanation for this hypertrophy of the impulse is that it has been accentuated by repression.[14] This explanation fails to take account of

---

depend less upon actual reality comparisons than upon unconscious 'irrational' reasons, generally feelings of great frustration and rage and the fear and guilt which the rage induces. . . . A supplementary function of alcohol drinking is the further repression of such feelings and memories, which threaten to emerge and become again conscious." Karl A. Menninger, *Man Against Himself*, p. 169.

[14]Thus a modern psychologist writes: "In the lower animals in a state of nature, and natively in man, the sex drive is a glandular and physiological one, satisfied by direct (though learned) mechanisms when it arises. In civilized man the direct satisfaction of the sexual urges is

the fact that the social disciplines, which civilized society has thrown about the satisfaction of the sex impulse, are made necessary by the very fact that the impulse has exceeded the necessities of the preservation of the species, from the very beginning; and that even in primitive man sex has never been merely "glandular and physiological." The sexual, as every other physical, impulse in man is subject to and compounded with the freedom of man's spirit. It is not something which man could conceivably leave imbedded in some natural harmony of animal impulses. Its force reaches up into the highest pinnacles of human spirituality; and the insecurity of man in the heights of his freedom reaches down to the sex impulse as an instrument of compensation and as an avenue of escape.

From the standpoint of "pure nature" the sex impulse is a natural basis of "alteregoism"; for it is the method by which nature insures that the individual shall look beyond himself to the preservation of the species. The fact that upon the purely instinctive basis both the self and the other are involved in sexual passion makes it possible for spirit to use the natural stuff of sex for both the assertion of the ego and the flight of the ego into another. The sexual act thus becomes, in human life, a drama in which the domination of one life over the desires of another and the self-abnegation of the same life in favour of another are in bewildering conflict, and also in baffling intermixture. Furthermore these corruptions are complexly interlaced and compounded with a creative discovery of the self through its giving of itself to another. Thus the climax of sexual union is also a climax of creativity and sinfulness. The element of sin in the experience is not due to the fact that sex is in any sense sinful as such. But once sin is presupposed, that is, once the original harmony of nature is disturbed by man's self-love, the instincts of sex are

---

thwarted at their appearance in infancy and at their strengthening in the glandular changes of adolescence by social conventions and economic obstacles. This thwarting directs attention to the drive and attaches it to many substitute stimuli and substitute responses." L. F. Shaffer, *The Psychology of Adjustment,* p. 105.

particularly effective tools for both the assertion of the self and the flight from the self. This is what gives man's sex life the quality of uneasiness. It is both a vehicle of the primal sin of self-deification and the expression of an uneasy conscience, seeking to escape from self by the deification of another. The deification of the other is almost a literal description of many romantic sentiments in which attributes of perfection are assigned to the partner of love, beyond the capacities of any human being to bear, and therefore the cause of inevitable disillusionment.[15] While the more active part of the male and the more passive part of the female in the relation of the sexes may seem to point to self-deification as the particular sin of the male and the idolatry of the other as the particular temptation of the woman in the sexual act, yet both elements of sin are undoubtedly involved in both sexes.

An analysis of sexual passion thus verifies the correctness of the seemingly contradictory Christian interpretation of the relation of sensuality to self-love. It contains both a further extension of the sin of self-love and an effort to escape from it, an effort which results in the futility of worshipping the "creature rather than the Creator." To complete the analysis it must be mentioned that sexuality is subject to the development of one further degree of sensuality. Sexual passion may, by the very power it develops in the spiritual confusion of human sin, serve exactly the same purpose as drunkenness. It may serve as an anodyne. The ego, having found the worship both of self and of the other abortive, may use the passion of sex, without reference to self and the other, as a form of escape from the tension of life. The most corrupt forms of sensuality, as for instance in commercialized vice, have exactly this characteristic, that personal considerations are excluded from the satisfaction of the sexual impulse. It is a flight not to a false god but to nothingness. The strength of the passion which makes this momentary escape possible is itself a consequence of sin primarily and of an uneasy conscience consequent

[15]*Cf.*, for a convincing analysis of this aspect of sexual attachment, Emil Brunner, *Man in Revolt*, Ch. 15.

upon sin secondarily. If this analysis be correct it verifies the Augustinian conception of sensuality as a further sin which is also a punishment for the more primary sin; and justifies his conclusion: "God does not compel men to do these things; He only leaves those alone who deserve to be forsaken."[16]

The proof that sex is a very crucial point in the spirituality of sinful man is that shame is so universally attached to the performance of the sexual function. The profundity of the account of the Fall in Genesis cannot be overestimated. For though the account describes sin as primarily disobedience to God through the temptation of pride and not as sensual passion, it understands that guilt becomes involved in sensual passion after the Fall, for man becomes suddenly conscious of his sexuality: "And the eyes of them both were opened, and they knew that they were naked; and they sewed fig leaves together, and made themselves aprons" (Gen. 3:7).

The idea of modern psychology, particularly Freudian psychology, that this sense of guilt is abnormal, unnecessary and entirely due to the repressions of civilization, is a consequence of a too superficial view of the complexities of the relationship of spirit to nature. The sense of shame in relation to sex antedates the conventions of civilized society, just as the inordinate expression of sexual passion is the cause and not the consequence of the social disciplines and restraints which society has set around this area of life. A sophisti-

[16]The flight of the self into the other and the escape into oblivion are recurring themes in D. H. Lawrence's analysis of sex. Thus for instance he describes the experience of a man and woman in *Sons and Lovers*: "To know their own nothingness, to know the tremendous living flood which carried them always, gave them rest within themselves. If so great a magnificent power could overwhelm them, identify them altogether with itself, so that they knew that they were only grains in the tremendous heave that lifted every grass blade its little height and living thing, then why fret about themselves? They could let themselves be carried by life and they felt a sort of peace each in the other" (p. 436). It will be noted that the motif of escape into subconscious nature is more dominant than the sense of loss in the other.

Sometimes Lawrence explicitly identifies the sex impulse with the longing for death.

cated effort to destroy modesty and the sense of shame by the simple
device of making the function of sex more public is therefore bound
to aggravate rather than alleviate the difficulties of man's sex life.[17]

On the other hand it must be admitted that Christian puritanism
and asceticism have usually been just as much in error in their effort
to eliminate the sin attached to and expressed in sex by undue repressions. Such efforts have not only aggravated the sexual problem but
have contributed to the self-righteous fury of those who sin covertly
in matters of sex against those who sin overtly.[18]

The problem of sex, sensuality and sin is very complex and for that
reason a constant source of confusion. Since sin is inevitably attached
to sex, the dualist and ascetic is tempted to regard it as sinful *per se*.
The anti-ascetic on the other hand, viewing the difficulties which
arise from morbidity and undue prurience, imagines he can solve the
problem by relaxing all restraints and by regarding minimal restraints only from the standpoint of social utility. The real situation
is that man, granted his "fallen" nature, sins in his sex life but not
because sex is essentially sinful. Or in other words, man, having lost
the true centre of his life in God, falls into sensuality; and sex is the
most obvious occasion for the expression of sensuality and the most
vivid expression of it. Thus sex reveals sensuality to be first another
and final form of self-love, secondly an effort to escape self-love by
the deification of another and finally as an escape from the futilities
of both forms of idolatry by a plunge into unconsciousness.

What sex reveals in regard to sensuality is not unique but typical
in regard to the problem of sensuality in general. Whether in drunk-

[17]The criticism of Augustine, directed against the Cynics, is strikingly
applicable to these modern theories: "It was against the modesty of natural shame that the Cynic philosophers struggled so hard in the error of
their astonishing shamelessness; they thought that the intercourse between husband and wife was indeed honourable and that therefore it
should be done in public. Such barefaced obscenity deserved to receive
a doggish name; and so they went by the title of 'Cynics' " (Κύνικοί—
doglike). From *On Marriage and Concupiscence,* Book I, Ch. 25.

[18]This is the point of criticism, for instance, in Ibsen's *The Wild Duck*
and Hawthorne's *The Scarlet Letter.*

enness, gluttony, sexual license, love of luxury, or any inordinate devotion to a mutable good, sensuality is always: (1) an extension of self-love to the point where it defeats its own ends; (2) an effort to escape the prison house of self by finding a god in a process or person outside the self; and (3) finally an effort to escape from the confusion which sin has created into some form of subconscious existence.

CHAPTER IX

ORIGINAL SIN AND MAN'S RESPONSIBILITY

THE Christian doctrine of sin in its classical form offends both rationalists and moralists by maintaining the seemingly absurd position that man sins inevitably and by a fateful necessity but that he is nevertheless to be held responsible for actions which are prompted by an ineluctable fate. The explicit Scriptural foundation for the doctrine is given in Pauline teaching. On the one hand St. Paul insists that man's sinful glorification of himself is without excuse: "So that they are without excuse: because that, when they knew God, they glorified him not as God" (Romans 1:20–21). And on the other hand he regards human sin as an inevitable defect, involved in or derived from the sin of the first man: "Wherefore, as by one man sin entered into the world, and death by sin; and so death passed upon all men, for that all have sinned" (Romans 5:12). Augustine manages to compress both of these assertions of inevitability and of responsibility into one statement when he writes: "Man's nature was indeed at first created faultless and without sin; but nature as man now has it into which every one who is born from Adam, wants the Physician, being no longer in a healthy state. All good qualities which it still possesses . . . it has from the most High God, its Creator and Maker. But the flaw which darkens and weakens all these natural goods, it has not contracted from its blameless Creator . . . but from that *original sin* which it committed *of its own free will*."[1]

Here is the absurdity in a nutshell. Original sin, which is by definition an inherited corruption, or at least an inevitable one, is nevertheless not to be regarded as belonging to his essential nature and therefore is not outside the realm of his responsibility. Sin is natural for man in the sense that it is universal but not in the sense that it is necessary. Calvin makes this distinction very carefully: "We say therefore that man is corrupted by natural pravity but which did not originate from nature. We deny that it proceeded from nature to signify that it is rather an adventitious quality or accident, than a substantial quality originally innate." But again: "We call it natural that no one may suppose it to be contracted by every individual from corrupt habit, whereas it prevails over all by hereditary right."[2]

Sin is to be regarded as neither a necessity of man's nature nor yet as a pure caprice of his will. It proceeds rather from a defect of the will, for which reason it is not completely deliberate; but since it is the will in which the defect is found and the will presupposes freedom the defect cannot be attributed to a taint in man's nature. Here again Calvin is most precise: "Wherefore as Plato has been deservedly censured for imputing all sins to ignorance, so also we must reject the opinion of those who maintain that all sins proceed from deliberate malice and pravity. For we too much experience how frequently we fall into error even when our intentions are good. Our reason is overwhelmed with deceptions in so many forms. . . ."[3] The doctrine of original sin never escapes the logical absurdities in which these words of Calvin abound. Calvin remains within speaking terms of logic by insisting that sin is "an adventitious quality or accident" rather than a necessity. But if this were true it could not be as inevitable as Calvin's own doctrine assumes. Kierkegaard

---

[1] *Treatise on Nature and Grace*, Ch. 3. *Anti-Pelagian Works*, Vol. I, p. 238.
[2] *Institutes*, Book II, Ch. 1, par. 11.
[3] *Institutes*, Book II, Ch. 2, par. 25.

is more correct in his assertion that "sin comes as neither necessity nor accident."[4] Naturally a position which seems so untenable from a logical standpoint has been derided and scorned not only by non-Christian philosophers but by many Christian theologians.[5]

The whole crux of the doctrine of original sin lies in the seeming absurdity of the conception of free-will which underlies it. The Pauline doctrine, as elaborated by Augustine and the Reformers, insists on the one hand that the will of man is enslaved to sin and is incapable of fulfilling God's law. It may be free, declares Augustine, only it is not free to do good. "How then do miserable men dare to be proud of free-will before they are liberated or of their own strength after they are liberated?" Yet on the other hand the same Augustine insists upon the reality of free-will whenever he has cause to fear that the concept of original sin might threaten the idea of human responsibility: "Only let no man dare so to deny the freedom of the will as to desire to excuse sin." Calvin is willing to accept Augustine's emphasis upon free-will when it is intended to emphasize human responsibility and yet he rejects Peter Lombard's definition, which is practically identical with Augustine's, because he suspects that it contains the Catholic heresy of belief in some native

---

[4]*Begriff der Angst*, p. 95. He advances psychological reasons for this assertion which are not immediately relevant but yet important. He believes that the anomaly of something which is neither necessity nor accident can be explained by the relation of sin to anxiety.

[5]Consider Pascal's frank acceptance of the logical absurdity of the doctrine of original sin:

"In fact if man had never been corrupt, he would enjoy in his innocence both truth and happiness with assurance; and if man had always been corrupt he would have no idea of truth and bliss. But wretched as we are, and more so than if there were no greatness in our condition, we have an idea of happiness and cannot reach it. We perceive an image of truth and possess only a lie. . . . For it is beyond doubt that there is nothing which more shocks our reason than to say that the sin of the first man has rendered guilty those who, being so removed from its source, seem incapable of participating in it. . . . Certainly nothing offends us more rudely than this doctrine, and yet without this mystery, the most incomprehensible of all, we are incomprehensible to ourselves." *Pensées*, 434.

endowment of man, which remains untainted by sin. Lombard's assertion that man is free not in the sense that he has an equal choice between good and evil but in the sense that he does evil voluntarily and not by constraint is accepted by Calvin sneeringly: "That indeed is very true; but what end could it answer to decorate a thing so diminutive with a title so superb?"[6]

One could multiply examples in the thought of theologians of the Pauline tradition in which logical consistency is sacrificed in order to maintain on the one hand that the will is free in the sense that man is responsible for his sin, and is not free in the sense that he can, of his own will, do nothing but evil. Sometimes, as in Luther, the vehemence of the attack upon doctrines of free-will which seem to deny the inevitability of sin, is such that the inconsistency is eliminated in favour of a position which retains nothing of the doctrine of free-will but the term. In the words of Luther, "Free-will lies prostrate . . . for it must either be that the Kingdom of Satan in man is nothing at all and thus Christ will be made to lie; or if the Kingdom be such as Christ describes, free-will must be nothing but a beast of burden, the captive of Satan, which cannot be liberated unless the devil be first cast out by the finger of God."[7] In this, as in other instances, Luther seems to heighten the Augustinian doctrine in the interest of a greater consistency but at the price of imperiling one element in the paradox, the element of human responsibility. Free-will is denied to the point of offering man an excuse for his sin. It is obviously not easy to state the doctrine of original sin without falling into logical pitfalls on the one hand and without obscuring factors in man's moral experience on the other. Before considering the conformity of the doctrine to actual experience it is, therefore, important to ascertain whether alternative doctrines, which may boast the virtue of a higher consistency, may also be regarded as more consonant with the facts of human experience.

[6]*Institutes,* Vol. I, Book II, Ch. 2, par. 7
[7]*On the Bondage of the Will,* trans. by Reverend Henry Cole, London, p. 298.

II

PELAGIAN DOCTRINES

The various alternative doctrines all may be regarded as variants of what has become known in the history of Christian thought as Pelagianism. The essential characteristic of Pelagianism is its insistence that actual sins cannot be regarded as sinful or as involving guilt if they do not proceed from a will which is essentially free. The bias toward evil, that is, that aspect of sin which is designated as "original" in the classic doctrine is found not in man's will but in the inertia of nature. It is in other words not sin at all. Actual sin is on the other hand regarded as more unqualifiedly a conscious defiance of God's will and an explicit preference of evil, despite the knowledge of the good, than in the classical doctrine. While traditional Pelagianism is not sharply defined until it takes form in the classic debates between Augustine and his critics, it is not unfair to regard all Christian thinkers before Augustine as more or less Pelagian. They may not define actual sin so explicitly as a perverse choice of the will as does Pelagius but they do define original sin as essentially some force of inertia in nature and history. They are in other words sufficiently under Platonic influence to find no real place for the myth of the Fall in their thought, though of course they seek to incorporate the Biblical story in their system. Kierkegaard thinks it significant that the Greek church defines original sin to this day as "the sin of the forefather" (ἁμάρτημα προπᾰτορικόν),[1] a concept which refers merely to an historical occurrence and has no other connotation. There is according to J. B. Mozeley no suggestion of an enslaved will in any Christian theology before Augustine.[2] Essentially Platonic doctrines of human nature could be brought into ostensible conformity with Pauline thought by the simple and natural expedient of stripping the Pauline *sarx* of its special connotation as

[1]*Begriff der Angst*, p. 21.
[2]*The Augustinian Doctrine of Predestination*, p. 125.

the principle of sinfulness in man and accepting merely the literal meaning of "the flesh" which wars against the spirit.

It is not surprising that wherever essentially classical views of man prevail, as for instance in both secular and Christian modern liberalism, the bias toward evil should be defined as residing not in man's will but in some sloth of nature which man has inherited from his relation to the brute creation. This remains true even when, as in the thought of men like Schleiermacher and in the theology of the social gospel, this sloth is attributed to the institutions and traditions of history rather than purely to sensual passion or to the finiteness of the mind.[3] By thus placing the inherited sloth in history rather than in each man's own sensual nature, some justice is done to the actual historical continuum in which every human action takes place, but the bias toward evil is always outside and never inside a particular will. The theory is thus virtually identical with the modern secular idea of the "cultural lag" as the explanation of evil in human actions.

Frequently the explicit purpose and always the inevitable consequence of this denial of individual responsibility for the bias toward evil is to increase the sense of responsibility for an individual evil

[3]Schleiermacher's explanation of original sin is: "Just as the Ego, with reference to each later generation, is due to the action of the one before it, so the sinful self-assertiveness of sense, proceeding as it does from its earlier development, has a more remote source than the individual's own life. But once God consciousness has emerged as a definite and effective agency and capable of growth, then every moment in which it does not manifest itself in comparison with earlier moments is an arrest originating in the doer himself and is veritable sin." Schleiermacher admits that this explanation destroys the connotation of "sin" and leaves only the idea of "original" (*Erb*) in the concept of original sin. *The Christian Faith*, par. 69. Walter Rauschenbusch places the primary emphasis on the transmission of sin through social institutions. He writes: "Theology has done considerable harm in concentrating the attention of religious minds on the biological transmission of evil. It has diverted our minds from the power of social transmission, from the authority of the social group in justifying, urging, and idealizing wrong, and from the decisive influence of economic profit in the defense and propagation of evil." *A Theology for the Social Gospel*, p. 67.

act. The argument by which this is done has not varied from the day of Augustine's critics. Every modern criticism of the Augustinian doctrine has been anticipated by Augustine's contemporaries. The logical inconsistency of the doctrine is emphasized. It is insisted that man cannot be held responsible for keeping a law or achieving an ideal if he lacks the capacity to do so. Thus the Kantian "I ought, therefore I can" is neatly anticipated in the argument of Cœlestius: "We have to inquire whether a man is commanded to be without sin; for either he is unable so to live and then there is no such commandment; or else if there be such a commandment he has the ability."[4]

The effect of such an effort to increase the sense of responsibility for individual sinful acts by emphasizing the freedom in which they are committed, is to make every sinful act appear as a conscious choice of evil in defiance of a known good. It is precisely to such acts of sheer perversity that F. R. Tennant confines the idea of sin in the most elaborate of modern Pelagian treatises.[5] Schleiermacher significantly makes no distinction between sin and the consciousness of sin. "We must insist on the fact," he writes, "that sin in general exists only insofar as there is consciousness of it."[6] Pelagianism in short ascribes all sins to "deliberate malice and pravity," to use Calvin's phrase.

The official Catholic doctrine of original sin, usually regarded as "Semi-Pelagian," does not greatly vary the emphasis of Pelagianism.

---

[4]Augustine, *Anti-Pelagian Works*, Vol. I, *Treatise on Man's Perfection in Righteousness*, p. 317. The logical difficulty in the doctrine of original sin is succinctly stated in Cœlestius' words: "We must ask whether sin comes from necessity or from choice. If from necessity then it is not sin; if from choice then it can be avoided." *Ibid.*, p. 315. Or again: "We must ask any one who denies man's ability to live without sin of what sort sin is. Is it such as can be avoided? Or is it unavoidable? If it is unavoidable then it is not sin; if it can be avoided then man can live without the sin which can be avoided." *Ibid.*, p. 315.

[5]Cf. F. R. Tennant, *The Concept of Sin*, and *The Origin and Propagation of Sin*.

[6]*Op. cit.*, par. 68.

The doctrine presupposes a distinction between the *pura naturalia,* the essential character of man as man and a "further gift" (*donum superadditum*) which God bestowed upon man in addition to his natural creation. This distinction, first suggested by Athanasius and achieving its final definition in the system of Aquinas, enables Catholic theology to incorporate the Biblical idea of the Fall without disturbing the concept of original sin as an inertia of nature. For in the Fall, the *donum superadditum.* is lost and, until restored by sacramental grace, man is subject to the natural limitations of his finite nature.[7] Original sin is thus described negatively. It is the privation of something which does not belong to man essentially and, therefore, cannot be regarded as a corruption of his essential nature. As in Pelagianism a basic purpose of the doctrine is to guard against conceptions of total depravity which destroy the idea of responsibility and thereby vitiate the very meaning of sin.[8] The logical difficulties of the Augustinian doctrine are thus avoided, and the peril of denying the structure of freedom in the assertion of its corruption is averted, as in Pelagianism. But the question remains whether either Pelagianism or Semi-Pelagianism is true to the psychological and moral facts in human wrong-doing.

III

AUGUSTINIAN DOCTRINES

The truth is that, absurd as the classical Pauline doctrine of original sin may seem to be at first blush, its prestige as a part of the Christian

[7]Thomas Aquinas writes: "The privation of original justice whereby the will is made subject to God, is the formal element in original sin, while every other disorder of the soul's powers is a kind of material element in respect to original sin. . . . Hence original sin is concupiscence materially and privation of original justice formally." *Summa theol.* Part Two (First Part), Second Number, Question 83, Art. I.

[8]Aquinas declares: "Sin cannot take away entirely from man the fact that he is a rational being, for then he would no longer be capable of sin. Wherefore it is not possible for this good of nature to be destroyed entirely." *Ibid.* Question 85, Art. 2.

truth is preserved, and perennially re-established, against the attacks of rationalists and simple moralists by its ability to throw light upon complex factors in human behaviour which constantly escape the moralists. It may be valuable to use a simple example of contemporary history to prove the point. Modern religious nationalism is obviously a highly explicit expression of the collective pride in which all human behaviour is involved and which Christian faith regards as the quintessence of sin. Inasfar as this pride issues in specific acts of cruelty, such as the persecution of the Jews, these acts obviously cannot be defined as proceeding from a deliberate and malicious preference for evil in defiance of the good. It is true of course that a modern devotee of the religion of race and nation regards his nation as the final good more deliberately than a primitive tribalist, who merely assumed that his collective life was the end of existence. Yet it would be fallacious to assume that a Nazi gives unqualified devotion to the qualified and conditioned value of his race and nation by a consciously perverse choice of the lesser against the higher good. But it would be equally erroneous to absolve the religious nationalist of responsibility merely because his choice is not consciously perverse.

He is obviously tempted to his attitude of self-glorification by feelings of inferiority which he shares with all mankind as a common fate but which in his case have been accentuated by historical vicissitudes to which his class and nation have been subjected. To understand this may prompt forgiveness but it cannot eliminate responsibility. For the general insecurity of man and the special sense of inferiority of his class and nation do not lead necessarily to the excessive self-assertion in which he is involved. They do not lead to sin unless sin is first presupposed. In other words actual sin is involved in the bias toward sin which issues in specific acts of cruelty.

If the sin of self-glorification is not an inevitable consequence of anxiety and insecurity it is even less the natural consequence of a primitive herd impulse which has not yet yielded to higher and more universal loyalties. The "cultural lag" theory of human evil is completely irrelevant to the analysis of his sin. For the sin of the religious nationalist represents a "conscious" defiance of more universal standards of loyalty which had been consciously established. In that sense it conforms perfectly to the Pauline doctrine of the relation of law to sin. Law makes sin more explicit: "I had not known lust, except the law had said, Thou shalt not covet." Sin is thus both unconscious and conscious. The degree of conscious choice may vary in specific instances of course. Yet even the more conscious choices do not come completely into the category of conscious perversity. Even particular acts of cruelty are probably not the consequence of a conscious love of evil, nor do they find an obvious satisfaction in inflicting pain upon others. They are, rather, the consequence of sin's pathetic vicious circle. The attempt to maintain one's own pride and self-respect by holding others in contempt adds an uneasy conscience to the general insecurity which the attitude of contempt is meant to alleviate. Stronger and stronger measures must therefore be taken to ward off the final breakdown. Here the Pauline psychology is more clarifying than any alternative analysis. The specific act of sin is the consequence of blindness: "Their foolish heart was darkened." But this blindness is not merely the blindness of man's natural ignorance. It is derived from a "vain imagination." It was because they "professed themselves wise" that they "became fools."

It is clear from such analysis of religious nationalism in terms of Pauline psychology that the distinction between original sin and actual sin cannot be made as clearly as is assumed in moralistic treatises on sin. The actual sin follows more inevitably from the bias toward sin than is usually assumed. On the other hand the bias toward sin is something more than a mere lag of nature or physical impulse or historical circumstance. There is, in other words, less freedom in the actual sin and more responsibility for the bias toward sin (original sin) than moralistic interpretations can understand.

The actual sin is the consequence of the temptation of anxiety in which all life stands. But anxiety alone is neither actual nor original sin. Sin does not flow necessarily from it. Consequently the bias toward sin from which actual sin-flows is anxiety plus sin. Or, in the words of Kierkegaard, sin presupposes itself. Man could not be tempted if he had not already sinned.

IV

TEMPTATION AND INEVITABILITY OF SIN

The full complexity of the psychological facts which validate the doctrine of original sin must be analysed, first in terms of the relation of temptation to the inevitability of sin. Such an analysis may make it plain why man sins inevitably, yet without escaping responsibility for his sin. The temptation to sin lies, as previously observed, in the human situation itself. This situation is that man as spirit transcends the temporal and natural process in which he is involved and also transcends himself. Thus his freedom is the basis of his creativity but it is also his temptation. Since he is involved in the contingencies and necessities of the natural process on the one hand and since, on the other, he stands outside of them and foresees their caprices and perils, he is anxious. In his anxiety he seeks to transmute his finiteness into infinity, his weakness into strength, his dependence into independence. He seeks in other words to escape finiteness and weakness by a quantitative rather than qualitative development of his life. The quantitative antithesis of finiteness is infinity. The qualitative possibility of human life is its obedient subjection to the will of God. This possibility is expressed in the words of Jesus: "He that loseth his life for my sake shall find it." (Mt. 10:39).

It will be noted that the Christian statement of the ideal possibility does not involve self-negation but self-realization. The self is, in other words, not evil by reason of being a particular self and its salvation does not consist in absorption into the eternal. Neither is the self divided, as in Hegelianism, into a particular or empirical and a universal self; and salvation does not consist in sloughing off its particularity and achieving universality. The Christian view of the self

is only possible from the standpoint of Christian theism in which
God is not merely the *x* of the unconditioned or the undifferentiated
eternal. God is revealed as loving will; and His will is active in
creation, judgment and redemption. The highest self-realization for
the self is therefore not the destruction of its particularity but the
subjection of its particular will to the universal will.

But the self lacks the faith and trust to subject itself to God. It
seeks to establish itself independently. It seeks to find its life and
thereby loses it. For the self which it asserts is less than the true self.
It is the self in all the contingent and arbitrary factors of its immediate situation. By asserting these contingent and arbitrary factors
of an immediate situation, the self loses its true self. It increases its
insecurity because it gives its immediate necessities a consideration
which they do not deserve and which they cannot have without
disturbing the harmony of creation. By giving life a false centre,
the self then destroys the real possibilities for itself and others.
Hence the relation of injustice to pride, and the vicious circle of injustice, increasing as it does the insecurity which pride was intended
to overcome.

The sin of the inordinate self-love thus points to the prior sin of
lack of trust in God. The anxiety of unbelief is not merely the fear
which comes from ignorance of God. "Anxiety," declares Kierkegaard, "is the dizziness of freedom,"[1] but it is significant that the
same freedom which tempts to anxiety also contains the ideal possibility of knowing God. Here the Pauline psychology is penetrating
and significant. St. Paul declares that man is without excuse because
"the invisible things of him from the creation of the world are clearly
seen, being understood by the things that are made, even his eternal
power and Godhead" (Romans 1:20). The anxiety of freedom leads
to sin only if the prior sin of unbelief is assumed. This is the meaning of Kierkegaard's assertion that sin posits itself.[2]

The sin of man's excessive and inordinate love of self is thus

[1]*Begriff der Angst,* p. 57.
[2]*Ibid.,* p. 27.

neither merely the drag of man's animal nature upon his more universal loyalties, nor yet the necessary consequence of human freedom and self-transcendence. It is more plausibly the consequence of the latter than of the former because the survival impulse of animal nature lacks precisely those boundless and limitless tendencies of human desires. Inordinate self-love is occasioned by the introduction of the perspective of the eternal into natural and human finiteness. But it is a false eternal. It consists in the transmutation of "mutable good" into infinity. This boundless character of human desires is an unnatural rather than natural fruit of man's relation to the temporal process on the one hand and to eternity on the other. If man knew, loved and obeyed God as the author and end of his existence, a proper limit would be set for his desires including the natural impulse of survival.[3]

The fact that the lie is so deeply involved in the sin of self-glorification and that man cannot love himself inordinately without pretending that it is not his, but a universal, interest which he is supporting, is a further proof that sin presupposes itself and that it is neither ignorance nor yet the ignorance of ignorance which forces the self to sin. Rather it "holds the truth in unrighteousness."

The idea that the inevitability of sin is not due merely to the strength of the temptation in which man stands by reason of his relation to both the temporal process and eternity, is most perfectly expressed in the scriptural words: "Let no man say when he is tempted, I am tempted of God: for God cannot be tempted with evil, neither tempteth he any man: But every man is tempted, when

[3]Failure to understand the difference between a natural and an unnatural though inevitable characteristic of human behaviour confuses otherwise clear analyses such as that of Bertrand Russell's: He declares: "Between man and other animals there are various differences some intellectual and some emotional. One chief emotional difference is that human desires, unlike those of animals, are essentially boundless and incapable of complete satisfaction." *Power,* p. 9.
Thus Mr. Russell is forced to regard the boundless will-to-power as natural in his analysis of human nature and as the very principle of evil in his analysis of society.

he is drawn away of his own lust, and enticed. Then when lust hath conceived, it bringeth forth sin: and sin, when it is finished, bringeth forth death."[4] But on the other hand the idea that the situation of finiteness and freedom· is a· temptation once evil has entered it and that evil does enter it prior to any human action is expressed in Biblical thought by the conception of the devil. The devil is a fallen angel, who fell because he sought ·to lift himself above his measure and who in turn insinuates temptation into human life. The sin of each individual is preceded by Adam's sin: but even this first sin of history is not the first sin. One may, in other words, go farther back than human history and still not escape the paradoxical conclusion that the situation of finiteness and freedom would not lead to sin if sin were not already introduced into the situation. This is, in the words of Kierkegaard, the "qualitative leap" of sin and reveals the paradoxical relation of inevitability and responsibility. Sin can never be traced merely to the temptation arising from a particular situation or condition in which man as man finds himself or in which particular men find themselves. Nor can the temptation which is compounded of a ·situation of finiteness and freedom, plus the fact of sin, be regarded as leading necessarily to sin in the life of each individual, if again sin is not first presupposed in that life. For this reason even the knowledge of inevitability does not extinguish the sense of responsibility.

[4] James 1: 13–15.

This word succinctly expresses a general attitude of the Bible which places it in opposition to all philosophical explanations which attribute the inevitability of sin to the power of temptation. One of the most ingenious of these is the theory of Schelling, who, borrowing from the mystic system of Jacob Boehme, declares that God has a "foundation that He may be"; only this is not outside himself but within him and he has within him a nature which though it belongs to himself is nevertheless different from him. In God this foundation, this "dark ground," is not in conflict with His love, but in man it "operates incessantly and arouses egotism and a particularized will, just in order that the will to love may arise in contrast to it." Schelling, *Human Freedom*, trans. by J. Gutman, pp. 51–53. Thus in this view sin is not only a prerequisite of virtue but a consequence of the divine nature.

V

RESPONSIBILITY DESPITE INEVITABILITY

The fact of responsibility is attested by the feeling of remorse or repentance which follows the sinful action. From an exterior view not only sin in general but any particular sin may seem to be the necessary consequence of previous temptations. A simple determinism is thus a natural characteristic of all social interpretations of human actions. But the interior view does not allow this interpretation. The self, which is privy to the rationalizations and processes of self-deception which accompanied and must accompany the sinful act, cannot accept and does not accept the simple determinism of the exterior view. Its contemplation of its act involves both the discovery and the reassertion of its freedom. It discovers that some degree of conscious dishonesty accompanied the act, which means that the self was not deterministically and blindly involved in it. Its discovery of that fact in contemplation is a further degree of the assertion of freedom than is possible in the moment of action.

The remorse and repentance which are consequent upon such contemplation are similar in their acknowledgment of freedom and responsibility and their implied assertion of it. They differ in the fact that repentance is the expression of freedom and faith while remorse is the expression of freedom without faith. The one is the "Godly sorrow" of which St. Paul speaks, and the other is "the sorrow of this world which worketh death." It is, in other words, the despair into which sin transmutes the anxiety which precedes sin.

There are of course many cases in which the self seems so deeply involved in its own deceptions and so habituated to standards of action which may have once been regarded as sinful that it seems capable of neither repentance nor remorse. This complacency is possible on many levels of life from that of a natural paganism in which the freedom of spirit is not fully developed, to refined forms of Pharisaism in which pride as self-righteousness obscures the sin of pride itself. It is not true, however, that habitual sin can ever destroy the uneasy conscience so completely as to remove the individual from the realm of moral responsibility to the realm of unmoral nature.[5]

The religious sacrifices of nature religions, in which primitive peoples express an uneasy conscience and assume that natural catastrophe is the expression of their god's anger against their sins, is a proof of the reality of some degree of freedom even in primitive life.[6] The brutality with which a Pharisee of every age resists those who puncture his pretensions proves the uneasiness of his conscience. The insecurity of sin is always a double insecurity. It must seek to hide not only the original finiteness of perspective and relativity of value which it is the purpose of sin to hide, but also the dishonesty by which it has sought to obscure these. The fury with which oligarchs, dictators, priest-kings, ancient and modern, and ideological pretenders turn upon their critics and foes is clearly the fury of an uneasy conscience, though it must not be assumed that such a conscience is always fully conscious of itself.

An uneasy conscience which is not fully conscious of itself is the root of further sin, because the self strives desperately to ward off the *dénouement* of either remorse or repentance by accusing others, seeking either to make them responsible for the sins of the self, or attributing worse sins to them. There is a certain plausibility in this self-defense, because social sources of particular sins may always be

[5]James Martineau erroneously regards the state of habitual sin as a reversion to natural necessity. He writes: "The forfeiture of freedom, the relapse into automatic necessity, is doubtless a most fearful penalty for persistent unfaithfulness; but once incurred it alters the complexion of all subsequent acts. They no longer form fresh constituents in the aggregate of guilt but stand outside in a separate record after its account is closed. . . . The first impulse of the prophets of righteousness when they see him thus is, 'he cannot cease from sin' and perhaps to predict for him eternal retribution; but looking a little deeper, they will rather say, 'he has lost the privilege of sin and sunk away from the rank of persons into the destiny of things." *A Study of Religion*, II, 108.

[6]*Cf.* W. E. Hocking, *The Meaning of God in Human Experience*, p. 235.

found and even the worst criminal can gain a certain temporary self-respect by finding some one who seems more deeply involved in disaster than he is. On the other hand such social comparisons always increase the force of sin, for they are efforts to hide a transaction between the self and God, even though God is not explicitly known to the sinner. While all particular sins have both social sources and social consequences, the real essence of sin can be understood only in the vertical dimension of the soul's relation to God because the freedom of the self stands outside all relations, and therefore has no other judge but God.[7] It is for this reason that a profound insight into the character of sin must lead to the confession, "Against thee, thee only, have I sinned, and done this evil in thy sight" (Ps. 51). All experiences of an uneasy conscience, of remorse and of repentance, are therefore religious experiences, though they are not always explicitly or consciously religious. Experiences of repentance, in distinction to remorse, presuppose some knowledge of God. They may not be consciously related to Biblical revelation but yet they do presuppose some, at least dim, awareness of God as redeemer as well as God as judge. For without the knowledge of divine love remorse cannot be transmuted into repentance. If man recognizes only judgment and knows only that his sin is discovered, he cannot rise above the despair of remorse to the hope of repentance.

The vertical dimension of the experience of remorse and repentance explains why there is no level of moral goodness upon which the sense of guilt can be eliminated. In fact the sense of guilt rises with moral sensitivity: "There are only two kinds of men," declares Pascal, "the righteous who believe themselves sinners; the rest, sinners, who believe themselves righteous." Pascal does not fully appreciate, at least as far as this statement is concerned, how infinite may be the shades of awareness of guilt from the complacency of those

---

[7] *Cf.* 1 Cor. 4:3f.: "But with me it is a very small thing that I should be judged of you, or of man's judgement: yea, I judge not mine own self. For I know nothing against myself; yet am I not hereby justified: but he that judgeth me is the Lord."

who are spiritually blind to the sensitivity of the saint who knows
that he is not a saint. Yet it is obviously true that awareness of guilt
arises with spiritual sensitivity and that such an awareness will be
regarded as morbid only by moralists who have no true knowledge
of the soul and God. The saint's awareness of guilt is no illusion.
The fact is that sin expresses itself most terribly in its most subtle
forms. The sinful identification of the contingent self with God is
less crass on the higher levels of the spiritual life but it may be the
more dangerous for being the more plausible. An example from the
realm of political life may explain why this is true. The inevitable
partiality of even the most impartial court is more dangerous to
justice than the obvious partiality of contending political factions in
society, which the impartiality of the court is intended to resolve.
The partiality of the contending forces is so obvious that it can be
discounted. The partiality of the court, on the other hand, is obscured by its prestige of impartiality. Relative degrees of impartiality
in judicial tribunals are important achievements in political life. But
without a judgment upon even the best judicial process from a higher
level of judgment, the best becomes the worst.[8]

The fact that the sense of guilt rises vertically with all moral
achievement and is, therefore, not assuaged by it nor subject to
diminution or addition by favourable and unfavourable social opinion, throws a significant light on the relation of freedom to sin. The
ultimate proof of the freedom of the human spirit is its own recognition that its will is not free to choose between good and evil. For
in the highest reaches of the freedom of the spirit, the self discovers
in contemplation and retrospect that previous actions have invariably
confused the ultimate reality and value, which the self as spirit senses,
with the immediate necessities of the self. If the self assumes that

[8]Surely this is the significance of the words of Isaiah: "He maketh the
judges of the earth as vanity" (Is. 40:23). In one of the great documents
of social protest in Egypt, "The Eloquent Peasant," the accused peasant
standing in the court of the Grand Visier declares: "Thou hast been set
as a dam to save the poor man from drowning, but behold thou art
thyself the flood." *Cf.* J. H. Breasted, *The Dawn of Conscience,* p. 190.

because it realizes this fact in past actions it will be able to avoid the corruption in future actions, it will merely fall prey to the Pharisaic fallacy.

This difference between the self in contemplation and the self in action must not be regarded as synonymous with the distinction between the self as spirit and the self as natural vitality. To regard the two distinctions as identical is a plausible error, and one which lies at the root of all idealistic interpretations of man. But we have already discovered that the sins of the self in action are possible only because the freedom of spirit opens up the deterministic causal chains of the self in nature and tempts the self to assume dignities, to grasp after securities and to claim sanctities which do not belong to it. The contemplating self which becomes conscious of its sins does not therefore view some other empirical self which is not, properly speaking, its true self. There is only one self. Sometimes the self acts and sometimes it contemplates its actions. When it acts it falsely claims ultimate value for its relative necessities and falsely identifies its life with the claims of life *per se*. In contemplation it has a clearer view of the total human situation and becomes conscious, in some degree, of the confusion and dishonesty involved in its action. It must not be assumed, however, that the contemplating self is the universal self, judging the finite and empirical self. At its best the contemplating self is the finite self which has become conscious of its finiteness and its relation to God as the limit and the fulfillment of its finiteness. When the self in contemplation becomes contritely aware of its guilt in action it may transmute this realization into a higher degree of honesty in subsequent actions. Repentance may lead to "fruits meet for repentance"; and differences between the moral quality in the lives of complacent and of contrite individuals are bound to be discovered by observers. But the self cannot make too much of them; for its real standard is not what others do or fail to do. Its real standard is its own essential self and this in turn has only God's will as norm. It must know that judged by that standard, the experience of contrition does not prevent the self from new dishonesties in subsequent actions. The self, even in contemplation, remains the finite self. In one moment it may measure its situation and discover its sin. In the next moment it will be betrayed by anxiety into sin. Even the distinction between contemplation and action must, therefore, not be taken too literally. For any contemplation which is concerned with the interests, hopes, fears and ambitions of this anxious finite self belongs properly in the field of action; for it is a preparation for a false identification of the immediate and the ultimate of which no action is free.

We cannot, therefore, escape the ultimate paradox that the final exercise of freedom in the transcendent human spirit is its recognition of the false use of that freedom in action. Man is most free in the discovery that he is not free. This paradox has been obscured by most Pelagians and by many Augustinians. The Pelagians have been too intent to assert the integrity of man's freedom to realize that the discovery of this freedom also involves the discovery of man's guilt. The Augustinians on the other hand have been so concerned to prove that the freedom of man is corrupted by sin that they have not fully understood that the discovery of this sinful taint is an achievement of freedom.

VI

LITERALISTIC ERRORS

The paradox that human freedom is most perfectly discovered and asserted in the realization of the bondage of the will is easily obscured. Unfortunately the confusion revealed in the debate between Pelagians and Augustinians has been further aggravated by the literalism of the Augustinians. In countering the simple moralism of the Pelagians they insisted on interpreting original sin as an inherited taint. Thus they converted the doctrine of the inevitability of sin into a dogma which asserted that sin had a natural history. Thereby they gave their Pelagian critics an unnecessary advantage in the debate, which the latter have never been slow to seize.[1]

[1]One can never be certain whether Pelagian and Semi-Pelagian criticisms of the Pauline doctrine are primarily directed against the literalistic

While Augustinian theology abounds in doctrines of original sin which equate it with the idea of an inherited corruption and which frequently make concupiscence in generation the agent of this inheritance, it is significant that Christian thought has always had some suggestions of the representative rather than historical character of Adam's sin. The idea of Adam as representative man allowed it to escape the historical-literalistic illusion. The very fountain-source of the doctrine of original sin, the thought of St. Paul, expresses the idea of original sin in terms which allow, and which possibly compel the conclusion that St. Paul believed each man to be related to Adam's sin in terms of "seminal identity" rather than historical inheritance. The Pauline words are: "Wherefore as by one man sin entered the world and death by sin; and so death passed to all men *for that all have sinned.*"[2] The idea of a mystical identity between Adam and all men is found in Irenæus and is explicitly formulated in Ambrose.[3] Even Augustine, who insists on the theory of an inherited corruption, inserts an interesting qualification which points in the same direction when he quotes the Pauline passage, Romans 3:23, so that it reads: " 'For all have sinned'—*whether in Adam or in themselves*—'and come short of the glory of God.' " The same idea struggles for, and achieves partial, expressions in some of the explana-

---

corruptions of it or against its basic absurd but profound insights. A good instance of such a criticism is to be found in a modern Anglo-Catholic treatise on the subject: "Nor is it necessary to do more than point out the absurdity of the theory of 'original guilt,' which asserts that human beings are held responsible to an all-just Judge for an act which they did not commit and for physiological and psychological facts which they cannot help. . . . Those (if there be any such) who demand formal disproof of the belief that what is *ex hypothesi* an inherited psychological malady is regarded by God in the light of a voluntarily committed crime, may be referred to the scathing satire of Samuel Butler's *Erewhon.*" N. P. Williams, *Ideas of the Fall and Original Sin,* p. 381.

[2]*Cf.* C. H. Dodd, *Epistle to the Romans,* p. 79.

[3]He writes: "So then Adam is in each one of us, for in him human nature itself sinned." *Apol. David altera,* 71.

tions of original sin in Calvin, even while he insists on the idea of inheritance.[4]

It is obviously necessary to eliminate the literalistic illusions in the doctrine of original sin if the paradox of inevitability and responsibility is to be fully understood; for the theory of an inherited second nature is as clearly destructive of the idea of responsibility for sin as rationalistic and dualistic theories which attribute human evil to the inertia of nature.[5] When this literalistic confusion is eliminated the truth of the doctrine of original sin is more clearly revealed; but it must be understood that even in this form the doctrine remains absurd from the standpoint of a pure rationalism, for it expresses a relation between fate and freedom which cannot be fully rationalized, unless the paradox be accepted as a rational understanding of the limits of rationality and as an expression of faith that a rationally irresolvable contradiction may point to a truth which logic cannot contain. Formally there can be of course no conflict between logic

[4]*Cf. Institutes,* Book II, Ch. i, par. 7. "We ought to be satisfied with this, that the Lord deposited with Adam the endowments he chose to confer on human nature; and therefore that when he lost the favours he had received *he lost them not only for himself* but for us all. Who will be solicitous about a transmission of the soul when he hears that Adam received the ornaments that he lost, *no less for us* than for himself? That they were given, not to one man only, *but to the whole human nature.*" It must be admitted that Calvin confines Adam's identity with human nature to the original endowments. The loss of these endowments is conceived in terms of an hereditary relation between Adam and subsequent men, for Calvin continues: "For the children were so vitiated in their parent that they became contagious to their descendants; there was in Adam such a spring of corruption that it is transfused from parents to children in a perpetual stream."

[5]Harnack declares: "The doctrine of original sin leads to Manichean dualism, which Augustine never surmounted, and is accordingly an impious and foolish dogma. . . . His doctrine of concupiscence conduces the same view." *History of Dogma,* Vol. V, p. 217. Harnack's criticisms must of course be discounted, as those of other Christian moralists, because he is as unable to understand the doctrine of original sin, when stripped of its literalistic errors, as when stated in its crude form. His assertion that "turn as he will, Augustine affirms an evil nature and therefore a diabolical creator of the world" is simply not true.

and truth. The laws of logic are reason's guard against chaos in the realm of truth. They eliminate contradictory assertions. But there is no resource in logical rules to help us understand complex phenomena, exhibiting characteristics which seem to require that they be placed into contradictory categories of reason. Loyalty to all the facts may require a provisional defiance of logic, lest complexity in the facts of experience be denied for the sake of a premature logical consistency. Hegel's "dialectic" is a logic invented for the purpose of doing justice to the fact of "becoming" as a phenomenon which belongs into the category of neither "being" nor "nonbeing."

The Christian doctrine of original sin with its seemingly contradictory assertions about the inevitability of sin and man's responsibility for sin is a dialectical truth which does justice to the fact that man's self-love and self-centredness is inevitable, but not in such a way as to fit into the the category of natural necessity. It is within and by his freedom that man sins. The final paradox is that the discovery of the inevitability of sin is man's highest assertion of freedom. The fact that the discovery of sin invariably leads to the Pharisaic illusion that such a discovery guarantees sinlessness in subsequent actions is a revelation of the way in which freedom becomes an accomplice of sin. It is at this point that the final battle between humility and human self-esteem is fought.

Kierkegaard's explanation of the dialectical relation of freedom and fate in sin is one of the profoundest in Christian thought. He writes: "The concept of sin and guilt does not emerge in its profoundest sense in paganism. If it did paganism would be destroyed by the contradiction that man becomes guilty by fate. . . . Christianity is born in this very contradiction. The concept of sin and guilt presupposes the individual as individual. There is no concern for his relation to any cosmic or past totality. The only concern is that he is guilty; and yet he is supposed to become guilty through fate, the very fate about which there is no concern. And thereby he becomes something which resolves the concept of fate, and to become that through fate! If this contradiction is wrongly understood it leads to false concepts of original sin. Rightly understood it leads to a true concept, to the idea namely that every individual is itself and the race and that the later individual is not significantly differentiated from the first man. In the possibility of anxiety freedom is lost, for it is overwhelmed by fate. Yet now it arises in reality but with the explanation that it has become guilty."[6]

[6]*Begriff der Angst*, p. 105.

CHAPTER X

JUSTITIA ORIGINALIS

"THE greatness of man," declares Pascal, "is so evident that it is even proved by his wretchedness. For what in animals is called nature we call wretchedness in man; by which we recognize that, his nature now being like that of animals, he has fallen from a better nature which once was his. For who is unhappy at not being a king except a deposed king? . . . Who is unhappy at having only one mouth? And who is not unhappy at having only one eye? Probably no man ever ventured to mourn at not having three eyes. But any one is inconsolable at having none."[1] No man, however deeply involved in sin, is able to regard the misery of sin as normal. Some memory of a previous condition of blessedness seems to linger in his soul; some echo of the law which he has violated seems to resound in his conscience. Every effort to give the habits of sin the appearance of normality betrays something of the frenzy of an uneasy conscience. The contrast between what man is truly and essentially and what he has become is apparent even to those who do not understand that this contrast is to be found in every human being and has its seat in the will of man himself. Those who do not understand the real nature of sin sometimes portray the contrast in terms of various levels of human culture. "The superman built the aeroplane," de-

[1]Pascal, *Pensées,* par. 409.

clared a modern scientist recently, "but the ape-man got ahold of it." Or sometimes they regard the contrast as one between the good man and his lagging and imperfect institutions.[2] The sense of a conflict between what man is and ought to be finds universal expression, even though the explanations of the conflict are usually contradictory and confused.

This universal testimony of human experience is the most persuasive refutation of any theory of human depravity which denies that man has any knowledge of the good which sin has destroyed. It is true of course, as Christian faith declares, that any human statement of the blessedness and perfection which are man's proper state and nature, are themselves coloured by sin, so that Christ, as the second Adam, is required to restore the image of the first Adam as he was before the Fall. The reason why there is a heightened sense of sin in Christianity is that the vision of Christ heightens the contrast between what man is truly and what he has become; and destroys the prestige of normality which sinful forms of life periodically achieve in the world. Yet faith in Christ could find no lodging place in the human soul, were it not uneasy about the contrast between its true and its present state; though this same faith in Christ also clarifies that contrast. Men who have fallen deeply into the wretchedness of sin are never easy in their minds; but their uneasiness is frequently increased by some vivid reminder of the innocency of their childhood or the aspirations of their youth.

There are no forms of disease or corruption, short of death, which do not reveal something of the healthful structure which they have corrupted. The blind eye is still an eye, though it may be completely sightless. The aberrations of an insane mind betray coherences in the very welter of incoherences which only a human and not an animal mind could conceive. The disorder of war would not be an evil did it not operate within and against some kind of harmony and interdependence of nations; and it could not be evil if it could not avail itself of the good of internal and domestic peace, from

[2]*Cf.* Robert Briffault, *Breakdown*

which it draws the capacity of conquest. "Even the thieves themselves that molest the world beside them," declared Augustine, "are at peace amongst themselves."[3]

Though Christian theology has frequently expressed the idea of the total depravity of man in extravagant terms, it has never been without witnesses to the fact that human sin cannot destroy the essential character of man to such a degree that it would cease being implied in, and furnishing a contrast to, what he had become. It is not surprising to find this emphasis in Thomas Aquinas, who does not hold to the doctrine of total depravity.[4] Yet even Luther, who believes that nothing but the name of the "image of God" is left to sinful man, animadverts upon the significance of man's uneasy conscience, a phenomenon which can be understood only as the protest of man's essential nature against his present state. Augustine is very explicit in his affirmation that the evil of sin cannot completely destroy the goodness of what God has created in man: "And it was manifested unto me that those things be good, which yet are corrupted; which neither were they sovereignly good nor unless they were good could be corrupted: for if sovereignly good, they were incorruptible, if not good at all there is nothing in them to be corrupted. . . . But if they be deprived of all good they would cease to be. . . . So long therefore as they are, they are good: therefore whatsoever is, is good."[5]

The problem of the relation of man's essential nature to his sinful state unfortunately has been confused in the history of Christian thought by a difficulty which we have previously observed in the doctrine of original sin: Christian theology has found it difficult to refute the rationalistic rejection of the myth of the Fall without falling into the literalistic error of insisting upon the Fall as an his-

---

[3]*De civ. Dei,* Book IV, Ch. 12.

[4]Aquinas writes: "Sin cannot take away entirely from man the fact that he is a rational being, for then he would no longer be capable of sin. Wherefore it is not possible for this good of nature to be destroyed entirely." *Summa,* First Part, Third Number, Question 85, Art. 1.

[5]*Confessions,* Book VII. Ch. 12.

torical event. One of the consequences of this literalism, which has seriously affected the thought of the church upon the problem of man's essential nature, is the assumption that the perfection from which man fell is to be assigned to a particular historical period, *i.e.* the paradisical period before the Fall. This chronological interpretation of a relation which cannot be expressed in terms of time without being falsified must not be attributed to the authority of the Biblical myth alone. The Stoics, after all, also believed in a golden age of innocency at the beginning of the world, and thought that the equality and liberty which their natural law enjoined, but which were beyond the possibilities of actual history, were realities of that blessed period. Furthermore every individual is inclined to give a chronological and historical version of the contrast between what he is and what he ought to be; for he regards the innocency of his childhood as a symbol and a reminder of his true nature. Yet the Biblical myth must be regarded as the primary source of the Christian belief in a chronological period in which man had a perfection which he has since lost.

The effect of this literalism has been to bring confusion into Christian thought on the relation of man's essential nature to his sinful condition. In Protestant thought it aggravated the tendency toward extravagant statements of man's depravity[6] and confused the effort to moderate such statements by the admission that some little power of justice remained to man. For the remnant of original perfection which was conceded to man was falsely identified with the capacity for "civil justice,"[7] a capacity which is as obviously corrupted by sin as any other human capacity. In Catholic thought, chronological literalism encouraged the definition of the state of original righteousness as a special supernatural gift, a DONUM SUPER-

[6]The most extreme statement of the doctrine of total depravity is probably found in the Lutheran Formulary of Concord, in which we read: "They are also likewise repudiated and rejected who teach that our nature has indeed been greatly weakened but nevertheless has not altogether lost all goodness relating to divine and spiritual things."

[7]Cf. *Augsburg Confession*, Art. 18.

NATURALE which was added to the PURA NATURALIA, that is to the essential humanity which Adam had as man. In consequence the paradox, that sin is a corruption of man's true essence but not its destruction, is obscured in both Protestant and Catholic thought. In Catholicism the Fall means the loss of something which is not essential to man and does not therefore represent a corruption of his essence. In radical Protestantism the very image of God in man is believed to be destroyed.[8] And when Protestant thought recoils from such extravagance, it looks for the remnant of man's original goodness in insignificant aspects of human behaviour.

The relation of man's essential nature to his sinful state cannot be solved within terms of the chronological version of the perfection before the Fall. It is, as it were, a vertical rather than horizontal relation. When the Fall is made an event in history rather than a symbol of an aspect of every historical moment in the life of man, the relation of evil to goodness in that moment is obscured.

II

ESSENTIAL NATURE AND ORIGINAL RIGHTEOUSNESS

It is impossible to do justice to the concept of the image of God and to the perfection of that image before the Fall without making a distinction between the essential nature of man and the virtue of conformity to that nature. Nothing can change the essential nature and structure, just as blindness of the eye does not remove the eye from the human anatomy. Not even the destruction of the eye can change the fact that the human anatomy requires two eyes. On the other hand the freedom of man creates the possibility of actions which are contrary to and in defiance of the requirements of this essential nature. This fact justifies the distinction between the essential structure and nature, and the virtue of conformity to it. Man may lose this virtue and destroy the proper function of his

[8] Karl Barth concedes only "that man is man and not a cat," when describing the sinful state of man. *Cf.* his brochure *Nein,* p. 27.

nature but he can do so only by availing himself of one of the elements in that nature, namely his freedom.

This fact prompted Irenæus to distinguish between the image and the likeness of God upon the basis of Genesis 1:26, a distinction which persisted in Christian tradition until the Reformation questioned its exegetical validity.[1] According to Irenæus the Fall destroyed the likeness but not the image of God. (In Greek the ὁμοίωσις but not the εἰκών: in Latin the *similitudo* but not the *imago*.) Luther was quite right in rejecting the theory from the standpoint of exegesis. The original text: "Let us make man in our image and after our likeness," represents no more than a common Hebraic parallelism. It certainly does not justify the later Catholic distinction between the *pura naturalia* and a *donum supernaturale,* the latter a special gift which God gave to man in addition to his natural endowment, a distinction which was reared upon Irenæus' original differentiation. Nevertheless, the distinction, properly limited and safeguarded, is helpful and even necessary.

It is important to distinguish between the essential nature of man and the virtue and perfection which would represent the normal expression of that nature. The essential nature of man contains two elements; and there are correspondingly two elements in the original perfection of man. To the essential nature of man belong, on the one hand, all his natural endowments, and determinations, his physical and social impulses, his sexual and racial differentiations, in short his character as a creature imbedded in the natural order. On the other hand, his essential nature also includes the freedom of his spirit, his transcendence over natural process and finally his self-transcendence.

The virtue and perfection which corresponds to the first element of his nature is usually designated as the natural law. It is the law which defines the proper performance of his functions, the normal harmony of his impulses and the normal social relation between himself and his fellows within the limitations of the natural order.

[1]*Cf.* Harnack, *History of Dogma,* II, p. 171.

Since every natural function of man is qualified by his freedom and since a "law" defining normality is necessary only because of his freedom, there is always an element of confusion in thus outlining a law of nature. It has nevertheless a tentative validity; for it distinguishes the obvious requirements of his nature as a creature in the natural order from the special requirements of his nature as free spirit.

The virtues which correspond to the second element in his nature, that is, to the freedom of his spirit, are analogous to the "theological virtues" of Catholic thought, namely faith, hope and love. They must be analysed at greater length presently. For the moment it is necessary to identify and validate them only provisionally as basic requirements of freedom. Faith in the providence of God is a necessity of freedom because, without it, the anxiety of freedom tempts man to seek a self-sufficiency and self-mastery incompatible with his dependence upon forces which he does not control. Hope is a particular form of that faith. It deals with the future as a realm where infinite possibilities are realized and which must be a realm of terror if it is not under the providence of God; for in that case it would stand under either a blind fate or pure caprice. The knowledge of God is thus not a supernatural grace which is a "further gift" beyond man's essential nature. It is the requirement of his nature as free spirit.

Love is both an independent requirement of this same freedom and a derivative of faith. Love is a requirement of freedom because the community to which man is impelled by his social nature is not possible to him merely upon the basis of his gregarious impulse. In his freedom and uniqueness each man stands outside of, and transcends, the cohesions of nature and the uniformities of mind which bind life to life. Since men are separated from one another by the uniqueness and individuality of each spirit, however closely they may be bound together by ties of nature, they cannot relate themselves to one another in terms which will do justice to both the bonds of nature and the freedom of their spirit if they are not related in terms of love. In love spirit meets spirit in the depth of the innermost essence of each. The cohesions of nature are qualified and transmuted by this relationship, for the other self ceases to be merely an object, serviceable to the self because of affinities of nature and reason. It is recognized as not merely object but as itself a subject, as a unique centre of life and purpose. This "I" and "Thou" relationship is impossible without the presupposition of faith for two reasons: (1) Without freedom from anxiety man is so enmeshed in the vicious circle of egocentricity, so concerned about himself, that he cannot release himself for the adventure of love. (2) Without relation to God, the world of freedom in which spirit must meet spirit is so obscured that human beings constantly sink to the level of things in the human imagination. The injunction, "love thy neighbour as thyself," is therefore properly preceded both by the commandment, "love the Lord thy God," and by the injunction, "be not anxious."

These ultimate requirements of the Christian ethic are therefore not counsels of perfection or theological virtues of the sort which merely completes an otherwise incomplete natural goodness or virtue. Nor can they be subtracted from man without making his freedom a source of sinful infection. They are indeed counsels of perfection in the sense that sinful man lacks them and is incapable of achieving them. But they are basic and not supplementary requirements of his freedom.[2]

This analysis of the matter leads to the conclusion that sin neither destroys the structure by virtue of which man is man nor yet eliminates the sense of obligation toward the essential nature of man, which is the remnant of his perfection. This sense of obligation is, in fact, the claim which the essential nature of man makes upon him in his present sinful state. The virtue which corresponds to the true nature of man therefore appears to sinful man in the form of law. It is the "good that I would" but which "I do not." It is "the commandment which was ordained to life" but which "I found to be unto death" (Romans 7), of which St. Paul speaks. It is unto death

[2]*Cf.* Emil Brunner, *Man in Revolt*, Ch. 5, c. 1.

because the law states the requirements without helping man to fulfill them. In fact it heightens sin by arousing sinful egotism to a
more conscious defiance of the essential nature of man (Romans
7:7). It may also arouse sinful pride by tempting man to assume that
he keeps the law because he knows it.[3] It is not possible for man to
understand himself merely from the standpoint of the law within
him, *i.e.,* from the perspective of the good which he knows he ought
to do. Fully to understand himself he must know that he violates the
law which he regards as his norm; but neither can he be fully
understood, if it is not recognized that this law is the claim of his
essential nature upon him.[4]

[3]This is the point of the Pauline passage: "Behold, thou art called a
Jew, and restest in the law, and makest thy boast of God, And knowest
his will, and approvest the things which are more excellent, being in-
structed out of the law; and art confident that thou thyself art a guide of
the blind, a light of them which are in darkness, an instructor of the foolish, a teacher of babes, which hast the form of knowledge and of the truth
in the law. Thou therefore which teachest another, teachest thou not thyself? thou that preachest a man should not steal, dost thou steal?" Romans 2:17–21.
  This challenge is remarkably relevant to the whole self-righteousness
of modern culture which imagines that a man's acceptance of ideals of
justice and peace proves that it is some one else and not he who is responsible for injustice and conflict.
[4]The utopian illusions and sentimental aberrations of modern liberal
culture are really all derived from the basic error of negating the fact of
original sin. This error, more fully discussed in Chapter 4, continually
betrays modern men to equate the goodness of men with the virtue of
their various schemes for social justice and international peace. When
these schemes fail of realization or are realized only after tragic conflicts,
modern men either turn from utopianism to disillusionment and despair,
or they seek to place the onus of their failure upon some particular social
group or upon some particular form of economic and social organization.
  Obviously there are varying degrees of sin and guilt and some men
and nations are more guilty than others of "disobedience to the heavenly
vision." Also there are specific evils in history, arising from specific
maladjustments in social and political organization. But these evils can
be dealt with most adequately, if men do not give themselves to the illusion that some particular organization of society might be found in
which men would no longer stand in contradiction to the law of their

Significantly Luther, who is so anxious to prove the destruction of the image of God in man, is just as emphatic in insisting that the law, and man's uneasy conscience, are the first point of contact between God and man. This conscience is the righteousness of the sinner (*justitia peccatoris*). Man's own heart accuses him (*cor accusator*). Without faith this accusation leads to despair and with faith it may lead to repentance.[5] Man's uneasy conscience is, in other words, an expression of the law which is written in his own heart. Man is most conscious of this law in terms of the contrast and tension between it and his sinful actions. There are in fact interpretations of conscience which practically limit its expression to the uneasiness which follows, rather than to any specific guidance which precedes, the act.[6] While such interpretations are too narrow, it is probably true that conscience is primarily known to man in terms of the disquiet, the sense of inner conflict which expresses itself in all moral life.

Following St. Paul, Christian thought has consistently maintained that the law must be regarded, not simply as something which is

---

own being. Furthermore, particular virulent forms and types of sin in particular men and nations can be checked most successfully if it is recognized that these types are but aggravations of a general human situation.

Both modern liberalism and modern Marxism are always facing the alternatives of moral futility or moral fanaticism. Liberalism in its pure form usually succumbs to the peril of futility. It will not act against evil until it is able to find a vantage point of guiltlessness from which to operate. This means that it cannot act at all. Sometimes it imagines that this inaction is the guiltlessness for which it has been seeking. A minority of liberals and most of the Marxists solve the problem by assuming that they have found a position of guiltlessness in action. Thereby they are betrayed into the error of fanaticism. The whole history of modern culture, particularly in its more recent efforts to defend itself against inferior and more demonic cultures, is a pathetic revelation of the weakness and confusion which result from these illusions about the character of man.

[5]*Cf.* M. A. H. Stromph, *Die Anthropologie Martin Luthers*, pp. 111–14.

[6]*Cf.* Rudolph Hoffmann, *Das Gewissen*, pp. 100 ff.

given man either by revelation, or for that matter by the authority of society, but as written in the heart.[7] This can only mean that the requirements of action, dictated by man's essential nature, are a part of his real self. They stand outside of the self in action; that is why they are "law," and appear in the guise of something imposed from without and are only the "form of knowledge and of truth" (Romans 2:20). The particular content of the voice of conscience is of course conditioned by all the relativities of history. Men may be mistaken in their interpretation of what life is essentially; and conscience may be, in its very content, a vehicle of sin. Yet even in its content the universalities of conscience are at least as significant as its varieties and relativities.[8] One must conclude that the real structure of life, the dependence of man upon his fellowmen for instance, which requires both organic and loving relations between them, asserts itself, in spite of all errors, against the confusion which human egotism and pride introduces into the relations of men.[9]

If this analysis be correct it follows that if Protestantism was right in rejecting the Catholic doctrine that the Fall had not altered man's essential nature because it had only destroyed a *donum supernaturale,*

[7]*Cf.* Romans 2:14-15: "For when the Gentiles, which have not the law, do by nature the things contained in the law, these, having not the law, are a law unto themselves: Which shew the work of the law written in their hearts, their conscience also bearing witness, and their thoughts the mean while accusing or else excusing one another."

[8]In the words of David Hume: "The epithets, sociable, good-natured, humane, merciful, grateful, friendly, generous, beneficent, or their equivalents are known in all languages and universally express the highest merits which human nature is capable of attaining." *An Enquiry Concerning the Principles of Morals,* Sec. II, Part i.

[9]There are of course instances in which practices which are almost universally condemned are actually enjoined by the customs of a particular group; and become the content of conscience for the individuals in that group through the prestige and influence of the custom. In such cases the moral life may be said to approach a state of total depravity. It is significant, however, that no group custom enjoins lying, stealing or murder indiscriminately, since such a law would lead to complete chaos within the group. There is thus always a limit to the relativity of law in the conscience of men.

it was wrong in asserting that man's essential nature had been destroyed. The Catholic doctrine presumably saw an alteration only in the virtue and not in the structure of man. But its definition of that virtue, namely man's communion with God and intimate contact with him, contains by implication a part of the essential structure of man, namely his transcendent freedom, which can be tolerable and creative only when it has found its source, end and norm in the will of God. This structure of freedom is revealed in the very bondage of sin; for it is by this capacity for the eternal that man transmutes his finite self into infinite proportions. It is by this capacity that he is able both to sin and to have some knowledge of his sin.

The disavowal of the historical-literalistic illusion, which places the original perfection of man in a period before an historical Fall, thus clarifies and corrects both Catholic and Protestant thought. Against Protestant thought it becomes possible to maintain that the image of God is preserved in spite of man's sin. In distinction from Catholic thought it is possible to eliminate the unwarranted distinction between a completely lost original justice and an uncorrupted natural justice. What is called original justice in Catholic thought really represents the requirements of human freedom in its most ultimate sense. Natural justice represents the requirements of man as creature. Both are corrupted by sin: but both are still with man, not indeed as realizations but requirements.

If however "before the Fall" is not an historical period the questions are: (1) Where is the locus of this perfection as requirement upon man; and (2) what is its character and content?

III

THE LOCUS OF ORIGINAL RIGHTEOUSNESS

If there is no historical period to which we may assign the *justitia originalis*, the original perfection, is it possible to find a locus for it? The complexity of this problem may be gauged in terms of an analogical but simpler question: Where is the locus of health in the life of a diseased organism? Obviously the seat of infection may be in one particular organ of the organism, so that the other parts are comparatively healthy. Yet disease in any part of the organism affects the whole. The whole organism is thus diseased. Yet there is some health as long as there is life. The very pains of disease are a testimony of this hidden health; for pain reveals that the normal harmony of the organism has been disturbed and is therefore health's indictment of disease. It is not possible to assign a particular locus to the residual health in the diseased body.

In the same way it is not possible to exempt "reason" or any other human faculty from the disease of sin. Since sin is the self's undue pride and exaltation, any force in human life which tends to keep the self in a normal position of subordination to God and coordination with its fellows must be regarded as an element of health, without which life would become completely self-destructive. While it is not possible to give such elements of health a particular locus, it is possible to find a locus for the consciousness and the memory of an original perfection. We have previously noted that the self which knows itself guilty is the transcendent self or, to speak more precisely, the self in the moment of transcending itself. The self in the moment of transcending itself exercises the self's capacity for infinite regression and makes the previous concretion of will its object. It is in this moment of self-transcendence that the consciousness and memory of original perfection arise. For in this moment the self knows itself as merely a finite creature among many others and realizes that the undue claims which the anxious self in action makes, result in injustices to its fellows.

The consciousness and memory of an original perfection in the self-as-transcendent must not be regarded as the possession of perfection. The fact is that the self-as-transcendent always assumes, mistakenly, that its present ability to judge and criticize the undue and unjust claims of the self in a previous action is a guarantee of its virtue in a subsequent action. This is not the case, for when the self acts it always uses the previous transcendent perspective partly as a "rationalization" and "false front" for its interested action. The action is therefore always sinful, even though it is important to recognize that there may be infinite gradations of interested and-disinterested action and of pretension and self-deception in covering these actions.

Perfection before the Fall is, in other words, perfection before the act; but it is important not to give too narrow a connotation to the concept of "act." The self may act even when the action is not overt. It acts whenever, as anxious self, it thinks or moves for its own protection in the welter of perils and passions which constitutes its world. Every thought, mood or action which proceeds from the self as anxious, finite, and insecure has some taint of sin upon it. But there is no consciousness of sin in such sinful action because the self is perfectly unified in its action. Without such inner unity it could not act at all. It is when, after the action, it takes a position outside rather than inside itself, that it becomes conscious of the inordinate character of its action.

The consciousness of original perfection is not in some universal self in distinction to an empirical self. There are obviously not simply two selves in conflict with each other. But in every moment of existence there is a tension between the self as it looks out upon the world from the perspective of its values and necessities and the self as it looks at both the world and itself, and is disquieted by the undue claims of the self in action. These two perspectives of the self are clearly revealed, for instance, in the Pauline process of self-searching. He declares on the one hand: "For we know that the law is spiritual; but I am carnal, sold under sin." Here the sinful self looks at a reality which seems to be outside the self. It is the law. But in almost the same breath St. Paul declares: "Now then it is no more I that do it, but sin that dwelleth in me" (Romans 7:14, 17). Here the self as ultimate subject looks at the sinful self and declares that it is not itself. It is "not I . . . but sin." *The "I," which from the perspective of self-transcendence, regards the sinful self not as self but as "sin," is the same "I" which from the perspective of sinful action regards the transcendent possibilities of the self as not the self but as "law." It is the same self; but these changing perspectives are obviously significant.*

The tendency of Augustinian thought, particularly as expressed in the Protestant Reformers, to deny these complexities in favour of a simpler emphasis upon the corruption of man, must be attributed not merely to the illusions of literalistic interpretations of the Fall, but also to the fear that any concessions to man's self-esteem would immediately aggravate the sin of pride. This is a justified fear, since the whole history of human self-righteousness proves that man always judges himself not from the standpoint of what he does but from the standpoint of his knowledge of what he ought to do. Assuming that he obeys "the law" because he knows it, he throws the onus of disobedience upon his fellowmen. That is why the strictures of St. Paul against the self-righteousness of the "good" people of his day have a relevance to the moral problems of our own day, though this relevance is not understood in liberal Christianity.[1] The greatest sin of moralistic Christianity is its tendency to encourage the assumption that men are as good as the ideals of justice and love which they entertain. This sin modern Christianity shares, of course, and also borrows from the general moralism of our culture. Nevertheless this confusion does not justify extravagant theories of total depravity, and such theories are not convincing refutations of the error in liberal moralism.

In placing the consciousness of "original righteousness" in a moment of the self which transcends history, though not outside of the self which is in history, it may be relevant to observe that this conforms perfectly to the myth of the Fall when interpreted symbolically. The myth does not record any actions of Adam which were

[1]The paradoxical relation between "original righteousness" and sin is perfectly expressed by Pascal in the words: "Vanity is so anchored in the heart of man that . . . those who write against it want to have the glory of having written well; and those who read it desire the glory of having read it. I who write this have perhaps this desire, and perhaps those who will read it." *Pensées*, p. 149.

sinless, though much is made in theology of the perfection he had before the Fall. Irenæus, with greater realism than most theologians, observes that the period was very brief, sin following almost immediately upon his creation. Adam was sinless before he acted and sinful in his first recorded action. His sinlessness, in other words, preceded his first significant action and his sinfulness came to light in that action. This is a symbol for the whole of human history. The original righteousness of man stands, as it were, outside of history. Yet it is in the man who is in history, and when sin comes it actually borrows from this original righteousness. For the pretension of sin is that its act is not in history but an act of impartiality, a deed of eternity.

IV

THE CONTENT OF JUSTITIA ORIGINALIS AS LAW

We have seen that the original righteousness or perfection is present with sinful man as "law" and we have tentatively defined this law as derived from man's essential nature and have distinguished between organic structure and freedom in man's essential nature. We have suggested that what is usually known as "natural law" in both Christian and Stoic thought is roughly synonymous with the requirements of man as creature and that the virtues, defined in Catholic thought as "theological virtues," that is the virtues faith, hope and love, are the requirements of his freedom and represent the *justitia originalis.* This righteousness, we have suggested, is not completely lost in the Fall but remains with sinful man as the knowledge of what he ought to be, as the law of his freedom.

(*a*) In making a more detailed analysis of the content of the law of original righteousness it is necessary to emphasize that the distinction between the natural law which states the requirements of man as creature and the *justitia originalis* which states the requirements of man's freedom can be only tentative and provisional. The primary mistake of Catholic theory is precisely the sharp and absolute distinction which it makes between the two. It speaks of an original righteousness which was lost in the Fall and a natural justice which remains essentially uncorrupted by the Fall. This distinction obscures the complex relation of human freedom to all of man's natural functions, and the consequent involvement of all "natural" or "rational" standards and norms in sin. There is therefore no uncorrupted natural law, just as there is no completely lost original justice. The freedom of man sets every standard of justice under higher possibilities, and the sin of man perennially insinuates contingent and relative elements into the supposedly absolute standards of human reason. Undue confidence in human reason, as the seat and source of natural law, makes this very concept of law into a vehicle of human sin. It gives the peculiar conditions and unique circumstances in which reason operates in a particular historical moment, the sanctity of universality. The confidence of medieval Catholicism in the ability of an unspoiled reason to arrive at definitive standards of natural justice thus became the very vehicle of the sinful pretensions of the age. The social ethics of Thomas Aquinas embody the peculiarities and the contingent factors of a feudal-agrarian economy into a system of fixed socio-ethical principles.

The relativizing effect of both freedom and sin upon all historical norms may be illustrated by a few specific examples. In Catholic natural law all social relations, including family relations, are precisely defined. *Inter alia* it is maintained that the natural law prohibits birth control and also that it enjoins the supremacy of the husband over the wife. The prohibition of birth control assumes that the sexual function in human life must be limited to its function in nature, that of procreation. But it is the very character of human life that all animal functions are touched by freedom and released into more complex relationships. This freedom is the basis of both creativity and sin. Freedom in relation to sex may occasion license and it may also provide for a creative relation between the sexual impulse and other more complex and refined spiritual impulses. In its teachings in regard to sex, Catholic theories of natural law might actually be more plausibly expressed in terms of the Lutheran concept of "order of creation" or *"Schoepfungsordnung."* For the concept of "order of creation" limits the law to a natural fact, such as natural bisexuality for instance, and does not introduce some specious universality of reason. It is not possible to escape the natural fact that the primary purpose of bisexuality in nature is that of procreation. But it is not easy to establish a universally valid "law of reason" which will eternally set the bounds for the function of sex in the historic development of human personality.

For the supremacy of the male over the female, all orthodox Christian theory finds additional support in Pauline-Biblical thought so that its assurance about its supposed absolute standard is made doubly sure, having the support of both the Bible and the law of reason. It is important to realize that no definition of the natural law between the sexes can be made without embodying something of the sin of male arrogance into the standard. The relation between the sexes is governed on the one hand by the natural fact of sex differentiation and on the other by the spiritual fact of human freedom. The natural fact that the woman bears the child binds her to the child and partially limits the freedom of her choice in the development of various potentialities of character not related to the vocation of motherhood. A rationalistic feminism is undoubtedly inclined to transgress inexorable bounds set by nature. On the other hand any premature fixation of certain historical standards in regard to the family will inevitably tend to reinforce male arrogance and to retard justified efforts on the part of the female to achieve such freedom as is not incompatible with the primary function of motherhood. The freedom, which is the unique capacity of humankind, makes it difficult to set precise standards for all time for any kind of relationship, including the relation between the sexes. The sinfulness of man, on the other hand, makes it inevitable that a dominant class, group, and sex should seek to define a relationship, which guarantees its dominance, as permanently normative. There are of course certain permanent norms, such as monogamy, which, contrary to the relativism of such Protestant sceptics as Karl Barth, are maintained not purely by Scriptural authority but by the cumulative experience of the race. About these universalities, amidst the relativities of standards, a word must be spoken presently.

The limitations of Catholic natural-law theories are revealed with equal clarity when applied to the field of international relations. The Catholic theory of a "just war"[1] is a case in point. The Catholic theory is infinitely superior to the Lutheran relativism and moral scepticism which finally leaves the Christian without any standards by which he might judge the relative justice of his nation's cause. Nevertheless, it assumes that obvious distinctions between "justice" and "injustice," between "defence" and "aggression," are possible. Contemporary history reinforces the clear lessons of the whole of history upon this point. Not all wars are equally just and not all contestants are equally right. Distinctions must be made. But the judgments with which we make them are influenced by passions and interests, so that even the most obvious case of aggression can be made to appear a necessity of defence; and even a war which is judged by neutral opinion to be wholly defensive cannot be waged with completely good conscience because the situations out of which wars arise are charged with memories of previous acts of aggression on the part of those now in defence.[2] This does not mean that the

[1]The Spanish Jesuit Suarez defines a just war as follows: "In order that a war may be justly waged, certain conditions must be observed and these may be brought under three heads. First it must be waged by a legitimate power. Secondly its cause must be just and right. Thirdly just methods should be used, that is equity in the beginning of war, in the prosecution of it and in victory." *Tractatus de legibus,* I, 9.

[2]The present European war is a case in point. The aggression of Germany is justified by the German rulers as nothing but a correction of the "injustices of Versailles." These claims are certainly spurious to a considerable degree and there are standards by which they may be judged to be so. Yet there is no "universal reason" to which an appeal may be made to arbitrate the point. Judgments upon the points at issue are relativized by geographic and political circumstances. And even those who are most certain that the German aggression is something more than a mere correction of a previous injustice cannot escape an uneasy con-

moralists who would refrain from all war, because the issues of any particular war are always filled with ambiguities, are right. The very same war which fails to yield an absolutely clear case of "justice" may yet concern itself with the very life and death of civilizations and cultures. Men do have to make important decisions in history upon the basis of certain norms, even though they must recognize that all historic norms are touched with both finiteness and sin; and that their sinfulness consists precisely in the bogus claim of finality which is made for them. The perennial mistake of rationalists, whether Stoic, Catholic or modern, is to exempt reason from either finiteness or sin or both and to derive universal rational norms from this confidence in reason.

While it is important to reject this error it is just as important to disavow the opposite error of the moral relativists, who deny every validity of general norms. In secular theory this relativism is the fruit of an extreme naturalistic empiricism. In the history of religious thought Lutheran orthodoxy tends to regard reason as so completely involved in the corruption of sin that it has no confidence in any "natural law" norms.[3] This conflict between a too simple rationalism and a too complete relativism may be resolved by a more dialectical analysis of the function of reason. Reason is in fact in an equivocal position between the self-as-subject and the self-as-agent of action, between the self as transcending itself and the anxious self in action. It is the servant of both. Its universal judgments, its effort to relate all things to each other in a system of coherence, can be alternately the instrument by which the self-as-subject condemns the partial and prejudiced actions of the sinful self, and the vehicle of the sinful self by which it seeks to give the sanctity of a false universality to its

_____

science about the injustices which were, in fact, involved in the peace which ended a previous war.

[3]W. Wiesner's chapter in the symposium *Christian Faith and the Common Life* (Oxford Conference) is an interesting example of a modern Lutheran's complete rejection of all rational or "natural law" norms of conduct.

particular needs and partial insights. An analysis of the complex facts which underlie the conception of "natural law," and of conscience in general, must do justice to both aspects of reason.[4]

(*b*) Thus far we have considered only the tendency of Catholic thought to derive too unqualified moral norms from a reason which is presumed to be limited but uncorrupted and pure as far as it goes. The discussion of this error is, however, only a negative approach to the problem of a *justitia originalis,* which Catholic theory regards as wholly lost in the Fall. A positive approach reveals that what is known as "natural law" and what is known as "original righteousness" are intimately related to each other, not only by reason of a common involvement in sin but by reason of the fact that human freedom places the requirements of "original justice" as ultimate possibilities over the requirements of the natural law. There is no justice, even in a sinful world, which can be regarded as finally normative. The higher possibilities of love, which is at once the fulfillment and the negation of justice, always hover over every system of justice.

The *justitia originalis* of Catholic theology is, as we have seen, the virtue of the soul's perfect communion with God, its perfect subordination to God's will and a consequent perfect co-ordination of all its impulses and functions with one another. This virtue is merely defined more fully when it is divided into the three virtues of "faith, hope and love" which, according to Catholic theory, are the "theo-

---

[4]Calvin's attitude toward reason stands between the Catholic and the Lutheran viewpoint. His position lacks consistency but it is probably more consistent with the facts than either the Catholic or the Lutheran position. He writes: "Reason, by which man distinguishes between good and evil, by which he understands and judges, being a natural talent, could not be wholly destroyed but is partly debilitated, partly vitiated, so that it exhibits nothing but deformity and ruin." *Institutes,* Book II, Ch. ii, par. 12.

It is hardly logical to claim that something which is only "partly vitiated" exhibits "nothing but deformity and ruin." But there is at least an approach in this inconsistency to the fact that reason is both a servant of sinful self-love and an organ of judgment upon it.

logical virtues" which divine grace supplies to sinful man, thereby completing a structure of virtue which the Fall had left incomplete. Whether these virtues are ever vouchsafed even to the redeemed man in as complete a form as Catholic theories of sanctification assume, is a question which we must consider later.[5] It is important at this point to establish that they are never as completely lost in the Fall as Catholic theory assumes. The original righteousness which sinful man has supposedly lost is in reality present with him as the ultimate requirement of his freedom. Because man is not merely creature but also free spirit, and because every moral norm stands under higher possibilities by reason of his freedom, there is no moral standard at which the human spirit can find rest short of the standard of "faith, hope and love."

This character of the theological virtues as "law" to sinful man is perfectly revealed in the "thou shalt" of the law of love: "Thou shalt love the Lord thy God with all thy heart, and all thy soul, and all thy mind. This is the first and great commandment. And the second is like unto it, Thou shalt love thy neighbour as thyself." Here something is commanded and demanded. That means law. But what is commanded is a state of heart and mind, a harmony between the soul and God ("Thou shalt love the Lord thy God"), a harmony within the soul ("with all thy heart, and all thy soul, and all thy mind"), and a harmony between the self and the neighbour ("thy neighbour as thyself") which, if attained, would exclude all commandment. Such a commandment can be understood as stating an ultimate condition of complete harmony between the soul and God, its neighbour and itself in a situation in which this harmony is not a reality. If it were a reality the "thou shalt" would be meaningless. If there were not some possibility of sensing the ultimate perfection in a state of sin the "thou shalt" would be irrelevant. It is significant that philosophical treatises on morals have universally misunderstood the "law of love" because they lacked the concept of sin as a basis for their analysis.

[5]See Vol. II, Ch. 4.

Whether it is possible for any man, either by nature or by grace, to fulfill this commandment and to heal the disharmony between himself and God, his neighbour and himself, is a question which we must postpone until we consider the Christian doctrine of redemption.[6] For the moment we are interested only in validating the law of love as a vision of health which even a sick man may envisage, as the original righteousness which man does not possess but which he knows he ought to possess, since the contradiction in which he stands, and the consequent compulsion and submission in his relations to God, the neighbour and himself, are obviously not an ideal state of health.

The relation of the law of love to law as such is perfectly comprehended in the story of Jesus' encounter with the rich young man. The young man had "kept all the commandments"; but the commandments, the "law" in the more restricted sense, did not satisfy him and his continued uneasiness prompted the question, "What lack I yet?" This question, "What lack I yet?" suggests that what lies in the uneasy conscience of the sinner is not so much a knowledge that the ultimate law of life is the law of love as the more negative realization that obedience to the ordinary rules of justice and equity is not enough.

Jesus defines the more ultimate possibility toward which the young man is yearning in the words: "If thou *wilt be perfect,* go and sell that thou hast and give to the poor." What is demanded is an action in which regard for the self is completely eliminated. All simple moralism, which assumes that the law of life needs only to be stated in order to be obeyed, is refuted by the response of the rich young ruler to this demand: "He went away sorrowful for he had great possessions." For the moment it would appear that only the extent of the young man's possessions made it impossible for him to obey the ultimate law, for Jesus observes: "Verily I say unto you that a rich man shall hardly enter into the kingdom of heaven." But the disciples quickly realize that the command runs counter to the

[6]See Vol. II, Chs. 5–6.

anxieties of all men about themselves and their possessions. Their question, "Who then can be saved?" quickly and justly extends the predicament of the rich young man to include all men, since all men are involved in the sin of establishing their own security by what they have and what they are.

The answer of Jesus to this despairing question implies a complete acceptance of the viewpoint of the disciples. Jesus admits that the ultimate possibility of human life is beyond the capacity of sinful man: "With man this is impossible." It is an ultimate possibility of divine grace: "But with God all things are possible." Modern liberal theology has made much of the difference between the attitude of Jesus toward human nature and that of St. Paul. But the thesis which is both implied and asserted in this story is the same as that which is the burden of Pauline soteriology. It is suggested that the contradiction between man's essential nature and his sinful condition is insoluble from the standpoint of man's own resources and can be solved only from the standpoint of God's resources.

The explicit and implicit views of human nature which this story yields, may therefore be summarized as follows: (*a*) Man as sinner is not unmindful of the ultimate requirements of his nature as free spirit. He knows that any particular historical concretion of law is not enough. (*b*) He is not fully conscious of the nature of these ultimate requirements, and (*c*) he is not ready to meet these requirements once they are defined. These three propositions give an accurate account of the typical relation of "original righteousness" to man as sinner (Matt. 22:37-39).

The specific content of this higher law, which is more than law, this law which transcends all law, this original righteousness which even sinful man has, not as a possession but in his sense of something lacking, has been tentatively defined, and this definition must now be further explicated. It contains three terms: (*a*) The perfect relation of the soul to God in which obedience is transcended by love, trust and confidence ("Thou shalt love the Lord thy God"); (*b*) the perfect internal harmony of the soul with itself in all of its desires and impulses: "With all thy heart and all thy soul and all thy mind"; and (c) the perfect harmony of life with life: "Thou shalt love thy neighbour as thyself."

(a) The first of these three requirements is the most basic one, just as unbelief or mistrust is the basic and primal sin. This basic requirement of the love of God is identical with the two terms in the Pauline triad, "faith" and "hope." Without faith in God's providence the freedom of man is intolerable. Hope is subordinate to and yet identical with faith. It is faith with regard to the future. The future is the symbol of the unpredictable possibilities of eternity which may appear in time. Without faith and hope these possibilities represent an intolerable threat to man's little universe of meaning. They may in any moment introduce uncalculated and incalculable elements into the little system of meaning by which men live and by which they seek to maintain their sense of domestic security. History is not rational. At least it does not conform to the systems of rational coherence which men construct periodically to comprehend its meaning. These systems are inevitably anchored in some specific anchor of meaning, which is itself subject to the vicissitudes of history. History can be meaningful, therefore, only in terms of a faith which comprehends its seeming irrationalities and views them as the expression of a divine wisdom, which transcends human understanding. Faith in the wisdom of God is thus a prerequisite of love because it is the condition without which man is anxious and is driven by his anxiety into vicious circles of self-sufficiency and pride. As we have previously noted, the admonition, "Be not anxious," has meaning only in conjunction with the faith expressed by Jesus: "Your heavenly father knoweth that ye have need of these things."

It is not to be supposed that the faith, hope and trust which eliminate anxiety are simple possibilities of human existence, not even for those who have some knowledge of God in Christ, that is for those in whom Christian revelation has penetrated through the confusion of sin. How little this commandment, "Be not anxious," is a simple possibility can be tested by any honest preacher who delivers a homily upon the text and searches his soul sufficiently to know how anxious he is to have the approbation of his congregation on his exposition of the admonition, not to be anxious. Freedom from anxiety, in other words, is an ultimate possibility which man as sinner denies in his action. Even the man of faith does so, inasfar as he is sinner. It belongs to the perfection before the Fall. The sinful self is anxious about itself and yet it knows that it ought not to be.

It might be argued that this knowledge, that faith and trust are a requirement of human freedom, is not a natural endowment of man, but becomes known to man only as Christian revelation discloses the full dimension of human freedom and the reality of God as the master of that freedom. In terms of Biblical symbolism this would mean that Adam's perfection before the Fall is not fully understood until the "second Adam" defines it. This thesis is, at least partially, correct. For the Christian faith is not only an answer to the human situation of self-contradiction; it is a fuller and clearer revelation of that contradiction. The revelation of God as redeemer accentuates a previous knowledge of God as judge, for the simple reason that the revelation of His redemptive love clarifies His character of holiness, in terms of which human sin is judged. The anthropological consequences of this paradox are that faith in God's ultimate resolution of the contradiction in which man stands clarifies man's knowledge of that contradiction. He sees that his anxiety is due to his unbelief.

Yet even when this is not clearly seen some echo of the commandment, "Be not anxious," comes to man in his anxiety. The serenity of faith is not his possession but he knows that it ought to be. It is instructive that the same Stoicism which elaborates a "natural law" and a doctrine of *"conscientia"* in which the "law" for man as creature is defined also has a doctrine of the "law" for man as free spirit. It is the Stoic doctrine of ἀπάθεια, which demands a state of indifference toward all vicissitudes of life which are beyond man's power. This doctrine may be regarded as a precise indication of what is possible within terms of natural theology for man to know about the commandment, "Be not anxious," and about the requirement of serenity as a condition of health for the freedom of man. It is significant, however, that it is not possible to achieve freedom from anxiety within the limits of Stoic pantheism without destroying creativity in history. The god of Stoicism is not himself free spirit and Creator. In consequence ἀπάθεια means, on the one hand, a self-sufficiency of the human spirit purchased at the price of withdrawing the soul into itself and cutting all its connections with the problems and obligations of history.[7] On the other hand, lacking a doctrine of Creation, and, therefore, having no distinction between God and the world and none between the world as created and the world in sin, Stoicism counsels freedom from anxiety in the false faith that all things are good.[8] Stoic freedom from anxiety is thus involved in both a self-sufficiency, which does not do justice to man's actual dependence upon the world about him, and also in a determinism which does not do justice to the evil in history.[9] These errors reveal the limits of a

---

[7]Epictetus expresses this idea in the words: "Of things some are in our power and others are not. In our power are opinion, pursuit, desire, aversion, and in one word whatever are our own actions. Not in our power are body, property, reputation, command, and, in one word, whatever are not our own actions. . . . If you suppose that only to be your own, which is your own; and what belongs to others, such as it really is; no one will compel you; no one will restrain you; you will find fault with no one; you will accuse no one, you will not do one thing against your will; no one will hurt you, you will not have an enemy, for you will suffer no harm." *The Enchiridion*, I.

[8]In the words of Marcus Aurelius: "If so be the gods have deliberated in particular of those things that should happen to me, I must stand to their deliberations, as discreet and wise. For that a god should be an imprudent god is hard to conceive.—But if so be they have not deliberated of me in particular, certainly they have on the whole in general, and those things which in consequence and coherence of this general deliberation happen to me in particular I am bound to embrace and accept." *Meditations*, VI, 39.

[9]Marcus Aurelius expresses both sides of the Stoic doctrine in one paragraph: "Thou must comfort thyself in the expectation of thy dissolu-

pantheistic rationalism, seeking to come to terms with the problem
of man's freedom and dependence. This problem can be solved only
in terms of the Christian conception of divine Providence. It is nevertheless important to recognize that Stoicism defines something of the
trust and serenity which even sinful man knows to be his ultimate
good. This is a part of the original perfection which man does not
have but knows he ought to have.

(*b*) The second requirement of *justitia originalis* is expressed in the
words, "with all thy heart and all thy soul and all thy mind," in the
Biblical law of love. This requirement and ideal possibility is that of
a complete inner accord within the soul. This inner accord is not a
reality in sinful man, because there is compulsion and submission
within the self just as between the self and God and the self and
society. But even sinful man knows that only such an inner harmony
would represent complete health. The sinful soul does nothing with
all its heart and soul and might. The effect of sin is that it would do
the good but does not do it, that "to will is present with me; but how
to perform that which is good I know not" (Romans 7:18), which is
to say that every action betrays a "defect of the will" (Augustine), an
inability to carry out a right general intention in the specific instance.

Idealists have traditionally explained this inner contradiction as
the tension between the intelligible and sensible self, or between the
universal and the empirical self. This explanation always has a certain
plausibility because there is an actual difference between the self as
transcendent and the self as agent of action. But the idealistic explanation disregards the unity of the self and obscures the fact that there is
only one will. This will stands in contradiction to itself because it
cannot do the good which it wills. The will is deficient in the specific
instance to carry out the transcendent purpose because the motive
power of the will in the specific instance is partly furnished by the

tion and in the meantime not grieve at the delay but rest contented in
these two things: First, that nothing shall happen unto thee which is not
according to the nature of the universe. Secondly, that it is in thy power
to refrain from doing anything contrary to thine own proper god and
inward spirit." *Meditations*, V, 10.

fears and anxieties of the anxious self; and these fears drive in a different direction from the transcendent general intention.

The anxious self invariably makes itself its own centre and end; but since the self transcends itself in infinite regression only God and not itself can be its centre and end. Thus there is an inner contradiction even in acts of obedience toward God. The fact that the act is one of obedience rather than of love means that it is not done with "all thy heart and all thy soul and all thy might." The self, inasfar as it is centred in itself, withholds perfect trust and faith and must be coerced. Yet it can never persuade itself that it is its own adequate centre and security. Therefore there is always a suggestion and memory of an ideal possibility in which this inner disharmony has been overcome. This memory refutes every doctrine of total depravity. But the actuality of inner tension refutes every doctrine of an unspoiled human goodness.

Inasfar as the self is centred in itself, it can offer only coerced obedience. Inasfar as the self transcends itself it knows the inadequacy of such reluctant attitudes. Therefore acts of obedience which fall short of love produce an uneasiness of conscience, only different in degree and not in kind from the uneasiness created by disobedience. The ideal possibility is always that "they may love the things which thou commandest and desire that which thou dost promise."

The perfect harmony of the soul with itself is thus a derivative of its perfect communion with, and love of, God. Where the love of God transcends obedience, the soul is centred in its true source and end without reservation. There are obviously no actions of sinful men which perfectly conform to this ideal possibility. The sense that an obedience which is less than love is not normative even though it is universal, is the *justitia originalis*. It is the sense that there ought not be a sense of ought; it is the "thou shalt" which suggests that there are no "thou shalts" in perfection.

(c) The love of the neighbour, the perfect accord of life with life and will with will, is, in the same manner, a derivative of perfect faith and trust in God. Without such trust man is involved in the vicious circle of anxiety and self-sufficiency which inhibits him from genuine concern for the needs of the neighbour. Love between man and man is thus but one facet of the total *justitia originalis*. It is also the final form of that righteousness. Love is the final requirement of human relations, if the freedom of the persons who are involved in mutual relations be considered.

Human personality has a depth and uniqueness which escapes the ordinary processes of knowledge. Those processes always tend to reduce the fellowman to a thing or object. Human as well as divine personality is obscured when the self seeks to understand the other merely as object of observation. The creative initiative of the other, the unique depth of personality in the other, is veiled by an approach which touches the surface of his life but does not penetrate to the secret of his being. The uniqueness of each individuality can be known in love but not in terms of general knowledge in which the self seeks to subordinate uniqueness in order to fit the "other" into the general categories of reason.[10]

Real love between person and person is therefore a relationship in which spirit meets spirit in a dimension in which both the uniformities and the differences of nature, which bind men together and separate them, are transcended. This is no simple possibility. Each soul remains, in a sense, inscrutable to its fellows. It is a possibility only by way of the love of God. All human love between person and person is frustrated by inscrutable mysteries in the heart of each person and by opaque "walls of partition" between man and man. Inasfar as human love is a possibility, therefore, it is always partly a relation between the soul and soul via their common relation to God. Inasfar as it is not a possibility it points to God as the final realization of the possibility. Where the love of God does not under-

---

[10]For a profound discussion of this problem see Martin Buber's *I and Thou* and also Nicolas Berdyaev's *Solitude and Society*. Berdyaev's treatment of the subject is partially vitiated by the dualistic assumption that the tendency to reduce the "thou" of the other self to "it" is but one aspect of the "degraded" character of all knowledge of objects. All external knowledge is thus regarded as an aspect of the "fallen" world.

gird and complete the relation of man to man, the differences which nature creates and sin accentuates, differences of geography, race, time, place and history, separate men from one another; and the similarities of nature and of reason may indeed unite men but not on the level of spirit and freedom.

The law of love is thus a requirement of human freedom; and the freedom of the self and of the other both require it. The freedom of the self is such that no rule of justice, no particular method of arbitrating the interests of the other with those of the self, can leave the self with the feeling that it has done all that it could. In its freedom it constantly rises above these laws and rules and realizes that they are determined by contingent factors and that they fall short of the ultimate possibility of loving the neighbour "as thyself." A sense of justice may prompt men to organize legal systems of unemployment insurance through which a general sense of obligation toward the needy neighbour is expressed. But no such system can leave the self satisfied when it faces particular needs among those who are the beneficiaries of such minimal schemes of justice. The freedom and uniqueness of the other also raise moral requirements above any scheme of justice. The other has special needs and requirements which cannot be satisfied by general rules of equity. It is significant that even in communist theory, the basic equalitarianism of the theory is transcended in its final vision of utopia. In that utopia even "bourgeois equality" is left behind for a state of perfection in which every one "will give according to his ability and take according to his need."

Love is thus the end term of any system of morals. It is the moral requirement in which all schemes of justice are fulfilled and negated. They are fulfilled because the obligation of life to life is more fully met in love than is possible in any scheme of equity and justice. They are negated because love makes an end of the nicely calculated less and more of structures of justice. It does not carefully arbitrate between the needs of the self and of the other, since it meets the needs of the other without concern for the self.

v

THE TRANSCENDENT CHARACTER OF JUSTITIA ORIGINALIS

Against pessimistic theories of human nature which affirm the total depravity of man it is important to assert the continued presence in man of the *justitia originalis,* of the law of love, as law and requirement. It is equally important, in refutation of modern secular and Christian forms of utopianism, to recognize that the fulfillment of the law of love is no simple possibility. Love is the law of freedom; but man is not completely free; and such freedom as he has is corrupted by sin. All historic schemes and structures of justice must take the contingencies of nature and history and the fact of sin into consideration. Since man transcends race and nation, time and place, no scheme of justice which regulates the interests of China and America, for instance, can stop short of affirming the interests of the individual in China less than the needs of the individual in America. But there is no simple possibility of relating these interests to each other in terms of a perfect coherence of love so that the man in China or America would affirm the interests of the man in America or China as much as he affirms his own. The human imagination is too limited to see and understand the interests of the other as vividly as those of the self. Furthermore the realization of any such system of harmony would require more than individual action. It would require the organization of vast economic and political structures in defiance of, and transcendence over, the contingencies of geography, the fortuitous differences of natural resources, etc. There is, therefore, no historic structure of justice which can either fulfill the law of love or rest content in its inability to do so.

The fact of sin introduces an even more stubborn force of corruption into the inertia of nature and finiteness. The man who is limited by time and place does not merely fail to sense the needs of others who live beyond the limits of his time and place. He resists the claim of their necessities upon his conscience and makes demands of his own which are incompatible with their interests. In both Stoic and Catholic theory special consideration was given to the situation created by the fact of sin by distinguishing between an absolute and a relative natural law. The former represents the demands of conscience without compromise with the fact of sin. The latter stated the legal and moral necessities of a sinful world. Thus the absolute natural law demanded complete liberty and equality. The relative natural law, on the other hand, defined the necessary coercion of government, the inequalities of property and class, including slavery, and the necessities of conflict. The absolute natural law outlawed war while the relative natural law recognized it as a necessary method of achieving justice in a sinful world.

Just as Catholic rationalism makes too complete a distinction between natural law and the *justitia originalis,* it also tends to differentiate too completely between a relative and absolute natural law. Nevertheless these distinctions correspond to actual realities in the moral experience, which modern secular and Christian utopianism disregards. The distinctions are too absolute because it is never possible to define the limits of the force of sin or of the ideal possibilities which transcend sin. One cannot, by definition, determine where and when an inequality of nature or history must be accepted as ineluctable fate and where it must be defied. Nor can one determine in advance where and when tyranny and injustice must be resisted even if such resistance results in overt conflict. If the distinction between relative and absolute natural law is made too sharp (as it is in medieval theory) the inequality and conflict which the relative law allows is accepted too complacently. There are no precise distinctions either between relative and absolute natural law, as there are none between natural law and the law of love, for the simple reason that the freedom of spirit is so enmeshed in the necessities of nature, and the health and sickness of that freedom are so involved in each other, that it is not possible to make rules isolating certain aspects of nature and sin without having them disturbed by the claims of the law of love as the requirement of freedom.

Yet it is better to make these distinctions, however arbitrary, than to dispense with them entirely as modern utopians do. The Christian utopians think they can dispense with all structures and rules of justice simply by fulfilling the law of love. They do not realize that the law of love stands on the edge of history and not in history, that it represents an ultimate and not an immediate possibility. They think they might usher in the Kingdom of God if only they could persuade men not to resist tyranny and thus avoid conflict. They do not recognize to what degree justice in a sinful world is actually maintained by a tension of competitive forces, which is always in danger of degenerating into overt conflict, but without which there would be only the despotic peace of the subordination of the will of the weak to the will of the strong.

The secular utopians of the eighteenth century added the love which transcends all law to the liberty and equality of a transcendent and absolute natural law, and fondly imagined that "liberty, equality and fraternity" constituted the law of "nature" in the exact sense of the word. They thought that these ultimate possibilities of human freedom transcending all history were not only simple possibilities of history but that they were actualities of nature as given. The combined influence of religious and secular utopianism has brought confusion into the whole problem of justice in the modern bourgeois-liberal world and incidentally complicated the problem of defending the genuine values of this world against the peril of a barbarism which has grown out of the decadence of our civilization.

Since Christianity measures the stature of man in terms of a freedom which transcends the necessities of nature but also finds that freedom corrupted by sin, it obviously has no simple answer to the question, whether the original righteousness, the perfection before the Fall, which sinful man retains as law, can finally become a realized fact of history. This is the problem which we shall analyse in its various facets and implications in the second volume of this treatise. In such an analysis it will be important to reconsider the almost forgotten issues which were once raised by the Protestant

Reformation. For the general answer of pre-Reformation Christianity was that the *justitia originalis,* the law of love, was not a possibility for natural man but that it could be realized by the redeemed man in whom "grace" had healed the hurt of sin. The Reformation took the fact of sin as a perennial category of historic existence more seriously and maintained that there is no point in history where history is fulfilled and where man's self-contradiction is ended. It therefore defined divine "grace" not so much as a divine power in man which completes his incompletion but as a divine mercy toward man which brings his uneasy conscience to rest despite the continued self-contradiction of human effort upon every level of achievement. This central issue of the Reformation has been forgotten in modern elaborations of Protestant thought in which even the reservations of Catholic theories of sanctification and perfection have disappeared. In consequence modern liberal Protestant interpretations of human nature and human destiny stand in as obvious contradiction to the tragic facts of human history, particularly contemporary history, as the more secular interpretations by which modern culture has been chiefly informed.

The complete contrast between the repudiation of Catholic optimism by the Protestant Reformation and the repudiation of both Catholic and Reformation pessimism about human nature in modern Protestantism is but one of many indications of the unresolved problems of Christian anthropology. As between Reformation pessimism and modern Protestant and secular optimism about the nature of man, the more moderate Catholic theories seem wise and reserved by comparison. Yet the Catholic synthesis broke down under the combined pressure of Renaissance and Reformation. The Renaissance regarded human nature and human history as a realm of unmeasured possibilities and felt that medieval religion failed to do justice to human freedom and human destiny. The Renaissance was right in this; but it was wrong in imagining that the possibilities of good would gradually eliminate the possibilities of evil. A false idea of progress was implicit in the curious compound of Christian eschatology and classical rationalism which was the foundation of Renaissance spirituality.

The Reformation on the other hand was obsessed with the fact that no historical distinctions between good and evil could have significance beside the fact that all these distinctions were eliminated at the final level of divine judgment, before which no man would be justified; and that the tremendous possibilities for realizing good in history had no meaning beside the fact that human nature and human history remained in terms of self-contradiction upon the highest as well as the lowest levels of moral and social achievement.

Both Renaissance and Reformation explored complexities of human nature beyond the limits understood in the "medieval synthesis." But the discoveries of each stood in contradiction to each other. Some of the confusions of modern culture about human nature arise from this unresolved contradiction. Others are derived from the fact that the Renaissance triumphed over the Reformation so completely that the insights of the latter were preserved only in a few backwaters and eddies of modern culture.

In how far and by what means it may be possible to bring Renaissance and Reformation insights about human nature into terms of fruitful interrelation is one of the primary problems to which we will address ourselves in the second volume of this treatise.

THE
NATURE AND DESTINY
OF MAN

II. Human Destiny

CHAPTER I

HUMAN DESTINY AND HISTORY

MAN IS, and yet is not, involved in the flux of nature and time. He is a creature, subject to nature's necessities and limitations; but he is also a free spirit who knows of the brevity of his years and by this knowledge transcends the temporal by some capacity within himself. Man "brings his years to an end as a tale that is told," having an even shorter life span than some dumb creatures. But the sense of melancholy which the anticipation of death induces in the human spirit is not known in the animal world. To brood either anxiously or with studied and learned serenity upon the fact that man is as "the grass which flourisheth in the morning and in the evening is cut down and withereth" is to reveal the whole dimension of existence which distinguishes man from the animal world.

Man's ability to transcend the flux of nature gives him the capacity to make history. Human history is rooted in the natural process but it is something more than either the determined sequences of natural causation or the capricious variations and occurrences of the natural world. It is compounded of natural necessity and human freedom. Man's freedom to transcend the natural flux gives him the possibility of grasping a span of time in his consciousness and thereby of knowing history. It also enables him to change, reorder and transmute the causal sequences of nature and thereby to *make* history. The very ambiguity of the word "history" (as something

I

that occurs and as something that is remembered and recorded) reveals the common source of both human actions and human knowledge in human freedom.[1]

There is no point in human history in which the human spirit is freed of natural necessity. But there is also no point at which the mind cannot transcend the given circumstances to imagine a more ultimate possibility. Thus the conflicts of history need not be accepted as normative, but man looks towards a reality where these conflicts are overcome in a reign of universal order and peace. History thus moves between the limits of nature and eternity. All human actions are conditioned on the one hand by nature's necessities and limitations, and determined on the other hand by an explicit or implicit loyalty to man's conception of the changeless principles which underlie the change. His loyalty to these principles prompts him to seek the elimination of contingent, irrelevant and contradictory elements in the flux, for the sake of realizing the real essence of his life, as defined by the unchanging and eternal power which governs it.

A basic distinction may be made between various interpretations of the meaning of life by noting their attitude towards history. Those which include history in the realm of meaning see it as a process which points and moves towards a fuller disclosure and realization of life's essential meaning. Those which exclude it, do so because they regard history as no more than natural finiteness, from which the human spirit must be freed. They consider man's involvement in nature as the very cause of evil, and define the ultimate redemption of life as emancipation from finiteness. In the one case history is regarded as potentially meaningful, waiting for the ultimate disclosure and realization of its meaning. In the other case it is believed to be essentially meaningless. It may be regarded as a realm of order; but the order is only the subordinate one of natural necessity which affects the meaning of life negatively. It is a mortal coil which must be shuffled off.

[1] *Cf.* Paul Tillich, *The Interpretation of History*, Part IV, Ch. 2.

The difference in the attitude of various cultures towards history is determined by contradictory estimates of man's transcendence over historical process, including his final transcendence over himself. In the one case it is assumed that since this capacity for self-transcendence represents the highest capacity of the human spirit, the fulfillment of life must naturally consist in man's emancipation from the ambiguities of history. His partial immersion in and partial transcendence over nature must be transmuted into a total transcendence. Some sort of *eternity* is therefore the goal of human striving in non-historical religions and philosophies; and the eternity which is man's end is the fulfillment of history to the point of being its negation. In this eternity there is "no separation of thing from thing, no part standing in isolated existence estranged from the rest and therefore nowhere is there any wronging of another." [2]

In religions which regard history as contributing to the meaning of life the attitude towards man's partial involvement in, and partial transcendence over, the process of nature and the flux of time, is totally different. This ambiguous situation is not regarded as the evil from which man must be redeemed. The evil in the human situation arises, rather, from the fact that men seek to deny or to escape prematurely from the uncertainties of history and to claim a freedom, a transcendence and an eternal and universal perspective which is not possible for finite creatures. The problem of sin rather than finiteness is, in other words, either implicitly or explicitly the basic problem of life. Yet the problem of finiteness is not eliminated. It is recognized that a man who stands in an historical process is too limited in vision to discern the full meaning of that process, and too limited in power to fulfill the meaning, however much the freedom of his knowledge and his power is one element in the stuff of history. Hence the temporal problem of human history and destiny in historical religions is: how the transcendent meaning of history is to be disclosed and fulfilled, since man can discern only

[2] Plotinus, *Enneads,* III, ii:1.

partial meanings and can only partially realize the meanings he discerns. In modern corruptions of historical religions this problem is solved very simply by the belief that the cumulative effects of history will endow weak man with both the wisdom and the power to discern and to fulfill life's meaning.

In the more profound versions of historical religion it is recognized, however, that there is no point in history, whatever the cumulations of wisdom and power, in which the finiteness of man is overcome so that he could complete his own life, or in which history as such does not retain the ambiguity of being rooted in nature-necessity on the one hand while pointing towards transcendent, "eternal" and trans-historical ends on the other hand.

Historical religions are therefore by their very nature prophetic-Messianic. They look forward at first to a point in history and finally towards an *eschaton* (end) which is also the end of history, where the full meaning of life and history will be disclosed and fulfilled. Significantly, as in the optimistic expectations of a "day of the Lord" which the first great literary prophet, Amos, found at hand and criticized, these Messianic expectations begin as expressions of national hope and expectations of national triumph. Only gradually it is realized that man's effort to deny and to escape his finiteness in imperial ambitions and power add an element of corruption to the fabric of history and that this corruption becomes a basic characteristic of history and a perennial problem from the standpoint of the fulfillment of human history and destiny. It is recognized that history must be purged as well as completed; and that the final completion of history must include God's destruction of man's abortive and premature efforts to bring history to its culmination.

The basic distinction between historical and non-historical religions and cultures may thus be succinctly defined as the difference between those which expect and those which do not expect a Christ. A Christ is expected wherever history is regarded as potentially meaningful but as still awaiting the full disclosure and fulfillment of its meaning. A Christ is not expected wherever the meaning of life is explained from the standpoint of either nature or supernature in such a way that a transcendent revelation of history's meaning is not regarded as either possible or necessary. It is not regarded as possible when, as in various forms of naturalism, the visions and ambitions of historical existence which point beyond nature are regarded as illusory; and nature-history is believed to be incapable of receiving disclosures of meaning which point beyond itself. It is not regarded as necessary when man's capacity for freedom and self-transcendence is believed to be infinitely extensible until the ambiguities of history are left behind and pure eternity is achieved. The significance of a Christ is that he is a disclosure of the divine purpose, governing history within history. Wherever it is believed that man's capacity to transcend self and history can be disassociated from his finiteness, the meaning of salvation is conceived as essen-tially redemption from history, obviating any necessity of, or desire for, the fulfillment of man in history, or for the disclosure of history's ultimate meaning.

A Christ is expected wherever history is thought of as a realm of fragmentary revelations of a purpose and power transcending his-tory, pointing to a fuller disclosure of that purpose and power. He is expected because this disclosure is regarded as both possible and necessary. It is regarded as possible because history is known to be something more than the nature-necessity in which it has its roots. It is regarded as necessary because the potential meaningfulness of history is recognized as fragmentary and corrupted. It must be completed and clarified.

The interpretation of the cultures of the world in this fashion according to their possession, or lack, of Messianic expectations, draws upon insights which are possible only after the logic of Messianic expectations has reached its culmination in the Christian belief that these expectations have been fulfilled in Christ. It is not possible to interpret cultures according to their expectation or want of expectations of *a* Christ without drawing upon the faith that *the* Christ has been revealed; for there can be no interpretation of the meaning of life and history without implicitly or explicitly drawing into the interpretation the faith which claims to have found the end of these expectations. This is to say, merely, that there can be no interpretation of history without specific presuppositions and that the interpretation which is being attempted in these pages is based upon Christian presuppositions. The Christian answer to the problem of life is assumed in the discussion of the problem. In that sense our interpretation is, as every interpretation must be in the final analysis, "dogmatic" or confessional. Yet it is not purely dogmatic or confessional; for it seeks to analyze the question and expectations for which a particular epic of history is regarded as the answer, and also to determine why these questions and expectations are not universal in history. Such an analysis must begin with a further inquiry into the character of non-historical forms of culture which regard Christ "as foolishness" because they have no questions for which Christ is the answer and no expectations and hopes for which his Cross is the fulfillment.

II

WHERE A CHRIST IS NOT EXPECTED

Nothing is so incredible as an answer to an unasked question. One half of the world has regarded the Christian answer to the problem of life and history as "foolishness" because it had no questions for which the Christian revelation was the answer and no longings and hopes which that revelation fulfilled. The cultures of this half of the world were non-Messianic because they were non-historical. Their failure to regard history as basic to the meaning of life may be attributed to two primary methods of looking at life which stand in contradiction to each other. The one is the method of regarding the system of nature as the final reality to which man must adjust himself. The other regards nature from the human perspective as either chaos or a meaningless order from which man will be freed either by his reason or by some unity and power within him higher than reason. There are systems of thought, of which Stoicism is the classic example, which combine both methods or which reveal a certain degree of ambivalence between the two; but the two most consistent methods of denying the meaningfulness of history are to reduce it to the proportions of nature or to regard it as a corruption of eternity.

1. *History Reduced to Nature*

The history of classical materialism from Democritus to Lucretius gives us a much more consistent view of life as seen from the perspective of nature than any modern form of naturalism; because there are few forms of modern naturalism which have not surreptitiously insinuated something of a Hebraic-Biblical view of life into their naturalism, thereby making nature the bearer and even the artificer of a meaningful history (as for instance when the fact of evolution in biology is made to bear the idea of progress in history). Only in classical thought, and in a few exceptional modern reversions to consistent classicism,[1] is the effort made to reduce history to the exact proportions of nature.

The attempt to deny the reality of history, by reducing it to the dimension of a meaningless natural sequence, is most perfectly expressed in classical thought in its meditations upon death and its protestations against the fear of death. The fact that man dies is indubitable proof of his organic relation to the world of nature and would seem to prove "that a man hath no preeminence above a beast"[2] for "all go unto one place; all are of the dust, and all turn to dust again."[3] Moreover, death is not only a revelation of human finiteness; but the endless sequence of life and death proves history, in one of its aspects at least, to be no more than a series of meaning-

---

[1] Modern forms of naturalism in which the moral values of history are conceived as standing in tragic defiance of the "trampling march of unconscious power" (Bertrand Russell) represent a significant departure from the more consistent naturalism of classicism.

[2] Ecclesiastes 3:19.   [3] *Ibid.,* 3:20.

less recurrences of the natural world. Classical naturalism seeks to reduce history to this simple dimension. "Consider," declares Lucretius, "how utterly unimportant to us was the past antiquity of infinite time, that elapsed before we were born. This then nature exhibits to us as a specimen of the time which will again be after our death. For what does appear terrible in it? Does anything seem gloomy? Is not all more free from any trouble than sleep?" [4]

Yet however inexorable death may be as law of nature, the fear of death is just as inevitable an expression of that in man, which transcends nature. It proves that he does have "preeminence above a beast"; because the fear of death springs from the capacity not only to anticipate death but to imagine and to be anxious about some dimension of reality on the other side of death. Both forms of fear prove man's transcendence over nature. His mind comprehends the point in nature at which his own existence in nature ends; and thereby proves that nature does not fully contain him. The fact that he fears extinction is a negative indication of a dimension in the human spirit, transcending nature. The fact that he is anxious about a possible realm of meaning on the other side of death, and speculates, in the words of Hamlet's soliloquy that "to die, to sleep" may mean "perchance to dream," is the positive indication of man's freedom transcending nature. The fear of death is thus the clearest embryonic expression of man's capacity as a creator of history.

Classical naturalism seeks to beguile man from this fear of death by attempting to persuade him that it is illusory and unwarranted. The argument contains two points. One is that there is nothing in history which man need to fear, since there is in fact no history, but only natural sequence and natural recurrence. "If universal nature," declares Lucretius, "should suddenly utter voice and thus upbraid

[4] *De rerum natura,* Book III, 955–80.
The thought of Lucretius contains inconsistent strains in which a minimal meaning is assigned to history either by regarding it as a process of degeneration (Book II) or as revealing progress (Book V).

any of us: 'What cause have you O Mortal thus excessively to indulge in bitter grief? Why do you groan and weep at the thought of
death? . . . Why do you not, O unreasonable man, retire like a guest
satisfied with life and take your undisturbed rest with resignation.
. . . . *Everything is always the same.* . . . All things remain the
same even if you should outlast all the ages in living; and still more
would you see them the same if you should never come to die.' " [5]

The other point in the argument is that there is no more to fear
in a possible super-history than in history itself, because man does
not transcend his temporal life and hence need not anticipate
judgment beyond death. Thus Epicurus writes: "There is nothing
terrible in living to a man who rightly comprehends that there is
nothing terrible in ceasing to live; so that it was a silly man who said
that he feared death not because it would grieve him when it was
present but because it did grieve him when it was future. . . . The
most formidable of all evils, death, is nothing to us, since, when we
exist, death is not present to us; and when death is present we have
no existence. It is no concern then to either the living or the dead;
since to the one it has no existence and the other class has no
existence itself." [6]

The fact that classical naturalism must seek to beguile men from
the fear of death not only by reducing history to the dimension of
natural sequence but also by denying the reality of any possible realm
of life and meaning beyond history is doubly significant. It proves
that there can be no sense of history at all (as embodied embryoni-
cally in the fear of death) without a further sense of an eternity
transcending history. The "partial simultaneity" of man by which
he comprehends the sequences of time into his consciousness inevitably carries with it, by way of implication, a sense of a divine "total
simultaneity" which comprehends the sequence of time beyond

[5] Book III, 925-55.
[6] Letter of Epicurus to Menæceus in Diogenes Laertius, *Lives and
Opinions of Eminent Philosophers,* Yonge's translation, p. 468.

man's own capacity of comprehension. A suprahistorical eternity is implied in history because the capacity by which man transcends temporal sequence, while yet being involved in it, implies a capacity of transcendence which is not limited by the sequence.

The fear of death also proves that the moral dimension of history, the distinction between good and evil is not annulled by the fact that the grave claims the righteous and the unrighteous; and the earth

> ". . . visits still
> With equalest apportionment of ill
> Both good and bad alike, and brings to one same dust
> The just and the unjust." [7]

The fear of death includes the fear of a possible punishment of evil; and consideration of the impartiality of death does not annul this fear. Nor is it destroyed by the argument that there is no reality beyond the fact of death, since the very fear which this argument is meant to quiet is an indication of height and depth in the human spirit which nature as such cannot contain. [8]

[7] Arthur Hugh Clough, "Easter."

[8] Virgil frequently testifies to the fear of punishment as a natural element in the fear of death as for instance in the words:

> "When at last the life has fled,
> And left the body cold and dead,
> E'en then there passes not away
> The painful heritage of clay;
> Full many a long contracted stain
> Perforce must linger deep in grain.
> So penal sufferings they endure
> For ancient crime to make them pure:
> Some hang aloft in open view
> For winds to pierce them through and through,
> While others purge their guilt deep-eyed
> In burning fire of whelming tide.
> Each for himself we all sustain
> The durance of our ghostly pain.
> *Aeneid,* Book VI.

The effort of classical naturalism to reduce history to the proportion of nature is, in short, abortive. It annuls the very meaning of life by its disavowal of history.

2. *History Swallowed Up in Eternity*

"Christ," declares St. Paul, is "to the Greeks foolishness" because "they seek after wisdom." This is to say that the expectation of the disclosure and fulfillment of the meaning of history at a point in history or at the end of history, has no meaning for the Greek world. It seeks after wisdom and therefore does not expect a Christ. It has no need of Christ because it finds a Christ in every man: the *logos* principle. If classical materialism reduces history to the proportions of natural sequence and temporal process, classical idealism and mysticism seek to flee the world of history precisely because they find no more meaning in history than classical naturalism finds. But they find something in man which classical naturalism does not find; and by that something man is to be emancipated from history. That something is either the intellectual principle of his soul, or something even more transcendent than his mind. Classical idealism and mysticism in short understand the transcendent freedom of the human spirit; but they do not understand it in its organic relation to the temporal process. The natural and temporal process is merely something from which man must be emancipated. That emancipation is the very fulfillment of the meaning of life. There is no yearning for fulfillment in history; there is only a desire to be freed from history

In Platonism the intellectual principle, the *logisticon,* is the organ of this emancipation. "The true lover of knowledge," declares Plato, "is always striving after being . . . that is his nature; he will not rest at those *multitudinous particular phenomena* whose existence is appearance only, but will go on . . . the keen edge will not be blunted nor the force of his passion abate until he have attained the true knowledge of every essence by a sympathetic and kindred power in the soul and by that power drawing near and *becoming in-*

corporate with very being, have begotten mind and truth, he will
know and truly live and increase; and then and not till then, will he
cease from travail." [9]

The important point in Platonism is that the "brightest and best
of being, in other words the Good" belongs to the world of "being"
and not to the world of "becoming," [10] and that a "power resides in
each of us" which enables us to reach that world. This is to say that
history is either an inferior or an illusory world: "the prison house
is the world of sight," the "Absolute Good" is the world of changeless essence underlying the changing world; and "the light of
reason only without the assistance of the senses" [11] is the power in
man which makes it possible for him to rise to this world of pure
being.

Since the human mind transcends itself in infinite regression,
and human reason is able to contemplate the fact of human reason,[12]
rational and intellectual methods of transcending, and escaping
from, history always finally give way to more mystical techniques in
which the effort is made to unite the soul with the Absolute, the

[9] *Republic*, 490–505.
There are many similar intellectualistic denials of the reality of the
"multitudinous particular phenomena" which are the very stuff of
history in Plato, though the general purpose of the *Republic* represents a
contradictory impulse towards historical concretion. There is not in Plato,
and there is not in any philosophy or religion, an absolutely consistent
denial of history. In Hinduism the Brahmin caste uses the prestige of its
superior ability to transcend history and transmutes it into a form of
social-political power with which to dominate historical society. The
prestige of its priestly skill in fleeing history becomes the basis of its
power to dominate society.

[10] *Republic*, 518.

[11] *Republic*, 532 B. All these quotations are taken from the *Republic*,
because the *Republic* reveals a dominant impulse towards historical concretion already referred to. The fact that the dominant note in Platonism
is not obscured in a book which departs somewhat from the Platonic
logic is therefore significant.

[12] See the discussion of the relation of "spirit" to "reason" in Vol. I,
Ch. V.

human with the divine, by isolating and cultivating a power of the soul, even higher and purer than reason. This is to say that Platonism finally culminates in neo-Platonism in the history and logic of otherworldly and non-historical cultures.

In the thought of Plotinus *nous* is not so much the rational principle in the soul as the power of self-consciousness. The *nous* does not contemplate the world, nor even the rational principle underlying the phenomenal reality. It contemplates itself until it is united and becomes identified with the "Authentic Being" of the final "Good" about which one must "not even say that it has intellection," for that "would be dividing it." [13]

The eternity to which the soul rises is an undifferentiated unity which finally swallows up all particularity. Plotinus is very precise in asserting that the eternity of the "Intellectual World" negates, rather than fulfills, history. "There can be no memory in the Intellectual World," he declares. "There will not even be memory of the personality, no thought that the contemplator is the self. In contemplative vision, especially when it is vivid, we are not at the same time aware of our own personality; the activity is toward the object of vision with which the thinker becomes identified." [14] Thus the end of life is the annulment of history and of the self in history. Whatever is involved in "process" never "possesses Being." [15]

It is hardly necessary to trace the logic of non-historical cultures in the oriental world; for Taoism, Hinduism, and Buddhism distinguish themselves from the non-historical tradition in Western classicism, chiefly by a more consistently mystical and less rationalistic disavowal of the meaningfulness of history.[16]

[13] *Enneads,* Book III, 10.
[14] *Ibid.,* Book II, 4.
[15] *Ibid.,* Book IV, 8.
[16] Even in Buddhism, though it is the most consistent of all a-historical religions, there are elements which are inconsistent with the dominant idea of redemption from history. The impulse towards history is particu-

The fact that there is a preliminary, rationalistic technique in Western non-historical cultures and that this technique should always result in tangents of thought which affirm rather than annul history (as in Plato's *Republic*) are indicative of a basic ambivalence towards history in the Western world, which culminates in the contrast and kinship of Hellenic and Hebraic culture. Reason is quite obviously a principle of order in history, though history-in-nature never fully conforms to rational principles. Reason is furthermore both a symbol of the freedom of man over nature and of his involvement in it. On this account only mystical forms of other-worldliness are completely consistent in denying the meaningfulness of history.

The conflict between materialism and idealism, between naturalism and supernaturalism in Greek classicism is partly bridged in Stoic thought, at the price, of course, of complete consistency. For Stoicism is never quite certain whether the *logos* principle, to which man is to conform, is an order imbedded in nature as such or whether it is a principle of human freedom; whether man is to conform to *physis* or to a principle unique to human nature, because the latter is peculiarly endowed with *logos*. "The end of life," declares Seneca, "is to act in conformity with nature, that is at once with the nature which is in us and with the nature of the universe." Since the "nature of the universe" includes both the determined order of *physis* and the peculiar freedom of man, this basic idea of Stoic ethics contains a fundamental confusion. The general tendency of Stoicism is, however, in the direction of the naturalistic side of the classical debate.

In that debate the *logos* principle is imbedded in nature for the naturalists and transcends nature in the unique freedom of the mind for the idealists. "The result [of the triumph of idealism in this

larly apparent in Mahayana Buddhism in which the Bodhisattvas renounce the final redemption from history in order to mediate redemption in history.

debate] was to vindicate the possibility of freedom, but at the cost of rehabilitating 'chance' or 'necessity' which thus once more emerged as the function of the (more or less) independent matter." [17]

There is in short no expectation of a Christ, no Messianic hope, in classical culture because the sovereignty to which man must be subordinated is not of the kind which is partly hidden and may be expected to be more fully revealed. In the one case Nature is god and obedience to that god requires the disavowal of all the unique fears, hopes, ambitions and evils which are the stuff of history. In the other case Reason is god; and the necessities and contingencies of history are, from the perspective of reason, reduced to pure "chance" or to a mechanistic necessity, which means that the history is essentially meaningless because it is partly imbedded in nature. There is no necessity or possibility in either case of a fuller revelation of the ultimate sovereignty of life in history and therefore of a fuller disclosure of the meaning of life. The only alternatives are either to reduce the meaning of life to the comparative meaninglessness of the natural order, or to emancipate life from this meaninglessness by translating it into the dimension of pure reason, which is to say, pure eternity.

III

WHERE A CHRIST IS EXPECTED

No Christ could validate himself as the disclosure of a hidden divine sovereignty over history or as a vindication of the meaningfulness of history, if a Christ were not expected. This is to say that if history is not regarded as potentially meaningful, the claim that potential meaning has been realized and that obscurities and ambiguities in

[17] The quotation is from *Christianity and Classical Culture* by Charles Norris Cochrane, p. 167. This work is a profound analysis of the inadequacies of the classical mind in coming to terms with the unique realities of history, in contrast to nature or reason.

history have been clarified would not be credible. Any Christ must be "foolishness to the Greeks," both ancient and modern. Christ may also be a "stumblingblock to the Jews"; but he is not "foolishness" to them. He may be a stumblingblock because, though expected, he proves not to be the kind of a Messiah who was expected. In fact one can assert dogmatically that the true Christ *must* be a stumblingblock in the sense that he must disappoint, as well as fulfill, expectations. He must disappoint some expectations because Messianic expectations invariably contain egoistic elements, which could not be fulfilled without falsifying the meaning of history. Every Messianic expectation contains an explicit or implicit assumption that history will be fulfilled from the particular locus of the civilization and culture which has the expectation.

The fact that there can be no Christ without an expectation of Christ relates Christianity as founded in a unique revelation to the whole history of culture; the fact that the true Christ cannot be the Messiah who is expected separates Christianity from the history of culture. In order to validate this view of the matter it is necessary to examine the history of Messianic expectations more fully.

1. *Types of Messianism*

The prophetic-Messianic interpretation of history culminates in Hebraic religion, and more particularly in the prophetic-apocalyptic, as against the legalistic tradition, of Hebraism. But Hebraic Messianism is not *sui generis* just as Greek classicism is only the most profound, and not the only elaboration, of a non-historical view of life. One can find some degree of Messianism in every culture in which history is taken seriously. The most explicit expressions of it are to be found in the cultures of the great early empires of Egypt, Mesopotamia and Persia. But even Roman imperialism is not without Messianic notes. The history of the Roman Empire is comprehended as a meaningful whole, and efforts are made to interpret universal history in relation to the history of the Roman Empire.

The idea in both Greek and Roman mythology of a "golden age," representing either a period of natural goodness and simplicity from which subsequent history has departed or a period of primitive crudeness from which subsequent ages have gradually risen to the achievements of civilization, lays a foundation for Roman Messianism. The Messianic age is regarded as a restoration of the primitive goodness. The idea that the fulfillment of history is, in some sense, a restoration of its early virtue is thus of very early origin.[1]

[1] The most significant Messianic note in Roman literature is the well known passage in Virgil's Fourth *Eclogue*:

> Bless him, the infant with whom
> discontinues the era of iron;
> Bless him with whom will arise
> the new race that is gloriously golden,
> Bless, chaste Lucina, the boy:
> now reigneth thy brother Apollo.

This Virgilian Messianic vision includes the hope of a transformed nature:

> Goats will return by themselves
> to our homesteads, with udders distended
> Nor any longer our cattle
> shall fear huge terrible lions.
> Then will the serpent die out
> and herbs disappear that bear poison.

The conception of a God-like Caesar who will rule the world is similar to the Egyptian hopes for the rule of a divine shepherd-King:

> But that boy will partake of the life of the Gods;
> he will meet them,
> Meet all the heroes; and he
> will in turn by the gods be beholden.
> Over a pacified world will he rule
> patriarchic in virtue.

For a full discussion of the relation of Roman Messianism and its indebtedness to other Messianic literature, see Eduard Norden, *Die Geburt des Kindes, Geschichte einer Religioesen Idee.*

To understand the logic of Messianism and its integral relation to the cultures for which history is included in the meaning of life it is necessary to include three elements or levels of Messianism, (*a*) the egoistic-nationalistic element, (*b*) the ethical-universalistic element and (*c*) a supra-ethical religious element as expressed in Prophetism. Of these three elements the first and second are expressed in pre-prophetic Messianism, while all three are present in the Messianism of the Hebrew prophets.

a. On the egoistic-nationalistic level Messianism looks forward to the triumph of the nation, empire or culture in which the Messianic hope is expressed. This means that history is regarded as obscure and that life is threatened with meaninglessness primarily because the collective life of nation or empire, which is the primary source of meaning, is known to be more finite than it pretends to be. The symbol of its insecurity is the power of its foes. The fulfillment of life's meaning is thus contained in the triumph of *our* nation or civilization over its foes. While this simple conception of the problem of life and history represents historical culture on its lowest level, it is an element which is not eliminated from even the highest level of prophetic Messianism. Even on that level the Messiah is expected to vindicate Israel against its enemies. Nor is this element ever completely eliminated from Christian conceptions of history in which the egoistic-nationalistic element is refuted in principle. In them it is understood that Christ does not vindicate a race or a nation. It is the sovereignty of God which is vindicated. But it is difficult to believe this without surreptitiously including the vindication of the righteous or of the believers, as against the unbelievers, in the divine vindication. This is a subtler form of egoistic corruption in the interpretation of history which we must analyse further presently. It must be added that it is not only impossible for the highest forms of Christian prophetism to remain free of egoistic corruptions; it is also impossible for the most advanced civilization to be safe against reversions to very primitive egoistic-nationalistic interpretations of history, as for instance in contemporary Nazism.

b. The ethical-universalistic level of Messianism.

On the second level of Messianism the problem of history is not the impotence of *our* race, empire or nation, and the answer to the problem of history, therefore, cannot be the triumph of *our* people over our foes. The problem of history is the impotence of the good against the evil forces in history. The momentary triumph of evil in history is seen as a threat to the meaningfulness of history and this threat is overcome by the hope of the coming of a Messianic king who will combine power and goodness. This is the significance of the figure of the Messianic "shepherd king," an important symbol not only in Hebraic but in Babylonian and Egyptian Messianism.[2]

The shepherd king is gentle despite his power. As a judge he rises to the heights of imaginative justice in which justice and mercy become one, for "he shall ,not judge after the sight of his eyes, neither reprove after the hearing of his ears; but with righteousness shall he judge the poor, and reprove with equity for the meek of the earth."[3]

It is sometimes assumed that it was the primary contribution of the Hebrew prophets to lift Messianism from the egoistic-nationalis-

---

[2] *Cf.* Isaiah 40:11: "He shall feed his flock like a shepherd: he shall gather the lambs with his arm, and carry them in his bosom, and shall gently lead those that are with young." Also Ezekiel 37:24: "And my servant David shall be king over them; and they all shall have one shepherd."

In the Egyptian Messianic tract "Admonitions of Ipuwer" the ideal king is described as follows: "He brings cooling to the flame. It is said he is shepherd of all. men. There is no evil in his heart. When his herds are few he passes the day to gather them together, their hearts being fevered." J. H. Breasted, *The Dawn of Conscience,* p. 198.

In the Messianism of the early empires, that of Persia comes nearest to transcending this egoistic-imperialistic element and achieving a genuine universalism in its interpretation of history. But since the fully formed Persian Messianism is Zoroastrianism, and Zoroastrianism is a prophetic reform movement in Parseeism, this universalism must be regarded as prophetic rather than pre-prophetic; the only prophetic Messianism, outside of Hebraism.

[3] Isaiah 11:3–4.

tic to the universalistic level, upon which the ethical meaning of history becomes the primary concern; and the seeming power of evil, and the seeming impotence of virtue in history is regarded as the greatest problem. It is true that prophetic Messianism moves, on the whole, on this level; and the first great prophet, Amos, undoubtedly challenges nationalistic elements in the current expectations of the "day of Yahweh." It is nevertheless erroneous to identify the universalistic element with prophetism, not only because that element was present in an undeveloped form in pre-prophetic Messianism (as we have noted in Egypt and Babylon as well as in Israel) but also, as will become apparent subsequently, because prophetic Messianism contains an even profounder element than the triumph of universalism over nationalism.

It is significant that the ethical Messianism, which overcomes the moral obscurities of history by the hope of an ultimately perfect conformity of power and goodness, contains by implication all the important and characteristic insights of cultures which take history seriously, as against those which do not.

The hope of an ideal king implies that the meaningfulness of history is obscured not primarily by the irrationalities, necessities and contingencies of nature; but by a uniquely historical phenomenon, the factor of "power." The injustices which threaten the moral meaning of history are derived from the power of will over will, of which nature as such knows very little. There are, indeed, slight forms of power in nature, as for instance the leadership of the oldest or strongest male in the herd; a form of power which is incidentally a nexus between animal and human social organization. But, in general, nature knows only competing impulses of survival and not competing wills to power.

Power is the product of spirit. It never exists without an alloy of physical force but it is always more than physical compulsion. This fact is symbolized by the importance of the priest, as distinguished from the soldier, as agent of social organization in all early societies.

The implied recognition of ethical Messianism, that the evils of history arise, not primarily from the contingencies of nature but from a uniquely historical phenomenon, the power of will over will, is thus to discover the moral enigma of history in history itself, and not primarily in history's relation to nature or in its corruption by natural contingencies.

But there is an even profounder understanding of history in ethical Messianism. Its strictures are directed particularly against unjust "rulers" and "elders." It recognizes that injustice flows from the same source from which justice comes, from the historical organization of life. The profoundest social tract of Egypt, "The Eloquent Peasant," pictures a peasant indicting the Grand Visier in the words: "Thou art set for a dam for the poor man to save him from drowning, but behold thou art his moving flood." [4] This indictment may be regarded not only as a shrewd expression of the moral ambiguity of all government, as both an instrument of, and a peril to justice; it is, more profoundly considered, a recognition of the basic paradox of history. It recognizes that the creative and destructive possibilities of human history are inextricably intermingled. The very power which organizes human society and establishes justice, also generates injustice by its preponderance of power.

The hope that the injustice of power may be overcome in a Messianic shepherd king might seem, at first blush, to be no more than the pious expectation of a "good Caesar" to which Christian political thought has occasionally degenerated.[5] But ethical Messianism is saved from this superficiality by the transcendent element in its Messianic expectations. The Messianic king who will combine power and goodness, strength and gentleness, justice and mercy, is never a purely historical figure. He is a god become earthly king. In Egyptian Messianism Re himself comes to earth to establish justice. This transcendent element is present in Babylonian and Hebraic Messianism as well.

[4] Breasted, *op. cit.*, p. 189.
[5] Most recently in the pietistic movement known as "Buchmanism."

To recognize that only God can perfectly combine power and goodness is to understand that power is not evil of itself; but that all power in history is in peril of becoming an instrument of injustice because it is itself one of the competing powers in human society, even while it seeks to become (as is the case of the power of government) a transcendent power through which subordinate conflicts are harmonized. A Messianism which recognizes that the inevitable egoistic corruption in all historical creativity cannot be eliminated if God Himself does not become the wielder of historical power, uses mythical symbols to express an insight into the character of human history which all modern utopian creeds have obscured.

On the other hand the hope of a shepherd king distinguishes Messianism as sharply from non-historical religions as from false interpretations of history. To look forward to an ideal harmony of life with life in human society, through the intervention of divine power, means that the fulfillment of life is sought in history and not in eternity. History is not regarded as evil by reason of being a realm of vitality; and perfection is not defined as some realm of devitalized forms, some eternal calm from which the vitalities of life have been abstracted.

The hope of the shepherd king is thus a very profound expression of the ethos of historical cultures. Its weakness lies in the fact that it hopes for an impossible combination of the divine and the historical. The God who is both powerful and good by reason of being the source of all power, and not some particular power in history, cannot remain good if he becomes a particular power in human society. Perfect goodness in history can be symbolized only by the disavowal of power. But this did not become clear until the One appeared who rejected all concepts of Messianic dominion and became a "suffering servant."

Prophetic Messianism did not arrive at this answer. But the great contribution of prophetic Messianism consists in the fact that it interpreted history too profoundly to allow the solution of the Messianic king to remain tenable. It saw history involved in the inevitable tragedy of tempting the rulers and the nations, who performed a special mission in history, to the sins of pride and injustice.

c. Thus a new religio-ethical dimension is introduced into the interpretation of history, which must be considered in terms of the relation of prophetism to Messianism.

2. *Prophetic Messianism*

Hebraic prophetism enters the history of culture with a strong criticism of current Messianism by the first of the literary prophets, Amos.[6] This criticism is sometimes interpreted as a rejection of the nationalistic implications of Messianism in favor of a more universalistic conception. This interpretation is correct as far as it goes; for Amos undoubtedly regarded the "Holy One of Israel" as a God who transcended the interests of Israel. Amos prophesied judgment upon other nations as well as upon Israel [7] and declares in Yahweh's name, that his sovereignty is manifested in the destiny of other peoples as well as in the history of Israel. Thus Amos' words: "Are ye not as children of the Ethiopians unto me, O children of Israel? saith Yahweh. Have not I brought up Israel out of the land of Egypt? and the Philistine from Caphtor, and the Syrians from Kir?" [8] have rightly been regarded as the first comprehension of universal history in human culture. Here history is seen not from the perspective of a nation but as a universal whole. And God is regarded as the sovereign of all peoples.

The anti-nationalistic emphasis in the oracles of Amos is heightened by his specific judgment of the destruction of Israel by the God of Israel, who is not dependent upon the triumph of his chosen

---

[6] Amos' strictures against current Messianism are contained in the words: "Woe unto you that desire the day of Yahweh! to what end is it for you? The day of Yahweh is darkness, and not light." Amos 5:18.

[7] Upon Damascus 1:3–5, upon Philistia 1:6–8, upon Ammon 1:13–15 and upon Moab 2:1–3.

[8] Amos 9:7.

nation for his glory.[9] Moreover the nationalistic priesthood regards his message as a threat to Israel. Amaziah, the priest, suggests that his prophesies of judgment upon the northern kingdom may be prompted by prejudices as a member of the southern kingdom.[10] Thus Amos' insights become the fountain source of the ethical-universalistic note in Hebraic prophecy. Viewed merely from the perspective of the history of ethics it is therefore not wrong to think of the prophetic movement as the consummation of the universalistic tendencies in the Hebraic interpretation of life and history, even if one recognizes, as one must, that prophetism is never completely purged of the nationalistic imperialistic interpretation of the meaning of history.

Nevertheless such an ethical interpretation of prophetism obscures its real profundity. Amos' predictions of judgment upon Israel are really only incidental to a more far-reaching criticism of all forms of optimistic Messianism. We cannot even be certain that the current Messianic ideas which Amos criticizes were purely nationalistic. They may have contained elements of universalism. The "day of Yahweh" may have been regarded as a triumph of God over the "dragon" or "serpent," symbol of the power of evil in history.[11] At any rate it is not so much the particularism as the optimism of the Messianic conceptions which comes under the prophet's strictures; and his criticisms make no concessions to the Messianic hope of the fulfillment of history in either nationalistic or universal terms.[12] For Amos' history is primarily a series of judgments, first upon

[9] Amos 3:2: "You only have I known of all the families of the earth: therefore I will punish you for all your iniquities."

[10] Amos 7:12: "Also Amaziah said unto Amos, O thou seer, go, flee thee away into the land of Judah, and there eat bread and prophesy there. But prophesy not again any more at Bethel; for it is the king's chapel and it is the king's court."

[11] Cf. *inter alia* W. O. E. Oesterley, *The Evolution of the Messianic Idea*, Ch. 16.

[12] If we assume, as most Old Testament critics do, that the hopeful words of Amos 9:11–15 are interpolated.

Israel and then upon all the nations. The judgment falls with particular severity upon Israel, precisely because it has been singled out for a special mission in history and has failed to perform it. Israel's special mission gives it no special security in history. On the contrary it is the assumption that it has a special security and can count upon a special divine favour, which represents the corruption of pride which must be punished.

If the implications of this conception of God's relation to history are fully analysed it will become apparent that Hebraic prophetism is not so much the triumph of universalism in the history of ethics as the beginning of revelation in the history of religion. It is the beginning of revelation because here, for the first time, in the history of culture the eternal and divine is not regarded as the extension and fulfillment of the highest human possibilities, whether conceived in particularistic or universalistic terms. God's word is spoken *against* both his favoured nation and against all nations. This means that prophetism has the first understanding of the fact that the real problem of history is not the finiteness of all human endeavors, which must wait for their completion by divine power. The real problem of history is the proud pretension of all human endeavors, which seeks to obscure their finite and partial character and thereby involves history in evil and sin.

When a word of God is spoken not only against a nation, but against all nations, because they are all involved in pride and injustice, human culture as an enterprise which seeks to comprehend the meaning of life and history from any or all human perspectives is transcended. Here revelation, with its correlate of faith, begins. The correlate is faith, because prophetism, unlike mysticism, does not make the effort to find the eternal and divine, which has eluded it in history, in some deeper level of human consciousness. It apprehends a divine word of judgment, spoken against the whole human enterprise, by faith. It can only be by faith because man can transcend himself sufficiently to know that an ultimate word may be spoken against him; but he cannot himself speak that word.[13]

a. The relation of prophetism to Messianism

The subsequent history of Hebraic prophetism and Messianism contains the two elements of nationalistic and universalistic Messianism in various compounds, together with the new dimension in the interpretation of history which was added by prophetism and for which Messianism never finds an adequate answer.

Contrary to evolutionary interpretations of prophetic thought, the conflict between the nationalistic and universalistic motifs in prophetism are not resolved by a gradual triumph of the latter over the former. The universalistic note is present, as we have seen, in the

[13] There is of course no absolute beginning for anything in history, including the beginning of "revelation." However sharply defined the idea of divine transcendence may be in Hebraic prophetism, Martin Buber plausibly maintains in his *Koenigtum Gottes* that this prophetic idea of divine transcendence is involved in the monotheism of Israel from the beginning. According to Buber the highly developed concept of transcendent majesty in Isaiah 45:5–10 is no different than the idea implied in the decalogue when God declares: "I am the Lord thy God, which brought thee out of the land of Egypt, from the house of bondage; thou shalt have none other gods before me" (Deuteronomy 5:6–7). "Nothing has been added or subtracted," writes Buber, "an unconditioned character implicit at first, now expresses itself explicitly" (p. 89).

There is of course no possibility of determining to what degree prophetic conceptions have been read back into Israel's history. But on the other hand Buber is right in seeing that something of the prophetic conception was implicit from the beginning, or the fully developed idea could not have gained credence.

This whole question is important because it reveals the very dialectical relation between "natural" and "revealed" religion. The whole relation is determined by the very character of human self-transcendence. Man transcends himself sufficiently to know that he cannot be the centre of his own existence and that his nation, culture or civilization cannot be the end of history. This is the "natural" ground for revelation. But he does not transcend himself in such a way as to be able to state the end of existence, except as, by faith, he apprehends the voice of God who speaks to him and "against" him.

first of the great prophets, Amos. It wins no gradual ascendancy over the nationalistic one. In the prophet Joel the nationalistic interpretation of history reaches extravagant proportions while the book of Jonah must be regarded as primarily a refutation of such nationalism. In Isaiah there are inconsistent elements of both nationalism and universalism.[14] In the apocalyptic books, which bring Hebraic Messianism to a consummation, history sometimes culminates in a general resurrection [15] while other apocalypses anticipate only the resurrection of Israel.[16] Purely nationalistic versions of Messianism were still powerful in Jesus' own day and his second temptation in the wilderness is presumably an account of his rejection of the political-nationalistic conception of the Messianic task.[17]

But this conflict is not the primary problem of prophetic Messianism. The real issue is between the highest form of Messianism (according to which history culminates in an age which resolves the problem of justice by combining power and goodness in the person of a Messianic king), and the insight of prophetism according to which all nations and peoples are involved in rebellion against God. The problem of the meaning of history according to prophetism is how history can be anything more than judgment, which is to say, whether the promise of history can be fulfilled at all.

This higher problem becomes the unsolved question of prophetic Messianism. For it is hardly too much to say that insofar as prophetism expresses itself in Messianic hopes it does not do very much more than refine and elaborate the ethical note which was present in preprophetic Messianism. It condemns the "rulers," the "judges"

[14] Isaiah predicts both a final judgment upon the Gentiles and the wicked in Israel (Isaiah 17:9–14) and a judgment upon the Gentiles and a vindication of Israel (Isaiah 13:9 to 14:2). The same ambiguity is to be found in Malachi (3:18 and 4:3) and in Zechariah (Ch. 12).

[15] As in the Book of Enoch, the Testament of the Twelve Patriarchs, the Apocalypse of Baruch and the Fourth Ezra.

[16] As in II Maccabees, Assumption of Moses and in portions of the Book of Enoch.

[17] Luke 4:5.

and the "princes" of Israel who "turn aside the poor in the gate from their right" [18] and who "swallow up the needy even to make the poor of the land to fail." [19] This is the note in Hebraic prophetism and Messianism which is the fountain and source of radical ethico-political criticism upon the pride of rulers and the injustice of the powerful.[20] The Messianic hope which corresponds to this prophetic criticism is the hope of the ideal Davidic, shepherd king in whose reign injustice and conflict will be overcome and justice and peace will be established. The hope is expressed in more or less transcendent terms. In the apocalyptic literature the transcendent note is heightened. The Davidic king is supplanted by the "son of man," who is a transcendent and heavenly figure; and the fulfillment of history becomes also the end of history; for the finite and natural basis of history is superseded.[21] There is, in other words, a consistent recognition of the sources of conflict and injustice and a realization of the fact that the ethical ideals of history transcend the limitations of nature and finiteness; but this realization becomes more pronounced and explicit in the apocalypses as compared with the Messianic hope of the prophets.

Yet this development in which the Messianic reign is conceived in more and more consistently transcendental terms does nothing to solve the problem which prophetism had introduced into Messianic thought. For the real problem of prophetism is not the finite char-

[18] Amos 5:12.

[19] *Ibid.*, 8:4.

[20] Cf. *inter alia,* Isaiah 3:16, Isaiah 5:8, Micah 2:1–2, Hosea 10:13, Isaiah 61:8 and many other passages too numerous to mention.

[21] The Messianic reign transcends the limitations of nature even in as early a version as that of Isaiah, according to which "the wolf also shall dwell with the lamb, and the leopard shall lie down with the kid" (Isaiah 11:6). In the vision of Ezekiel the hope of peace and justice carries with it the expectation of a change in nature: "Therefore will I save my flock, and they shall no more be a prey; and I will judge between cattle and cattle. And I will set up one shepherd over them . . . And I will make with them a covenant of peace, and will cause the evil beasts to cease out of the land" (Ezekiel 34:22–25).

acter of all historical achievement, though that remains one of the subordinate problems. The real problem is presented by the prophetic recognition that all history is involved in a perennial defiance of the law of God.

The prophets believe that Israel is especially guilty before God precisely because it is uniquely commissioned by God and seeks falsely to derive a special security from this mission. According to Micah, Israel declares: "Is not the Lord among us? None evil can come upon us." And this presumption leads to a terrible judgment: "Therefore shall Zion for your sake be plowed as a field." [22] This sin rises higher than the injustices which flow from power, and the wars which issue from competing will-to-power. It is the more primal sin of pride.[23]

The failure of Israel to fulfill its special historical destiny is regarded by the prophets as an ineluctable fate, though they do not for that reason excuse it. Here the prophetic interpretation of history approaches the Christian doctrine of original sin.[24]

If taken seriously, the consummation of history cannot be a Messianic reign which helps the righteous to triumph over the unrighteous, or which resolves the conflicts of history in a reign of peace, or which abases the mighty and exalts the poor and the meek. The consummation of history can only be in a divine mercy which makes something more of history than merely recurring judgment. The problem of history, according to prophetism, is not that God should be revealed as strong enough to overcome the defiance of

---

[22] Micah 3:11–12.

[23] See Chs. V and VII in Vol. I.

[24] Jeremiah expresses his pessimism in the words: "Can the Ethiopian change his skin, or the leopard his spots? Then may ye also do good, that are accustomed to do evil" (Jeremiah 13:23). And Isaiah has an even more deeply pessimistic conception of the effect of the divine word upon Israel. The consequence of the divine word is to "make the heart of this people fat, and make their ears heavy and shut their eyes"; and this spiritual obtuseness will not yield to anything but a judgment in which the "cities be wasted without an inhabitant" (Isaiah 6:9 ff.).

the evil against His will; but as having resources of mercy great enough to redeem as well as to judge all men.

It is significant that, though the prophets begin by the realization of the sin of pride in the life of Israel, the idea is gradually expanded to become a principle of interpretation for the whole of history. All the nations are regarded as being in rebellion against God. Each in its turn receives some special mission from God or enjoys some special privilege and makes its momentary eminence or security the basis of a pride which must finally destroy it.[25]

It is this level of prophetic insight for which prophetic Messianism has no answer. The prophets do of course affirm the mercy of God as well as the awfulness of His wrath and the certainty of His judgments. But there is no certainty about the relation of mercy to judgment. On the whole the prophetic recognition of this ultimate problem is most perfectly expressed in the longing for mercy recorded in Isaiah 64: "Oh that thou wouldest rend the heavens, that thou wouldest come down, that the mountains might flow down at thy presence. . . . When thou didst terrible things which we looked not for, thou camest down, the mountains flowed down at thy presence. . . . But we are all as an unclean thing, and all our righteousnesses are as filthy rags. . . . For thou hast hid thy face from us, and hast consumed us, because of our iniquities. . . . Be not wroth very sore, O Lord, neither remember iniquity for ever."[26] The distinction between the righteous and the unrighteous disappears in the discovery that "all our righteousnesses are as filthy rags" and that "we are all as an unclean thing." The assurance that God will complete history by overcoming the ambiguity of the momentary triumph of evil yields to the question of how God will complete history by overcoming the perennial evil in every human good. The "hidden" sovereignty of God, which demands a fuller disclosure in the Messianic reign, is hidden, not because the divine power is not

[25] See particularly Ezekiel's series of judgments upon the nations. Ezekiel 26–34.

[26] Isaiah 64:1–9.

fully disclosed but because the relation of divine mercy to divine wrath remains a mystery.

b. The failure of Messianism to answer the prophetic problem

If we are to understand why the true Christ was a "stumbling-block" to the Jews, that is to those who expected a Christ, as well as foolishness to the Gentiles who did not expect him, and why Christian faith regards him as the true Christ both because he was expected and because he was not the Christ who was expected, it is necessary to see why Hebraic Messianism (though able to rise from particularism to universalism, and from an inchoate to an explicit recognition of the fact that the fulfillment of history transcended the finite and natural basis of history), was never able to come to terms fully with the issue which prophetism had raised. There were two reasons for this failure.

The first reason was that the misery of Israel during and after the exile made it difficult and well-nigh impossible to face the ultimate issue of history before the pressing perplexities of the penultimate issue. The people of Israel had been judged by God for their sins, and history had executed His terrible wrath. But when they reflected upon their fate they were overwhelmed by the incongruity of the fact that the jailers and executors of divine judgment were worse than they. The prophets might well insist that the nemesis of each proud nation would come in turn; but that did not change the immediate impression of a very unjust history which obscured the justice of God. This is to say that a "vertical" interpretation of history in which all men and nations are judged for falling short of the divine demands still leaves the problem of the relative good and evil of any short span of history unsolved, and more particularly the seeming triumph of the relatively evil over the relatively good.[27]

[27] Our own generation would have faced this same perplexity in the event of the triumph of tyranny over the forces of democratic civilization. Such a triumph would undoubtedly reveal all the weaknesses and vices of the democratic civilization and in that sense would have been

Inevitably, the Messianic hope, which holds out the prospect of a triumph of the good over evil in history, will gain the ascendancy over a more ultimate hope in any catastrophic period in which the momentary triumph of the relative evil over the relative good threatens history with meaninglessness. The questions, "Why do the righteous suffer?" and "Why do the wicked triumph?" were bound to pre-occupy the mind of Israel in the exilic and post-exilic period.

But there is an even profounder reason why the more ultimate issue raised by prophetism could not be answered in prophetic Messianism. It is an affront to human self-righteousness. We shall see to what degree the Christian faith, though explicitly accepting the ultimate issue, is subject to covert denials of it.[28] It is comparatively easy for man to recognize his weakness and to know that he is too inextricably involved in history as process and flux to be able to complete it. But it is not so easy to recognize that his premature and pretentious efforts to fulfill what he cannot fulfill involve human history in tragic realities of sin, which only a divine mercy can purge. For this reason the most plausible culmination of Messianism is one which substitutes the "righteous" for a particular race or nation and then looks forward to the culmination of history and the vindication of God through the triumph and the vindication of the righteous of all nations.

Furthermore, it is a question whether it is possible to interpret life and history consistently in terms of a problem for which the answer is not known. The final problem of prophetism is one for which Messianism had no answer. It is natural, therefore, that it should justified as a divine judgment upon the sins of civilization. But the question would still remain: Why should the tyrants triumph? Why should those who are more evil than ourselves be the executors of judgment? Under the pressure of that perplexity every vital religion will deal with proximate as well as with ultimate problems of history. It will hope for the destruction of tyranny as a mediate goal of history, whatever may be its insights into the ultimate problem of life and history.

[28] Chs. V–VII.

revert to the problem for which it had the answer. It was certain that the hidden sovereignty of God would guarantee the .ultimate triumph of good over evil in history. But it was not certain how the divine mercy is related to the divine wrath and how the perplexity of a total history standing in defiance of God would be resolved.

It is particularly interesting to note how the apocalyptic writings (in which Hebraic Messianism culminates and in which, despite a fantastic imagery, the logic implied in this Messianism is really driven to its final conclusion) [29] deal with this issue. The apocalyptic books generally look forward to the final disclosure of the "hidden" Messiah, which is to say that the Messianic reign is regarded as the final revelation of the obscured sovereignty of God and the confused meaning of history.[30] This final disclosure is conceived, on the whole, as a vindication of God and the righteous. The unrighteous will be destroyed; and some of the apocalyptic books imaginatively and proleptically indulge in a veritable orgy of vindictive triumph. Yet the more ultimate problem appears again and again as an afterthought.[31] The most remarkable relation between the ultimate and penultimate problem of history is to be found in one of the latest and certainly one of the profoundest books of apocalyptic literature:

[29] The idea that Hebraic apocalypse is a corruption rather than a logical culmination of the Messianic hope has gained currency in secularized schools of criticism which do not understand the basic significance of the problem of time and eternity, of history and super-history with which the apocalyptic writings are concerned.

[30] In the Similitudes of Enoch the hidden Messiah is described as follows: "Before the suns and the signs were created and before the stars of the heavens were made his name was uttered before the Lord of spirits. . . . He hath been chosen and *hidden,* before him before world was created."

[31] In the Book of Enoch there are interpolations which dwell upon the necessity of mercy as well as of judgment. Both in the Psalms of Solomon and the Similitudes of Enoch the final problem of the relation of judgment to mercy is alluded to. *Cf.* J. Wicks, *The Doctrine of God in Jewish Apocryphal and Apocalyptic Literature.*

the Ezra Apocalypse. In the so-called Salathiel vision of this late apocalypse the questions of the "seer" are always put in terms of the ultimate problem, while God's answers always reassure the seer by assurances taken from the conventional Messianic hope. He is told that the righteous will triumph and the unrighteous will perish and that it is not his business to worry about the fate of the latter. But this answer does not resolve his perplexities; for his problem is whether there are any righteous who deserve to triumph.[32]

This apocalyptic book, actually written, or at least compiled, in the Christian era, leaves a profound impression with its invariably right questions and its usually wrong answers. Here is the perfect symbol of how Hebraic prophetism overreaches itself with an ultimate question for which it has no answer, and which it seeks to suppress because it lacks the answer.

This must be understood, if the Christian answer to the Messianic question is to be appreciated; and if we are to realize how the Christ validates himself as the true Christ both by fulfilling and by disappointing Messianic expectations.

[32] *Cf.* IV Ezra 7:45: "And now I see that the coming age shall bring delight to the few but torment to the many. For the evil heart has grown up in us which has estranged us from God, and brought us to destruction, . . . *and not a few only but well nigh all that have been created.*"

iv Ezra 7:118–120: "O thou Adam what hast thou done? For though it wast thou that hast sinned, the fall was not thine alone but also ours who are thy descendants. For how does it profit us that the eternal age is promised us whereas we have done the works that bring death? And that there is foretold us an imperishable hope whereas we are so miserably brought to futility."

CHAPTER II

THE DISCLOSURE AND THE FULFILLMENT OF THE MEANING OF LIFE AND HISTORY

CHRISTIANITY ENTERS the world with the stupendous claim that in Christ (that is in both the character of Christ and the epic of his life) the expectations of the ages have been fulfilled. The specific form of this claim was the belief that the Kingdom of God had come, or in the words of Jesus, "This day is this scripture fulfilled in your ears." [1] The claim was that in the life, death and resurrection of Christ, the expected disclosure of God's sovereignty over history, and the expected establishment of that sovereignty had taken place. In this disclosure of the power and will which governs history, both life and history had found their previously partly hidden and partly revealed meaning, though it is not denied that God remains, despite this revelation, partly *Deus absconditus*.

Before analysing the import of this "absurd" claim further,[2] it is necessary to explore the relation of the meaning of life, the meaning of history, and the sovereignty of God. The prophetic-Messianic hope anticipates the disclosure and fulfillment of the meaning of history through the revelation and establishment of God's sov-

[1] Luke 4:21.
[2] St. Paul admits the absurdity of the claim. It is "foolishness" to the Greeks, a "stumblingblock" to the Jews: it is the "foolishness of God" which is "wiser than men." 1 Cor. 1:25.

ereignty. This expectation is explicit in including the meaning of history in the meaning of life. Implicitly it assumes that the meaning of life transcends the meaning of history. If history cannot find its meaning except in the disclosure of a divine sovereignty, which both governs and transcends it, it is implicitly, though not explicitly, assumed that history, however meaningful, cannot give life its full meaning. Each individual transcends and is involved in the historical process. In so far as he is involved in history, the disclosure of life's meaning must come to him in history. In so far as he transcends history the source of life's meaning must transcend history.

This is covertly or implicitly recognized in prophetic Messianism because of the element of transcendence in its expectations. It is always looking toward the fuller disclosure of a God who transcends and is yet immanent in the historical process. Furthermore the ultimate level of prophetic Messianism states the problem of human existence in terms which history cannot solve. Each life and each portion of history are found to stand in proud and rebellious contradiction to the divine and eternal purpose; which means that only a transcendent mercy can overcome this contradiction.

The fact that the meaning of life transcends the meaning of history is only implicitly recognized in prophetic Messianism, for the "Kingdom of God" is expected on earth, however much it is a transmuted and sublimated "earth" or nature which becomes the scene of the Kingdom. This lack of explicitness is partly overcome in the apocalyptic culmination of the prophetic movement, in which it is literally a "new heaven" and a "new earth" which become the scene of the Messianic kingdom. It is particularly significant that in this expected fulfillment of the Messianic kingdom, the individuals of previous ages are resurrected to participate in the culmination of history. This is symbolic of the fact that each individual is believed to stand in a direct relation to the eternal by reason of transcending the historical process; and are also known to stand in an indirect relation to it, by reason of being involved in the historical process.

The Christian belief that the meaning of both life and history is disclosed and fulfilled in Christ and his Cross, is in a sense a combination of Hellenic and Hebraic interpretations of life. It conforms to the Hellenic interpretations of life because in these there is an understanding of the fact that the meaning of life transcends history; but in them history tends to be excluded from the realm of meaning, and life is fulfilled by escaping from the historical process. In Christianity it is fulfilled, though not wholly, within the historical process. New Testament faith conforms to the Hebraic interpretations of life because in them life is fulfilled in history, though in Christianity the implicit difference between "life" and "history" is made explicit. That is why Christianity is preached to both "Jews and Greeks" though it develops on the ground of Hebraism and not on the ground of Hellenism. It is a greater "foolishness" to the Greeks who do not expect a Christ at all, than it is a "stumblingblock" to the Jews, who expect a different kind of Christ.[3]

To the Greeks the Christ is foolishness because he represents a disclosure of the eternal in history. In so far as history participates in flux and in "becoming" it is not able, according to Greek opinion, to anticipate or entertain a disclosure of the eternal will which underlies it. In so far as man has within himself some element of the eternal "being" which transcends flux and finiteness, no disclosure of the eternal will is necessary. To declare, as Christian faith does,

[3] There is of course no completely consistent merging of Hellenic and Hebraic, of mystic and apocalyptic viewpoints in the New Testament, nor a consistent dominance of the latter over the former. Broadly speaking the synoptic gospels are consistently apocalyptic and the conception of the Kingdom of God, which dominates synoptic thought, is one which expresses the historical-apocalyptic approach to life. In the thought of St. Paul apocalyptic and mystic viewpoints stand in uneasy tension to each other, but the apocalyptic predominates. The Fourth Gospel on the other hand represents a tension of the two viewpoints under the dominance of the mystic. The Johannine conception of "eternal life" is a slightly Hellenized version of the synoptic "Kingdom of God." But it is significant that the Fourth Gospel is not consistently Greek in its presuppositions. Its retention of the idea of the resurrection is indicative of its organic relation to the synoptic-Hebraic viewpoint.

that a disclosure of the eternal will and purpose is both possible and necessary is to accept the paradox of man and history fundamentally. It is to understand that man is, even in the highest reaches of his transcendent freedom, too finite to comprehend the eternal by his own resources. But it is also understood that man is, even in the deepest involvement of process and nature, too free of nature to be blind to the possibilities of a disclosure of the Eternal which transcends him.

II

JESUS' OWN REINTERPRETATION OF PROPHETIC MESSIANISM

The Christian community came into being by the faith that Jesus was the Christ who had fulfilled the expectations of the ages. But this belief runs counter to the actual expectations of the prophetic movement in the period of its culmination. The Christ whom Christian faith accepts is the same Christ whom Messianism rejects, as not conforming to its expectations. The acceptance would not have been possible if Jesus had not himself transformed the Messianic expectation in the process of negating and fulfilling it.[1]

In tracing how Jesus himself reinterpreted prophetic Messianism, it is necessary to begin with an aspect of his teaching which concerns not the reinterpretation but the acceptance of the prophetic-Messianic tradition.

[1] The final truth about life is always an absurdity but it cannot be an absolute absurdity. It is an absurdity inasfar as it must transcend the "system" of meaning which the human mind always prematurely constructs with itself as the centre. But it cannot be a complete absurdity or it could not achieve any credence. In this sense Kierkegaard goes too far in his statement: "Anything that is almost probable or probable, or extremely and emphatically probable, is something he [man] can almost know, or as good as know, or extremely and emphatically almost know —but it is impossible to believe. For the absurd is the object of faith, and the only object that can be believed." *Concluding Unscientific Postscript,* translated by D. F. Swenson and W. Lowrie, p. 189. The relation between Kierkegaard's view and Barth's theory of the relation of revelation to culture is obvious. *Cf.* Karl Barth, *The Doctrine of the Word of God,* pp. 226 ff.

1. *Jesus' Rejection of Hebraic Legalism*

The most obvious conflict in the gospels is not between types of Messianism but between the Messianism in terms of which Jesus interprets his life and ministry, and the official legalism of his day. His conflict with the Pharisees is, in a sense, a final conflict in the heart of Hebraism between two facets of Hebraic spirituality: legalism and Messianism. They existed side by side, partly contradicting and partly supplementing each other from the very beginning of known Hebraic history. The Deuteronomic code was an effort to place legalism in the service of prophetism and to give to prophetic insights the permanence of legal codes. Beginning with the restoration of the second temple and ending with its destruction in 70 A.D. legalism gained a gradual ascendancy over prophetism, so that in Jesus' own day the apocalyptic movement, which informed his thought, was borne by unofficial rather than official Judaism. There was, of course, no absolute distinction between them, since Phariseeism had its own apocalyptic tendencies.

Legalism is a kind of arrested and atrophied religion of history. In Hebraism it rests upon the idea that the God, who delivered Israel out of the land of Egypt, made the decalogue a part of the covenant between Himself and the nation. This legalism is therefore type and symbol of every form of legalistic religious consciousness which binds the counsels of God prematurely to a law which is contingent to time and place. The Talmudic reinterpretations, applications and extensions of the Torah seek to do justice to the endless variety of problems and occasions for which the original law seems to be inadequate. But the policy of adding law to law cannot solve the essential weakness of law as the disclosure of the divine purpose in history. Jesus observed that the glosses, footnotes and reinterpretations of the elders actually had the effect of diluting the original force of the law.[2]

The criticisms of legalism in both the gospels and epistles give

---

[2] Mt. 15:6. "Thus have ye made the commandment of God of none effect by your tradition."

an indirect insight into a prophetic rather than legalistic interpretation of life. The criticisms take the following forms:

(*a*) No law can do justice to the freedom of man in history. It cannot state the final good for him, since in his transcendence and self-transcendence no order of nature and no rule of history can finally determine the norm of his life. This may be the import of Jesus' statement: "Except your righteousness shall exceed the righteousness of the scribes and Pharisees, ye shall in no case enter the kingdom of heaven." [3] In the Pauline epistles this emphasis upon the transcendence of the human spirit over any particular law is expressed in the Pauline word: "Stand fast therefore in the liberty wherewith Christ hath made us free, and be not entangled again with the yoke of bondage," [4] which is to say that no proximate law, but only an ultimate law, represented by a disclosure of God's own nature can be normative for man.

(*b*) No law can do justice to the complexities of motive which express themselves in the labyrinthine depths of man's interior life. This is the burden of Jesus' paradoxical extension of the law to the point of its abrogation in the Sermon on the Mount [5] in which the demands of the law are extended so that hate as well as murder, lust as well as divorce are prohibited. But this means in effect that law is relativized as social law, since the demands exceed anything which could be enforced by society upon the individual. Law becomes a matter between God and the individual.

(*c*) Law cannot restrain evil; for the freedom of man is such that he can make the keeping of the law the instrument of evil. He can screen evil motives by outward conformity to the law: "For ye make clean the outside of the cup and of the platter, but within they are full of extortion and excess." [6] He can also use observance of the law as the vehicle of sinful pride.[7] These criticisms, whether indicating the law's inability to define the ultimate good or to restrain

---

[3] Mt. 5:20.   [5] Mt. 5:27–48.
[4] Gal. 5:1.   [6] Mt. 23:25.
[7] The parable of the Pharisee and Publican, Lk. 18:9 ff.

the ultimate evil, namely, man's use of virtue as the vehicle of pride, all reveal Christ's understanding of life and history in terms of the heights of its freedom.[8] They are criticisms which are possible only from a perspective which assumes the dimension of Eternity in human history, knows the height and depth of good and evil in each moment of existence and realizes the futility of capturing the vitalities of human existence in any system or of fixing the infinite possibilities of life upon any particular level.

The conflict between Jesus and the Pharisees is thus a final conflict between the prophetic-Messianic and the legalistic facets in Hebraism. In modern Judaism there are both legalistic and mystical tendencies but no strong forward-looking historical tendencies. The sense of history expresses itself retrospectively. In modern Jewish life Messianic and apocalyptic tendencies, still surviving in the ethos of Hebraism, have been forced to find expression in secularized versions of Messianism, such as the liberal idea of progress and Marxism or in slightly heterodox movements such as Hassidism. Christianity appropriated the prophetic Messianic tradition, though, of course, not in such a way as to render the Christian tradition immune to recurring fallacies of legalism. The tendency to find a premature security, a premature righteousness and a superficial sense of meaning in law, is a recurring tendency in all life and culture.

2. *Jesus' Rejection of Nationalistic Particularism*

While it is wrong to assume, as is sometimes done, that Jesus' rejection of the nationalistic element in prophetic Messianism represents his primary emphasis in the reinterpretation of prophetic Messianism, it is obviously true that the Messianic interpretations which verge on nationalistic idolatry are rejected, despite such remnants of nationalistic interpretations as are found in his encounter with the

---

[8] The Pauline attitude towards the law includes most of these criticisms but adds the significant idea that the law is powerless. It states a norm without giving power to fulfill it.

Syrophenician woman. There the assertion that "I am sent but to
the lost sheep of the house of Israel" may be regarded as a tentative
and testing remark which is refuted by Jesus' own assurance to the
alien woman: "O woman, great is thy faith: be it unto thee even as
thou wilt." [9]

The story of the Good Samaritan obviously implies the rejection
of nationalistic Messianism and the account of the temptation in the
wilderness includes the rejection of the idea of a national triumph
as a legitimate Messianic hope.[10] One of the most perfect disavowals
of nationalism in the gospels is to be found in a word of John the
Baptist: "And think not to say within yourselves, We have Abraham
to our father; for I say unto you, that God is able of these stones to
raise up children unto Abraham." [11] Here the freedom of God over
the instruments of his will, very specially over the one chosen instrument, the nation of Israel, is asserted according to highest insights
of prophetic universalism, as against the lower level of nationalistic
Messianism. It is significant, however, that Christianity does not
finally purge itself of nationalistic particularism until St. Paul asserts
the right to preach the gospel to the Gentiles, rejects the validity of
the Jewish law for Christians, and substitutes the church for the
nation as the "Israel of God." However important it may be to
recognize the rejection of nationalism in Jesus' interpretation of
prophecy, it is quite wrong to imagine that this represents the final
achievement of Jesus' Messianism, though modern interpretations of
Christianity, which see no more in Jesus' life and ministry than the
culmination of a certain moral development, frequently confine
Jesus' Messianism to these proportions.

3. *Jesus' Rejection of the Answer of Hebraic Messianism for the Problem Presented by Prophetism*

We have previously noted that prophetism presents a problem for
which Messianism has no adequate answer; and that this problem

[9] Mt. 15:21 ff.; Mk. 7:24 ff.   [10] Mt. 4:1 ff.   [11] Mt. 3:9.

became obscured again and again, partly because the vicissitudes of Israel's history accentuated the necessity of the vindication of the righteous over the unrighteous to the exclusion of the more ultimate problem; partly because the ultimate problem of prophetism is an affront to human self-esteem; and partly because it is a problem for which there is no answer within the limits of Messianism. This ultimate problem is given by the fact that human history stands in contradiction to the divine will on any level of its moral and religious achievements in such a way that in any "final" judgment the righteous are proved not to be righteous. The final enigma of history is therefore not how the righteous will gain victory over the unrighteous, but how the evil in every good and the unrighteousness of the righteous is to be overcome.

This enigma is involved in the prophetic interpretation of history, beginning with Amos' rigorous analysis of the pride of nations and running through the whole of prophetic literature. But it remains a mystery only partly disclosed and not at all solved until Jesus makes it the basis for his reinterpretation of Messianism. Jesus' parable of the Last Judgment [12] reveals the logic of this reinterpretation most perfectly. The symbolism of the parable, the picture of the Messianic judge separating the sheep from the goats, the righteous from the unrighteous, is a recurring motif of apocalyptic literature. Jesus accepts it and on one level of his own interpretation it would appear that history culminates in the Messianic vindication of the righteous and the destruction of the wicked. But a significant new note is added. The righteous are humble and do not believe themselves to be righteous. They accept the judge's commendation with the confession, "Lord, when saw we thee an hungred, and fed thee? or thirsty, and gave thee drink? When saw we thee a stranger, and took thee in? or naked, and clothed thee? or when saw we thee sick, or in prison, and came unto thee?" [13] While the righteous are contritely aware of their unworthiness of this vindication, the unrighteous are equally unconscious of their guilt. The distinction

[12] Mt. 25: 31–46.   [13] Mt. 25:37–39.

between the righteous and the unrighteous is significantly not obscured. There are those who serve their fellowmen and there are those who do not. But the ones who do are conscious of the fact that in any final judgment they are discovered not to have fulfilled the law of life; while the ones who do not are too self-centred to know of their sin. Thus the final judgment, as Jesus sees it, actually includes both levels of prophetic Messianism, the more purely moral and the supra-moral. The distinction between good and evil in history is not destroyed; yet it is asserted that in the final judgment there are no righteous, i.e., in their own eyes. Jesus' conflict with Pharisaic self-righteousness is governed by the same conviction. It is the contrite publican who is "justified" before the righteous Pharisee, for "whosoever shall exalt himself shall be abased; and he that shall humble himself shall be exalted." [14]

Here then is the first reason why Jesus' Messianism was an offense and was bound to be rejected. The fact that it affronted the egotism of a nation was insignificant beside the greater offense of outraging the pride of man as man. The second reason for the "offensive" character of Jesus' Messianism was in the answer which he gave to the problem emphasized by this reinterpretation of life and history. This answer is most succinctly stated in his own words, "The Son of man must suffer." [15] The answer introduces the outrageous idea of a suffering Messiah into the Messianic thought, which had not entertained any other conception than that of a triumphant Messiah. The idea that the "Son of man must suffer" represents a combination of the "son of man" idea taken from the apocalypses of Daniel and Enoch and the idea of the "suffering servant" taken from Isaiah 53. The figure of the "son of man" is that of a heavenly conqueror and judge, through whom history is brought to culmination. The suffering servant figure is not a Messianic symbol; or, if so, only in a very secondary sense. Most probably it was meant to designate the nation rather than any individual. If so, it represented a profound effort to give the sufferings of Israel a higher meaning by the

[14] Mt. 23:12.   [15] Mk. 8:31.

suggestion that its mission and triumph in the world would not be achieved by the usual triumph over others but by its vicarious suffering for the sins of others. To declare, as Jesus does, that the Messiah, the representative of God, must suffer, is to make vicarious suffering the final revelation of meaning in history. But it is the vicarious suffering of the representative of God, and not of some force in history, which finally clarifies the obscurities of history and discloses the sovereignty of God over history.

This synthesis of the suffering servant idea in Isaiah and the son of man figure in apocalyptic literature, as Rudolf Otto rightly observes, "was not made bit by bit in the gradual growth of post-humous apologetics in some unknown church but . . . was due to an incomparably original conception on the part of one who could also conceive that the Kingdom was actually coming as he himself has conquered Satan." [16]

The synthesis represents something more than the collation of two hitherto unrelated concepts, the one Messianic and the other quasi-Messianic. It represents a profound reinterpretation of the meaning of history. If the revelation of history's meaning is given through vicarious suffering of a guiltless individual or nation this means one of two things. It may mean that vicarious love is a force in history which gradually gains the triumph over evil and therefore ceases to be tragic. This is the optimistic interpretation which liberal Christianity has given the Cross of Christ. According to this interpretation the power of love in history, as symbolized by the Cross, begins tragically but ends triumphantly. It overcomes evil. But the idea of the suffering servant in history may also mean that vicarious love remains defeated and tragic in history; but has its triumph in the knowledge that it is ultimately right and true. Such a tragic conception still leaves the problem of the evil in history unresolved. How is the evil of history overcome? Does the power of the guilty, under which the guiltless suffer, go on indefinitely? Is history a constant repetition of the triumph of evil on the plane

[16] *The Kingdom of God and the Son of Man*, p. 255.

of the obvious and is the triumph of the good merely the inner triumph of its own assurance of being right?

The synthesis of Jesus, according to which the suffering servant is not merely a character of history, but is the representative of the divine, transcends both the simple optimism of the first interpretation and the purely tragic implication of the second conception. It is God Who suffers for man's iniquity. He takes the sins of the world upon and into Himself. This is to say that the contradictions of history are not resolved in history; but they are only ultimately resolved on the level of the eternal and the divine. However, the eternal and the divine which destroys evil is not some undifferentiated eternity which effaces both the good and evil of history by destroying history itself. God's mercy must make itself known in history, so that man in history may become fully conscious of his guilt and his redemption. The Messiah must give his life "a ransom for many." [17]

Thus Jesus' own reinterpretation of Messianism contains the two offensive ideas that the righteous are unrighteous in the final judgment and that God's sovereignty over history is established and his triumph over evil is effected not by the destruction of the evil-doers but by his own bearing of the evil. It must be noted that the second, as well as the first, idea is implied in prophetism, however offensive it may be in its explicit form. Just as the idea that the distinction between the righteous and the unrighteous disappears in the final judgment, is implicit in the most radical prophetic analyses of history, so also the idea that God suffers in history is implicit in the whole Hebraic-prophetic idea that God is engaged and involved in history, and is not some unmoved mover, dwelling in eternal equanimity.[18]

[17] Rudolf Otto calls attention to the fact that *lutron* (ransom) had a unique religious connotation before it had a commercial-juridical meaning. It was a sacrifice by which religious guilt was covered or removed. *Ibid.,* p. 259.

[18] Though implicit in Old Testament theology the idea never became explicit in Judaism. C. G. Montefiore writes: "Rabbinic Judaism, as all

The absurd and offensive nature of Jesus' reinterpretation of Messianism not only prompted his rejection by the Jews. It aroused baffled incredulity in the small circle of his disciples. Peter's reaction to Jesus' prediction of his suffering: "Be it far from thee, Lord: this shall not be unto thee" [19] may be regarded as symbolic of the resistance to the truth of Christianity which develops not only outside, but inside of, the Christian faith. The eschatological fellowship surrounding Jesus could not understand the idea until it had been transmuted into a fact of history. Yet even when transmuted into a fact, the final truth of Christianity is not easily accepted. Nor can it be accepted once and for all. The history of Christianity is the history of the truth of Christ contending constantly against the truth as men see it.

4. *Jesus' Reinterpretation of the Eschata*

Prophetic and apocalyptic hopes anticipated an end which would both disclose and establish the sovereignty of God; which would both reveal the meaning of life and fulfill it. In Jesus' own reinterpretation, these two facets of history's culmination are, at least partially, separated. The indication of this separation is given in the double affirmation that on the one hand the "Kingdom of God has come" and on the other hand that "the Kingdom of God will come." On the one hand, history has reached its culmination in the disclosure of the hidden sovereignty of God and the revelation of the meaning of life and history. On the other hand history is still waiting for its culmination in the second coming of the triumphant

subsequent Judaism, denied in its fullness the doctrine of a 'suffering God.' Perhaps this denial may be the reason why Rabbinic Judaism had little to say upon the subject of suffering which supplements or enlarges or goes beyond the Old Testament. The Rabbis went willingly to martyrdom and they extolled it. But the perception of a certain splendor in suffering or in the endurance of suffering, which most of us would now acknowledge, is wanting in them." Introduction to *A Rabbinic Anthology*, p. xli.

[19] Mt. 16:22.

Messiah. In combining the conceptions of the "suffering servant" and the "Son of man," Jesus, in effect, attributed the qualities of the suffering servant to his first coming and the qualities of the triumphant Son of man to a second coming,[20] either his own or another.

This separation of two aspects of Messianic fulfillment was not altogether new in the thought of Jesus. In later apocalyptic literature the coming of the Messiah and the final judgment, resurrection and culmination of history are not synchronous.[21] In Jesus' own interpretation there was indeed a victory over Satan and the power of evil in the first coming as a suffering servant. Yet ultimate victory was postponed until "The Son of man shall come in the glory of his Father with his angels; and then he shall reward every man according to his works." [22] "The modern theory of 'realized eschatology' according to which the coming of Christ effectively fulfills Messianic prophecies and reduces the promises of a second coming in the New Testament to insignificance, must be challenged. The strain of thought embodied in the New Testament hope of a 'second coming' is indispensable for the Christian interpretation of history and for a true understanding of New Testament thought."[23]

The full implication of the double idea that the "Kingdom of God has come" and that it is "coming" is that history is an interim. Whatever may be the meaning of Jesus' parables of the leaven and the mustard seed, he certainly does not present the "Kingdom"

[20] In a profound analysis of this problem F. D. V. Narborough declares: "Just as our Lord accepted the rôle of the Servant . . . in the present age, so he seems to have accepted the 'Son of man' as, to some extent, an indication of his rôle in the age to come." Narborough's essay in Ch. 2 of *Essays on the Trinity and Incarnation* edited by A. E. J. Rawlinson.

[21] W. O. E. Oesterley declares: "In the Old Testament and Apocalyptic writings the 'last times' by no means always or necessarily imply the end of all things. Although when the last times are to come about is never stated definitely, they are always presented as a process upon which shall follow the inauguration of a new age." *Doctrine of Last Things,* p. 195.

[22] Mt. 16:27.

[23] For exposition of idea of "realized eschatology," see C. H. Dodd, *The Gospel and History.*

which has entered into history through his suffering and death as a force which will gradually transmute history into something quite different from what it is. In obvious contradiction to modern liberal interpretations of the power of love in history, Jesus discourages the hope that the preaching of the gospel will banish evil from history. "In this rejoice not," he warns his disciples, "that the spirits are subject unto you; but rather rejoice, because your names are written in heaven." [24] The love which enters history as suffering love, must remain suffering love in history. Since this love is the very law of history it may have its tentative triumphs even in history; for human history cannot stand in complete contradiction to itself. Yet history does stand in actual contradiction to the law of love; and Jesus anticipates the growth of evil as well as the growth of good in history. Among the signs of the end will be "wars and rumours of wars" and the appearance of false Christs.[25]

In thus conceiving history after Christ as an interim between the disclosure of its true meaning and the fulfillment of that meaning, between the revelation of divine sovereignty and the full establishment of that sovereignty, a continued element of inner contradiction in history is accepted as its perennial characteristic. Sin is overcome in principle but not in fact. Love must continue to be suffering love rather than triumphant love. This distinction becomes a basic category of interpreting history in all profound versions of the Christian faith, and has only recently been eliminated in modern sentimentalized versions of that faith.

One seemingly serious, but actually superficial, change in Jesus' own interpretation must be made. He expected the historic interim between the first and second establishment of the Kingdom to be

[24] Lk. 10:20.
[25] Mt. 24:6. This element in Jesus' own eschatology finally achieves its definitive expression in the figure of the "Anti-Christ" in the Johannine epistles, who appears at the end of history. Taken seriously, as it should be, this symbol refutes every modern liberal interpretation of history which identifies "progress" with the Kingdom of God. We shall deal with this issue more fully in Chapter X.

short.[26] In this error he was followed both by St. Paul and the early church, with the consequent false and disappointed hope of the *parousia* in the lifetime of the early disciples. This error was due to an almost inevitable illusion of thought which deals with the problem of the relation of time and eternity. The *eschata* which represent the fulfillment and the end of time in eternity are conceived literally and thereby made a point in time. The sense that the final fulfillment impinges on the present moment, the feeling of urgency in regard to anticipating this fulfillment, expresses itself in chronological terms and thereby becomes transmuted into a "proximate futurism," into the feeling that the fulfillment of history is chronologically imminent.

In reinterpreting the New Testament idea of the *parousia* (and, as we shall see later, all other ideas dealing with the relation of history and super-history, such as resurrection and judgment) it is important to take Biblical symbols seriously but not literally. If they are taken literally the Biblical conception of a dialectical relation between history and superhistory is imperiled; for in that case the fulfillment of history becomes merely another kind of time-history. If the symbols are not taken seriously the Biblical dialectic is destroyed, because in that case concepts of an eternity are connoted in which history is destroyed and not fulfilled.

This single adjustment in the New Testament view is defined as superficial rather than serious to distinguish the idea of "interim" as here used from that of Albert Schweitzer.[27] According to his conception the whole ethic and religion of Jesus is based upon his illusion of his proximate return. The absolute character of his ethic is due, in the opinion of Schweitzer, to the belief that the "time is short." The real fact is that the absolute character of the ethic of Jesus conforms to the actual constitution of man and history, that

[26] Mt. 10:23: "Ye shall not have gone over the cities of Israel till the Son of man be come." Mt. 16:28: "Verily I say unto you, There be some standing here, which shall not taste of death, till they see the Son of man coming in his kingdom."

[27] Cf. *The Quest of the Historical Jesus.*

is, to the transcendent freedom of man over the contingencies of nature and the necessities of time, so that only a final harmony of life with life in love can be the ultimate norm of his existence. Yet man's actual history is subject to contingency and necessity and is corrupted by his sinful efforts to escape and to deny his dependence and his involvement in finiteness. The idea that the time is short expresses Christianity's understanding that these limitations and corruptions of history are not finally normative for man.

Thus reconstructed, the idea that history is an "interim" between the first and the second coming of Christ has a meaning which illumines all the facts of human existence. History, after Christ's first coming, has the quality of partly knowing its true meaning. In so far as man can never be completely in contradiction to his own true nature, history also reveals significant realizations of that meaning. Nevertheless history continues to stand in real contradiction to its true meaning, so that pure love in history must always be suffering love. But the contradictions of history cannot become man's norms, if history is viewed from the perspective of Christ. For the Christian, the anticipation of a final judgment and fulfillment means an emancipation from the proximations of good and the concretions of evil which represent the "standards" of history. Thus the absolute ethical and religious demands of the gospel are not irrelevant, though the expectation of Christ's imminent return has only occasionally been a living hope within the church since the second century. Even the idea of a proximate second coming is not irrelevant when understood symbolically; for it expresses the idea that every moment of time makes not only for the fulfillment of life, but hastens man towards the dissolution of death. This fact of death threatens life with meaninglessness unless man is "saved by hope" and understands life in such a way that neither his involvement in history nor his transcendence over it destroys the meaning of life. To understand life and history according to the meaning given it by Christ is to be able to survey the chaos of any present or the peril of any future, without sinking into despair. It is to have a vantage point from which one may realize that momentary securities are perennially destroyed both by the vicissitudes of history and by the fact of death which stands over all history.

This faith is perfectly expressed in the Pauline confession: "Who shall separate us from the love of Christ? Shall tribulation, or distress, or persecution, or famine, or nakedness, or peril, or sword? . . . Nay in all these things we are more than conquerors through him that loved us. For I am persuaded, that neither death nor life, nor angels, nor principalities, nor powers, nor things present, nor things to come, nor height, nor depth, nor any other creature, shall be able to separate us from the love of God, which is in Christ Jesus our Lord." [28]

III

THE ACCEPTANCE BY CHRISTIAN FAITH OF THE EXPECTED
AND THE REJECTED MESSIAH

The correlate of revelation is faith. The mutual relation between the two is so close that revelation cannot be completed without faith. The revelation of God in Christ, the disclosure of God's sovereignty over life and history, the clarification of the meaning of life and history, is not completed until man is able, by faith, to apprehend the truth which is beyond his apprehension without faith. The truth is not completely beyond his apprehension; otherwise Christ could not have been expected. It is nevertheless beyond his apprehension, or Christ would not have been rejected. It is a truth capable of apprehension by faith; but when so apprehended there is a consciousness in the heart of the believer that he has been helped to this apprehension. This consciousness is summed up in the confession: "No man can say that Jesus is the Lord, but by the Holy Spirit" [1] and is suggested in Christ's acknowledgment of Peter's

[28] Romans 8:35, 37, 38.　　　[1] 1 Cor. 12:3.

confession: "Flesh and blood hath not revealed it unto thee, but my Father which is in heaven." [2]

The revelation of Christ is not completed until the little Christian community surveys the whole Christian epic, which includes the life and the teachings of Christ, but also and supremely the sacrificial death upon the Cross, understood by Christ as a necessary "ransom for many." Included in this history is not merely the immediate epic but also the history of expectation. Christ could not be the Christ, if he had not been expected; which is why the gospels (particularly St. Matthew) make a great deal of the fulfillment of prophecy, though the correlations between expectation and fulfillment are sometimes conceived in a mechanical and literalistic fashion. It is by the contemplation of the whole of this history in terms of expectation and fulfillment that Christian faith arrives at the confession, "Surely this was the Son of God." If the revelation in Christ had been merely the record of a high form of "God consciousness," or merely the culmination of man's search after God, or the portrayal of a high type of virtue, if Christ had merely revealed God to us by symbolizing divine goodness in his own goodness (which are the interpretations of Christian revelation in liberal Christianity), the revelation would have stood complete in itself. It would have been an historic fact or a form of historic striving which man comprehends and apprehends by his reason and appropriates for the sake of his growing wisdom and his developing culture. But such interpretations of life and faith do not proceed from a radical or profound analysis of the problem of life. They assume that the problem of life is to discover the highest form of goodness; to learn what is "worthy of man's highest devotion." They do not understand life in its twofold character of involvement in finiteness and transcendence over it; or the further complication of the corruption of sin which is the consequence of premature and self-sufficient efforts to escape from the weakness, dependence and insufficiency of the human situation.

[2] Mt. 16:17.

Wherever history is understood as solving its own problems by the cumulation of knowledge and wisdom and the consequent increase of virtue; whenever the complexities of history's relation to eternity are not known to be characteristic of history on every level of its development, the Christian claim that God has been revealed in Christ cannot be taken seriously. This is why liberal Christianity can give no satisfactory answer to the question why Christ, rather than some other "good" character of history, should be revered as divine, or how we can have the assurance that an evolutionary development may not produce a higher form of "goodness" more worthy of our "highest devotion."

1. *Christ Crucified as the "Wisdom of God and the Power of God"*

The faith of the Christian community, that the expectations of the ages have been fulfilled in Christ, that the hidden sovereignty of God has been fully revealed, and the meaning of life disclosed and fulfilled, is most accurately expressed in the succinct phrase of St. Paul, that this Christ who was not expected by the Greeks ("unto the Greeks foolishness"), and who was not the Christ the Jews expected ("unto the Jews a stumblingblock") is nevertheless "unto them which are called both Jews and Greeks, the power of God and the wisdom of God." [3] The Johannine assertion that "the law was given by Moses but *grace* and *truth* came by Jesus Christ" [4] makes the same affirmation, correlating two slightly different, but almost identical definitions of the significance of Christ.

The *wisdom* and the *truth* in Christ is the purpose and the will of the divine sovereign of life and history, which had been partially revealed and partially obscured in life and history. The Christian affirmation is that it is now fully disclosed. The *power* and *grace* in Christ is the dynamic authority of the divine sovereign of life and history, which had been partly revealed by the actualization of good in history and partly obscured by the defiance of sin. The Christian

---

[3] 1 Cor. 1:23-24.   [4] John 1:17.

affirmation is that this divine power is now established and disclosed in such a way that there can be no question about any other power being able to overcome it.

From the perspective of human history, which cannot be fully comprehended from its own perspective or fulfilled by its own power, the *wisdom* and the *power* in Christ is what gives life its meaning and guarantees the fulfillment of that meaning.

But what is it in this revelation of Christ which gives the final answer to the problem of man, who is both free and bound, both involved in finiteness and transcending it; and betrayed into sin by this situation? It can certainly not be the simple assurance that God is merciful rather than vindictive, to which some modern sentimental versions of the Christian faith have reduced the Christian revelation. This simple and sentimental contrast between the Old and the New Testament answers no significant or ultimate question. In the New Testament the Atonement is the significant content of the Incarnation. To say that Christ is the "express image of his person" [5] is to assert that in the epic of this life and death the final mystery of the divine power which bears history is clarified; and, with that clarification, life and history are given their true meaning.

It will be remembered that the prophets were certain about the wrath and the justice of God. They were less certain about His mercy. They knew that there was mercy; for history in its processes disclosed God's "longsuffering" as well as His wrath. But they could not be certain about mercy for it seemed to stand in contradiction to the divine justice. Did the one abrogate the other? The *wisdom* apprehended in Christ finally clarifies the character of God. He has a resource of mercy beyond His law and judgment but He can make it effective only as He takes the consequences of His wrath and judgment, upon and into Himself.

Thus the insistence of Christ that the Son of man must suffer is, quite accurately, elaborated and completed in the faith of the church, that the sufferings of this Son of man are the disclosure of God's

[5] Heb. 1:3.

suffering. The suffering of God is on the one hand the inevitable consequence of sin's rebellion against goodness; and on the other hand the voluntary acceptance by divine love of the consequence of sin. The classical Christian idea of Atonement emphasizes that God is both the propitiator and the propitiated.[6] The Father sends the Son into the world to become a sacrifice for sin. But it is also the wrath of the Father which must be propitiated. There can be no simple abrogation of the wrath of God by the mercy of God. The wrath of God is the world in its essential structure reacting against the sinful corruptions of that structure; it is the law of life as love, which the egotism of man defies, a defiance which leads to the destruction of life. The mercy of God represents the ultimate freedom of God above His own law; but not the freedom to abrogate the law. All the various efforts of theology to rationalize the mystery of the Atonement in commercial and juridical theories of God's justice or even the absurd patristic theory which had credence before Anselm (according to which God played a trick upon the devil by confronting him with the divine in the shape of a man) are efforts to state the paradox of the divine mercy in relation to the divine wrath. Implausible as many of the theories are and much as they may obscure rather than clarify the ultimate mystery, none of them completely effaces the central truth embodied in the doctrine of the Atonement. The justice and the forgiveness of God are one, just as Father and Son are equally God. For the highest justice of God is the holiness of His love. It is love as law which man affronts and defies. Yet forgiveness and justice are not one, just as Father and Son are two. The fact that God cannot overcome evil without displaying in history His purpose to take the effects of evil upon and into Himself, means that the divine mercy cannot be effective until the seriousness of sin is fully known. The knowledge that sin causes suffering to God is an indication of the seriousness of sin. It is by that knowledge that man is brought to despair. Without this despair there is no possibility of the contrition which appropriates the divine

6 *Cf.* G. Aulen, *Christus Victor.*

forgiveness. It is in this contrition and in this appropriation of divine mercy and forgiveness that the human situation is fully understood and overcome. In this experience man understands himself in his finiteness, realizes the guilt of his efforts to escape his insufficiency and dependence and lays hold upon a power beyond himself which both completes his incompleteness and purges him of his false and vain efforts at self-completion.

It must be emphasized that this final revelation of the divine sovereignty over life and this final disclosure of the meaning of life in terms of its dependence upon the divine judgment and mercy is not simply some truth of history which is comprehended by reason, to be added to the sum total of human knowledge. It must be constantly apprehended inwardly by faith, because it is a truth which transcends the human situation in each individual just as it transcended the total cultural situation historically. "Forgiveness," declares Kierkegaard quite rightly, "is a paradox in the Socratic sense insofar as it involves a relationship between the eternal truth and the existing individual. . . . The individual existing human being must feel himself a sinner; not *objectively* which is nonsense but *subjectively* which is the most profound suffering. . . . He must try to understand the forgiveness of sins and then despair of understanding. With the understanding directly opposed to it, the inwardness of faith must lay hold of this paradox." [7]

2. *The Relation of the "Wisdom of God" to the "Power of God"*
a. The identity of Wisdom and Power

The assertion of Christian faith is that the knowledge of God through the crucified Christ is both "wisdom" and "power," both "grace" and "truth"; which is to say that not only are life and history now fully known by having found their true end and meaning beyond themselves but they are also completed and fulfilled. Christ as "power" and as "grace" can be mediated to the individual only if the truth of the Atonement is appropriated inwardly. In that case

[7] Søren Kierkegaard, *Concluding Unscientific Postscript*, p. 201.

the alternate moods of despair and false hope are overcome and the individual is actually freed to live a life of serenity and creativity.

The understanding of the intimate relation between wisdom and power is constantly imperiled by Christian interpretations of the doctrine of the Atonement which seek to make it merely a disclosure of wisdom. This is particularly true on the Hellenic side of Christian faith. It will be remembered that Christ was not expected among the Greeks either because it was thought impossible for God to reveal Himself in history (since history was regarded as no more than temporal succession and natural sequence); or because it was thought unnecessary (since each man's reason was each man's Christ). When the gospel is finally preached to the Gentiles the general tendency is to appropriate its truth only in so far as it conforms to their problem. Their problem is the problem of finiteness and eternity and their conviction is that the chasm between the two is unbridgeable. What they appropriate from the gospel therefore is the affirmation that this chasm can be bridged. Thus Clement declares that, "The word of God became man in order that thou mayst learn from man how man becomes God." [8] Origen, the greatest of the Alexandrian theologians, thought of Christ primarily as the mediator between the "uncreated One and the created many" and Prophyry passed the judgment upon him that "though his outward life was that of a Christian . . . he thought like the Greeks." [9]

[8] *Protrepticus* I, 8.

[9] A. Harnack, *History of Dogma,* Vol. II, p. 341. Such a judgment does not do justice to the Scriptural content in Origen's thought, particularly his emphasis upon grace as a power which philosophy could not give, upon the necessity of the forgiveness of sins and upon the hope of the resurrection as against the Greek idea of immortality.

Nevertheless Origen, and the Greek Fathers generally, were inclined to regard Christ, not so much as an answer to the problem of sin as the Bible defined it, but as an answer to the problem of death. Sometimes Christ seemed no more than a supplement to the answer which Plato and the philosophers had already given. Sometimes he was regarded as

The obsession of the Greek mind with the problem of finiteness and eternity had two consequences, as Greek thought sought to appropriate the "foolishness" of the gospel. One was that it exhausted itself in accepting an un-Greek answer to a Greek problem. It did accept the Christian affirmation that the eternal had made itself known in history. But it regarded that fact, of itself, as the answer to the final problem of life. It did not fully understand that the particular content of the divine disclosure was the knowledge of the mercy and the justice of God in their paradoxical relationship, in other words, the Atonement. The specific theological formulation of this error lies in the emphasis upon the Incarnation, to the exclusion of the doctrine of the Atonement or, at least, its relegation to a subordinate position. This error persists in certain types of Catholic and Anglican thought, sometimes more particularly in the latter because of its great dependence upon patristic theology.

Hastings Rashdall, a typical Anglican rationalist, takes satisfaction in the fact that the doctrine of the Atonement was "never heartily accepted" in the church before St. Augustine and that it was "sometimes wholly ignored." [10] One might add that one possible reason why Christian thought before Anselm had nothing but an implausible theory of the Atonement when it did give the doctrine attention (the theory that God played a trick upon the devil and caught the

a more adequate bridge between the historical and the eternal than Greek philosophy afforded.

Irenæus, though no pure Hellenist, described salvation through Christ as a way of attaining "incorruptibility and immortality" which could not have been attained in any other way than by man's becoming united in Christ with incorruptibility and immortality" (*Against Heresies,* III, xix, 1).

Gregory of Nyssa's entire "Great Catechism" is essentially devoted to the refutation of the two typically Hellenic objections to the gospel, namely that philosophy made the coming of Christ unnecessary and that the revelation of the eternal in the finite was impossible.

[10] *The Idea of the Atonement,* p. 206. For Rashdall the final idea in Christian revelation is truly a "stumblingblock."

devil by "baiting the hook with Christ"), is because the doctrine was of no sufficient importance really to engage its mind. In typical Hellenistic Christianity doctrines of the Atonement are essentially irrelevant because the disclosure of God in history does not require a specific content. It is sufficient that God should make Himself known against the scepticism of the Greek mind that this is not possible. He need not make known His wrath and mercy, since it is not sin but finiteness which troubles man.

Greek thought tends to develop another error when the Christian idea of the relation of "power" to "wisdom" is stated in Greek terms. When Greek thought seeks to express the idea that "God was in Christ" and made Himself known in history in the Incarnation, it tries to state this truth in metaphysical terms. This means in effect that an ultimate truth, transcending all human wisdom and apprehended by faith, is transmuted into a truth of human wisdom and incorporated into a metaphysical system.

The effect of this procedure is clearly seen in the Christological controversies of the early Christian ages. These controversies end in the formula of Chalcedon and the Nicene creed in which the affirmation of Christian faith is made in defiance of Greek thought but within the limitations of Greek terms. The Greek idea that there is an absolute gulf between the "passible" and the "impassible," between the temporal and the eternal is refuted and transcended. But the Christian affirmation that God makes Himself known in history through Christ is partly obscured by the terms used to affirm it. The indication of this tendency is the theory of the two natures of Christ, in terms of which early Christian thought is forced to state its conviction about Jesus' historical and human character on the one hand, and his significance as the revelation of the divine on the other. By stating this double facet of Christ in ontic terms, a truth of faith, which can be expressed only symbolically, is transmuted into a truth of speculative reason. Christ is, according to these statements of faith, both God and man. It is asserted that his humanity does not derogate from his divinity or his divinity from his humanity. All definitions of Christ which affirm both his divinity and humanity in the sense that they ascribe both finite and historically conditioned and eternal and unconditioned qualities to his nature must verge on logical nonsense. It is possible for a character, event or fact of history to point symbolically beyond history and to become a source of disclosure of an eternal meaning, purpose and power which bears history. But it is not possible for any person to be historical and unconditioned at the same time. But the logical nonsense is not as serious a defect as the fact that the statement tends to reduce Christian faith to metaphysical truths which need not be apprehended inwardly by faith. The relation between "power" and "wisdom" is thereby destroyed because the final truth about life is not apprehended in such a way that the "existing individual" (Kierkegaard) is shattered in his self-esteem at the very center of his being; his insecurity as a finite individual in the flux of time is not robbed of all false securities of power or pride; his anxiety is not heightened until it reaches despair. Out of such despair contrition is born; and of contrition faith is conceived; and in that faith there is "newness of life," which is to say "power."

b. The difference between Wisdom and Power

Despite the intimate relation between the "wisdom of God" and the "power of God" which, according to Christian faith, is revealed in Christ, despite the confidence that a full understanding of the meaning of life also leads to the fulfillment of life, and that a full disclosure of the mercy of God also means the effective accretion of "grace" in the life of the believer, it must be emphasized that Christian faith has a more unambiguous confidence in Christ's full disclosure of life, history and God, than in the fulfillment of life's meaning. The idea of "power" and "grace" in Christian thought is ambiguous. On the one hand the believer is regarded as capable of fulfilling life as it has been disclosed to him. On the other hand he remains in both the finiteness of history and in the corruption of sin. The "grace" of God is on the one hand a power of God in man which completes his incompleteness. It is on the other hand the merciful power of God over man, whereby sin is overcome by God's mercy, but not by human goodness. The fulfillment of history, according to Christian faith, has two facets. According to the one there is fulfillment in every moment in which man establishes relation to God in contrition and faith. According to the other, life waits for its fulfillment and "we are saved by hope." These two aspects of fulfillment are in conformity with Christ's own interpretation of the Kingdom as having come and as coming.[11]

3. *The Foolishness of God and the Wisdom of Men*

St. Paul defines the truth revealed in "Christ crucified" as the "foolishness of God which is wiser than men" as the "hidden wisdom" which "none of the princes of this world knew, for had they known it they would not have crucified the Lord of glory." Yet this foolishness, this wisdom which could not be anticipated by human wisdom, becomes to "them which are called" the "power of God and the wisdom of God."[12] In these Pauline paradoxes we have a very exact and succinct definition of the relation of revelation to human culture. The truth which is revealed in the Cross is not a truth which could have been anticipated in human culture and it is not the culmination of human wisdom. The true Christ is not expected. All human wisdom seeks to complete itself from the basis of its partial perspective. The pride of nations and of national and imperial cultures is only a primitive form of the pride of man as man, who will seek to complete the meaning of life from the standpoint of some human virtue or achievement and who will confuse and corrupt life's meaning by that very attempt.

But on the other hand when the Christ is accepted, the truth embodied in him becomes the basis of a new wisdom. This is to say that while *Heilsgeschichte* is not merely an aspect of general history, nor its natural culmination, neither is it a completely sepa-

[11] We shall deal with this problem more fully in Chapters IV and V.
[12] I Cor. 1 and 2.

rate history. Its revelations are what give history meaning. It is not true that life would be meaningless but for the revelations embodied in *Heilsgeschichte*. Life and history are filled with suggestions of meaning which point beyond themselves; and with corruptions of meaning due to premature solutions.

The truth as apprehended by faith is not something which simple men believe upon authority and wiser men deduce from experience. For there is an element in the truth of faith which defies the wisdom of both wise and foolish, more particularly of the wise. But on the other hand a truth of faith is not something which stands perpetually in contradiction to experience. On the contrary it illumines experience and is in turn validated by experience. The finiteness of the human mind does not completely exclude the truth of faith for the reason that the finite mind is sufficiently free to transcend itself and to know something of its own finiteness. It is this capacity of self-transcendence which gives rise to both the yearning after God and to the idolatrous worship of false gods. It leads both to the expectation of Christ and to the expectation of the false Christ, who will vindicate us, but not our neighbour. Neither the finiteness of the human mind nor the sinful corruption of the mind or the "ideological taint" in all human culture can completely efface the human capacity for the apprehension of the true wisdom. Since there can be no total corruption of truth or virtue[13] there is always a residual desire for the true wisdom, and the real God and the final revelation of the meaning of life, below and above the sinful tendency to build a world of meaning around ourselves as the center. It is this residual virtue which emerges in true contrition. Faith and contrition are so closely correlated because it is the apprehension of the truth beyond ourselves in faith which makes us contritely conscious of our previous effort to complete the structure of truth from within ourselves; and this contrition in turn validates the truth of faith. It becomes "the power of God and the wisdom of God" to "them that are called." This circular relation between

[13] *Cf.* Vol. I, Ch. X.

contrition and faith in the interior complexities of the soul gives partial justification to both the theologies which regard "grace" as a completion of "nature" and those which set "grace" in contradiction to nature. Protestant theology is right in setting grace in contradiction to nature in the sense that the vicious circle of false truth, apprehended from the standpoint of the self, must be broken and the self cannot break it. In that sense the apprehension of the truth in Christ is always a miracle; and "flesh and blood have not revealed it unto us." But Protestant theology, more particularly radical Protestant theology (Barth), is wrong in denying the "point of contact" (*Anknuepfungspunkt*) which always exists in man by virtue of the residual element of *justitia originalis* in his being.[14]

The relation between the truth, apprehended in God's self-disclosure, and the truth about life which men deduce through a rational organization of their experience, might best be clarified through the analogy of our knowledge of other persons. We know what we know about other persons, partly through an observation of their behaviour. But human personality, unlike animal life, has a depth and uniqueness which cannot be understood purely in terms of external behaviour. The depth is partly comprehended by assuming that the depths of self-consciousness within ourselves correspond to that in the other person. The uniqueness of the other person is partly falsified, however, by our effort to understand him in terms which we have drawn from the knowledge of ourselves. This represents the sinful corruption in human intercourse, the projection of ourselves into the life of the other, our effort to understand the uniqueness of the other by a false assumption that our

[14] See Emil Brunner's *Nature and Grace* and Karl Barth's answer, *Nein*. In this debate Brunner seems to me to be right and Barth wrong; but Barth seems to win the debate because Brunner accepts too many of Barth's presuppositions in his fundamental premises to be able to present his own position with plausibility and consistency. Barth is able to prove Brunner inconsistent, but that does not necessarily prove him to be wrong.

own desires, hopes and ambitions are identical with those of the other.

The other self cannot be understood until he speaks to us. Only the "word" of the other self, coming out of the depth or height of his self-transcendence can finally disclose the other "I" as subject and not merely as object of our knowledge. Only this communication can give the final clue to the peculiar behaviour of the other. This behaviour always contains contradictory elements which make the real meaning of the behaviour something of a mystery. When the other self finally speaks, the self-disclosure of his words partly clarifies obscurities in his previously observed behaviour and partly negates false conclusions which the self has made by trying to understand the other self in terms of its own characteristic prejudices and passions. The knowledge gained from this self-disclosure of the other self does not stand in complete contradiction to the knowledge gained from the observation of his behaviour. It could stand in such contradiction only if the depths of self-transcendence of the other self were in complete contradiction to the life of the self as involved in its physical organism. There is contradiction between the knowledge gained from the observation of the behaviour and the knowledge gained from the self-disclosure of the other person only in so far as the self has interpreted the other falsely. Finally, the knowledge gained by such self-disclosure completes incomplete knowledge, previously known through the study of behaviour. The word of self-disclosure is thus partly a completion of incomplete knowledge, partly a clarification of obscurities and contradictions and partly a correction of falsifications.

This is exactly the relation of the self-disclosure of God as received by faith to such other knowledge as man has about the "hidden" God. When prophetic Messianism affirms that life and history are under the sovereignty of a hidden God it declares, not that life and history are meaningless, but that they can be understood only in terms of a dimension deeper and higher than the system of nature, that there are obscurities and contradictions in the "behaviour" of history which can be clarified only if the unique purpose of God is more fully disclosed; and that human explanations of this behaviour must be corrected since they contain sinful elements. These sinful elements in the knowledge of God are more pronounced than in the knowledge of the other self because they involve the pride of the finite self seeking to understand, not merely another self, but the eternal ground and source of existence in terms of itself.

This whole analogy implies the concept of divine "personality" which is indeed an invariable implication of prophetic and Christian interpretations of life and history, in contrast to more rationalistic and pantheistic philosophies. While the concept of personality cannot be cleansed completely of anthropomorphic elements, inasmuch as all human personality implies limitations of the senses and a tension between freedom and finiteness which are not applicable to the divine,[15] it is nevertheless a serviceable analogical concept because it connotes precisely that height of freedom on the one hand and that relation to organic process on the other which prophetic and Christian faith assumes in understanding God's transcendence over, and his immanent relation to, the world.[16]

[15] See Francis H. Bradley's rigorous analysis of these anthropomorphic elements in the concept of personality, leading him to the rejection of the concept in his definition of the Absolute. *Appearance and Reality,* particularly pages 413 ff. and 531 ff.

[16] Though Karl Barth protests against all forms of analogical reasoning when dealing with the "wholly other," he nevertheless avails himself of the analogy of the concept of personality when defining the character of the divine. He seeks to hide his analogic logic by inverting it. He declares that concepts of human personality are derived from the concept of divine personality. "Personalness," he writes, "means being the subject not only in the logical but in the ethical sense, being a free subject, free even in respect of the periodical limitations which are given with its individuality as such, able to dispose of its own existence and nature. If we represent to ourselves what this means, it will not occur to us to see in this personalizing of the word of God a case of anthropomorphism. The problem is not whether God is a person but whether we are. Or shall we find among us one who in the full and real sense of this concept

The self-disclosure of God in Christ is significantly regarded by Christian faith as the final "word" which God has spoken to man. The revelation of the Atonement is precisely a "final" word because it discloses a transcendent divine mercy which represents the "freedom" of God in quintessential terms: namely God's freedom over His own law. Yet this freedom is not capricious. It is paradoxically related to God's law, to the structure of the world. This is the paradox of the Atonement, of the revelation of the mercy of God in its relation to the justice of God.

When this word of revelation is spoken it completes incomplete knowledge, in so far as human history is a realm of reality having its final basis in eternity. There are elements in the "behaviour" of history which point to this "hidden" source of its life. It is in that sense that history is meaningful but pointing beyond itself. Secondly, the word of revelation clarifies obscurities and contradictions in history. In that sense history is meaningful but its meaning is threatened by meaninglessness. Finally the "word" of God corrects falsifications which have been introduced into the human interpretations of life's meaning by reason of man's effort to explain history from the standpoint of himself as its center. In that sense the word of revelation stands in contradiction to human culture and is "foolishness" to the wise.

But precisely because it is such foolishness, transcending human wisdom, it becomes, once accepted, the basis for a satisfactory total explanation of life. It becomes truly wisdom. Revelation does not remain in contradiction to human culture and human knowledge. By completing the incompleteness, clarifying the obscurities and correcting the falsifications of human knowledge it becomes true wisdom to "them that are called."

---

we can call a person. But God is really a person, really a free subject." *Doctrine of the Word of God*, p. 157. Barth's logic cannot hide the fact that, however imperfect human personality is in contrast to divine personality, he has taken the very concept of personality from human life and has applied it to the divine. From what other source could he have derived it?

CHAPTER III

THE POSSIBILITIES AND LIMITS OF HISTORY

THE CHRISTIAN faith affirms that the same Christ who discloses the sovereignty of God over history is also the perfect norm of human nature. He is the "second Adam" as well as the "Son of God." As the revelation of the paradoxical relation of the divine justice and mercy He discloses the ultimate mystery of the relation of the divine to history. This revelation clarifies the meaning of history; for the judgment of God preserves the distinction of good and evil in history; and the mercy of God finally overcomes the sinful corruption in which man is involved on every level of moral achievement by reason of his false and abortive efforts to complete his own life and history.

Christ as the norm of human nature defines the final perfection of man in history. This perfection is not so much a sum total of various virtues or an absence of transgression of various laws; it is the perfection of sacrificial love. The same Cross which symbolizes the love of God and reveals the divine perfection to be not incompatible with a suffering involvement in historical tragedy, also indicates that the perfection of man is not attainable in history. Sacrificial love transcends history. It does not transcend history as a thought transcends an act. It is an act in history; but it cannot justify itself in history. From the standpoint of history mutual love is the highest good. Only in mutual love, in which the concern of one person for the interests of another prompts and elicits a reciprocal affection, are the social demands of historical existence satisfied. The highest good of history must conform to standards of coherence and consistency in the whole realm of historical vitality.[1] All claims within the general field of interests must be proportionately satisfied and related to each other harmoniously. The sacrifice of the self for others is therefore a violation of natural standards of morals, as limited by historical existence.

Furthermore the sacrifice of the interests of the self for others is psychologically impossible when life is conceived only in terms of nature-history. If the self identifies its life with physical existence the basic ethical paradox of the gospel ethic: "Whosoever loseth his life shall find it" can have no meaning. This paradox can have meaning only if the dimension of life is known to transcend historical existence. The rewards which Jesus promises to those who follow him are therefore identified with "the resurrection." Sacrificial love thus represents a tangent towards "eternity" in the field of historical ethics. It is nevertheless the support of all historical ethics; for the self cannot achieve relations of mutual and reciprocal affection with others if its actions are dominated by the fear that they may not be reciprocated. Mutuality is not a possible achievement if it is made the intention and goal of any action. Sacrificial love is thus paradoxically related to mutual love; and this relation is an ethical counterpart of the general relation of super-history to history.

The relation of sacrificial to mutual love cannot be defined as a truth of revealed religion of which nothing is known apart from the revelation of God in Christ. Any rigorous analysis of the ethical problem of history discloses that history transcends itself in such a way that the highest good transcends historical canons and possibilities. For this reason the popular imagination fastens upon the Cross as the symbol of the highest ethical norm, even when and if

[1] *Cf.* L. T. Hobhouse, *The Rational Good.*

the full profundity of the religious meaning of the Cross is not understood. Human experience constantly yields some knowledge of the fact that concern for the other rather than the self leads inevitably to consequences which cannot be justified in purely historical and this-worldly terms. Nevertheless the ethical truth embodied in the Cross is clarified by the religious revelation contained in the Cross. For without the latter's disclosure of the relation of God to history ethical life tends to degenerate either into an egoistic utilitarianism which makes self-regarding motives ethically normative; or into a mystical ethics which flees from the tensions and incomplete harmonies of history to an undifferentiated unity of life in eternity.

II

SACRIFICIAL LOVE AND THE SINLESSNESS OF CHRIST

The paradoxical relation of sacrificial to mutual love clarifies the Christian doctrine of the sinlessness of Christ. Furthermore it makes the doctrine that Jesus was both human and divine religiously and morally meaningful and dispenses with the necessity of making the doctrine metaphysically plausible. The impossibility of doing the latter is fully attested by the ages of Christological controversy in which Christian thought sought futilely to express the idea that Christ was fully human and yet transcended the human. This controversy produced a long series of heresies in which either the human or the divine quality of the life of Christ was denied or obscured. The heresies were refuted by orthodox affirmations which were forced to commit themselves to metaphysical absurdities. Since the essence of the divine consists in its unconditioned character, and since the essence of the human lies in its conditioned and contingent nature, it is not logically possible to assert both qualities of the same person. It is even more impossible to affirm that the divine nature of Christ does not qualify the human qualities, or that the conditioned character of human existence is not in contradiction to the unconditioned character of the divine. The chasm between the human and the divine, between the historical and the eternal cannot be bridged by metaphysical speculations which begin with absolute distinctions between them.

The significance of the affirmation that God is revealed in Christ, and more particularly in his Cross, is that the love (*agape*) of God is conceived in terms which make the divine involvement in history a consequence of precisely the divine transcendence over the structures of history. The final majesty of God is contained not so much in His power within the structures as in the power of His freedom over the structures, that is, over the *logos* aspects of reality. This freedom is the power of mercy beyond judgment. By this freedom He involves Himself in the guilt and suffering of free men who have, in their freedom, come in conflict with the structural character of reality.[1] The *agape* of God is thus at once the expression of both the final majesty of God and of His relation to history.

The love of Christ, His disinterested and sacrificial *agape,* as the highest possibility of human existence, stands in paradoxical, rather than contradictory, relation to the majesty of God, so conceived. The assertion that Christ is both human and divine is contradictory when defined in terms which Christian orthodoxy used to refute the heresies which denied, from one side or the other, that there could be a relation between the historical and the eternal. These contradictions were asserted, nevertheless, because they expressed, though inadequately, what Christian faith has always apprehended beyond all metaphysical speculations, about the paradoxical relation of a divine *agape,* which stoops to conquer, and the human *agape,* which rises above history in a sacrificial act.

[1] Professor Charles Hartshorne's *The Vision of God* gives a very profound analysis of this problem and presents the thesis that God's perfection must be defined primarily in terms of His capacity for self-transcendence, or in his phrase in His "self-surpassing" character rather than in the traditional concepts of omnipotence, if the Christian doctrine of His ability to enter into loving relationship with suffering men is to have any meaning.

Though the relation between the divine and human in Christ is not contradictory, it is paradoxical. The final majesty, the ultimate freedom, and the perfect disinterestedness of the divine love can have a counterpart in history only in a life which ends tragically, because it refuses to participate in the claims and counterclaims of historical existence. It portrays a love "which seeketh not its own." But a love which seeketh not its own is not able to maintain itself in historical society. Not only may it fall victim to excessive forms of the self-assertion of others; but even the most perfectly balanced system of justice in history is a balance of competing wills and interests, and must therefore worst anyone who does not participate in the balance.

The significant contrast between the divine and the human in Christ is not, as Greek thought assumed, the contrast between the "impassible and the passible." It is a contrast between the perfect coincidence of power and goodness in the divine. It is impossible to symbolize the divine goodness in history in any other way than by complete powerlessness, or rather by a consistent refusal to use power in the rivalries of history. For there is no self in history or society, no matter how impartial its perspective upon the competitions of life, which can rise to the position of a disinterested participation in those rivalries and competitions. It can symbolize disinterested love only by a refusal to participate in the rivalries.[2] Any participation in them means the assertion of one ego interest against another.

In apprehending the Cross as the symbol of this ultimate perfection Christian faith has always been profounder than the theologies

---

[2] For this reason the ethics of nonresistance as taught in the Sermon on the Mount is in perfectly consistent relation with the love symbolized in the Cross. Modern Christianity is wrong, however, in presenting this ethic as one which might, if generally practiced, become successful in history. It is even more mistaken if it declares that a non-violent participation in all the claims and counterclaims of historical social life preserves the essentials of the gospel ethic of nonresistance. *Cf.* Richard B. Gregg, *The Power of Non-Violence.*

which sought to rationalize it. For faith has consistently regarded the Cross as the point in history where the sinful rivalries of ego with ego are transcended; and it has not tried with too much consistency to fit every action of the historical Jesus into the symbol of this perfection. The theologians on the other hand have attempted to give either metaphysical or legalistic interpretations of this perfection. If they attempted the former they leaned heavily upon the doctrine of the Virgin birth to prove that the divine perfection was not tainted by ordinary human nature. The flaw in the logic of the Virgin birth apologetics is amply revealed by the need of the corollary Catholic doctrine of the immaculate conception of the Virgin Mary. The son of a human mother, even though born without a human father, is still organically related to the whole human situation; and the doctrine of the immaculate conception of his mother is a mere gesture in overcoming the dilemma; for even an infinite regression of immaculate conceptions would hardly serve to remove the taint.

The more moralistic liberal Protestant interpretations of the sinlessness of Christ are probably most perfectly expressed in Schleiermacher's conception of the perfection of Christ's "God-consciousness." But Schleiermacher is forced by his conception into a very unscriptural denial that Christ was "in all points tempted like as we are" yet without sin.[3] Schleiermacher is quite right of course in suggesting that to be tempted means in a sense to have sinned; for temptation is a state of anxiety from which sin flows inevitably. And this anxiety is a concomitant of finite and insecure existence.[4] It is not possible for this reason to assert the sinlessness of every individual act of any actually historical character. It is possible to assert that in Jesus there is a remarkable coincidence and consistency of doctrine, of purpose and of act. His ethical doctrine contains an uncompromising insistence upon conformity to God's will without reference to the relativities and contingencies of historical situations.

[3] Friedrich Schleiermacher, *The Christian Faith,* pp. 415 ff.
[4] *Cf.* Vol. I, Ch. VII.

The animating purpose of his life is to conform to the *agape* of God. His life culminates in an act of self-abnegation in which the individual will ceases to be a protagonist of the individual life; and the life ends upon the Cross. The Cross could not have the symbolic significance for Christian faith if the life and the doctrine were not consistent with it. But on the other hand the Cross symbolizes the perfection of love more consistently than any cumulation of individual acts. The moralistic conception of sinlessness is inevitably betrayed into a legalistic interpretation of life. Perfection or sinlessness is interpreted as conformity to a given code of conduct. But how is the ultimacy of that code determined?

The Cross symbolizes the perfection of *agape* which transcends all particular norms of justice and mutuality in history. It rises above history and seeks conformity to the Divine love rather than harmony with other human interests and vitalities. This harmony is a desirable end of historical striving; but it can never be a final norm. For sinful egoism makes all historical harmonies of interest partial and incomplete; and a life which accepts these harmonies as final is bound to introduce sinful self-assertion into the ethical norm.

The interpretations which define the sinlessness and perfection of Christ in either metaphysical or legalistic terms can have no real illumination for human conduct. If only a God-man, who transcends the conditions of finiteness absolutely, can define and delineate the norm of human existence, the contrition which contemplation of such a norm may prompt is quickly transmuted into complacency. For we must live our life under the conditions of finiteness; and may therefore dismiss any ideal or norm as irrelevant which does not have to meet our conditions.

But the actual situation is that, though we are subject to the conditions and limitations of nature, we are not absolutely conditioned or limited. The human spirit rises in indefinite transcendence over the natural conditions of life; and there is no particular point at which conscience can be made easy by the assurance that an action beyond this point would mean loss of life or sacrifice of our interests. There is always the possibility of sacrificing our life and interest; and this possibility always has the corresponding assurance that to lose our life thus is to gain it. But such a gain cannot be measured in terms of the history which is bound to nature. The gain can only be an integrity of spirit which has validity in "eternity." It can have meaning only when life is measured in a dimension which includes the fulfillment of life beyond the present conditions of history. But life can be measured in that dimension only "by faith," just as the perfection of Christ can be discerned only "by faith." The effort to reduce that perfection to a simple historical fact, which can be measured in terms of historical norms and standards, is to reduce paradox to absurdity. The perfection of *agape* as symbolized in the Cross can neither be simply reduced to the limits of history, nor yet dismissed as irrelevant because it transcends history. It transcends history as history transcends itself. It is the final norm of a human nature which has no final norm in history because it is not completely contained in history.

All this has been understood by the wisdom of faith, though it has been withheld from the wise. Theologies continue to elaborate systems which either claim the authority of the Cross for the relative norms of history or which raise the perfection of the Cross and the sinlessness of Christ to a position of irrelevance. But meanwhile Christian faith has always understood, beyond all canons of common sense and all metaphysical speculations, that the perfection of the Cross represents the fulfillment—and the end—of historical ethics.

The ethical implications of the Cross illumine the actual character of human history. This insight is possible only after the religious implications of the Cross have given the answer to the problem which is presented by the character of history. There are ultimate problems of life which cannot be fully stated until the answer to them is known. Without the answer to them, men will not allow themselves to contemplate the full depth of the problem, lest they be driven to despair. The Christian doctrine of Christ as the "second Adam," as normative man, is thus a doctrine which hovers between natural and revealed religion. It belongs to natural religion in the sense that any rigorous analysis of the moral life of man will, partially disclose the tangents towards the eternal in all morality. It belongs to revealed religion because it is not possible, without faith, to follow these implications through to their final logical conclusion. Without faith the ethical life of man is always haunted by the sceptical reflection that "a living dog is better than a dead lion," [5] which is to say that all moral imperatives are limited by the survival impulse which lies at the foundation of historical existence.

III

THE RELATION OF CHRIST'S PERFECTION TO HISTORY

A complete analysis of the relation of Christ's perfection to history would result in a comprehensive statement of the Christian interpretation of history. Some aspects of this interpretation have already been considered and others remain to be discussed. It is nevertheless advisable and necessary to consider the most important characteristics of this interpretation in the present connection. Upon the basis of the Christian conviction that the *agape* of Christ is the disclosure of both the divine love which bears history and the human love which is history's "impossible possibility," one may define the main principles of the Christian interpretation of history. This can be done most simply by considering (*a*) The perfection of Christ in relation to innocency, or to the beginning of history; (*b*) The perfection of Christ in relation to mutual love or to the substance of history; and (*c*) The perfection of Christ in relation to eternal fulfillment, or the end of history

1. *The Perfection of Christ and Innocency*

The idea that Christ is the "essential" man, the perfect norm of human character, is expressed scripturally in the Pauline phrase that Christ is the "second Adam." [6] Christ's perfection reestablishes the

---

[5] Ecclesiastes 9:4.

[6] *Cf.* 1 Cor. 15:22 and Romans 5:12 ff. The actual phrase is used sparingly. But the whole New Testament consistently regards Christ as the final norm of human character. The Johannine prologue regards

virtue which Adam had before the fall. We have previously noted that Christian theology has difficulty in defining the perfection before the fall and that its definitions frequently border on the fantastic.[7] But the doctrine of the second Adam, when taken seriously, is a protection against these confusions and fantasies. Christian thought understands (even though it does not always realize the full implications of the doctrine) that it is not possible to define the lost perfection of Adam, the ideal possibilities of human life, except in terms drawn from the perfection of Christ. It is significant, however, that whenever it states this conviction it is forced into the corollary belief that the perfection of Christ not only reestablishes but exceeds the primitive perfection.[8]

To say that the innocency of Adam before the fall can be restored only in terms of the perfection of Christ is to assert that life *can approach its original innocency only by aspiring to its unlimited end.*

Christ as the historical manifestation of the divine *logos* which is the pattern of the whole creation.

[7] Vol. I, Ch. X.

[8] Irenæus is very fond of the idea that Christ "recapitulates Adam in Himself." He believed that the "plasm of the first man never lost the image of God," that Christ restored this image, that he is the "first man" walking once more upon the earth "at the end of a long line which was from the beginning," but that He exceeds the goodness of Adam before the Fall as perfection transcends innocency (*Against Heresies,* Book III, xix and xxiv).

Gregory of Nyssa describes salvation as being "restored to the fashion of the pure Adam, man attains the stature of the last, and becomes even higher than he was because he becomes deified." *The Great Catechism,* par. 37.

Thomas Aquinas asks the question whether if man had not sinned God would have become incarnate and answers in the affirmative, giving as the reason that in Christ "the last creature, *viz.,* man, is joined to the first principle: *viz.,* God." It belongs to God, he declares, "to manifest Himself by some infinite effect." If man had not sinned, he might have been united to God "in a natural manner as to an end"; but to be united to God in person exceeds the limits of the perfection of nature." (*Summa Theologica,* Part III, Q. 1, Art. 3.) The argument is somewhat artificial; but the underlying conception of unlimited possibilities for human nature is important.

The paradoxical character of the interpretation of history involved in this affirmation is already implied in the tentative confusion of defining Adam's state before the fall as both "perfection" and "innocency." Primeval goodness represents innocency in so far as it is a harmony of life with life which has not yet been disturbed or disrupted by freedom. This is why there is some justification for the thought which runs from Irenæus to Hegel, according to which the primeval goodness is a kind of prehistoric state from which both historic virtue and evil finally emerge. In Hegel's thought, the fall is a necessary prerequisite of virtue; for in it the individual comes to self-consciousness; and sinful self-assertion is a necessary prelude to the harmonious and loving relationship of life with life in terms of freedom. Innocency is thus the harmony of life with life without freedom. Mutual love is the harmony of life with life within terms of freedom; and sacrificial love is harmony of the soul with God beyond the limitations of sinful and finite history.

But it is impossible to use the symbol of primeval or prehistoric innocency exactly for the reason that the uniqueness of man consists in his freedom and self-transcendence; and there is therefore no possible historical state of man, however primitive the society, or however undeveloped the child, in which there is harmony without freedom. An inchoate freedom has already disturbed the harmony of nature. This is one reason why it is not possible to assign a historical locus to the perfection before the fall; [9] and also why the ideal possibility of life, symbolized in the first Adam, cannot be defined consistently as "innocency" but must always contain some connotation of "perfection."

In terms of social history there are no primitive societies in which life is related to life in the frictionless harmony of the ant-hill. We do know something about the character of primitive societies; a great deal more, at least, than the eighteenth century philosophers who used the idea of a "state of nature" as a foil for their interpretation of historical society. We know that on the one hand primitive

[9] *Cf.* Vol. I, Ch. X.

societies were held together by natural impulses of gregariousness and consanguinity and that in them the individual is never com-pletely emancipated from the "primeval we" consciousness.[10] In this characteristic, primitive society is organically related to animal herds and families. Its history must be regarded as prehistory. But on the other hand we know of no primitive society which does not adopt various stratagems to achieve the unity which the animal herd has by nature. Political artifice supplies some cement of its social cohesion.[11] The very strictness with which primitive custom binds the individual to the group and prohibits individual deviations from established norms (however capricious the origin of such norms may be) is the mark of the primitive community's fear of anarchy. The primitive community has no freedom in its social structure, not because the individual lacks an embryonic sense of freedom but precisely because he does have such a sense; and the community is not imaginative enough to deal with this freedom without suppressing it. This means that the brotherhood of even the most primitive community cannot be a completely "innocent" mutual relation of life to life. In so far as freedom has arisen to destroy the harmony of nature, the community seeks to suppress it for the sake of preserving the social unity. There are thus elements of tyranny in the social cohesion of the primitive community. Furthermore the relation of the primitive community to other communities are minimal at first; and when they develop they begin as conflict relations. The innocency of primitive life thus embodies the twin evils of the tyrannical

[10] *Cf.* Fritz Kunkel, *Charakter, Einzelmensch und Gruppe.*

[11] Henri Bergson regards the "static religion" of the primitive community as the "defensive reaction of nature against the dissolvent power of intelligence." But this religion is obviously not purely a stratagem of "nature." It represents a partly conscious and partly unconscious reaction to the situation created by human freedom and the religion is itself a product of that freedom. It is because there are conscious elements in the strategy of primitive religion that some interpreters are able to regard the priest as a conscious imperialist who manipulates religion for the purpose of gaining social power in the primitive community. See Bergson, *Two Sources of Morality and Religion,* p. 112.

subordination of life to life and the anarchic conflict of life with life.

Where there is history at all there is freedom; and where there is freedom there is sin. Yet the mutualities of the primitive community are inexact symbols of the loving relation of life to life. There is a certain validity in the perennial inclination of men to focus upon the past, whether in terms of the prehistory of the human race, or in terms of some imagined innocency and simplicity in the life of their own nation, as symbol of the brotherhood which they intend to achieve in history.

The same symbolic inexactness becomes apparent in analysing the innocency of a child. A child does not enter the world with a developed self-consciousness. It is held within the "primeval we" consciousness of the family. As its self-consciousness develops it reveals a self-centeredness which is akin to the self-sufficiency of the primitive community. But as it relates itself to other lives it also betrays impulses to dominate them, tendencies toward jealousy and envy which reveal its developing freedom, the anxieties which are concomitants of that freedom, and the usual abortive strategies intended to overcome these anxieties. A child is thus never completely innocent; and yet its innocency is an inexact symbol of the goodness towards which all life should move. This ambiguity of childlike innocency gives a certain plausibility to the contradictory approaches to the symbol of the child in Christian thought. Jesus consistently uses the symbol of childlike goodness for the perfection to be achieved in the Kingdom of God; while orthodox theologians, beginning with Augustine, regard childhood as involved in sinful corruption and as therefore in need of redemption.

The whole character of human history is thus implicitly defined in the Christian symbolism of the "first" and "second" Adam. To define the norm of history provisionally in terms of prehistoric innocency is to recognize that a part of the norm of man's historic existence lies in the harmonious relation of life to life in nature. To define it ultimately in terms of a sacrificial love which transcends history is to recognize the freedom of man over his own history without which historical creativity would be impossible. The actual historic achievements of man in history, his creation of larger and larger units of "brotherhood," the building of city-states, nations and empires, are always corrupted by the twin evils of the tyrannical subordination of life to life and the anarchic conflict of life with life. There is therefore no pure ethical norm in history; nor any hope of history gradually purifying itself so that it will achieve this norm. The "essential," the normative man, is thus a "God-man" whose sacrificial love seeks conformity with, and finds justification in, the divine and eternal *agape,* the ultimate and final harmony of life with life. Yet this eternal norm is not presented without a provisional glance at the primitive harmony of life in nature. The Christian faith appreciates what is valid in romantic primitivism as a part of the Christian affirmation of the goodness of creation. But the Christian interpretation of life and history has a too lively sense of the freedom which reaches into eternity to interpret life merely in terms of primitive innocency. To this innocency it relates the tragic perfection of the Cross.

2. *The Perfection of Christ and Possibilities of History*

We have previously noted[12] that the disclosure of the character of God and the meaning of history in Christ has a threefold relation to the conceptions of the meaningfulness of history as established in historic cultures and their Messianic hopes. It (*a*) completes what is incomplete in their apprehensions of meaning; (*b*) it clarifies obscurities which threaten the sense of meaning; and (*c*) it finally corrects falsifications of meaning which human egoism introduces into the sense of meaning by reason of its effort to comprehend the whole of life from an inadequate centre of comprehension.

The perfection of Christ, the transcendent *agape* symbolized in the Cross, has exactly this same threefold relation to the ethical realities of history. The ethical norm of history as comprehended by the "natural" resources of man, by his sober examination of the facts and requirements of life in human society, is mutual love. Man

[12] Vol. II, Ch. II.

knows both by experience and by the demand for coherence in his rational nature, that life ought not to be lived at cross purposes, that conflict within the self, and between the self and others, is an evil. In that sense love is the law of life according to the insights of natural religion and morality. It is normative, at any rate, in any religion or culture which takes socio-historic existence seriously and does not seek immediate flight into a non-historical·unity of life.

The sacrificial love of the Cross has a threefold relation of transcendence to these accepted norms of mutuality in history.

a. Sacrificial love (*agape*) completes the incompleteness of mutual love (*eros*), for the latter is always arrested by reason of the fact that it seeks to relate life to life from the standpoint of the self and for the sake of the self's own happiness. But a self which seeks to measure the possible reciprocity which its love towards another may elicit·is obviously not sufficiently free of preoccupation with self to lose itself in the life of the other. Considerations of prudence thus inevitably arrest the impulse towards, and concern for, the life of the other. Aristotle's chapters on friendship [13] reveal these difficulties in the logic of mutuality very clearly, though it is only fair to say that Aristotle has his own tangent towards transcendence; for in the final instance the friend in Aristotle's Ethics affirms the interests of the other for the sake not of some obvious advantage to the self but for the sake of the "happiness" of the self, in its transcendent integrity of spirit.

David Hume's discussion of the same problem [14] brings out the issue very clearly. He begins by envisaging a possible mutual love in history which would obviate all the defenses against, and restrictions upon, human egoism which systems of justice establish. "Suppose," he declares, "that the necessities of the human race continue as at present, yet the mind is so enlarged and so replete with friendship and generosity, that every man has the utmost tenderness for every man, and feels no more concern for his own interest than for

---

[13] In *Nicomachean Ethics,* Chs. VIII and IX.
[14] In *An Inquiry Concerning the Principle of Morals.* Sec. III, Part 1.

that of his fellows; it seems evident that the use of justice would, in that case, be suspended by an extensive benevolence; nor would the divisions and barriers of property and obligation have been thought of. Why should I find another by deed or promise to do me a good office when I know that he is already prompted by the strongest inclination to seek my happiness; and would of himself perform the desired service, except the hurt he thereby receives be greater than the benefit accruing me? . . . Why raise landmarks between my neighbor's field and mine, when my heart has made no division between our interests; but shares his joys and sorrows with the same force and vivacity as if originally my own? . . . And the whole human race would form only one family where all would live in common and everything be used freely without regard to property."

Here we have a vision of the perfect love of the Kingdom of God; and it is significant that Hume defines it partly in terms of actual achievements in family life. "We may observe," he declares, "that the case of families approaches to it; and the stronger the mutual benevolence is among individuals, the nearer it approaches, till distinctions of property be lost and confounded among them." But Hume does not understand the paradoxical relation between sacrificial and mutual love at all. He is certain that love can justify itself only "from its necessary use to the intercourse and social state of mankind." Therefore if it should not be able to validate itself by consequences of perfect mutuality; if the "returning or disguised selfishness of men" proved the "inconvenience" of a social state in which the self had no protection against the selfishness of others, even "imprudent fanatics" would be persuaded to return "anew to ideas of justice and of separate property."

Hume is quite right, of course, in insisting that social morality must seek the best possible harmony of life with life, given the egoism of man, and that men do, in fact, elaborate systems and restraints of justice to protect themselves and each other against human egoism. Even the "imprudent fanatics" of our own day, the Christian perfectionists, who think that *agape* is a simple possibility of history, avail themselves of such schemes of justice. But Hume does not understand that whatever achievements of mutuality actually exist in history have never been established by the cool calculations of social usefulness which he suggests. For such calculations would inevitably be too impressed by the peril of the "disguised selfishness" of men to encourage any venture of real brotherhood towards them.

History does contain an indefinite series of achievements in the organization of larger realms of brotherhood. The Biblical warning "if ye love them which love you, what reward have ye" [15] is certainly relevant to historic realities; for the failure of pure love to calculate possible reciprocal responses to it is the force which makes new ventures in brotherhood possible. The consequence of mutuality must, however, be the unintended rather than purposed consequence of the action. For it is too uncertain a consequence to encourage the venture towards the life of the other. According to the ethic of Jesus the actual motive of *agape* is always conformity to the will of God: "that ye may be children of your Father in heaven." Thus the harmonies which are actually achieved in history always are partly borrowed from the Eternal.[16]

[15] Mt. 5:46.
[16] Professor Anders Nygren's profound analysis of this problem in his *Agape and Eros* (S. P. C. K., London) has the virtue of revealing the contrast between the pure and disinterested love which the New Testament regards as normative and the egoistic element which is connoted in all love doctrines (*eros*) of classical thought. But he makes the contrast too absolute. Non-Christian conceptions of love do indeed seek to justify love from the standpoint of the happiness of the agent; but the freedom of man is such that he is not without some idea of the virtue of love which does not justify itself in terms of his own happiness. It is significant that Jesus does not regard the contrast between natural human love and the divine *agape* as absolute. He declares: "If ye then, being evil, know how to give good gifts unto your children, how much more shall your Father which is in heaven give good things to them that ask him" (Mt. 7:11).

Rudolf Bultmann makes the contrast between the demands of the Kingdom of God and the ethical possibilities of history even more absolute. He denies that the rigorous demands of the Sermon on the Mount

There are no limits to be set in history for the achievement of more universal brotherhood, for the development of more perfect and more inclusive mutual relations. All the characteristic hopes and aspirations of Renaissance and Enlightenment, of both secular and Christian liberalism are right at least in this, that they understand that side of the Christian doctrine which regards the *agape* of the Kingdom of God as a resource for infinite developments towards a more perfect brotherhood in history. The uneasy conscience of man over various forms of social injustice, over slavery and war, is an expression of the Christian feeling that history must move from the innocency of Adam to the perfection of Christ, from the harmony of life with life in unfree nature to the perfect love of the Kingdom of God. The vision of universal love expressed by St. Paul in the words: "There is neither Jew nor Greek, there is neither bond nor free, there is neither male nor female, for ye are all one in Christ Jesus," [17] is meant primarily for the church. But it cannot be denied that it is relevant to all social relationships. For the freedom of man makes it impossible to set any limits of race, sex, or social condition upon the brotherhood which may be achieved in history.

Even the purest form of *agape,* the love of the enemy and forgiveness towards the evil-doer, do not stand in contradiction to historical possibilities. Penal justice can achieve more and more imaginative forms; and these more imaginative and generous treatments of the evil-doer can be historically justified by the reclamation of the criminal. But they cannot be initiated purely by considerations of

---

have any relation to " 'the highest good' in the ethical sense." He declares that the "Kingdom of God is something miraculous, in fact absolute miracle, opposed to all the 'here and now; it is 'wholly other.' " (*Jesus and the Word,* pp. 35–37.) His insistence that the ethical injunctions of the New Testament have no relation to the observable ethical good of human experience but must be merely accepted in faith, may be regarded as excessive Hebraism and deficient in the Greek sense of the relation between God and the structural aspects of historic reality. His position is nicely refuted in the Johannine prologue in which Christ is regarded as the very foundation of the structures of history.

[17] Gal. 3:28.

their social value; for a considerable risk is always involved in such treatment. Furthermore every society will mix concern for the safety of society and sinful elements of vindictive passion with whatever elements of forgiving *agape* may be insinuated into its penological procedures. But there is no limit to the possible admixture of forgiving love in criminal justice, except of course the absolute limit that no society will ever deal with criminals in terms of pure forgiveness or achieve a perfect relation between justice and forgiveness.[18]

b. The Cross represents a transcendent perfection which clarifies obscurities of history and defines the limits of what is possible in historic development.

Every interpretation of human history which has some understanding of the transcendent norm of historical ethics is inclined to fall into the error of regarding the transcendent norm as a simple possibility. This error runs through the thought of most sectarian versions of Christianity and through the secularized forms of Christianity in the Renaissance and the Enlightenment. It is an error to which American liberal Protestantism has been particularly prone because sectarian and secular perfectionism have been compounded in this form of the Christian faith. Marxist apocalypticism also shares in this error. Whether by sanctifying grace (as in sectarian interpretations) or by the cumulative force of universal education (as in secular liberalism) or by a catastrophic reorganization of society (as in Marxism), it is believed possible to lift historic life to the plane upon which all distinctions between mutual love and disinterested and sacrificing love vanish. The Marxist version of this perfection, in which all rules of justice are transcended, is vividly

---

[18] W. Wiesner in his chapter in the Oxford Conference Report, *The Christian Faith and the Common Life,* presents a radical Lutheran version of the relation of forgiveness to the necessities of retributive justice and declares that they stand in contradiction to each other. There is as much truth, and as little, in this position as in the Tolstoyan perfectionism which imagines that there is a possibility of eliminating judge, jailor, and executioner from the historic schemes of retributive justice.

expressed by Lenin: "Every right," he declares, "is an application of the same measure to different people who are not the same and not equal to each other. This is why 'equal right' is really a violation of equality and an injustice. . . . Different people are not alike. One is strong and another weak. One is married and another not. . . . The first phase of communism can therefore still not produce justice and equality. Unjust differences in wealth will still exist; but the unjust exploitation of man by man will become impossible. . . . Immediately upon attainment of formal equality for all members of society . . . there will inevitably arise before humanity the question of going further from formal equality to real equality, *i.e.,* to realizing the rule: 'From each according to his ability and to each according to his need.' " [19]

This is a significant secular vision of the "Kingdom of God," where even the highest form of equal justice is transcended in an uncoerced and perfect mutuality. The Marxist finds such a vision plausible because he imagines that sinful egoism is derived merely from the class organization of society. The secular liberal finds similar visions plausible, primarily because he thinks that universal education will progressively universalize the mind until each person will be able (and willing?) to affirm the interests of others as much as his own. The sectarian and perfectionist Christian finds it plausible because he believes that sanctifying grace can destroy sin in fact as well as in principle. We shall have to deal with these errors more fully in subsequent chapters. In this context we need only to call attention to the fact that the Christian faith in its profoundest versions has never believed that the Cross would so change the very nature of historical existence that a more and more universal achievement of sacrificial love would finally transmute sacrificial love into successful mutual love, perfectly validated and by historical social consequences.

The New Testament never guarantees the historical success of the "strategy" of the Cross. Jesus warns his disciples against a too

[19] N. Lenin, *The State and Revolution,* Ch. 5, Par. iii and iv.

sanguine historical hope: "In this rejoice not, that the spirits are subject unto you; but rather rejoice because your names are written in heaven." [20] In that warning we have a telling refutation of the utopian corruptions of Christianity. Whatever the possibilities of success for *agape* in history (and there are possibilities of success because history cannot be at complete variance with its foundation) the final justification for the way of *agape* in the New Testament is never found in history. The motive to which Christ appeals is always the emulation of God or gratitude for the *agape* of God.

Thus the Cross clarifies the possibilities and limits of history and perennially refutes the pathetic illusions of those who usually deny the dimension of history which reaches into Eternity in one moment, and in the next dream of achieving an unconditioned perfection in history.

Since this possibility does not exist, it is not even right to insist that every action of the Christian must conform to *agape,* rather than to the norms of relative justice and mutual love by which life is maintained and conflicting interests are arbitrated in history. For as soon as the life and interest of others than the agent are involved in an action or policy, the sacrifice of those interests ceases to be "self-sacrifice." It may actually become an unjust betrayal of their interests. Failure to understand this simple fact and this paradoxical relation between individual and collective action has resulted in the unholy alliance between Christian perfectionism and cowardly counsels of political expediency in dealing with tyrants in our own day.

The preservation of cultures and civilizations is frequently possible only as individuals disregard their own success and failure and refuse to inquire too scrupulously into the possibilities or probabilities of maintaining their own life in a given course of action. Thus effective collective historical action depends to a considerable degree upon the individual's contempt for, or indifference to, his own fate; an indifference which is possible only if the individual possesses an

[20] Luke 10:20.

implicit or explicit faith in a dimension of existence which is deeper and higher than physical life and which makes it possible for him to confess: "Whether we live, we live unto the Lord; and whether we die, we die unto the Lord: whether we live therefore, or die, we are the Lord's." [21]

c. The Cross represents a perfection which contradicts the false pretensions of virtue in history and which reveals the contrast between man's sinful self-assertion and the divine *agape*.

Just as the Cross symbolizes the meaning of life which stands in contradiction to all conceptions of the "truth," seeking to complete the meaning of history from the inadequate centre of the hopes and ambitions of a particular nation or culture, so also it symbolizes the final goodness which stands in contradiction to all forms of human goodness in which self-assertion and love are compounded.

There are no forms of historical reality which do not contain this sinful admixture. There are no forms of remedial justice from which the egoistic element of vindictiveness has been completely purged. The coming decades of post-war reconstruction will offer us ample proof of this tragic fact. There are no political strategies for extending the realms of mutuality in the human community which remain immune to the egoistic corruption of imperialism. Every human community must be organized from a given centre of power; and that centre of power must try to be an impartial adjudicator of the interests of others even while it remains an interested and partial social force, individual or collective, international or intranational, among the many social forces which must be brought into an equilibrium. We cannot be complacent about this imperial corruption in all forms of political justice and social organization. The Cross is a constant source of contrition in regard to the corruption. But neither does history, even on its highest levels, achieve a purity which removes the contradiction between the divine *agape* and the egoistic element in the human community. That tragic aspect of history will be illumined anew when the world powers which have

[21] Romans 14:8.

defeated tyranny seek to organize the community of nations.[22] This is an aspect of historical reality which has been almost completely obscured by modern interpretations of history. Radical Reformation thought frequently emphasizes it to the exclusion of the other aspects we have considered. Recognition of this aspect of history has the distinction of being a unique Christian insight; for practically all other forms of interpreting history, whether classical or modern, whether mystical or legalistic, find some way of destroying the ultimate contradiction between the self-assertion of the human life and the divine *agape*.

IV

THE RELATION OF CHRIST'S PERFECTION TO ETERNITY

If the Christian doctrine of Christ as the "second Adam" refutes both the romantics, who think a return to primeval innocency possible, and the evolutionary optimists who think that history moves towards a perfection in which nature-history is transcended without ceasing to be grounded in nature, it also refutes the mystics who seek perfection by contemplation of, and final incorporation into, an eternity from which all vitalities and particularities of history have been subtracted. In Meister Eckhardt's heretical Christian mysticism, the goal of life is significantly unrelated to the innocency of Adam but is like the state of unity which preceded creation itself. "The poor man," he declares, "is not he who wants to do the will of God but he who lives in such a way as to be free of his own will and from the will of God, *even as he was when he was not.*"[1] In the slightly less heretical and more Christian mysticism of Jacob Boehme the unity, defined as perfection, is not placed in an eternity preceding creation. But the perfection of Adam in the created world

---

[22] The Christian answer to the problem of the perennial and inevitable character of this corruption will be considered in Chapters VIII and IX.

[1] *Meister Eckhardt* by Franz Peiffer, translated by D. de B. Evans, Vol. I, p. 220.

is defined as an androgynic unity which is free of the tension and disunity of sexual differentiation. In common with Platonism and Hellenic Christianity, Boehme believes that bisexuality is a consequence of sin. Furthermore he thinks that Adam's perfection must have meant that he had a body which was "without intestines and without stomach," a rather vivid symbol of the mystic aversion to the physical basis of life.[2]

There is a tendency in all forms of rationalism and mysticism, including Christian rationalism and mysticism, to define perfection in history as the contemplation of the Eternal, rather than as a love which co-ordinates will to will under the will of God; and to define the perfection which transcends history as absorption into an Eternal Logos or an eternal unity, purer than *Logos* and form itself. Even the naturalistic Aristotle defines the ultimate good as the contemplation of eternal perfection,[3] and the Aristotelian and Platonic influence in medieval Christianity has frequently prompted it to define the perfection towards which life must move as contemplation rather than loving action; that is, to make *gnosis* rather than *agape* the final norm.

It is important to realize that the Christian doctrine of an incarnated *Logos* who becomes the "second Adam" is as rigorously opposed to dualistic doctrines which seek escape from history, as to romantic and naturalistic ones, in which history fulfills itself too simply. Man is neither a unity without freedom, nor freedom without vitality. Rooted in the necessities and limitations of nature he has a freedom which can only find its final security in God. Significantly St. Paul distinguishes love as sharply from *gnosis* as from law. To distinguish it from law is to emphasize the freedom of man, for which no law can be the final norm. To distinguish it from *gnosis* is to emphasize the difference between a contemplation of the eternal

---

[2] *Cf.* Ernst Benz, *Der Vollkommene Mensch nach Jacob Boehme*, pp. 51–70. Benz calls attention to the fact that the mystic aversion towards biological function rather justifies Nietzsche's remark that man's abdomen might well dissuade him from thinking himself a God.

[3] *Nicomachean Ethics*, Bk. X, vii, 7 and 9.

and a vital emulation of the divine love in which all the emotions and volitions of life are included.[4] The God whom Christians worship reveals his majesty and holiness not in eternal disinterestedness but in suffering love. And the moral perfection, which the New Testament regards as normative, transcends history not as thought transcends action but as suffering love transcends mutual love. It is an act rather than a thought which sets the Christ above history, and being an act, it is more indubitably in history than a mere thought.

In the Pauline conception there is a legitimate *gnosis,* a knowledge of God "in part," which is transcended in the consummation when "I shall know even as I am known."[5] But the elements in the historical which really abide are "faith, hope, and love, and the greatest of these is love."

While the Christian conception of love has had too great an authority in the church to allow any but heretical mystics, such as Eckhardt, to transmute the idea of ultimate perfection into one of pure contemplation, Christianity nevertheless has difficulty in preserving the Biblical conception of love against mystical and rationalistic tendencies to interpret this love in such a way that it becomes purely the love towards God and ceases to be related to brotherhood and community in history. If sectarian and liberal versions of Christianity are inclined to forget that the perfection of Christ transcends history, the mystical tradition in medieval Christianity forgets that the perfection of love revealed in Christ is relevant to history.

"There is nothing in the world to be compared with God," de-

---

[4] The *locus classicus* of the Pauline rejection of *gnosis* is in 1 Cor. 13. "Though I speak with the tongues of men and of angels and . . . though I have the gift of prophecy and understand all mysteries and all knowledge . . . and have not love, it profiteth me nothing." The argument is probably directed particularly against the *gnosis* promised in the mystery cults; but it is equally valid against gnosticism in the broader sense, which would include emancipations from evil promised in all forms of rationalism and mysticism.

[5] 1 Cor. 13:12.

clares St. John of the Cross, "and he who loves any other thing together with Him wrongs Him." [6] This sentiment clearly contradicts Christ's own interpretation of the love commandment, with its affirmation that the "second" commandment, enjoining the love of the neighbour, is "like unto" the first, which enjoins love of God. This medieval mystic in whom the mystical version of Christianity is expressed in the most classic form, goes so far as to exclude the love of the neighbour specifically from the ultimate perfection. He writes: "As long as the soul has not attained unto the state of union of which I speak, it is good that it should exercise itself in love, in the active as well as the contemplative life. But once it is established there it is no longer suitable that it should occupy itself with other works or with exterior exercises which might raise the slightest possible obstacle to its life of love with God, and I do not even except those works most relevant to God's service." [7]

Significantly this logic drives the great mystic into a virtual dualism in which the innocency of Adam, the essential goodness of the created world, is completely obscured as a relevant truth, and the final perfection of man becomes identical with a final absorption into the divine. St. John of the Cross declares: "For since the soul has been made one thing with God it is after a certain manner God by participation; for though this is not so as perfectly as in the next life, the soul is, as it were, the shadow of God. And since the soul by means of this substantial transformation is the shadow of God, it does in and through God that which He does through Himself in the soul, *in the same way as he does it.*" [8]

Though Catholic mysticism exceeds the limits usually maintained by a Catholic rationalism in this emphasis, the renowned modern neo-Thomist, Jacques Maritain, is probably not wrong in declaring that there is no contradiction between anything implied by St. Thomas and more explicitly asserted by St. John of the Cross. Mari-

---

[6] *Ascent of Mount Carmel*, Bk. I, v. 4.
[7] St. John of the Cross, *Canticles* 2d redaction, str. 28.
[8] *Canticles,* str. 38.

tain himself speaks of the mystical experience as proving that the soul can "break through the entanglements of created things and establish itself in the nudity of spirit." [9]

The Biblical dialectic which is imperiled, if not destroyed, by this type of Christian thought is succinctly expressed in the words of St. Paul in which he admonishes the faithful to "walk worthy of the vocation wherewith ye are called, with all lowliness and meekness, with long suffering, forbearing one another in love, endeavouring to keep the unity of the Spirit in the bond of peace." He justifies this admonition by the observation that there "is one God and Father of all, who is above all, and through all and in you all," in other words by an affirmation of the basic Christian belief in the transcendence of God over, and His immanence in, the world. The dialectic is strengthened still further by attributing the grace of unity to the ascended Lord but with the observation "that He that ascended what is it but that he also descended first into the lower parts of the earth? He that descended is the same also that ascended up far above all heavens, that he might fill all things." [10] In this Pauline statement the Biblical conception of the relation of history to the perfection of Christ is stated symbolically in very clear terms. It is a conception which is constantly imperiled by theories which either place the norm of history too simply within history or which conceive of an eternal perfection as irrelevant to history and achieved only when thought transcends action, or when mystical consciousness transcends thought; and when the soul, freed of will and impulse, of distractions and responsibilities, contemplates the eternal.

These mystical heresies reveal by contrast to what degree the Christian conception of the love of Christ is ethically normative in Christian life because of the prior conception of the character of God, as revealed in Christ. The God of Christian revelation is not disengaged from, but engaged in, the world by His most majestic attributes; it is consequently not the highest perfection for man to achieve a unity of being from which all natural and historical

---

[9] *Degrees of Knowledge*, p. 394.   [10] Eph. 4:1–10.

vitalities have been subtracted. The highest unity is a harmony of love in which the self relates itself in its freedom to other selves in their freedom under the will of God.

v

SUMMARY

An analysis of the full implications of the Christian doctrine of the "second Adam" and the perfection of Christ yields principles for interpreting historical reality which illumine, and are validated by, the facts of history. The paradoxical relation of perfection to innocency, to maturity and to eternity comprehended in terms of the relation of the Cross to history, illumines all the complex relations of history.

The state of innocency towards which the Christian doctrine of perfection casts a provisional glance is a state of nature or prehistory in which the harmony of life with life, as nature knows it, has not yet been broken. In this state neither the individual nor the community has achieved sufficient freedom over historical process to be "anxious" or insecure, or to be tempted by this insecurity to the abortive strategies of sin. Yet, in so far as human history knows no absolute state of nature, it is not possible to find any such locus of innocency in the life of either the individual or the race.

As freedom develops, both good and evil develop with it. The innocent state of trust develops into the anxieties and fears of free dom; and these prompt the individual and the community to seek an unjust security at the expense of others. On the other hand it is possible that the same freedom may prompt larger and larger structures of brotherhood in human society. This brotherly relation of life with life is most basically the "law of life." It alone does justice to the freedom of the human spirit and the mutual dependence of men upon each other, their necessity of fulfilling themselves in each other.

There is, however, no development towards larger realms of brotherhood without a corresponding development of the imperial cor-

ruption of brotherhood. There is, therefore, no historical development which gradually eliminates those sinful corruptions of brotherhood which stand in contradiction to the law of love. The law of
love is, therefore, not a norm of history, in the sense that historical
experience justifies it. Historical experience justifies more complex
social strategies in which the self, individual and collective, seeks
both to preserve its life and to relate it harmoniously to other lives.
But such strategies of mutual love and of systems of justice cannot
maintain themselves without inspiration from a deeper dimension
of history. A strategy of brotherhood which has no other resource
but historical experience degenerates from mutuality to a prudent
regard for the interests of the self; and from the impulse towards
community to an acceptance of the survival impulse as ethically
normative.

The *agape,* the sacrificial love, which is for Christian faith revealed upon the Cross, has its primary justification in an "essential
reality" which transcends the realities of history, namely, the character of God. It does not expect an immediate or historical validation but looks towards some ultimate consummation of life and history. On the other hand the Christian doctrine of Creation does not
set the eternal and divine into absolute contradiction to the temporal and the historical. There are, therefore, validations of *agape* in
actual history, in so far as concern for the other actually elicits a
reciprocal response.

This interpretation of the possibilities and limits of history is the
fruit of natural experience and a natural (rational) analysis of experience. For any rigorous examination of the problems of man in
nature-history clearly reveals that history points beyond itself and
that it does so by reason of the freedom and transcendence of the
human spirit. It is never completely contained in, or satisfied by, the
historical-natural process, no matter to what level this process may
rise.

But this interpretation is the fruit of faith and revelation in so far
as there is no experience which points irrefutably to the particular

divine ground and end of history which Christian faith discerns in Christ and the Cross. In the realm of ethics as in the realm of truth, the revelation of Christ is foolishness, in the sense that experience does not lead us to expect or anticipate the answer which it makes to the ethical problem. But it is "wisdom to them that are called" in the sense that, once accepted, it becomes an adequate principle for interpreting the ethical problem in history. It is the only principle of interpretation which does justice to the two factors in the human situation: Man's involvement in natural process, including the imperative character of his natural impulse of survival; and his transcendence over natural process, including his uneasy conscience over the fact that the survival impulse should play so dominant a role in all his ethical calculations.

CHAPTER IV

WISDOM, GRACE AND POWER
(THE FULFILLMENT OF HISTORY)

EVERY FACET of the Christian revelation, whether of the relation of God to history, or of the relation of man to the eternal, points to the impossibility of man fulfilling the true meaning of his life and reveals sin to be primarily derived from his abortive efforts to do so. The Christian gospel nevertheless enters the world with the proclamation that in Christ both "wisdom" and "power" are available to man; which is to say that not only has the true meaning of life been disclosed but also that resources have been made available to fulfill that meaning.[1] In Him the faithful find not only "truth" but "grace."[2]

The whole of Christian history is filled with various efforts to relate these two propositions of the Christian faith to each other, in such a way that the one will not contradict the other. These efforts are never purely academic; for the two sides of the gospel correspond to two aspects of historic reality. The two emphases are contained in the double connotation of the word "grace" in the New Testament. Grace represents on the one hand the mercy and forgiveness of God by which He completes what man cannot complete

[1] Cf. 1 Cor. 4:19: "The Kingdom of God is not in word but in power."
[2] John 1:17.

98

and overcomes the sinful elements in all of man's achievements. Grace is the power of God over man. Grace is on the other hand the power of God in man; it represents an accession of resources, which man does not have of himself, enabling him to become what he truly ought to be. It is synonymous with the gift of the "Holy Spirit." The Spirit is not merely, as in idealistic and mystical thought, the highest development of the human spirit. He is not identical with the most universal and transcendent levels of the human mind and consciousness. The Holy Spirit is the spirit of God indwelling in man. But this indwelling Spirit never means a destruction of human self-hood. There is therefore a degree of compatibility and continuity between human self-hood and the Holy Spirit. Yet the Holy Spirit is never a mere extension of man's spirit or identical with its purity and unity in the deepest or highest levels of consciousness. In that sense all Christian doctrines of "grace" and "Spirit" contradict mystical and idealistic theories of fulfillment.

The conception in Christian thought of a fulfillment and completion of life by resources which are not man's own, prevents Christian ideas of fulfillment by grace from standing in contradiction to the more fundamental conviction that human life and history cannot complete themselves; and that sin is synonymous with abortive efforts to complete them. It is furthermore in consistent relation with the proposition that man perceives the completeness beyond his incompleteness and the holiness beyond his sin only by faith. For if it is possible to become aware of the limits of human possibilities by a faith which apprehends the revelation of God from beyond those limits, it must also be possible to lay hold of the resources of God, beyond human limits, by faith. And this certainly is reinforced by the character of the Christian revelation, according to which God is not a supernal perfection to which man aspires, but has resources of love, wisdom and power, which come down to man. The very apprehension of the "wisdom of God," the completion of the structure of meaning by faith, must have connotations of "power" in it. For if we understand the possibilities and limits

[margin, handwritten:] Grace aids man in doing what is impossible for man — it overcomes the sinful elements in all of man's achievements.

Grace synonomous with Holy Spirit.

of life from beyond ourselves, this understanding has some potentialities of fulfilling the meaning of life. It breaks the egoistic and
self-centred forms of fulfillment, by which the wholesome development of man is always arrested and corrupted. For this reason it is
not possible to give a fully logical or exactly chronological account
of the relation of faith to repentance, of the apprehension of truth
which is beyond our comprehension to the shattering of the self by
a power from beyond ourself. If a man does not know the truth
about God, who is more than an extension of his self (a truth to
be known only by faith), he cannot repent of the premature and
self-centred completion of his life around a partial and inadequate
centre. But it can be, and has been, argued with equal cogency, that
without repentance, that is, without the shattering of the self-centred self, man is too much his own god to feel the need of, or to
have the capacity for, knowing the true God. The invasion of the
self from beyond the self is therefore an invasion of both "wisdom"
and "power," of both "truth" and "grace." The relation of insight
to will, of wisdom to power in this experience is too intricate to be
subject to precise analysis.

Yet whatever "newness of life" flows from the experience of repentance and faith is, when governed by true Christian faith, conscious of a continued incompleteness and a certain persistence of
the strategy of sin. For this reason the peace which follows conversion is never purely the contentment of achievement. It is always,
in part, the peace which comes from the knowledge of forgiveness.

II

THE BIBLICAL DOCTRINE OF GRACE

When we turn to the New Testament doctrine of grace, more particularly to the Pauline interpretation of it, it becomes apparent that
both facets of the experience of grace—the conquest of sin in the
heart of man on the one hand, and the merciful power of God over
the sin which is never entirely overcome in any human heart, on
the other—are fully expressed in the Pauline doctrine. The relation

between them is not always made explicit. It is therefore possible for the various Christian traditions, which emphasize the one or the other facet of grace, to find support in this or that Scriptural text. In this way St. Paul's thought has become the fountain source of both perfectionist theories of grace and of the protest of Reformation thought against them.[1]

Schlatter describes the twofold aspect of the Pauline experience of grace with the right circumspection and impartiality: "He has a sense of sin, as including and comprehending all his actions, and yet at the same time and in the same consciousness he has a good conscience which is at peace with itself and is conscious of the normality of its actions. Both of these aspects of his consciousness are rooted and united in the awareness of the divine forgiveness and the sense of a righteousness which divine grace has imparted."[2]

There are texts in the Pauline epistles which lean to the one or the other side of the interpretation of grace. The contrast between the old life and the new is described again and again in terms which seem to make an absolute [3] distinction between the two

But it must be observed at once that some of the very assertions

---

[1] Paul Wernle observes quite correctly: "All gnostic and methodistic sects which have insisted upon or sought after the sinlessness of the redeemed, have merely exaggerated a true element in the Pauline tradition." *Der Christ und die Suende bei Paulus,* p. 24.

[2] A. Schlatter, *Der Glaube im Neuen Testament,* p. 503.

[3] Cf. *inter alia*: Romans 6:8 ff. "Now if we be dead with Christ we believe that we shall also live with him. Knowing that Christ, being raised from the dead, dieth no more; death hath no more dominion over him. For in that he died, he died unto sin once; but in that he liveth he liveth unto God. Likewise reckon yourselves dead indeed unto sin but alive unto God through Jesus Christ our Lord." The death and resurrection of Christ as symbolic of the death of sin and the resurrection of the new life of righteousness is a perennial theme in Pauline thought.

Romans 8:6. "To be carnally minded is death; but to be spiritually minded is life and peace."

Romans 6:22. "But now, being made free from sin and become servants to God, ye have your fruit unto holiness and the end everlasting life."

Eph. 4:24. "That ye put on the new man, which after God is created in righteousness and true holiness."

which lend themselves to perfectionist interpretations are immediately followed by injunctions which cast doubt upon such an exposition. These injunctions declare in effect: you are now sinless. Therefore you must not sin any more. The exhortation implies that the original statements have a slightly different meaning than their obvious connotation. They really mean: self-love has been destroyed in principle in your life. See to it now that the new principle of devotion to God in Christ is actualized in your life.[4] The qualifying statements, following immediately upon affirmations which suggest, or might suggest, complete holiness, raise the question whether St. Paul's conception of holiness ever connotes complete freedom from sin. He does undoubtedly maintain that there is a radical difference between "carnal-mindedness" and "spiritual-mindedness" and this difference might be defined as the contrast between the life which is governed by the *principle* of self-centredness and one which is governed by the *principle* of devotion and obedience to God. But his injunction to the sinless, not to sin any more, implies that he understands the possibility of sinning for those who have broken with sin in principle.[5]

[4] Cf. *inter alia*: Romans 6:11-12. "Likewise reckon ye also yourselves to be dead indeed unto sin . . . *let not sin therefore reign* in your mortal body."

In Eph. 4: 17-32, the logic of the Christian life is said to demand that "ye henceforth walk not as the other Gentiles walk, in the vanity of their mind." The fact that they have renounced sin in principle demands that they break with it in fact, and the redeemed are admonished to conquer very obvious sins: "Let him that stole steal no more," etc.

Eph. 5:8: "For ye were sometimes darkness but now are ye light in the Lord: walk as children of the light."

Gal. 5:24-26: "And they that are Christ's have crucified the flesh with the affections and lusts. If we live in the spirit, *let us also walk* in the spirit. Let us not be desirous of vainglory, provoking one another, envying one another."

[5] The Johannine epistles state the idea of sinlessness more unqualifiedly and have, therefore, always been favorite sources of proof texts for sanctificationist doctrines, particularly in the Eastern church. Cf. 1 John 3:6: "Whosoever abideth in him sinneth not." 1 John 3:9: "Who-

This interpretation is reinforced by the well-known Pauline disavowal of perfection: "Not as though I had already attained, either
were already perfect; but I follow after, if that I may apprehend
that for which also I am apprehended of Christ Jesus," [6] in which
the newness of life in principle is regarded as a gift, which
must subsequently be realized progressively in volition and aspira-
tion.

These qualifications make it quite apparent that there are no
essential contradictions in Pauline thought, however much the emphasis may shift from one to the other aspect of grace. The insistence
upon the radical difference between the old and the new life is not
in conflict with what must be regarded as the primary Pauline emphasis; his idea of grace as "justification," as the assurance of divine
forgiveness. On this side of Pauline thought the disavowal of perfection is explicit and precise. The very burden of the Pauline message is that there is no peace in our own righteousness. The final
peace of the soul is gained on the one hand by the assurance of
divine forgiveness; and on the other hand by "faith." The Christ
who is apprehended by faith, *i.e.* to whom the soul is obedient in
principle, "imputes" his righteousness to it. It is not an actual possession except "by faith." [7]

[Handwritten margin note: Two elements in Paul: 1. Insufficiency of our own righteousness. 2. Assurance of divine forgiveness.]

---

soever is born of God doth not commit sin; for his seed remaineth with
him; and he can not sin because he is born of God." The Johannine
literature asserts sinlessness of actual acts because its conception of the
new life, influenced by Hellenistic thought, connotes an almost metaphysical distinction between the new and the old life. Yet even here we
find important reservations. Cf. *inter alia*: 1 John 1:8: "If we say we
have no sin we deceive ourselves and the truth is not in us."

[6] Phil. 3:12.

[7] Cf. *inter alia*: Romans 5:1: "Therefore being justified by faith, we
have peace with God, through our Lord Jesus Christ."
Romans 3:22 ff.: "There is no difference: for all have sinned and come
short of the glory of God; being justified freely by his grace through the
redemption that is in Christ Jesus, whom God has set forth as a propitiation through faith in his blood, to declare his righteousness for the
remission of sins that are past, through the forbearance of God."
Eph. 2:8: "For by grace are ye saved through faith. . . . It is the

This doctrine of the "imputation of righteousness" has always been offensive to moralistic interpreters of Christian faith. They have made much of the non-moral character of such imputation. But forgiveness, as a form of love which is beyond good and evil, is bound to be offensive to pure moralists. The Pauline doctrine really contains the whole Christian conception of God's relation to human history. It recognizes the sinful corruption in human life on every level of goodness. It knows that the pride of sin is greatest when men claim to have conquered sin completely. ("Not of works lest any man should boast.") It proclaims no sentimentalized version of the divine mercy. It is possible to appropriate this mercy only through the Christ, whose sufferings disclose the wrath of God against sin, and whose perfection as man is accepted as normative for the believer, by the same faith which sees in Him, particularly His Cross, the revelation of the mystery of the divine mercy triumphing over, without annulling, the divine wrath. The doctrine is, of course, subject to corruption, and has been corrupted innumerable times in the Christian ages. It can become a vehicle of complacency, prompting men to "continue in sin that grace may abound." It may be interpreted in juridical and legalistic terms in such a way that it never conveys the religious truth which strikes man in the very centre of his spiritual being. But all this does not change the profundity of the conception of "justification by faith" and its complete conformity with the conception of life, God and history as we have it in the gospels.

There is a possibility that the balance which St. Paul maintains between the two facets of the experience of grace—the power of

---

gift of God, not of works, lest any man should boast. For we are his workmanship, created in Christ Jesus unto good works."

Gal. 5:4: "Christ is become of no effect unto you, whosoever of you are justified by the law; ye are fallen from grace."

Phil. 3:8–11: "I have suffered the loss of all things, and . . . do count them but dung . . . that I may win Christ, and be found in him not having my own righteousness, which is of the law, but that which is through the faith of Christ, the righteousness which is of God by faith."

God within the life of man, making for newness of life, and the power of God's love over man, annulling his sin by His mercy—is slightly imperiled in some Pauline ideas, which are strongly influenced by his polemic against Jewish legalism. In these he suggests that the forgiveness of sins applies particularly to the sins of the past [8] and seems to identify the "works" of the law which justify no man, particularly with the works of the historic Jewish law.[9]

The Pauline emphasis upon forgiveness of past sins lies at the basis of the whole Catholic-Medieval interpretation of the relation of justification and sanctification, in which justification is made the prelude of subsequent sanctification, and in which the complex and paradoxical relation between the two is imperiled or destroyed, thus leading to a new form of self-righteousness. Possibly, St. Paul did not carry his own thought through to its ultimate conclusion and ages of Christian experience were required to disclose that a righteousness "by grace" may lead to new forms of Pharisaism if it does not recognize that forgiveness is as necessary at the end as at the beginning of the Christian life.

The profound confession of St. Paul in Romans 7 has sometimes been used to refute the interpretation of Pauline thought, according to which justification applies only to past sins in the state before conversion. These refutations argue that a man who confesses to such inner tensions as are expressed in the words: "For the good that I would I do not: but the evil which I would not, that I do," could certainly not have believed that the forgiveness of sins applied only to sins before conversion. The difficulty with this refutation is that there is no certainty that St. Paul intended to describe his spiritual state after conversion in the words of Romans 7. Whether this con-

---

[8] *Cf.* Romans 3:24: "Being justified freely by His grace through the redemption that is in Christ Jesus: whom God hath set forth to be a propitiation . . . for the remission of sins *that are past.*"

[9] Gal. 3:11: "But that no man is justified by the law in the sight of God it is evident: for the just shall live by faith."

Romans 3:20: "Therefore by the deeds of the law there shall no flesh be justified in his sight; for by the law is the knowledge of sin."

fession was intended to be purely retrospective, or was meant to express a tension which even the redeemed experience, is an exegetical problem which is answered according to previous doctrinal presuppositions. With our own doctrinal preconceptions of the problem involved we cannot believe St. Paul meant to confine his confession to the state before conversion. The record of Christian history proves that no living man is ever completely emancipated from the inner contradictions, which the chapter so eloquently portrays.

As for the suggestion that St. Paul meant to confine the "deeds of the law," which failed to justify, merely to the Jewish law and suggested thereby that the righteousness of grace fulfilled a more perfect law, namely the law of love, this theory is refuted by the fact that contrast in the relevant passages is between "law" and "faith." Undoubtedly St. Paul was thinking particularly of Jewish legalism, when he elaborated the thesis that law, of itself, was a curse, since no man fulfilled it; and that "deeds of the law" were a source of delusion, since they pretended to a perfection which no man could achieve. But there is no reason why the condemnation of legalistic righteousness should be interpreted in the thought of St. Paul as applying only to the explicit Jewish law. He, himself, extends the whole principle of the law beyond the Jewish legal and moral tradition and asserts that "when the Gentiles, which have not the law, do by nature the things contained in the law, these, having not the law, are a law unto themselves." [10]

It is true of course that a higher than the traditional law is implied in the "gospel." The New Testament is critical of the law not only because it does not furnish the resources to fulfill its own demands, but also because its demands are not high enough and do not exhaust the possibilities of good in any given situation. These possibilities are comprehended only in the law of love, which transcends and fulfills all law. But this is not the point which St. Paul is

[10] Romans 2:14. This argument significantly precedes the discussion of the relation of "law" and "faith" in Romans 3.

making when he criticizes the deeds of the law, though it may be
implied in the criticism. It may be implied because the keeping of
the law may give men a false sense of virtue and obscure the unrighteousness of those who are legally righteous.

A survey of Pauline thought must thus lead to the conclusion
that there is no contradiction in his elaboration of the doctrine of
grace. There is, at least, no final contradiction. There is, on the
contrary, a profound understanding of the complexities of the
spiritual life of man with its possibilities of genuine newness of
life in "love, joy and peace" for those who have broken with self-
love in principle; and yet of the possibility of sin even on this new
level of righteousness.

[margin handwritten note: Pauline thought realizes the spiritual possibilities of man as a saved individual and yet the possibility of sin in this new state]

III

GRACE AS POWER IN, AND AS MERCY TOWARDS, MAN

An analysis of the relation of grace as power and grace as pardon
in Biblical thought, though it may prove Biblical doctrine to be
essentially consistent, will hardly convince modern man of the relevance of the doctrine. All modern theories of human nature whether
Christian, semi-Christian or non-Christian, have arrived at simpler
solutions for the moral problem. These simpler solutions are, broadly
speaking, comprehended in the one strategy of increasing the power
and the range of mind and reason against the narrower impulses of
the body. It is necessary therefore to apply the Biblical doctrine to
the facts of experience in order to establish its relevance. This can
be done most conveniently in terms of the application of a very
comprehensive and profound Pauline text to the moral and spiritual
experience of men: "I am crucified with Christ: nevertheless I live;
yet not I, but Christ liveth in me: and the life which I now live in
the flesh I live by the faith of the Son of God who loved me, and
gave himself for me." [1]

[1] Gal. 2:20.

It will be well to consider the implications of this description of the process of regeneration in order:

1. *"I am Crucified with Christ"*

We have previously noted that St. Paul is fond of interpreting the destruction of the old life and the birth of the new in the symbolism of the death and resurrection of Christ. The first assertion of his interpretation is that the old, the sinful self, the self which is centred in itself, must be "crucified." It must be shattered and destroyed. It cannot be redeemed merely by extending the range of mind against the inertia of the body. The Christian doctrine of grace stands in juxtaposition to the Christian doctrine of original sin and has meaning only if the latter is an accurate description of the actual facts of human experience. It will not be necessary to reconsider this doctrine here.[2] But it may be helpful to restate the human situation very briefly in terms of the doctrine. The plight of the self is that it cannot do the good that it intends.[3] The self in action seems impotent to conform its actions to the requirements of its essential being, as seen by the self in contemplation. The self is so created in freedom that it cannot realize itself within itself. It can only realize itself in loving relation to its fellows. Love is the law of its being. But in practice it is always betrayed into self-love. It comprehends the world and human relations from itself as the centre. It cannot, by willing to do so, strengthen the will to do good. This weakness is partly due to finiteness. The propulsive powers of the self, with its natural survival impulse, do not suffice to fulfill the obligations which the self as free spirit discerned. But the weakness is not merely one of "nature." It is also spiritual. The self never follows its "natural" self-interest without pretending to be obedient to obligations beyond itself. It transcends its own interests too much

[2] We have sought to do this in Vol. I, Chs. VII–IX.
[3] "For to will is present with me: but how to perform that which is good I find not." Romans 7:18.

to be able to serve them without disguising them in loftier pretensions. This is the covert dishonesty and spiritual confusion which is always involved in the self's undue devotion to itself.[4]

The self in this state of preoccupation with itself must be "broken" and "shattered" or, in the Pauline phrase, "crucified." It cannot be saved merely by being enlightened. It is a unity and therefore cannot be drawn out of itself merely by extending its perspective upon interests beyond itself. If it remains self-centred, it merely uses its wider perspective to bring more lives and interests under the dominion of its will-to-power. The necessity of its being shattered at the very centre of its being gives perennial validity to the strategy of evangelistic sects, which seek to induce the crisis of conversion.[5] The self is shattered whenever it is confronted by the power and holiness of God and becomes genuinely conscious of the real source and centre of all life. In Christian faith Christ mediates the confrontation of the self by God; for it is in Christ that the vague sense of the divine, which human life never loses, is crystallized into a revelation of a divine mercy and judgment. In that revelation fear of judgment and hope of mercy are so mingled that despair induces repentance and repentance hope.[6]

[margin notes: The self-centered self must be broken or shattered   The self is shattered by confrontation with God, through Christ.]

[4] Described by St. Paul in the words: "Their foolish heart was darkened." Romans 1:21.

The Augustinian definition of the plight of the self as a "defect of the will" is correct in pointing to the necessity of an accession of power from beyond the self; but it is incorrect, or at least subject to misinterpretation, in so far as it suggests mere weakness, rather than spiritual confusion as the cause of the vicious circle of self-centredness.

[5] There is of course no absolute necessity for a single crisis. The shattering of the self is a perennial process and occurs in every spiritual experience in which the self is confronted with the claims of God, and becomes conscious of its sinful, self-centred state.

[6] While Christians rightly believe that all truth necessary for such a spiritual experience is mediated only through the revelation in Christ, they must guard against the assumption that only those who know Christ "after the flesh," that is, in the actual historical revelation, are capable of such a conversion. A "hidden Christ" operates in history.

2. *"Nevertheless I Live"*

The Christian experience of the new life is an experience of a new selfhood. The new self is more truly a real self because the vicious circle of self-centredness has been broken. The self lives in and for others, in the general orientation of loyalty to, and love of, God; who alone can do justice to the freedom of the self over all partial interests and values. This new self is the real self; for the self is infinitely self-transcendent; and any premature centring of itself around its own interests, individually or collectively, destroys and corrupts its freedom.

The possibility of a reconstruction of the self is felt to be the consequence of "power" and "grace" from beyond itself because the true analysis of the plight of the self revealed it to be due to impotence rather than to lack of knowledge. The current and contemporary ideas of salvation by knowledge (even as the gnostic ways of salvation in the ancient world) rest upon a dualistic interpretation of human personality, which separates mind from body, and spirit from nature. They obscure the unity of selfhood in all its vital and rational processes. Wherever this dualism prevails "spirit" is devitalized, and physical life is despiritualized.

The assertion, "nevertheless I live," may be taken to refute two alternative schemes of salvation. In the one the self is indeed invaded by "spirit" as "power" but it is not the "Holy Spirit" and therefore it destroys the self. In the other the spirit of the self seeks to extend itself into its most universal and abstract form until all power, and ultimately the self itself, is lost.

The possession of the self by something less than the "Holy Spirit" means that it is possible for the self to be partly fulfilled and partly destroyed by its submission to a power and spirit which is greater than the self in its empiric reality but not great enough to do justice

---

And there is always the possibility that those who do not know the historical revelation may achieve a more genuine repentance and humility than those who do. If this is not kept in mind the Christian faith easily becomes a new vehicle of pride.

to the self in its ultimate freedom. Such spirit can be most simply defined as demonic. The most striking, contemporary form of it is a religious nationalism in which race and nation assume the eminence of God and demand unconditioned devotion. This absolute claim for something which is not absolute identifies the possessing spirit as "demonic"; for it is the nature of demons to make pretensions of divinity; just as the devil "fell" because he sought the place of God.[7] The invasion and possession of the self by spirit, which is not the Holy Spirit, produces a spurious sense of transfiguration. The self is now no longer the little and narrow self, but the larger collective self of race or nation. But the real self is destroyed. The real self has a height of spiritual freedom which reaches beyond race and nation and which is closer to the eternal than the more earthbound collective entities of man's history. Such demonic possession therefore destroys and blunts the real self and reduces it to the dimensions of nature.[8]

However terrible the consequences of modern demonic possessions, particularly in political life, they furnish the useful lesson of proving that human life is actually subject to power and not merely to mind. Modern political religions captured men partly because our liberal culture had become devitalized and "rationalized" to the point where salvation or the fulfillment of life was universally regarded as no more than the extension of mind. Men felt certain that they possessed themselves; and sought in the complacency of their self-possession to extend the range of the self and to make it more inclusive. But a self which possesses itself in such a way never escapes from itself. Human personality is so constructed that it must be possessed if it is to escape the prison of self-possession. The infinite regression of its self-transcendence represents possibilities of freedom

[7] *Cf.* Vol. I, p. 180.

[8] *Cf.* Erich Fromm, *Escape from Freedom* for a psychological discussion of what is involved in modern demonic politics. It goes without saying that loyalty to nation and other historical communities is not destructive of freedom when these do not make final and absolute claims upon the human spirit.

which are never actualized in self-possession; for self-possession means self-centredness. The self must be possessed from beyond itself.

Yet such possession of the self is destructive if the possessing spirit is anything less than the "Holy Spirit." For in that case spirit represents some partial and particular vitality in life and history and therefore does not deserve the unconditioned devotion which is consequent upon being thus possessed. According to the Christian faith, Christ is the criterion of the holiness of spirit.[9] He is the criterion of holiness because the revelation of God in Christ is on the one hand an historical focus of the divine, through which the mystery of the divine becomes morally and socially relevant to human nature, involved in finiteness and unable to comprehend the eternal. On the other hand it is the unique character of the revelation of God in Christ that it makes the divine and eternal known in history without giving any particular or partial force, value or vitality of history a sanctity or triumph which its finite and imperfect character does not deserve. Christ is thus both the criterion of the holiness of spirit and the symbol of the relevance between the divine and the human.

The Pauline word, "nevertheless I live," is set not only against the fulfillment of self by demonic possession through which the self is really corrupted and destroyed; it also marks the contrast between Christian conceptions of fulfillment and mystic doctrines of salvation in which the final goal is the destruction of the self. We have previously considered the tendencies towards self-destruction in various types of naturalistic, idealistic and mystic philosophies and religions.[10] We need only to emphasize at this point that the contrast between mystic-idealistic and Christian conceptions of self-fulfillment is determined by the "existential" character of the

---

[9] *Cf.* 1 John 4:1–2: "Beloved, believe not every spirit, but try the spirits whether they are of God; because many false prophets are gone out into the world. Hereby know ye the Spirit of God. Every spirit that confesseth that Jesus Christ is come in the flesh *is* of God."

[10] *Cf.* Vol. I. Ch. III.

self in Christian doctrines. The self is a unity of finiteness and free-dom, of involvement in natural process and transcendence over process. There is, therefore, not one particular level of the self, either in its consciousness or its reason, which can be extricated from flux and thereby achieve redemption. But on the other hand the unity of the self is so conceived in the Christian faith that it is not destroyed in the process of its fulfillment. Mystic doctrines of salva-tion might be expressed in a paraphrase of the Pauline word: "The Christ in me has been resurrected; therefore I have ceased to live." [11] According to these doctrines the real self is never threatened, judged, crucified or destroyed in any first step of salvation. Yet it is destroyed and lost in the final step. According to these doctrines there are various selves, and more particularly two: one immersed in finiteness and the other transcending it; [12] yet neither is a real self.

According to the Christian doctrine the sinful self must be de-stroyed from beyond itself because it does not have the power to lift itself out of its narrow interests. It cannot do so because all of its transcendent powers are intimately and organically related to its finiteness. It is tempted by this situation to pretend emancipation; but this pretension is its sin. Yet when the sinful self is broken and the real self is fulfilled from beyond itself, the consequence is a new

[11] This contrast between Christian and mystic doctrines is analysed profoundly in James Denney's *The Christian Doctrine of Reconciliation* and summarized in his phrase: "I would rather be saved in Christ than lost in God."

[12] One could multiply examples of this destruction of selfhood in various idealistic and mystic schools of thought. It may be helpful to offer a single example from the thought of Francis H. Bradley: "The finite is more or less transmuted and as such disappears in being accomplished. This common destiny is assuredly the end of the good. The ends sought by self-assertion and *self-sacrifice* are each alike unat-tainable. The individual can never himself become a harmonious system. In the complete gift and dissipation of his personality *he as such* must vanish; and with that the good as such is transcended and submerged. . . . Most emphatically no self-assertion or self-sacrifice nor any goodness or morality has as such any reality in the absolute." *Appearance and Reality,* pp. 419–20.

life rather than destruction. In the Christian doctrine the self
is therefore both more impotent and more valuable, both more
dependent and more indestructible than in the alternate doctrines.[13]

3. *"Yet not I; but Christ Liveth in Me"*

The last of the Pauline assertions about the reconstruction of the
self in the experience of conversion and "self-realization" could be
defined as a "negation of a negation"; for the denial that the self
has been destroyed is now made subject to another denial on another
level. Just what does St. Paul mean by this final denial "Yet not I;
but Christ liveth in me"?

There is an ambiguity in this final explication of the relation of
the self to Christ which may well be an expression of the double
aspect of the Christian experience of grace, to which we have previously alluded, and with which all the Christian ages are concerned. The "yet not I" could be intended to assert merely the
"priority of grace," to be a confession by the converted self that its
new life is the fruit, not of its own power and volition, but of an
accretion of power and an infusion of grace. It could also be intended as an affirmation that the new self is never an accomplished
reality; that in every historic concretion there is an element of sinful
self-realization, or premature completion of the self with itself at
the centre; that, therefore, the new self is the Christ of intention
rather than an actual achievement. It is the self only by faith, in
the sense that its dominant purpose and intention are set in the
direction of Christ as the norm. It is the self only by grace, in the
sense that the divine mercy "imputes" the perfection of Christ and
accepts the self's intentions for achievements.

The double negation could mean either one or the other of these
two affirmations. But why could it not mean both? Is it not fun-

---

[13] We shall have to consider in a later chapter how this Christian
conception of selfhood is emphasized, guarded and expressed in the
paradoxical Christian hope of the "resurrection of the body."

damental to Pauline thought that these two aspects of grace are
always involved, in varying degrees of emphasis in the various interpretations of the life of the spirit? And is it not the testimony
of human experience that in the final experience of "love, joy and
peace," it is not possible to distinguish between the consciousness
of possessing something which we could not have possessed of ourselves and the consciousness of not possessing it finally but having
it only by faith?

We shall proceed upon the assumption that both affirmations are
contained in the Pauline "negation of the negation" and scrutinize
them in turn.

a. Grace as the power not our own.

Whenever the power of sinful self-love is taken seriously there is
a concomitant sense of gratitude in the experience of release from
self. It is felt that this is a miracle which the self could not have
accomplished.[14] The self was too completely its own prisoner by
the "vain imagination" of sin to be able to deliver itself. Just as the
truth of God which breaks the vicious circle of false truth, apprehended from the self as the false centre, can never be other than
"foolishness" to the self-centred self until it has been imparted by
"grace" and received by faith; so also the power which breaks the
self-centred will must be perceived as power from beyond the self;
and even when it has become incorporated into the new will, its
source is recognized in the confession: "I, yet not I."

Yet a difficult problem confronts us in this confession. If divine

*The self
was too
completely
its own
prisoner
to deliver
itself.*

[14] Augustine expresses this continued sense of gratitude and humility
in the new life in a classic passage: "How is it then that miserable men
dare to be proud, either of their free will before they are freed; or of
their own strength, if they have been freed? . . . If therefore they are
slaves of sin, why do they boast of free will? For by what a man is
overcome to the same is he delivered as a slave. But if they have been
freed why do they vaunt themselves as if it were by their own doing and
boast as if it had not been received?" "On the Spirit and the Letter,"
Ch. 52, in *Nicene and Post-Nicene Fathers*, First Series, Vol. V.

If only God can save us, than individual responsibil-ity is threatened.

grace alone were the source of the new life Christian faith would be forced to accept a doctrine of divine determinism which would seem to imperil every sense of human responsibility. This is exactly the danger which Reformation theology, and more particularly Calvinistic theology, runs in its doctrines of predestination; and this tendency has been reaffirmed in the modern radical Reformation thought of Barth. It cannot be denied that the doctrine has some Scriptural authority. St. Paul did not hesitate to affirm, on occasion, the almost capricious character of the divine mercy.[15]

The possible consequences of moral irresponsibility which may arise from such conceptions of the divine determinism are illustrated by an example admitted by Augustine himself. He reports that a group of monks, upon being taken to task for their moral sloth into which their piety had degenerated, declared: "Why do you preach to us about our duties and exhort us to fulfill them, since it is not we who act but God who worketh in us both to will and to do? . . . Let our superiors be satisfied to point out our duties . . . but let them not reprove us when we are at fault, since we are such as God has foreseen us to be and his grace has not been given us to do better."[16]

The moral and spiritual irresponsibility of these monks is an example of a constant peril to the spiritual life arising from too deterministic conceptions of redemption, though it is fair to observe that some Christian traditions have achieved a sense of responsibility in practice which their own doctrines of predestination denied.

It may be relevant to note that the Pauline text, of which the monks availed themselves in part, contains in its full form a more paradoxical statement of the relation of grace and free will. St. Paul writes: "Work out *your own* salvation with fear and trembling; for *it is God* which worketh in you both to will and to do of his

[15] Cf. *inter alia*: Romans 9:18: "Therefore hath he mercy on whom he will have mercy, and whom he will he hardeneth."

[16] St. Augustine, *De corruptione et gratia*, 4–10.

good pleasure." [17] This statement of the relation of divine grace to human freedom and responsibility does more justice to the complex facts involved than either purely deterministic or purely moralistic interpretations of conversion.

If it be true, as we have maintained,[18] that no sinful self-centredness can ever destroy the structure of freedom and self-transcendence in man, it must follow that there is some inner testimony from the very character and structure of the human psyche against the strategy of sinful egotism. The finite mind has some understanding of its own finiteness; and therefore it cannot escape an uneasy conscience over its sinful effort to complete its own life about "itself and its own" (Luther). This is the "point of contact" between grace and the natural endowments of the soul, which even Luther, despite his doctrine of total depravity, admits and which Karl Barth seeks desperately to deny. As long as there is such a point of contact there is something in man to which appeal can be made; though it must be admitted that men may be driven to despair, rather than repentance, either by the events or the appeals which shake the self-confidence of the sinful self.

The careful effort of Catholic theology to do justice to both grace and free will would therefore seem to be more correct than the tendency in Augustinian and Reformation theology to deny all human activity in, and responsibility for, repentance or faith. Thomas Aquinas defines the relation between the two in the well-known metaphor of the light of the sun and the seeing of the eye. The analogy for grace is the light which comes from the sun and without which man could not see at all. But the necessity and possi-

---

[17] Phil. 2:12–13. A word of the Book of Revelation contains the same double emphasis: "Behold, I stand at the door and knock; if any man hear my voice and *open the door*, I will come in to him, and will sup with him, and he with me." Rev. 3:20.

[18] Particularly in the discussion of *Justitia Originalis* in Vol. I, Ch. X.

[margin, handwritten:] There is some inner testimony from the very structure of the human psyche against the strategy of human egotism.

There is much truth in the "activism" of Catholicism, but it goes astray by defining too narrowly the limits of human activity and responsibility

bility of human action is expressed in the analogy: "He who has his eyes turned away from the light of the sun prepares himself to receive the light of the sun by turning his eyes thither." [19]

The weakness of this Catholic "synergism" is that it defines the limits of human activity and responsibility and of divine grace too precisely and exactly, and places them too much on the same level; a weakness which pertains to all Thomistic analyses of the final mysteries. Thereby the profundity of the experience of conversion tends to be obscured. The real situation is that both affirmations— that only God in Christ can break and reconstruct the sinful self, and that the self must "open the door" and is capable of doing so— are equally true; and they are both unqualifiedly true, each on its own level. Yet either affirmation becomes false if it is made without reference to the other.

The sinful self is responsible for becoming aware of the undue character of its self-love.

From the level of the sinful self, surveying its own situation, it is always true that it has the possibility of, and therefore responsibility for, becoming conscious of the undue character of its self-love. But when the self stands beyond itself "by faith," it is conscious of the fact that nothing it has done or can do is free of debt to the miracle of grace. It cannot explain why this tragic event, or that impulse towards the life of another, or this word of truth from the gospel should have shattered its old self-confidence and made conversion and reconstruction possible. From that perspective everything is a miracle of grace and every form of newness of life justifies the question: "What hast thou that thou hast not received?"

From man's point of view, however, this appears to be totally a gift of God.

Whenever this apprehension of the situation by faith becomes dimmed, a careful balancing of the two factors of redemption on the same level easily, and almost invariably, leads to new forms of self-righteousness. Thus St. Gregory, the theologian, began a description of his father's Christian life with a nice balance of the two factors: "I do not know which to praise more: the grace which called him or his own choice." But he ended his appreciation of his father's Christian faith with an analysis in which grace and gratitude for

[19] *Treatise on Grace*, Question 109, Art. 6.

mercy have really disappeared: "He belonged to those who anticipate faith by their disposition; and possessing the thing itself, lacked
only the name. . . . He received faith itself as a reward for his
virtue." [20]

The conception of the relation of grace and human resources in
Reformation theology does justice to the ultimate and religious level
of the problem; but it is in danger of obscuring the complexity of
the relation by denying the reality of human freedom. The Catholic
conception on the other hand seeks to do justice to both elements in
the relation but it tends to comprehend them upon the same level
and to measure the exact limits of each.

b. Grace as the forgiveness of our sins.

We have proceeded upon the assumption that the "negation of
the negation" in the Pauline text: "Yet not I, but Christ liveth in
me" has a double connotation; the second suggests that the new life
is not an achieved reality. It is directed to Christ as the norm of
life "by faith," and it accepts the divine grace which imputes his
perfection to the believer. This second meaning is supported by the
words with which the passage continues: "And the life which I now
live in the flesh I live by the faith of the Son of God, who loved me,
and gave himself for me." [21]

It may be prudent to note that whether or not the particular text
under review contains both connotations is of no great importance,
though there is no reason to assume that it does not. The thought
of St. Paul, taken as a whole, certainly illumines both aspects of the
experience of grace. But at the moment our concern is not with
Pauline thought but rather with the relevance of the Biblical doctrine of grace to the experiences of life. Does experience validate this
double conception?

It would be wrong to look for validation of the Biblical doctrine

[20] Quoted by Nicholas N. G. Gloubosky, Ch. II in the symposium,
The Doctrine of Grace, S. C. M. Press, London, p. 78.
[21] Gal. 2:20.

in some natural experience of grace. If our analysis of the relation of faith to reason, and of the "Holy Spirit" to the spirit of man be correct, the experience which validates the doctrine can only be prompted by the doctrine itself. For without the "wisdom of God" apprehended in faith, and standing partly in contradiction to human wisdom, men are never conscious of the seriousness of sin; for the judgment of God against their sinful pride and self-assertion is not perceived.

There is indeed a counterpart of the doctrine of justification by faith in idealistic philosophy which illustrates the precise limits of concurrence and difference between "natural theology" and a theology which rests upon a Biblical basis. According to this doctrine there must be some kind of consummatory experience in life, some sense of achieved perfection, even when it has not been achieved, some anticipation of the goal, even while still involved in process. But none of these doctrines takes sin seriously. The consummatory experience bridges the gap between the imperfection which is involved in process and the transcendent goodness. In them man justifies himself by anticipating the eternity, to which the eternal element in his spirit entitles him.[22]

Without the radical sense of judgment in Biblical religion it is always possible to find some scheme of self-justification. Man may judge himself; but this capacity for self-judgment supposedly proves the goodness of that self which pronounces the judgment upon the empirical self. This judging self can, therefore, declare, "I am thereby justified." It is the self for which the end of evolution is already attained. It lays hold on eternity. Man's ability to judge

[22] B. Bosanquet's version of the doctrine is: "Religion justifies the religious man. It does not abolish his finiteness, his weakness or his sin. It denies that they are real." In *What Is Religion,* p. 49.

Francis H. Bradley's conception is similar. He says: "For the faith of religion the end of evolution is already evolved." *Ethical Studies,* p. 279.

J. Caird expresses the same idea in the words: "Religion rises above morality in this, that whilst the ideal of morality is only progressively realized, the ideal of religion is realized here and now." *Introduction to Philosophy of Religion,* p. 284.

himself is proof of a goodness in him which has final justification. But according to Biblical faith the confession always runs: "I know nothing by myself; yet am I not hereby justified; but he that judgeth me is the Lord." [23]

Such an experience is itself the fruit of grace in the sense that it represents a "wisdom" about life which is "foolishness" in prospect and wisdom only in retrospect. Experience as such may not yield it, and yet justify it in the end. In this context we must inquire particularly whether experience justifies the assertion that the conscience remains uneasy even in the highest reaches of achievement in the new life. Is it true that sin, though broken "in principle," is never broken in fact in the new life? Is it true that peace is never solely a sense of having realized what life should be; but always contains an element of hope and an assurance of forgiveness? Is the final peace dependent upon the certainty that there are divine resources which are able to cope with the continued contradiction between human self-love and the divine purpose?

Modern Christianity has not been concerned with the relevance of this interpretation of human experience, for reasons which we shall have occasion to examine more thoroughly presently. The study of the relevance of this doctrine must therefore confront the indifference and even hostility of "modern" men, whether Christian or unChristian.

The real question is not whether we are able to achieve absolute perfection in history; for even the most consistent perfectionist sects do not deny that human life remains in process. The question is whether in the development of the new life some contradiction between human self-will and the divine purpose remains. The issue is whether the basic character of human history, as it is apprehended in the Christian faith, is overcome in the lives of those who have thus apprehended it.

That question would seem to find one answer in logic and another in experience. It is logical to assume that when man has be-

[23] I Cor. 4:4.

come aware of the character of his self-love and of its incompatibility with the divine will, this very awareness would break its power. Furthermore, this logic is at least partially validated by experience. Repentance does initiate a new life. But the experience of the Christian ages refutes those who follow this logic and without qualification. The sorry annals of Christian fanaticism, of unholy religious hatreds, of sinful ambitions hiding behind the cloak of religious sanctity, of political power impulses compounded with pretensions of devotion to God, offer the most irrefutable proof of the error in every Christian doctrine and every interpretation of the Christian experience which claim that grace can remove the final contradiction between man and God. The sad experiences of Christian history show how human pride and spiritual arrogance rise to new heights precisely at the point where the claims of sanctity are made without due qualification.

Christians have tended to forget the reality of man's egotism, and this has led to perfectionism.

A tragic and revealing aspect of the experience of the Christian ages is that, again and again, "publicans and sinners" have had to rescue an important aspect of truth about life, and restore wholesomeness into human relations, against the fanaticism of Christian saints, who had forgotten that sainthood is corrupted whenever holiness is claimed as a simple possession. A full appreciation of the profundities of the Christian faith must therefore prompt gratitude to these "publicans and sinners" for their periodic testimony against the Christian Church whenever it has forgotten the full truth of its gospel and has allowed itself to be betrayed into new forms of self-righteousness. The publicans and sinners do not, of course, have the full truth either. For when they turn from the moral scepticism, which enables them to challenge religious fanaticism, they develop fanatic furies of their own. They have no principle of interpreting life which can save them from alternate moods of scepticism and fanaticism. But that does not change the fact that a moral sceptic, who regards all truth and all goodness as merely a cloak of self-interest, does at least understand the perennial egoistic corruption of truth and goodness. He is finally betrayed into moral nihilism because he knows nothing of the truth and goodness, not so corrupted, which are the possession of faith alone. The protest of secularism against Catholicism in all national cultures, in which Catholicism has played the dominant rôle and has invariably compounded the relativities of politics and history with the ultimate sanctities, is particularly instructive in this connection.

If we examine any individual life, or any social achievement in history, it becomes apparent that there are infinite possibilities of organizing life from beyond the centre of the self; and equally infinite possibilities of drawing the self back into the centre of the organization. The former possibilities are always fruits of grace (though frequently it is the "hidden Christ" and a grace which is not fully known which initiates the miracle). They are always the fruits of grace because any life which cannot "forget" itself and which merely makes brotherhood the instrument of its "happiness" or its "perfection" cannot really escape the vicious circle of egocentricity.[24] Yet the possibilities of new evil cannot be avoided by grace; for so long as the self, individual or collective, remains within the tensions of history and is subject to the twofold condition of involvement in process and transcendence over it, it will be subject to the sin of overestimating its transcendence and of compounding its interests with those which are more inclusive.[25]

[24] This "dialectical" element in the anatomy of morals is not understood at all in Mortimer Adler's neo-Thomist treatise, *A Dialectic of Morals*. Adler fails to comprehend the difference between *agape* and *eros*. He therefore does not see that the quest for happiness does not emancipate from egocentricity, even if perfection is regarded as the way to happiness. The individual who seeks his happiness through his perfection is still centred within himself.

[25] It is frequently asserted in Christian, particularly in Reformation, thought, that we will continue to sin so long as we are "in the body." This would make it appear that sin is the consequence of finiteness. But, whether explicitly or implicitly, Christian thought gives this phrase the same connotation as the Pauline conception of *sarx*. Historical existence

There are thus indeterminate possibilities of redeeming parent-hood from the lust of power and making the welfare of the child the end of family life. But there are also many possibilities of using the loving relationship of the family as an instrument of the parental power impulse on a higher or more subtle level. The "saints" may not be conscious of this fault; but the children who have to extricate themselves from the too close and enduring embrace of loving parents know about it. There are indeterminate possibilities of re-lating the family to the community on higher and higher levels of harmony. But there is no possibility of a family escaping the fault of regarding its own weal and woe as more important to the whole than it really is. There are unlimited opportunities of relating "our" nation more harmoniously to the lives of other nations; but there is no possibility of doing so without some corruption of national egoism.[26]

It is not easy to express both these two aspects of the life of grace, to which all history attests without seeming to offend the canons of logic. That is one reason why moralists have always found it rather easy to discount the doctrine of "justification by faith." [27] But

---

is never mere finiteness but finiteness and freedom; and a part of his-torical existence is therefore the temptation, and a yielding to the tempta-tion, of claiming ultimate significance for partial values and ultimate validity for partial perspectives.

[26] Even now genuine hopes for a new world order are compounded with anticipatory pride over the eminence which "Anglo-Saxon" civiliza-tion will have in it; or of the possibilities of achieving an "American Century" through American power.

[27] Emil Brunner defines the twofold character of grace as: "It is a having and yet not having, a standing beyond the contradiction and yet standing in it. It is justification of the sinner, who, though justified, con-tinues to the last days of his earthly life to be a sinner and is as much in need of forgiveness as on the day of his conversion." *Theology of Crisis,* p. 63.

Martin Luther expresses the paradox in many ways, as for instance: "The beneficiary of justification knows that now he serves the law of God and asks for mercy because he serves the law of sin" or "Both things are true, no Christian has sin and all Christians have sin" or "The saints are

here, as in many cases, a seeming defiance of logic is merely the consequence of an effort to express complex facts of experience. It happens to be true to the facts of experience that in one sense the converted man is righteous and that in another sense he is not.

The complexity of the facts not only makes it difficult to comprehend them in a formula which does not seem to offend canons of consistency. It is also difficult to express both aspects of the experience of grace without unduly suppressing one or the other side of it. The theologies which have sought to do justice to the fact that saints nevertheless remain sinners have frequently, perhaps usually, obscured the indeterminate possibilities of realizations of good in both individual and collective life. The theologies which have sought to do justice to the positive aspects of regeneration have usually obscured the realities of sin which appear on every new level of virtue. This has been true particularly of modern versions of Christian perfectionism; because in them evolutionary and progressive interpretations of history have been compounded with illusions which have a more purely Christian source.

We must trace the course of this debate in detail presently; for it embraces the whole history of western Christendom and it involves all the issues which are crucial for an understanding, and a possible reorientation, of the spiritual life of our day.

At the moment it is important to emphasize that the two sides of the experience of grace are so related that they do not contradict, but support each other. To understand that the Christ in us is not a possession but a hope, that perfection is not a reality but an intention; that such peace as we know in this life is never purely the peace of achievement but the serenity of being "completely known and all forgiven"; all this does not destroy moral ardour or responsibility. On the contrary it is the only way of preventing premature completions of life, or arresting the new and more terrible pride

[right margin, handwritten:] Theologies have overstressed either the sinfulness or the goodness of man

Thus, man exists in tension in that transcendance of egotism is both: the gift of God and the effort of man

---

always intrinsically sinners; that is why they are declared righteous extrinsically," or "We are sinners in reality but are righteous in hope." Quoted from *Works,* Ficker, ed., Vol. II, pp. 104, 105 and 176.

which may find its roots in the soil of humility, and of saving the Christian life from the intolerable pretension of saints who have forgotten that they are sinners.

The simple moralists will always regard this final pinnacle of the religious experience with little or no comprehension. They will assert that it is merely a formula which allows us "to continue in sin that grace may abound." But if the "foolishness of God" has been truly incorporated into the wisdom of faith the simple answer to this charge can be: "God forbid. How shall we, that are dead to sin, live any longer therein?" [28]

[28] Romans 6:2.

CHAPTER V

THE CONFLICT BETWEEN GRACE AND PRIDE

IF OUR analysis up to this point be, in any fundamental sense, a correct one, the Pauline interpretation of grace and the new life is not a unique dogma which could or could not have been added to the gospels. Its significance lies in its explicit formulation of the problem of life and history, as it was apprehended negatively in the prophetic interpretation of history and as it was positively affirmed in Jesus' reinterpretation of prophetic expectations. It is closely related to Jesus' insistence that the righteous are not righteous before the divine judgment; and to his conception of the suffering Messiah as a revelation of the justice and the mercy of God.

If we now address ourselves to the task of tracing the interpretation of the central dogma of Christian faith through the Christian ages it becomes increasingly apparent that human self-esteem resists the truth of the Christian gospel almost as vigorously within the bounds of a faith which has ostensibly accepted it, as it was resisted by the pre-Christian ages. They expected a Christ but not the Christ who would vindicate God in his justice and mercy without including any man in that vindication. The Christian ages seek a new way of vindicating men who have become righteous through Christ.

This resistance takes many forms and avails itself of many current philosophies in various ages. While it is important to note the particular causes which prompted Christian theologians to deny or to obscure the fundamental paradox of the gospel's interpretation of life and history, it is more important to recognize that the motive which underlies all these various formulations is essentially the same. It is the unwillingness of man to admit the curious predicament of his existence by reason of his simultaneous involvement in, and transcendence over, temporal flux and finiteness; or, more exactly his unwillingness to admit that there is no escape from this predicament even on the level of the new life. The favourite strategy for denying the perennial character of the contradiction between the human and the divine is to interpret the revelation of God in Christ as the disclosure of the eternal in history resulting in a consequent translation of the believer from the historical and temporal to the eternal. Such a redemption involves the apprehension of the eternal truth; and this knowledge of the truth also presumably guarantees the realization of it in life; in other words, the achievement of perfection.

It is well to recognize at the outset that the perennial revolt in the Christian ages against the whole truth of the Christian gospel is the cause of the fanaticisms and religiously sanctified imperial lusts which have disfigured the history of Western civilization. In this revolt the invariable strategy is to set one part of the Christian truth against the whole of it. This revolt explains why a civilization, informed by a religious faith, which, alone among the faiths of the world, both encouraged historic creativity and responsibility and yet set the limits upon man's historic possibilities, must appear from the perspective of the more earthbound (Confucianism) and the more world-denying (Buddhism) religions of the East as a civilization of unbridled ambitions and heaven-storming passions.

This does not mean that the corruption of Christian truth by human self-esteem could have been avoided if this or that theological tendency had not gained ascendency, in this or that epoch. To say that the self-confidence of classical culture is the primary source of this corruption is to explain a general tendency historically but not profoundly. For human pride is more powerful than any instruments of which it avails itself. It must be regarded as inevitable that a religion which apprehends the truth about man and God by faith alone should be used as the instrument of human arrogance. This is done whenever the truth which is held by faith, because it is beyond all human attainment, comes to be regarded as a secure possession. In this form it is no longer a threat to man. It does not mediate judgment upon the false and imperial completions of human life. It becomes, rather, the vehicle of the pretension that the finiteness and sin of life have been overcome. The New Testament understands how inevitable this misuse of the gospel is. Its conception of the false Christs and of the Antichrist, who appear at the end of history expresses this understanding. But this tragic aspect of Christian history is understood only occasionally outside of the New Testament. For everywhere else in the Christian ages, the saints seek to refute the justified jeers of sceptics and sinners by pointing to the blamelessness of the life of Christians or by seeking to prove that the virtues of the church outweigh its vices. Yet Christianity can validate its truth about life and history only when it is possible, from the standpoint of that truth, to comprehend the rise of the false truths which use Christianity itself as their vehicle.

II

PRE-AUGUSTINIAN CONCEPTIONS OF GRACE

In tracing the resistance which the truth of the gospel meets in the ages we might begin with a period of Christian thought, from the Apostolic age to Augustine, in which the Pauline formulation of the ultimate religious problem was only imperfectly, if at all, apprehended. The thought of the period was moulded by the necessity of establishing and defending the Christian faith in, and against, the Græco-Roman culture. That culture regarded the time-eternity problem as the crucial issue in man's life and sought salvation in mystery religions, Gnostic sects, Mantic arts, Platonic and Neo-Platonic philosophies, in all of which the temporal could be translated into the eternal or the eternal purged of the temporal.

Christian faith had enough power to challenge the Hellenic doctrine of the chasm between the divine and the historical and to
elaborate Christologies which broke with Greek dualism. But it did
not have enough power to come to a clear perception of the problem
of sin which was involved in the Christian interpretation of historical reality; or of the doctrine of the Atonement, which was the
Christian answer to this problem. "Attempts at deducing the
church's doctrinal position," writes Harnack, "from the theology
of Paul . . . will always miscarry; for they fail to note that to the
most important premises of the Catholic doctrine of faith belongs
an element which we cannot recognize as dominant in the New
Testament, viz. the Hellenic spirit." [1] The idea that baptism cured
the believer of sin, a fruitful source of perfectionist illusions, had a
very early beginning.[2] Salvation was frequently equated with the
true knowledge of God through Christ, as contrasted with the errors
of heathendom. The deeper problems of the Christian faith were
partially obscured in some of the Apostolic Fathers and totally so
in others.[3] The ideas of "eternal life," knowledge (*gnosis*) and law,
particularly the new law of Christ, exhausted the meaning of the
gospel. Nor does the situation change in the thought of the Apologists who follow the Apostolic Fathers. Justin Martyr regards
Christianity as a "new law" and a "new philosophy." In this conception he does not simply capitulate to Platonism; for he does not
believe that man has inherent capacities to arrive at the truth and
to achieve virtue. These are gifts of grace. But the paradox of our
having and not having them is not understood. The Biblical idea
of the forgiveness of sins is of course never denied. But forgiveness

[1] *History of Dogma*, Vol. I, p. 48. Harnack's understanding of the loss
of Pauline profundities in pre-Augustinian Christianity is the more
remarkable and impressive because he, himself, does not fully appreciate
the implications of Pauline thought.

[2] The Epistle of Barnabas (70–79 A.D.) gives the idea special prom-
inence.

[3] Partially so in Clement, Barnabas, Polycarp and Ignatius; totally so
in Hermas and the second epistle of Clement. *Vide,* Harnack, Vol. I,
p. 172.

(margin note: Perfection through gnosis)

becomes a single remission *of sins that are past*[4] at a very early date. The Catholic formula of subordinating justification to sanctification is thus of very early origin.

The position of Tertullian on these issues is particularly significant. He was the protagonist of Biblical, particularly of Hebraic thought, against the Hellenizing tendencies of the early Christian philosophers and he sought to preserve the prophetic-eschatological interpretation of history against the corrosion of Hellenic interpretations. Furthermore he understood the doctrine of original sin. Yet he was confused in his understanding of the Christian doctrine of the justice and mercy of God. He regarded the idea of divine forgiveness as irrational and unjust, and declared that, "if we really needed to ascribe to God a goodness so at variance with reason, it would be better that there should be no God at all."[5]

The tendency to regard Christianity as a way to achieve the eternal and to realize perfection was even more pronounced in the Eastern than in the Western church. Origen, the greatest of Eastern theologians, as indeed the most original of all pre-Augustinians, was both perfectionist and moralistic in his conception of the method of attaining holiness.[6] His predecessor, Clement of Alexandria, expressed the idea of the deification of man through Christ, which characterized all Alexandrian thought, in the words: "When we are reborn we receive straightway that perfect thing for which we are

---

[4] This limit upon grace is explicit in Barnabas 5:9 and 11 Clem. 2: 4–7.

[5] *Adv. Marcionem,* i, 25. Despite his polemic against Hellenizing tendencies Tertullian paid inadvertent tribute to the power of these ideas in the church by occasionally defining the significance of Christ in essentially Hellenic terms, as for instance: "God lived among us, that man might be taught to do the things of God. God acted on the level with man, that man might be able to act on the level with God." *Adv. Marcionem,* ii, 27.

[6] Origen declared: "The perfection of God's likeness a man must acquire for himself by his own zealous endeavors in imitation of God; because the possibility of being perfect is given to man at the beginning through the dignity of God's image; but the perfect likeness he must accomplish for himself through the fulfillment of works. *De princ,* III, vi, 1.

striving. For we are enlightened and that is to know God; he can therefore not be imperfect who has known that which is perfect." [7] The gnostic formulation of the way of salvation echoes in these words. Gregory of Nyssa believed that, "Man, restored to the fashion of pure Adam, attains the measure of the stature of the last and becomes even higher because he becomes deified." [8]

While the Biblical-Pauline conceptions are more prominent in the thought of less consistent Hellenists, such as Irenæus and Athanasius, it cannot be affirmed that the full meaning of the Biblical conception of sin and grace was understood by them. A modern historian is probably not far from the truth in the assertion that "the (pre-Augustinian) church never heartily accepted St. Paul's doctrine of justification by faith. . . . Sometimes it was wholly ignored; at other times even when the formula was respected it was interpreted in a way which would have been expressed more naturally by saying that men are saved by repentance." [9]

The Greek idea of *gnosis* thus dominated the pre-Augustinian centuries; and, though the church rejected the more explicitly dualistic forms of it as heresy, it capitulated to more modified Hellenistic conceptions of the way of salvation. [10] Greek Christianity sometimes capitulated so completely to Hellenism that the gospel became merely a higher form of knowledge. When more Biblical it recognized the necessity of "grace" and "power"; which is to say, it understood the human problem in volitional rather than in purely rationalistic terms. But even then it never rose to a full comprehension of the problem of man's historical existence as viewed in prophetic-Biblical thought and as culminating in the New Testament conceptions of sin and grace. Thus an Egyptian father writes: "The

---

[7] *Pædagogus*, I, vi.

[8] *De instituto Christiano.*

[9] Hastings Rashdall, *The Idea of Atonement in Christian Theology,* p. 206.

[10] Harnack writes: "It is therefore no paradox to say that Gnosticism, which is just Hellenism, obtained half a victory in Catholicism." *History of Dogma,* I, p. 227.

grace of God can purify a man in an instant and make him perfect; for all is possible to God; as happened in the case of the robber, who was transformed by faith in a moment of time and brought into paradise."[11]

Perfectionist illusions reach their most consistent proportions in the thought of St. John of Chrysostom, who, confining divine grace to the sacrament of baptism, declares: "Grace touches the soul itself and tears up sin by the roots. . . . The soul of him who is baptized . . . is purer than the rays of the sun, and such as it was originally begotten; nay rather far better than this; for it enjoys the Spirit which sets it on fire on all sides and extends its holiness. . . . The Holy Spirit recasting it by baptism as in a furnace and consuming its sins causes it to shine more purely than any pure gold."[12]

While the thought of the Latin church is never as consistently perfectionist as that of the Eastern church, and while subsequent developments lead the Western church to further modification of its position, the thought of the Eastern church bears the stamp of complete consistency from the Greek fathers to the dogmas of the contemporary Orthodox church. In terms of the history of culture this represents the triumph of Hellenism over Hebraism. In terms of religion it is the failure of the church to understand that part of the gospel which is directed against itself and its saints.[13]

[handwritten margin note: Eastern church went all the way in accepting Gnostic Christianity.]

[11] The Blessed Marcarius of Egypt, *De custodia cordis,* xii.

[12] Homil: In Epist. I and Cor. 15:1–2.

[13] As we shall not have occasion to trace perfectionist thought in the Greek church through the centuries to the present it may be relevant to quote a modern Orthodox theologian upon this dominant tendency in the Eastern church. He writes that "the Greek Fathers do rightly believe that when once God is acting through the sacraments, His action cannot have only temporary character or partial effect. The power of Divine Grace is manifested through the Sacraments and its effect is eternal." Hamilcar S. Alivisatos in symposium, *The Doctrine of Grace,* S. C. M. Press, London, p. 267.

One of the most authoritative Orthodox theologians of recent times, Chrestos Androustos, states the Greek doctrine of sanctification in most unequivocal terms. He writes: "The two elements of forgiveness of sins and justification are not separate from each other, as if sanctification

III

THE CATHOLIC CONCEPTION OF GRACE

The realization within the post-apostolic church that the primary issue of life and history is the relation of grace to sin, rather than the subordinate problem of eternity to time, comes to its first clear and explicit expression in the thought of Augustine. Scriptural authority had prevented the prophetic-Biblical concepts from ever being completely lost; but they had certainly been obscured in the preceding centuries. With Augustine's elaboration of the Pauline doctrine of original sin, the Christian ages arrive at a full consciousness of the fact that it is not finiteness but the "false eternal" of sin, the pretension that finiteness has been or can be overcome, which brings confusion and evil into history.[1]

[margin note: Augustine realizes that finiteness can never can be fully overcome]

----

followed upon cleansing from sin, but they are two aspects of the same thing. . . . The remission of sin is not the mere imputation of freedom from sin,—but the actual effacement of it. . . . God, in judging a sinner, does not regard him as righteous while he remains a sinner, but makes him actually righteous. The state of sin is removed entirely by God's power in the act of justification. . . . The principle and basis of sin in the perversion of the will is entirely removed and the regenerate will is born godward." In his "Dogmatike" quoted in Frank S. B. Gavin's *Some Aspects of Contemporary Greek Thought*, p. 227.

It may be relevant to call Tolstoi to witness against the moral consequences and spiritual confusion which results from such perfectionist pretensions. He writes in *"My Confession"*: "The Orthodox church: with this word I no longer connect any conception than that of a few hirsute men, extremely self-confident, deluded and ignorant, in silk and velvet with diamond panagias, called bishops and metropolitans; and other thousands of hirsute men, who under the guise of performing certain sacraments are busy fleecing the people. Instead of humility there is grandeur; instead of poverty there is luxury, instead of forgiving offenses, hatred and wars. And all men deny one another but not themselves."

These strictures are not entirely fair because Tolstoi was a perfectionist of sectarian persuasion who was convinced that, if only a more rigorous strategy were adopted, men could be freed of sin. He understood the perennial factors of historic existence as little as the sacramental perfectionists.

[1] *Cf.* Vol. I, Ch. VI.

The neo-Platonic influence in Augustine's thought slightly obscures the Biblical paradoxes. His analysis of the human situation is Biblical, though his conception of sin as a "defect" of the will—as a lack of power to do good—is partly derived from Plotinus and is not in complete conformity with his profound understanding of the inevitable tendency towards self-love in the expression of human freedom. Perhaps this slight admixture of Hellenistic thought in his doctrine of sin contains the roots of his error in the doctrine of grace, which is the Biblical answer to the problem of sin. For Augustine's doctrine of grace blunts and obscures the complex relation between grace as power and grace as pardon. He does not question the traditional conception of the relation between the two. We have seen that the idea of God's forgiveness and justification, preceding and laying the foundation for sanctification, began very early. According to this theory, the divine mercy, mediated through Christ, destroys the sinful contradiction between man and God, and turns the soul from self-love to obedience; whereupon it may grow in grace and achieve constantly higher stages of sanctification. This subordination of justification to sanctification becomes definitive for the whole Catholic conception of life and history. It contains the roots of a new self-righteousness and a new pretension that man is able to complete life and history. The difference between it and Hellenistic conceptions is that it expresses man's consciousness of his inability to realize the good by his own power; but it assumes that it can be accomplished by the aid of divine power. "It is certain," declares Augustine, "that we can keep the commandments if we so will; but because the will is prepared by the Lord we must ask him for such force of will as to make us act by willing. It is certain that it is we who will when we will but it is he who makes us will what is good; . . . it is he who makes us act by supplying efficacious power to our will." [2] It must be quite apparent that this exposition does full justice to the relation of a power not our own to our own power. In his polemic against Pelagian moralism, this is the point

[2] *On Grace and Free Will*, xvii, 32.

which Augustine is intent upon guarding. But he does not fully recognize the persistent power of self-love in the new life. He knows that love is no simple possibility for human nature; but he is certain that it is God's possibility in the heart of man.

Man's seeking of perfection may be perfect.

His classical treatise on the subject of Christian perfection is an exposition of the Pauline text: "Not as if I had already attained, either were already perfect." In expounding this text he recognizes, as do most Christian perfectionists, that there is no possibility for finite nature of arriving at a goal; for man is in history and history is a process of becoming. But he is convinced that the seeking of the goal may be perfect. "Let us," he says, "as many as are running perfectly, be thus resolved that, being not yet perfected, we pursue our course to perfection along the way which we have thus far run perfectly." [3]

While Augustine doesn't believe that man can wholly overcome sin, he believes that the sins which remain are venial, rather than mortal.

He does not, of course, affirm the sinlessness of Christians. He sees no possibility of conquering sin absolutely. He is certain that concupiscence remains and that consequently divine forgiveness is necessary up to man's last hour. [4] But he is convinced that the sins which remain are "venial" rather than "mortal"; which is to say that he regards expressions of self-love, after redemption, as incidental, and not as the expression of a basic attitude. "He is not unreasonably said to walk blamelessly," according to Augustine, "not who already has reached the end of his journey, but who is pressing on to the end in a blameless manner, free from damnable sins and at the same time not neglecting to cleanse by almsgiving such sins as are venial." [5] The distinction between damnable and venial sins is, and remains, an important one in Catholic thought. The idea that almsgiving can cleanse the soul of venial sins is the camel's nose of "righteousness by works" entering into the tent of grace.

The important point at issue in the Augustinian conception is whether the destruction of sin "in principle" means that the power

[3] *On Man's Perfection in Righteousness*, Ch. 19.
[4] *Enchiridion*, lxiv.
[5] *On Man's Perfection in Righteousness*, Ch. 20.

of inordinate self-love is broken in fact. It is the thesis of both
Augustine and all the Catholic ages that this is the case; and that
residual sin represents the eruption of vagrant desires and impulses
which have not yet been brought completely under the control of
the central will. The thesis is plausible enough; for if destruction
of self-love "in principle" does not also mean "in fact" in some basic
sense, what does it mean? Certainly there must be some facts which
reveal the new principle by which the soul lives. Surely there must
be "fruits meet for repentance"!

But here the complexities of the moral life are obscured by too
simple statement of them. The actual situation is that man may
be redeemed from self-love in the sense that he acknowledges the
evil of it and recognizes the love of God as the only adequate motive
of conduct; and may yet be selfish in more than an incidental sense.
The pride of a bishop, the pretensions of a theologian, the will-to-
power of a pious business man, and the spiritual arrogance of the
church itself are not mere incidental defects, not merely "venial"
sins. They represent the basic drive of self-love, operating upon
whatever new level grace has pitched the new life. Pure love is "by
faith" in the sense that only when man, in prayer and contemplation, is lifted beyond himself does he have a vantage point from
which self-love does not operate. In action the power of self-love
is mixed with the new power of the love of God which grace has
established.

This tragic quality of the spiritual life was never clearly apprehended until the Reformation. Its apprehension gives the Reformation its particular and unique place in the history of the Christian
life. Augustine's failure to understand it had the consequence of
making him the father of Catholicism in his doctrine of grace;
while he became at the same time the ultimate source of the Reformation in his doctrine of sin. The Reformation discovered that there
was in the Pauline-Biblical and in the Augustinian analysis of the
human situation a problem too profound to be solved by the Augustinian answer to that problem.

[margin, handwritten: Actually, man may be redeemed from sin (through repentance) and still be selfish in more than an incidental sense.]

The Augustinian portrayal of the collective, as well as the individual, historical situation remains within the limits of this qualified perfectionism. The conflict in history is between the *civitas Dei* and the *civitas terrena,* the one being animated by the "love of God" to the point of contempt for the self, the other by "the love of self" to the point of contempt of God. He acknowledges that in history the two cities are "commingled" and he has no simple perfectionist solutions for the problems of relative justice which arise even for the Christian in a sinful world. But on the whole he identifies the *civitas Dei* with the historical church, of which he asserts that only there is true justice to be found. He does surround this identification with all kinds of qualifications, which later Catholic ages did not have the prudence to maintain. He distinguishes between the *civitas Dei* as it is here on earth and the *civitas superna* as it is in heaven. He differentiates between the church as it is and as it will be.[6] He declares explicitly that "wherever in these books I have mentioned the church as not having a spot or wrinkle, it is not to be taken as now existing but of the church whose existence is being prepared."[7]

Nevertheless the church is, despite these qualifications, in some sense the Kingdom of God on earth. It had not achieved the ultimate perfection; and moreover there is, in his thought, no guarantee that all members of it are saved. But the conception of its perfection corresponds essentially to his idea of the perfection of the saints. He thought of it as "pursuing its course to perfection" along the way which it has "thus far run perfectly."[8] But he could not con-

---

[6] "*Ecclesia qualis nunc est*" and "*ecclesia qualis tunc erit.*" *De civitas Dei,* Book XX, Ch. 9.

[7] *Retract,* II, xvii.

[8] Bishop Gore rightly affirms that Augustine did not originate the idea of the visible church; or the belief that salvation is by the church alone; or the conviction that "he cannot have God for his Father who has not the church for his Mother." In all these convictions he merely entered into the general Catholic heritage. Charles Gore, *The Church and the Ministry,* pp. 13 ff.

A. Robertson agrees with Gore that Augustine did not originate the idea of the visible church and adds that "it would be truer to say that

ceive of it as standing itself under divine judgment. In other words the church was the historic *locus* where the contradiction between the historical and the divine was overcome in fact; rather than that *locus* where the judgment and the mercy of God upon the historical are mediated, and where, therefore, the contradiction of the historical and the holy is overcome in principle. This conviction governs Augustine's whole philosophy of history. The historical conflict between self-love and the love of God is essentially a conflict between the church and the world; and the commingling of church and world never means that the church might, as an historic institution, become the vehicle of evil. The church does not, in other words, really stand under the judgment of God. Rather it reigns with Christ. "Even now," he declares, "the church is the Kingdom of Christ, and the Kingdom of heaven. That is to say even now *his saints reign with him,* not indeed in the same way as they will reign then. Nor yet do the tares reign with him, although in the church they are growing with the wheat." [9]

It may well be that subsequent Catholic ages weakened the Augustinian analysis of the human situation and transmuted it into semi-Pelagian doctrine. But they did not have to change his conception of the Christian solution of the human situation. For the Augustinian and the Catholic doctrine of grace are one; and the one doctrine runs consistently through the Catholic centuries. According to it sin is essentially the loss of an original perfection, rather than the corruption of the image of God in man; and grace is the completion of an imperfect nature. The fulfillment of what is good but incomplete in nature is emphasized, as against the element of cor-

---

he originated the idea of the invisible church." A. Robertson, *Regnum Dei,* p. 187.

Augustine's reservations about the church did contain the Reformation idea of the invisible church, which became the instrument of placing the historic church under divine judgment; just as his basic idea about the church, without reservations, was in conformity with accepted Catholic belief before and after his time.

[9] *De civ. Dei,* Book XX, Ch. 9.

ruption which always places "nature" and "grace" in contradiction. In the analysis of the situation of man in history the Biblical-paradoxical element is slightly stronger in Augustine than in the official Catholic doctrine as ultimately defined by Thomas Aquinas; but in the definition of what grace accomplishes there is no difference between Augustine and Aquinas.

In this definition the self-esteem of classical man and the Biblical sense of the contradiction between man and God are nicely merged. The Biblical view of man-in-history overcomes the classical concept of the sufficiency of human (particularly rational) powers. In the Catholic view it is always through grace that man is able to do the good. But the classical view overcomes the Biblical in the sense that the redeemed man actually stands beyond the sin of history in fact as well as in principle. The precise formulation of this qualified uneasiness about the human situation is the subordination of justification to sanctification and the assertion that forgiveness is needed and meant primarily for "sins that are past."

The final and symbolically most revealing form of this new Catholic self-righteousness is the belief held in Catholic faith that in the final judgment man is saved by merit; only he must realize that the merit is achieved by the grace of God. On this point Aquinas is able to agree perfectly with Augustine. He writes: "Man by his own will performs works which are worthy of eternal life; but, as Augustine says, for this it is necessary that the will of man should be prepared by grace. As the gloss on the 'Grace of God is life eternal' (in Augustine) says: 'It is certain that eternal life is given as a reward for good works; but those works for which it is granted belong to the grace of God.' " [10]

The point at issue may seem academic to the casual student. It may even appear to the critical as a case of that futile theological hairsplitting, which seems to make theological debate so fatuous. But all important issues, whether in philosophy or theology, are finally defined in very precise distinctions, which may easily hide

[10] Thomas Aquinas, *Treatise on Grace*, Quest. 109, Art. v.

Can man, on the basis of his own merits, ever stand before a divine judgement with an easy consciousness?

from the unwary, even as they reveal to the initiated, the importance of the issue which is at stake. The issue at stake here is whether man's historical existence is such that he can ever, by any discipline of reason or by any merit of grace, confront a divine judgment upon his life with an easy conscience. If he can it means that it is possible for a will centred in an individual ego to be brought into essential conformity with the will and power which governs all things. On this question the Catholic answer is a consistently affirmative one.[11]

Catholic synthesis says, "Yes!"

There were Catholic mystics who tended to go beyond the bounds of the Catholic synthesis in their assertion of the perfectibility of man by grace. This strain of medieval thought must be considered presently as one of the roots of modern perfectionism. At the moment it is not important to consider it but rather to recognize the significance of the Catholic doctrine in which a balance is struck between the Biblical idea that man cannot complete his own life and history, and that he involves himself in evil in the pretense of doing so; and the classical (and generally non-Biblical) confi-

---

[11] It must be emphasized that the Catholic doctrine never asserts absolute but essential conformity between the redeemed will and the will of God.

Aquinas asserts that "the gift of habitual grace is not given us that we may be in no further need of divine help; for every creature needs that God should preserve it in that goodness which it received from him."

He declares, however, that in the redeemed state, "man can keep from mortal sin, which is grounded in reason, yet he cannot avoid venial sins because of the disorder of the *lower sensual desires,* the movements of which the reason can indeed severally repress . . . but he cannot repress all, for while he represses one, another perchance arises." According to this formulation the conformity of the human to the divine will is well nigh absolute, and the only sin which remains is occasioned by vagrant impulses below the level of the will. This conception might seem to be purely classical rather than Biblical. But Aquinas' syntheses of the two are always as perfectly proportioned as it is possible to make them. Thus he saves this interpretation of the residue of sin from purely classical connotations by declaring that the vagrancy of the lower desires is due to lack of perfect submission of the will to God: "Because man's will is not wholly subject to God it follows that there must be many disorders in the acts of reason." From *Treatise on Grace,* Quest. 109, Art. ii.

dence that some capacity in man, which transcends finiteness and process, is able to realize the vision which he apprehends by such transcendence.

The Catholic synthesis is expressed in many ways. It is summarized perfectly in Bernard of Clairvaux's assertion that man has freedom from necessity in the state of nature, freedom from sin in the state of grace and freedom from misery in the state of glory.[12] This is to say that the difference between the consummation of life in history and the consummation of life beyond history is merely that the former is still subject to the conditions of finiteness.

The Catholic synthesis.

The only explicit variation from this consistent Catholic doctrine is contained in the Formula of Ratisbon, in which the desire to come to terms with the Reformation prompted the, from the Catholic standpoint, remarkable thesis that, "We are not just or accepted of God on account of our own works of righteousness, but are reputed just on account of the merits of Jesus Christ only." But after possibilities of compromise with the Reformation had been dissipated the Catholic church defined its position in different terms at the Council of Trent. Then it declared: "If any man shall say that the good works of man that is justified are in such wise the gifts of God that they are not also *the good merits* of him that is justified, or that the said justified by the good works that are performed . . . does not *truly merit increase of grace and eternal life,* . . . let him be anathema."[13]

[12] St. Bernard of Clairvaux, *Concerning Grace and Free Will*, Ch. iii. Trans. by Watkins Williams, SPCK.

[13] Council of Trent, Canon xxvii. It would be wrong to create the impression that the Council of Trent was always wrong in defining its position in opposition to the Reformation. Very frequently it was rightly concerned to guard one side of the paradox of grace: that it is a power of righteousness, against the tendency towards moral defeatism and antinomianism in the Reformation. Canon xxii is thus rightly directed against Protestant antinomianism: "If any shall say that Christ Jesus was given to men as redeemer and in whom they should trust and not also as legislator whom they should obey, let him be anathema."

Canon xi contains an equally valid protest against the idea that grace

It took its position solidly on the ground that no real contradiction remained for the redeemed between what man is and what he ought to be, and insisted that: "If any man shall say that the commandments of God are, even for a man that is justified and constituted in grace, impossible to keep, let him be anathema." [14]

Whatever reservations Catholic thought may make in regard to "venial" sins, it never has any serious question about the actual coincidence of grace as pardon and grace as power or about the essential sinlessness of the redeemed man. In the words of Cardinal Newman, it believes that, "Justification is the fiat of Almighty God which breaks upon the gloom of our earthly state as the Creative Word upon chaos. It declares the soul righteous and in that declaration on the one hand conveys pardon *for its past sins* and on the other makes it actually righteous." [15]

The Catholic doctrine of grace is the foundation of a total theological structure, which exhibits the same consistent logic in all of its parts. In all of them the Biblical-prophetic view of life and history is provisionally accepted, though frequently weakened by the definition of sin as the privation of an original perfection, rather than as a positive corruption. But even when the definition of the human situation is more Biblical than classical (as in the case of Augustine) the proposed solution of the situation defies the limits

[right margin handwritten note:] Sin is the privation of an original perfection, rather than a positive corruption

---

is pardon only: "If any man shall say that men are justified either by the sole imputation of the righteousness of Christ, or by the sole remission of sins to the exclusion of the grace and charity which is shed abroad in their hearts by the Holy Ghost, and is inherent in them, or even that the grace by which we are justified is *only the favour of God,* let him be anathema."

[14] Canon xviii.

[15] Lectures on Justification, p. 83. It might be added that the Anglo-Catholic position never varies significantly from the Roman one. In one of the ablest treatises on grace from an Anglo-Catholic theologian, Robert C. Moberly writes: "There is no ultimate distinction between 'to justify' and 'to make righteous'; between a man's being pronounced righteous by the Truth of God and being in the Truth of God righteous." *Atonement and Personality,* p. 335. Moberly's book is a masterly analysis of the relation of grace to the freedom of human personality.

of human possibilities, as the Bible conceives them. It seeks for a place in history where sin is transcended and only finiteness remains. In seeking for that place it runs the danger of falling prey to the sin of spiritual pride and of illustrating in its own life that the final human pretension is made most successfully under the aegis of a religion which has overcome human pretension in principle.

All Catholic errors in overestimating the sinlessness of the redeemed reach their culmination, or at least their most vivid and striking expression, in the doctrine of the church. Here the reservations of Augustine are forgotten; and the church is unreservedly identified with the Kingdom of God. It is the *societas perfecta*. It is the sole dispenser of grace. Its visible head assumes the title: "Vicar of Christ" which appears blasphemous from the perspective of a prophetic view of history.[16] The title and the claim of papal infallibility reach such heights of human pretension that the Reformation indictment of the Pope as "Anti-Christ" may be regarded as something of an historical inevitability. Indeed political opponents of the Pope anticipated the Reformation in making the indictment during the Catholic ages. Non-Roman Catholics may regard papal, and indeed hierarchical pretensions in general, as corruptions, rather than expressions of, essential Catholic doctrine. It is indeed true that the councils once held the authority which the Pope now claims; and that Augustine's conception of the "saints who reign with Christ" was less pretentious than the claims of actual political dominion which Hildebrand derived from these words. But this merely means that the rulers of a perfect society have usurped the sanctity which was once claimed for the society as such. In the final religious analysis either claim is equally monstrous, though the earlier is more plausible than the later one.

The deification of the church is spiritually dangerous, however conceived. The Catholic doctrine that the church is an "extension

[handwritten margin note: Catholic errors meet their highest point when the Church is declared to be perfect as it exists on earth.]

---

[16] The title dates from Innocent III. In earlier centuries it was the Holy Spirit who was Vicar of Christ and the Pope was only St. Peter's Vicar.

of the Incarnation" represents a significant shift of emphasis from the Pauline-Biblical doctrine that the church is the "body of Christ." For when conceived as the body it is clear that it remains subject to the laws of historical reality. Its ideal and norm is, that all its members should be perfectly coordinated to one another by being subordinated to the "head" which is Christ.[17] But the actual realities always betray some of the contradictions which characterize historical existence. In history there is always "another law in my members, warring against the law of my mind."[18] This war is certainly as apparent in the collective, as in the individual, life of the redeemed.

When an institution which mediates the judgment of God upon all the ambiguities of historic existence claims that it has escaped those ambiguities by this mission, it commits the same sin which the prophets recognized so clearly as the sin of Israel. This sin becomes particularly apparent—and intolerable—when it expresses itself in political will-to-power; and it is mitigated only slightly by the achievements of universality which the historic church and papacy have to their credit. A "Vicar of Christ," who represents one among many competing social and political forces in history, cannot be a true representative of the Christ, who was powerless in history and in whom no particular cause or force in history triumphed or was vindicated. The fact that the papal-ecclesiastical power actually achieved a measure of impartiality and transcendence over warring nations and competing social forces and was thereby enabled to play a creative rôle in the history of the Western world may be recorded with gratitude. But it does not prove that the church was able to escape the mixture of creativity and corruption which characterizes all historic striving.

History clearly reveals how curiously and tragically the "spirit of Christ" and the "genius of Caesar" were compounded in the motives and methods of the great popes and in the whole history of ecclesiastical achievement and pretension. The ecclesiastical-religious con-

[17] I Cor. 12.   [18] Romans 7:23.

[Margin annotation:] In the Pauline concept of the body of Christ, the members are subordinated to the "head". Catholicism makes the justified and sanctified individual (i.e. the Pope) equal with Christ, who is the head.

[Margin note, handwritten:] Middle classes came to resent the social and political injustices of the papacy & resultant medieval society. Must overthrow religious authority which supported it.

trol of economic life was at once a harmonization of conflicting economic interests from an impartial perspective; and an intolerable alliance between priestly and feudal forces. The rising middle classes found this religious sanctification of the justice and injustice of the feudal order vexatious; and they came to the inevitable conclusion that the order could not be changed without challenging the religious authority which supported it.

The papal political control of Europe was on the one hand an effort to bring the self-will of nations under the dominion of the "law of Christ"; and it was on the other hand a claim of dominion shared with, and precariously maintained against, the empire. In this contest with the empire the alleged superiority of the "spiritual" over the "temporal" power was constantly used as a weapon of the ecclesiastical authority for the purpose of establishing "temporal" dominion. But this claim was not sufficient to maintain the precarious eminence of the papacy. It also availed itself of very "temporal" diplomatic and political strategies. These were finally subordinated to the primary pattern of using the rising French power as a counterweight against the German emperors. The religious collapse of the imposing structure was caused by the revolt against the religious pretensions inherent in the papal power. The political collapse was occasioned by the increasing subservience of papal power to these same French interests, which served originally as a counter-weight against the empire. The details and complexities of this struggle go beyond our present interest. It is important to recognize, however, that the ultimate outcome corresponds to the prophetic prediction of doom upon historical dominions which seek to usurp the majesty of God.[19]

The theological-religious control over the cultural life of Europe exhibited the same ambiguities as the economic and political dominion of the church. It was on the one hand an effort to bring all

[19] It may be relevant in this connection that in Ezekiel's impressive prophecies of doom upon all the nations of the world because "they have set their heart as the heart of God," ends with a prophecy of doom upon the spiritual leaders, "the shepherds of Israel," because they "fed themselves, and fed not my flock." Ezekiel 34:8.

truth of science, philosophy and culture under the authority of the truth of the gospel, in which partial truth finds its fulfillment and the sinful corruptions of truth are revealed and purged. It was on the other hand the expression of the pride of priests, seeking to transmute an ultimate religious position, which can be held only by faith, into a human possession and into an instrument of authority over other types of knowledge.

One need not be a fatalist to regard this whole development of Catholic doctrine as practically inevitable in the history of Christian thought and life. It was inevitable because man's self-esteem resists that part of the truth of the gospel which is set against all human achievements and discovers the sinful element of self-aggrandisement in them. That resistance was obvious before Christ came in the inadequacy of the solutions offered by Messianic hopes for the problem of history as disclosed by prophetic interpretation. They could not find a solution because they looked for a vindication of God which would include the vindication of the hopeful. The resistance was obvious in the circle of Jesus' own disciples, who found the idea of a suffering, rather than triumphant, Messiah offensive.[20] It was apparent in the early church which found the part of the gospel, which promised the completion of incomplete human life, more sympathetic than the Atonement, as an answer to the problem of sin.

Furthermore the complexities of the religious life, particularly the twofold aspect of grace, were sufficiently perplexing, even without the confusion prompted by human pride. Reason was bound to find difficulty in understanding that the faith and the grace by which we stand beyond the contradictions and ambiguities of history is no simple possession; that it is a having and not having; and that, claimed as a secure possession, it becomes a vehicle of the sin from which it ostensibly emancipates. For all these reasons the effort to achieve a perfection which stands beyond the contradictions of history was inevitable in Christian life; and it was equally inevitable

[20] *Cf.* Mk. 8:31-38.

[margin handwritten note:] Mistake of R.C.C. was inevitable, because man's self-esteem rebells against that part of the Gospel which points to his own sinfulness.

(granted the actual problem of man-in-history) that this effort should involve the church in new sins on the very pinnacle of its spiritual achievements. This is the pathos of the glory and the decline of medieval Christianity.

IV

THE DESTRUCTION OF THE CATHOLIC SYNTHESIS

The historic reaction to these achievements and pretensions was equally inevitable. In a sense the full truth of the gospel was never fully known, or at least never explicitly stated in the church until history had furnished incontrovertible proof of the error of simpler interpretations. Here lies the significance of the Reformation. It is the historical locus where that side of the gospel, which negates and contradicts historical achievements, became more fully known. This truth invaded the historical consciousness of Western man with a tempestuous fury and changed the whole history of Christendom. The polemical interests of the historic controversy, which was thereby initiated, were bound to prompt a frequently one-sided presentation of the rediscovered truth of the gospel. In this one-sided emphasis the other side of the gospel, embodied in the Catholic "synthesis" was frequently obscured or lost. But no polemic or other weaknesses of the Reformation can derogate from the fundamental character of the insights embodied in the Reformation doctrine of "justification by faith." This doctrine, which appears so irrelevant to modern men, who are strangers to both the Catholic and the Reformation interpretations of the Christian faith, represents the final renunciation in the heart of Christianity of the human effort to complete life and history, whether with or without divine grace. It represents the culmination of the prophetic interpretation of history; for it admits those aspects of historic reality without reservation, which the prophets first disclosed. It understands that human history is permanently suspended between the flux of nature and finiteness and its eternal source **and end**; that every effort to

[handwritten margin note: Justification by faith marks the historic moment when man realized the sinfulness which is part off his nature.]

escape this situation involves man in the sinful pride of seeking to obscure the conditioned character of his existence; and that even the knowledge of this fact, which man may have "by grace" is no guarantee of immunity from sin.

The Reformation understands that therefore we are "justified by faith" and "saved in hope"; that we must look forward to a completion of life which is not in our power and even beyond our comprehension. It realizes that the unity of human existence, despite its involvement in, and freedom from, natural process, is such that it cannot be "saved" either by disavowing its freedom in order to return to nature, or by sloughing off its creaturely character so that it may rise to the "eternal." This is a final enigma of human existence for which there is no answer except by faith and hope; for all answers transcend the categories of human reason. Yet without these answers human life is threatened with scepticism and nihilism on the one hand; and with fanaticism and pride on the other. For either it is overwhelmed by the relativity and partiality of all human perspectives and comes to the conclusion that there is no truth, since no man can expound the truth without corrupting it; or it pretends to have absolute truth despite the finite nature of human perspectives.

But before considering the meaning of Reformation doctrine more fully it is important to recognize that that curious compound of human self-confidence and gospel humility which was effected in the "medieval synthesis" was challenged not merely by the Reformation but also by the Renaissance. The spiritual life of recent centuries is determined by interactions between these two forces. Modern historians of culture have had some difficulty in relating these two great spiritual movements to each other. Frequently they are presented as merely two concurrent movements of "emancipation" from ecclesiastical control and superstition. At other times they are interpreted as successive movements of emancipation; and in that case the Renaissance is usually regarded as the more thorough. In such interpretations the logical order does not agree with the chronological one; for the Renaissance began two centuries earlier than the Reformation. It is significant, moreover, that it developed in the heart of Catholicism. Fifteenth-century Vatican life was the very centre of Renaissance spirituality. The fact is that the Renaissance was at once more Catholic and more "modern" than the Reformation.

This fact will seem paradoxical if it is not recognized that the Renaissance and Reformation represent partly contradictory historical forces, released by the disintegration of the medieval synthesis. For the Renaissance the Catholic interpretation of the human situation is too pessimistic; and for the Reformation it is too optimistic. But since the Catholic synthesis is more optimistic than pessimistic there is more affinity between the Renaissance and Catholicism than between Reformation and Renaissance or between the Reformation and Catholicism. The line between Catholic and Renaissance perfectionism is comparatively unbroken, though the Renaissance dispenses with "grace" as a prerequisite power for the fulfillment of life. It finds the capacities for fulfillment in human life itself. The Reformation on the other hand represents a more complete break with the medieval tradition; for it interprets "grace" primarily, not as the "power of God" in man; but as the power (forgiveness) of God towards man. It denies that either an individual life or the whole historical enterprise can be brought to the degree of completion which Catholic theories of grace imply.

The Renaissance opposes the ecclesiastical control of all cultural life in the name of the autonomy of human reason and thereby lays the foundation for the whole modern cultural development. The Reformation opposes the dogmatic control of religious thought by the church in the name of the authority of Scripture, insisting that no human authority (not even that of the church) can claim the right of possessing and interpreting the truth of the gospel, which stands beyond all human wisdom and which is invariably corrupted (at least in detail) by these interpretations. Each one of these protests against the church's pretended sole right or ability to interpret

[marginal handwritten note:] For the Renaissance the Catholic interpretation of the human situation was too pessimistic.

For the Reformation, the Catholic position was too optimistic.

and to apply the final truth has its own validity. But they are drawn from completely different levels of experience.

The Renaissance protest, in the name of the autonomy of reason, is much less conscious of the ultimate human problem. It knows that human perspectives are partial and finite; but it would overcome this finiteness progressively by the extension of the power of mind. It does not understand how invariably the paradox of finiteness and freedom leads to the more serious problem of sin. Its protest against ecclesiastical authority is nevertheless valid upon its own level. For religious dogma always tends to regard the ultimate sense of meaning, which it embodies, as a substitute for all the subordinate realms of meaning which the human mind discerns and discovers by tracing the causal sequences of nature and by bringing all phenomena into some realm of meaning by the power of coherence inherent in human reason.

Renaissance plead for the autonomy of human reason.

It is significant that the greatest achievement of Renaissance culture lay in directing rational inquisitiveness towards the elaboration of modern natural science. For in the study of nature the human mind may really approximate that god-like objectivity which it fondly, but erroneously, imagines itself to possess when it studies the facts of human history. In the field of history it is no pure mind which observes the facts, but an anxious reason, organically related to an anxious ego, reacting with pity or scorn, with fear or pride, to the greatness or the weakness, to the promised support or the threatened peril, of this or that competitive expression of human vitality.

The Reformation protest against ecclesiastical authority is conscious only of the ultimate human problem which transcends all the particular and subordinate realms of meaning in human life. It knows that human life cannot complete itself; that "the world by its wisdom knew not God"; and that the world involves itself in evil by finding some inadequate centre of meaning for its whole realm of coherence. It detects in the church control of religious dogma a new form of idolatry on the Christian level. Here a human institution centres life and history around itself; it does this by "possessing" the truth which transcends all truth and by pretending to dispense the "grace" which is a power beyond all human power and is operative only when human powers recognize their own limits.

Danger of Bible-olotry in Reformation.

The Reformation insistence upon the authority of Scripture, as against the authority of the church, bears within it the perils of a new idolatry. Its Biblicism became, in time, as dangerous to the freedom of the human mind in searching out causes and effects as the old religious authority. But rightly conceived Scriptural authority is meant merely to guard the truth of the gospel in which all truth is fulfilled and all corruptions of truth are negated. This authority is Scriptural in the sense that the Bible contains the history, and the culmination in Christ, of that *Heilsgeschichte* in which the whole human enterprise becomes fully conscious of its limits, of its transgressions of those limits, and of the divine answer to its problems. When the Bible becomes an authoritative compendium of social, economic, political and scientific knowledge it is used as a vehicle of the sinful sanctification of relative standards of knowledge and virtue which happen to be enshrined in a religious canon.

The Bible.

The Renaissance and Reformation conceptions of liberty which emerge from this struggle with authority also move on different levels, but they are not as diametrically opposed to each other as are the conceptions of life which underlie them. The Renaissance is interested primarily in freeing human life, and more particularly the human quest for knowledge, from inordinate social, political and religious restraints and controls. It is, therefore, the direct source of the struggle for freedom in human society, which has characterized the modern age. The Reformation means by freedom primarily the right and the ability of each soul to appropriate the grace of God by faith without the interposition of any restrictive institution of grace. It is interested in a freedom which transcends all social situations and may express itself even within and under tyranny.

Since, however, the same religious authority which claims to dispense "grace," and to control and mediate the divine mercy, also claims ultimate authority in the social-historical situation, the struggles for religious and social liberty tend to converge and to support each other. It is this fact which gives a certain plausibility to those interpretations of Renaissance and Reformation according to which both are diverse expressions of a common impulse towards liberty.

The struggle of the Renaissance and Reformation against religious authority, though more opposed to each other in basic principle than in actual expression, do not, however, reveal the full contrast between the two types of spirituality generated in each movement. That contrast may well be defined in terms of the "sanctification" and "justification" aspects of the Christian doctrine of grace.

The Renaissance is, when considered from the standpoint of Christian doctrine, "sanctificationist" in principle. In it all the reservations upon the hope of fulfilling life and realizing its highest possibilities, expressed in the prophetic-Christian consciousness, are brushed aside. If Catholic doctrine unduly subordinates the element of Christian truth symbolized in the concept of "justification," the Renaissance dismisses the idea completely, because it does not seem to correspond to any reality in its experience. One might add that on this issue the Renaissance has been definitive for the spirituality of modern man. For no typical modern man has any appreciation of the truth about life and history contained in the doctrine.

[margin handwritten note: Rennaissance does not recognize any barrier between the knowledge of the good and the power to do it.]

But the Renaissance goes further. It not only destroys the paradox of "justification" and "sanctification" but it dismisses the whole idea of "grace"; for it does not recognize any hiatus between the knowledge of the good and the power to do it. On that issue it represents a conscious return to classical conceptions of the human situation. It believes that man has capacities within himself (either rational or mystical) adequate for the fulfillment of life's most transcendent goals.[1] Here the Renaissance is equally definitive for modern spirit-

---

[1] The early Italian Renaissance expressed this confidence in human capacities in many forms: "I have made myself," said Potano. "Man can

uality. The only exception to this general tendency is to be found in "sectarian" Protestantism. Though the sects of the Reformation define salvation in essentially Renaissance and "perfectionist" terms, rather than in terms of the Reformation, they do retain the Christian concept of grace. The pietist sects believe that grace is required for the realization of individual perfection; and the apocalyptic sects depend upon the interposition of divine providence for the culmination of the whole historical process in an ideal society.[2]

It must be observed that while the perfectionism of the Renaissance was consciously based upon classical interpretations of the human situation it unconsciously added a Christian-Biblical element to its world view. Without this element it could not have taken its optimistic attitude towards the whole historical process. Its concept of history as a meaningful process, moving towards the realization of higher and higher possibilities is derived from Biblical-Christian eschatology. But the Renaissance, and with it the whole of modern culture, changed the Biblical conception of history at two important points. It did not conceive the fulfillment of history as transcending history and as therefore representing also its "end." Nor did it regard an ultimate "judgment" as a part of the "end" as in Biblical eschatology. It had, in other words, no consciousness of the ambiguous and tragic elements in history; or at least it knew of none which would not be progressively eliminated by the historical process itself. The whole of modern utopianism is thus implicit in Renaissance spirituality. The "idea of progress," the most characteristic and firmly held article in the *credo* of modern man, is the inevitable philosophy of history emerging from the Renaissance. This result was achieved

---

make whatever he will of himself," declared Alberti. "The nature of our spirit is universal," boasted Palmieri; and Ficino believed that "man seeks everywhere and always to be like God."

This assertion of human powers is less conscious or explicit in the later Renaissance because it is no longer under the necessity of stating it in opposition to Christian conceptions of grace.

[2] The relation of sectarian Christianity to Renaissance spirituality will be considered more fully in the next chapter.

[margin note: Renaissance concept of progress goes back to the Biblical-Christian idea of eschatology]

by combining the classical confidence in man with the Biblical confidence in the meaningfulness of history. It must be observed, however, that history is given a simpler meaning than that envisaged in the prophetic-Biblical view.

One of the tasks which confront us in re-assessing the human situation today is to reject what is false and to accept what is true in the Renaissance world view. Human history is indeed filled with *endless possibilities*; and the Renaissance saw this more clearly than either classicism, Catholicism or the Reformation. But it did not recognize that history is filled with endless possibilities *of good and evil.* It believed that the cumulations of knowledge and the extensions of reason, the progressive conquest of nature and (in its later developments) the technical extension of social cohesion, all of which inhere in the "progress" of history, were guarantees of the gradual conquest of chaos and evil by the force of reason and order. It did not recognize that every new human potency may be an instrument of chaos as well as of order; and that history, therefore, has no solution of its own problem.

Renaissance realized the limitless possibilities of human history, but it did not realize that these possibilities included both good and evil.

This tragic aspect of history, towards which the Renaissance was partly oblivious, was precisely that aspect of history which the Reformation most fully comprehended. This comprehension is contained in the Reformation polemic against all doctrines of sanctification, whether Catholic, secular or sectarian-Christian, in which it detects a too-simple confidence in historical possibilities. Its doctrine of "justification by faith" contains implications for an adequate interpretation of history which have never been fully appropriated or exploited, probably because most Protestant theologies which are interested in the historical problem, have drawn their inspiration from the Renaissance rather than from the Reformation.

It must be noted, however, that the understanding of the Reformation for the ultimate problem of historic existence was not (and probably could not) be elaborated without tendencies towards moral and cultural defeatism. Its consciousness of the ultimate frustration which faces every human enterprise inclined it towards indifference when dealing with all the proximate problems. When confronting these problems every moral situation, whether individual or collective, actually discloses, when fully analysed, unending possibilities of higher fulfillment. There is no limit to either sanctification in individual life, or social perfection in collective life, or to the discovery of truth in cultural life; except of course the one limit, that there will be some corruption, as well as deficiency, of virtue and truth on the new level of achievement.

This moral pessimism and cultural indifferentism of the Reformation was one cause of its defeat by the forces of the Renaissance. It must be recognized that the spiritual life of modernity has been primarily determined by this defeat. The indifference of the Reformation to the proximate problems and the immediate possibilities of human existence was, however, only one cause of this defeat. The other was that the phenomenal development of all the sciences and social techniques, of the conquest of nature and of the general extension of human capacities in the modern period were bound to emphasize what was true, and to hide what was false, in the Renaissance estimate of life.

In order to justify this interpretation of the modern situation it will be necessary to consider the Renaissance and the Reformation more fully. It is particularly important to understand why and how those aspects of the truth about human nature and destiny in which the Renaissance and the Reformation contradict each other, represent valuable insights into human nature and history, which are partially blunted and obscured in the medieval synthesis in which both were contained. The question is whether they can be so conceived and defined that they will not contradict or tend to defeat each other. If this were possible a philosophy of human nature and destiny could emerge which would reach farther into the heights and depths of life than the medieval synthesis; and would yet be immune to the alternate moods of pessimism and optimism, of cynicism and of sentimentality to which modern culture is now so prone.

CHAPTER VI

THE DEBATE ON HUMAN DESTINY IN MODERN
CULTURE: THE RENAISSANCE

OUR ANALYSIS of the human situation in the light of Christian faith has brought us to the conviction that both the Renaissance and the Reformation embody insights which must enter into an adequate redefinition of the possibilities and limits of man's historical existence. In order to do this effectively it is necessary to reopen a debate which was brought to a premature conclusion in modern culture by the almost complete triumph of the Renaissance over the Reformation. This triumph was so great that the most characteristic insights of the Reformation were lost even to the consciousness of large sections of Protestant Christianity. Modern Protestantism frequently betrays greater indifference to, and ignorance of, the ultimate problems for which the doctrine of justification by faith was the answer than either Catholic Christianity or secular culture. The former may have solved the problem too easily; but it has never ceased to be aware of it. Secular spirituality, on the other hand, is frequently prompted by a wholesome commonsense to recognize the inevitable relativities and frustrations of history more generously than the perfectionist presuppositions of many modern Protestants permit them to do. Sometimes it develops a secularized version of the doctrine of justification to meet the

problem of historical frustration; while liberal Protestantism remains enmeshed in sentimental and illusory historical hopes.[1]

Liberal Protestantism belongs, on the whole, to the Renaissance
rather than the Reformation side of the debate on human destiny.

The spiritual situation in the Anglican church conforms to neither
the Renaissance nor Reformation pattern of the other churches.
Though its Thirty-nine Articles and the prayer book are informed
by Reformation theology and piety, the characteristic insights of the
Reformation are frequently obscured. The spiritual tension in the
Anglican communion in recent centuries has been between Catholic
emphases and a pre-Renaissance liberalism which is at least partly
derived from the preoccupation of Anglican theology with patristic
thought. The emphasis upon classical learning in the older English
universities and the dependence of Anglican clergymen upon general university training rather than upon special theological studies,
tends to increase the classical content of Anglican thought and to
obscure the issues in which there is a contrast between Biblical and
classical perspectives.

The debate within Anglicanism is thus between a pre-Augustinian
theology and a post-Augustinian Catholicism. In this debate both
parties betray strong perfectionist tendencies. The former group has
affinities with modern liberalism; but prayer-book piety and the
influence of Christian history prevent the secularization of this semi-
Pelagianism. The Reformation content of the prayer book is meanwhile a constant resource, influencing the thought of the church
in various ways. It would be difficult to assess how many sermons
defy, and how many are inspired by, the spirit of the prayer of

---

[1] This judgment is more applicable to the spiritual situation in America than in Europe. European Protestantism has, generally speaking,
remained in closer contact with its own Reformation roots. American
Protestantism is predominantly sectarian in origin and has therefore
inherited the perfectionism of the sects of the Reformation. This perfectionism belongs spiritually to the Renaissance rather than the Reformation. In America it is frequently compounded with the secular perfectionism, derived from the French enlightenment.

general confession in which the devout are prompted to confess that "there is no health in us."

At its worst Anglican thought is a compound of liberalistic moralism and traditional piety. At its best it manages to combine all facets of the Christian doctrine of grace more truly than other churches.

The Renaissance was not as right, and the Reformation was not as wrong, as the outcome of the struggle would seem to indicate.

The conviction that the debate between Renaissance and Reformation must be reopened does not imply that the former was wholly wrong and the latter wholly right in defining the human situation. It implies only that the Renaissance was not as right, and the Reformation not as wrong, as the outcome of the struggle between them would seem to indicate. The debate has indeed been reopened already with the rise of "dialectical theology." This theology was a part of the general revolt against modern culture when the first World War prompted men to suspect that the facts of contemporary history were at variance with their interpretation in contemporary culture. But unfortunately this theological movement proceeded upon the assumption that the Renaissance was wholly wrong and that the Reformation was wholly right. In elaborating this conviction it stressed the most negative aspects of Reformation thought, even to the point of suppressing the emphasis upon sanctification and the fulfillment of life which the Reformation had retained.[2] In consequence the theological movement, initiated by Karl Barth has affected the thought of the church profoundly, but only negatively; and it has not challenged the thought outside of the church at all. It defied what was true in Renaissance culture too completely to be able to challenge what was false in it.

It seems necessary, therefore, to reopen the debate between Renaissance and Reformation by a different strategy, and to appreciate what was Christian and true in the Renaissance interpretation of life and history before we convict it of its errors.

[2] Adolf Koeberle's *The Quest of Holiness* is a significant Lutheran polemic against Barthian theology on the ground that it destroys the Reformation impulse towards sanctification.

II

THE MEANING OF THE RENAISSANCE

The Renaissance as a spiritual movement is best understood as a tremendous affirmation of the limitless possibilities of human existence, and as a rediscovery of the sense of a meaningful history. This affirmation takes many forms, not all of which are equally consistent with the fundamental impulse of the movement. But there is enough consistency in the movement as a whole to justify the historian in placing in one historical category such diverse philosophical, religious and social movements as the early Italian Renaissance, Cartesian rationalism and the French enlightenment; as the liberal idea of progress and Marxist catastrophism; as sectarian perfectionism and secular utopianism. In all of these multifarious expressions there is a unifying principle. It is the impulse towards the fulfillment of life in history. The idea that life can be fulfilled without those reservations and qualifications which Biblical and Reformation thought make is derived from two different sources; from the classical confidence in human capacities and from the Biblical-Christian impulse towards sanctification and the fulfillment of life, more particularly the Biblical-eschatological hope of the fulfillment of history itself.

These two sources determine the double connotation of the very word Renaissance. Just as the Renaissance is a conscious return to classical learning and to classical conceptions of the human situation, so also the more obvious connotation of the word "renaissance" is merely the "rebirth" of learning in general and of classical learning in particular. Though this is the only connotation recognized in most modern histories of culture, the word also meant something much more significant. It meant the rebirth of the earth and of human society. It was an expression of Christian eschatological hopes. This profounder meaning may have been less conscious than the former; but it must be observed that, in the early Renaissance

at least, the more profound and far-reaching connotation of "renaissance" was more explicit than later theories of the meaning of the
word and of the movement implied.[1]

Renaissance conceptions of both individual and historical fulfillment drew partly upon resources of the Catholic ages. The Renaissance idea of the infinite possibilities of individual life was ostensibly based upon classical conceptions; but these classical conceptions
were never completely lost in Catholic rationalism, and they expressed themselves with particular force in the perfectionism of
Catholic mysticism and monasticism. An unbroken line runs from
the medieval mystics to Protestant pietists. The Renaissance idea of
the fulfillment of history, which was finally elaborated in the idea
of progress of the seventeenth and eighteenth century, was at least
partly derived from Franciscan radicalism.

Franciscan piety, arising in the thirteenth century, has the distinction of being both the final flower of monastic perfectionism
and the beginning of a new sense of historical fulfillment. The
charm of its individual perfectionism was derived from the absolutism of the gospel ethic rather than from the world-denying dualism
and mysticism which partly informed traditional medieval monasticism. Its sense of a dynamic and meaningful history, moving towards the establishment of the Kingdom of God on earth, was the
result of a merger between the apocalypticism of Joachim of Flores
and St. Francis' ideas of sanctification. Joachim of Flores may be
regarded as the first thinker of the medieval period who challenged
the static conception of history which had resulted from the identification of the church with the Kingdom of God in Catholic doctrine. According to Joachim, the history of the world was divided

---

[1] Konrad Burdach in his *Reformation, Renaissance, Humanismus*
adduces convincing proof of the conscious intention of Renaissance
thinkers to indicate something much more than a revival of learning by
their hope of rebirth. When they spoke of *"nova vita,"* of *"renovatio,"*
"renovari," *"renasci"* and *"regeneratio"* they thought of the regeneration,
sometimes of the individual life, sometimes of the church, sometimes of
Roman and Italian civilization and sometimes of the world.

into three periods, that of the Father, of the Son and of the Holy Spirit. The period of the Son was his own contemporary ecclesiastical epoch and was drawing to a close. But he looked forward to the epoch of the Holy Spirit in which the law of Christ, only contained as a promise in Catholic sacramentalism, would be inwardly fulfilled.

The radical wing of Franciscanism claimed that the apocalyptic hopes of Joachim had been realized in the perfection of Francis' life and would be fulfilled in the ideal order which Franciscan monasticism would establish. The thought of the "spirituals" of the type of Frater Peter John Olivi, who frequently claimed a spiritual eminence for Francis which challenged the very centrality of Christ in Christian dogma, may be regarded as the real emergence of historical consciousness from the a-historical and non-historical piety of mysticism. This is where Biblical eschatological thought, long submerged by the classical and ecclesiastical ingredients in the medieval synthesis, came into its own once again. It is significant, however, that a new modern element is subtly compounded with Christian eschatology. According to Olivi, history itself is *Heilsgeschichte*. The modern confidence in the redemptive power of the historical process itself is evident in embryonic form in the thought of the Franciscan spirituals.[2]

Franciscan theologians mediated both the individual perfectionist urge and the hope of historical fulfillment to the Renaissance. The greatest of Franciscan theologians, Bonaventura, was the special mediator of the one, and Roger Bacon of the other. Bonaventura's ambitious words: "He who loves God with perfect love is transformed into Him" were re-echoed, and frequently secularized in the "titanism" of the Renaissance. Bonaventura always remained

---

[2] The most authoritative historical analysis of this extraordinary merger of mystical and eschatological-historical consciousness in the confluence of the Joachimite and Franciscan thought is to be found in Ernst Benz, *Ecclesia spiritualis*.

conscious of man's dependence upon grace; while the Renaissance regarded the marvellous intellectual powers, inherent in human nature, as the source of all those limitless possibilities of human life which its literature celebrated. The relation between Franciscan perfectionism and Renaissance hopes is nevertheless real.

Roger Bacon's passion for learning frequently prompts modern historians to celebrate him as the "first modern," as the harbinger of the spring of a new age in the winter of the Middle Ages. But it is not always observed that he justifies learning primarily as the best method of providing men with weapons for meeting the peril of the Anti-Christ, who is to appear in the fullness of time. Thus Franciscan eschatology and the new passion for learning are united in the thought of Bacon. Naturally the sense of a dynamic history, moving towards its fulfillment in the present and the future, is not of purely Christian or Franciscan-Joachimite origin. The general awakening of the Renaissance, its sense of new powers and potencies, prompted a spontaneous generation of the sense of the fulfillment of history. Yet without the Christian eschatological presuppositions, the classical conceptions to which the Renaissance ostensibly returned, would not have provided adequate vehicles for this mood.

Actually the new and the old are strangely mingled in Dante's vision of both individual and political rebirth, in Petrarch's symbols of awakening from sleep, and in the sketches of utopia in the later Renaissance; Francis Bacon's *New Atlantis,* Sir Thomas More's *Utopia,* and Campanella's *Civitas solis.* There are echoes of Franciscan eschatology in the political Messianic pretensions of Carlo Rienzo, the unifier of Rome [3] and even in the ludicrous Messianic consciousness of Emperor Frederick II, pretensions which prompted ecclesiastical authorities to level the charge of Anti-Christ against him. [4]

The heightened sense of individuality and the urge towards the fulfillment of the highest possibilities of individual life in Renais-

[3] Burdach, *op. cit.,* Ch. II.   [4] Benz, *op. cit.,* p. 225.

ance spirituality have been considered in another connection.[5] It is therefore necessary to complete the picture of Renaissance thought here by sketching the development of theories of history through which Christian eschatological conceptions were transmuted into the modern idea of progress.

The chief agent of this development was undoubtedly the new confidence in developing reason, in cumulative knowledge and experience and in the rational conquest of nature. In this historical trend the classical confidence in rational man was disassociated from the historical pessimism of classical culture and made the instrument of historical optimism.[6] Even when, as in the case of Descartes, problems of the meaning of history were not consciously or explicitly considered, the passion for science is subtly related to historical optimism.[7]

Whatever form this confidence in reason as a force of historical progress may take, all the forms are expressions of a unified philosophical mood. The guiding principle of the philosophy which underlies the idea of progress is that of an immanent *logos* which is no longer believed to transcend history as an eternal form, but is thought of as operating in history, bringing its chaos gradually under the dominion of reason. Sometimes, as in the thought of Fichte and Hegel, this idea is profoundly conceived as a part of a whole metaphysical system; and history becomes, as in Fichte's thought, an indeterminate approximation of the receding goal of rational freedom, or, as in Hegel's thought, it is the gradual development of the self-consciousness of the eternal Spirit. Sometimes, as in the French enlightenment, the historical optimism merely rests upon the certainty that reason will generate individual virtue, or

---

[5] In Vol. I, Ch. III.

[6] This is particularly clear in the thought of Francis Bacon who protests against the cyclical interpretation of history, inherited from classicism, declaring that it is an obstacle to the advancement of learning.

[7] Descartes had originally intended to give his *Discourse on Method* the title: "The Project of a Universal Science, which can elevate our Nature to its highest degree of Perfection."

destroy the superstitions which hinder social progress,[8] or will prompt wise rather than foolish government.[9] Sometimes, particularly in the eighteenth-century Enlightenment, which was a less profound second chapter of the Renaissance, the historical hope rests altogether upon the idea that the rational conquest of nature will enhance physical welfare and increase physical comforts.[10]

Though the idea of progress as the most dominant and characteristic article in the creed of modernity is powerful enough to use the most diverse philosophies as its instruments, this basic confidence in an immanent *logos* principle never really varies. Even when Darwinism is used to express the mood of historical optimism in the nineteenth century, and the biological idea of the survival of the fittest becomes the bearer of historical optimism, a very naturalistic version of the *logos* principle is operative. For the law of survival in nature is thought of as a force of harmony and progress which will transmute even the most tragic conflicts of history into means of historical advance.

Neither the nineteenth nor twentieth century adds anything of importance to the general dogma of progress, as conceived from the

[8] Condorcet looks forward to the day "when tyrants and slaves, priests and their stupid hypocritical tools will have disappeared" and when men will be freemen with "no master save reason."

[9] Voltaire hopes for a period when "prejudices . . . will gradually disappear among all those that govern nations" and when "philosophy universally diffused, will give some consolation to human nature for the calamities which it will experience in all ages." Voltaire, unlike many of his contemporaries, is never a consistent optimist.

[10] Sébastien Mercier asked: "Where will the perfectability of man stop, armed with geometry and the mechanical arts and chemistry?"

Priestley expressed this more vulgar idea of progress perfectly in the words: "Nature, including both its materials and its laws, will be more at our command; men will make their situation in this world abundantly more easy and comfortable; they will prolong their existence in it and will grow daily more happy. . . . Thus whatever the beginning of the world, the end will be glorious and paradisiacal beyond what our imagination can now conceive." Quoted by J. B. Bury, *The Idea of Progress*, pp. 197 and 221.

early Renaissance to the eighteenth century. Most modern socio-logical-historical philosophies take the idea for granted and elaborate it in terms which are derived from, or at least similar to, the thought of Comte or Spencer.

The relation between these modern ideas of progress and Christian eschatology is that in both cases history is conceived dynamically rather than statically or retrogressively.[11] The difference between them is twofold. The first difference is that the Renaissance thinks of the fulfillment of life, whether individually or in terms of total history, without "grace." It neither needs nor expects either an infusion of power for the fulfillment of individual life or the operation of "providence" in the fulfillment of history. The "laws" of nature and the "laws" of reason are its surrogates for providence. They give meaning to the whole of history, for they guarantee its growth. It does not deal with the problem of power, because it accepts the classical thesis that *logos,* reason, law or any forming principle of life inevitably bring the vitalities of history under its dominion.

The second difference is of even greater importance. The Renaissance regards history as dynamic; but it generally disregards the twofold dynamic in it. It assumes that all development means the advancement of the good. It does not recognize that every heightened potency of human existence may also represent a possibility of evil. The symbol for this difference is that in Christian eschatology the *end* of history is both judgment and fulfillment. The modern conception sees the end as only fulfillment.[12] Sometimes it is purely

[11] The identification of the church with the Kingdom of God led to a static conception of history in the middle ages. An even more dominant medieval idea, that the world was degenerating was probably compounded of classical pessimism and the negative side of the Christian expectation of the "end" of the world. The early Renaissance was continually engaged in the refutation of this retrogressive view of history.

[12] Marxist catastrophism comes considerably closer to Christian eschatology by its idea of a catastrophic judgment upon the evils of a capitalistic society which will usher in the period of fulfillment. But it cannot conceive of a judgment upon this new period of fulfillment.

utopian and anticipates the realization of the unconditioned good within the conditions of nature-history. But even when there are conceptions of an infinitely regressive goal, as for instance in the thought of Fichte,[13] the relation between the historical and the eternal is regarded as primarily the relation between "becoming" and "being." There is no sense of the historical being involved, on every level of achievement, in contradiction to the eternal. This tragic idea is expressed in Christian faith by its doctrine of a "final judgment," to which all history is subject.

The contradiction between the historical and the divine is created by the inevitable tendency of every individual and collective comprehension and realization of the meaning of history to complete the system of meaning falsely, with the self, individual or collective, as the premature centre, source, or end of the system. The inability of any age, culture or philosophy to comprehend the finiteness of its perspectives and the limit of its powers always produces a presumptuous claim of finality.

There is a curious pathos in the fact that modern interpretations of history almost invariably exhibit this tendency in their incidental errors and miscalculations. They identify their own age or culture, or even their own philosophy with the final fulfillment of life and truth and history. This is the very error which they have not taken into account or discounted in their basic principle of interpretation. It is not possible for any philosophy to escape this error completely. But it is possible to have a philosophy, or at least a theology, grounded in faith, which understands that the error will be committed and that it is analogous to all those presumptions of history which defy the majesty of God.[14]

[13] Cf. *Die Grundzuege des Gegenwaertigen Zeitalters* (1806).

[14] Benedetto Croce calls attention to the "fantastic idolization of France" in the thought of the French historian and philosopher of history, Michelet (Croce, *History as the Story of Liberty*, p. 24). Fichte believed that history would move from the fourth period of conscious reason and science to the fifth period of "regnant reason and art" chiefly through the mediation of German philosophy. Hegel was less nationalistic in his

"Our age," declared the French historian, Charles Perrault in 1687, "is, in some sort, arrived at the very summit of perfection. And since for some years the rate of progress has been much slower and appears almost insensible—as the days seem to cease lengthening when the summer solstice draws near—it is pleasant to think that there are probably not many things for which we need envy future generations." [15]

Historical fulfillment is not always claimed for the present. In its profounder moods modern philosophy of history makes the future rather than the present the surrogate for God and calls upon it to assume the divine functions of judging and redeeming the present. In this form it expresses the pride merely of man in general and not of a particular age and culture But even in this form the future is usually regarded as but a further extension of the present; and no further historical development is expected which might stand in contradiction to the achievements of the present.

In short the common and most grievous error in modern interpretations of history is their too simple conception of historical progress. They are right in conceiving history dynamically. Their understanding of the indeterminate possibilities of both individual and collective human existence is profounder than the alternate Catholic and Reformation conceptions; and this insight must be taken into account in any reformulation of the problem of human destiny. But they are wrong in conceiving the dynamic aspects of

---

conception but even more presumptuous. He believed that "the Germanic spirit is the spirit of the new world, whose object is the realization of absolute truth as endless self-determination of freedom which has its absolute form itself for content. The vocation of the Germanic peoples is to furnish bearers of the Christian principle" (*Philosophie der Geschichte* in *Werke*, Vol. ix, p. 415). The conception is not nationalistic for "Germanic peoples" means something more than "German." But it is more presumptuous than Fichte's thought, for it does not look forward to a final period of history. Rather it seems to contemplate present culture as having achieved the final good of history.

[15] Quoted by Bury, *op. cit.*, p. 87.

history too simply. They hope for an ever increasing dominance of "form" and "order" over all historical vitalities, and refuse to acknowledge that history cannot move forward towards increasing cosmos without developing possibilities of chaos by the very potencies which have enhanced cosmos.

III

SECTARIAN PROTESTANTISM AND THE RENAISSANCE

It is not possible to conclude the discussion of Renaissance spirituality without considering a form of Protestantism which has some remarkable affinities with the basic Renaissance attitude towards history, namely sectarian Protestantism. The Protestant sects, which arose contemporaneously with the Reformation, are critical of Catholicism for reasons which are in almost complete contrast to those of the Reformation. They do not protest against the claims of perfection which Catholicism makes. They are, themselves, usually extravagantly perfectionist. Their primary quarrel with Catholicism is that they suspect sacramentalism of achieving a pseudo-perfection and of "piping" and infusing grace too painlessly into the soul of the sinner and thus failing to induce a genuine change towards a new life.[1]

Sectarian Protestantism draws its inspiration from more Biblical sources than the Renaissance, though some forms of it have a common root in medieval mysticism. But it expresses a common impulse toward the completion of life and history.

In order to explore the genius of sectarianism more fully it is advisable to distinguish between two types of sects, or at least between two impulses in sectarianism: (*a*) The impulse towards the

---

[1] Robert Coachman, a sectarian leveller of the Cromwellian period, makes this typical criticism of sacramental grace: "When all manner of graceless men are fed with seales and pledges of God's favor and are invested with the full privileges and highest prerogatives of the most godly in the church, and are daily told that here is the body and blood of Christ given for them, how presumptuous they grow." *The Glory of the Stone* (1641), p. 15.

perfection of individual life expressed in the pietistic sects and
(b) the impulse towards the fulfillment of history expressed particularly in the Anabaptist and socially radical sects.

a. The Pietistic Sects. The pietistic-mystical sects combine a mystical and a Biblical element in varying proportions. Where the
mystical element is strongest, redemption is conceived as a restoration of some original unity of life, which must be achieved by
contemplation. Where the Biblical element is strongest conversion
is by "grace." The emphasis on grace is strongest in the evangelistic
sects. Here the conversion experience is regarded not so much as
the development of some inner power within the self as a shattering
of the old and sinful self and its reconstruction by the Holy Spirit.
The belated pietistic-evangelistic sect of Methodism insisted most
consistently on the strategy of creating a conversion crisis by confronting the soul with the spirit of Christ. This crisis affects the total
self and generates that creative despair, that "Godly sorrow" which
makes it possible for the "power" of the Holy Spirit to reconstruct
the self on a higher level.

The perfectionist impulse in sectarian Christianity is informed
by the same logic which we have studied in pre-Augustinian Christianity. Sometimes it is expressed in extravagant terms, as in the words
of George Fox: "For all the sects of Christendom that I discoursed
with I found none that could bear to be told that any should come
to Adam's perfection, into the image of God, that righteousness
and holiness that Adam was in before he fell; to be pure and clean
without sin as he was. Therefore how shall they be able to bear being told that any shall grow up into the full measure of the stature
of Christ, when they cannot bear to hear that any shall come, while
on earth, into the same power and spirit that the prophets and
apostles were in." [2]

[2] George Fox, *Journal*, p. 101. Fox does not hesitate to make explicit
sanctificationist claims for his own redeemed state: "I knew nothing,"
he writes of his conversion, "but pureness and innocency and righteousness, being renewed in the image of Christ Jesus so that I say I was come
up to the state of Adam, which he was in before he fell. . . . But imme-

Sectarian perfectionism is constantly in peril of destroying the paradox of sanctification and justification in Biblical religion. Its experience of grace is conceived entirely as *"Christus in nobis"* and not as *"Christus pro nobis."* In common with George Fox, most sectarian perfectionists imagine that orthodox Christians, whether Catholic or Protestant, fail to achieve perfection only because they do not try hard enough or do not define perfection as the goal of the Christian life with sufficient rigour and consistency.[3]

If we study the conceptions of human nature which underlie sectarian doctrines and isolate the mystical, rationalistic and Biblical elements which are expressed there, it becomes quite apparent that the perfectionist idea of salvation is intimately related to and dependent upon previous conceptions of human nature. These conceptions, though influenced by Biblical thought in varying degrees, are essentially mystical or rationalistic. In common with both classicism and medieval mysticism, pietism believes in a universal and divine element in human nature which can be freed from the temporal. It has little understanding of the paradox that sin is the fruit of spirit and is possible only in that freedom; for it regards spirit the divine quality in man.[4] In terms of the symbols of Christian doctrine this mistake could be defined as mistaking the image of God in man for God Himself. "The Kingdom of God is within

---

diately I was taken up in spirit to see another and more steadfast state than Adam's innocency, even into the state of Christ Jesus that should never fall." *Ibid.,* p. 286.

[3] In Rufus M. Jones' *Spiritual Reformers,* the most eminent contemporary Quaker philosopher assumes that the perfectionist sects represent the real Reformation and that the actual Reformation movement was arrested by its refusal to follow the logic of Christian sanctification to its real conclusion.

[4] A contemporary critic of Fox saw this error very clearly; he wrote: "The light within, say they, is the only judge we must follow, the only Pilot we must steer by, the voice whereunto we must give ear, the only sanctuary to which we must fly for resolution, never remembering how this sanctuary is profaned by continual acts of idolatry and fornication therein committed." Richard Sherlock, *The Quakers Wilde Questions* (1654), p. 66.

you," declared Hans Denck, the father of both pietistic and apocalyptic sectarianism, "and he who searches outside himself will never find it, for apart from God no one can either seek or find him, for he who seeks God already in truth has him." [5]

The idea of the "inner light" and of the "hidden seed" always suggests that the divine element in human life may be found at the deepest level of consciousness or the highest level of mind. The idea is sometimes more mystical and sometimes more rationalistic. Sebastian Franck gives it a purely mystical connotation: "This inner light," he declared, "is nothing else than the word of God, God himself, by whom all things are made and by whom all men are enlightened. . . . No one can know God outside himself, outside of that region where *he knows himself in the ground of himself.*" [6]

The typical mystical strategy of introversion, the "journey towards the centre", is again and again commended as the way of salvation. Peter Balling, leader of the Dutch sectarian "Collegiant" movement, defined the technique of introversion in terms known in every type of mysticism: "We direct thee to within thyself," he wrote. "Thou oughtest to turn into, to mind and have regard to, that which is within thee, to wit, the light of truth, the true light which enlighteneth every man that cometh into the world." [7] Peter Sterry, one of Cromwell's court preachers, has a similar conception of the divine element in man lying at the depth of human consciousness, which is to be found by introversion. He wrote: "There is a spiritual man which lies hid under the natural man as seed under the ground. . . . If thou *go into thyself* beyond the natural man, thou shalt meet the Spirit of God." Any one who "would know the soul to its depths would know God." [8]

In the thought of the Dutch pietist and humanist, Cornhert, the

[5] Rufus M. Jones, *Spiritual Reformers of the Sixteenth and Seventeenth Centuries,* p. 24.

[6] *Ibid.,* p. 54.

[7] Peter Balling, *The Light of the Candlestick* (1662). Balling was in intimate relation with Spinoza.

[8] Rufus M. Jones, *op. cit.,* p. 283.

divine principle in man is interpreted in more purely rationalist terms. He believed that "through reason man partakes of the word of God which is reason itself, revealed and uttered. Therefore man may know of his own salvation with a certainty which far transcends the lower knowledge which we possess of external things." [9]

The Quaker, John Norris, defined the inner light with a confused combination of Biblical and rationalistic terms: "I think," wrote Norris, "that (a) that there is a light in man otherwise how can he know or perceive anything; (b) that he is not his own light or a light unto himself; and (c) that God is his light. That divine light is to be consulted and its answers carefully attended to." [10]

The confusion appears again and again in Quaker thought. The treatises do not always make clear whether "Christ" and "Spirit" are meant in the Biblical or the mystical sense. Sometimes they are used to designate merely native endowments of the soul; and sometimes they are used ambiguously, as for instance in Barclay's "Apology," one of the ablest of Quaker systematic treatises. "By this seed," he writes, ". . . we understand a spiritual and heavenly and invisible principle in which God as Father, Son and Spirit dwells, *a measure of which divine and glorious life is in all men as a seed* which of its own nature draws and *invites us to God;* and this we call *vehiculum Dei* or the spiritual body of Christ because it is never separated from God nor Christ . . . therefore as it is resisted God is said to be resisted; and on the contrary as it is received in the heart and suffered to bring forth its proper and natural effect, Christ comes to be formed and raised." [11]

In the thought of the various sectarian perfectionists, Wesley's conception, despite his indebtedness to such mystics as Thomas à Kempis, William Law, Theologia Germanica and Tauler, contains the largest Biblical element. Wesley is quite clear that deliverance must be from sin and not from finiteness; and he thinks of the

[9] *Ibid.,* p. 108.
[10] William C. Braithwaite, *Second Period of Quakerism,* p. 392.
[11] Robert Barclay, *An Apology for the True Christian Divinity,* p. 136.

process in existential rather than in purely contemplative terms. Furthermore his thought is rooted in the New Testament doctrine of forgiveness and justification. However, he regards justification in essentially Augustinian terms: as forgiveness for sins that are past; and he thinks of sanctification as the higher stage of redemption.

Wesley was in continual debate with the German pietists, particularly the Moravians, in regard to the doctrines of justification and sanctification, the latter, particularly Zinzendorf, being strongly under the influence of Reformation thought. Wesley records a debate with Zinzendorf in his journal as follows: Z: "I acknowledge no inherent perfection in this life. This is the error of errors. I pursue it through the world with fire and sword. Christ is our sole perfection. Whoever follows inherent perfection denies Christ." W: "But I believe that the spirit of Christ works this perfection in true Christians." Z: "By no means; all our perfection is in Christ. Our whole Christian perfection is faith in the blood of Christ. All Christian perfection is imputed and not inherent. We are perfect in Christ. In ourselves we are never perfect." W: "We strive about words." [12]

In this debate between Wesley and the Moravians all the significant issues between Reformation and perfectionist spirituality emerge. Wesley is primarily intent to guard against antinomianism in Reformation thought. He protests against the doctrine that "there is only one commandment in the New Testament, *viz.* to believe." He calls this assertion a "gross, palpable contradiction to the whole tenor of the New Testament, every part of which is full of commandments from St. Matthew to Revelation." [13] In a letter to the church at Herrnhut he writes: "I have heard that some of you affirm that it [salvation] implies liberty from the commandments of God so that one who is saved through faith is not obliged to obey them." In this same letter in which the moral tension of sectarian Christianity is rightly set against the antinomianism, to which Reforma-

[12] Wesley's *Journal*, Vol. II, p. 487.   [13] *Journal* II, p. 356.

tion thought is prone, he also wrongly attacks what is true in
Reformation thought and declares: "I have heard some of you
affirm that it [salvation] does not imply the proper taking away
of our sins, the cleansing of our souls from all sin but only the
tearing of the system of sin to pieces." [14]

This debate, in which each side is right on one point and wrong
on the other, may be taken as a miniature of the whole controversy
between the Renaissance and Reformation.[15] The one rightly maintains the moral imperatives of the gospel and wrongly imagines that
they can be completely realized; the other rightly understands the
limits of historic existence but is wrongly tempted to an antinomianism, which allows men "to continue in sin that grace may
abound."

[14] *Ibid.,* II, 491. The same issue arises in a conversation with two
Moravians, Boehler and Spangenberg. The latter asserts that "the old
creature or old man remains with us till the day of our death." But "the
new man is stronger than the old; so that while corruption continually
strives, yet while we look to Christ it cannot prevail." Wesley asked him:
"Is there then corruption in your heart?" and Spangenberg answered
with the proper paradox: "In the heart of my old man there is but not
in the heart of my new man. . . . Inward corruption cannot be taken
away till our bodies are in the dust." Wesley records this conversation
and adds the observation: "Was there inward corruption in our Lord;
And cannot the servant be as his master?" *Ibid.,* p. 452.

[15] It is not possible to consider all the complexities of Wesley's perfectionism. It ought to be mentioned, however, that some of his perfectionist claims arise from a Pelagian doctrine of sin. He defined it as a "voluntary defiance of a known law." Perfection as conscious compliance
with known laws is of course possible. Meanwhile Wesley was too much
of a realist to be able to deny the reality of those sinful elements in the
life of the redeemed which are neither fully conscious nor yet completely
unconscious. (Cf. *Nature and Destiny of Man,* Vol. I, Chs. VII and
VIII.) There is thus a conflict in Wesley's thought between his realism
and his defective doctrine of sin, which results in such equivocal statements as "I do not contend for the term sinless though I do not object
against it." He resolved the conflict by a rather neat theological device.
He declared that there was no moment in life for which real perfection
could be claimed except the moment just before death. His disciples have
not always had the prudence to set the same limits.

Sectarian pietism, representing an amalgam of Biblical and mystical presuppositions, never externalizes the fulfillment of life in the manner of secular spiritual movements which had their rise in the Renaissance. It is significant nevertheless that it makes perfectionist claims which obscure the realities of historic existence as effectively as secular utopianism; and sometimes it indulges in even more deleterious sentimentalities. The root of the error of sectarian perfectionism is to be found in a conception logically and historically related to those held by secular perfectionists. The "hidden seed" and the "inner light" is an immanent Christ, which corresponds to the immanent *logos* of the main stream of Renaissance thought. The immanent Christ may be conceived more dynamically than the immanent *logos;* and conversion and redemption may therefore involve the total personality to a larger degree than the various secular *logos* doctrines do. But the idea of an immanent Christ in man, just as a completely immanent *logos* in history, obscures the real dialectic between the historical and the eternal. It fails to recognize that the freedom of man in history, whether conceived in rational or mystical terms contains possibilities of both good and evil.

b. The Eschatological Sects. The perfectionist impulse of the Reformation sects was not confined to the hope of individual sanctification in the pietistic-individualistic sects. It expressed itself also in the eschatological hopes for the fulfillment of history and the realization of a perfect society of the social radical sects, particularly the Anabaptists of the continent and the Cromwellian sects of seventeenth century England. Some of these were "suffering" sects and some were "fighting," to adopt Troeltsch's distinction. This is to say that some were more purely apocalyptic, waiting upon God to usher in the "Kingdom of Christ," while others were ready to engage the enemy in order to bring in the Kingdom of God upon earth. Whatever the differences between them they are all expressions of the impulse towards the fulfillment of life and history, which belongs to Renaissance spirituality.

If the pietist sects revealed the Biblical element in their thought and life by their idea of individual conversion through "grace" and "power," the eschatological sects betrayed their relation to the Biblical thought-world by conceiving of the historical process as moving towards a critical conflict between Christ and Antichrist rather than as a gradual process of the triumph of good over evil.[16]

The conceptions of continental Anabaptists of the sixteenth century and the "Fifth Monarchy" men of seventeenth century England were explicitly apocalyptic.[17] This led on the continent to absurd attempts at the realization of the Kingdom of God upon earth, the best known of which was the experiment at Münster, where Jan Bockelson, finally proclaimed himself "King of the whole earth." [18] The apocalyptics of England, unfortunately, or perhaps fortunately, were never able to claim the realization of the Kingdom. They had, in consequence, a much more creative relationship to all the democratic and equalitarian movements initiated in Cromwellian England. This distinction between continental and English apocalyptics

[16] The Quakers, in so far as they hoped for the social realization of the Kingdom of Christ on earth, came nearest to an evolutionary or progressive view of history, for they regarded the realization of love in individual life as at the same time the force which would gradually redeem society. The continental pacifist sects, on the other hand, particularly the Mennonites, were more purely apocalyptic. Menno Simons initiated the protest against the "fighting" sects of the Anabaptist movement on the continent. But he was never under the illusion that "suffering love" would gradually become historically successful and would overcome the world. He thought of it rather as a sign and symbol of the Kingdom of God, which God would have to usher in in his good time. The problem of historical evil was, according to his faith, beyond the comprehension and the power of man.

[17] The "Fifth Monarchy" men discerned five great periods of history, four of which had been dominated by the great empires of history and the fifth of which would be the period in which all kingdoms of the world would be subordinated to the Kingdom of Christ. This apocalyptic idea was not confined to a closely knit sect but spread through the other Cromwellian sects. *Cf.* George P. Gooch, *Democratic Ideas in Seventeenth-Century England.*

[18] *Cf.* E. B. Bax: *The Rise and Fall of the Anabaptists,* and Eduard Bernstein, *Cromwell and Communism.*

prompts the observation that what is legitimate in the perfectionist urge is always most perfectly expressed *in spe*. It is a good thing to seek for the Kingdom of God on earth; but it is very dubious to claim to have found it. In that claim some new relativity of history and some new egoistic force make pretensions of sanctity which, at best, are merely absurd and, at worst, unleash new furies and fanaticisms. That is why Marxism is so much better as leaven in history than the realized Marxism of Stalinism.

Even when the apocalyptic mood was less explicit in sectarian life, most of the English sects, who constituted the left-wing of Cromwell's army were implicitly eschatological. They were inclined to regard the political and economic system from which they suffered as the final form of historical evil and to hope, therefore, that victory over it would usher in the final period of social perfection.

Thus while Biblical eschatology was responsible for their view of history, as moving towards a final crisis, the general mood of historical optimism prompted them to seek for the Kingdom of God, without reservation, in history. They disregarded the Biblical idea of a "final" judgment and a "final" fulfillment beyond all possible historical realizations.

Their affinity with Renaissance thought is furthermore revealed in their inclination to identify God and "Spirit" with reason, and reason with the "natural law" of justice, which they used as a principle of criticism against historic forms of injustice. Gerrard Winstanley, the leader of the Diggers, wrote: ". . . the spirit which will purge mankind is pure reason. . . . Though men esteeme this word reason to be too meane to set forth the Father by, yet it is the highest name that can be given him. . . . For it is reason that made all things and it is Reason that governs the whole creation." [19]

Winstanley, who is probably the profoundest as well as the most radical of the Cromwellian sectaries, exhibited another extremely

[19] *The Saint's Paradise*, p. 78.

significant conflict between Biblical and modern conceptions in his thought. He had on the one hand a Biblical conception of the fall, according to which the fall is synonymous with the rise of "particular love," against the principle of "universal love." His other theory makes him the real progenitor of the Marxist interpretation of history. The idea is that sin comes into the world through the rise of property; for "this particular propriety of mine and thine has brought in all misery upon the people. For first it has occasioned people to steal from one another. Secondly it hath made laws to hang those that did steal." [20] According to this theory it will be possible to abolish sin by returning to those conditions of "common treasury" which existed in the beginning of history.[21] Here, in the second interpretation is one of the first of the modern interpretations of historical evil, which seeks its origin in some specific *locus* of history and in a special historical "fall." Winstanley anticipates the Marxist interpretation of history.

All of the radical sects of the Cromwellian period looked forward towards an ideal society, though they did not define it in identical terms. The Levellers were more libertarian and the Diggers more equalitarian. Between them they anticipated the modern bourgeois ideals of liberty and the proletarian ideals of equality.

The insistence of sectarian Christianity that the Kingdom of God is relevant to all historical social problems, and that brotherhood is a possibility of history is certainly a part of the Christian gospel. The debate between the Reformation sects and the Reformation itself joins the issue between the Renaissance and the Reformation within the heart of Biblical Christianity. The sects prove how thoroughly

[20] *The New Law of Righteousness*, p. 61.
[21] For recent studies of Cromwellian left-wing thought see: A. S. P. Woodhouse, *Puritanism and Liberty*; David W. Petegorsky, *Left-Wing Democracy in the English Civil War*; and Professor G. H. Sabine's *The Works of Gerrard Winstanley*. Petegorsky is inclined to emphasize the secular-social theory of the origin of sin in Winstanley's thought and Professor Sabine the more religious-Biblical one.

Christian the impulse is to fulfill the will of God and to realize the possibilities of man in history. These impulses express, at least, one part of the gospel. But there is a part of the Christian interpretation of life which the sects do not understand; and it is precisely that side of the truth which the Reformation had rediscovered and which it guarded with such devotion that it became oblivious to the truth which the sects embodied and expressed.

The impulse to fulfill God's law in history and to bring the realities of history into greater conformity with the Kingdom of God related sectarian Christianity fruitfully to the whole history of political and economic democracy. Calvinism, which as Troeltsch rightly observes, is semi-sectarian in many of its characteristics, also made its contributions to the democratic cause, as did the combination of Catholic and Renaissance thought which became embodied in the Anglican church. The Lutheran reformation was betrayed meanwhile into the hands of social reaction.

But sectarian radicalism also expressed all the utopian illusions of modern culture, proving thereby that the whole truth of the gospel is not to be found here. The eschatological sects were superior to the main stream of Renaissance thought in possessing both a more social and more radical interpretation of historical tasks and possibilities. Both its social and its radical notes were undoubtedly derived from Bible prophetism. But the sects failed to comprehend the meaning of the profoundest element in this prophetism. They did not see that all history and all historic achievements must remain under the judgment of God; that the "Kingdom of God" which we achieve in history is never the same as the Kingdom for which we pray. The sectarians sought for an ideal society in which every contradiction to the law of love would be eliminated. But such a society is no more possible in history than are sanctified individuals who have no law in their members warring against the law that is in their mind.

IV

THE TRIUMPH OF THE RENAISSANCE

It is possible even before we consider Reformation thought more carefully to establish one of the causes of the remarkable triumph of the Renaissance over the Reformation in the past three centuries. Even if the Reformation had not failed to do full justice to those aspects of history which the Renaissance illumined, the latter would probably have triumphed because of the special circumstances of modern history. Since the dawn of modern history, the advance of science, the phenomenal increase of wealth and comfort which the applied sciences have made possible, the revolutionary changes in government and industry, the discovery and settlement of new continents, the expansion of commerce to the point where it encircles the globe, all these developments were conducive to the support of the spirit of historical optimism. It is not easy to understand that the perennial problems of man's existence in history will reappear on every level of historical achievement in a period when the changes in the conditions of his life are so great as to create the illusion that new conditions and achievements have eliminated the perennial problems.

While the bourgeois classes were in the process of establishing our democratic capitalistic society, it was natural that they should assume that all injustice had disappeared or would disappear when feudalism had been completely vanquished. It was equally natural, when the democratic dreams of the seventeenth and eighteenth century turned into the sorry realities of the nineteenth and twentieth century, that new revolutionists and utopians should arise who imagined that if only bourgeois injustice could be eliminated, it would be possible to establish perfect justice. This particular proletarian dream has, incidentally, not been completely subjected to historical disillusionment, though the contradiction between Marxist hopes and Russian realities has certainly initiated that process. The whole optimism of our culture is as natural as the sanguine spirit of the youth who imagines that the awakening of his mind and imagination, the growth of physical powers and the enlargement of responsibilities, all guarantee the successful realization of his life. The youth can hardly be expected fully to realize that each new power and potency of life creates its own new problem.

It was natural that when modern technology increased the intensity and extent of social cohesion and established something like brotherhood on wider and wider areas, men would be so enamoured of this achievement that the other side of the picture would not be discerned. It was not recognized that the same technology which would create a potential world community, might also produce international chaos, if the world community lacked adequate political instruments for the organization of its life. No one anticipated that, before such a world community could be created, mankind might be driven to the very edge of the abyss of destruction; that efforts would be made to harness modern technology to purely destructive and imperial ends; that nations would use these destructive possibilities of a technical society in an effort to unify the world upon a tyrannical basis; that they would come perilously near to success; and that part of their success would be due to a false sense of security and a parasitic dependence upon comforts created by a technical society in the remnants of the civilized world.

We are still so completely immersed in these tragic historic realities that it is not possible even to chart the course by which we may emerge from them. We can only know that the twentieth century has refuted the dreams of the earlier centuries of the modern era in the most tragic terms, and that modern culture is immersed in pathetic confusions by reason of this refutation. The confusion is so great partly because modern culture has no alternate perspectives upon life and history to which it might turn, when it finds the certainties of yesterday dissipated by the realities of today.

No alternate perspectives are available because the triumph of the Renaissance was so complete that it destroyed not only particular interpretations of the Christian religion, but submerged the Christian religion itself, as, in any sense, a potent force in modern culture. The Catholic form of the religion became discredited by the fact that all the liberties of modern life and all the achievements of social and political justice were established in defiance of Catholicism's premature identification of its feudal society with the sanctities of the Kingdom of God. The Reformation form of the religion was not so much discredited as simply lost. It lives on of course after a fashion; for nothing in history ever seems to die completely. It certainly does not live with any such vestigial vitality as Catholicism boasts.

If we inquire why the characteristic insights of the Reformation were lost to modern man so completely we must determine to what degree what was true in the Reformation was overwhelmed by what was false in the Renaissance by reason of the peculiar illusions of modern history. For the contemporary refutation of these illusions might also provide a contemporary validation of the truth of the Reformation.

But we have suggested that the Reformation did not present its truth without error; that it was inclined to destroy the paradoxical Biblical conception of grace, and the twofold aspect of historical fulfillment as much from one side as did the Renaissance from the other. For this reason our inquiry must be particularly careful to approach the affirmations of the Reformation critically. Otherwise we merely shall harness contemporary disillusionment to historical defeatism; even as past decades placed their characteristic optimistic illusions in the service of an historical utopianism. In that case we should not learn anything from our total experience; we should merely permit the alternate vicissitudes of history to prompt alter nate moods of illegitimate hope and unjustified despair.

CHAPTER VII

THE DEBATE ON HUMAN DESTINY IN MODERN CULTURE: THE REFORMATION

THE ANALYSIS of the contemporary religious situation has prompted several anticipatory appreciations and criticisms of the Reformation which must now be more fully examined. We have assumed that the Reformation has a more significant place than is generally realized in the history of Christian thought and life. It was the historical *locus* where the Christian conscience became most fully aware of the persistence of sin in the life of the redeemed. This realization, and the consequent refutation of alternate and more optimistic conceptions, resulted in a new appreciation of that part of the gospel which found the final completion of life in divine mercy.

We have suggested that the Reformation was frequently tempted to destroy the Biblical paradox of *"Christus in nobis"* and *"Christus pro nobis,"* of grace as power within us, and grace as power over us from one side, while sectarian Christianity destroyed the paradox from the other side. This criticism must be considered more fully.

It would be presumptuous to make such a criticism without a full appreciation of the effort of the Reformation to be true to the twofold Biblical conception of grace. Nor will the criticism stand without a careful discrimination between the Lutheran and the Calvinistic approaches to this central problem; for the two sides of the Reformation did not arrive at identical conclusions on this issue. It will be advisable therefore to consider each in turn.

II

THE LUTHERAN REFORMATION

Luther's approach to the ultimate problem of the Christian life was dominated by two considerations. The primary one was his conviction, established after bitter experience, that no final peace could be found by the effort to achieve righteousness. He had tried the method of monastic perfectionism and had failed; and the assurance of the Pauline word that "the just shall live by faith," therefore came to him as a happy release from the bondage of "the law," from the intolerable tension of an uneasy conscience which came the nearer to despair, the more imperious the demand for perfection appeared to it. The secondary consideration was the result of historical observation, rather than inner experience. He was convinced that the pretention of finality and perfection in the church was the root of spiritual pride and self-righteousness. His belief that the mystic-ascetic attempt at perfection was futile prompted his polemic against monasticism. His conviction that the pretension of finality was dangerous motivated his polemic against ecclesiasticism.

In elaborating his own theory of grace and the Christian life he was far from excluding that side of the paradox of grace according to which it is the source of a new life, of "love, joy and peace." Luther has his own relation to the mystical tradition,[1] and he followed the tendency of those who converted the classical mystical effort at union with God into a "Christ-mysticism." The soul of the believer, he claimed, became so united with Christ that all his virtues flow into it: "Since the promises of God are words of holiness, truth, righteousness, liberty and peace, and are full of universal goodness, the soul, which cleaves to them with a firm faith, is so united to

[1] *Cf.* Rudolf Otto, *Mysticism, East and West.*

them, nay thoroughly absorbed by them, that it not only partakes of, but is thoroughly saturated by all their virtues." [2]

Luther interprets the power of righteousness, psychologically, primarily as the motive of love and gratitude to God. This motive dispenses with the necessity of considering the gratitude or ingratitude, the praise or blame of fellowmen: "Thus from faith flow forth love and joy in the Lord, and from love a cheerful willing free spirit, disposed to serve our neighbour voluntarily, without taking into account any gratitude or ingratitude, praise or blame, gain or loss. Its object is not to lay men under obligation, nor does it distinguish between friends or enemies . . . but most freely spends its goods, whether it loses them through ingratitude or gains goodwill." [3] Here Luther comprehends the whole beauty and power of Christian *agape,* particularly its transcendent freedom over all the prudential considerations of natural ethical attitudes.

He does not deny, in other words, that the new life is capable of a new righteousness. He only insists that it is not justified by them: "A Christian, being consecrated by his faith, does good works; but he is not by these works made a more sacred person or more a Christian. This is the effect of faith alone." [4]

Luther does not deny that the new life is capable of a new righteousness. He only insists that it is not justified by them.

[2] *On Christian Liberty,* p. 261. Luther very frequently used the mystical, as also Pauline metaphor of marriage to describe the union of the soul with Christ: "The third incomparable grace of faith is this: that it unites the soul to Christ, as the wife to the husband, by which mystery as the Apostle teaches, Christ and the soul are made one flesh. Now if they are one flesh, and if a true marriage . . . is accomplished between them . . . then it follows that all they have becomes theirs in common, as well good things as evil things; so that whatsoever Christ possesses that the believing soul may take of itself and boast of as its own, and whatever belongs to the soul, that Christ claims as his." . . . "Christ is full of grace, life and salvation. The soul is full of sin, death and hell. These will belong to Christ and grace, life and salvation to the soul." It will be noticed that in the final phrases the imputed righteousness is integrally related to an achieved righteousness. *Ibid.,* p. 264.

[3] *Ibid.,* p. 270.

[4] This correct formulation in regard to the reality of good works also contains one of Luther's errors. For it is by "faith alone" rather than by

Many of the emphases in Luther's thought combine the classical Christian doctrine shared by Catholicism and the Reformation, on the priority of grace, with a new emphasis on the place of forgiveness in grace. The soul is the "poor little harlot" who brings nothing to the spiritual marriage but a "sackfull of sins" and her "rich bridegroom Christ" brings all the goodness. Or the soul is the "parched earth" which can bring forth no fruit unless grace as the "rain from heaven" water it. But with this rain the Christian will "as a good tree bring forth good fruits. For the believer has the Holy Spirit; and where He is He will not allow me to be idle but incites him to all exercises of piety, to the love of God, to patience in affliction, to prayer, thanksgiving and the showing of love towards all." [5]

In picturing the possibilities of this love towards all Luther displays the most profound understanding of the meaning of Christian *agape,* particularly of its completely disinterested motives. He regards the ethic of the Sermon on the Mount as definitive for Christians, always so long as he is dealing with personal attitudes and relationships.[6]

Despite these great merits of the Lutheran position there are quietistic tendencies in it, even when Luther is analysing the intricacies of personal religion, where he is on the whole most faithful to the Biblical paradox. Sometimes he lapses into mystic doctrines of passivity or combines quietism with a legalistic conception of the imputation of righteousness. "Without works" degenerates into "without action" in some of his strictures against the "righteousness

---

"grace alone" that peace is found. This means that man's acceptance of grace by faith, rather than grace itself, becomes determinative. This error betrayed Luther into a rejection of whatever goodness may be realized outside the Christian life. For he continues: "Nay, unless he has previously been a Christian, none of his works would have any value at all; they would really be impious and damnable sins." *Ibid.,* p. 275.

[5] *Works* (Weimar, ed.), Vol. 40, p. 265.

[6] *Cf.* Werner Betcke, *Luther's Socialethik.* Luther's understanding of the primacy of the love commandment in Christian ethics is certainly much profounder than Calvin's.

In its rejection of works righteousness, Lutheranism has exhibited a fear of action of any kind.

of works." He writes: "This most excellent righteousness of faith . . . which God through Christ imputeth to us without works, is neither political nor ceremonial, nor the righteousness of God's law, nor consisteth in works, but is clean contrary: that is to say, a *mere passive* righteousness. . . . For in this we work nothing unto God, but only receive and suffer another to work in us, that is to say, God. Therefore it seemeth good to me to call this righteousness of faith, or Christian righteousness, the passive righteousness." [7]

The mystic fear of action, because all action is tainted with sin, has its counterpart in the Lutheran fear of action, because it may tempt to a new pride. So Emil Brunner warns that "all energetic ethical activity carries with it a great danger. It may lead to the opinion that by such activity deliverance from evil is being accomplished." [8] The danger cannot be denied. But if moral action is discouraged on that ground, the Reformation theologian is in no better position than the monastic perfectionist who disavows particular moral and social responsibilities because of the taint of sin which attaches to them. Ideally the doctrine of justification by faith is a release of the soul into action; but it may be wrongly interpreted to encourage indolence. The barren orthodoxy of seventeenth-century Lutheranism, in which the experience of "justification by faith" degenerated into a "righteousness of belief," was not an inevitable, but nevertheless a natural, destruction of the moral content of the Christian life, for which there was a certain warrant in Luther's own thought.

According to Luther, the peace of the redeemed erases the sense of coming short of the Law.

Possibly a greater weakness in the Lutheran analysis of grace is found in Luther's idea of the relation of grace to the law. His difficulty here is derived not so much from his theory of justification as from his idea of sanctification. Luther's vision of the "love, joy and peace" which the redeemed soul has in Christ, is of an ecstatic transcendence over all the contradictions of history, including the inner contradictions of the "ought," the sense of moral obligation.

[7] In Commentary on Galatians, xciii.
[8] Emil Brunner, *The Divine Imperative*, p. 72.

Agape, as the fulfillment of the law, results in a complete disappearance of the sense of obligation to the law, and in a consequent elimination of all the careful discriminations of justice which belong to "law" in the broadest sense.[9]

Emil Brunner's exposition of Reformation ethics leads to exactly the same result. He writes: "The chief emphasis of Scriptural ethics lies not in victory over lawlessness but in the fight against legalism. . . . If I feel that I ought to do right it is a sign that I cannot do it. . . . Willing obedience is never a fruit of the sense of 'ought' but only of love. . . . Freedom means release from the sense of 'ought' from the bondage of the law."[10]

In this exposition of a highly personal and interior sanctification, the Reformation obscures the wisdom inhering in its doctrine of justification. For according to the doctrine of justification the inner contradiction of the soul is never completely healed. There are undoubtedly ecstatic moments when the conflict between self-love and the love of God, between conscience and the anxious survival impulse of the ego are transcended. But these moments are merely "earnests" of the final fulfillment of life; and they do not describe the general condition of the life of the redeemed. In that condition the relation between law and grace is much more complex; for by the inspiration of grace the law is extended as well as overcome. Repentance and faith prompt a sense of obligation towards wider

[9] Luther's conception of the relation of grace to law is most clearly expressed in his Commentary upon Galatians in which he writes: "For when Paul saith that we are delivered from the curse of the law by Christ, he speaketh of the whole law and principally of the moral law, which only accuseth, curseth and condemneth the conscience, which the other two [judicial and ceremonial] do not. Wherefore we say that the Moral Law or the Law of the Ten Commandments has no power to accuse or terrify the conscience in which Jesus Christ reigneth by his grace, for he hath abolished the power thereof." Gal. 2:21.

Luther thinks of the law primarily in negative terms. Its purpose is "to reveal unto man his blindness, his misery, his impiety, ignorance, hatred and contempt of God, death, hell, the judgment and deserved wrath of God." *Ibid.*

[10] Emil Brunner, *The Divine Imperative,* pp. 72–78.

As man enters the realm of Christian living, he becomes aware of greater and greater demands to be satisfied. Thus, there can be no complete fulfillment.

and wider circles of life. The need of this neighbour, the demands of that social situation, the claims of this life upon me, unrecognized today may be recognized and stir the conscience to uneasiness to-morrow. There is a constantly increasing sense of social obligation which is an integral part of the life of grace. To deny this is to be oblivious to one aspect of historic existence which the Renaissance understood so well: that life represents an indeterminate series of possibilities, and therefore of obligation to fulfill them. It is pre-cisely because this is so that there can be no complete fulfillment; for "a man's reach should exceed his grasp" (Browning). The con-ception of the relation of grace to law in Luther need not lead to antinomianism, as is sometimes charged; but it is indifferent to rela-tive moral discriminations. It does not relax moral tension at the ultimate point of moral experience; for there it demands the love which is the fulfillment, and not the negation of law. But it relaxes the tension at all intermediate points and does not deal seriously with all the possible extensions of justice to which men ought to be driven by an uneasy conscience.[11]

[11] In analysing this problem Brunner continually confuses the sense of moral obligation with "legalism," that is, with the limitation of moral ob-ligation to a specific code of conduct. Thus he knows no middle ground between perfect love and legalism. He writes: "The legalistic type of person finds it impossible to come into real human personal contact with his fellow-man. Between him and his neighbor there stands something impersonal, the 'idea,' the 'Law' . . . something abstract which hinders him from seeing the other person as he really is." This might be a just condemnation of legalism in the narrow sense but Brunner subsumes all experiences of moral obligation under the term and continues: "The good that one does simply from a sense of duty is never the good. Duty and genuine goodness are mutually exclusive." *Ibid.*, pp. 73–74.

There would be little goodness in history by that standard. Suppose we grant that there is not much goodness in which all sense of obligation has been swallowed up in perfect love. It would still be important to achieve higher and higher forms of goodness by the extension of the sense of obligation. When we confront the claims of our fellow men we may not be "legalistic" at all in the sense that we do not try to measure those claims by some fixed standard of justice. Yet we might with uneasy con-

The weakness of the Lutheran Reformation in dealing with the problem of law and grace in it becomes even more apparent when the issue is transferred from the inner life to the complexities of culture and civilization, and all expressions of the collective life of man. Here the "defeatism" of the Reformation becomes much more apparent. Its understanding of the ultimate problem of historical existence seems to preclude any understanding of all the proximate problems. The Reformation understands that every possible extension of knowledge and wisdom falls short of the wisdom which knows God. It realizes that the "world by its wisdom knew not God" and it rejoices in the grace, apprehended by faith, which overcomes the sinful ego-centricity of all human knowledge. But it has no interest in the infinite shades and varieties of the amalgam of truth and falsehood which constitutes the stuff of science and philosophy, and of all human striving after the truth. The Renaissance was undoubtedly wrong in imagining that the final truth could be found by the cumulative process of the history of culture. It did not recognize the peril of new errors on each new level of wisdom; most particularly the error of assuming that an age which had a point of vantage over all preceding ages would thereby arrive at the final truth.

But was it not right, in comparison with the Reformation, to take the obligation towards the truth seriously? And was not the Reformation delivered into the sin of cultural obscurantism by its indifference towards the relative distinctions of truth and falsehood which are so important in the history of culture: Did it not put itself essentially in the position of the unprofitable servant who declared: "Lord I knew thee that thou art an hard man, reaping where thou hast not sown, and gathering where thou has not

———

science weigh those claims against our own interests and decide to do some justice to them. This whole moral process might proceed without any reference to any known "law." It could be extremely personal and individual too. But it would still fall short of that perfect love, which Brunner seems to regard as the only release from "legalism."

[margin notes, handwritten:] The Reformation says that we can't know truth so why bother?

[margin notes, handwritten:] Was not the Reformation guilty of cultural obscurantism by its indifference towards the relative distinction of truth and falsehood which are so important in the history of culture.

strawed; and I was afraid and went and hid thy talent in the earth; lo, there thou hast that is thine." [12]

In confronting the problems of realizing justice in the collective life of man, the Lutheran Reformation was even more explicitly defeatist. Human society represents an infinite variety of structures and systems in which men seek to organize their common life in terms of some kind of justice. The possibilities of realizing a higher justice are indeterminate. There is no point in historical social achievement where one may rest with an easy conscience. All structures of justice do indeed presuppose the sinfulness of man, and are all partly systems of restraint which prevent the conflict of wills and interests from resulting in a consistent anarchy. But they are also all mechanisms by which men fulfill their obligations to their fellow men, beyond the possibilities offered in direct and personal relationships. The Kingdom of God and the demands of perfect love are therefore relevant to every political system and impinge upon every social situation in which the self seeks to come to terms with the claims of other life.

Luther denies this relevance explicitly. He declares: "The way to discern the difference [between law and gospel] is to place the gospel in heaven and the law on the earth: to call the righteousness of the gospel heavenly, and the righteousness of the law earthly and to put as great a difference between [them] as God hath made between heaven and earth. . . . Wherefore if the question be concerning the matter of faith and conscience let us utterly exclude the law and leave it on earth. . . . Contrariwise in civil policy obedience to law must be severely required. There nothing *must be known* concerning the conscience, the Gospel, grace, remission of sins, heavenly righteousness or Christ himself; but Moses only with the law and the works thereof." [13]

[12] Mt. 25:24–25.

[13] Commentary upon Galatians. It is interesting to compare this complete severance between the religious and the civil idea of liberty with the observation of John Milton: "It will not misbecome the meanest Christian to put in mind Christian magistrates, and so much more freely

Here we have the complete severance between the final experience of grace and all the proximate possibilities of liberty and justice, which must be achieved in history. This principle of separation leads to a denial that liberty can have any other meaning for the Christian than liberty from "God's everlasting wrath. For Christ hath made us free not civilly nor carnally but divinely; that is to say our conscience is now made free and quiet, not fearing the wrath of God to come." Social antinomianism is guarded against by the injunction, "Let every man therefore endeavour to do his duty diligently in his calling and help his neighbour to the utmost of his power." [14] But evidently no obligation rests upon the Christian to change social structures so that they might conform more perfectly to the requirements of brotherhood. In his attitude towards the peasant revolt Luther rigorously applied this separation between the "spiritual kingdom" and the "worldly" one; and met the demands of the peasants for a greater degree of social justice with the charge that they were confusing the two.[15] He took a complacent

---

by how much they desire to be known as Christians, that they meddle not rashly with Christian liberty the birthright and outward testimony of our adoption, lest they . . . be found persecuting them that are free born of the spirit . . . bereaving them of that sacred liberty which our Saviour by his own blood purchased for them." From *Of Civil Power in Ecclesiastical Causes.*

Milton declares it "impertinent to endeavor to argue us into slavery on the example of our Saviour" who did indeed take "in our stead the form of a servant but he always retained his purpose of being a deliverer." . . . "He asked for the tribute money. 'Whose image and superscription is it?' says he. They tell him it was Caesar's. 'Give then to Caesar,' says he, 'the things that are Caesar's.' . . . Our liberty is not Caesar's. It is a blessing we have received from God himself." From *Pro populo Anglicano defensio.*

This is another instance in which the sectarian conception of the relation of the gospel to social problems is right and the Reformation is wrong.

[14] *Ibid.*, 5, 2.

[15] Luther declared that the peasant demand for the abolition of serfdom "would make all men equal and so change the spiritual Kingdom of Christ into an external worldly one. Impossible! An earthly kingdom

attitude towards the social inequalities of feudalism and observed that on earth there will always be masters and slaves. Luther added an element of perversity to this social ethic by enlarging upon the distinction between an "inner" and an "outer" kingdom so that it became, in effect, a distinction between public and private morality. The rulers, as custodians of public morality, were advised to "hit, stab, kill" when dealing with rebels. For Luther had a morbid fear of anarchy and was willing to permit the *Obrigkeit* any instrument to suppress it. The peasants on the other hand, as private citizens, were admonished to live in accordance with the ethic of the Sermon on the Mount. They were told that their demand for justice violated the New Testament ethic of nonresistance.[16]

By thus transposing an "inner" ethic into a private one, and making the "outer" or "earthly" ethic authoritative for government, Luther achieves a curiously perverse social morality. He places a perfectionist private ethic in juxtaposition to a realistic, not to say

---

cannot exist without inequality of persons. Some must be free, others serfs, some rulers, others subjects." *Works* (Weimar, ed.), Vol. 18, p. 326. "It is a malicious and evil idea that serfdom should be abolished because Christ has made us free. This refers only to spiritual freedom given to us by Christ in order to enable us to withstand the devil." *Ibid.*, p. 333.

[16] "You will not bear," Luther wrote to the peasants, "that anyone inflict evil of injustice upon you, but you want to be free and suffer only justice and goodness. . . . If you do not want to bear such a right [the right of suffering] you had better put away your Christian name and boast of another name in accordance with your deeds or Christ himself will snatch away his name from you." *Works* (Weimar, ed.), Vol. 18, p. 309.

To the princes he wrote: "It will not help the peasants to claim (Genesis I and II) that all things were created free and common and that they are all equally baptized. . . . For in the New Testament Moses counts for nothing; but there stands our master Christ and casts us with body and possessions under the Kaisers and worldly law when he says, 'Give unto Caesar the things that are Caesars.' " *Ibid.*, p. 361.

In the one case Biblical perfectionism is avowed without reservation and in the other case it is as completely disavowed.

Officials don't have to be just

Individual does have to be just.

cynical, official ethic. He demands that the state maintain order without too scrupulous a regard for justice; yet he asks suffering and nonresistant love of the individual without allowing him to participate in the claims and counter-claims which constitute the stuff of social justice. The inevitable consequence of such an ethic is to encourage tyranny; for resistance to government is as important a principle of justice as maintenance of government.

Luther's inordinate fear of anarchy, prompted by his pessimism, and his corresponding indifference to the injustice of tyranny has had a fateful consequence in the history of German civilization. The tragic events of contemporary history are not unrelated to it. His one-sided interpretation of the socio-political problem was also influenced by the exaggerated emphasis which he placed upon the Pauline injunction: "Let every soul be subject unto the higher powers. For there is no power but of God; the powers that be are ordained of God. . . . For rulers are not a terror to good works but to the evil." [17]

Even without this particular error, the Lutheran political ethic would have led to defeatism in the field of social politics. Its absolute distinction between the "heavenly" or "spiritual" kingdom and the "earthly" one, destroys the tension between the final demands of God upon the conscience, and all the relative possibilities of realizing the good in history. The spiritual and moral significance of various progressive realizations of justice is denied from two angles. On the side of its realism the Lutheran ethic finds all historical achievements equally tainted with sin and the distinctions between them therefore unimportant. On the side of its gospel perfectionism it finds them falling equally short of that perfect love of the Kingdom of God, which is alone the earnest of salvation.[18]

[17] Romans 13:1–3.

[18] The defeatism in the realm of social morality, prompted by radical Reformation thought, is strikingly illustrated by a modern dialectical theologian, Hans Asmussen, who writes: "As long as it is the message of the churches that this home [the world] shall be made as beautiful as possible through ethical action so long are we tools of secularism. . . . It

The Lutheran Reformation is thus always in danger of heightening religious tension to the point where it breaks the moral tension, from which all decent action flows. The conscience is made uneasy about the taint of sin in all human enterprise; but the conviction that any alternative to a given course of action would be equally tainted, and that in any case the divine forgiveness will hallow and

would be a better confession of faith if the churches said to the world and to the heathen: We wait. Put an end to all social injustice. Eliminate war. After you have done all that, we still wait. All this is not enough for us. Purify mankind to the highest degree of perfection, morally and spiritually. That also is not enough for us. . . . I will remain as one who waits. For I have a gospel, good news. I await the resurrection of the dead and life in the world to come." In *Zwischen den Zeiten,* July, 1930. Here quite obviously the eschatological tension, which belongs to the Christian view of history, is allowed to destroy the meaningfulness of history and to rob all historic tasks and obligations of their significance.

Emil Brunner who is more interested in ethical action than the other dialectical theologians arrives nevertheless at similar defeatist conclusions. On the one hand he allows the ultimate religious perspective upon the sinful taint in all human actions to destroy all proximate distinctions: "We see," he says, "how the real purpose of life is being thwarted at every turn in all the 'orders' which constitute the framework of human life; the ends sought are so futile and empty and the means used to achieve these ends are so utterly contemptible."

On the other hand he interprets the doctrine of "justification by faith" in such a way as to lead to a complacent acceptance of all this injustice. "The judge," he declares, "must deliver his sentence in accordance to the law in its present state, even though he may be personally convinced that the law is unjust. He does not make a 'compromise' when he acts in this way, if he is acting in the spirit of faith. For he knows that he cannot create a better law and that in this world law is necessary; but he also knows that so long as the people who frame the laws are unjust . . . that is to the end of life on earth . . . there will be no truly just system of law." *Divine Imperative,* pp. 253–255.

The whole history of jurisprudence reveals the importance of maintaining life in a legal tradition by an imaginative juridical application of the law to new situations. Fortunately there have always been judges who have never heard of this doctrine of justification by faith and who have therefore been prompted by a sensitive conscience to apply the law as justly as possible.

sanctify what is really unholy,[19] eases the uneasy conscience prematurely. Thus the saints are tempted to continue in sin that grace may abound, while the sinners toil and sweat to make human relations a little more tolerable and slightly more just.

The weakness of the Lutheran position in the field of social ethics is accentuated to a further degree by its inability to define consistent criteria for the achievement of relative justice. Despite its conception of sanctification as an ecstatic love which transcends all law, and of its doctrine of justification which eases the conscience in its inability to realize the good perfectly, it is forced, nevertheless, to find some standards of relative good and evil. Since it rightly has less confidence than Catholicism in the untainted character of reason, it relegates the "natural law" that is, the rational analysis of social obligations, to the background, as an inadequate guide. But it has only odds and ends of systems of order to put in the place of "natural law." These consist primarily of two conceptions. The one is the order and justice which any state may happen to establish. This order is accepted uncritically precisely because a principle of justice, by which the justice of a given state could be criticized, is lacking. The other is the idea of a *Schoepfungsordnung* an "order of creation," which is presumably, the directive given by God in the very structure of the created world. The difficulty with this concept is that human freedom alters and transmutes the "given" facts of creation so much that no human institutions can be judged purely by the criterion of fixed principles of "creation."

In the field of sex-relations for instance, bi-sexuality and those vocations of mother and father which are unalterably related to biological differentiation are the only factors which may rightfully be placed in the category of "order of creation." Monogamy can certainly not be placed there, or for that matter any other form of marital union or standard of sex-relation. In political relations Luther sometimes regarded government as belonging to the "order

[19] *Cf.* Brunner, *ibid.*, p. 246.

of creation," and at other times seemed to think that its authority was derived from a special "divine ordinance," Scripturally validated, particularly in Romans 13. Government, however, can be regarded as belonging to "creation" only in the sense that both human freedom and the abuse of human freedom require that human society have a cement of cohesion transcending the natural sociality of animal existence. But no particular government can be derived from the "order of creation"; nor is the uncritical obedience to government, which Luther demanded, a part of the requirement of such an "order."

III

THE CALVINISTIC REFORMATION

It is an indication of the complexity of the problem which the Reformation confronted, that while the Lutheran side of the Reformation always walks on the edge of the precipice of supramoralism, not to say antinomianism, the Calvinistic Reformation is imperilled by the opposite danger of a new moralism and legalism. Puritanism may be regarded as the historic capitulation to this danger. The inability of Reformation thought to sail perfectly between the Scylla of the one and the Charybdis of the other danger, must prompt us to diffidence and modesty in dealing with the ultimate problem with which the Reformation is concerned. It is no easy task to do justice to the distinctions of good and evil in history and to the possibilities and obligations of realizing the good in history; and also to subordinate all these relative judgments and achievements to the final truth about life and history which is proclaimed in the gospel. Every effort to do it involves the whole paradoxical conception in Biblical faith, of the character of history, of its meaningfulness on the one hand, and of the completion of its meaning only in the judgment and mercy of God, on the other.

When Calvin confronts Roman doctrines he elaborates Reformation thought in terms which are hardly distinguishable from the

Lutheran position. He insists that, "there never was an action performed by a pious man, which if examined by the scrutinizing eye
of divine justice would not deserve condemnation." He thinks that,
"this is the principal hinge on which our controversy with the
papists turns" for "there is no controversy between us and the
sounder schoolmen, concerning the beginning of justification"; but
the Catholics believe, "that a man, once having been reconciled to
God through faith in Christ, is accounted righteous with God on
account of his good works, the merit of which is the cause of his
acceptance" while "the Lord on the contrary declares that faith was
reckoned unto Abraham for righteousness." [1]

He believes that, "there still remains in a regenerate man a fountain of evil, continually producing irregular desires. . . . that sin
always exists in the saints till they are divested of their mortal
bodies." [2] Perhaps his finest insight into the complexities of perfection and sin is expressed in the words: "When we denominate
the virtue of the saints perfect, to this perfection belongs the acknowledgment of imperfection both in truth and in humility." [3]

But when he develops his own doctrine of sanctification, he arrives
at conclusions hardly to be distinguished from the Catholic ones.
"Do you wish," he asks, "to obtain the righteousness of Christ?
You must first possess Christ; but you cannot possess him without
becoming partaker of his sanctification; for he cannot be divided.
. . . Union with Christ by which we are justified contains sanctification as well as righteousness." [4] He thinks that the rejection of
the idea of justification by works means, "not that no good works
can be done or that those which are performed may be denied to
be good but that we may neither confide in them nor ascribe our
salvation to them." [5]

Sometimes he comes rather close to the Catholic distinction between venial and mortal sins, as for instance when he declares that

[1] *Inst.*, III, xiv, 11.
[2] *Inst.*, III, iii, 10.
[3] *Inst.*, III, xvii, 15.

[4] *Inst.*, III, xvi, 1.
[5] *Inst.*, III, xvii, 1.

the state of sanctification means that, "our carnal desires are daily more and more mortified, and we are sanctified, that is consecrated unto the Lord unto real purity of life, having our hearts moulded to obey his law so that our *prevailing inclination* is to submit to his will." [6]

Here perhaps lies the crux of the matter. Whenever the Christian, in whom sin is broken "in principle," claims that the sins which remain are merely incidental "carnal desires" without recognizing that the sin of self-love is present in a more basic form, there is a corresponding dissipation of the "broken spirit and the contrite heart." The fulfillment of life is no longer subject to the paradox of having and not having it. Sometimes Calvin defines the paradox in Augustinian terms and believes saints to be essentially righteous though lacking the final attainment of perfection. The believers, he declares, "are denominated righteous from the sanctity of their lives; but as they rather devote themselves to the pursuit of right-eousness than actually attain righteousness itself, it is proper that this righteousness, such as it is, should be subordinate to justification by faith, from which it derives its origin." [7]

The definition of the Christian paradox of justification and sanc-tification is probably made more carefully in Calvin's *Institutes* than in any other system of thought. If he errs on the side of claiming too much in the end it is an error which is difficult to correct with-out committing the opposite error. But that Calvin committed an error, in feeling too secure in the sanctification of the Christian, is attested not only by his other writings, where he does not always make such careful qualifications and reservations, but also by his own actions.

His frequent tendency to define sin as carnal desire rather than as primarily self-love, contributes to a new self-righteousness; for sainthood in terms of a completely disciplined life which has sub-ordinated all desires to a dominant purpose is a simpler possibility than a perfection which has excluded all egoistic elements from the

[6] *Inst.*, III, xiv, 9.   [7] *Inst.*, III, xvii, 11.

Claims
that
Calvin
is a
perfect-
ionist.

dominant purpose. The history of Puritan self-righteousness reveals
the weakness of Calvinism on this point. Calvin does not fully
understand the law of love as the final law. That is at least one
reason why he thinks of himself a little too confidently as standing
on the other side of the sinful contradictions of existence, despite
his protestations that he will not ascribe salvation to the goodness
of the saints. He interprets the Pauline assertion, that love is the
greatest of the three virtues of faith, hope and love, as meaning
only that "charity is serviceable to more people since only a few can
be justified by faith." [8] He places love not only under faith, but
under "purity of faith" in his hierarchy of virtues. The purpose of
this ordering is to justify his rigour against heretics. Yet it is precisely in his loveless attitude towards heretics, who are, in his opinion, guilty "of dishonouring the majesty of God," a sin more heinous
than "to kill an innocent man or to poison a guest or to lay violent
hands on one's own father" [9] that he reveals that lack of pity, which
is the particular sin of the self-righteous, who do not know themselves as, in some sense, in the same condemnation with those whom
they indict.[10] The final proof of the genuine spirit of humility in
the "elect," of their "brokenness of spirit," is their capacity for mercy
and forgiveness. Without consciousness of their own need of forgiveness, "good" people never show mercy towards "bad" people.

[8] *Opera,* I, 798. Calvin thinks that, "as our liberty should be subject to
charity so our charity should be subservient to purity of faith. It becomes
us indeed to have regard to charity, but we must not offend God for the
love of the neighbor." *Inst.,* III, xix, 13.

[9] Commentary on Zech. 13:3.

[10] This matter will be dealt with more fully in the following chapter.
Calvin's emphasis upon the suppression of carnal desires, his identification of righteousness with self-discipline is not in perfect conformity
with his more Scriptural definition of sin as pride. (*Cf.* Vol. I, p. 187.)
He is not completely lacking in an appreciation of love as the final good.
"His is the best and most holy life," he writes, "who lives as little as
possible for himself." *Inst.,* II, viii, 54.

But in his total thought both his passion for right doctrine and for the
discipline of sensual impulses, outweigh his appreciation of the love
commandment.

The difference between Calvin's conception of the relation of grace to law and the Lutheran doctrine of grace and law conforms to the general divergence between the two theologies; Calvin inclines towards legalism rather than supra-moralism. He does not, as Luther, believe that grace abrogates the law, for he does not think of sanctification as an ecstatic experience of love which transcends all law. He thinks of it rather as a rigorous obedience to law. But since it is impossible for the soul in its sinful state to know the perfect law, it is necessary for it to be guided by the "divine law," particularly as it is revealed in the Bible.

"Though the law of God," he says, "contains in it that newness of life by which His image is restored in us, yet since our tardiness needs much stimulation and assistance, it will be useful to collect from various places in Scripture a rule for the reformation of life, that they who cordially repent may not be bewildered in their pursuit."[11]

Calvin guilty of Biblicism

Calvin's "divine law," in which he finds an answer to every moral and social problem, is nicely defined here. For it is a compendium collected from "various places in Scripture," without reference to the historical relativities which are enshrined in a sacred canon. This is the ethical corollary in Calvin's system of his general Biblicism, not to say Bibliolatry. Just as Luther regards the Bible primarily as the "cradle of Christ" and therefore has a principle of criticism of Scripture itself in the Christ of Scripture, so he also understands that the love commandment transcends all other commandments in the Bible. He is thereby saved from the error of Biblicism in both theology and ethics. Calvin, on the other hand, commits both errors.

Calvin's conception of "divine law" has the advantage of consistency over Luther's sketchy directives in the field of social and political life. But it nevertheless combines the errors of both obscurantism and pretension. It is obscurantist in that it does not sufficiently engage man's rational capacities in determining what is just and unjust in his relation to his fellows. It appeals prematurely to Biblical

[11] *Inst.*, lll, vi, 1.

authority for answers to every conceivable moral and social problem. Catholic social ethics, though informed by an unjustified confidence in the ability of a universal reason to define the norms of justice, are sometimes more discriminating than the Calvinistic appeal to "divine law." Calvin's ethical system is pretentious as well as obscurantist; for it gives the Christian an unjustified confidence in the transcendent perfection of the moral standards which he has derived from Scripture and obscures not only the endless relativities of judgment, involved in applying a Scriptural standard to a particular situation, but also the historical relativities which are imbedded in these Scriptural standards themselves.

Though Calvinism made some genuine contributions to the advance of democratic justice, as we shall see shortly, it is not surprising that possibly greater contributions towards higher justice in recent centuries were derived from the sectarianism and various versions of the Renaissance movement. These movements may have been even blinder than Catholicism to the egoistic corruption in every historic system of justice; but they did understand both the possibility and the obligation of rational men to use their reason in estimating the needs of their fellowmen and in defining tolerably just standards of division between "mine" and "thine." Both sides of the Reformation on the other hand either regarded the problem of justice as insoluble by reason of human sinfulness; or they solved it too simply by appeals to presumably transcendent standards of justice, which were supposedly untainted by human sinfulness. But appeals to these standards merely resulted in one more human effort to find an absolutely secure and safe position, beyond historical ambiguities and contradictions.

A survey of these various aspects of Reformation thought and life leads to the conclusion that, despite its polemic against the premature transcendence over history in Catholicism, it is as frequently tempted to commit the same error as Catholicism (though with the use of different instruments of pretension) as it is to commit the opposite error.

This fact suggests that Reformation insights must be related to the whole range of human experience more "dialectically" than the Reformation succeeded in doing. The "yes" and "no" of its dialectical affirmations: that the Christian is *"justus et peccator,"* "both sinner and righteous"; that history fulfills and negates the Kingdom of God; that grace is continuous with, and in contradiction to, nature; that Christ is what we ought to be and also what we cannot be; that the power of God is in us and that the power of God is against us in judgment and mercy; that all these affirmations which are but varied forms of the one central paradox of the relation of the Gospel to history must be applied to the experiences of life from top to bottom. There is no area of life where "grace" does not impinge. There are no complex relations of social justice to which the love of the Kingdom of God is not relevant. There are on the other hand no areas or experiences where historical insecurity and anxiety are completely transcended, except in principle. There are indeed moments of prayer and, perhaps, ecstatic achievements of *agape* in which men are caught up in the "seventh heaven"; but these moments are merely an "earnest" of the fulfillment of life and must not be claimed as a possession. There is, finally, the transcendence of man over history and sin by faith. But that is also an "earnest"; and is corrupted like the manna in the wilderness when stored up as a secure possession.

IV

A SYNTHESIS OF REFORMATION AND RENAISSANCE

The defeatism of the Lutheran, and the tendency towards obscurantism in the Calvinist, Reformation must be regarded as a contributory cause of defeat of the Reformation by the Renaissance. It failed to relate the ultimate answer of grace to the problem of guilt to all the immediate and intermediate problems and answers of life. Therefore it did not illumine the possibilities and limits of realizing increasing truth and goodness in every conceivable historic and social situation.

This defeatism is only a contributory cause of its defeat because the general atmosphere of historical optimism in the past centuries seemed to refute even what was true in the Reformation; just as it seemed to validate what was both true and false in the Renaissance. There was, therefore, little inclination to discriminate between the true and the false emphases in the Reformation; between the truth of its ultimate view of life and history and its failure to relate this truth helpfully to intermediate issues of culture and social organization.

But when we are confronted with the task of reorienting the culture of our day, it becomes important to discriminate carefully between what was true and false in each movement. There is of course a strong element of presumption in the effort to make such judgments which will seem intolerable to those who disagree with them; and which can be tolerable even to those who find them validated, at least partially, by contemporary history, only if it is recognized that they are made in "fear and trembling."

The course of modern history has, if our reading of it be at all correct, justified the dynamic, and refuted the optimistic, interpretation contained in the various modern religious and cultural movements, all of which are internally related to each other in what we have defined broadly as "Renaissance." It has by the same token validated the basic truth of the Reformation but challenged its obscurantism and defeatism on all immediate and intermediate issues of life.

The "logic" of modern history, for which this rather large claim is made, can be simply defined. On the one hand the extension of all forms of knowledge, the elaboration of mechanical and social techniques, the corresponding development of human powers and historical potencies and the consequent increase of the extent and complexity of the human community have indubitably proved that life is subject to growth in its collective and total, as well as in its individual, forms. On the other hand the course of history, particularly in the past two centuries, has proved the earlier identification of growth and progress to be false. We have, or ought to have, learned, particularly from the tragedies of contemporary history, that each new development of life, whether in individual or social terms, presents us with new possibilities of realizing the good in history; that we have obligations corresponding to these new possibilities; but that we also face new hazards on each new level and that the new level of historic achievement offers us no emancipation from contradictions and ambiguities to which all life in history is subject. We have learned, in other words, that history is not its own redeemer. The "long run" of it is no more redemptive in the ultimate sense than the "short run." It is this later development of modern history which has given the Reformation version of the Christian faith a new relevance. No apology is necessary for assigning so great a pedagogical significance to the lessons of history. The truth contained in the gospel is not found in human wisdom. Yet it may be found at the point where human wisdom and human goodness acknowledge their limits; and creative despair induces faith. Once faith is induced it becomes truly the wisdom which makes "sense" out of a life and history which would otherwise remain senseless. This is possible for individuals in any age, no matter what its historical circumstances.

But it cannot be denied that historical circumstances may be more or less favourable to the inducement of the "Godly sorrow" which worketh repentance. There are periods of hope in history in which the Christian faith would seem to be irrelevant, because history itself seems to offer both the judgment and the redemption which the Christian faith finds in the God who has been revealed in Christ. There are other periods of disillusionment when the vanity of such hopes is fully revealed. We have lived through such centuries of hope and we are now in such a period of disillusionment. The centuries of historical hope have well nigh destroyed the Christian faith as a potent force in modern culture and civilization. We do not maintain that the period of disillusionment in which we now find ourselves will necessarily restore the Christian faith. It has merely reestablished its relevance. There is always the alternative of despair, the "sorrow of the world" to the creative despair which induces a new faith.

If, however, the modern generation is to be helped to find life meaningful without placing an abortive confidence in the mere historical growth, it is incumbent upon those who mediate the truth of the gospel to this generation, to accept and not to reject whatever truth about life and history has been learned in these past centuries of partial apostasy. This is the more important because the lessons which have been learned are implied in the whole Biblical-prophetic view of history, which, in its pure form, has always regarded history in dynamic terms, that is, as moving towards an *end*.

A new synthesis is therefore called for. It must be a synthesis which incorporates the twofold aspects of grace of Biblical religion, and adds the light which modern history, and the Renaissance and Reformation interpretations of history, have thrown upon the paradox of grace. Briefly this means that on the one hand life in history must be recognized as filled with indeterminate possibilities. There is no individual or interior spiritual situation, no cultural or scientific task, and no social or political problem in which men do not face new possibilities of the good and the obligation to realize them. It means on the other hand that every effort and pretension to complete life, whether in collective or individual terms, that every desire to stand beyond the contradictions of history, or to eliminate the final corruptions of history must be disavowed.

Because both Renaissance and Reformation have sharpened the insights into the meaning of the two sides of the Christian paradox, it is not possible to return to the old, that is, to the medieval synthesis, though we may be sure that efforts to do so will undoubtedly be abundant.

The medieval-Catholic synthesis is inadequate because it rested upon a compromise between the twofold aspects of grace. It arrested

the fullest development of each aspect. Its conception of the fulfillment of life was marred by its confinement of the power of grace
to a human-historical institution. In the realm of the spiritual and
moral life this meant that grace was bound to sacraments, institu-
tionally controlled and mediated. Since "grace" stands for powers
and possibilities beyond all human possibilities, this represents an
intolerable confinement of the freedom of God within human limits.
"The wind bloweth where it listeth,"[1] said Jesus to Nicodemus;
and that is a picturesque description of the freedom of divine grace
in history, working miracles without any "by your leave" of priest
or church. Since some of the most significant developments in the
field of social morality have taken place in modern life in defiance
of a sacramental church, which had limited social justice unwit-
tingly to the essential conditions of feudal life, it is understandable
that modern culture should still be informed by a strong resentment
against the pretensions of such a church.

In the field of culture the Catholic synthesis is equally unavailing.
It is one thing to believe that no elaboration of philosophy or science can carry us beyond the truth which is contained in the gospel;
and another to allow a human institution to control the whole cultural process in order to prevent science and philosophy from defying the authority of the gospel. When the final authority of the
gospel over all human culture is thus transmuted into the authority
of a historical and human institution, the pride of priests is inevitably mixed with an authority which can be ultimate only when
it stands beyond all human situations and achievements. If a human
authority sets the limits and defines the conditions under which the
pursuit of truth shall take place, it is quite inevitable that significant
truth should be suppressed and valuable cultural ambitions should
be prematurely arrested under the guise of keeping them within the
confines of the final truth about life and history as apprehended by
faith.

The real situation is that the human mind can, in the various

[1] John 3:8.

disciplines of culture, discover and elaborate an indeterminate variety of systems of meaning and coherence by analysing the relation of things to each other on every level of existence, whether geological or biological, social or psychological, historical or philosophical. If these subordinate realms of meaning claim to be no more than they are they will add to the wealth of our apprehensions about the character of existence and the richness of our insights into reality. They are furthermore valuable guides to conduct and action, whether it be in the exploitation of nature, or the manipulation of social forces, or the discipline of individual life. If the effort is made to establish any one of these subordinate realms of meaning as the clue to the meaning of the whole, the cultural pursuit becomes involved in idolatry. A premature source and end for the meaning of life is found; which is to say that a god is found who is not truly God, a principle of final judgment is discovered which is not really final; or a process of salvation and the fulfillment of life is claimed which is not finally redemptive.

It is perhaps inevitable that the free pursuit of knowledge should lead to such various forms of idolatry. There will be philosophies, claiming to have comprehended the world in a system of meaning, superior to the tragic and paradoxical meaning which the Christian faith finds in it. There will be social philosophies certain that they have found a way to achieve perfect brotherhood in history. There will be psychiatric techniques which pretend to overcome all the anxieties of human existence and therefore all its corruptions. There will even be engineering schemes for fulfilling life by the mere multiplication of comforts.

The truth of the gospel cannot be maintained against these pretensions by the interposition of any human authority. The attempt thus to restrain culture from idolatry is unwise because truth is bound to be suppressed with the suppression of error. Here the injunction in the parable of the wheat and tares is relevant: "Let both grow together until the harvest; and in the time of harvest I will say to the reapers, Gather ye together first the tares, and bind them in bundles to burn them; but gather the wheat into my barn." [2]

The attempt must also prove abortive, for there is no way of validating the truth of the gospel until men have discovered the error which appears in their final truth; and are threatened with the abyss of meaninglessness on the edge of their most pretentious schemes of meaning. Christian faith must, in other words, be in a much freer play with all the powers and ambitions of the cultural life of man than was permitted in that synthesis of culture and faith which the medieval church established.

But on the other hand the inclination of the Reformation to disavow all intermediate cultural tasks on the ground that the final wisdom is not to be found there; and to be indifferent to the obligations for achieving a more tolerable brotherhood in history, on the ground that such achievements fall short of salvation, is equally inadmissible. The Renaissance spirits of our day have vaguely equated what they regard as the cultural and social obscurantism of the Catholic and the Protestant church. They have seldom understood how different the strategies of the two forms of Christianity are. If the one is obscurantist it is because it places premature limits and unjustified restraints upon the pursuit of knowledge and the development of social institutions. If the other is obscurantist, it is because it is either indifferent towards the problems of thought and life which all men must consider though they are short of the ultimate problem of salvation; or because it interposes a new authority, that of Scripture, in such a way as to make the ultimate meaning of life, as contained in the gospel a substitute for all subordinate realms of meaning or as obviating the necessity of establishing these subordinate realms.

Any workable synthesis between culture and the Christian faith, which is also a synthesis between the two aspects of grace, must not abstract the ultimate human situation from immediate and intermediate ones. There is no social or moral obligation which does

[2] Mt. 13:30.

not invite us on the one hand to realize higher possibilities of good and does not on the other reveal the limits of the good in history. There is no mystery of life, or complexity of causal relations, which do not incite the inquisitive mind to try to comprehend them; and which do not upon careful scrutiny point to a mystery beyond themselves. There is, therefore, no way of understanding the ultimate problem of human existence if we are not diligent in the pursuit of proximate answers and solutions. Nor is there any way of validating the ultimate solution without constantly relating it to all proximate possibilities. On this issue Renaissance perspectives are truer than either Catholic or Reformation ones.

The one point at which the Reformation must make its primary contribution to the synthesis is in refuting both Catholic and Renaissance pretensions of fulfilling life and history either by grace or by natural capacities inhering in human nature or in the historical process. Here the Reformation has rediscovered the final truth about life and history, implied in Old Testament prophetism and made explicit in the New Testament. In this sense the Reformation has an insight which goes beyond the truth embodied in the Catholic synthesis, and which cannot be stated in the compromises between Hellenism and prophetism which that synthesis achieved.

The double aspect of grace, the twofold emphasis upon the obligation to fulfill the possibilities of life and upon the limitations and corruptions in all historic realizations, implies that history is a meaningful process but is incapable of fulfilling itself and therefore points beyond itself to the judgment and mercy of God for its fulfillment. The Christian doctrine of the Atonement, with its paradoxical conception of the relation of the divine mercy to the divine wrath is therefore the final key to this historical interpretation. The wrath and the judgment of God are symbolic of the seriousness of history. The distinctions between good and evil are important and have ultimate significance. The realization of the good must be taken seriously; it is the wheat, separated from the tares, which is gathered "into my barn," which is to say that the good within the finite flux has significance beyond that flux.

On the other hand the mercy of God, which strangely fulfills and yet contradicts the divine judgment, points to the incompleteness of all historic good, the corruption of evil in all historic achievements and the incompleteness of every historic system of meaning without the eternal mercy which knows how to destroy and transmute evil by taking it into itself.

The Christian doctrine of the Atonement is therefore not some incomprehensible remnant of superstition, nor yet a completely incomprehensible article of faith. It is, indeed, on the other side of human wisdom, in the sense that it is not comprehensible to a wisdom which looks at the world with confident eyes, certain that all its mysteries can be fathomed by the human mind. Yet it is the beginning of wisdom in the sense that it contains symbolically all that the Christian faith maintains about what man ought to do and what he cannot do, about his obligations and final incapacity to fulfill them, about the importance of decisions and achievements in history and about their final insignificance.

CHAPTER VIII

HAVING, AND NOT HAVING, THE TRUTH

IF THE CHRISTIAN conception of grace be true then all history remains an "interim" between the disclosure and the fulfillment of its meaning. This interim is characterized by positive corruptions, as well as by partial realizations and approximations of the meaning of life. Redemption does not guarantee elimination of the sinful corruptions, which are in fact increased whenever the redeemed claim to be completely emancipated from them. But the taint of sin upon all historical achievements does not destroy the possibility of such achievements nor the obligation to realize truth and goodness in history. The fulfillments of meaning in history will be the more untainted in fact, if purity is not prematurely claimed for them. All historical activities stand under this paradox of grace.

These activities may be roughly placed into two general categories: the quest for the truth and the achievement of just and brotherly relations with our fellowmen. These two categories comprise the cultural and the socio-moral problems of history. It will be well to study each of these forms of historical activity in turn to see how the paradox of our having, and yet not having either truth or justice in history conforms to the facts; and how our understanding of the paradox influences, or may influence, our actions.

II

THE PROBLEM OF THE TRUTH

The ideal possibilities and the sinful realities in the realm of culture have been previously discussed.[1] We know that the freedom of the human spirit over the flux of nature and history makes it impossible to accept *our* truth as *the* truth. The capacity for rational self-transcendence opens up constantly new and higher points of vantage for judging our finite perspectives in the light of a more inclusive truth. On the other hand our involvement in natural and historical flux sets final limits upon our quest for the truth and insures the partial and particular character of even the highest cultural vantage point. Thus human culture is under the tension of finiteness and freedom, of the limited and the unlimited.

Two complicating factors must be added to this tension: since human personality is an organic unity of its vital and rational capacities, rational apprehensions are subject not merely to the limits of a finite mind but to the play of passion and interest which human vitalities introduce into the process. Knowledge of the truth is thus invariably tainted with an "ideological" taint of interest, which makes our apprehension of truth something less than knowledge of *the* truth and reduces it to *our* truth. The cultural quest is furthermore confused by the premature claims of finality which men invariably make for their finite perspectives. This pretension is the sinful element in culture. It includes not merely the effort to deny the finiteness of our perspectives but to hide and obscure the taint of interest and passion in our knowledge. This pride is the real force of "ideology." Without it the partial character of all human knowledge would be harmless and would encourage men to invite the supplementation and completion of their incomplete knowledge from other partial perspectives. In so far as sin has not, and cannot, destroy the rational capacities of men or reduce them to

[1] *Cf.* Vol. I, Ch. VII.

a state of total depravity, such supplementation is a continuing factor in the cultural process.

The denial of the finiteness of our knowledge and the false claim of finality is always partly the ignorance of our ignorance. It is a failure in our capacity for self-transcendence. But since this capacity belongs to man's native endowment, the sinful claim of finality is always partly a conscious or semi-conscious effort to obscure the partial and interested character of our knowledge of the truth. We are not merely ignorant of our ignorance but we "hold the truth in unrighteousness."

The Christian answer to this problem is the apprehension of the truth "in Christ." This is a truth about life and history which fulfills what is valid and negates what is sinful in our knowledge of the truth. It fulfills what is valid, because man's self-transcendence enables him to hope for and desire the disclosure of a meaning which has a center and source beyond himself. It negates what is sinful because it disappoints that element in all human hopes and expectations, which seeks to complete the meaning of life around the self, individual or collective, as the inadequate center of the realm of meaning. Thus the true Christ is both expected and rejected. When the *logos* is made flesh it is the light that "shineth in darkness and the darkness apprehended it not." [2] Yet it is possible to accept this truth despite, and because of, its contradiction of all sinful truth. By such acceptance the believer is lifted in principle above the egoistic corruptions of the truth in history: "as many as received him, to them gave he the right to become children of God." [3]

We have already considered the difference between this Christian conception of the *logos* who is revealed in history and overcomes the darkness of the lie in history ("the light shineth in darkness") and the *logos* doctrines, particularly of classical culture, according to which the truth is achieved by the emancipation of the *logos* in man from the conditions of finiteness in history.

[2] John 1:1, 5–11. (Rev. ed.)   [3] John 1:12. (Rev. ed.)

At this point it is necessary to set the Biblical doctrine in contrast to two alternative doctrines which have emerged on the soil and ground of the Christian interpretation of life. The classical *logos* doctrine is an alternative to the Biblical doctrine only in those forms of Christian mysticism in which the eternal and divine element in man is abstracted from the conditions of finiteness in history. The more potent modern alternatives are subtly compounded with the Christian interpretation of the problem of truth. According to the one, truth is established not only *in principle* but in fact in the heart of those who have accepted Christ. They are no longer sinners in their apprehension of the truth. According to the other, more and more perfect truth is apprehended by the cumulative processes of culture in history. The first alternative is quite obviously the Catholic version of "sanctification" in the realm of culture, though one must hasten to add that it is fairly defined as "Catholic" only if it is understood that this pretension of achieving the truth without sinful corruption in history is not limited to the institution in which it has been most precisely defined. It is a perennial error in all forms of Christianity.

The second alternative is also obviously the "Renaissance" version of the answer to the cultural problem. Classical and Christian concepts are combined in it. It is a *logos* doctrine which has been changed by historical consciousness. The *logos* is no longer purified by emancipation from history. It is purified by the process of history itself. History is, in fact, the record of the gradual emergence and purification of the *logos*. Hegelianism is, in a sense, the most perfect statement of this "Renaissance" solution of the problem of the truth in history, though there are naturalistic versions of the cumulation of wisdom and truth in history which are also expressions of it, despite their rejection of "idealism."

If we set these alternatives in contrast to the "Biblical" doctrine it must be understood that the term "Biblical" is meant to embrace the explication of the Biblical paradox of grace in Christian history particularly in the Reformation. Christian history is filled not only with all kinds of pretensions that Christians stand completely beyond the egoistic corruption of the truth; it also contains, partly as reaction to these pretensions, forms of awareness, in varying degrees of explicitness, that "redemption" in the realm of culture and truth is a having and a not-having of the truth; and that the pretension of having it leads to a new lie. This is the paradox of grace applied to the truth. The truth, as it is contained in the Christian revelation, includes the recognition that it is neither possible for man to know the truth fully nor to avoid the error of pretending that he does. It is recognized that "grace" always remains in partial contradiction to "nature," and is not merely its fulfillment.

The very apprehension of this paradox is itself an expression of the twofold aspect of grace. It is a thought beyond all human thought and can affect thinking only indirectly. For it is not possible to remain fully conscious of the egoistic corruption in the truth, while we seek to establish and advance it in our thought and action. But it is possible in moments of prayerful transcendence over the sphere of interested thought and action to be conscious of the corruption; and it is also possible to carry this insight into our interested thoughts and actions so that it creates some sense of pity and forgiveness for those who contend against our truth and oppose our action. But "grace" enters and purifies our thought and action fully only if the contradiction between it and "nature" (in this case corrupted truth) is understood. Here lies the secret of forgiveness. Mercy to the foe is possible only to those who know themselves to be sinners.[4]

---

[4] Professor Tillich's analysis of this problem, to which I am greatly indebted, arrives at a formal transcendence over the ambiguity of all historical truth by the following logic: "The doctrine of the character of knowledge as a decision, like everything that makes truth relative, elicits the objection that this doctrine makes itself relative and thus refutes itself. . . . What is true, however, of all knowledge cannot be true of the knowledge of knowledge, otherwise it would cease to have universal significance. On the other hand, if an exception is admitted, then for one

But the same uneasiness, which prompts pity and forgiveness towards the protagonist of an opposing "truth," must also incite the soul to the most diligent possible purification of the truth which it holds and by which it acts. Thus the twofold aspects of grace,

---

bit of reality the equivocal character of being is broken. . . . Is that possible? It would be impossible if the removal of the ambiguity of existence were to occur at any place in existence. Whatever stands in the context of knowledge is subject to the ambiguity of knowledge. Therefore such a proposition must be removed from the context of knowledge. . . . It must be the expression of the relation of knowledge to the Unconditioned. . . . The judgment that is removed from ambiguity . . . can be only the fundamental judgment of the relationship of the Unconditioned and Conditioned. . . . The content of this judgment is just this—that our subjective thinking never can reach the unconditioned Truth. . . . This judgment is plainly the absolute judgment which is independent of all its forms of expression, even of the one by which it is expressed here. It is the judgment which constitutes truth as truth." Paul Tillich, *The Interpretation of History*, pp. 169, 170.

Professor Tillich's analysis of the thought which transcends all conditioned and finite thought, and proves its transcendence by its realization of the finiteness of thought, is a precise formulation of the ultimate self-transcendence of the human spirit, revealed in its capacity to understand its own finiteness. It is a philosophical formulation of this reality, and therefore deals with the problem of finiteness and not of sin. Sin is the refusal to admit finiteness. This refusal is sinful precisely because spirit has the capacity to recognize its finiteness. But when it refuses to do so its sinful self-glorification must be broken by the power of "grace."

What Professor Tillich describes could therefore be equated with what I have defined at another point (Vol. I, Ch. X) as "perfection before the fall," the perfection which hovers as possibility but not as actuality over all action. If this possibility is realized at all, it belongs to the realm of "grace" and cannot be merely ascribed to the native endowment of spirit: that is its capacity for self-transcendence. Without such a capacity there would indeed be no "point of contact" for "grace," that is, without a shattering of the false sense of self-sufficiency and universality of spirit, the effort would be made (as it is made in idealistic philosophy) to extend the pinnacle of self-transcendence in the human spirit until it becomes universal spirit, that is God.

This is why the real "dialectic" of the conditioned and the Unconditioned in human culture is taken seriously in principle only in the Christian faith.

defined traditionally as "sanctification" and "justification" are no more in contradiction to each other in the field of culture, and in the search for truth, than in any other field.

If this approach to the problem of truth be defined as Biblical, and the Biblical paradox of grace be comprehended in the light of Christian history which culminated in the Reformation, it is necessary to add immediately that no claim is made for the success of the Reformation, as a particular historical movement, in dealing with the problem of truth and culture. The test of how well this paradox of the gospel is comprehended, and how genuinely it has entered into human experience is the attitude of Christians towards those who differ from themselves in convictions which seem vital to each. The test, in other words, is to be found in the issue of toleration. To meet the test it is necessary not merely to maintain a tolerant attitude towards those who hold beliefs other than our own. The test is twofold and includes both the ability to hold vital convictions which lead to action; and also the capacity to preserve the spirit of forgiveness towards those who offend us by holding to convictions which seem untrue to us. Judged by that standard, the Reformation has little advantage over other versions of the Christian faith. Furthermore we must admit that Christian history in general has frequently generated fanaticisms as grievous as the idolatries of other cultures.

The history of Christianity proves that such grace as is manifested in Christian life does not lift men above the finiteness of the mind; nor yet save them from the sin of claiming to have transcended it. The divisions in the church, caused by geographic and climatic conditions, by class distinctions and economic circumstances, by national and racial particularities and by historical qualifications of every kind, are proof of the continued finiteness of those who live by grace.[5] The fanatic fury of religious controversies, the hatred engendered in theological disputes, the bitterness of ecclesiastical

[5] *Cf.* H. R. Niebuhr, *The Social Sources of Denominationalism.*

rivalries and the pretentious claims of ecclesiastical dominion all reveal the continued power of sin in the life of the "redeemed"; and the use which sin makes of the pretension of holiness.

It is in fact not surprising that the enemies of Christianity should frequently regard it as the tool of inordinate historical claims and pretensions; rather than as a religion in which all such pretensions are broken in principle, and should sigh and hope for the destruction of religion as the only way of emancipating mankind from fanaticism. The enemies of religion do not, of course, understand that they are dealing with a more fundamental problem than anything created by this or that religion; that it is the problem of the relative and the absolute in history; that the problem is solved by Christian faith "in principle"; that Christian faith may aggravate the problem if it claims more than that; but that alternative solutions, as they are evolved in secular culture, present us either with the abyss of scepticism or with new fanaticisms.

III

THE TEST OF TOLERANCE

If we apply the test of toleration to the various versions of the Christian faith, in order to determine how closely they approximate to the wisdom of the gospel, we meet with some obvious results and with others which will seem surprising until they are more fully explored. The foregone conclusion is that the Catholic version of the Christian faith is intolerant in principle. This is not surprising because the Catholic idea of sanctification in regard to the problem of truth is consistent with its general theories of grace. The more surprising result of such an historical investigation is that Reformation theology has not, in fact, brought forth fruits of the contrite spirit and the broken heart in the field of intellectual controversy which would be consonant with its theory of grace and its doctrine of justification. The reason for this failure has been partially anticipated in our general survey but must be considered in the light of the test of toleration. The chief source· of toleration in modern history has been in the various forces of the Renaissance movement, both sectarian and secular. But it is necessary to inquire whether the tolerant attitude of the "liberal" spirit meets both, or only one, of the two aspects of the test of toleration. Does it also maintain a vital and organic relation between thought and action while it achieves forbearance of contrary and contradictory views and opinions?

1. *Catholicism and Toleration*

Catholicism is impelled by its whole history and by its peculiar doctrine of grace to claim unconditioned possession of the truth. In this claim in the realm of culture it obviously destroys the Biblical paradox of grace. It pretends to have as a simple possession, what cannot be so possessed. It may vary its attitude slightly towards other versions of the Christian faith from time to time, but it is completely consistent and unyielding in its conviction that it alone possesses the truth and the whole truth.

One of the ablest exponents of Augustinian thought in contemporary Catholicism, Erich Przywara, writes about the Inquisition: "The Dominican order had become, willy-nilly, the servants of the Inquisition, not on account of a sort of fanaticism (the great Dominicans were all men of child-like humility and even tender sensitiveness) but on account of an utter abandonment of all individualism to the service of the everlasting truth. . . . God is just *the* Truth (a genuine Augustinian phrase) and so service to the Truth is service to God. . . . The Dominican type regards itself as entrusted by an inscrutable providence with the sacred guardianship of the one Truth in the midst of the world. It is of the type which stands in the world . . . but yet while in the world it stands there with the single task of subjecting the world . . . to the dominion of this one everlasting truth. Truth remote from all fluctuations due to individuality and existence."[1] The difficulty with this essentially

[1] Erich Przywara, *Polarity*, p. 106.

high-minded justification of the Inquisition is that it does not understand that the one everlasting truth of the gospel contains the insight that mere men cannot have this truth "remote from all fluctuations due to individuality and existence." This error is the root of all Inquisitions.

Catholics may indeed be individually humble and contrite, as Przywara avers; and may therefore compare favorably with Protestant individualists who have a fanatic zeal for their own individual interpretation of truth. But Catholicism is collectively and officially intolerant. Its intolerance expresses itself not only in blindness towards possible facets of truth contained in other than its own interpretations of the truth; but also in efforts to suppress the profession of other religions, including the profession of other versions of the Christian religion.

The Jesuit protagonist of intolerance in Elizabethan England, Robert Parsons, defined the logic of the Catholic position with rigorous consistency: "If every man which hath any religion and is resolved therein must needs suppose this only truth to be in his own religion, then it followeth necessarily that he must likewise persuade himself that all religions beside his own are false and erroneous; and consequently all assemblies, conventicles, and public acts of the same are wicked and dishonorable to God." Parsons carried this logic to the point of asserting that even if the other religions were really true, "yet would I be condemned for going among them, for that in my sight and judgment and conscience, by which only I must be judged, they must need seem enemies to God." [2]

The Catholic doctrine, which forces the church to seek for the monopoly of the public profession of religion in a state, is officially defined in the encyclical *Immortale Dei* of Pope Leo XIII: "Since no one is allowed to be remiss in the service due to God, and since the chief duty of all men is to cling to religion in both its teaching

---

[2] Quoted by W. K. Jordan, *The Development of Religious Toleration in England,* Vol. I, p. 390. Jordan's great work is invaluable for students of this problem.

and practice . . . not such religion as they may have preference for but the religion which God enjoins, and which certain and most clear marks show to be the only true religion . . . it is a public crime to act as if there were no God. So too it is a sin in the state not to have care of religion . . . or out of the many forms of religion to adopt that one which chimes in with the fancy, for we are bound absolutely to worship God in that way which He has shown to be His will." A modern Catholic theologian, commenting on these official words, underscores them as follows: "If the state is under moral compulsion to profess and promote religion it is obviously obliged to promote and profess only the religion that is true; for no individual, no group of individuals, no society, no State is justified in supporting error or in according to error the same recognition as to truth." [3]

The simple distinction between "truth" and "error," consonant with similar simple distinctions in Catholic teachings between "justice" and "injustice" is a convenient tool of the terrible and pathetic illusion that "our" truth must use every instrument of coercion, as well as persuasion, to destroy and suppress the "false-

---

[3] John A. Ryan and Francis J. Boland, *Catholic Principles of Politics,* p. 314. The authors admit that this position is "intolerant but not therefore unreasonable." For "error has not the same rights as the truth." They call attention to the fact that the official position requires the suppression of other religions only if the nation is Catholic by an overwhelming majority and that therefore, "Its practical realization is so remote in time and in probability that no practical man will let it disturb his equanimity." They warn Catholics in non-Catholic nations against denying this doctrine for the sake of averting animus against the church; for they believe that, "the majority of our fellow citizens will be sufficiently honourable to respect our devotion to the truth and sufficiently realistic to see that the danger of religious intolerance towards non-Catholics in the United States is so improbable and so far in the future that it should not occupy their time and attention." *Ibid.,* p. 321.

This curious and pathetic logic implies an admission that the intolerance to which the church is forced by its presuppositions is really dangerous to both civil peace and civil liberty. Non-Catholics are consoled with the assurance that religious diversity, once established historically, will prevent the church from putting its theory into practice.

hood" of an opposing belief. For the distinction ignores the ambiguous character of all knowledge in history and obscures the residual error in even the purest truth, and the saving truth in even the most obvious error. It supports Catholicism in its fury against the "enemies of God" and the "enemies of Christ." The church does not understand that rebellions and revolutions against its authority may be prompted not by hatred of God or Christ, but by resentment against the unjustified use of Christ as a "cover" for the historical relativities of culture and civilization in which it happens to be involved.[4] It is not the Christ but "my" Christ who arouses this fury.

The Greek Orthodox version of this Catholic error differs slightly from the Roman one. The difference is in the more mystical conception of "grace" which, in Eastern thought, is regarded as the triumph of eternity over time and finiteness. Thus an Orthodox theologian defines the unconditioned truth possessed by the church as the achievement of the eternal in time: "The Catholic nature of the church is seen most vividly in the fact," he writes, "that the experience of the church belongs to all times. In the life and

---

[4] The Pastoral of the Spanish Bishops during the Spanish Civil War (published September 1937) contains a vivid expression of this Catholic illusion. The Bishops described the hatred of the church among the communists as follows: "The hatred against Jesus Christ and the Blessed Virgin reached paroxysms . . . in the vile literature of the red trenches, ridiculing the divine mysteries, in repeated profanations of the Sacred Host we can glimpse the hatred of hell incarnated in our poor communists. . . . 'I have sworn to be revenged on you,' said one [soldier] to our Lord, enclosed in the tabernacle, and aiming at Him with a pistol, he fired at Him saying: 'Surrender to the reds. Surrender to Marxism.' "

The identification of Christ with the "Sacred Host" on the altar is the perfect fruit of the Catholic error. The host on the altar is an historically conditioned symbol of the ultimate sanctity. All historical symbols contain the taint of profanation; for they insinuate the partial and particular values of "my" civilization, culture, and values into the sphere of absolute sanctity. The profanation of the sacred by the enemy against which we complain is therefore always, at least partly, a protest against our own profanation of the sacred.

existence of the church time is mysteriously overcome and mastered.
Time so to speak stands still. It stands still because of the
power of grace which gathers together in catholic unity of life
that which has become separated by walls built by the course of
time." [5]

Anglo-Catholicism has been saved, by the lack of such actual
historical universality as the Roman church can boast, from making
as consistent pretensions as the Roman church. But it has the same
difficulty in recognizing the contingent and sinful elements in the
truth which the Church possesses. Due to this error it has introduced confusion into the ecumenical movement of the non-Roman
churches by insisting that the basis of ecumenical unity must include
both a common faith and a common "order." But the "order" of
a church, its rites and its polity, belong clearly to the realm of the
historically contingent. Failure to recognize this fact naturally leads
the Catholic wing of the non-Roman churches to insist that its
order is the only possible one for an ecumenical church. The logic
of this sinful spiritual imperialism conforms to the logic of sin
generally. It is the unconscious ignorance, and the conscious denial,
of the finiteness of its own perspective. Anglo-Catholicism is not
alone in displaying this sin, but it has been particularly blind to
the finite perspectives in the realm of "grace" and therefore especially prone to refute its sanctificationist interpretations of the
Church by its own actions. [6]

[5] Rev. G. V. Florovsky, quoted by J. H. Oldham in the symposium:
The Church of God: An Anglo-Russian Symposium, p. 62.

[6] The pathos of this whole problem is most vividly portrayed in efforts
to make the sacrament of the Lord's Supper into a genuine symbol of
the unity of the church, above and beyond all distinctions and relativities
which divide it. Any insistence that this sacrament must be administered
according to a particular "order" inevitably leads either to new display
of the division of the church, by preventing the common observance of
the sacrament; or to a new display of imperialism, by forcing Christians
of different persuasion to accept one order of administration as the price
of unity. The Scriptural observation: "There are differences of admin-
istrations, but the same Lord; and there are diversities of operations,

2. *The Reformation and Toleration*

We have maintained that the Reformation doctrine of "justification by faith" in its relation to the doctrine of sanctification represents the final recognition within the Christian faith of the twofold
aspect of grace in Biblical religion. Logically the paradox of grace,
that it is a having and not having, applies to the realm of culture
and truth with the same validity as to any other realm of life. But
the Reformation failed to apply it to this realm. Its fanaticisms
disturbed the peace of both the church and civil society no less than
did Catholic intolerance. In its treatment of those who differed from
its interpretation of the Gospel it was singularly barren of the
"fruits meet for repentance," of the humility which betrays the
"broken spirit and the contrite heart." It gave little indication of
any consciousness that error might be mixed with the truth which
it possessed; though the truth which it possessed contained the
recognition of this very paradox.[7]

Martin Luther had some misgivings about the use of the death
penalty for heretics as late as 1526 and declared: "I can in no wise

---

but it is the same God which worketh all in all" (1 Cor. 12:5-6) is
clearly not heeded.

It may be observed that this sacrament can never become the effective
symbol of the unity of the church if its original eschatological motif does
not receive new emphasis. ("For as often as we eat this bread and drink
this cup, ye do show forth the Lord's death, *till he come.*" (1 Cor.
11:26.) This eschatological emphasis in the sacrament is a true expression of the eschatological character of the church. It does not have the
unity in fact which it desires in principle. The divisions of history and
the chasms of nature and sin leave their mark upon it. It cannot overcome them completely in fact; but it would overcome them more completely than it does if it would recognize its inability to overcome them
more contritely. It would thus live in memory ("This do in remembrance of me") and in hope ("till he come"). Such memory and such
hope would not leave the present unaffected. The church could have the
more of grace, if it admitted that the truth was subject to the paradox of
having and not having.

[7] Professor Tillich has expressed this failure in the significant phrase
that it never submitted the doctrine of justification by faith to the experience of justification by faith.

admit that false teachers ought to be put to death. It is sufficient to banish them." But only a year later the lust of battle against the Anabaptists had dissipated these scruples and he was urging the use of the sword to suppress them. In dealing with both the mystic and the radical-apocalyptic forms of sectarianism, Luther and Calvin were equally pitiless; and the Swiss reformer Zwingli had a similar attitude towards them. Calvin, writing to the Duke of Somerset (Protector during Edward VI's minority), demanded the suppression of heresy by the civil arm: "There are two kinds of rebels who have arisen against the king," he declared. "The one is a fanatical sort of people who under the color of the gospel would put everything to confusion. The other are those who persist in the superstitions of the papal Antichrist. Both alike deserve to be repressed by the sword, which is committed to you, since they not only attack the King but strive with God, who has placed him on his throne."

In the long history of religious controversy in England from the reign of Elizabeth to that of Cromwell, Presbyterianism pursued a policy very similar to that of Catholicism. It pled for liberty of conscience when it was itself in danger of persecution; and threatened all other denominations with suppression when it had the authority to do so. A contemporary Anglican critic of Presbyterianism charged that, "these men cried out for liberty of conscience and boasted that the oppression which was levied against them was the hallmark of their own sainthood. But directly they gained even partial authority, they instantly renounced their former tenderness of conscience and accomplished the destruction of the church with every instrument that a persecuting zeal could recommend." [8]

An impartial historian summarizes the position of both Catholics and Puritans in this long religious controversy: "It has been said that Puritans and Catholics were contending for liberty of conscience. To put it so seems misleading, if not altogether untrue. They were contending for the liberty of their own consciences, not for those of other people. . . . What they both claimed was freedom

[8] Quoted by Jordan, *op. cit.,* Vol. II, p. 365.

to dominate. So far as they were concerned it was merely an accident in the vast process of things, that their efforts to free themselves
helped to enlarge human freedom." [9]

The intolerance of theologians of the orthodox Reformation was
the more reprehensible because the sectaries, against which their
fanaticism was particularly directed, emphasized the very truths
which supplemented the insights of the Reformation. While it
would be wrong to give a purely economic interpretation of the
differences between the Reformation and sectarianism, it cannot be
denied that the theological differences were partly occasioned by,
and the expressions of, social and economic conflicts. Sectarianism
was on the whole the religion of the poor; and their insistence that
religious ideals were socially relevant was occasioned by the pressure
of their economic and social disabilities. Meanwhile the orthodox
Reformation frequently became the religious screen for higher
middle class economic interests, as generally as Catholicism was
involved politically and economically with the older feudal classes.
The mixture of theological and economic perspectives, which
theologians are prone to deny and which economic determinists
emphasize to the point of making religion a mere tool of economic
interest, is one aspect of historical reality which refutes the pretensions of pure idealists, whether religious or secular. Even the most
abstract theological controversy, as also the seemingly most objective
scientific debate, is never free of accents which interest and passion
have insinuated into the struggle. These interests are, it must be
observed, much more complex and never as purely economic as
Marxism assumes.

If the Reformation had observed the debates and conflicts in
which it was involved in the light of its own ultimate insights into
the imperfect character of all human ambitions and achievements,
it could have used contemporary experience to validate its doctrines
and to mitigate the fury with which it supported them.

[9] J. W. Allen, *A History of Political Thought in the Sixteenth Century,* p. 209.

Perhaps it is idle to search for particular causes of the failure of the Reformation to do this; for we have previously noted that sinful pride is able to use as instruments the very doctrines which are intended in principle to overcome it. Yet it is necessary to look for particular causes of this failure; because there were other spiritual movements, both secular and religious, which did, in fact, approach a tolerance consonant with the Christian spirit of forgiveness, though they possessed less searching doctrinal insights into the contingencies of history and the sinful corruptions of culture than the Reformation.

Undoubtedly one cause of the failure of the Reformation in the field of culture was that its Bibliolatry implied "sanctificationist" principles in the realm of culture and truth, despite its generally more paradoxical conception of grace. Thomas Hobbes was one, among many, critics of the church, who observed this effect of the Reformation: "After the Bible was translated into English," he wrote, "every man, nay, every boy and wench that could read English, thought they spoke with God Almighty . . . and every man became a judge of religion, and an interpreter of the scriptures to himself." [10] The certain conviction of the faithful that the Bible gave them the final truth, transcending all finite perspectives and all sinful corruptions, thus contributed to individual spiritual arrogance, no less intolerable than the collective arrogance of the older church. This pride expressed itself despite the fact that contrary interpretations of scripture, against which the arrogance was directed, contradicted the pretension of an absolutely valid interpretation. For they proved that men interpreted Scripture variously, according to the variety of social and historical perspectives from which they severally approached it.

Though Reformation Bibliolatry (to which, as we have previously observed, Calvinism was more prone than Lutheranism) is thus one explanation of the fanaticism of the Reformers and their disciples, it is an explanation which must itself be explained.

[10] Thomas Hobbes, *Behemoth, Works,* VI, 190.

Perhaps it was possible for the Reformation to take this simple jump out of the relativities and ambiguities of history, because it did not labour with sufficient earnestness and seriousness on those ultimate problems of human culture, where both the possibiltiies and the limits of human wisdom are discovered and defined. When this is done the gospel truth, which both negates and fulfills human wisdom, cannot be claimed as a simple possession. For men are persuaded to the contrite recognition that their effort to explicate this truth by human wisdom (which is the task of theology) is subject to historical contingencies, influenced by egoistic passions, corrupted by sinful pretensions and is, in short, under the same judgment as philosophy.

Theology may differ from philosophy in that it has broken with the principle of self-centredness in culture "in principle." It has done so in principle because it recognizes that the "world by its wisdom knew not God"; that it is not possible to complete the structure of meaning from any particular human perspective, or with any finite value as the centre and source of meaning. But the whole history of theology proves that this "in principle" does not mean "in fact." When the truth which transcends all partial and particular perspectives is made relevant to the truths of history and culture (a task which theology must perform despite its perils) these applications are subject to the same contingent elements which the history of philosophy reveals. Luther's contemptuous attitude towards philosophy is therefore without justification; more particularly because in practice philosophy sometimes achieves a greater spirit of humility than theology. It is saved from *hybris* by its lack of any quick means of escape from the obvious limitations of all human knowing. It has no Jacob's ladder upon which the angels of grace rightly ascend and descend, but which is used falsely when the theological Jacob imagines it an instrument for climbing into heaven.[11]

[11] *Cf.* Genesis 28:12.

In short, the intolerance of the Reformation is the consequence of a violation of its own doctrinal position. Its doctrine of justification by faith presupposed the imperfection of the redeemed. Logically this includes the imperfection of "redeemed" knowledge and wisdom. Its intolerant fanaticism sprang from its failure to apply this insight to the cultural problem so that it would mitigate the spiritual pride of man. Its actions thus proved its theory to be correct; but they also revealed it to be ineffective. It is a theory which must not only be apprehended by the mind but which must enter into the heart and break its pride. The authority of the Bible was used to break the proud authority of the church; whereupon the Bible became another instrument of human pride. The secularists may be pardoned if, as they watch this curious drama, they cry "a plague o' both your houses"; and if they come to the conclusion that all ladders to heaven are dangerous. It must be observed, however, that these ladders cannot be disavowed so simply as the secularists imagine. Pride may ascend the ladder which was meant for the descent of grace; but that is a peril which inheres in the whole human cultural enterprise. The secularists end by building ladders of their own; or they wallow in a nihilistic culture which has no vantage point from which "my" truth can be distinguished from "the" truth.

3. The Renaissance and Toleration

The toleration, whether in religious or in socio-economic disputes, which has made life sufferable amidst the cultural and social complexities of the modern world, and which enabled modern society to achieve a measure of domestic tranquility without paying the price of tyrannical suppression, is obviously the fruit, primarily, of the movement which we have defined broadly as "Renaissance." The heroes of science who defied religious authority and reopened prematurely solved problems, stood in that tradition. The Renaissance generated a wholesome attitude of scepticism which made for sanity wherever human pride had exceeded the limits of human certainty. The achievement of toleration in modern culture is sometimes regarded as due to the destruction of religious fanaticism through the destruction of religion itself.[12] In so far as this is the case modern culture solves the problem of toleration only when the conflicts were explicitly religious; and offers no antidote for the implicitly religious fanaticism generated in ostensibly secular political and social movements.

It must be observed, however, that sectarian Protestantism, which is, as we have previously noted, intimately related to Renaissance spirituality, also made very substantial contributions to the spirit of liberty and toleration.

The rationalist-humanist wing of the Renaissance made its contributions to toleration by challenging particular prejudices with the supposed universalities of reason; and by dissolving the false universalities of dogmatic religion by the force of empirical observations, proving the wide variety and relativity of all historical forms of culture. The two strategies frequently operated side by side and receive varying degrees of emphasis in the typical champions of toleration in Renaissance humanism. Bruno leans to the one, Montaigne to the other mode of attack; Descartes to the first and Locke and Voltaire to the second.

Sectarian Christianity meanwhile challenged Christian fanaticism from within the presuppositions of Christian faith. Its mystic certainties transcended the historically conditioned certainties of dogmatic faith. Its individualism challenged the orthodox passion for religious uniformity; and its social radicalism set the absolute ethical demands of the gospel against the social compromises which religious authority had prematurely sanctioned. Hans Denck, the father of Reformation pietism, in whose thought are the germs of

---

[12] As for instance in W. E. H. Lecky's *The Rise and Influence of the Spirit of Rationalism in Europe*. Lecky regards the religious doctrine of "exclusive salvation" as the primary, if not sole, cause of the spirit of persecution; and "rationalism" as its sole cure.

both mystic-pietistic and radical-apocalyptic sectarianism, was a champion of toleration, as was also Schwenkfeld.[13]

While the Independents and the Levellers were the particular champions of toleration among seventeenth-century English sects, all the English sects made some contribution to the ideals of liberty. Lilburne and Walwyn, Winstanley and Roger Williams, these and many lesser known champions of liberty, are equally or more important in the history of English toleration, than the champions of liberty on the humanist side of the Renaissance.

The most distinguished of all champions of toleration, John Milton, combines Renaissance humanism and sectarian Christianity in a remarkable synthesis. Less profoundly Thomas Jefferson also achieved this synthesis, though the rationalist element in his thought is more pronounced and the Christian content more minimal.[14]

Sectarianism was not, of course, universally tolerant. It had its own source of fanatic fury. Its simple perfectionism made it blind to the inevitability of the compromises in which it saw its opponents involved. It therefore poured the fury of its self-righteous scorn upon them without recognizing that their compromises were but the obverse side of responsibilities, which the perfectionists had simply disavowed.[15] Sometimes its individualism (and this applies to secular libertarianisms as well) rendered its preaching of toleration too cheap; for it assumed no responsibility for, nor understood the

[13] Denck's last words before death were: "God is my witness that I desire things to go well with me only for the sake of one sect: the communion of saints, let be where it will."

[14] In English history the only important group which does not conform to these two general categories were the Cambridge Platonists and the moderate Anglican champions of toleration, particularly W. Chillingworth and Jeremy Taylor. The latter's *Liberty of Prophesying* is a classic on the subject. These Anglicans combine Renaissance insights with more orthodox rather than sectarian-Christian conceptions. Thomas More is an earlier exponent of the same general viewpoint.

[15] The modern counterpart of this sectarian fury is the self-righteousness of some pacifists who think it easy to love a tyrant but find it hard to preserve a decent Christian charity towards fellow-Christians who differ with them on the proper method of destroying tyranny.

necessity of, social peace and order. It did not therefore recognize the necessity of minimal coercion in even the most liberal society.[16]

But despite these sectarian fanaticisms, the history of sectarianism in general is as important as the more secular movement of the Renaissance in the development of toleration in the Western world.

The agreement upon this issue between secularists and sectarians rests upon two common approaches to the problem of truth, in which other differences are transcended. Both recognize the peril to truth in the coerced acceptance of it. And both are conscious of the finite character of human perspective and the variety of human viewpoints, which make perfect agreement in the search for truth impossible.

On the first point the secularists emphasize the futility of maintaining truth by coercion. "The truth," declared John Locke, "would certainly do well enough if she were left to shift for herself. She seldom has received, and I fear never will receive, much assistance from the power of great men. . . . If truth makes not her way into the understanding by her own light, she will be but weaker for any borrowed force violence can add to her." [17] The sectarian Christians give this same idea a slightly more moral-religious content. They do not see how coerced acceptance of the truth can redeem the soul. A letter of Flemish Baptists, under persecution in Elizabethan England, was a moving expression of the idea: "We testify before God and your majesty that were we in our conscience able by any means to think or understand the contrary, we would with all our hearts receive and confess it; since it were a great folly in us not to live rather in the exercise of a right faith, than to die perhaps in a false one. . . . It is not in our power to believe this or that as evil doers who do right or wrong as they please. But the true faith must

---

[16] The conflict between Oliver Cromwell and sectarian fanatics is instructive on this point. Cromwell agreed in principle more with the spirit of Independency than with Presbyterian policy. But he understood the difficulties of maintaining social order and peace as his sectarian critics did not.

[17] From *A Letter on Toleration*.

be planted in the heart by God, and to Him we pray daily that he would give us His spirit to understand His word and the Gospel." [18]

The second point of agreement between secular and sectarian theories of toleration is derived from the appreciation and understanding by the Renaissance of the cultural task as an historical process. It understands the contingent character of all historical knowledge and appreciates the wide variety of perspectives which history and nature, geography and climate introduce into human culture.[19] Here the Renaissance is more thoroughly in agreement with the Biblical understanding of man as "creature" and the Christian appreciation of the limits of human knowledge in history than alternative and more orthodox Christian doctrines. The Renaissance had its own ways of surmounting this historical relativity, which must be considered presently. It was led into new errors by many of them. But its provisional understanding of historical relativity gave it a great advantage over Christian orthodoxy.

This recognition of the fragmentary character of all historical apprehension of the truth is superbly expressed in Milton's *Areopagitica,* though in symbolism more Biblical than modern culture as a whole uses: "Truth indeed came once into the world with her Divine Master and was a perfect shape most glorious to look upon; but when He ascended and His Apostles after him were laid asleep, then straight arose a wicked race of deceivers . . . who took the Virgin truth, hewed her lovely form into a thousand pieces and scattered them to the four winds. From that time ever since the sad

[18] Roger Williams makes the same point, as indeed it is continually made by sectarian Christianity: "The ordinances and discipline of Jesus Christ, though wrongfully and profanely applied to unregenerate men, may cast a blush of civility and morality upon them . . . yet withal I affirm that the misapplication of ordinances to unregenerate and unrepentant persons, hardens up their souls in a dredful sleep . . . and sends millions of souls to hell in the secure expectation of a false salvation." From *The Bloudy Tenent of Persecution.*

[19] This insight was Montaigne's particular contribution to modern thought but it is proliferated in many forms and varieties of thought.

friends of Truth, such as durst appear, imitating the careful search that Isis made for the mangled body of Osiris, went up and down, gathering up limb by limb, still as they could find them. We have not yet found them all, Lords and Commons, nor ever shall do till the Master's second coming." [20]

The same idea is the frequent preoccupation of sectarian and independent thought. "Let us not," wrote John Saltmarsh, ". . . assume any power of infallibility to each other; . . . . for another's evidence is as dark to me as mine to him . . . till the Lord enlighten us both for discerning alike." [21]

This provisional understanding of the relativity of human knowledge, including the relativity of various interpretations of religious revelation, is an integral part of the recovery of the sense of the historical in Renaissance thought. It is the primary cause of the ability of the Renaissance to meet one of the two tests of the problem of toleration: the willingness to entertain views which oppose our own without rancour and without the effort to suppress them.

It is in meeting the other test: the ability to remain true to and to act upon our best convictions, that modern culture most frequently fails. It finds difficulty in avoiding irresponsibility and scepticism on the one hand and new fanaticisms on the other.

Its position is safe from illusion so long as it simply seeks to preserve the free commerce of opinion, in the hope that a higher truth will emerge in the process. In the words of John Stuart Mill: "Though silenced opinion be an error, it may, and very commonly does, contain a portion of the truth; and since the general or prevailing opinion on any subject is rarely or never the whole truth, it

[20] Milton's use of Biblical and oriental symbolism is indicative of the combination of Christian and humanist elements in his thought. The statement is nevertheless a perfect expression of the Christian doctrine of history as an "interim" between the revelation of the truth and its fulfillment. It encourages the gathering up of the truth "limb by limb" on the one hand; and yet expects no completion of the truth in history on the other.

[21] From *Smoke in the Temple* (1646).

is only the collision of adverse opinion that the remainder of the truth has a chance of being supplied." [22]

The hope that fragmentary portions of the truth will finally be pieced together into the whole truth, or the belief that intellectual intercourse is a kind of competition in which the truth will finally prevail against falsehood, are admirable provisional incentives to tolerance. They are, moreover, provisionally and relatively true. The intellectual life of mankind is a process in which truth is constantly being sifted from falsehood; and the confidence that truth will finally prevail in history robs falsehood of its seeming immediate peril and mitigates the anxious fanaticism with which "our" truth is defended.

The difficulty with this solution is that it is only a provisional and not a final answer to the question of the relation of the "whole truth" to the fragmentary truths of history. Obviously this issue is a segment of the whole problem of time and eternity. The belief that history is moving towards the disclosure of the whole truth is a part of an entire conception of the relation of time to eternity, in which it is assumed that history transmutes itself into eternity, and progressively devours its own finiteness. It is typical of the combination of classical and historical viewpoints in the Renaissance, according to which the *logos* in history is not emancipated from finiteness and history but gradually prevails within history.[23]

[22] From Essay on *Liberty*.

[23] A typical modern statement of this belief and hope is to be found in Professor John Dewey's *A Common Faith*. According to Dewey the divisive elements in human culture are vestigial remnants of outmoded religious prejudices which will yield to the universal perspectives which modern education will inculcate. This education will create practical unanimity among men of good will. Modern culture was generating new and fierce ideological conflicts, not remotely connected with traditional religious concepts, while Professor Dewey was writing this book.

The hope of establishing an intellectual position free of ideology springs up eternally in modern culture and takes many forms too numerous to mention. A particularly striking form is found in Professor Karl Mannheim's *Ideology and Utopia*. His contribution is striking because his "sociology of knowledge" is so much more conscious of the all-

In so far as modern tolerance has been achieved by disavowing religion it may rest merely on indifference towards the ultimate problems of life and history, with which religion is concerned. Since religious questions have been a particularly fecund source of fanaticism and conflict, the gain in provisional toleration has therefore been great. But the weakness in the modern position is also quite apparent. Either it achieves toleration by taking an irresponsible attitude towards ultimate issues; or it insinuates new and false ultimates into views of life which are ostensibly merely provisional and pragmatic. Here are the twin perils of scepticism and a new fanaticism.

It is significant that so much of modern toleration applies merely to the field of religion; and that the very champions of toleration in this field may be exponents of political fanaticism. It is simple enough to be tolerant on issues which are not believed to be vital.[24] The real test of toleration is our attitude towards people who oppose truths which seem important to us, and who challenge realms of life and meaning towards which we have a responsible relation. Tolerance in religion, therefore, frequently means an irresponsible attitude towards the ultimate problem of truth, including particularly the problem of the relation of *the* truth to the fragmentary truths of history. In the same way tolerance in political struggles may merely reveal irresponsibility and indifference towards the problem of political justice.

This irresponsible attitude may degenerate into complete scepticism, though there are very few consistent sceptics in the world. Absolute scepticism is rare because the very lack of confidence in the possibility of achieving any valid truth in history presupposes some

___

pervasive character of ideology than most similar analyses. He nevertheless hopes to eliminate ideology by developing a high degree of consciousness of the conditioned character of human knowledge. Such a consciousness may indeed purge knowledge of many overt ideologies, but it cannot produce an unconditioned mind.

[24] "Tolerance," said Gilbert Chesterton, "is the virtue of people who don't believe anything."

criterion of truth by which all fragmentary truths are found wanting. Nevertheless, complete scepticism is always a possible consequence of the spirit of toleration; for no toleration is possible without a measure of provisional scepticism about the truth we hold.[25] The Christian position of contrition in regard to "our" truth, the humble recognition that it contains some egoistic corruption, degenerates into irresponsibility as soon as we disavow the obligation to purge the truth we hold of its egoistic corruption. The irresponsibility degenerates into more complete scepticism if we come to the conclusion, that since history contains nothing but partial perspectives and fragmentary viewpoints, there is no possibility of discerning truth from falsehood. Complete scepticism represents the abyss of meaninglessness, a pit which has constantly threatened modern culture and into which it occasionally tumbles. Frequently, as in pre-Nazi German culture, it precedes the subordination of truth to political power. Scepticism thus becomes the forerunner of cynicism.

But new fanaticisms are the much more probable consequence of the modern position than complete scepticism. In these fanaticisms an ultimate position and a final truth are implicitly or explicitly insinuated into what was provisionally regarded as a realm of partial and fragmentary truths. Thus new religions emerge in an ostensibly irreligious culture.

In the main current of Renaissance thought, the belief that the intercourse between fragmentary truths will culminate in the realization of the whole truth becomes itself a religious position as soon as it is changed from a merely provisional and tentative attitude towards the immediate problem of dealing with fragmentary truths, into an answer to the final problem of truth and falsehood. Such a religion can and does maintain tolerance towards all religious beliefs except those which challenge this basic assump-

[25] "The only foundation for toleration," said Charles James Fox, "is a measure of scepticism and without it there can be none."

Oliver Cromwell, facing the peril to the state of conflicting religious absolutes, expressed the same idea in religious terms: "By the bowels of Christ," he said, "remember that you may be mistaken."

tion. The idea of progress is the underlying presupposition of what may be broadly defined as "liberal" culture. If that assumption is challenged the whole structure of meaning in the liberal world is imperiled. For this reason the liberal world is intolerant in regard to this article of its creed. It does not argue about its validity, precisely because it has lost every degree of scepticism in regard to it.

The creed is nevertheless highly dubious. It is true in so far as all historical processes, including the intellectual and cultural process, are meaningful and lead to fulfillment. It is false in so far as all historical processes are ambiguous. In the field of culture this means that the realization of a higher truth can lead to a new falsehood. Penetration into the mysteries of nature, for instance, may lead to false analogies between nature and history; or the discovery of the dynamic character of history may lead to the error of assuming that growth means progress.

The erroneous belief that history is its own fulfillment has been previously considered. The very structure of the human spirit refutes confidence in history as a process of cultural fulfillment as certainly as it refutes the general confidence in history. Man being a creature who both transcends and is involved in historical process cannot find perfect fulfillment in that process. His freedom over the process can be used on any level to introduce new error into the discovery of truth. But even if this were not the case his transcendence over history makes it impossible to complete his structure of meaning within the limits of history. He must ask how historical truth is related to ultimate, that is, "eternal" truth. And if he knows that historical truth is not merely imperfect but also corrupted truth, he faces a problem for which there is no answer but a divine mercy which purges the historical of its corruptions and completes its incompleteness.

But other fanaticisms grow up on the ground of the modern position baser than the mild fanaticism of the religion of progress. All of them, despite their variety, may be defined as political fanaticisms, generated by political religions. Thomas Hobbes and the French protagonist of political absolutism, Jean Bodin, may be regarded as the most typical historical exemplars of this tendency in modern culture, which finally culminated in the Nazi creed of race and nation. The tendency begins with a sceptical and irresponsible attitude towards the religious problem and an aversion to religious controversy because it imperils the tranquility of the national state. In the case of Bodin, the fratricidal religious conflict in France persuaded him to renounce his Huguenot faith for a syncretistic religion. His new religious position nicely reveals the perils of scepticism. For his highminded effort to find the truth in all religions ends with the poorly concealed conviction that all religions are equally true and *equally false.*[26] But Bodin's real concern was the unity of France; and he solved that problem by conceiving an absolute state, which had the power and the right to suppress all opinions and vitalities which might imperil its unity. In the thought of both Hobbes and Bodin, this demand for unconditioned loyalty to the state is implicitly rather than explicitly religious. It is implicitly religious because it demands unconditioned loyalty; but not explicitly so because it does not make the overt claim that the whole meaning of life and existence is fulfilled in the individual's relation to the national community. It was left to the Nazis to illustrate one possible kind of progress in history, by developing the logic of this state absolutism to its final conclusion. Thus they achieved the final corruption of cynicism on the soil of religious scepticism.

Thomas More, who was a Renaissance nationalist when his sovereign Henry VIII imperiled the interests of England by sub servience to papal politics, and who was a Catholic universalist when the king sought to establish royal supremacy in spiritual matters, proved the validity and availability of the Christian position as a resource against this new political fanaticism. Despite its own corruption of fanaticism, the Catholic version of the Christian faith is at least a bulwark against the idolatry of political and national absolutisms. Challenged by the king to submit to his

[26] *Cf.* Jean Bodin, *Colloquium Heptaplomeres*

authority spiritually as well as politically, and presented with the futility of defiance in view of the submission of all other English leaders, More appealed to the authority of the universal church which had not submitted. "For," said he, "though some nations fall away, yet likewise as how many boughs fall from the tree, though they fall more than be left thereon, yet they make no doubt which is the very tree, although each of them were planted in another place and grew to a greater tree than the stock he came first of." [27]

This Christian universalism, despite its corruptions in both the Protestant and Catholic versions of the Christian faith, has proved as resourceful in our own day as in the day of Henry VIII. It has defied the cynical solution of the cultural problem, more successfully than any other position.

The Marxist solution of the problem of truth stands on a higher ground than the subordination of all culture to the power of the state. But it is nevertheless a political religion; and must be regarded as one of the late fruits on the soil of Renaissance thought. According to its faith the particular perspective of the proletarian class is not a relative but a transcendent vantage point for the apprehension of the truth. All truth but its own is therefore tainted with the "ideological" taint of interest. But obviously the pretension of any class or nation, of any culture or civilization, that it alone has escaped from the finiteness of human knowing. and the corruption of interest and passion, is merely another form of the taint of pride which confuses all quests for the truth. It is a secularized version of

[27] *A Dialogue concerning heresyes and matters of religion* (1528). When More was told that "the bishops, universities and best learned of this realm" had submitted to the king he replied significantly: "For I nothing doubt that, though not in this realm yet in Christendom about . . . they be not the fewer part that are of my mind therein. But if I should speak of those already dead, of whom many now be holy saints in heaven, I am sure that it is far the greater part . . . of them that thought in this case the way that I think now. Therefore am I not bound to conform my conscience to the council of one realm against the general council of Christendom." Cf. *Thomas More* by R. W. Chambers, p. 341.

the pretension of complete sanctification. The fruit of fanaticism is the natural consequence of this claim.

However we twist or turn, whatever instruments or pretensions we use, it is not possible to establish the claim that we have the truth. The truth remains subject to the paradox of grace. We may have it; and yet we do not have it. And we will have it the more purely in fact if we know that we have it only in principle. Our toleration of truths opposed to those which we confess is an expression of the spirit of forgiveness in the realm of culture. Like all forgiveness, it is possible only if we are not too sure of our own virtue.

Loyalty to the truth requires confidence in the possibility of its attainment; toleration of others requires broken confidence in the finality of our own truth. But if there is no answer for a problem to which we do not have the answer, our shattered confidence generates either defeat (which in the field of culture would be scepticism); or an even greater measure of pretension, meant to hide our perplexities behind our certainties (which in the field of culture is fanaticism).

CHAPTER IX

THE KINGDOM OF GOD AND THE STRUGGLE
FOR JUSTICE

THE STRUGGLE for justice is as profound a revelation of the possibilities and limits of historical existence as the quest for truth. In some respects it is even more revealing because it engages all human vitalities and powers more obviously than the intellectual quest.

The obligation to build and to perfect communal life is not merely forced upon us by the necessity of coming to terms with the rather numerous hosts, whom it has pleased an Almighty Creator to place on this little earth beside us. Community is an individual as well as social necessity; for the individual can realize himself only in intimate and organic relation with his fellowmen. Love is therefore the primary law of his nature; and brotherhood the fundamental requirement of his social existence.

Since man is a unity of vitality and reason, the social coherence of life can never be purely rational. It includes an interpenetration of all powers and potencies, emotional and volitional as well as rational. But the power of rational freedom gives human communities a higher dimension than those of nature. Man's freedom over the limits of nature in indeterminate regression means that no fixed limits can be placed upon either the purity or the breadth of the brotherhood for which men strive in history. No traditional attainment of brotherhood is secure against criticism from a higher historical perspective or safe from corruption on each new level of achievement.

The indeterminate character of these possibilities of both good and evil in social and political relations justifies the dynamic interpretation of the social process. The facts of history may not support the conclusion that historical process has continually purified and perfected social relations; but they certainly prove that the breadth and extent of historical communities have been consistently increased. Every age, and more particularly the age of technics, has confronted men with the problem of relating their lives to a larger number of their fellowmen. The task of creating community and avoiding anarchy is constantly pitched on broader and broader levels.

These facts have presented modern culture with what seemed irrefutable proofs of its progressive view of the social task. The "Kingdom of God" seemed to be an immanent force in history, culminating in a universal society of brotherhood and justice. The secular and liberal-Protestant approaches to the socio-moral problem, based upon this presupposition, are too numerous to mention. Modern sociological treatises are practically unanimous in assuming this view of history. The Marxist interpretation of history deviates from it. But the deviation is only provisionally radical. Its catastrophism is finally subordinated to a progressive and utopian concept of history. The liberal-Protestant version has added little but pious phrases to the interpretation.

The definition of the Christian view of human destiny as presented must lead to other, and partly contrary, conclusions. The conclusions are not completely contrary because they do not refute the dynamic character of history or the significance of its continually expanding tasks and obligations. They do, however, challenge the identification of historical growth with moral progress. According to our interpretation, "grace" is related to "nature" partly as fulfillment and partly as negation. If the contradiction between "nature" and "grace" is not recognized, and the continued power of "nature" in the realm of "grace" is not conceded, new sins are brought into history by the pretension that sin has been progressively eliminated.

II

THE RELATION OF JUSTICE TO LOVE

If we apply this formula of the Christian interpretation of life to human society it may be well to begin by translating the terms so that they will be relevant to the socio-moral issue. "Nature" in this case represents the historical possibilities of justice.[1] "Grace" would correspond to ideal possibility of perfect love, in which all inner contradictions within the self, and all conflicts and tensions between the self and the other are overcome by the complete obedience of all wills to the will of God.

Translated into these terms the Christian conception of the relation of historical justice to the love of the Kingdom of God is a dialectical one. Love is both the fulfillment and the negation of all achievements of justice in history. Or expressed from the opposite standpoint, the achievements of justice in history may rise in indeterminate degrees to find their fulfillment in a more perfect love and brotherhood; but each new level of fulfillment also contains elements which stand in contradiction to perfect love. There are therefore obligations to realize justice in indeterminate degrees; but none of the realizations can assure the serenity of perfect fulfillment. If we analyse the realities of history in terms of this formula it will throw light on aspects of history which would otherwise remain obscure and perplexing; and will obviate mistakes which are inevitably made under alternative interpretations. Higher realizations of historic justice would be possible if it were more fully

---

[1] It may be helpful to recall that in Christian usage "nature" when set in juxtaposition to "grace" never means the finite or natural process as distinguished from rational freedom. It means the "sinful nature" of man, as distinguished from the state of emancipation from sin.

understood that all such realizations contain contradictions to, as well as approximations of, the ideal of love. Sanctification in the realm of social relations demands recognition of the impossibility of perfect sanctification.

The paradoxical relation between justice and love is expressed on various levels. We have previously explored the relation between sacrificial and mutual love.[2] In that analysis it became apparent that mutual love (in which disinterested concern for the other elicits a reciprocal response) is the highest possibility of history in the sense that only such love is justified by historical consequences; but also that such love can only be initiated by a type of disinterestedness (sacrificial love) which dispenses with historical justification. Thus the pinnacle of the moral ideal stands both inside and beyond history: inside in so far as love may elicit a reciprocal response and change the character of human relations; and beyond history in so far as love cannot require a mutual response without losing its character of disinterestedness. The love commandment is therefore no simple historical possibility. The full implications of the commandment illustrate the dialectical relation between history and the eternal.

III

LAWS AND PRINCIPLES OF JUSTICE

The relation of justice to love contains complexities analogous to the dialectical relation of mutual to sacrificial love. These complexities may be clarified by considering them in two dimensions. The first is the dimension of rules and laws of justice. The second is the dimension of structures of justice, of social and political organizations in their relation to brotherhood. The difference between the first and second dimension obviously lies in the fact that laws and principles of justice are abstractly conceived, while structures and organizations embody the vitalities of history. The contradiction between actual social institutions and arrangements and the ideal

[2] Vol. II, Ch. III.

of brotherhood is obviously greater than between love and the rules and laws of justice.

All systems, rules and laws governing social relations are on the one hand instruments of mutuality and community; and they contain on the other hand mere approximations of, and positive contradictions to, the ideal of brotherhood. These aspects of the character of rules of justice must be examined in turn.

Systems and principles of justice are the servants and instruments of the spirit of brotherhood in so far as they extend the sense of obligation towards the other, (*a*) from an immediately felt obligation, prompted by obvious need, to a continued obligation expressed in fixed principles of mutual support; (*b*) from a simple relation between a self and one "other" to the complex relations of the self and the "others"; and (*c*) finally from the obligations, discerned by the individual self, to the wider obligations which the community defines from its more impartial perspective. These communal definitions evolve slowly in custom and in law. They all contain some higher elements of disinterestedness, which would not be possible to the individual self.

In these three ways rules and laws of justice stand in a positive relation to the law of love. It is significant that the rational element is constitutive in each of them. An immediately felt obligation towards obvious need may be prompted by the emotion of pity. But a continued sense of obligation rests upon and expresses itself in rational calculations of the needs of others as compared with our own interests. A relation between the self and one other may be partly ecstatic; and in any case the calculation of relative interests may be reduced to a minimum. But as soon as a third person is introduced into the relation even the most perfect love requires a rational estimate of conflicting needs and interests. Even the love within a family avails itself of customs and usages which stereotype given adjustments between various members of the family in such a way that each action need not be oriented by a fresh calculation of competing interests.

The definitions of justice arrived at in a given community are the product of a social mind. Various perspectives upon common problems have been merged and have achieved a result, different from that at which any individual, class or group in the community would have arrived. The fact that various conceptions of a just solution of a common problem can be finally synthesized into a common solution disproves the idea that the approach of each individual or group is consistently egoistic. If it were, society would be an anarchy of rival interests until power from above subdued the anarchy.

Interests may indeed clash to such a degree that no arbitration of the conflict is possible, in which case the conflict is ended either by the victory of one side or the other, or by the submission of both to a superior coercive force. Martin Luther's and Thomas Hobbes' political views are informed by the belief that all conflicts of interest are of such a nature.

The achievements of democratic societies refute this pessimism; and with it the purely negative conception of the relation of government and systems of justice to the ideal of brotherhood. History reveals adjustments of interest to interest without the interposition of superior coercive force to be possible within wide limits. The capacity of communities to synthesize divergent approaches to a common problem and to arrive at a tolerably just solution proves man's capacity to consider interests other than his own. Nevertheless, the fact that a synthesis of conflicting interests and viewpoints is not easy, and may become impossible under certain conditions, is a refutation of a too simple trust in the impartial character of reason. It would be as false to regard rules and principles of justice, slowly elaborated in collective experience, as merely the instruments of the sense of social obligation, as to regard them merely as tools of egoistic interest.

An analysis of the development of social conscience on any current social issue, as for instance the community's sense of obligation to the unemployed, may clarify the complex factors involved in this development. The unemployment benefits which the community pays to those who are out of work is partly an expression of the sense of obligation of the more privileged members of the community towards those who are less fortunate. They find an advantage in meeting this obligation according to fixed principles instead of relying upon their own occasional feeling of pity for this or that needy person. They know furthermore that their own knowledge of comparative needs is very inadequate and that they require the more impartial and comprehensive perspective of the total community, functioning through its proper agencies. This function of principles of unemployment relief presents the most positive relation between specific rules and the sense of brotherhood.

On the other hand the benefits which are paid to the unemployed are almost always higher than the privileged would like to pay, even though they may be lower than the poor would like to receive. Some members of the privileged classes in modern communities have in fact obscured the issue of justice in regard to this problem by the most obvious and transparent of all ideologies. They have sought to maintain that the unemployed are the victims of sloth rather than of the caprices of an intricate industrial process; and that the fear of hunger might cure their sloth. The actual schedule of payments upon which the community finally decides represents the conclusions of the social, rather than any individual, mind, and is the consequence of a perennial debate upon the subject. It is probably a compromise between conflicting viewpoints and interests. It certainly is not an unconditionedly "just" solution of the social problem involved. The privileged may in fact accept it for no better reason than that they fear the revolt of the poor. This aspect of the situation proves the impossibility of completely separating the concept of "principles of justice" from the hopes and fears, the pressures and counter-pressures, of living communities, expressed below the level of a rational calculation of rights and interests.

The solution may nevertheless become a generally accepted social standard; and some privileged members of the community may welcome it, because it expresses their considered sense of social obligation upon which they would prefer to rely rather than upon the momentary power of pity. The poor as a whole may receive less from these benefits than an individual needy person might secure by appealing to a given sensitive and opulent individual. But they will certainly receive more than if all of them were dependent upon nothing but vagrant, momentary and capricious impulses of pity, dormant unless awakened by obvious need.

This positive relation between rules of justice and the law of love must be emphasized in opposition to sentimental versions of the love commandment, according to which only the most personal individual and direct expressions of social obligation are manifestations of Christian *agape*. Both sectarian and Lutheran analyses of the relation of love to justice easily fall into the error of excluding rules of justice from the domain of love.[3]

Laws and systems of justice do, however, have a negative as well as a positive relation to mutual love and brotherhood. They contain both approximations of and contradictions to the spirit of brotherhood. This aspect of their character is derived from the sinful element in all social reality. They are merely approximations in so far as justice presupposes a tendency of various members of

---

[3] Emil Brunner succumbs to this error when he writes: "The believer's most important duty . . . always remains that of pouring the vitality of love into the necessarily rigid forms of the order [structure of justice]. . . . The end is the personal relation itself. . . . To improve it [the order] is not a hopeless task, nor is it unnecessary but it is still only a matter of *secondary importance.* The one thing that matters is to do what can be done only from the standpoint of faith, namely, to love our neighbour 'In Christ,' and to serve him in any way we can. . . . It is supremely important to emphasize the truth that what is decisive always takes place in the realm of personal relations and not in the political sphere, save where we are concerned with preserving the whole order from a general breakdown." *The Divine Imperative,* p. 233.

Brunner's consistently negative interpretations of the political task and his idea of its secondary importance is a Lutheran heritage in his thought. He is, of course, correct in asserting that no systems and schemes of justice fulfill the law of love so that the possibility of giving them a higher content by personal attitudes and actions is obviated.

a community to take advantage of each other, or to be more concerned with their own weal than with that of others. Because of this tendency all systems of justice make careful distinctions between the rights and interests of various members of a community. The fence and the boundary line are the symbols of the spirit of justice. They set the limits upon each man's interest to prevent one from taking advantage of the other. A harmony achieved through justice is therefore only an approximation of brotherhood. It is the best possible harmony within the conditions created by human egoism. This negative aspect of justice is not its only characteristic, as has been previously observed. Even if perfect love were presupposed, complex relations, involving more than two persons, require the calculation of rights. The negative aspect is nevertheless important.

The more positive contradiction to brotherhood in all schemes of justice is introduced by the contingent and finite character of rational estimates of rights and interests and by the taint of passion and self-interest upon calculations of the rights of others. There is no universal reason in history, and no impartial perspective upon the whole field of vital interests, which compete with and mutually support each other. Even the comparatively impartial view of the whole of a society, as expressed particularly in the carefully guarded objectivity of its juridical institutions, participates in the contingent character of all human viewpoints.

Such rules of justice as we have known in history have been arrived at by a social process in which various partial perspectives have been synthesized into a more inclusive one. But even the inclusive perspective is contingent to time and place. The Marxist cynicism in regard to the pretended moral purity of all laws and rules of justice is justified. Marxism is right, furthermore, in regarding them as primarily rationalizations of the interests of the dominant elements of a society. The requirements of "natural law" in the medieval period were obviously conceived in a feudal society; just as the supposed absolute and "self-evident" demands of eighteenth-century natural law were bourgeois in origin.

The relative and contingent character of these ideals and rules of justice refutes the claim of their unconditioned character, made alike by Catholic, liberal and even Marxist social theorists.[4] Both Catholic and liberal social theories (and for that matter the Stoic theories in which both had their origin) make a distinction between "natural law" and the "positive" or "civil" law. The latter represents the actual and imperfect embodiment of the rules of justice in specific historical communities. The contingent and relative character of the latter type of law is recognized; but finality is ascribed to the former. This fundamental distinction must be challenged. It rests upon an untenable faith in the purity of reason; and it is merely another of the many efforts which men make to find a vantage point of the unconditioned in history. The effect of this pretended finality of "natural law" is obvious. It raises "ideology" to a higher degree of pretension, and is another of the many illustrations in history of the force of sin in the claim of sinlessness.[5]

There is of course a tenable distinction between ideals of justice and their embodiment in historical or "civil" law. The latter is the consequence of pressures and counter-pressures in a living community. It is therefore subject to a greater degree of historical relativity than "natural law." In so far as thought is purer than action

---

[4] Marxist theory as usual detects the taint of interest in theories other than its own. But it also has the equivalent of a "natural law." In that law the dominance of the ideal of equality is, for instance, clearly "ideological." It is informed by a justified resentment of the poor against inequality but fails to recognize the inevitability of functional inequalities in society.

[5] Catholic theories of "natural law" are no less pretentious than secular theories, even though they subordinate the virtue of justice, enjoined in the natural law, to the virtue of love, achieved by grace. According to Catholic theory "natural law" is the part of the "divine" or the "eternal" law which is manifested in human reason. The endless relativities of historical rational perspectives are obscured. This unconditioned claim for an essentially universal reason is the basis of the remarkable degree of certainty with which Catholic moral theology is able to define "justice" and "injustice" in every possible situation. *Cf.* Vol. I, Ch. X.

"natural law" is purer than "civil law." Furthermore it is important to recognize the validity of principles of justice, rationally conceived, as sources of criticism for the historical achievements of justice in living communities. If the medieval and modern secular theories of natural law claim too much for these rational principles of justice, both secular and Reformation relativists frequently dismiss them as irrelevant or dangerous. Karl Barth's belief that the moral life of man would possess no valid principles of guidance, if the Ten Commandments had not introduced such principles by revelation, is as absurd as it is unscriptural.[6]

The practical universality of the prohibition of murder for instance in the moral codes of mankind is just as significant as the endless relativities which manifest themselves in the practical application of the general prohibition. There are essentially universal "principles" of justice moreover, by which the formulation of specific rules and systems of justice is oriented. Both "equality" and "liberty" are recognized in Stoic, medieval and modern theories of natural law as transcendent principles of justice; though the modern theories (both bourgeois and Marxist) falsely regard them as realizable rather than as transcendent principles. An analysis of one of them, the principle of equality, will serve to reveal the validity of both as transcendent principles of justice.

The perpetual recurrence of the principle of equality in social theory is a refutation of purely pessimistic conceptions of human nature, whether secular or religious. Its influence proves that men do not simply use social theory to rationalize their own interest. Equality as a pinnacle of the ideal of justice implicitly points towards love as the final norm of justice; for equal justice is the approximation of brotherhood under the conditions of sin. A higher justice always means a more equal justice. Special privilege may be

---

[6] It is in conflict with the Pauline assertion: "For when the Gentiles which have not the law, do by nature the things contained in the law, these, having not the law, are a law unto themselves." Romans 2:14. Barth's exegetical effort to eliminate the force of this Pauline doctrine is tortuous. *Cf.* his *Epistle to the Romans,* pp. 65–68.

frowned upon more severely by those who want it than those who have it; but those who have it are uneasy in their conscience about it. The ideological taint enters into the discussion of equality when those who suffer from inequality raise the principle of equality to the definitive principle of justice without recognizing that differences of need or of social function make the attainment of complete equality in society impossible.[7] The beneficiaries of special privilege emphasize, on the other hand, that inequalities of social function justify corresponding inequalities of privilege. They may also assert, with some, but less, justification, that inequality of reward is a necessary inducement for the proper performance of social function. But they will seek to hide the historic fact that privileged members of the community invariably use their higher degree of social power to appropriate an excess of privileges not required by their function; and certainly not in accord with differences of need.

The validity of the principle of equality on the one hand and the impossibility of realizing it fully on the other, illustrates the relation of absolute norms of justice to the relativities of history. The fact that one class will tend to emphasize the absolute validity of the norm unduly, while another class will be inclined to emphasize the impossibility of achieving it fully, illustrates the inevitable "ideological taint" in the application of a generally valid principle, even if the principle itself achieves a high measure of transcendence over partial interest.[8]

[7] This is the aspect of the problem recognized in Stoic and medieval theories, according to which equality belongs to the golden age or to the perfection before the fall.

[8] The Stoic and Catholic distinction between relative and absolute natural law is a helpful recognition of the necessity of accommodating absolute principles to relative and "sinful" historic situations. But the idea that the requirements of "relative" natural law can be stated absolutely proceeds from the failure to include the human mind in the relativities of history. Here Emil Brunner's criticisms of this distinction are admirable. *Cf. The Divine Imperative,* pp. 626–632.

Brunner, however, erroneously follows the Reformation disparagement of the function of reason in the realm of social ethics and arrives

The complex character of all historic conceptions of justice thus refutes both the relativists who see no possibility of finding valid principles of justice, and the rationalists and optimists who imagine it possible to arrive at completely valid principles, free of every taint of special interest and historical passion.

The positive relation of principles of justice to the ideal of brotherhood makes an indeterminate approximation of love in the realm of justice possible. The negative relation means that all historic conceptions of justice will embody some elements which contradict the law of love. The interests of a class, the viewpoint of a nation, the prejudices of an age and the illusions of a culture are consciously and unconsciously insinuated into the norms by which men regulate their common life. They are intended to give one group an advantage over another. Or if that is not their intention, it is at least the unvarying consequence.

IV

STRUCTURES OF JUSTICE

If rules and principles of justice ideally conceived and transcending the more dubious and ambiguous social realities of living societies have an equivocal relation to the ideal of brotherhood, this twofold

---

at a consequent dismissal of the ideal of equality as merely a "rational" and therefore unchristian norm. He writes: "The egalitarian law of nature does not belong to the world of the Bible but to the context of Stoic rationalism. The egalitarian ideal does not arise out of reverence for the Creator but out of the desire to dictate to the Creator how things ought to be, or the presupposition that the Creator ought to treat every one alike." *Ibid.,* p. 407.

Any parent who has sought to administer justice and to compose childish disputes will know how spontaneously children appeal to the principle of equality as the correct principle of arbitrament, and with what difficulty they must, on occasion, be persuaded that differences of age, function and need, render the principle inoperative, or make it only indirectly relevant. The children may lack proper reverence for the Creator of inequalities; but on the other hand they have certainly never heard of, or been spoiled by, "Stoic rationalism."

character is even more obvious and apparent in the structures and systems, the organizations and mechanisms, of society in which these principles and rules are imperfectly embodied and made historically concrete. We have already noted the distinction between "natural law," as a rational statement of principle of justice, and "positive" law, which designates the historic enactments of living communities. But an analysis of the equivocal character of the "structures" of justice must include more than a mere consideration of "civil" or "positive" law. It must look beyond legal enactments to the whole structure and organization of historical communities. This structure is never merely the order of a legal system. The harmony of communities is not simply attained by the authority of law. *Nomos* does not coerce the vitalities of life into order. The social harmony of living communities is achieved by an interaction between the normative conceptions of morality and law and the existing and developing forces and vitalities of the community. Usually the norms of law are compromises between the rational-moral ideals of what ought to be, and the possibilities of the situation as determined by given equilibria of vital forces. The specific legal enactments are, on the one hand, the instruments of the conscience of the community, seeking to subdue the potential anarchy of forces and interests into a tolerable harmony. They are, on the other hand, merely explicit formulations of given tensions and equilibria of life and power, as worked out by the unconscious interactions of social life.

No human community is, in short, a simple construction of conscience or reason. All communities are more or less stable or precarious harmonies of human vital capacities. They are governed by power. The power which determines the quality of the order and harmony is not merely the coercive and organizing power of government. That is only one of the two aspects of social power. The other is the balance of vitalities and forces in any given social situation. These two elements of communal life—the central organizing principle and power, and the equilibrium of power—

are essential and perennial aspects of community organization; and no moral or social advance can redeem society from its dependence upon these two principles.

Since there are various possibilities of so managing and equilibrating the balance of social forces in a given community that the highest possible justice may be achieved and since the organizing principle and power in the community is also subject to indeterminate refinement, communal order and justice can approximate a more perfect brotherhood in varying degree. But each principle of communal organization—the organization of power and the balance of power—contain possibilities of contradicting the law of brotherhood. The organizing principle and power may easily degenerate into tyranny. It may create a coerced unity of society in which the freedom and vitality of all individual members are impaired. Such a tyrannical unification of life is a travesty on brotherhood. Again, the principle of the balance of power is always pregnant with the possibility of anarchy. These twin evils, tyranny and anarchy, represent the Scylla and Charybdis between which the frail bark of social justice must sail. It is almost certain to founder upon one rock if it makes the mistake of regarding the other as the only peril.

No possible refinement of social forces and political harmonies can eliminate the potential contradiction to brotherhood which is implicit in the two political instruments of brotherhood—the organization of power and the balance of power. This paradoxical situation in the realm of social life is analogous to the Christian conception of the paradox of history as discerned in other realms of life. In order to explore the meaning of the paradox more fully it will be well to begin with an analysis of the nature and meaning of "power" in communal life.

1. *The Unity of Vitality and Reason*

The perennial importance of power in social organization is based upon two characteristics of human nature. The one is the unity of vitality and reason, of body and soul. The other is the

force of human sin, the persistent tendency to regard ourselves as
more important than any one else and to view a common problem
from the standpoint of our own interest. The second characteristic
is so stubborn that mere moral or rational suasion does not suffice
to restrain one person from taking advantage of another. Legal
authority may be more sufficing; but there is no legal authority
which does not imply sanctions or the threat of coercive action
against recalcitrance. The first characteristic, the unity of vitality
and reason in human nature, guarantees that egoistic purposes will
be pursued with all vital resources which an individual or collective
will may control. Therefore social restraints upon these anti-social
purposes must be equally armed with all available resources.

Disputes may of course be composed and conflicts arbitrated
without recourse to all such resources. Conscience may appeal to
conscience and reason to reason. There are in fact no conflicts in
which these appeals are not made, even when the conflict has
become physical. But in every conflict of interest the possibility of
marshalling every possible resource on either side is implied. Most
human conflicts are composed, or subdued, by a superior authority
and power, without an overt appeal to force or without the actual
use of force, either violent or non-violent. But the calculation of
available resource on each side is as determinative in settling the
outcome of the struggle as more purely rational or moral considerations.[1]

The threat of force, whether by the official and governmental
representatives of a community or by the parties to a dispute in a
community is a potent instrument in all communal relations. It
may not be frequently used in a stable and well-ordered community;
but if either government, or a party to a dispute, explicitly dis-

---

[1] A strike in industry is a case in point. It may be arbitrated but the
compromise between the two sides or the yielding of one side to the
other is partly determined by the shrewd calculation of either side of the
resources of social and economic power of which the other side could
avail itself in case the conflict became overt, and of the possible position
which government and public would take towards it.

avowed any resource at its disposal, it would upset whatever equilibrium of social forces existed at that moment; it would thereby increase the possibility of successful recalcitrance or resistance on the part of the group or interest, prepared to use every available resource. The prospect of successful resistance naturally also increases the probability that a venture in resistance will be made.[2] The rational calculation of the powers and vitalities, involved in a social situation, is thus an inevitable accompaniment of the rational calculation of rights and interests, involved in a socio-moral problem. The invariable correlation of the two is a nice symbol of the unity of vitality and reason in all social existence.

2. *Types of Power in Social Life*

The spiritual and physical faculties of man are able, in their unity and interrelation, to create an endless variety of types and combinations of power, from that of pure reason to that of pure physical force. Though reason is commonly supposed to be transcendent, rather than partial, it is hardly necessary at this point to prove that reason may be the instrument of the ego in advancing its claims against another. When it is so used it is a "power" which supports

---

[2] This is how a liberal democratic world, dreaming of progress towards purely rational and moral resolutions of all social conflicts, stumbled into a "total war." A sensitive conscience may be revolted by the tragic and brutal realities of man's social life and decide to disavow all power. But if this powerlessness is not accompanied by a concomitant disavowal of social responsibility it leads to the moral confusions in which secular and religious perfectionists are usually involved. Complete nonresistance may have moral meaning, if it is understood that unprotected rights and privileges will probably be lost and that in many social situations they are practically certain to be lost. Non-violent resistance has meaning as a pragmatic technique; for it is well to explore all methods of achieving justice and maintaining peace, short of violent conflict. But non-violent resistance as a moral or political absolute is a source of moral and political confusion. The implicit and explicit aversion of the democratic world to violent forms of dispute was a factor upon which proponents of "total war" calculated. It increased the probability of their success and therefore the certainty of their venture.

the claims of one life against another. The shrewd do take advantage of the simple. A rational solution of a conflict may be a very unjust one, if the more robust has "overpowered" the weaker intellect. But there are other spiritual faculties which may serve the same purpose. One man may keep another enslaved purely by "soul" force.[3] Such soul force may consist of spiritual vitalities of various kinds, mental and emotional energy, the possession or the pretension of virtue, the prestige of an heroic life, or of a gentle birth. Pure physical force is always a last resort in individual relations. It is determinative in these relations only on primitive levels. All civilized relations are governed more by spiritual, than by physical, facets of power. It is significant that they are not, for that reason, naturally more just.

The forms of power which are developed collectively display an even wider variety of types. On the whole social power rests upon differentiations of social function. The soldier is the bearer of physical force in advanced societies, not because he is physically strong, but because he has the instruments, and masters the techniques, of physical conflict. The priest has social power (especially potent in the organization of early empires) because he mediates the authority of some ultimate majesty and endows the political authority of a given oligarchy with this sanctity. The ownership and the control of property and economic process represents partly physical and partly spiritual power. It is physical in so far as the wealth created by the economic process is physical. It is spiritual in so far as the right to use and control this physical force is derived from law, custom, the prestige of function and other similar considerations. The modern belief that economic power is the most basic form, and that all other forms are derived from it, is erroneous. The first landlords were soldiers and priests who used military

---

[3] Gandhi's identification of "soul force" with non-egoistic motives and "body force" with egoistic ones, is almost completely mistaken. The type of power used by the will to effect its purposes does not determine the quality of the purpose or motive.

and religious forms of social power to possess and to acquire land. Economic power, before the modern period, was derivative rather than primary. It was used to enhance the comforts of the oligarchs of society and to insure the perpetuation of their social eminence from generation to generation. But it did not give them their initial eminence. In modern Germany, Nazi political oligarchs transmute political power into economic power. In the bourgeois period economic power did tend to become more fundamental and to bend other forms to its purposes. In democratic societies it was, however, always under some restraint from the more widely diffused political power of the common man, inhering in the universal right of suffrage.[4]

All historic forms of justice and injustice are determined to a much larger degree than pure rationalists or idealists realize by the given equilibrium or disproportion within each type of power and by the balance of various types of power in a given community. It may be taken as axiomatic that great disproportions of power lead to injustice, whatever may be the efforts to mitigate it. Thus the concentration of economic power in modern technical society has made for injustice, while the diffusion of political power has made for justice. The history of modern democratic-capitalistic societies is on the whole determined by the tension between these two forms of power. In this history the economic oligarchy has sought to bend political power to its purposes, but has never done so with complete success. On the other hand the political power of the common man

[4] It has been an error in both liberal and Marxist social interpretations to identify ownership with economic power. The control and manipulation of economic process is also a form of economic power. It gives workers minimal power resources to set against the power of ownership; and the managers of economic process are acquiring an even larger share of power. James Burnham's *The Managerial Revolution* is a one-sided correction of the error of identifying ownership with economic power too simply. The error contributes to the political miscalculations of Marxism. For when it abolishes economic ownership it may merely merge both economic and political power in the hands of an oligarchy which controls both political and economic processes.

has been an instrument of political and economic justice; but it has also not succeeded completely in eliminating flag.ant forms of economic injustice. This tension is unresolved, and may never be completely resolved. At the moment the justice achieved by this tension in the democratic world is under attack from a tyranny created by the mergence of political, economic and religious power in a Nazi oligarchy and by its more or less intimate partnership with an older military oligarchy.

Political power deserves to be placed in a special category, because it rests upon the ability to use and manipulate other forms of social power for the particular purpose of organizing and dominating the community. The political oligarchy usually possesses at least two forms of significant social power. In all early empires these two forms were the priestly and the military power, which were either merged in one class, or which were combined through intimate collaboration between the military and the priestly class. Modern democracies tend towards a more equal justice partly because they have divorced political power from special social functions. They endowed all men with a measure of it by giving them the right to review the policies of their leaders. This democratic principle does not obviate the formation of oligarchies in society; but it places a check upon their formation, and upon the exercise of their power. It must be observed, however, that the tyrannical oligarchy, which now challenges the democratic world, arrived at its eminence by the primary use of political power (the demagogic manipulation of the masses) and then gradually acquired the other forms of power: the control of economic process, the pretension of religious sanctity, and the control of, or collaboration with, military power.

The shifting interrelations of various types of power in human society are determined by a wide variety of historical developments from the technical to the religious level of social existence. Thus the development of modern commerce gave the middle classes new economic power. They used it to challenge the priestly-military oligarchy of feudal society. They undermined the power of land-

ownership with the more dynamic economic power of the ownership of bank stock. The development of modern technical industry
had a twofold effect. It both enhanced the economic power and
wealth of the owners and manipulators of economic process, and it
gave industrial workers a form of power (exercised for instance by
their refusal to co-operate in an interrelated economic process) which
the common men of agrarian societies did not have. Sometimes a
shift in power relations has a much more spiritual origin. Who can
deny that the development of prophetic religion, which challenges
rather than supports political majesty in the name of the majesty
of God, helps to destroy priestly-military oligarchies and to create
democratic societies? In this way the prophetic elements in Christianity have contributed to the rise of modern democratic societies,
just as conservative elements in the Christian tradition have
strengthened the pretensions of oligarchies by their uncritical identification of political power with the divine authority.

   The complexity of the technical, rational and prophetic-religious
factors which contributed to the rise of modern democracies, illustrates the complex and intimate involvement of all these factors
in the whole historical process. The interweaving of these various
strands in the total fabric of historical development refutes both
vitalists and rationalists, who would interpret the social process
either as merely a chaos of vital forces or as a simple progressive triumph of reason over force. "Reason" and "force" may be the "end
terms" of human spirituality and vitality. But no sharp distinction
can be made between them at any point. Nor are there absolute
distinctions between any of the intermediate manifestations of
human vitality, which history elaborates in endless variety. No form
of individual or social power exists without a modicum of physical
force, or without a narrow pinnacle of "spirit" which transcends
the conflict and tension of vital forces. But the tension and balance
of such forces in any given social situation include vitalities and
powers which manifest the complex unity of spirit and nature, of
reason and force, in the whole of human existence.

3. *The Organization and Balance of Power*

Our primary concern is with the twofold relation of structures of justice or various forms of communal organization to the principle of brotherhood. These structures invariably contain, according to our analysis, both approximations and contradictions to the ideal of love. This thesis must now be examined more closely in the light of the conclusion that all social life represents a field of vitality, elaborated in many forms, which are related to each other in terms of both mutual support and of potential conflict. Since human history defies, rather than observes, the limits, in which nature confines both mutual dependence and conflict, it becomes a task of conscious political contrivance in human history to mitigate conflict and to invent instruments for the enlarging mutualities of social existence.

Human brotherhood is imperiled by two, and possibly three, forms of corruption. Will seeks to dominate will. Thus imperialism and slavery are introduced into history. Interest comes in conflict with interest and thus the relations of mutual dependence are destroyed. Sometimes the self, individual or collective, seeks to isolate itself from the community and to disavow communal responsibilities. This evil of isolationism is, however, a negative form of the evil of conflict, and therefore does not deserve a special category.

The domination of one life by another is avoided most successfully by an equilibrium of powers and vitalities, so that weakness does not invite enslavement by the strong. Without a tolerable equilibrium no moral or social restraints ever succeed completely in preventing injustice and enslavement. In this sense an equilibrium of vitality is an approximation of brotherhood within the limits of conditions imposed by human selfishness. But an equilibrium of power is not brotherhood. The restraint of the will-to-power of one member of the community by the counter-pressure of power by another member results in a condition of tension. All tension is covert or potential conflict. The principle of the equilibrium of power is thus a principle of justice in so far as it prevents domination and enslavement; but it is a principle of anarchy and conflict in so far as its tensions, if unresolved, result in overt conflict. Furthermore social life, when not consciously managed and manipulated, does not develop perfect equilibria of power. Its capricious disproportions of power generate various forms of domination and enslavement. Human society therefore requires a conscious control and manipulation of the various equilibria which exist in it. There must be an organizing centre within a given field of social vitalities. This centre must arbitrate conflicts from a more impartial perspective than is available to any party of a given conflict; it must manage and manipulate the processes of mutual support so that the tensions inherent in them will not erupt into conflict; it must coerce submission to the social process by superior power whenever the instruments of arbitrating and composing conflict do not suffice; and finally it must seek to redress the disproportions of power by conscious shifts of the balances whenever they make for injustice.[7]

It is obvious that the principle of government, or the organization of the whole realm of social vitalities, stands upon a higher plane of moral sanction and social necessity than the principle of the balance of power. The latter without the former degenerates into anarchy. The former is, moreover, a more conscious effort to arrive at justice than the latter. It belongs to the order of the historical while the former belongs, on the whole, to the order of the natural.[8]

---

[7] This is done in the democratic state, for instance, when the taxing power is used not merely for securing revenue but also to counteract the tendency towards centralization of power and privilege which inheres in the technical and highly centralized industrial process.

[8] Rousseau's and Hobbes' social contract theories of government have such contradictory estimates of the "state of nature" because both fail to understand the ambiguous character of social equilibrium without the interference of government. Rousseau sees only the elements of harmony within it, and Hobbes only the elements of conflict and anarchy. Rousseau on the other hand sees only the principle of domination in government and Hobbes only the principle of order.

It is nevertheless important to recognize that government is also morally ambiguous. It contains an element which contradicts the law of brotherhood. The power of the rulers is subject to two abuses. It may actually be the dominion which one portion of the community exercises over the whole of the community. Most governments until a very recent period were in fact just that; they were the consequence of conquest by a foreign oligarchy.[9] But even if government does not express the imperial impulse of one class or group within the community, it would, if its pretensions are not checked, generate imperial impulses of its own towards the community. It would be tempted to destroy the vitality and freedom of component elements in the community in the name of "order." It would identify its particular form of order with the principle of order itself, and thus place all rebels against its authority under the moral disadvantage of revolting against order *per se*. This is the sin of idolatry and pretension, in which all government is potentially involved. This evil can be fully understood only if it is recognized that all governments and rulers derive a part of their power, not only from the physical instruments of coercion at their disposal, but also from the reality and the pretension of "majesty." The uncoerced submission which they achieve, and without which they could not rule (since coerced submission applies only to marginal cases and presupposes the uncoerced acceptance of the ruler's authority by the majority) is never purely "rational" consent. It always includes, explicitly or implicitly, religious reverence for "majesty." The majesty of the state is legitimate in so far as it embodies and expresses both the authority and power of the total community over all its members, and the principle of order and justice as such against the peril of anarchy. The legitimate majesty of government is acknowledged and affirmed in the Christian doctrine of government as a divine ordinance.

[9] The Norman unification of England, the Tartar conquest of Russia and the Manchu conquest of China are a few of the many examples of foreign conquest as the agent of the unification of a society.

But there are no historic expressions of the majesty of state and government without an admixture of illegitimate pretensions of majesty and sanctity. These can be most simply defined as the tendency of states and governments to hide and obscure the contingent and partial character of their rule and to claim unconditioned validity for it.

The whole development of democratic justice in human society has depended upon some comprehension of the moral ambiguities which inhere in both government and the principle of the equilibrium of power. It is the highest achievement of democratic societies that they embody the principle of resistance to government within the principle of government itself. The citizen is thus armed with "constitutional" power to resist the unjust exactions of government. He can do this without creating anarchy within the community, if government has been so conceived that criticism of the ruler becomes an instrument of better government and not a threat to government itself.[10]

The achievements of democracy have been tortuously worked out in human history partly because various schools of religious and political thought had great difficulty in fully comprehending the perils to justice in either one or the other instrument of justice— the organization of power and the balance of power. Usually the school of thought which comprehended the moral ambiguities of government did not understand the perils of anarchy inhering in uncontrolled social life; while those who feared this anarchy were uncritical of the claims and pretensions of government. History had to stumble by tortuous process upon the proper techniques for avoiding both anarchy and tyranny, against the illusions of idealists and of realists who understood only one or the other side of the problem. In this process the Christian tradition itself seldom

---

[10] The Presbyterian constitutionalist of seventeenth-century Scotland, Samuel Rutherford, expresses the distinction in the words: "We teach that government is natural not voluntary; but the way and manner of government is voluntary." *Lex Rex* (1644), Question IX.

stated the full truth of its twofold approach to the political order in such a way that it would give guidance in the complexities of political and social life. The mistakes which were made in comprehending the paradox in the political sphere conform to the limitations of the various Christian and secular traditions, which we have examined in other spheres. They can therefore be stated fairly briefly.

v

THE CHRISTIAN ATTITUDE TO GOVERNMENT

The development of Christian and of modern secular theories of politics is determined by an interplay of one classical and of two Biblical approaches to stuff of the political order. The Bible contains two approaches, which taken together and held in balance, do justice to the moral ambiguities of government. According to the one, government is an ordinance of God and its authority reflects the Divine Majesty. According to the other, the "rulers" and "judges" of the nations are particularly subject to divine judgment and wrath because they oppress the poor and defy the divine majesty. These two approaches do justice to the two aspects of government. It is a principle of order and its power prevents anarchy; but its power is not identical with divine power, It is wielded from a partial and particular locus and it cannot achieve the perfect union of goodness and power which characterizes divine power. The pretension that its power is perfectly virtuous represents its false claim of majesty. This claim elicits alternate moods of reverent obedience and resentful rebellion in history.[1]

---

[1] It is significant that the first Biblical record of the institution of monarchy is interpreted from two perspectives according to two traditions embodied in the book of Samuel. According to the one, Samuel anointed Saul King at the behest of Yahweh (1 Sam. 8:22). According to the other the desire of the people for a king was regarded as an affront to God, who was himself king of his people: "And ye have this day rejected your God, who himself saved you out of all your adversities

The double approach of prophetic criticism and of priestly sanctification of royal or state authority, have armed both conservative and
radical schools of Christian thought with plausible proof-texts for
their respective positions. Only occasionally is the truth in each
position properly appreciated. Unfortunately a single text from St.
Paul has done much to destroy the force of the Biblical paradox. St.
Paul's very "undialectical" appreciation of government in Romans
13 has had a fateful influence in Christian thought, particularly in
the Reformation.[2] But its influence was fortunately never able to

---

and your tribulations; and ye have said unto him, Nay, but set a king
over us." 1 Sam. 10:19.

The various expressions of these two approaches towards government
cannot be fully traced here. The critical attitude of the prophets towards
government has been considered in another context. On the other hand
the idea that the King is the Lord's anointed runs through the whole
Old Testament as does the appreciation of the necessity of government
(*Cf.* Judges 17:6: "In those days there was no king in Israel, but every
man did that which was right in his own eyes.").

In the New Testament Jesus on the one hand recognizes the legitimate authority of government ("Render therefore unto Caesar the things
that are Caesar's." Mt. 22:21) but on the other hand he sets the dominion
of kings in contrast to the mutual love and service of the Kingdom of
God ("The kings of the Gentiles exercise lordship over them . . . but
ye shall not be so: but he that is greatest among you, let him be as the
younger; and he that is chief, as he that doth serve." Luke 22:25-26).

[2] Romans 13:1-3: "Let every soul be subject unto the higher powers.
For there is no power but of God: the powers that be are ordained of
God. Whosoever therefore resisteth the power, resisteth the ordinance
of God . . . for the rulers are not a terror to good works, but to the
evil."

This unqualified endorsement of government and the unqualified
prohibition of resistance to its authority is justified by the mistaken assertion that government is no peril to virtue but only to vice. History proves
that the power of government is morally ambiguous. It may on occasion
imperil not evil but "good works." The best possible government cannot
completely escape from such a possibility. It must be recognized that
the Pauline justification of government was valid enough in the particular historical context in which it was made. It was undoubtedly a
warning against the irresponsibility towards government which the
eschatological mood of the early church encouraged. The fact that it

extinguish the power of prophetic criticism upon the evils of government in Christian history.

As against these two approaches to the political order in the Bible the classical world thought of politics in simpler and more rational terms. Government was primarily the instrument of man's social nature. Its function of preventing anarchy, so strongly emphasized in Christian thought, and so unduly stressed in the Reformation, was appreciated only indirectly. For Aristotle the purpose of government was fellowship (κοινωνία); and Plato studied the state in his *Republic* as a macrocosm which would reveal all the laws of harmony in larger outline relevant to the microcosm of the individual soul.

In both Aristotle and Plato the harmony of society is practically identified with the constitutional structure, the principles by which it is governed. The approach is, in the parlance of modern philosophy, "non-existential." [3] They are always looking for forms and principles of justice, for constitutions and arrangements which will bring the rough vitalities of life under the dominion of the

---

became a vehicle for a too uncritical devotion to government by its indiscriminate application in subsequent centuries illustrates one of the perils of Biblicism. Biblical observations upon life are made in a living relation to living history. When they are falsely given an eminence which obscures this relation, they can become the source of error and confusion.

[3] Aristotle declares that "the constitution (πολιτεία) is the life of the *polis*" (*Politics* VI, iv, 11). In Plato's *Laws* the Athenian Stranger declares: "When there has been a contest of power, those who gain the upper hand so entirely monopolize the government as to refuse all share to the defeated party. . . . Now according to our view such governments are not polities at all nor are laws right which are passed for the good of particular classes and not for the good of the whole state. . . . That state in which the law is subject and has no authority, I perceive to be on the highway to ruin; and that state in which the rulers are the inferiors of the law has salvation."

The idea that the practices of states must conform to rules and principles of justice is of course tenable and necessary. But both Plato and Aristotle underestimate the dynamic and vital elements in the political order. They obscure the fact that political life is a contest of power, no matter by what laws it is governed.

logos. They do not of course trust the mere force of law to do this. But when they look for the best human agencies to interpret, apply and enforce the principles of law, and try to construct some transcendent vantage point from which government may operate against the conflicts of partial interests (in the case of Aristotle particularly against the conflict between rich and poor) they find it in some class of virtuous and rational men. It is the superior reason of such men or their specialized knowledge in affairs of government, which endows them with the virtue of disinterestedness. Greek political theory believes in other words in an *élite class.* The perils of anarchy according to classical thought arise primarily from the ignorance of common citizens who are unable to comprehend the total needs of the community. Plato seeks to cultivate the disinterestedness of the rulers by semi-ascetic disciplines, as well as by rational excellency. In any case the realm of politics, as a field of vitality and as a contest of power is inadequately comprehended. The Stoic theory, particularly in its distinction between the absolute and the relative natural law, comes closer to the realities of politics. But even the Stoics, and particularly the Roman Stoics, have a too optimistic conception of the political order. Cicero gave a highly moralistic account of politics in general and of Roman imperialism in particular. He regarded the state as a compact of justice, and had little understanding of the power realities which underlie the compact.

The Christian ages, after the dissipation of the eschatological hope and the concomitant political irresponsibility of the early church, worked out a political ethic in which gospel perfectionism and Biblical realism were combined with classical (particularly Stoic) optimism. Augustine was the first to introduce a new and more Pauline note into this field of thought, as he did in so many other fields. Making the criticism of Ciceronian rationalism and optimism his point of departure he denied that the state is a compact of justice, and insisted that "there is not any justice in any commonwealth whatsoever but in that whereof Christ is the founder and ruler." [4] He regarded the peace of the world as an uneasy armistice between contending social forces. It is "based on strife." It is not so much justice as "the harmonious enjoyment of that which they love" which holds the *civitas* together.[5] Such a morally neutral definition of political cohesion allows Augustine to compare the harmony of the state with the harmony which thieves maintain among themselves and to suggest that there may be little difference except size, between a state and a robber band.[6]

Augustine sees the social life of man as constantly threatened either by conflict between contending forces, held in an uneasy equilibrium, or by the tyranny of the dominant power which "lays a yoke of obedience upon its fellows." This interpretation may not do full justice to the constructive elements of order in either the Roman Empire or in any *res publica* or commonwealth of history. He may

[4] *De civ. Dei,* Book II, ch. 21.

[5] *De civ. Dei,* Book XIX, ch. 24.

[6] *Ibid.,* IV, 4. See A. J. Carlyle's *Medieval Political Theory in the West.* Vol. I, pp. 165-170. C. H. McIlvain is not certain that Carlyle's interpretation of Augustine's departure from the political theories of St. Ambrose and the other Fathers is correct. *Cf.* McIlvain: *The Growth of Political Thought in the West,* p. 155. However, Augustine's position is made clear in other than the particular passages in which he distinguishes between Cicero's conception of the *res publica* and his own. For instance he compares the social order of the state with the divine order, not in terms of justice but in terms of order created by power: "For herein is perverse pride the imitator of the goodness of God, laying a yoke of obedience upon its fellows under itself instead of God; thus hates it a just peace of God and builds an unjust one for itself." *De civ. Dei,* XIX, 12. This is the same point made by Biblical prophetism against the pretension of kings.

He regards the peace established in various earthly realms as good, so far as it goes, but as unstable. "Wretched are they that are strangers to God; and yet have they a kind of allowable peace, but they will not have it forever for they used it not well while they had it" (*Ibid.,* XIX, 26). It is always threatened either by civil war or by imperialistic ventures which know no limits: "For any part [of the civitas terrena] which wars against the other desires to be the world's conqueror. . . . And if it conquer it extols itself and so becomes its own destruction." *Ibid.,* XV, 4.

have taken the conditions of a declining, rather than a more healthy, Roman Empire as definitive; and he may have sharpened the contrast too much between the *civitas Dei* and the *civitas terrena,* so as to produce a perfect antithesis between the love of God in the one and the love of self in the other. But despite these errors of overemphasis, the Augustinian conception of the political order gives a much truer picture of both the dynamic and the anarchic elements in political life than classical political theories.

Despite Augustine's great authority, his political realism had only a moderate influence on the course of medieval political theory. The latter incorporated a much larger classical element than is evident in Augustine's thought. Medieval Catholicism succeeded in fact in creating as imposing a synthesis in the realm of political theory as in other fields of thought. The synthesis is still superior to many alternative systems which have developed since the destruction of the synthesis; but it is, of course, subject to the general limitations of its larger principles of synthesis.

Medieval political theory manages to incorporate both strands of Biblical thought with classical perspectives. The prophetic-Biblical criticism upon the injustice and the pride of rulers is never lacking; but unfortunately it becomes the instrument of the papal-ecclesiastical claim of dominion. The Stoic-Christian idea that government is a requirement of the relative, rather than of the absolute, natural law, prevents the inequalities and the coercive necessities of government from being regarded as finally normative. The distinction preserves a minimal note of criticism upon government. There is thus a moderate medieval constitutionalism which makes the ruler subject to both natural law and to civil law.[7]

The authority of the ruler and the idea of necessity of govern-

[7] To civil law because the natural law implies a covenant of justice between the ruler and the people. According to Carlyle medieval constitutionalism represents an unbroken tradition until the fifteenth century and does not allow the idea of the absolute and unconditioned rights of the ruler to arise. Carlyle, *op. cit.,* Vol. VI.

ment is upheld at the same time both by Biblical authority and by the Stoic idea of government as a necessity in an imperfect world. The more classical element in medieval political thought is revealed in an essentially rationalistic approach to political problems, tending to obscure the tension of vitalities and interests as a perennial factor in all social life. The peril of tyranny, inherent in the power of the state, is not regarded as arising inevitably from its nature as a centre of power, and from the natural inclination of power, including state power, to become excessive. Instead medieval theory makes moralistic and too absolute and clear-cut distinctions between the justice and tyranny of rulers.[8] It does not comprehend that the justice and peace which the power of the state achieves is always subject to some degree of corruption by reason of the inordinate character of this power, and the particular interests of the ruler.

Medieval constitutionalism contains abundant moral justification for resistance to tyranny but the idea is not implemented politically and Lord Acton is therefore slightly extravagant in regarding Aquinas as the fountain of democratic theory.[9] Medieval theory failed to comprehend the political order as a vast realm of mutually dependent and conflicting powers and interests, and to appreciate the contingent and relative character of any "justice" which might be achieved at a given moment by the power of government and by the specific equilibria of forces existing at that moment. This failure was one cause of its inability to deal realistically with the new

[8] Aquinas defines tyranny as "ruling which is not directed to the common good of the multitude but rather to the private good of the ruler." *De regimine principum.*

[9] Aquinas did believe that the people had the right to appoint the king and therefore an equal right to depose him (*De regimine principum* I, 6). John of Salisbury even justified regicide as a remedy for tyranny. This critical attitude towards the injustices of government is far superior to modern theories of state absolutism; but it is not democratic in the sense that it provides no constitutional means of resisting the inordinate claims of government or of placing its power under continued popular scrutiny. *Cf.* McIlvain, *op. cit.,* pp. 326–28.

forces, and the consequent disbalances introduced into the medieval political economy by rising commerce.[10]

With the decay of the medieval synthesis, the various elements in the compound of political thought took their own more consistent way, as was the case in other realms of thought. Many of the new political theories may be less true, and are certainly less balanced, than the more comprehensive medieval interpretation of the political order. But most of them contain facets of truth which do more justice to the highest possibilities and the darkest realities of the political order than was possible in the medieval synthesis.

The Renaissance in its secular streams of thought developed two fundamental tendencies. The one embodied the rationalistic-optimistic approach to the problem. We cannot trace this tendency in all of its elaborations. It is expressed in the many varieties of the "liberal" approach to politics. In some of them the *laissez-faire* thesis predominates. It is believed to be a simple matter to achieve a stable equilibrium of social interests if only the inordinate power of government is eliminated. In others the power of government is regarded as a simple rational authority over rational men, which will become more just and more universal as reason is extended.

One contemporary fruit of this stream of Renaissance thought consists in theories of world government, according to which the self-will and moral autonomy of nations could be destroyed by the

[10] A modern Catholic historian regrets that Catholicism was so long in overcoming the influence of Augustinian pessimism, and thinks that the essential optimism of Thomas Aquinas came just a little too late to save the structure of medievalism (*Cf.* Alois Demph, *Sacrum Imperium,* p. 30). An absolutely contradictory thesis would come as near to the truth. The optimism of medievalism prevented it from comprehending the tendency towards decay and disintegration in any social structure. The medieval church sought, according to Troeltsch, for "a perpetuation of the relatively satisfactory situation in which the relative values of the social order are crowned by the absolute values of the institution of grace." Ernst Troeltsch, *Social Teachings of the Christian Churches,* Vol. I, p. 326.

simple expedient of depriving the sovereignty of nations of its legal sanctity.[11] Other theorists are slightly more realistic and hold that international government must be supported by predominant power. But they would create the central pool of power abstractly by some kind of social contract between the nations, without reference to the organic and vital processes through which equilibria of power and the centralization of power are actually effected in history.

The Renaissance movement, however, developed another stream of thought which appropriated some of the insights of Christian realism and pessimism. It recognized the perils of conflict in the dynamic elements of social existence; but it was prompted by these insights to elaborate absolutistic theories of the state. It failed, in other words, to appropriate any of the prophetic-critical elements in the Christian tradition. To this strain of thought we must, in cursory terms, assign Machiavelli, Thomas Hobbes, Jean Bodin, in some respects Hegel and Bosanquet, and of course a host of other lesser men. Sometimes as in the case of Machiavelli, the political pessimism degenerates into moral cynicism. Marxism has the distinction of being the only pessimistic-realistic school of thought in the modern period which directs its realism against the moral ambiguities of the power of government, rather than upon the perils of social anarchy which government is designed to mitigate.

The strong Biblical basis of sectarian radicalism makes it advisable to consider it in this context in juxtaposition to the orthodox Reformation, rather than in relation to the Renaissance movement. So conceived Protestant Christian theories of politics, in their totality, describe a full arc from the extreme pessimism of the Lutheran Reformation to the extreme optimism of the more radical sects; from the uncritical sanctification of government in Luther to the uncritical rejection of government, as such, in the anarchistic sects; from the uncritical acceptance of inequality as a consequence and

[11] *Cf. inter alia*, G. Niemeyer, *Law Without Force.*

remedy for sin in Luther, to the uncritical belief in equality as a simple historical possibility in the communistic sects. In this wide variety of thought the greatest contribution to democratic justice was made by those Protestant groups which came closest to an understanding of both the vice and the necessity of government and both the peril and the necessity of a free interplay of social forces. Among those who came nearest to this understanding were moderate Anglicans who combined Catholic with Renaissance perspectives and whose political theories are most systematically expressed in the thought of Thomas Hooker; semi-sectarian movements like English Independency; and finally the later Calvinists, who rescued Calvinism from its earlier and too consistent pessimism.

This rather sweeping judgment demands historical substantiation, though the limits of this treatise necessarily restrict the analysis of the vast historical material.

Luther's uncritical moral and religious sanctification of the power of government (particularly based upon Romans 13) has been previously considered. It prevented Lutheranism from having any vital relationship with the development of democratic justice in the modern world, with the possible exception of the Scandinavian countries.[12] The development of political theory in modern radical Reformation thought is instructive because Barth is on the whole more Lutheran than Calvinistic in his approach to political questions. He has been Lutheran, at least in his general indifference towards problems of political justice, though he has not quite shared Luther's uncritical acceptance of political authority. His strong emotional reaction to Nazi tyranny has, however, persuaded him to change his emphasis. He now criticizes the Reformation for having regarded government as an ordinance of divine providence without at the same time setting it under the judgment of God. Nevertheless

---

[12] I say "with the possible exception of the Scandinavian countries" because I have been unable to find authoritative material on the relation between the impressive development of constitutional democracy in Scandinavia and the dominant Lutheran religion.

the influence of Reformation perspectives is so powerful in his thought that his doctrinal justification for his opposition to Nazi tyranny is hardly sufficient to explain that opposition.[13]

As against the uncritical sanctification of established political authority, and the pessimistic acceptance of coercion, inequality and conflict as necessary conditions in a sinful world in Lutheranism, sectarian Protestantism in its many forms manages to express all the various aspects of the critical-prophetic strain of Christian thought.

In the more extreme sects this is done to the point of obscuring the other side of the truth. The perils of government are appreciated, but not its necessity. The contradiction between the majesty of government and the majesty of God is emphasized; but the legitimate majesty of government is not apprehended.[14] Usually the failure to appreciate the necessity of government is derived from per-

[13] Barth defines a just state [*Rechtsstaat*] as follows: "It will realize its own potentialities insofar as it gives the church the freedom [to preach the gospel of justification]. . . . What human justice is cannot be measured by some romantic or liberal conception of natural rights but purely by the concrete right of the freedom which the church must claim for its word, insofar as it is God's word." *Rechtfertigung und Recht,* p. 46.

This is a very minimal contribution to the problem of justice in the state. The freedom to preach the gospel of justification means of course that the state would thereby permit the word of divine judgment to be spoken against its pride and pretensions. But none of the intermediate problems of justice are illumined by this final word of judgment.

In his letter to British Christians Barth declares that "it was probably wise of the government to *allow* [*sic*] the British public to discuss peace aims" but he thinks that "British Christians should . . . take as little advantage of this *permission* as possible." *This Christian Cause.*

[14] In the "Certain Queries Presented by Many Christian People" to Lord Fairfax, Lord General of the Army of Parliament, he is warned: "not to take that honour to yourselves that is due to Christ, nor be instrumental in setting up a mere natural and worldly government . . . whereby the public interest of Jesus Christ will be banished." Quoted by Arthur S. Woodhouse: *Puritanism and Liberty,* p. 242.

George Fox's indictment of the "magistrates" as "usurpers" reveals the same uncritical lack of appreciation of the necessity of government.

fectionist illusions in regard to human nature and human society.[15] Sometimes government is accepted; but the libertarian emphasis is so strong that all coercive acts of government are morally repudiated.[16]

Sometimes the requirements of the absolute natural law, the ideals of liberty and equality, were rightly restored as principles of criticism and final judgment upon all relative justice and injustice in history; but the inevitability of relative distinctions in history is usually not understood. The eighteenth-century secular theory of equality as a simple "law of nature" is rooted in seventeenth-century sectarian theory.[17] The sect of "Diggers" anticipated, and may have inspired, the Marxist theory of government as primarily a tool of the privileged classes.[18]

Though the extremer sects always went too far in challenging either the pessimism of the Reformation or the circumspection of

[15] Many forms of American liberal-Protestant perfectionism are implicitly anarchistic in their social theories, as they are explicitly sanctificationist in their theories of redemption. *Cf. inter alia:* E. Stanley Jones, *Christ's Alternative to Communism.*

[16] This position is taken for instance by the "Leveller" sect. Its leader, John Lilburne, declared: "It is unnatural, irrational, sinful, wicked, unjust, devilish and tyrannical for any man whatsoever spiritual or temporal, clergyman or layman, to appropriate or assume unto himself power, authority and jurisdiction to rule, govern, or reign over any sort of men in the world without their free consent." From a *Freeman's Freedom Vindicated* (1646). The idea is legitimate if it means the "free" acceptance of the authority of government in general. But in sectarianism it frequently excluded the coercive power of government in specific instances, thus making for anarchism.

[17] *Cf.* Woodhouse, *op. cit.,* pp. 68–69.

[18] *Cf.* David Petegorsky, *Left-Wing Democracy in the English Civil War.* The theory is of course partly right in the sense that oligarchies tend to seek their own advantage. It is wrong, however, in the sense that the corruption of a principle cannot explain the principle. The special privileges of a ruling class were the fruits of their special power. Their special power was partly derived from the necessity of government in the community, which they supplied, however imperfectly. The necessity of government, by which special privilege is created, is antecedent to the corruption of government.

Catholic theories, they did of course provide much of the leaven of modern democratic development. But the more inclusive and comprehensive conceptions of political life were developed by the semisectarian Separatists (Roger Williams), the Independents (John Milton) and by the later Calvinists.

The development of Calvinistic thought from a conservative justification of political authority to a living relation with democratic justice deserves special consideration because, in its final form, Calvinistic theory probably came closest to a full comprehension of all the complexities of political justice.

The earlier Calvin was almost as uncritical as Luther in his sanctification of state authority and in his prohibition of resistance to it.[19] Fortunately he permitted some exceptions to this position. He, himself, extended these to some degree under the stress of history, and later Calvinists developed them into a full-orbed democratic outlook. He allowed disobedience, though not resistance, if the political authority came in conflict with God's demands upon the conscience;[20] and he objected only to private and not official resistance to the authority of the ruler. The "lower magistrates" were not only allowed, but enjoined, to resist the tyranny of kings. It was a simple matter for later Calvinists to think of any elected representatives of the people as lower magistrates, who resisted tyranny officially and not privately.

The later Dutch, French and Scottish Calvinists distinguished

[19] *Cf. Inst.,* IV, xx. "Wherefore if we are cruelly vexed by an inhuman prince or robbed and plundered by one avaricious . . . let us remember our offenses against God which are doubtless chastised by these plagues . . . and let us consider that it is not for us to remedy these evils . . . but to implore the aid of God in whose hands are the hearts of kings . . ."

[20] *Inst.,* IV, xx, 32. "But in that obedience . . . due to rulers . . . we must always make this exception . . . that it be not incompatible with obedience to Him, to whose will . . . kings should be subject."
It must be admitted that this qualification did not have the force it might have had because it was applied narrowly. It meant that men must not allow rulers to interfere with their profession of the right religion.

between government as an ordinance of God's providence and the particular form of government which might obtain at a given moment. Thus they freed the religious conscience from undue reverence for any particular government and established a critical attitude towards it; while yet preserving religious reverence for the principle of government. They understood, as the proponents of the secular social contract theory of government did not, that it is not within the power of conscious human will to create government. The formation of government and statehood belongs to the slow processes of the ages and its roots are antecedent to any human decision. Government deserves reverence not only because it is necessary but because it is a gift which man did not consciously contrive. But unlike Calvin the later Calvinists did understand the importance of human action in the formation of particular governments and the responsibility of men for the achievement of justice.[21]

Calvin believed that kings had a covenant with God to rule justly and the people had a covenant with God to obey. But he denied that this double covenant implied a contract between the ruler and the people. It was a simple matter for later Calvinists to insist that this covenant was triangular, between the ruler, the people, and God; that it was a covenant of justice; and that if the ruler broke it by injustice, the people were absolved of obedience.[22] Thus justice,

---

[21] Calvin declared that "the correction of unbridled governments" is a "revengement of the Lord" and "it is not committed to us to whom is given no other commandment but to obey and to suffer" (*Inst.,* IV, xx). In contrast Samuel Rutherford, the Scottish constitutionalist, declared: "It is not in men's free will that they have government or no government . . . or to obey or not to obey the acts of the court of nature, which is God's court." But he advised that we must "distinguish between the power of government and the power of government by magistracy." The latter the people may "measure out by ounce weights . . . no more and no less, so that they may limit, moderate and set banks and marches to the exercise," . . . they "may give it out . . . upon this and this condition." *Lex Rex,* iii, iv (1644).

[22] In the words of Rutherford: "There is an oath betwixt the king and his people laying on by a reciprocation of hands, mutual civil obligation of the people to the king and the king to the people." *Ibid.*

In the important French Huguenot, anonymous tract *Vindiciae con-*

rather than mere order and peace, became the criterion for government; and democratic criticism became the instrument of justice.[23] The difference between the democratic temper of later Calvinism and the undue and uncritical reverence for political authority in the early Reformation, both Lutheran and Calvinistic, is well illustrated in John Knox's interpretation of Romans 13. Being asked how he could square his defiance of royal authority with this scriptural injunction in Romans 13, he answered: "The power in that place is not to be understood as the unjust commandment of men but the just power wherewith God hath armed his magistrates and lieutenants to punish sin." Advised that this interpretation implied that subjects could control and judge their rulers, he replied: "And what harm should the commonwealth receive if the corrupt affection of ignorant rulers be moderated and bridled by the wisdom and discretion of Godly subjects so that they would not do violence to any man?"[24]

Too much must not be claimed for either later Calvinism or Independency in establishing democratic justice in the Anglo-Saxon world. The vindication of the right of self-government and the elaboration of effective constitutional forms for the expression of the right, was the fruit of many secular, as well as religious, movements. But the secular movements were inclined to libertarianism in their reaction to the evils of government; or to base their democratic theories upon the idea of the goodness of human nature; and

---

tra tyrannos (1579) the same argument is advanced: "It is certain that the people require a performance of covenants . . . The people ask the king whether he will govern justly. He promises he will. Then the people answer, and not before, that whilst he govern uprightly, they will obey faithfully. The king promises . . . the which failing to be accomplished the people are quit of their promises."

[23] It is not possible in this context to trace the development of the idea of democratic election of rulers from the idea of the right of resistance. Samuel Rutherford argues that since even royalists admit the right of the people to elect inferior magistrates in the cities, "ergo many cities have the power to create a higher ruler; for royal power is but the united and superlative power of inferior judges." *Ibid.*

[24] Iohn Knox, *History* II, 282.

consequently to underestimate the perils of anarchy, while they directed their attention to the perils of tyranny.[25]

Whatever may be the source of our insights into the problems of the political order, it is important both to recognize the higher possibilities of justice in every historic situation, and to know that the twin perils of tyranny and anarchy can never be completely overcome in any political achievement. These perils are expressions of the sinful elements of conflict and dominion, standing in contradiction to the ideal of brotherhood on every level of communal organization. There is no possibility of making history completely safe against either occasional conflicts of vital interests (war) or against the misuse of the power which is intended to prevent such conflict of interests (tyranny). To understand this is to labor for higher justice in terms of the experience of justification by faith. Justification by faith in the realm of justice means that we will not regard the pressures and counter pressures, the tensions, the overt and the covert conflicts by which justice is achieved and maintained, as normative in the absolute sense; but neither will we ease our conscience by seeking to escape from involvement in them. We will know that we cannot purge ourselves of the sin and guilt in which we are involved by the moral ambiguities of politics without also disavowing responsibility for the creative possibilities of justice.

VI

JUSTICE AND WORLD COMMUNITY

In the crisis of world history in which we stand, we have a particularly vivid example of the twofold character of all historic political tasks and achievements. The economic interdependence of the world places us under the obligation, and gives us the possibility,

[25] American constitutionalism owes more to the circumspection of James Madison's essentially Calvinistic approach to the problems of government than to Thomas Jefferson's simple libertarianism. Jefferson as a statesman more frequently acted, in fact, upon Madison's presuppositions than upon his own.

of enlarging the human community so that the principle of order and justice will govern the international as well as the national community. We are driven to this new task by the lash of fear as well as by the incitement of hope. For our civilization is undone if we cannot overcome the anarchy in which the nations live. This new and compelling task represents the positive side of historical development and reveals the indeterminate possibilities of good in history.

Unfortunately, however, many of the idealists who envisage this new responsibility think they can fulfill it best by denying the perennial problems of the political order. They think that world government is possible without an implied hegemony of the stronger powers. This hegemony is inevitable; and so is the peril of a new imperialism, which is inherent in it. The peril can best be overcome by arming all nations great and small with constitutional power to resist the exactions of dominant power. This is to say that the principle of the balance of power is implied in the idea of constitutional justice. But if the central and organizing principle of power is feared too much, and the central authority is weakened, then the political equilibrium degenerates once more to an unorganized balance of power. And an unorganized balance of power is potential anarchy.

Thus we face all the old problems of political organization on the new level of a potential international community. The new international community will be constructed neither by the pessimists, who believe it impossible to go beyond the balance of power principle in the relation of nations to each other; nor by the cynics, who would organize the world by the imposition of imperial authority without regard to the injustices which flow inevitably from arbitrary and irresponsible power; nor yet by the idealists, who are under the fond illusion that a new level of historic development will emancipate history of these vexing problems.

The new world must be built by resolute men who "when hope is dead will hope by faith"; who will neither seek premature escape from the guilt of history, nor yet call the evil, which taints all their achievements, good. There is no escape from the paradoxical relation of history to the Kingdom of God. History moves towards the realization of the Kingdom but yet the judgment of God is upon every new realization.

CHAPTER X

THE END OF HISTORY

EVERYTHING IN human life and history moves towards an end. By reason of man's subjection to nature and finiteness this "end" is a point where that which exists ceases to be. It is *finis*. By reason of man's rational freedom the "end" has another meaning. It is the purpose and goal of his life and work. It is *telos*. This double connotation of end as both *finis* and *telos* expresses, in a sense, the whole character of human history and reveals the fundamental problem of human existence. All things in history move towards both fulfillment and dissolution, towards the fuller embodiment of their essential character and towards death.

The problem is that the end as *finis* is a threat to the end as *telos*. Life is in peril of meaninglessness because *finis* is a seemingly abrupt and capricious termination of the development of life before it has reached its true end or *telos*. The Christian faith understands this aspect of the human situation. It shares an understanding of the tension between time and eternity with all other religions. But it asserts that it is not within man's power to solve the vexing problem of his subjection to, and partial freedom from, the flux of time. It holds, furthermore, that evil is introduced into history by the very effort of men to solve this problem by their own resources.

The evil thus introduced by the "false eternals" of human pride complicates the problem of historical fulfillment. The culmination of history must include not merely the divine completion of human incompleteness but a purging of human guilt and sin by divine judgment and mercy.

We have previously considered the implications of the revelation of God in Christ for the interpretation of history, and sought to establish that the Kingdom of God as it *has come* in Christ means a disclosure of the meaning of history but not the full realization of that meaning. That is anticipated in the Kingdom which *is to come,* that is, in the culmination of history. It must be remembered that a comprehension of the meaning of life and history from the standpoint of the Christian revelation includes an understanding of the contradictions to that meaning in which history is perennially involved.

Such an understanding by faith means that the world is in a sense already "overcome"; for none of the corruptions of history, its fanaticisms and conflicts, its imperial lusts and ambitions, its catastrophes and tragedies, can take the faithful completely unaware.[1] The light of revelation into the meaning of life illumines the darkness of history's self-contradictions, its fragmentary realizations of meaning and its premature and false completions. But obviously such a faith points to an *end* in which history's incompleteness and corruption is finally overcome. Thus history as we know it is regarded as an "interim" between the disclosure and the fulfillment of its meaning. Symbolically this is expressed in the New Testament in the hope that the suffering Messiah will "come again" with "power and great glory."[2] Men shall "see the Son of man sitting on the right hand of power, and coming in the clouds of heaven."[3]

---

[1] *Cf.* 1 Thess. 5:3-6. "For when they shall say, Peace and safety: then sudden destruction cometh upon them, as travail upon a woman with child. . . . But ye, brethren, are not in darkness, that *the day should overtake you* as a thief. Ye are all the children of light. . . . Therefore . . . let us watch and be sober."

[2] Mt. 24:30.

[3] Mt. 26:64 and Mk. 13:26.

II

THE NEW TESTAMENT IDEA OF THE END

This hope of the *parousia* in New Testament thought is sometimes dismissed as no more than a projection of those elements of Jewish apocalypse to which the first coming of Christ did not conform and for the satisfaction of which a "second coming" had to be invented. On the other hand they have frequently been taken literally and have thus confused the mind of the church. The symbol of the second coming of Christ can neither be taken literally nor dismissed as unimportant. It participates in the general characteristic of the Biblical symbols, which deal with the relation of time and eternity, and seek to point to the ultimate from the standpoint of the conditioned. If the symbol is taken literally the dialectical conception of time and eternity is falsified and the ultimate vindication of God over history is reduced to a point in history. The consequence of this falsification is expressed in the hope of a millennial age. In such a millennial age, just as in a utopian one, history is supposedly fulfilled despite the persisting conditions of finiteness. On the other hand if the symbol is dismissed as unimportant, as merely a picturesque or primitive way of apprehending the relation of the historical to the eternal, the Biblical dialectic is obscured in another direction. All theologies which do not take these symbols seriously will be discovered upon close analysis not to take history seriously either. They presuppose an eternity which annuls rather than fulfills the historical process.

The Biblical symbols cannot be taken literally because it is not possible for finite minds to comprehend that which transcends and fulfills history. The finite mind can only use symbols and pointers of the character of the eternal. These pointers must be taken seriously nevertheless because they express the self-transcendent character of historical existence and point to its eternal ground. The symbols which point towards the consummation from within the temporal flux cannot be exact in the scientific sense of the word.

They are inexact even when they merely define the divine and eternal ground of history in terms of contrast to the temporal. They are even more difficult to understand when they seek to express the Biblical idea of an eternity involved in, and yet transcending, the temporal.

The *eschata* or "last things" in New Testament symbolism are described in three fundamental symbols: the return of Christ, the last judgment and the resurrection. They must be considered in order.

1. *The Parousia*

The idea of the return of the triumphant Christ dominates the other two symbols. The judgment and the resurrection are a part of the vindication of God in the return of Christ. To believe that the suffering Messiah will return at the end of history as a triumphant judge and redeemer is to express the faith that existence cannot ultimately defy its own norm. Love may have to live in history as suffering love because the power of sin makes a simple triumph of love impossible. But if this were the ultimate situation it would be necessary either to worship the power of sin as the final power in the world or to regard it as a kind of second God, not able to triumph, but also strong enough to avoid defeat.[1]

The vindication of Christ and his triumphant return is therefore an expression of faith in the sufficiency of God's sovereignty over the world and history, and in the final supremacy of love over all the forces of self-love which defy, for the moment, the inclusive harmony of all things under the will of God.

This return of Christ stands at the "end" of history in such a way that it would sometimes appear to be a triumph in history and to mean a redeemed temporal-historical process. But according to

[1] In Zoroastrianism, the only other historical religion beside Judaism and Christianity, this dualistic conclusion is actually drawn and history is conceived as an equal battle between the good and evil God. But even in Zoroastrianism the good God triumphs in the end.

other, and usually later, interpretations, the fulfillment of the historical process is also its end in the quantitative sense; and the redemption of history would appear to be its culmination also. This twofold aspect of the final vindication of Christ implies a refutation in Biblical faith of both utopianism and a too consistent other-worldliness. Against utopianism the Christian faith insists that the final consummation of history lies beyond the conditions of the temporal process. Against other-worldliness it asserts that the consummation fulfills rather than negates, the historical process. There is no way of expressing this dialectical concept without running the danger of its dissolution. The dissolution has, in fact, taken place again and again in Christian history. Those who believed in the simple fulfillment of history have been arrayed against those who believed that historical existence was robbed of its meaning in the final consummation. Both parties to the debate used Christian symbols to express their half-Christian convictions.

If we analyse the meaning of the two subordinate symbols of the "last judgment" and the resurrection it becomes clear that, according to Biblical faith, some aspects of history are refuted more positively while the meaning of historical existence as such is affirmed more unequivocally than in alternative conceptions.

2. The Last Judgment

The symbol of the last judgment [2] in New Testament eschatology contains three important facets of the Christian conception of life and history. The first is expressed in the idea that it is Christ who will be the judge of history. Christ as judge means that when the

---

[2] *Cf.* Mt. 25:31 ff. "When the Son of man shall come in his glory, and all the holy angels with him, then shall he sit upon the throne of his glory: and before him shall be gathered all nations; and he shall separate them one from another, as a shepherd divideth his sheep from the goats."

11 Cor. 5:10: "For we must all appear before the judgment seat of Christ; that every one may receive the things done in his body, according to that he hath done, whether it be good or bad."

historical confronts the eternal it is judged by its own ideal possibility, and not by the contrast between the finite and the eternal character of God.[3] The judgment is upon sin and not finiteness. This idea is in logical accord with the whole Biblical conception of life and history, according to which it is not the partial and particular character of human existence which is evil, but rather the self-love by which men disturb the harmony of creation as it would exist if all creatures obeyed the divine will.

The second facet in the symbol of the last judgment is its emphasis upon the distinction between good and evil in history. When history confronts God the differences between good and evil are not swallowed up in a distinctionless eternity. All historical realities are indeed ambiguous. Therefore no absolute distinction between good and evil in them is possible.[4] But this does not obviate the necessity and possibility of a *final* judgment upon good and evil. To be sure the righteous, standing before the last judgment, do not believe themselves to be righteous,[5] and their uneasy conscience proves the final problem of history to be that, before God, "no man living is justified." There is no solution for this final problem short of the divine mercy and the "forgiveness of sins." We have already noted the import of the Christian doctrine of the Atonement. It affirms that the ultimate mercy does not efface the distinctions between good and evil; for God cannot destroy evil except by taking it into and upon Himself. The very rigour with which all judgments in history culminate in a final judgment is thus an expression of mean-

[3] Augustine interprets the idea that we must be "made manifest before the judgment seat of Christ" as follows: "God the Father will in his personal presence judge no man, but He has given His judgment to His Son who shall show himself *as a man* to judge the world, even as he showed himself as a man to be judged of the world." *De civ. Dei,* Book XIX, ch. 27.

[4] This is the point of the parable of the wheat and the tares, both of which must be allowed to grow until the harvest (final judgment) because they cannot always be distinguished from one another. Mt. 13:24–30.

[5] *Cf.* Vol I, Ch. II.

ingfulness of all historic conflicts between good and evil. Yet the necessity of a "final" judgment upon all other judgments is derived from the ambiguity of these conflicts.

The third facet in the symbol of the last judgment is to be found in its locus at the "end" of history. There is no achievement or partial realization in history, no fulfillment of meaning or achievement of virtue by which man can escape the final judgment. The idea of a "last" judgment expresses Christianity's refutation of all conceptions of history, according to which it is its own redeemer and is able by its process of growth and development, to emancipate man from the guilt and sin of his existence, and to free him from judgment.

Nothing expresses the insecurity and anxiety of human existence more profoundly than the fact that the fear of extinction and the fear of judgment are compounded in the fear of death. The fear of extinction is the fear of meaninglessness. When life is "cut off" before any obvious completion; when *finis* so capriciously frustrates the possibility of achieving *telos,* the very meaningfulness of life is called into question. But before faith can apprehend the divine mercy which completes our incompleteness and forgives our sins it must confront the divine judge. In that confrontation it is not death but sin as the "sting of death" which is recognized as the real peril. For the ending of our life would not threaten us if we had not falsely made ourselves the centre of life's meaning.[6]

[6] In one of the profoundest of the later Jewish apocalypses, the Fourth Ezra, the fear of extinction is compared with the fear of judgment. Judgment is regarded as preferable to mere extinction because it is a part of the consummation of life: "Woe unto those who survive in those days! But much more woe unto those who do not survive. For they that do not survive must be sorrowful knowing, as they do, what things are reserved in the last days but not attaining unto them. But woe also unto them that survive, for this reason, that they must see great peril and many distresses even as these dreams do show. Yet it is *better to come into these things* incurring peril, than to *pass away as a cloud out of the world* and not see what shall happen in the last time." IV Ezra 13:15 ff.

Literalistic conceptions of the allegedly everlasting fires of hell have frequently discredited the idea of a final judgment in the minds of modern Christians. But moral sentimentality in modern Christianity would have probably dissipated the significance of the idea of judgment, even if a literalistic orthodoxy had not seemed to justify the dissipation. It is unwise for Christians to claim any knowledge of either the furniture of heaven or the temperature of hell; or to be too certain about any details of the Kingdom of God in which history is consummated. But it is prudent to accept the testimony of the heart, which affirms the fear of judgment. The freedom of man, by which he both transcends and is creative in history, makes the fear of a judgment beyond all historical judgments inevitable. Many a court of opinion may dismiss us with a: "Well done, thou good and faithful servant"; but we will deceive ourselves if we believe such a judgment to be final. If men are fully aware, they will discern an accent of the fear of judgment in the fear of death. The fear of death arises merely from the ambiguity of finiteness and freedom which underlies all historical existence; but the fear of judgment is prompted by awareness of the mixture of sin and creativity which is the very substance of history.

3. *The Resurrection*

The idea of the resurrection of the body is a Biblical symbol in which modern minds take the greatest offense and which has long since been displaced in most modern versions of the Christian faith by the idea of the immortality of the soul. The latter idea is regarded as a more plausible expression of the hope of everlasting life. It is true of course that the idea of the resurrection transcends the limits of the conceivable; but it is not always appreciated that this is equally true of the idea of an immortal soul. The fact is that the unity of historical existence, despite its involvement in and transcendence over nature, makes it no more possible to conceive transcendent spirit, completely freed of the conditions of nature, than to conceive the conditions of nature transmuted into an eternal consummation. Either idea, as every other idea, which points to the consummation beyond history, is beyond logical conception. The hope of the resurrection nevertheless embodies the very genius of the Christian idea of the historical. On the one hand it implies that eternity will fulfill and not annul the richness and variety which the temporal process has elaborated. On the other it implies that the condition of finiteness and freedom, which lies at the basis of historical existence, is a problem for which there is no solution by any human power. Only God can solve this problem. From the human perspective it can only be solved by faith. All structures of meaning and realms of coherence, which human reason constructs, face the chasm of meaninglessness when men discover that the tangents of meaning transcend the limits of existence. Only faith has an answer for this problem. The Christian answer is faith in the God who is revealed in Christ and from whose love neither life nor death can separate us.

In this answer of faith the meaningfulness of history is the more certainly affirmed because the consummation of history as a human possibility is denied. The resurrection is not a human possibility in the sense that the immortality of the soul is thought to be so. All the plausible and implausible proofs for the immortality of the soul are efforts on the part of the human mind to master and to control the consummation of life. They all try to prove in one way or another that an eternal element in the nature of man is worthy and capable of survival beyond death. But every mystic or rational technique which seek to extricate the eternal element tends to deny the meaningfulness of the historical unity of body and soul; and with it the meaningfulness of the whole historical process with its infinite elaborations of that unity.[7] The consummation of life in these terms

[7] Professor John Baillie has called attention to the fact in his profound study of the Christian hope of everlasting life that the Platonic conception of immortality is but a more philosophical version of the primitive and animistic sense of a shadowy survival after death. Such a survival, according to Professor Baillie, may be convincing but not comforting. *And the Life Everlasting,* Ch. 4.

The Christian faith knows it to be impossible for man or any of man's historical achievements to transcend the unity & tension between the natural & eternal in human existence.

does not mean the preservation of anything significant in either the individual or the collective life of man in history.

As against these conceptions of consummation in which man denies the significance of his life in history for the sake of affirming his ability to defy death by his own power, the Christian faith knows it to be impossible for man or for any of man's historical achievements to transcend the unity and tension between the natural and the eternal in human existence. Yet it affirms the eternal significance of this historical existence from the standpoint of faith in a God, who has the power to bring history to completion.

In the symbol of the resurrection of the body, the "body" is indicative of the contribution which nature makes to human individuality and to all historical realizations. We have previously noted that human individuality is the product of both the self-consciousness of spirit and the particularity of a finite natural organism.[8] In the same way every cultural and spiritual achievement, every social and political organization in history embodies both natural conditions and normative concepts which transcend and defy the particular and unique situation in which they develop.

If only the soul survives, then you have no personal characteristics in eternity

Climate and geographic limits, poverty and plenty, the survival impulse and sexual desires, and all natural conditions leave their indelible mark upon the spiritual constructions of history. Yet historical achievements transcend these limits in varying degrees of freedom. The doctrine of the immortality of the soul implies that eternal significance can be ascribed only to that element in the historical synthesis which transcends finite conditions. If this implication is followed to its logical conclusion nothing remains in eternity but an undifferentiated unity, free of all particularity and distinctions. We have previously observed how this conclusion is rigorously drawn, particularly in Buddhism and Neo-Platonism.

The doctrine of the resurrection of the body implies that eternal significance belongs to the whole unity of an historical realization in so far as it has brought all particularities into the harmony of the

[8] *Cf.* Vol. I, Ch. III.

whole. Consummation is thus conceived not as absorption into the divine but as loving fellowship with God. Since such a perfect relation with God is not a human possibility it depends upon the mercy and power of God. Christian faith can only trust His mercy to deal with the recalcitrance of sin, even as it trusts His power to overcome the ambiguity of man's finiteness and freedom.

It is important to recognize that the rational difficulties which confront us in the doctrine of the resurrection are not all derived from literalistic corruptions of the doctrine; and they are, therefore, not all surmounted, if literalism is disavowed. Even if we do not believe that, "the earth will give back those that it treasured within it and Sheol will give back that which it had received and hell will return that which it owes" [9] we are still confronted with the formidable difficulty of asserting, what seems logically inconceivable, namely, that eternity will embody, and not annul, finiteness, or, in the words of Baron von Hügel, that the "total abidingness of God" will not destroy our "partial abidingness."

[margin note: If finiteness can be embodied in eternity, then we are faced with a paradox]

This rational difficulty partly explains the inconsistencies of Jewish apocalyptic writings, which furnished the background of New Testament conceptions. Sometimes they presented the consummation of history as something which occurred on this side of the "end of time." In that case the "resurrection of the just" was believed to usher in a millennial age upon this earth. Sometimes, particularly in the later apocalypses, the fulfillment and the end of history were conceived as coinciding; and all limitations of nature and time were believed to be transcended in the consummation.[10]

The second idea is of course more tenable than the first. But if the

[9] Similitudes of Enoch, 51:2.

[10] Edwyn R. Bevan observes: "As time went on, and the thought of the religious Jews became mature, it was largely realized that no Kingdom of God limited by the essential conditions of earthly life could satisfy the spirit of man." *The Hope of the World to Come*, p. 26.

R. H. Charles makes the same point, believing that eschatological thought gradually yielded to the conviction that "the earth, however purified is no fitting place for an eternal Messianic kingdom." *A Critical History of the Doctrine of the Future Life in Israel*, p. 220.

first had not preceded, and left its mark upon the second, the latter might well have had little to distinguish it from Greek conceptions of immortality. The whole Hebraic-Biblical conception of the unity of body and soul and of the meaningfulness of the historical process was bound to lead to this wrestling of the mind of later Judaism with this insoluble problem. New Testament thought wrestled with it too. St. Paul was convinced that "flesh and blood cannot inherit the kingdom of God; neither doth corruption inherit incorruption." [11] But this conviction did not drive him to the conclusion that everlasting life annuls all historical reality for which "the body" is the symbol. He believed rather that "it is sown a natural body and is raised a spiritual body" and that the consummation means not to "be unclothed, but clothed upon." [12] In that succinct phrase the Biblical hope of a consummation which will sublimate rather than annul the whole historical process is perfectly expressed. It is not possible to give a fuller or more plausible account of what is implied in the Christian hope of the fulfillment of life; and it is well to remember that the conditions of finiteness make a more explicit definition of the consummation impossible. It is therefore important to maintain a decent measure of restraint in expressing the Christian hope. Faith must admit "that it doth not yet appear what we shall be." But it is equally important not to confuse such restraint with uncertainty about the validity of the hope that "when he shall appear, we shall be like him; for we shall see him as he is." [13] The Christian hope of the consummation of life and history is less absurd than alternate doctrines which seek to comprehend and to effect the completion of life by some power or capacity inherent in man and his history. It is an integral part of the total Biblical conception of the meaning of life. Both the meaning and its fulfillment are ascribed to a centre and source beyond ourselves. We can participate in the fulfillment of the meaning only if we do not seek too proudly to appropriate the meaning as our secure possession or to effect the fulfillment by our own power.

[11] i Cor. 15:50.   [12] ii Cor. 5:4.   [13] i John 3:2.

III

THE END AND THE MEANING OF HISTORY

If there are partial realizations of meaning in history, as well as corruptions and distortions, it ought to be possible to discern them from the vantage point of the true end. For this reason a Christian interpretation of human destiny requires one further view of the meaning of history in the light of what is believed about the character of the ultimate consummation. If the final consummation fulfills, rather than annuls, historical meaning, the real content of this meaning must be illumined by the light of faith. Furthermore it must be possible to gain some insight into the character of the sinful corruptions of meaning, particularly since they are mostly derived from the error of regarding partial realizations as the final fulfillment.

Such an examination of history in the light of the Christian interpretation of the end must begin with a distinction between two dimensions in the relation of eternity to time. Eternity stands over time on the one hand and at the end of time on the other. It stands over time in the sense that it is the ultimate source and power of all derived and dependent existence. It is not a separate order of existence. For this reason the traditional connotation of the concept, "supernatural," is erroneous. The eternal is the ground and source of the temporal. The divine consciousness gives meaning to the mere succession of natural events by comprehending them simultaneously, even as human consciousness gives meaning to segments of natural sequence by comprehending them simultaneously in memory and foresight.

Eternity stands at the end of time in the sense that the temporal process cannot be conceived without a *finis;* and eternity cannot be conceived as having a *finis.* Eternity outlasts time, though we know nothing about either an abrupt ending of the world or of the gradual dissipation of its natural energies. Our efforts to picture the relation in spatial terms always leads us astray and prompts us to

[margin handwritten note: Eternity stands over time on the one hand and at the end of time on the other]

project a particular point in future time which will also be the end of time. This effort to picture the end of time from inside the time process is the cause of most of the literalistic corruptions of the Christian conception.

The two dimensions of the relation of eternity to time result in two perspectives upon the meaning of history. From the one perspective we discern those qualities and meanings of history which seem to have absolute significance without reference to their relation to the continuum of history. An act of martyrdom or of perfect sacrifice may or may not have discernible historical consequences, and may be appreciated without reference to the consequences. It may "be recorded in heaven" without being obviously recorded on earth. There may also be a "final" judgment upon particular evils in history without waiting for a "last" judgment, *i.e.,* suspending judgment until all its historical consequences have been recorded. On the other hand a "final" judgment about any historical matter may be a judgment which seeks to comprehend a particular event, act or quality in history in the light of its consequences in history. It is not possibile, of course, for finite minds to reach a vantage point from which they could deliver final judgment from either perspective. But their effort to do so is illustrative of the two dimensions of history in its relation to the eternal.[1]

In so far as the freedom of man to be creative in history implies a freedom over history itself, there are tangents of freedom which

[1] It might be well to observe at this point that the synoptic symbol of "The Kingdom of God" is more "existential" than the Johannine and Greek conception of "eternal life." To place "eternity" and "time" in juxtaposition is to distinguish primarily between the flux of process and the principle which underlies the process. The juxtaposition of "Kingdom of God" and history implies a more religious and existential definition of the relationship. The sovereignty of God over all creaturely wills has the same two relations as eternity has to time. It is on the one hand the authority of the source of life over all life at any moment. It is on the other hand a sovereignty which is finally vindicated in "the end."

stand in direct relation to eternity. This dimension of history prompts, and would seem to justify, Leopold von Ranke's famous dictum [2] that each moment of time and history is equidistant from eternity. But the dictum is only partially justified, for it leaves the other dimension of history out of account. History is also a total process which requires understanding of its totality from some "last judgment." [3] In so far as every act and event, every personality and historical construction is immersed in an historical continuum it takes its meaning from the whole process. If we look at history only from "above" we obscure the meaning of its "self-surpassing growth." If we look at it only from a spatially symbolized end we obscure all the richness and variety which is expressed in its many parts.

IV

THE DIVERSITY AND UNITY OF HISTORY

An effort to comprehend the meaning of history from the standpoint of the Christian faith must include three aspects of it: (1) The partial fulfillments and realizations as we see them in the rise and fall of civilizations and cultures; (2) The life of individuals; and (3) The process of history as a whole. In considering these three aspects it will become apparent that the view "from above" must predominate, though it cannot be exclusive, in the consideration of the first two aspects. The view from the "end" must predominate but not be exclusive in viewing history as a whole.

[2] *Cf. Ueber die Epochen der Neueren Geschichte.*
[3] Benedetto Croce seeks to do justice to the two dimensions of the historical in the words: "Every act stands altogether in relation to itself and altogether in relation to something else; it is both a point of repose and a stepping stone; and if it were not so it would be impossible to conceive the self-surpassing growth of history." *History as the Story of Liberty,* p. 90. An act cannot stand only in relation to itself. It must be related to some realm of meaning, but it can transcend the meaning of the historical process.

1. *The Rise and Fall of Cultures and Civilizations*

History is filled with many achievements and constructions which "have their day and cease to be." The rise and fall of empires and civilizations are the most obvious examples of the pluralistic aspect of history, but they are not, by any means, the only manifestations of this aspect. The rise and fall of particular governments and oligarchies within a given civilization, the growth and decline of specific cultural traditions, or of eminent families in a community, or of various types of voluntary associations, or of even more minor historical concretions, are equally illustrative of the pluralism of history.

Whatever meaning is to be found in this pageant of recurring life and death must be discerned primarily, though not wholly, "from above." Each historical configuration may be regarded as an integral realm of meaning, for its relation to the whole historical process is minimal or, at any rate, obscure.

The pluralistic interpretation of history has received a new impetus in recent years by the work of Oswald Spengler and, more recently by Arnold Toynbee's monumental inquiry into the rise and fall of civilizations.[1] These and similar pluralistic interpretations conform to Ranke's principles of historical interpretation, summarized in his conception of the equidistance of all temporal events from the eternal. But even historical pluralism cannot escape the question of comprehensive meaning. It seeks to find some principle of coherence in the rise and fall of various civilizations. Spengler believes that the processes of nature are the only clue to the meaning of the growth and decline of various world cultures. According to his thesis there is no unity in history but the common fate of diverse and incommensurate civilizations. This common fate is governed by the laws of nature. All civilizations pass through ages analogous to spring, summer, autumn and winter; which is to say

[1] Oswald Spengler, *The Decline of the West.* Arnold J. Toynbee, *The Study of History.*

that historical organisms are equated with natural ones. Thus the freedom of history is regarded as either wholly illusory or at least as completely subordinate to nature. It cannot be denied that, since the freedom of history rises on the ground of nature-necessity, historical destiny is always partly determined by the vitality and decay of the natural factors underlying any historical achievement. Empires and cultures may "grow old"; and fail to survive perils in their age which they could have surmounted in their youth.

Yet, as Toynbee points out, the failure of civilizations always involves something more than mere weakness of age. They perish because they make mistakes in meeting some new challenge or complexity of history. Every civilization makes some fatal mistake in the end and perishes. But these mistakes are not under the law of natural necessity. Unlike individual life, the collective and social organisms of history could ideally be perpetually replenished by new life and strength. But this would require that they be perpetually adapted to new historical situations. Their final failure to do so is always a fate into which they are tempted by their freedom and is not due to natural necessity.[2] Sometimes they perish because pride of power prompts them to extend themselves beyond the limits of human possibilities. Sometimes the oligarchy which has been instrumental in organizing a society becomes purely repressive and destroys what it has created. Sometimes the strategies and techniques

[2] It is Toynbee's great merit to see this element of tragic destiny in history where Spengler sees only the organic growth and decay of historical organisms. *Cf. The Study of History,* Vol. IV, particularly pp. 260 ff. Toynbee unnecessarily emphasizes the rôle of a minority, in the period of creativity; and of the degeneration of this minority into a "dominant" minority, maintained by repression, in a period of decay. There are undoubtedly such minorities in all social and political organisms; and in so far as failure and decay is caused by errors in judgment and action they must be attributed particularly to the portion of the community in which its will and mind are articulated. But the causes of the failure are always many. Could the decay of contemporary France be ascribed to the faults of any particular minority only? Does not history point to a much more complex source of such a breakdown?

of yesterday are falsely applied to new situations and problems to which they are not relevant. This mistake may be regarded as a form of the intellectual pride which falsely raises contingent factors in history to the eminence of false absolutes.[3] Sometimes civilizations perish because they are beguiled by philosophies of "detachment." Their spiritual leaders flee prematurely to some illusory realm of supra-historical serenity and equanimity and betray their responsibilities in history.[4] Modern technical civilization may perish because it falsely worshipped technical advance as a final good. One portion of a technical society may harness techniques to the purpose of destruction and vent its fury upon another portion of the civilization, which has grown soft by regarding the comforts yielded in such great abundance by a technical age, as the final good.

If we sought to do full justice to all the various possibilities of decline and causes of decay we would find ourselves merely recapitulating the various types of human sin.[5] They would fall into the two general categories of the sins of sensuality, and the sins of pride. In the former the freedom of history is denied and men creep back to the irresponsibility of nature. In the latter the freedom of man is overestimated. Men seek to complete history without regard to the contingent and finite character of the self, individual or collective, of the culture or civilization, which they make the basis

---

[3] Toynbee's analysis of this "nemesis of creativity" is very convincing. He defines the confusion of the contingent and the absolute as the "idolization" of "an ephemeral self," of "an ephemeral institution" and "an ephemeral technique." *Ibid.*, Vol. IV, pp. 261 ff.

[4] The weaknesses of the rule of Marcus Aurelius in the declining days of Rome belong in this category. It is significant that the most "saintly" of Roman emperors should have hastened, though he certainly did not initiate, the decline of Rome, under the influence of Stoic idealism which made *apatheia* the final good. Some of the "Christian idealism" of our own day, dreaming of a Kingdom of God which is completely irrelevant to the tragic facts and problems of history, stands in the same relation to the decline of Western civilization. There are other, and profounder, causes of our difficulties. But modern "idealism" has certainly aggravated our problems.

[5] *Cf.* Vol. I, Chs. VII and VIII.

of their pretension. This is the sin of imperialism. Or they seek to abstract human freedom from history. This pride of mystic other-worldliness makes the human spirit, not the master of history but the agent of its own emancipation from history.

All these various forms of historical decline and destruction have one common characteristic. They are not merely biological death. The Augustinian dictum: "It is not by death that we sin but by sin that we die," may be partly untrue when applied to individual life; for individual existence is rooted in a natural organism subject to the conditions of finiteness.[6] But it is a very apt description of the death of civilizations. It is by "sin that they die." They are not determined by absolute natural necessity. Their mistakes and errors are made in the same freedom, out of which their creativity arises. The mistakes are never prompted by mere ignorance. The "vain imagination" of sin is in them.

It would be wrong, however, to view the history of the world's many cultures and civilizations with an eye only upon their decline. They die in the end; but they also live. Their life is a testimony of the creativity of history, even as their death is a proof of the sin in history. The vast variety of historic organisms, the richness of their elaborations of human potentialities, the wealth of their many cultural forms and social configurations are as certainly a testimony to the divine providence under which they have grown, as their destruction is a vindication of the eternal judgment, which they are unable to defy with impunity. In their weakness and youth, while making their way in history against all the perils of life, they are revelations of the power of God who "hath chosen . . . the things which are not, to bring to nought things that are."[7] In their glory, when the disintegration of evil is already apparent in their life and yet ultimate destruction is so long postponed, their fate reveals the "longsuffering" of the divine mercy. For God's judgments are never precipitate and the possibilities of repentance and turning from the evil way are many. According to the degree with which

[6] *Cf.* Vol. I, Ch. VI.   [7] I Cor. 1:28.

civilizations and cultures accept these possibilities of renewal, they may extend their life indeterminately. But at some point or other they make the fatal mistake, or a whole series of fatal mistakes. Then they perish; and the divine majesty is vindicated in that destruction.[8]

It is not possible to make some simple distinction between the period of creativity in a civilization and the period of decline, because every civilization and culture, every empire and nation, reveals destructive elements in its period of creativity, even as there are creative elements in its period of decline.[9] But we know that

[8] Here we must recall the relevance of the prophetic conception of the rise and fall of empires and the belief that their destruction represents a vindication of the divine majesty against the pretensions of false majesty. *Cf.* Ezekiel 28:17–18: "Thine heart was lifted up because of thy beauty, thou hast corrupted thy wisdom by reason of thy brightness: I will cast thee to the ground. . . . I will bring thee to ashes upon the earth in the sight of all them that behold thee." This and many similar predictions of doom upon the various empires is always followed with the refrain: "In that day shall they know that I am the Lord."

[9] The tendency towards nationalistic Messianism is a case in point. Every culture at some time or other makes explicit Messianic pretensions and conceives the ambition of making itself the centre of the universal community. This Messianism is the overt form of the pride which is covert in all particular human communities. Sometimes this Messianism is a last gasp of life in a decaying world. A culture seeks to obscure its mortal fate by this pretension. Thus it was a decaying Egyptian sacerdotal state (after 1600 B.C.) which made the most extravagant Messianic-imperial pretensions; and Dante's vision of a Holy Roman Empire was the swan song of Ghibelline imperialism. The Messianic pretensions of the idea of the Russian nation as "Christophorus" developed after the Russian church had ceased to exercise a decent restraint upon the political will-to-power of the state and was unconsciously intended to hide that failure.

But on the other hand a very youthful and creative American civilization compounded the Christian vision of the Kingdom of God with the "American dream." It was in the early part of the nineteenth century (circa 1800–40) that American culture expressed its contempt for a "decadent" Europe by hoping that history would be fulfilled on American soil.

In between these pretensions of youth and of age are such aberrations as Lionel Curtis' identification of the British Empire with the

there are periods in which creativity predominates; and other ages in which corruption and destruction predominates.

If the whole of history is viewed from inside a period of creativity it is given a false meaning; because the entire historical process is falsely identified with a tangent in a particular age of a particular culture. If the whole of history is viewed from the vantage point of a period of decline it is threatened with meaninglessness. For the course of history is falsely identified with the doom of a given civilization. Whatever meaning there is in the rise and fall of civilizations can be known only "by faith"; for it must be viewed from the vantage point of an eternity above history, which no man has as a possession but only by faith. From such a vantage point history is meaningful, even if it should be impossible to discern any unity in its continuing processes. It is meaningful because eternal principles are vindicated in both the life which overcomes death in rising civilizations, and in the death which overtakes proud life in dying ones.[10]

"City of God" (*cf.* Curtis, *Civitas Dei*). How can we know until we have more historical perspective whether the Messianic pretensions of Anglo-Saxon imperialism (which are frequently made more extravagantly in America than in Britain) are the swan song of a dying Anglo-Saxon world, or the egoistic corruption in the creative function of this world in organizing a world community?

[10] It is impossible to write about the life and death of civilizations in a period when it is still uncertain whether we are in the throes of death or the birth pangs of a new life in the history of Western civilization, without a special word about the relevance of the Christian interpretation of human destiny to our own situation. The genius of the Christian faith makes it impossible either to view the trials and tumults of a civilization with detached and irresponsible equanimity nor yet to identify the meaning of life with the preservation of our culture and civilization.

We are at the moment engaged in the limited task of warding off a great peril which arose when a virulent form of corruption challenged the remnants of our civilization. Our obtuseness in understanding the relation between this virulence and the more static corruption out of which it developed, our tardiness in meeting the peril, the domestic disharmonies and nationalistic prejudices which made a united action

2. *The Individual and History*

The plight of the individual in his relation to the whole process of history is derived from his twofold relation to the historical process. His creativity is directed towards the establishment, perpetuation and perfection of historical communities. Therefore the meaning of his life is derived from his relation to the historical process. But the freedom which makes this creativity possible transcends all communal loyalties and even history itself. Each individual has a direct relation to eternity; for he seeks for the completion of the meaning of his life beyond the fragmentary realizations of meaning which can be discerned at any point in the process where an individual may happen to live and die. The end of an individual life is, for him, the end of history; and every individual is a Moses who perishes outside the promised land. But each individual also has an indirect relation to eternity. In so far as he takes historical responsibilities seriously he must view the problem of fulfillment from the standpoint of the ultimate and final "end." [11]

[margin annotations: The end of an individual is, for him, the end of history; and every individual is a Moses who perishes outside the promised land. But each individual has an indirect relation to eternity.]

against a common peril difficult and halting: all these weaknesses place the outcome of even the limited struggle in doubt. The outcome of larger issues is even more problematic. We do not know whether Western civilization has the resources to transcend nationalistic parochialism sufficiently to fashion a world community, compatible with the interdependence of a technical age; or whether it can solve the domestic-economic problems, aggravated by the dynamics of a technically advanced industrial process.

Standing inside such a civilization our responsibilities are obvious. We must seek to fashion our common life to conform more nearly to the brotherhood of the Kingdom of God. No view of history *sub specie æternitatis* dare beguile us from our historical obligations. But if we should fail, as well we may, we can at least understand the failure from the perspective of the Christian faith. In so far as we understand the failure we will not be completely involved in it, but have a vantage point beyond it. We could not deny the tragic character of what we discern but we would not be tempted to regard it as meaningless.

[11] The Ezra Apocalypse (Fourth Ezra) states this problem of individual life succinctly: "But lo O Lord thou art ready to meet with thy blessing those that survive *in the end;* but what shall our predecessors

If the eternal fulfillment of individual life is comprehended merely from "above," the social and historical meaning of life is destroyed. Individual life is regarded as an end in itself. This is precisely the effect not only of mystic doctrines of fulfillment but also of many orthodox Protestant versions of eschatology, in which the "end" stands only above history and the Biblical idea of the "end" is obscured.[12]

On the other hand modern protests against these Christian (and sometimes non-Christian) forms of "other-worldliness" make the mistake of trying to fulfill the meaning of life in the historical process itself. Thereby they not only obscure the reality of individual freedom in its transcendence over history but also deny the finite character of the historical process.

In their crudest forms the purely social and historical interpretations of life bid the individual to fulfill his life in his community. The breadth of the communal life and the majesty of its power supposedly complete and fulfill the partial interests and inadequate power of the individual. The relative immortality of the community is intended to compensate for the brevity of an individual's life. The difficulty with this solution is that each individual is so much more, even while he is so much less, than the community. His years are briefer than those of his community; but both his memories and anticipations have a longer range. The community knows only of its own beginnings but the individual knows of the rise and fall of civilizations before his own. The community looks forward to the victories, and fears the defeats of history; but the individual

(margin annotations, handwritten):
Many moderns who deny the Christian hope make the mistake of trying to fulfill the meaning of life in the historical process itself.

Thus, one's life is fulfilled through his contribution to the ongoing life of the community.

The trouble with this is that each individual is so much more, even while he is so much less, than the community.

---

do, or we ourselves or our posterity?" (5:41). Or again: "How does it profit us that an eternal age is promised us, whereas we have done works that bring death? And that there is foretold us an imperishable hope, whereas we are so miserably brought to futility?" (7:119–20).

[12] Reformation theology is on the whole defective in failing to preserve the Biblical conception of the end; and modern Barthian eschatology accentuates this defect. It pays little attention to a possible meaning of history as a continuum and speaks of eschatology in terms of the eternity which impinges upon every moment of time.

discerns a more final judgment. If the nations stand before that last judgment too, they do so in the conscience and mind of sensitive individuals. The brotherhood of the community is indeed the ground in which the individual is ethically realized. But the community is the frustration as well as the realization of individual life. Its collective egotism is an offense to his conscience; its institutional injustices negate the ideal of justice; and such brotherhood as it achieves is limited by ethnic and geographic boundaries. Historical communities are, in short, more deeply involved in nature and time than the individual who constantly faces an eternity above and at the end of the time process.

More refined forms of social and historical schemes of redemption bid the individual to fulfill his life and compensate for the brevity of his years by his relation, not to any particular historic community, but to the historical process itself.[13]

We have previously considered the reasons why it is impossible to regard history as redemptive and why the hope of an adequate judgment and a sufficient fulfillment of the life of the individual in the historical process must lead to the most pathetic disillusionment. It may suffice at this point to illustrate and recapitulate previous analyses of this problem by the simple expedient of imagining ourselves the "posterity" to which the eighteenth century appealed

---

[13] An historian of the eighteenth century describes the substitution of "posterity" for eternity in eighteenth-century thought as follows: "For the love of God they substituted love of humanity; for vicarious atonement the perfectibility of man through his own efforts, and for the hope of immortality in another world the hope of living in the memory of future generations. . . . The thought of posterity was apt to elicit from eighteenth century philosophers and revolutionary leaders a highly emotional and essentially religious response." Carl L. Becker, *The Heavenly City of Eighteenth-Century Philosophers,* p. 130.

The essentially religious character of this appeal to posterity is perfectly expressed in the words of Diderot: "O posterity, holy and sacred! Supporter of the oppressed and unhappy, thou who art just, thou who art incorruptible, thou who wilt revenge the good man and unmask the hypocrite, consoling and certain idea, do not abandon me. Posterity is for the philosopher what the other world is for the religious."

and noting the incongruity of being regarded as the "supporters of the oppressed," as "holy and sacred," in short as worthy or capable of being the final judges or redeemers of those who have gone before us. We are furthermore so deeply involved in and preoccupied with our own perplexities that we are as disinclined, as we are unworthy, to act as surrogates for God.

Yet there is always an element of truth in these simple appeals to history as the fulfillment of life; for the meaning of life is to be found partly in man's involvement in historical tasks and obligations.

The New Testament answer to the problem of the individual is given from the standpoint of both the eternity which is "above" and the eternity which is at the end of history. The idea of a "general resurrection," in which all those who perished before the fulfillment of history, are brought back to participate in the final triumph, does justice to both the value of individual life, without which the fulfillment of history would be incomplete; and to the meaning of the whole course of history for the individual, without which his life cannot be fulfilled.[14]

The symbol of the resurrection of the body is, even without the conception of a general resurrection at the end of history, both more individual and more social in its connotations than the alternative

[14] The idea of a general resurrection in later apocalyptic literature in which New Testament conceptions of the resurrection are rooted, is sometimes erroneously regarded as an indication of the triumph of individualistic religion over previous tribal or nationalistic ideas of the fulfillment of life. R. H. Charles, in his otherwise authoritative work in this field, commits this error (*Cf.* R. H. Charles, *Eschatology*). The idea of a general resurrection in Jewish apocalypse which permits those who perished before the final triumph to participate in it, does of course recognise the problem of individuals who die before the social meaning of life is fulfilled. But on the other hand it also implies a mutual relation between individual and social fulfillment and makes each dependent upon the other.

The participation of individuals of all ages in the age of fulfillment is implausible when taken literally; but it is symbolically profound. It relates the eternity which stands over each moment of time to the eternity in which the time process is fulfilled.

[margin handwritten note:] Yet there is always an element of truth in these simple appeals to history as the fulfillment of life; for the meaning of life is to be found partly in man's involvement in historical tasks and obligations.

Immortal of a "nous" is far less personal than a resurrection of the body.

idea of the immortality of the soul. It is more individual because it asserts eternal significance, not for some impersonal *nous* which has no real relation to the actual self; but for the self as it exists in the body. This self bears within it the anxiety and insecurity of finite existence on the one hand, and the capacity to touch the horizons of the eternal on the other hand. The hope of the resurrection affirms that ultimately finiteness will be emancipated from anxiety and the self will know itself as it is known.

The idea of the resurrection is more social because the historical constructions of human existence, the cultures and civilizations, the empires and nations and finally the whole historical process, are, just as individual life, the product of a tension between natural conditions and the freedom which transcends nature. The idea of the resurrection implies that the historical elaborations of the richness of creation, in all their variety, will participate in the consummation of history. It gives the struggles in which men engaged to preserve civilizations, and to fulfill goodness in history, abiding significance and does not relegate them to a meaningless flux, of which there will be no echo in eternity.[15]

Neither utopian nor purely other-worldly conceptions of fulfillment do full justice to the paradoxical relation of the individual to the historical process. The individual faces the eternal in every moment and in every action of his life; and he confronts the end of history with his own death. The dimension of his freedom transcends all social realities. His spirit is not fulfilled in even the highest achievements of history; his conscience is not eased by even the most unequivocal approbation of historical courts of judgment; nor need it be finally intimidated by historical condemnations. On the other hand the individual's life is meaningful only in its organic relation to historical communities, tasks and obligations.

[15] It is significant that radical sectarianism frequently recognized the relevance and meaning of the idea of the resurrection in its polemic against a too individualistic orthodox Christianity. *Cf.* particularly *Man's Mortality* by Richard Overton, the leader of seventeenth-century Levellers.

The relation of the meaning of life to parenthood is a convenient microcosmic example of this double dimension of individual life. No individual parent fulfills the total meaning of his life in his relation to his children. There are innumerable facets of meaning which are comparatively irrelevant to the vocation of parenthood. But on the other hand it is not possible to divorce the meaning of life from the vocation of parenthood. Parents must be "justified" in the lives of their children. But children are hostages held by the future. The fulfillment of the life of the parents depends upon the realization of character in their children. Thus the present must wait upon the future for its final fulfillment.

3. *The Unity of History*

However meaningful life may be in the individual patterns and collective configurations which are appreciated "from above," or from the standpoint of their direct relation to the eternal source and end of meaning, history as such represents a total realm of coherence which requires comprehension from the standpoint of its ultimate *telos*.

Even without any explicit principle of comprehension, or any adequate philosophy or theology of history, the most cursory examination of history will yield certain tangents of coherence and reveal minimal relations of unity. A consistently pluralistic conception of history is not tenable, or even plausible. It may be, as Aristotle observed, that the arts are lost and found many times in the course of history. It may be that a Roman civilization must realize certain social standards completely *de novo,* without reference or dependence upon the achievement of these standards in a Babylonian or Egyptian civilization. But on the other hand there is always a residual minimum of social and cultural experience which is deposited by one civilization and used by another. The history of science cannot be traced without beginning with the mathematics and astronomy of Egyptian priests. The science and philosophy of Western civilization obviously rest upon Greek foundations; and

There are Cumulative effects in history.

Western statecraft is inexplicable without an understanding of its Roman-Stoic presuppositions. The Hebraic-Christian interpretation of history, which we have sought to elucidate in these pages, has its roots in Babylonian, Egyptian and Persian forms of Messianism. There are, in short, cumulative effects in history. Even Spengler is forced to admit that, when new civilizations are built upon the ruins of old ones, their character is partly determined by the way new life absorbs, adapts itself to, and grows around the old ruins.

The inner relation of successive civilizations to each other may be described as "unity in length" or in time. The inner relation of contemporary civilizations to each other may be described as "unity in breadth" or in space. The former unity is more obvious than the latter one. The history of Western civilization is, for instance, more clearly related to Greece and Rome than it is to its own contemporary China. Yet there are minimal relations of mutual dependence even in "breadth." While the Western world has elaborated science and techniques to a greater extent than the oriental world, it would not be possible to comprehend our Western scientific development without understanding the contributions of oriental scientific discoveries towards it.[16]

Perhaps the most significant development of our own day is that the cumulative effects of history's unity in length is daily increasing its unity in breadth. Modern technical civilization is bringing all civilizations and cultures, all empires and nations into closer juxtaposition to each other. The fact that this greater intimacy and contiguity prompts tragic "world wars" rather than some simple and easy interpenetration of cultures, must dissuade us from regarding a "universal culture" or a "world government" as the natural and inevitable *telos* which will give meaning to the whole historical process.

But on the other hand it is obvious that the technical interdependence of the modern world places us under the obligation of elaborating political instruments which will make such new intimacy and

[16] *Cf.* Lewis Mumford, *Technics and Civilization.*

interdependence sufferable. This new and urgent task is itself a proof of the cumulative effects of history. It confronts us with progressively difficult tasks and makes our very survival dependent upon their solution. Thus the development of unity in breadth is one aspect of the unity of length in history.

These facts seem obvious enough to occasion some agreement in their interpretation, even when the presuppositions which govern the interpretations are divergent. It must be agreed that history means growth, however much the pattern of growth may be obscured by the rise and fall of civilizations. Though one age may have to reclaim what previous ages had known and forgotten, history obviously moves towards more inclusive ends, towards more complex human relations, towards the technical enhancement of human powers and the cumulation of knowledge.

But when the various connotations of the idea of "growth" are made more explicit a fateful divergence between the Christian and the modern interpretation of human destiny becomes apparent. As we have previously noted, the whole of modern secular culture (and with it that part of the Christian culture which is dependent upon it) assumes that growth means progress. It gives the idea of growth a moral connotation. It believes that history moves from chaos to cosmos by forces immanent within it. We have sought to prove that history does not support this conclusion. The peril of a more positive disorder is implicit in the higher and more complex order which human freedom constructs on the foundation of nature's harmonies and securities. The spiritual hatred and the lethal effectiveness of "civilized" conflicts, compared with tribal warfare or battles in the animal world, are one of many examples of the new evil which arises on a new level of maturity.

Two other examples of this aspect of history may be cited. The sanity of a mature individual incorporates psychic complexities and tensions into a tolerable unity, richer and finer than the simple unity of childhood. But it is also subject to aberrations to which children are immune. Children may be abnormal but are usually not subject to insanity. The political cohesion of a great national or imperial community has a breadth and extent beyond that of a primitive tribe. Furthermore it embodies social complexities of which tribal unity is innocent. The achievement of unity within this complexity represents growth toward "maturity." But every such realm of political order is filled with tensions which may become overt conflicts if not carefully "managed." The communities of history are political artifacts. They lack the security of nature and are exposed to the perils of human errors, and the aberrations of human freedom. No conceivable historical growth can therefore make a possible world government of the future as stable and secure as the order of a national community; just as no national community is as immune to disorder as the family or the tribe.

The New Testament symbol for this aspect of historical reality, this new peril of evil on every new level of the good, is the figure of the Antichrist. The Antichrist belongs to the *eschata,* to the "last things" which herald the end of history. The most explicit denial of the norm of history must be expected in the most ultimate development of history.[17] Closely related to this idea of the final evil at the end of history, is the general anticipation of evils in the course of

---

[17] The specific term of Antichrist is found only in the Johannine epistles. 1 John 2:18; 4:3; 11 John 7. In these references the figure is not particularly identified with the end. But the Johannine epistles provide an explicit term for a general New Testament idea, which is variously expressed. Jesus' vision of the end includes the appearance of those who "shall come in my name, saying, I am Christ" (Mt. 24:5); and of "false Christs and false prophets" who will "shew great signs and wonders, insomuch that, if it were possible, they shall deceive the very elect" (Mt. 24:24 and Mk. 13:22). Not only the most explicit form of pride, but also final conflicts and wars belong to the end of history (Mt. 24:6).

In the apocalyptic sections of the epistles Christians are assumed to have insights into history which will make it possible for them to understand "sudden destruction" when other men say "peace and safety" (1 Thess. 5:2); and "perilous times" are predicted when "men shall be lovers of their own selves, covetous, boasters, proud," etc. (11 Tim. 3:2). *Cf.* also Revelation 16:16–18; 19:19.

history, which believers will understand but by which the world will be taken unawares.

The New Testament symbol of the Antichrist was appropriated by Catholicism primarily for the purpose of designating potent foes of the church. This polemic use of the symbol obscured the fact that the ultimate evil might be not the denial, but the corruption, of the ultimate truth. This is the point which the Protestant Reformation made in levelling the charge of Antichrist against the church itself. But neither Catholicism nor the Reformation used the symbol of the Antichrist effectively as a principle of general historical interpretation. Modern Protestantism has not understood the significance of the symbol for obvious reasons. It has, therefore, been used and misused primarily by literalists who have sought to prove that some current and contemporary Napoleon, Hitler, or Cæsar conformed to the prophecies of Antichrist or had a name, the letters of which could be tortured to yield the number 666.[18]

The inclination of contemporary millenarian literalism to identify some current embodiment of evil with Antichrist, corresponds to a recurrent tendency in all apocalypses. It is probably as natural for an age to think of the evil against which it contends as the final form of evil as to make the mistake of regarding the good which it embodies as the final good.[19] The belief of an age that it has reached

[18] *Cf.* Rev. 13:18 "Let him that hath understanding count the number of the beast: for it is the number of a man; and his number is six hundred threescore and six." The "Beast" of the book of Revelation is quite rightly related in Christian eschatology to the conception of the Antichrist for it also is a symbol of the final form of evil, demanding blasphemous worship of itself. *Cf.* Rev. 13:4.

[19] Thus the book of Daniel places the Babylonian Empire in the position of the ultimate evil, believing that, "when the wickedness of the empire has gone so far as to deify itself and deny all reverence to anything higher, it demands and brings the divine intervention. Its hour has struck and with it the hour of the world's salvation." Adam Welch, *Visions of the End*, p. 124.

In later Jewish and Christian apocalypses it is the Roman, rather than the Babylonian Empire which has this unenviable position. In the "Eagle Vision" of the Ezra Apocalypse the sins of Rome are regarded

the end of history is pathetic, even though understandable. If we must have such illusions the apocalyptic versions of it have the merit, at least, of picturing history as moving towards a climax, and of regarding the consummation not as the mere display of the triumph of the good over evil but as a desperate conflict between the two.

But an adequate Christian philosophy of history requires better use of the symbol of the Antichrist than as a polemic weapon against contemporary foes or as the bearer of inadvertent insights, scattered among literalistic illusions. In the New Testament the symbol is integral to a total and consistent view of history, according to which the future is never presented as a realm of greater security than the present or as the guarantor of a higher virtue. The Antichrist stands at the end of history to indicate that history cumulates, rather than solves, the essential problems of human existence.

This does not mean that evil has its own independent history, culminating in the final idolatries and blasphemies of the Antichrist. Both the *civitas Dei* and the *civitas terrena* grow in history, as Augustine observed. But they do not have their separate histories. The evil which appears at the end of history is either a corruption of the final good or it is an explicit denial and defiance of that good which would be impossible without the juxtaposition of the good. This is to say that evil is negative and parasitic in origin, even though its effect is positive and its power something more than inertial resistance. Modern tyrannies are not the end product of a long history of tyranny in which ancient evils have been consciously refined to their present consistency of evil. They are rather characteristic corruptions of a mature civilization in which technical instruments have become more effective tools of tyrannical purpose. Modern idolatrous religions, which conform so perfectly to the

---

as embodying and accentuating all previous evils and thus pointing to the end of history (IV Ezra 12:15).

The idea of Marxist apocalypse that capitalism is the final evil, the defeat of which will mean the destruction of evil in history, is a secularized version of this same illusion.

vision of the "Beast" who demands religious worship for himself; and of the "false Christs" who "deceive the very elect," are not the final fruit of an independent history of idolatry. They are explicit forms of self-worship which gain their power by consciously defying higher religious and moral standards. Modern international anarchy is not the fruit of a long history of anarchy. It is, rather, the corruption and disintegration of a system of order. It is so terrible because it presupposes potential or actual mutualities on a larger scale, than those achieved in previous civilizations.[20]

The final evil is thus dependent upon the final good. Either it consciously and explicitly defies the Christ, in which case it requires Christ as a foil; or it is a lesser good, claiming to be the ultimate one, in which case it requires Christ as a cloak. The one form is the Antichrist of the sinners and the other the Antichrist of the righteous. But in either case the force of the Antichrist, though parasitic and negative in origin, is so positive in effect, and so stubborn in purpose that no force, immanent in history, is capable of encompassing its defeat. The Antichrist who appears at the end of history can be defeated only by the Christ who ends history.

All the known facts of history verify the interpretation of human destiny implied in New Testament eschatology. Yet most of the philosophies of history, both ancient and modern, have sought to obscure either one or the other aspect of history which Biblical eschatology illumines. Ancient philosophies of history either denied the meaningfulness of history entirely or they saw only the limited meaningfulness of its allegedly recurring cycles. Modern philosophies have emphasized the unity of history and its cumulative tendencies; but they sought to obscure and deny the perils and evils in the cumulations of history, so that they might regard history itself as the God of redemption.

If we inquire more closely why these mistakes were made, our consideration of the end of human destiny brings us back to the

[20] Paul Althaus emphasizes the negative character of the Antichrist in relation to Christ in his *Die Letzten Dinge,* p. 273.

problems of the beginning. For the most plausible explanation of the mistakes is that they were prompted by the desire to find a way of completing human destiny which would keep man's end under his control and in his power. The ancient world sought to do this by emancipating the spirit of man from the flux of finiteness or by subordinating his freedom to that flux. The modern world has sought redemption by regarding the process of history itself as a guarantor of the fulfillment of human life.

In every case the "vain imagination" of human pride entered into these calculations and determined the result. "Honest" mistakes may account for some confusion. The freedom of man transcends the flux of nature in such a way that the hope of completely severing the spirit from the integuments of nature is an understandable illusion. The processes of growth in history are, furthermore, so obvious that the modern error of confusing growth with progress may be regarded as an equally inevitable mistake. Yet both these mistakes also rested upon a wilful disregard of some of the obvious evidences. It is obvious that man does not have the power to extricate himself from flux and finiteness, as idealists and mystics of the ancient and the modern world believed. It is equally obvious that history does not solve the basic problems of human existence but reveals them on progressively new levels. The belief that man could solve his problem either by an escape from history or by the historical process itself is a mistake which is partly prompted by the most universal of all "ideological" taints: the pride, not of particular men and cultures, but of man as man.

For this reason it is possible to make a truer analysis of human destiny upon the basis of a religious faith which has disavowed human pride in principle, though it must not be assumed that any particular Christian analysis will not exhibit in fact what it has disavowed in principle. But if the Christian faith really finds its ultimate security beyond all the securities and insecurities of history; if it is really "persuaded, that neither death, nor life, nor angels, nor principalities, nor powers, nor things present, nor things to come, nor height, nor depth, nor any other creature, shall be able to separate us from the love of God, which is in Christ Jesus our Lord," [21] it may dissuade men from the idolatrous pursuit of false securities and redemptions in life and history. By its confidence in an eternal ground of existence which is, nevertheless, involved in man's historical striving to the very point of suffering with and for him, this faith can prompt men to accept their historical responsibilities gladly. From the standpoint of such a faith history is not meaningless because it cannot complete itself; though it cannot be denied that it is tragic because men always seek prematurely to complete it.

Thus wisdom about our destiny is dependent upon a humble recognition of the limits of our knowledge and our power. Our most reliable understanding is the fruit of "grace" in which faith completes our ignorance without pretending to possess its certainties as knowledge; and in which contrition mitigates our pride without destroying our hope.

[21] Romans 8:38–39.

FINIS

COMBINED INDEX TO

VOLUMES I AND II

SCRIPTURAL PASSAGES

PROPER NAMES

SUBJECTS

INDEX OF PROPER NAMES

INDEX OF SUBJECTS